The Selected Journals of
L.M. Montgomery
VOLUME II

At the end of her life L.M. Montgomery (1874–1942) expressed the wish that most of her handwritten journals could be published eventually, after suitable time had elapsed. She turned over her journals to her younger son, Dr E. Stuart Macdonald, and charged him with their care, and with seeing to their eventual publication in whatever form he deemed best. Before he died in 1982, Dr Macdonald turned over the handwritten volumes of his mother's journals, a much abridged version of them which she had typed, her scrapbooks and photographic collection, account books and publishing records, her personal library of some 264 books, and various memorabilia to the University of Guelph.

The entire journals comprise ten large legal-size volumes containing almost two million words and spanning the years 1889 to 1942. This second Oxford volume—which includes material from the handwritten volumes 3, 4, and 146 pages of volume 5—is a selection of representative entries, showing all her preoccupations and activities between 1910 and 1921.

L.M. Montgomery, c.1919

The Selected Journals of L.M. Montgomery

VOLUME II: 1910–1921

EDITED BY

Mary Rubio & Elizabeth Waterston

TORONTO
OXFORD UNIVERSITY PRESS
1987

DRAWINGS BY ERIC BARTH

CANADIAN CATALOGUING IN PUBLICATION DATA

Montgomery, L. M. (Lucy Maud), 1874-1942.

The selected journals of L.M. Montgomery

Includes indexes.

Partial contents: v. 1. 1889-1910 — v. 2. 1910-1921

ISBN 0-19-540503-X (v. 1). – ISBN 0-19-540586-2 (v. 2).

1. Montgomery, L. M. (Lucy Maud), 1874-1942 – Diaries.
2. Novelists, Canadian (English) – 20th century – Diaries. * I. Rubio, Mary, 1939–
II. Waterson, Elizabeth, 1922– III. Title.

PS8526.045Z53 1985   C813'.52   C85-099705-4
PR9199.2.M6Z468 1985

OXFORD is a trademark of Oxford University Press

1 2 3 4 – 0 9 8 7

Printed in Canada by
Webcom Limited

Contents

14465

Illustrations

Acknowledgements

We wish to acknowledge gratefully the unfailing support, encouragement, and assistance that has been offered by our husbands: Gerald Rubio, of the Department of English at the University of Guelph, and Douglas Waterston, former Director of the Department of Information, University of Guelph. Throughout the project Evan W. Siddall has given outstanding help as researcher, proofreader, photographer, and computer specialist. Barbara Conolly has brought unflagging enthusiasm and exceptional care to every phase of our work. A legion of other people at Guelph have given us much appreciated help: David Murray, Dean of Arts; Douglas Killam, English Department Chairman; Nancy Sadek, Archivist, and her staff; Dr. Ruth Tatham; Bernard Katz, McLaughlin Library; Elizabeth Waywell; Dan Waterston; Glenys Stow; Joel Duncan; Erich Barth; Jan Walker, Gail McGinnis, and Bonnie Hulse. Our other assistants have included Sharon Nancekivell, Ramona Montagnes, Lenie Ott, and Jennifer Rubio.

Gracious help has come from colleagues and friends elsewhere: in Boston, Bill Amlie; in the Maritimes, Orlo Jones (Prince Edward Island Heritage Foundation), Professor Malcolm Ross (Dalhousie University), Allan Dunlop (Public Archives of Nova Scotia, Halifax), Professors David Weale and F.P. Bolger (University of PEI), Mary Furness (Vernon Bridge, PEI), and Ruth and George Campbell (Park Corner, PEI); in the Uxbridge/Leaskdale/Zephyr area, Wilda Clark, Isabel St. John, Mary Stiver, Lily Meyers Cook, Cameron and Jessie Leask, Fred Leask, Rae Fleming and Allan McGillivray (Curator, Uxbridge-Scott Museum), whose local history (*Decades of Harvest*, 1986) is an excellent source of information about Leaskdale; in Quebec, Professor Helen Neilson and Janet Finlayson of Macdonald College, John Robert Sorfleet (Concordia University); in Toronto and district, Professor John Moir and Kim Moir of Knox College, Rea Wilmshurst, the Rev. Eoin Mackay, Marion Webb Laird, Anita Webb, David Macdonald, Marian Hebb, Don McLean; in England, Anne Stow (Cambridge University), Valerie Mays, and Nick Whistler. Ruth Macdonald of Toronto again rates a special thank you for her continuing encouragement. We are indebted to New Concept (Toronto) for their skill in surmounting the technical problems presented by the design of this volume.

At Oxford University Press, Pat Sillers gave meticulous help, and above all we appreciate the co-operation, participation, and editorial guidance of William Toye, Editorial Director of Oxford University Press.

Finally, we gratefully acknowledge a Research Grant from the Social Sciences and Humanities Research Council of Canada and the general use of facilities and space generously proffered by the University of Guelph.

Introduction

On 11 February 1910, when L.M. Montgomery wrote the first entry in this volume, she had recently become a world-famous author. *Anne of Green Gables*, published in April 1908, quickly went into a second printing; and in the entry dated 19 February 1910 she says she has received over $7,000 in royalties—an enormous figure in a province where the average yearly income for a working woman was less than $300. Writing a bestseller is what every author dreams of; for L.M. Montgomery the overwhelming success of her first novel seemed to change her world.

In 1910 Lucy Maud Montgomery was thirty-five years of age. She had behind her three years as a country school teacher in Prince Edward Island, one year in a newspaper office, and a decade of apprenticeship as a writer. Since 1898 she had made a good living by turning out stories and poems for church and women's magazines, while keeping house for her ageing grandmother. She was soon to face some major changes: the death of her grandmother (March 1911); marriage (July 1911) to the man who had been patiently waiting for her since their engagement in 1906; and a subsequent move to Ontario where she was to live for the second half of her life. This second Oxford volume of her journals chronicles her mixed feelings as she anticipates and adjusts to her new life. She describes her thoughts and emotions as she leaves a landscape and home she has loved; goes on a honeymoon in Scotland and England where she visits famous literary sites and her ancestors' homes; becomes mistress of her own home, the Presbyterian manse in Leaskdale, Ontario, and the centre of activity in that community; achieves motherhood (1912 and 1915); agonizes over the Great War and its impact on peoples' lives; becomes embroiled in two unpleasant lawsuits with her publisher in Boston; and discovers that her husband is subject to mental illness.

By 1910, although she dreaded uprooting herself from Prince Edward Island, she knew that she had already lost most of what made Cavendish so congenial. Many of the old people she loved and respected had died. Some of her childhood friends had married and become absorbed in personal domestic concerns; many of the energetic ones had left the Island to seek their fortunes elsewhere. (Although the Island had been settled early, and had been the cradle of Canadian Confederation, it could not support the population of the 1890s and there had been a steady exodus of the most enterprising young people to the mainland.) Maud Montgomery herself had become an anomaly in the community, set apart by her intellectual interests, her reserved personality, her confined life with her feeble but demanding grandmother, her position as an unmarried woman, and inevitably, by her new and exotic status as a famous author.

Unfortunately her money and fame had not altered her relationship with her grandmother, who set the rules of the house—which rooms were to be heated, how late the lamps could burn, how often bathing was permitted, and so on. Maud looked to a different life in the future, one she hoped would bring her another kind of fulfilment.

Throughout her life Maud Montgomery bore the psychic scars of a child who had not been given enough emotional warmth since babyhood, raised as she was by her dour and rigid maternal Macneill grandparents after her young mother's death. Change and loss were frequent features of her existence. She suffered the deaths of people extremely important to her: her kindly grandfather Montgomery in 1893; her stern grandfather Macneill in 1898; Herman Leard, a young man to whom she had been deeply attached but did not consider marrying, in 1899; and her beloved father, Hugh John Montgomery, in 1900. Each of these deaths affected her deeply. Maud well knew that when her grandmother died the house in which they lived, and in which she had been raised, would go to her Uncle John Macneill, who lived on the adjacent property. She would then be dispossessed of the only home she had ever known.

From this accumulation of psychic loss and loneliness, together with her sense that the Cavendish world of her childhood was slipping away, Montgomery had "brooded up" the compelling story of "Anne of Green Gables", an orphan desperately seeking love and a permanent home. Montgomery had taken her own longings and imaginativeness, created a vivacious little heroine, bundled her into a heartwarming and humorous plot, and set all this in a highly atmospheric P.E.I. landscape. Redheaded Anne Shirley, with her gingery, impulsive, and lovable personality, had an immediate impact. When L. M. Montgomery's publisher requested a sequel, she rapidly produced three more bestsellers: *Anne of Avonlea*, written in 1908; *Kilmeny of the Orchard*, written in 1909; and *The Story Girl*, written in 1910. Readers began writing to Miss Montgomery from all over the world. Foreign publishers were seeking translation rights. Her fans included young and old, schoolgirls and distinguished statesmen, such as the Governor-General of Canada, Earl Grey. In rural Prince Edward Island, Montgomery had found all the ingredients for gentle but effective satire of human types, religious beliefs, and cultural mores. She had also found ways to help readers enjoy an intense idealistic response to nature, and had enunciated a universally acceptable theme: that courage, cheerfulness, imagination, and determination can reconstruct disordered lives and ease the way to responsible maturity.

But though L. M. Montgomery's novels and stories are grounded in a real time and place and in real personalities, the author's experience and awareness of darknesses and depths, both in society and in private experience, are given scant place in her fiction. One must turn to the journals for a more complete picture of her background, her time, and her society.

The author L.M. Montgomery moved consciously between the golden world she created for her readers and the iron necessities of her daily life. Part of her complex psychological make-up required her to construct a public image of herself as someone who was always dignified, cheerful, and self-controlled. Given the explosive tension between her strong character and her powerlessness within the fabric of her Cavendish family, clan, and community, it is not surprising that she needed the private outlet of a personal journal. She writes: "Temperaments such as mine *must* have some outlet, else they become poisoned and morbid by 'consuming their own smoke'. And the only safe outlet is in some record such as this" (11 February 1910).

Her word-choice is significant: by 1910 she knew that she was constructing a culturally important and psychologically rich "record", a life-document. As a child she had begun to keep a diary for at least two reasons: she loved word-play, and the keeping of a little diary fed her childish sense of a future destiny as a writer. Later, in the long period of caring for her grandmother, she became more introspective, and thus aware of the tensions in her own personality— between the "Puritan Macneill conscience" and the "hot Montgomery blood", between the controlled exterior and the churning interior. Her journals, in their psychological function, often provided a refuge for "sick soul", and a place where she could risk showing a side of her personality she preferred to hide, even from herself. This very human inner self could by turns be depressed, proud, vulnerable, distant, uncharitable or compassionate. As L. M. Montgomery became an increasingly public person, she needed more than ever a secret release for her thoughts. Thus she writes that she means "to try ... to paint my life and deeds—ay, and my thoughts—truthfully, no matter how unflattering such truth may be to me. No life document has any real value otherwise" (11 February 1910). Also, by 1910, when her career as a novelist took off, she began to see how important the journals were to her writing, how they could help her recover her lost world of childhood. The journals became a professional source book. After she married and moved to Ontario in 1911 she copied the early journals as a way of maintaining her access to the life she continued to recreate in successive novels.

Her new home, the Ontario village of Leaskdale, was little more than a convergence of roads, about sixty miles north east of Toronto, where farmhouses, the small Presbyterian Church, its manse, and a store formed the nucleus of a community. The Leaskdale congregation had been founded in 1862; a first church was built in 1864 and a new one in 1909. When her husband, the Rev. Ewan Macdonald, first accepted the charge at Leaskdale, there were twenty-one families in regular attendance, many of whom had been settled in this gently rolling area for several generations. Big farmhouses and lofty elms contributed to an attractive pastoral landscape, and some of the views resembled the undulating P.E.I. roadside panoramas. But the quaint picturesque quality of Cavendish was lacking; furthermore, there was no seashore, no sparkling gulf, and the people were not her own folk. The move to Ontario created an enormous upheaval in her life, as had the adjustment to fame.

The new checks on her self-expression were many. First, she had married a minister, and ministers' wives in the early twentieth century were fettered to a life of circumspect utterance. The church was the centre of the community and

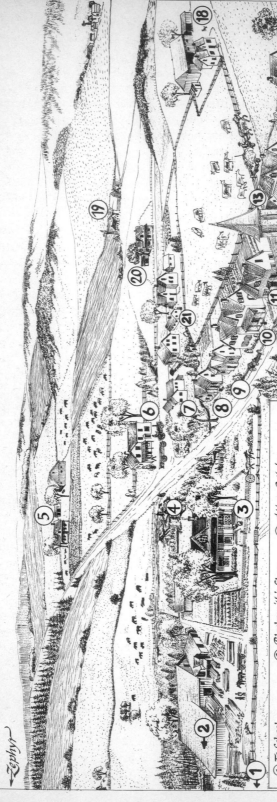

The Village of Leaskdale, Ontario

ca. 1919

Zephyr

① To School
② Saw-mill
③ George Leask
④ Grist-mill Site
⑤ Shier Farm
⑥ Harrison's Store (formerly Cook's)
⑦ Slaughterhouse
⑧ Blacksmith's Shop
⑨ Albert Cook (formerly Colling' Store)
⑩ Manse (L.M.M.'s home)
⑪ Isaac Warner
⑫ Presbyterian Church
⑬ James Cook (formerly Glide's Carriage works)
⑭ Misses Oxtoby
⑮ Lyons' old log house
⑯ James Blanchard Farm
⑰ To Mustards; Lapps'
⑱ Oxtoby Farm
⑲ Collins' Homestead
⑳ Richard Colwell
㉑ Cheese Factory

UXBRIDGE

the minister was its focus: he baptized the infants, instructed the children, married the young people, organized social gatherings and community projects, mediated disputes between members of the community, engaged in pastoral visitations to encourage and strengthen social bonds among the flock, prayed and preached to stiffen their faith, dispensed comfort in times of loss, and presided at the burials. The minister's wife was his helpmate in keeping the community running smoothly. Neither of them could show favoritism to any members of the congregation without upsetting others—and there were grave consequences if the minister's wife indulged in gossip or betrayed confidences that came to her because of her husband's position. Maud Montgomery Macdonald saw clearly the role she had to play and played it well, for she had a genuine compassion for people, born of her own capacity to suffer. But anyone reading her Leaskdale journal can see that she often felt inner rebellion over the many demands made on her. She *had* to keep her inner life very private. With her tongue not much in her cheek, she wrote: "Those whom the gods wish to destroy they make ministers' wives."

A second reason for turning inward and writing in her journal was that she had married a man whose mental orientation was totally different from her own and, despite his many abilities and good personal qualities, he provided scant intellectual companionship: he did not enjoy reading literature and he did not respond to beauty in nature or to any kind of aesthetic experience. Once Maud remarked sadly that the only subject on which he talked well was theology; and since she held rather heterodox views on religion, she did not encourage this topic of conversation. After his mental illness developed he became increasingly unable to furnish even emotional companionship for his wife, despite his deep affection for her.

For Maud Macdonald, no alternative companionship was at hand. Having suffered the trauma of being uprooted from an extended family of articulate Campbell cousins, with whom she had been accustomed to "rinse out her soul", she found that she could not release tensions in heart-to-heart discussions either with the new neighbours, or with literary colleagues in Toronto such as Marshall Saunders, Nellie McClung, and Marian Keith.

Another check on her self-expression was the mere fact of her womanhood. In the early years of the twentieth century, women's success was ultimately measured by how well they fulfilled their biological destiny. The dominant status of men was enshrined in church liturgy and the Bible. Girls grew up to the realization that life would always offer them less status and fewer possibilities—for the simple reason that they were not male. Society expected them to pour their energies into raising children and caring for the mate they had promised to honour and obey. At best a strong woman could hope to marry a gifted man and help him achieve greatness. The teaching profession was only then opening up for women, and it was poorly paid. Women could own property, but they rarely did; and they did not have the legal right to vote. Unmarried women had little status. An unhappily married woman had no dignified course but to bear her pain in silence—unless, of course, she was a skilful writer who could sublimate her tensions by creating fiction and express her personal feelings in a journal. Unlike the average woman of her time, Montgomery managed to find a voice. In her fiction it was indirect: her novels, which appear on the surface to be lighthearted, even effervescent, sometimes contain a serious subtext; even her humour is often derived from anger and frustration. But in her journals she gave direct vent to her feelings, believing that she herself, and those discussed, would be in their graves before her words were heard.

Montgomery's journals—her "life document"—offer unique rewards to anyone interested in the history of women. We find here, first, an extraordinary study of marriage. Montgomery enjoyed reading books about women who made unusual adjustments to marriage, books such as Countess von Arnim's *Elizabeth and her German Garden* and Olive Schreiner's *The Story of an African Farm*. Montgomery's journals also reveal a woman's frustration at being married to a man who did not share her intellectual and physical energy. In her own romantic novels she often seemed reluctant to end courtship stories with the conventional closure of "and then they were married"; when her independent heroines marry, she suggests a veiled but perceptible disharmony between their early aspirations and their eventual situations. In Montgomery's journals we find accounts of unfortunate marriages, her own and her contemporaries'. We see the stress that silence, service, and subservience occasionally created in women. This journal also unfolds the story of Montgomery's talented cousin Frederica Campbell, poised to face the hard choice between a beloved profession and a less-loved, hastily married husband returning from the war. We also begin to see (between the lines of the journal) the tragic price that men sometimes paid, innocently and unwittingly, for living in a society that expected them to be stronger, more capable, and more stable than women, especially the women they married. Ewan Macdonald's story emerges as a sub-plot. Perhaps only psychiatrists can unravel the complexity of his ailments and eccentricities, and only social counsellors can assess the dynamics of this stressful marriage.

The journal also gives a rich record of motherhood, in a time when child-raising was undergoing radical change in theory and practice. These were the days of the kindergarten movement, of emphasis on parenthood as fostering rather than tutelage. Changes in pediatric medicine brought new ways to cope with childhood disease and reduce childhood mortality. Montgomery's account of her life during three pregnancies and births—her psychological response to motherhood, her record of her babies' development in speech, movement, health, food, and discipline—enriches our knowledge of the history of child care.

Household management too was being reshaped, with the development of new equipment and new theories about woman's work in the home. Under the influence of Adelaide Hoodless, and with the financial help of Sir William Macdonald, "Household Science" had been established as an academic discipline in 1903 at Guelph, Ontario, and in 1905 at Macdonald College, Quebec. Montomery's cousin Frederica took a McGill degree in Household Economics at Macdonald College and went on to work at Red Deer College, University of

Alberta. Women's magazines reflected the shift towards a new view of home management. Montgomery's journals fill out the picture of how these changes seeped into home life. She writes of the management of meals, children, maids, clothes, furniture, decorating, and entertaining. "I do not honestly know whether I have sufficient strength to do all that seems expected of me," she writes on 29 November 1915.

With Montgomery's wry discovery of her first grey hair (recorded 3 August 1913), we are reminded of another aspect of a woman's life: concern for her appearance. The photographs that accompany the journals make their own claim to a place in the history of dress; discussions of materials and hairstyles supplement the knowledge we have of the vagaries of fashion.

Montgomery's journals also illuminate the life of a working writer, for she was a professional. She surveyed the requirements of the market and wrote for it, maintaining the necessary discipline for a prodigious output of poems, articles, and stories for magazines as well as of novels. At the same time the journals prompt us to think about the deeper sources of her writing. It becomes clear that the yearly novels are drawn from remembered life, from life newly experienced, and also from reading and a sense of world affairs. Montgomery's exact accounts of royalties attest to her business acumen, and document the publishing conditions of the day. She kept her earnings separate, under her own management, rather than following the normal practice of handing them over to her husband.

One tangled thread running through the diaries is the reference to lawsuits against the L.C. Page Company of Boston. In 1919 L.M. Montgomery launched one suit over payment of royalties. Later she launched another over Page's exploitation of the popularity of Anne: after she changed to another publisher, Page unscrupulously tied a group of inferior previously published early stories to "Avonlea" and suggestively used a red-haired girl in a cover picture. Behind the details lie two facts: copyright laws were being radically revised, as Canada prepared to join the Berne Convention governing international publishing; and big publishers did tend to exploit popular writers, especially women, who were unlikely to complain. Montgomery's cases make good dramatic reading; they also shed light on a general professional sore-spot.

Direct engagement in her own professional battles coincides with Montgomery's vicarious engagement in those of the Great War. The journals contain a vivid account of her highly emotional response to the war—its possibility, its frightening actuality, and its aftermath. Historians have furnished many accounts of the battle front; Montgomery offers a woman's record of the changing texture of daily life on the home front—the life of ordinary people in times of crisis. As a minister's wife, Montgomery was at the nerve centre of the community, responding with uncommon sensibility to the world events that brought deaths and breakdowns to soldiers and their families. (Twenty-one young men from the parish served in the armed forces; six were killed in action.) Her war-time journals unwittingly demonstrate the role that newspapers had begun to play, keeping the war in front of everyone daily, and recounting enemy "atrocities" (whether real or propagandized) in a way that

L.M. Montgomery's Europe:
Honeymoon Trip; Battles in the Great War

North Sea

English Channel

Amsterdam
Dixmude Antwerp
Passchendaele Ypres Brussels
Messines
Dover Bailleul Armentières Mons
Calais Arras Vimy Douai
Courcelette Cambrai
Montdidier St. Quentin
Amiens Reims
SOMME Soissons
SEINE Paris
Paris MARNE Verdun
Meuse

Tigris
Baghdad
Kut

Jerusalem

Riga
Dvina

Warsaw
Łódź
Przemysl
Tarnow
Dniester

Buzau
Bucharest
Dobruja

Dardanelles
Gallipoli

Sarajevo

Berlin

Gorizia
Venice Piave

Rome

Skagerrak
Jutland

Orkney
Scapa Flow

Edinburgh

London

Paris

Stuffa Iona
Oban
Inverness
Kirriemuir
Tullybody
Alloa Edinburgh
Trossachs Berwick
Glasgow Abbotsford Skayts.
Ayr Carlisle
Windermere
Haworth York
Leeds
Liverpool
Chester
Dunwich
Dunstan
Warwick Oxford
Stratford
LONDON

mobilized the public into productive war rallies and other activities. The story of women's war effort from 1913 to 1918 is important: Prime Minister Borden stated that these activities led to women's enfranchisement. Montgomery used her war-time journals as a source for her romantic novel, *Rilla of Ingleside* (1920); but the journals themselves record reality. There is no comparable "war book" by a woman.

Women's interests, however, do not dominate the journals. Montgomery depicts public interest in spiritualism, developments in transportation and communication, changes in medicine and psychiatry, the beginning of "church union" disputes, and current events such as the burning of the Houses of Parliament in 1916 and the Halifax Explosion in 1917. We learn about life in horse-and-buggy days when roads were unpaved and carriages were open to snow, sleet, and rain; about hot bricks being used to keep feet warm in the carriage, just as hot-water bottles were taken to bed to warm icy sheets. We witness the effect that illness had on physical stamina and mental equilibrium, in a pre-antibiotic era when a cold might bring on pneumonia and death, and when the daily irritations of cystitis and ulcerating teeth simply had to run their course over days and weeks. We see the problems of keeping a house warm in the days before modern insulation. And we watch a world-famous author endlessly correcting multiple carbon copies of manuscripts before the day of automated copying.

In short, Montgomery's valuable journal documents the mainstream of life among ordinary people. Its geography includes Ontario, Prince Edward Island, Boston, and the American Mid-West—and the many places in Flanders and Poland and Turkey and Romania where battles engaged the imagination of those who were not at the front. Though the period of these journal entries is 1910 to 1921, we are shown the effects of "future shock" in a small rural community. Electronic and mechanical developments—the car, the aeroplane, the phonograph, the machinery developed during the war—produced rapid change. L.M. Montgomery was not alone in feeling that she was being violently propelled into a future that frightened her. Having begun her life in a static and rather idyllic rural community, she watched the pace of people's lives quicken because of technological change and the spreading influence of urban centres. The experience was disorienting and often terrifying, and she surely spoke for many in her generation when she wrote: "Our old world is passed away forever—and I fear that those of us who have lived half our span therein will never feel wholly at home in the new" (June 1916).

Once Montgomery left the Leaskdale community (in 1926) she spoke of it with great warmth and called her early married days a very full and happy period of her life. While at Leaskdale she travelled regularly to the nearby town of Uxbridge for "Hypatia Club" meetings, and became an honorary member of this club founded years earlier by a group of women university graduates. She also made a number of trips to Toronto, sometimes to speak, sometimes to visit friends and to attend movies or plays, sometimes to attend meetings, such as those of the Canadian Women's Club. On the whole her life between 1910 and 1921—deficient as it may have been for a woman of her

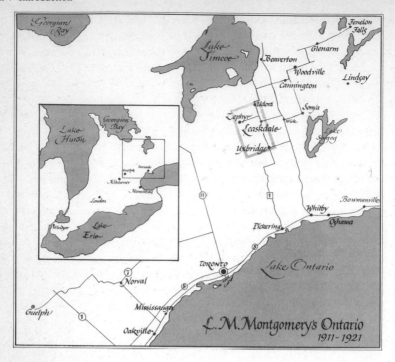

L. M. Montgomery's Ontario
1911-1921

wide-ranging interests and reading—offered more intellectual stimulation than she could at that time have found in Cavendish. The pleasures of Cavendish, and indeed the village she knew in her youth, existed by this time only in her imagination. Return visits depressed Montgomery because they forced her to acknowledge change and decay. The old-timers who gave Cavendish its character were gone, along with her favourite rows of trees and hedges and many well-loved houses. Although she maintained a few close ties in Cavendish, she knew she could no longer live there happily. But she could recapture it in her books, escaping into a fantasy as a welcome respite from the trials in her immediate life. Her memory trips were perhaps a curse as well as a blessing; though they gave her a break from real life, they may have made it more painful to return to a daily existence where she could not control the script.

Ultimately the journals hold our interest because Montgomery is such a gifted storyteller. Her impeccable timing, her telling use of detail, and her sense of narrative continuity give them the same compelling quality that induces her fans to read her novels over and over throughout their lives. The Anne series, which has reached around the world, has become a secret source of encouragement for dreams of liberty in Poland, and an inspiring example of insurgent will in Japan. The power of the novels inheres not only in their plots, messages, and characters, but in the swing of the style. That style lends the same readability to the journals, where Montgomery's insights into human personality are keen, often cutting, and her satiric sketches are delivered with a sparkling sense of the inappropriate and the comic, and a sensitivity to the nuances of relationships. In the journals, as well as in her novels, her essential goodwill usually moderates the portraits of those she satirizes—the pompous, the self-righteous, the affected, the small-minded, the bigoted, the self-important, and the merely misguided. Real anger flares up only rarely, and it often seems to dissipate as soon as she has skewered someone with words.

Although over seventy-five years have passed since Montgomery began this segment of her journals in 1910, her words still have power. They may in some places irritate or disappoint descendants of people who were a part of her life. All communities have assorted embarrassments and oddities in the closet, and hers was no exception. She was perspicacious and judgemental. She could be very tart (and very funny), but ultimately her comments describe her as much as they do the person being analysed. No doubt her journals will spark debate about whether the various periods of distress she registers were the result of genuine physical and mental fatigue arising from circumstances beyond her control, or were the product of an overwrought mind. Skimming the ten volumes of the handwritten journals, we note how Montgomery put off writing down something that was hard for her to handle emotionally. She seemed to feel threatened by the idea that to write it down was to make it real. On the other hand, she acknowledged that the only way to move beyond a difficult experience was to put it into words, giving it a fixed temporal reality, so that she could proceed with her life. Yet she often tells us that she would never choose to be like those who live lives of complacent engagement with the surface detail of daily life. "One cannot have imagination and the gift of wings, along with the placidity and contentment of those who creep on the earth's solid surface and never open their eyes on aught but material things. But the gift of wings is better than placidity and contentment after all" (31 January 1920).

A Note on the Text

In preparing this volume, we have preserved Montgomery's idiosyncrasies in capitalization, hyphenation, and placement of quotations marks unless these interfere with the reader's understanding of the text, and we have commented on any such alterations in the Notes. We have maintained her spelling of words ending in -or/-our, to show the change in her practice: in the Maritimes she had been trained in the American convention (color, honor, etc.), but soon after moving to Ontario, she began to adopt the British way of spelling such words (colour, honour, etc). Another interesting feature of her orthography—preserved in this book—is her inconsistency in spelling Scottish names. On a single page she may use the variants McFarlane/Macfarlane, or Mackay/McKay. A comparable irregularity appears widely on tombstones, wills, and other documents in Prince Edward Island, indicating that in earlier times people did not distinguish between such variants as McKenzie, MacKenzie, Mackenzie, and Mackensie. We have silently corrected most other spelling errors—there are many more in these volumes than in the earlier ones—and have also corrected misspellings of proper names such as George Eliot and *Macbeth*.

We have deleted some entries about the war; some accounts of sleepless nights and of her maladies (recurrent attacks of cystitis, mammitis, flu, cold, ulcerating teeth); part of the story of a trip to Warsaw, Indiana (where Ewan's brother was a successful physician); and several accounts of routine annual visits in Prince Edward Island to old friends and acquaintances. We deleted a long section, written after she first arrived in Leaskdale, in which Montgomery took a mental walk up and down Cavendish, giving anecdotal commentary on the people. We shortened some sections of her honeymoon trip, and an account (pp. 38-45) of the originals of people and places in her books, because these are already available in *The Alpine Path* (1975). We have pruned some sections of armchair philosophizing to maintain the narrative force, although these accounts of her response to books she was reading are always interesting, and indicate the complete flux of her mental life. All such excisions are indicated by ellipses (...) and all entries totally or partially excised are listed at the end of this book. We have corrected some dates to accord with a perpetual calendar.

This volume of Montgomery's journals has been designed to reflect her positioning of photographs within the text. From her collection of over 1500 snapshots and studio photographs (which are now at the University of Guelph) she chose pictures of people and places to illustrate her entries, and we have included a generous selection of them.

We have added several footnotes to clarify Montgomery's method of creating the final copy of her journals. When she was travelling or exceptionally busy or distressed, she made brief entries in a notebook. Later, writing a retrospective narrative, she would transcribe some of these notes into the journal, setting the insertions within quotation marks. This practice appears in four entries in the present volume: 28 January 1912, 27 September 1913, 1 December 1918, and 1 September 1919. We have indicated the openings of the flashbacks with the dagger symbol (†) and have marked the return to retrospective narrative with an asterisk (*).

What stands in the handwritten journals from which we have worked was in fact slightly edited by L.M. Montgomery herself. She carefully razored several pages and substituted other pages. (The blank books she used had 500 numbered pages; if a page was removed it had to be replaced and renumbered by hand.) The excised and replaced pages usually appear when she begins to discuss people who are very close to her—for instance, her husband, sons, and other relatives. Since numerous comments that would have been distressing to them still stand in the later as-yet unpublished journals, we can only guess at what may have been removed in these places. Her decision to remove these pages seems to declare that when she first wrote her entries she spoke with a frankness not designed for outside eyes, but that she later made the excisions because she had come to think of her handwritten journals as documents that would be read by posterity.

1910

Friday, Feb. 11, 1910
Cavendish, P.E.I.

Somehow, it is with a curious feeling of reluctance that I begin this new volume of my journal. Why I feel so I do not know. Perhaps it is because the last volume—or rather, the life it reflected—was so bitter and tragic; and hence there is a subconscious impression that the next volume must be so, too, and therefore I shrink from entering on it. Yet this is foolishness; and even if it were so I must go on with it. I could not live without my journal now. Temperaments such as mine *must* have some outlet, else they become morbid and poisoned by "consuming their own smoke". And the only *safe* outlet is in some such record as this.

I have just been reading over my first two volumes; and the thought uppermost in my mind is that, after all, in spite of my free confessions and self-analysis, a stranger perusing these journals would receive from them a quite misleading impression of my real character and life.

The first volume seems—I think—to have been written by a rather shallow girl, whose sole aim was to "have a good time" and who thought of little else than the surface play of life. Yet nothing could be falser to the reality. As a child and young girl I had a strange, deep, hidden inner life of dreams and aspirations, of which hardly a hint appears in the written record. This was partly because I had not then learned the art of self-analysis—of putting my real thoughts and feelings into words; and partly because I did not then feel the need of a confidant in my journal. I looked upon it merely as a record of my doings which might be interesting to me in after years. Hence, I kept to the surface of existence and thought, in the writing of it, and never attempted to sound the deeps below.

Again, the second volume gives the impression of a morbid temperament, generally in the throes of nervousness and gloom. Yet this, too, is false. It arises from the fact that of late years I have made my journal the refuge of my sick spirit in its unbearable agonies. The record of pain seems thus almost unbroken; yet in reality these spasms came at long intervals, when loneliness and solitude had broken down my powers of endurance. Between these times I was quite tolerably happy, hopeful and interested in life.

Well, I begin the third volume. I am going to try to strike a better balance in it—to write out my happiness as well as my pain. And I mean to try, as far as in me lies, to paint my life and deeds—ay, and my thoughts—truthfully, no matter how unflattering such truth may be to me. No life document has any real value otherwise; the worst as well as the best must be written out—*and*

1

the best as well as the worst, since we are, every one of us, whether we own to it sincerely or not, angel and devil mixed up together, now the one predominating, now the other—in the endless struggle of Ormuzd and Ahrimanes. In one mood we are strongly tempted to acknowledge only the angel and disown the devil; in another mood we grovel and lash ourselves in the miserable conviction that we are *all* devil. But one mood is as false to truth as the other. The only thing to do is to look the matter squarely in the face—and then to try to keep the devil in subjection—starve him out eventually by giving all the nourishment of our nature to the angel. Yet he can live on so little—this demon of sense and hate and anger—and often when we think him dead, or at least so weakened as to be shorn of his power, he will rise up in seemingly renewed might and rend our souls with his bestial impulses.

So, for good or evil, I begin this volume. I turn over its blank pages with a shrinking wonder. *What will be written in them?*

I have been fairly well since my last entry until yesterday, when I had a very dreadful day of nervous unrest. Today I felt much better; and, according to an unwilling promise I went in to Mayfield to spend the afternoon with Amanda Macneill—now the wife of George Robertson. She married him last July. How she *could* do it I do not know. He is a most ignorant, uncouth man, lacking little of being absolutely hideous and in intellect so sub-normal as to narrowly escape being in the class of pronounced mental defectives. I know that she neither loved nor respected him.

He used to try to go with her off and on since they were grown up. In her early girlhood she would have none of him and snubbed him most unsparingly and openly. He was then a gaunt awkward creature, short-sighted and uncanny looking, the butt of the community. As long as Amanda had any hope of getting anybody else—she had a couple of unhappy love affairs which came to nothing, both the men jilting her after leading her to think them in earnest— she would have nothing whatever to do with him. She told me once that she could never spend her life with him. Why her two affairs petered out I don't exactly understand but I have reason to believe that Amanda disgusted her lovers with over-eagerness. She did too much of the courting! However it was, she lost them and then she fell back on George, who meekly accepted her, knowing he could not get a wife anywhere else.

I was at the wedding and it was a weird performance. Amanda was deucedly cranky and mysterious. She was a ghastly-looking bride for when she stood up in the parlor to be married she turned—not pale but the most gruesome *livid green*. I never saw such a color in a face in my life before. As for George, he looked as much like a monkey, short of the tail, as any supposedly human creature could. But they were married and Amanda went to live in at Mayfield, about three miles from here.

Her departure from Cavendish was a decided relief to me, since I would no longer be compelled to meet her frequently. She has of late years developed such a dreadful disposition that any intercourse with her was a real misery to me. It is impossible to realize that she is the same Amanda Macneill I loved in childhood and young girlhood. But she is *not* the same. She is not the same in *any* respect. *That* Amanda does not now exist. I think of *her* as of a dead and buried friend of youth.

But some slight intercourse has still to be kept up. Amanda was here one afternoon lately and I promised to return the visit. I went today to get it over. There was no pleasure in the afternoon. I cannot even talk gossip with Amanda. I am oppressed by the spirit of malice with which she seems to utter and hear every word. And there is nothing else she can talk of. The only pleasure of the outing came when I was walking home alone with my good friends the stars. I also had the delight of seeing for the first time the mysterious, phantom-like Zodiacal Light.

"Amanda's Home"
[*Amanda Macneill Robertson, holding Chester*]

But recently I have had to drop my studies in astronomy for a time. In my present nervous condition they had a bad effect on me. The effort to realize those dreadful, enormous distances between the stars crushed me. In the midst of such an unthinkable assemblage of suns, *what was I* that God should be mindful of me? I felt lost—I felt like *nothingness*. And, as such feelings were intolerable in my present condition, I have stopped trying to plumb the universe until I return to my normal state.

Yet my study of the stars has a great and indescribable fascination for me. I never took up anything that gained such a hold on me or that gave me such strange, eerie, unearthly pleasure—the most purely spiritual pleasure I have ever known since there is indeed nothing of earth about it!

Saturday, Feb. 19, 1910
Cavendish, P.E.I.

After a very miserable week I feel slightly better to-day though very dull and tired. I received my publisher's report today and the year's royalty check—over seven thousand dollars! It seems like mockery that this money should come to me now when I am perhaps too broken ever to enjoy it. If I could only have had one tenth of that sum when I was a young girl, struggling for an education and enduring many humiliations and disappointments because of my lack of money. A little of it then would have saved me much. Nevertheless, I suppose it is not to be despised even now, if I ever regain health and spirit to enjoy it.

There are as yet very few days when I can work. My new book is at a standstill and my correspondence is very far behind. But all this matters little if I can regain a measure of health and energy. The trouble is, that when I cannot work there is nothing else here to take up my thoughts or pass the time, and then I am apt to fall into morbid brooding. I cannot even get out for a walk.

Saturday, March 19, 1910
Cavendish, P.E.I.

I have, as a rule, continued very miserable this past fortnight. Some days I was able to work and therefore able to endure. Other days I could not work and then it seemed that I could *not* endure. I have had a very bad cold and sore throat and I cannot get rid of it.

Have been busy reading the proof of *Kilmeny*. It is to be out in May. Recently I received a copy of the Swedish edition of *Anne*—interesting as a curiosity. Anne is portrayed on the cover as a black-and-white damsel, lugging a huge carpet-bag, and having hair of a literally *scarlet* hue—a startling contrast to the black and white. Of course I cannot judge as to the merits of the translation since I know no Swedish.

Oh, I am so very tired! If I could only feel *rested* once more. It does not seem to me just now that I would ever ask anything else. But of course I would! If I felt like my old self there are many, many things I would ask—and keenly desire.

Wednesday, March 23, 1910

It is dreadful to feel so tired all the time as I do. This afternoon I went to the

"Frede"
[*Frederica Campbell*]

Sewing Circle at Alec Macneills and sat and sewed little dresses and trousers for small heathen in Trinidad when it seemed to me I would fall from my chair with sheer weariness if I relaxed a muscle. Then we had choir practice in the evening and after it I walked home alone hardly able to drag one foot after another.

Tuesday, Mar. 29, 1910

Frede Campbell came up from Cape Traverse—where she is teaching—on Tuesday to spend Easter with me. I believe that all I need is companionship. I felt like a different being when she was here. We talked out all our difficulties and worries and they did not loom so blackly and menacingly when put into words. I feel strengthened and able to go on. I think if Frede had not come to see me I must have given up completely. What a great blessing faithful friendship is—the friendship of a true woman on whom one can depend and in whom one can trust. I fear it is a rare thing. Yet I have found some such friends—not many but enough. I do not, since girlhood passed, make friends easily or lightly. But I no longer desire many friends or a superficial popularity. Rather do I wish a few, kin to me of soul, whom I can grapple to my life with bonds not to be broken, on whose honor I can rely, and in whose companionship I can find satisfaction. For such friends I say "Thank God," with all my heart.

Monday, Apr. 4, 1910
Cavendish, P.E.I.

To-day, in going through an old trunk I came upon a "crazy quilt." And I took it out and unfolded it and sat me down to study it and the memories of the past it recalled. When I was about twelve years old "crazy patchwork" had just come into vogue. It was "all the rage." Everybody made at least a "crazy" cushion. Some few attempted quilts. I was among the latter.

The name was certainly an inspired one. "Crazy" such work certainly was— nay, more, rankly insane. To my present taste it is inexpressibly hideous. I find it hard to believe it possible that I could ever have thought it beautiful. But I did so think it; and I expended more "gray matter" devising ingenious and complicated "stitches" than I ever put into anything else.

I was from twelve to sixteen completing the quilt—five years; and verily it was "Love's Labor's Lost" for by the time I had finished it crazy patchwork was out of the fashion. My crazy quilt has been lying folded in that trunk ever since—and will continue to lie folded. Perhaps future generations may regard it as a curiosity as we look upon old samplers now.

Nevertheless, I felt many a tug at my heart as I looked over it to-day. It was compact of old memories; almost every gay piece or bit of embroidery called up some long-ago incident or place or face. As for the dreams sewn into that quilt, they were as thick as Autumn leaves in Vallambroso.

A great part of the delight of "crazy" work was the excitement of collecting pieces for it—silks, satins, velvets—for of no meaner materials might genuine crazy patchwork be made. Old boxes and drawers were ransacked and long hidden bits of finery joyfully found and used. Contributions were levied on all my friends. Did one get a new dress or hat a bit of the trimming must be begged. Sometimes the work was at a standstill for weeks because of lack of scraps. But eventually enough were collected and the quilt completed—a quaint cipher of many and many an old gayety and vanity and heartbeat. Sometimes I sent away a dollar to an American silk firm and received a package of pieces about four inches square cut from remnants. They were always very rich and beautiful, with the glamor of the outer world about them—the world of wealth and fashion where "grande dames" disported themselves in whole robes of these materials. It was a never failing diversion of my chums and me to "choose out" the various dresses we would have if given our pick of those gay samples.

There are many pieces from dresses of my mother and aunts in that quilt. Many wedding dresses figure there. And all are covered with intricate stitching. The result is a very nightmare of jumbled hues and patterns. And once I thought it beautiful!

Well, after all, it gave me pleasure in the making and so what matters if the result was not worth while? I had "the joy of the working" and that was the essence of heaven.

Monday, Apr. 25, 1910
To-day was beautiful. We have had a very early and very lovely spring. I began housecleaning to-day. I have always enjoyed housecleaning. There is something very pleasant in getting rid of the winter's dust and grime and making the rooms sweet and fresh.

I did the north room to-day. It is an unfinished room, rough plastered, and has always been used as a store-room for clothes, blankets, and cast-offs. It looks out on a wilderness of young poplars and spruces. I remember when I first began to take charge of the housecleaning what a task it was to clean that room, so full of useless odds and ends it was, not one of which would grandmother suffer to be disposed of. They might "come in handy sometime." It was vain to argue with her so I took matters into my own hands and quietly burned some of the trash at each successive housecleaning, with the happy result that in a few years it was all gone and cleaning the north room simplified by half.

Tonight I walked over the hill and washed my soul free from dust in the aerial bath of a spring twilight.

Tuesday, April 26, 1910
Cavendish, P.E.I.
To-day was the turn of the "look-out." This little room was where I used to sleep in summer until I was about twelve or thirteen. I remember that I was always very careful—in my thoughts and diary, *not* in my conversation—to call it "my boudoir"—as a "boudoir" figured largely in all the fashionable fiction of that day. One never hears of "boudoirs" now. But I had mine and in it I kept my few books and magazines, my dolls and work-box and all my little knick-knacks. There was a beautiful view from the low window over the trees of the "front" garden to the far green hills and woods of western Cavendish.

Nowadays the little "look-out" serves as a trunk-room and Daffy looks upon it as his "boudoir," for he spends most of his time there, sleeping on the bed. Poor little room! I dreamed many a bright dream there—and none but the dream of fame has ever been fulfilled!

"View from the hill"
[*Cavendish, PEI*]

Wednesday, Apr. 27, 1910
Cavendish, P.E.I.

To-day I cleaned my own dear room. It is a white peaceful nest tonight. Alas, that I should ever have to leave it! No spot on earth can ever be to me what it is. Here, by its window I have sat in grief and joy and looked afar to those green hills in rapture and in heartbreak. Many a night I have wept myself to sleep here and many nights I have been happy here. But there have been many more sorrowful nights than happy ones; and perhaps that is why I love it so— as we love what comforts us in sorrow more than what merely shares in joy. Oh, little room, when I leave you I fear my heart will break.

This evening I walked up to the barrens and picked an armful of Mayflowers. They are even more beautiful than usual this year. I never saw such large pink-and-white clusters. As somebody said of strawberries so say I of Mayflowers, "God might have made a sweeter blossom but God never did." I enjoyed my walk and gathering so much. There was a sweetness in it not to be put into words. Like the Mayflowers, it had the sweetness of the past and the dream of the future commingled.

Monday, May 2, 1910

To-day I cleaned the parlor and "spare room"—those solemn rooms of state which seemed such princely apartments to my childish eyes. Never in my recollection was the parlor much used. After Aunt Emily went away it was never used at all. Her wedding was the last festivity ever held in it. The spare room was quite frequently used however. I remember when I was a child I had an avid desire to sleep in it—just because it *was* the spare room and such a wonderful-seeming place. My desire was never given me. And when I grew old enough to compass it if I had wished—lo, the desire was not.

The parlor was a large, pleasant room, with south and west windows, with green slat-blinds of a kind I have never seen elsewhere. It had also long lace curtains which were considered very elegant in those days and which very few people in Cavendish then had. The carpet was very gorgeous—all roses and ferns. It is not "my idea" of a carpet now but once on a time I thought it left nothing to be desired. There is an old black "colonial" mantel piece which I admire now; but in those long ago days it did not appeal to me. I thought much more highly of the "lambrequined" mantels in other people's parlors. The furniture was simple and old-fashioned. A horsehair sofa and rocker were thought quite elegant. The rest of the chairs were plain, cane-bottomed ones. There were many gay tidies and cushions. The old room has never changed. Every chair stands precisely where it always did and every tidy is placed on the same cushion at the same angle. There always seems to me a certain pleasing dignity about the room, born of its very simplicity and old-fashionedness. I like occasionally to step in there and sit on the old rocker and just dream.

8

May 4, 1910
Cavendish, P.E.I.

My third book "Kilmeny of the Orchard" came to-day. Like the others it is nicely gotten up. Who would have thought that a book of my own would so soon become a commonplace to me? The advent of "Anne" in cold type seemed a wondrous event. But *Kilmeny* is "all in the day's work"—nothing more.

Monday, May 23, 1910
Cavendish, P.E.I.

To-night I succeeded in seeing Halley's comet. It was a sorry spectacle—little more than a dull white star. There has been so much concerning it in the newspapers and periodicals of the past 6 months that everyone expected a wonderful sight and we have been proportionately disappointed. Tonight I gazed at it and tried to feel enthusiastic, remembering that this self-same star I gazed at hung over doomed Jerusalem during its memorable siege and lighted Norman William to his English conquest ere the fatal day of Senlac Hill. It will be seventy-five years before this comet "calls" again. By that time I shall not be searching for it in the tremulous spring-time skies. I shall be lying somewhere under the grasses and eyes now unborn will be gazing at the famous vagabond of space.

> "Get leave to work;
>   In this world 'tis the best you get at all,
>   For God in cursing gives us better gifts
>   Than men in benediction."

So wrote Elizabeth Barrett Browning—and truly. It is hard to understand why work should be called a curse—until we remember what bitterness forced or uncongenial labor is. But the work for which we are fitted—which we are sent into the world to do—what a blessing it is and what fulness of joy it holds! I felt this to-day as I wrote a chapter of my new book and experienced the creator's subtle, all-embracing joy in creating. "Leave to work"—one would think everyone could obtain so much. But sometimes suffering and trouble forbid us the leave. And then we realize what we have lost and know that it is better to be cursed by God than forgotten by Him. If God had punished Adam and Eve in the old myth by sending them away to idleness—by *forbidding* them to work, then indeed would they have been outcast and accursed. But He sent them out from Eden to *labor*—and not all their dreams of Paradise, "whence the four great rivers flow" could have been as truly sweet as those which crowned their days of toil.

Oh God, as long as I live give me "leave to work"—thus pray I—leave and courage!

Monday, July 11, 1910
Cavendish, P.E.I.

In April our minister, John Stirling, married Margaret Ross of Stanley and they are now living in the manse. This means a great deal to me. Margaret has been an intimate friend of mine for the past two years and it is very pleasant to have her so near me. I like her very much and we have "awfully good times" together. She is what may be called "a sweet woman". She is rather lacking in strength and a certain reticence which I would like to see in her; and I am far from thinking it is wholly safe to tell her *everything*. But she is a very congenial companion.

"Margaret" (x)
[Margaret Ross Stirling]

She does not love John Stirling. She likes him very well—and she is "getting on". For the matter of that I somehow can't fancy any woman *loving* John Stirling. He is one of the nicest men I've ever met—clever—absolutely good and *sincere*—which is a rarer thing among ministers than I once fondly believed; so that in spite of his marked homeliness of feature everyone likes him. I like him tremendously—and I could never have the slightest fancy for him as a man. Not because of his marked homeliness, either. He *is* very homely; but the refinement and goodness of his features prevent his plainness from being in any way repulsive. When you come to know him well you never think of it. But he simply isn't one of the men whom women love though they may marry them from some other motive.

In spite of his fine mentality he is a poor preacher and is rather lazy, too—which things will always militate against him. But his extreme *likeableness* is a huge asset. I think he and Margaret will get on very nicely in the parish and I am exceedingly glad to have them near me.

This evening I was invited to tea at the manse to meet Dr. Pringle of Yukon fame. He is a voluble talker and as his conversation is wholly about life in the Yukon it is very entertaining. But I do not think he can talk of much except Yukon life and I am sure he is very egotistical. He is not a man with whom other people can be conversationally at their best. He is one of those men who listen absently to anything you may say, as if they were just waiting for you to finish to break in with what they are thinking of saying. You feel that your remarks have slipped over their consciousness without making the slightest impression on it, as a pebble might slide over ice. Dr. Pringle complained several times that I "wouldn't talk"—he kept calling me "Anne" and seemed to think I must or should be as big a chatter box as she was. But the truth was he didn't give me or anyone else the slightest chance to talk.

Uncle Leander, Aunt Mary and Kennedy are here for the summer.

Sunday, Aug. 14, 1910
Cavendish, P.E.I.
I feel quite "played out". Small wonder! This morning in church I encountered Sophy Simpson. She told me she was coming to see me before she went home on Wednesday and, as I did not want her either Monday or Tuesday, when I

expected other company I decided to sacrifice the nice, restful afternoon and evening I had planned for myself and asked her over from church. I put in a quite terrible afternoon. Sophy is more Sophyan than ever. She seems to be the concentrated essence of Simpsonism and nothing else. I had to take her through Lover's Lane—may jackals sit on her grandmother's grave for asking it! It desecrated the place. Faugh! The flavor of Sophy Simpson must hang around it for weeks. She is increasingly difficult to talk with and has lost none of her old aptness for saying the wrong thing at every possible opportunity. I had to go up to the Baptist Church this evening with her but glory be, I got rid of her after the service. And how blissful was my walk home alone in the moonshine of the summer night. Sophy would make anyone in love with solitude.

She remarked condescendingly as we passed through Lover's Lane, "After all, I think there is nothing so pretty as Nature".

How flattered Nature must feel!

Sunday, August 21, 1910
Cavendish, P.E.I.
Frede has been here since Thursday. We enjoyed every minute of the time. She went home today and I miss her terribly. She is going to Macdonald College this fall to take the course in Household Science. I am going to give her the money for it. Frede is too clever a girl to be wasted any longer teaching rural schools in P.E. Island. She must be given a chance to do something with her brains. I wanted her to go to McGill and take an Arts course, telling her I would put her through. But she finally decided against it. I think she feels she is rather too old for that and perhaps she is right. When a girl nears twenty five she does not feel like going into the classes with sixteen year olds. My good fortune came a little too late for Frede, as far as the B.A. is concerned.

Friday, Aug. 26, 1910
Cavendish, P.E.I.
Uncle L's went this morning. It is a relief. He is a very unpleasant guest, poor man, and grandmother is always more or less upset during their sojourn. I hope I shall be able to get some work done now. I have accomplished almost nothing these past six weeks. If I had been having a *real* vacation that would not matter. But to be prevented from working merely by constant petty happenings and worries is very unsatisfactory....

Tuesday, Sept. 6, 1910
Yesterday evening I spent at Alec Macneill's. I came home about ten o'clock and found the following rather disconcerting telegram from Lieutenant Governor Rogers awaiting me.

"His Excellency Earl Grey will be in Ch'town on Sept. 13th and wishes to meet you."

Earl Grey is our present Governor General. This was something of an honor—but rather an unwelcome one and one with which I would rather have dispensed. Not that I had any foolish dread of meeting "lords and ladies of high degree"—who are just human beings who have to wash behind their ears as I do—but because, circumstanced as I am, I foresaw a great deal of preliminary bother and worry over the matter and that, too, when I had a worrisome summer and was hoping for a quiet fall. However, there it was—almost "a royal command"—certainly not to be disregarded if it could be obeyed. There seemed to be no way out of it, short of breaking my leg or taking the smallpox. So I must; but I did not sleep much last night—and it was not gratified vanity that kept me awake either.

This morning I went to the manse and talked the matter over with Margaret—which cleared my ideas somewhat. I had, like the celebrated "Miss Flora Macflimsy", nothing to wear—at least nothing suited to any vice-regal function, however informal. And as I did not know just what the function would be I hardly knew what to get.

I decided to go up to Mr. Hillman's forthwith and see if Bertie Hillman could make me a dress before Saturday night. I went and found that she could. Then I had to scurry around arranging for a rig to take me to the station tomorrow and cancelling some engagements I had made for the rest of the week. I feel very tired tonight and not at all in good fettle for what will be certainly a tiresome expedition tomorrow.

Wednesday, Sept. 7, 1910
Cavendish, P.E.I.
This morning it threatened to rain; but rain or not "needs must" etc. I started for the station at eight o'clock, rattling along in Pierce Macneill's old wagon which is decidedly the worse for wear and giggling to myself over what Earl Grey and his staff would think if they could see my equipage and steed! I arrived at Hunter River just in time to escape the rain which began to come down heavily as the rain started. I was lucky enough to meet my cousin Will Sutherland and his wife on the train. They are home from British Columbia on a visit and I was very curious to meet her for

"Will and Lilian"
[*Sutherland*]

reasons connected with Frede. Will S. is the man Frede loved and I am inclined to think he cared a good deal for her. But he was engaged to Lilian Donahue and eventually married her, thereby destroying Frede's chance for the highest happiness. Well, there are few who have that, I think, and there are I hope many things in life for Frede besides Will Sutherland's love. But, judging from my impressions of Lilian, Will has made a mistake. Lilian seems a pleasant but very "common" person with nothing at all distinctive or charming about her. She was very nice to me—overdid it in fact. But I think if I had not written *Anne* she would not have bothered her head much about me and I am sure I should find a prolonged dose of her society very wearisome.

I dined with them at the Victoria. Then, as it was still raining heavily, I hired a carriage to do my shopping in. I got a piece of pretty brown silk with other necessary accoutrements and managed by dint of "hustling" to finish my shopping before train time. Then I scurried down to the station and had an agitated half hour's chat with Bertie. I reached home at night, dead tired.

Yesterday I had a letter from Dr. Macphail of Montreal who is in town and who is going to entertain the Earl's party at his old homestead in Orwell. Dr. Macphail himself is a brilliant man and a noted writer. He wrote that Earl Grey was "an ardent admirer" of my books and wished to meet the author. This is flattering, I suppose. Yet I do not think it is really half as flattering as the opinion of many an obscure individual who may yet be a better literary critic than Earl Grey. Dr. Macphail's own opinion is probably of more real importance than His Excellency's. Yet it speaks something for "Anne" too, that she should have been sufficiently delightful to a busy statesman to cause him to single her out in his full life and inspire him with a wish to meet her creator.

Saturday, Sept. 10, 1910
Cavendish, P.E.I.
This has certainly been a nerve-racking week, flying about attending to a score of different things, answering letters, and making arrangements. At present the programme stands thus:—I go to town Monday. At eleven o'clock Tuesday morning the Vice-Regal party leave for Orwell on a special train, where a luncheon will be served at the Macphail place. I am to join the party at the station. This will mean an informal meeting and I am very glad, since it will be much easier.

This afternoon, feeling tired and a little nervous, I went to Lover's Lane. It made me my own woman again....

Sunday Night. Sept. 11, 1910
Cavendish, P.E.I.
To-day was very beautiful. We had service in the morning. Almost everyone has heard of the "Grey affair" and most of the folks in church looked at me as if they found it rather hard to believe. My friends are all pleased—and those who are *not* my friends seem rather uncomfortably speechless. There is nothing for them to say. They cannot deny or belittle it—and they will not admit it. I confess that in regard to them I do feel a little bit of triumph.

Aunt Mary Lawson, who is visiting in Cavendish, came over with me from church. She is far more excited over the matter than I am. She looks upon it as a tremendous honor done to the clan and it warms the cockles of her Macneill heart. I had to show her the telegram and the letters and put on my dress for her. My dress is really quite pretty and I think it is suitable and becoming. I leave tomorrow morning for town. I wish it were all well over.

Friday, Sept. 16, 1910
It is all over—and I'm very thankful—and besottedly glad to get back to my own quiet life again. This does not mean that I have not had a pleasant and interesting time. I had; but there has been a great nervous strain with it all, and I am relieved that this has come to an end and I can return to my books and pen, and homely simple tasks and pleasures.

Monday morning I drove to Hunter River and went to town. It was a very beautiful day of summer air and sunshine mingled with autumnal mellowness and I looked longingly to the purple woods on the western hill where I would much rather have spent the day.

Bertie met me at the train and I went with her to her room at Mrs. Sutherland's, Upper Prince. She gave up housekeeping in the spring—a wise course. I am glad she did, for the double responsibility of teaching and housekeeping was far too heavy for her. But I miss the old home in town very much. Dear Aunt Mary! How proud she would have been over the compliment that has been paid me! How pleased to do anything that might help me!

*L.M. Montgomery in dress
worn to meet Earl Grey*

But Bertie has a very nice room and her kindness and thoughtfulness and general unselfishness were beyond my power to express. I shall never forget it and I don't know how I could have got along in all the consequent worry and fuss without going clean crazy had it not been for her.

When I came in from downtown Monday afternoon I found a note from Mrs. Rogers (Lieutenant Governor's wife) saying that a wireless from Earl Grey had informed her that the *Earl Grey*—the Government steamer, named after him, on which he travelled would not get into town until three o'clock Tuesday afternoon. This, she supposed, would upset Dr. Macphail's arrangements and the Orwell expedition would not come off until Wednesday.

This upset the arrangement of other people than Dr. Macphail. My own carefully laid little plans were scattered to the winds. On second thoughts, however, I was well pleased. I was tired and I would have Tuesday to rest in and complete my preparations at leisure. It would involve staying in town another day than I had allowed for but I had got Judy Gallant to stay with grandmother in my absence so I did not have to worry over that.

Therefore, I put off all finishing touches till Tuesday, spent the evening calling on friends and finally went to bed without even putting my hair in "crimpers", as was necessary for the style I wanted to wear. Then, rashly thinking that I would have plenty of time to get my "beauty sleep" for the Orwell Expedition the next night I began reading Dr. Macphail's new book

"Fallacies", not wishing to encounter him with it unread. I began it as a duty but continued it as a pleasure for it was a very fascinating and stimulating volume, with a good deal of disagreeable truth in it.

Tuesday morning I went placidly down town to do some shopping but presently had to come flying up again in anything but a placid fashion—and a long walk it was, too. I had called in at the Bank of Nova Scotia where Cuthbert informed me that Mrs. Sutherland had telephoned to him that there was a letter from Mrs. Rogers at the house for me. When I got back I found to my dismay that we were to leave for Orwell that afternoon as soon as the *Earl Grey* got in.

"Then and there was hurrying to and fro." I had to go down to the Queen's and call on Mrs. Rogers. Then I met Bertie at the Plaza for dinner and then hurriedly added the last touches to my dress. Then I dressed, Bertie patiently playing the part of lady's maid. I was to be at the station at three and the Earl's party was expected to arrive soon after. I was there at three—but I had to wait until four before they came. Mrs. Rogers fished me out of the waiting room and took me over to where the Earl's party stood. I was presented. It was very informal and there was nothing at all terrifying. Earl Grey shook hands with me and began at once to talk about *Anne* and the pleasure it had given him.

He is a tall genial elderly man, with a frank pleasant face, and a most unaffected "homely" manner. He has bright dark eyes, very prominent teeth and is only passably good looking. I was then presented to "Her Excellency",

"*Lady Grey, Earl Grey*"

the Countess, and her daughter, Lady Evelyn. The countess is a big "blowsy" woman, not in the least pretty and possessed of no charm whatever of manner or expression. She wasn't in the least "Vere de Vereish" in appearance. Bertie MacIntyre, woman for woman, looks ten times more like the traditional countess.

Lady Evelyn is young and quite pretty, with fresh rosy cheeks and her father's dark eyes. Lady Evelyn was very nice to me and her mother tried to be, but neither of them has his trick of putting you perfectly at your ease. I felt at home with him from the first and could talk to him freely.

The special left at once. In "our" car were also the Governor and Mrs. Rogers, Judge and Mrs. Fitzgerald, Premier and Mrs. Hazard. They were all very nice to me. I liked the Fitzgeralds very much. Did not care much for the Hazards.

When we reached Orwell we were all met by carriages and driven half a mile to the old Macphail homestead, a quite pretty place. There we had afternoon tea served in the glass veranda built across the front of the house. Then we strolled about in groups and amused ourselves. The evening was delightful. Mrs. Macphail, the doctor's mother, and his sister Janetta seemed very nice people. The doctor himself is a strange-looking man—looks like a foreigner.

Presently Earl Grey asked me to go for a walk, saying he wanted to hear all about my books etc. We went through the orchard and followed a little winding path past the trees until we came to a small white building. "Let's sit down here," said His Excellency, squatting down on the steps. Accordingly, I "sat", too—since there did not exactly seem to be anything else I could do. I could not say to Earl Grey "This is the Macphail water closet"—although that is what it was!! I suppose Earl Grey didn't know there were such places in existence. It was a neat little building, painted white, and even had a lace curtain in the window—likely put on for the occasion. And that is where His Excellency and I sat for half an hour and had our heart to heart talk. He never let the conversation lag, for he could ask a "blue streak" of questions. He asked me to send him an autographed copy of *Kilmeny* and my poems and was altogether delightful to me. But I was suffering so acutely from a suppressed desire to laugh that I hardly knew what I was saying. The Earl thought I was nervous and asked me if I had been rather dismayed at the idea of meeting him and when I said, "Yes, I've been in a blue funk," he laughed and said "But you won't feel that way any more, will you." I said "No", but I really think if we had sat there much longer I would have gone into hysterics—and never been able to explain why. I was mortally afraid that some poor unfortunate was cooped up in the house behind us, not able to get out; and I beheld with fascinated eye straggling twos and threes of women stealing through the orchard in search of the W.C. and slinking hurriedly back when they beheld the Earl and me gallantly holding the fort!

Finally the Earl got up and we went back to the house, I internally thanking my gods. Dinner was served. There were three tables—one in the dining room and two on the veranda. I was at one of the latter. Beside me on the left was Judge Fitzgerald. Opposite us were Mrs. Fitzgerald and a Mr. Armory, Canadian correspondent of *The Times*—a very clever fellow. At one end of the table was a man I did not know and at the other, just at my right hand was a homely, red-haired, insignificant individual who, I had been told by someone, was a human being named Brock, of the Ottawa geological survey. Accordingly, I held him in no awe and talked to him quite "sassily", laying down the law on the politics of Ancient Egypt (the history of which I have been studying lately) and the ultimate fate of the British Empire, contradicting him flatly as to Germany's designs and telling him the story of how I once got "drunk" on a medicinal dose of whisky. Later on I was somewhat horrified to discover that he was really Lord Percy, the A.D.C.-in-waiting of the Earl's suite. Had I known who he was I would have been tongue-tied. Not because he was Lord Percy—after the Earl and the W.C. a mere Lord at a dinner table had no terrors for me—but because I would have supposed he must know vastly more of the subjects we were discussing than I could.

After dinner we had a pleasant half hour in the parlor and then left. I drove
to the station with Lady Evelyn. Her manner is more like her father's than her
mother's but she cannot "make talk" as he can. She told me she was "shy" so
perhaps she was more ill at ease than I was.

We reached town at 10.30 and I bade them all good-bye and thankfully got
into my cab and drove to Prince St. I was very glad it was all over. As I told
Bertie I felt as if I had been for a flight in an airship. It was very interesting
and delightful, but the best part was in getting back to good firm earth again.

I was so tired I did not sleep well. Next morning I went down town shopping.
I made an engagement with my dentist for three and another to take tea with
Perle Taylor at six. Then I met Bertie at the Plaza for dinner. After dinner we
went up to Prince St. promising ourselves a pleasant two hours of rest and
chat. Alas for our delusive hopes! Mrs. Sutherland met us with the information
that the Earl of Lanesborough had called when I was out and left a letter. This
proved to be an invitation to dine with their Excellencies on board the Earl
Grey that evening at 7.30.

I did not want to go—that was all there was to it. I had thought I was through
with the whole "Grey" matter. But help there was none. I had to fly to the
telephone, cancel my engagements, order a cab, flowers, etc. etc. Then I lay
down until five but could not sleep. At five I began to dress, aided by the
patient Bertie. At seven my cab came and I went down to the marine wharf,
where Lord Lanesborough had said a boat would be waiting for me. It was—
at least some boat was, though I discovered later on that it was not the boat
which had been sent to meet me. Mr. Armory and Dr. Macphail were in it also
and we were rowed out to the *Earl Grey* in a pouring rain. Lord Percy came
and took my wraps and Lord Lanesborough and Mr. Brock (the real Brock
who *looks* much more like a "lord" than Percy) talked to me until the other
members of the party came—Lieutenant Governor Rogers and Mrs. Rogers,
Mayor Rogers and his wife, Judge and Mrs. Fitzgerald, Professor and Mrs.
McNaughton, Colonel and Mrs. Ogilvie. Then "the Greys" came in, and
presently we all went down to dinner. Professor McNaughton took me down.
He is Professor of Classics at McGill and the only man I ever met who talks
as people do in books. His conversation was brilliant but somewhat too continuous. I had no time to look about me and not much time to eat. The menu was
quite elaborate but none of the food tasted any better than many a dinner I've
eaten in old country farmhouses and some of it not nearly as well. The pudding
in particular was a vile concoction. We drank the King's health in champagne.
It was all interesting but I was really too tired to enjoy it fully. However, the
memory will always be a pleasant one. The only disagreeable part was in
curtseying ourselves backward out of the Vice-Regal presence. However, I
think I managed it as gracefully as the rest, though I narrowly escaped falling
over the high doorstep and my train combined. I kept my eye on Mrs. Rogers
and did just as she did.

Upstairs we had a rather dull time until the gentlemen rejoined us. Then we
had a pleasant half hour. Earl Grey came and chatted to Mrs. McNaughton and
me very interestingly, squatted on the floor between our chairs. He asked me

all about grandmother and told me to give her his "very special regards". I thought that little act of thoughtfulness betokened the real nobility of the man more than anything else. I do not wonder that he is a popular Governor General.

We left at ten in a pouring rain and were rowed ashore. The *Earl Grey* left for Pictou soon after. Cuthbert met me at the wharf with a carriage and I eventually reached "home" in a rather damp plight, so wretchedly tired that I could not sleep at all well. Next morning I spent shopping and then Bertie and I went to dinner at the Taylors. We had a drive about town afterwards but I did not enjoy it. The Taylors, in spite of their advantages in wealth and social position, are stupid, uninteresting people. Perle has not given any sign of remembering my existence since we sojourned together in Halifax until this Grey affair has given her memory a sudden jog. Perle was always a bit of a snob.

I left town at 5.30. Got to Hunter River at seven and drove home, getting here at nine. Stella Campbell was here. At any other time I would have been glad to see her but now I did not want to see *anyone*. I only wanted to get to bed in silence. This was not possible. I had to recount the details of my trip to Stella and what with laughing and talking got "past my sleep" again and spent a restless night. Stella went home this afternoon—and I am going to bed at six o'clock! I never felt so tired in my life. Physical weariness and nerve fatigue combined have made a wreck of me!!

Wednesday, Sept. 21, 1910
Cavendish, P.E.I.
Until yesterday I was very ill ever since Saturday with a bad cold and an attack of cholera morbus. Had grandmother not been sick in just the same way I should have blamed my recent excursion into "high life" for my collapse. And indeed, no doubt the nervous strain of the past three weeks has left me less able to cope with physical ills.

Sunday and Monday grandmother and I were both so ill that we could not do anything, not even wait on each other. I could not lift my head without vomiting painfully. I was so thankful yesterday to feel better and be able to do something. But there is so much to do, for everything has got so behind hand these past three weeks. I certainly ought to keep a servant. To do the housework I do in connection with my increasing literary work is too much for me. But grandmother would never hear of such a thing and would think me crazy if I suggested it.

Sometimes I feel as if I could *not bear* for one day longer this ceaseless tyranny in petty things to which she subjects me. It is a useless waste of time and nerves to make any protest. Nothing has the slightest influence on her. One might as well talk to a pillar of granite. If asked why she does this or behaves thus she simply denies it flatly. If I show any resentment she cries for hours together and—in plain English—sulks. Many times I feel at my wits' end between the chains which bind me on all sides and the numerous calls and claims which my literary success has brought forth. My life was hard enough before I became "a celebrity". My success, instead of making it easier, has made it twice as hard by doubling the worries and mortifications which attend my circumstances here. I am well off and tolerably famous—but the conditions of my life are not even physically comfortable and I am beset with difficulties on every side—and all, or mainly, because I must live in subjection to a woman who, always inclined to be domineering and narrow-minded, has had those qualities intensified by age until life with her means the utter suppression of all individuality in those who live with her.

Well—well—well! I went for a walk in Lover's Lane tonight and forgot all these worries for a time in its ideal beauty. It is always lovely but tonight it seemed more beautiful than I had ever known it. The soft, warm rain of the afternoon had extracted all the woodland odors until the air was dripping with fragrance—dying fir, frosted ferns, wet leaves. That walk this evening gave me such exquisite pleasure as is impossible to express in clumsy words and furnished me with a little strength to go on with life and work.

Sunday, Sept. 25, 1910
Cavendish, P.E.I.
I felt a little better to-day. This evening I spent at the manse. Margaret and I sat before the grate fire in the library and talked. How I do love an open fireplace. I love it so much that I feel sure I shall never have one of my own. No, I shall be doomed to stuffy stoves or—worse still!—a radiator all my life.

"The Manse. X is library window"
[*Home of John and Margaret Stirling*]

To sit before an open fire with a "kindred spirit" and talk of "cabbages and kings" is about as good a thing as life can offer.

Thursday, Sept. 29, 1910
Cavendish, P.E.I.
Have been gradually improving and am able to eat again. My cold still clings to me however. I cannot shake it off.

To-day I received a very bright, amusing, interesting letter from a girl of sixteen in faraway Australia. It was a pleasure to read. I get so many such letters—two or three almost every day. Some of them are lovely, all are kind but some are rather monotonous. So far I have answered all with a note at least but I am finding it a good deal of a tax. In future I must make post-cards do duty instead. But the little Australian must have a real good answer to hers. What a small big world it is! And how far little red-haired Anne has travelled!...

Tuesday, Nov. 29, 1910
Cavendish, P.E.I.
Two months since my last entry—and it really seems more like ten years. In those two months, or rather in fourteen days of those two months, I have

"lived" more than I've done in the past twelve years—lived more, learned more, enjoyed more. For those fourteen days I was re-bathed in youth. And now I must write all about it in this poor old journal which has been blotted with so many dismal entries and now must receive the unaccustomed entry of a joyous one.

It began in an odd fashion on October 13th. Through September and October I had been having a rather agitated correspondence with Mr. Page over some complaints the Musson Book Co. of Toronto had made to me in regard to Mr. Page's business methods. The matter was eventually cleared up—to a certain extent at least—after a vast deal of typewriting and scribbling.

Then on October 13th I received from Mr. Page the final letter on the subject. He said that I should be personally acquainted with my publishers and that this affair which had involved so much correspondence could have been settled in ten minutes' conversation—that it was almost necessary to have a personal interview regarding my new book; and finally that he and Mrs. Page would be delighted if I could go to them for a visit in October or November.

When I read the letter I had not the slightest notion of going. It seemed to me that I might as well try to go to the moon. It would be impossible to get away; my wardrobe was not ready for such a trip and to make it so, especially at this time of year and under existing conditions, was also impossible; and, finally, I did not want to go. I dreaded meeting new people—I dreaded new surroundings—I dreaded what I believed would be the demand for nervous energy and exertion—a demand which I felt I could not meet, so physically miserable had I been ever since September. No, I laughed at the very idea of going to Boston; and I sat me down and wrote a letter to Mr. Page, saying I could not possibly go this fall; but I added that I would try to go up for a brief visit in the spring—for he had concluded his letter by saying that if I did not go up he thought he would have to come down to P.E.I. To have him come *here*, under present conditions was unthinkable. So I flung out the spring suggestion to head him off in that idea, trusting to luck that by the spring he would have forgotten all about the matter.

I sealed the letter and left it in my portfolio for the next day's mail. Then I went to tea at the manse, met "the Greens"—Rev. Mr. Green and his wife, a most uninteresting couple—and afterwards went to prayer-meeting. Then I went home and went to bed.

Now comes an odd little psychological incident. I was almost asleep—in that dreamy state between sleeping and waking, when suddenly a thought flashed vividly into my brain, exactly as if a voice had spoken it to me—"Go to Boston". I sat up, wide-awake, tingling all over with some strange electric inrush of energy and determination. In a few moments the whole plan unrolled itself before me like a scroll or picture. "I *will* go. Stella Campbell is going up to visit Lucy Ritchie. I will go when she goes. Judy Gallant is a steady trusty French girl and is just now out of employment. I'll hire her to stay with grandmother while I'm away. And I'll get what clothes I need after I go up".

There it all was, resolved on. I lay down again and went to sleep. In the morning I tore up the letter to Mr. Page and wrote another accepting his invitation.

Then remained to carry out our plans. I knew that this would mean a good deal of bother and worry but somehow I faced it all undauntedly—nay, with positive enjoyment. I felt strangely blithe and joyous—as I had not felt for years.

I had finished my book "The Story Girl." I was sorry to finish it. Never, not even when I finished with *Anne*, had I laid down my pen and taken farewell of my characters with more regret. I consider "The Story Girl" the best piece of work I have yet done. It may not be as popular as *Anne*—somehow I don't fancy it will. But from a literary point of view it is far ahead of it. It is an idyl of childhood on an old P.E. Island farm during one summer. I have written it from sheer love of it and revised it painstakingly—up there by the window of my dear white room. It may be the last book I shall ever write there.

I wished to get the typewriting done before I left. The first half I had done in town, the second half I did myself. From that time until I left for Boston I was a busy mortal.

As soon as I heard from Stella when she was going (I had offered before this, by the way, to pay the expenses of her trip, because I felt that she was bitterly jealous of Frede's going to Macdonald), I walked back to "Toronto" to see Judy. By the road it would be nearly five miles. But I took a "short cut" back through Lover's Lane and over the fields beyond to "Toronto", as the little French settlement back among the hills is called. I did not know the exact way and several times lengthened the cut by wandering around looking for a path through some thick growing spruce grove. But it was an exquisite day and I enjoyed my walk through those golden fields and green dreaming woods.

Finally I reached Judy's home and secured the promise of her services during my absence. Before arriving there reason told me not to count too surely on getting her. She might be going to another place—she might not be able to come—but nothing worried me. I *felt* that I was to go to Boston. I *knew* that all my plans were going to be carried out. Judy would agree to come. And she did.

I had quite an experience getting back. Judy's mother assured me that the "shortest" cut was a road that led through the woods back of their house. I rashly decided to go that way, found the road—*a* road at all events—and trod it blithely. But alas, it dwindled away and away till it was a mere cow-path—and then, lo, it was not! To turn back would mean loss of time. I plunged blindly on. I knew I would come out in time if I kept on—but such a woeful scramble as it was, through a trackless wilderness of maple scrub and underbrush. I tore my skirt and ruined my rubbers and lost my temper. I was just "plain mad" when I finally did come out and found myself after a full hour's pilgrimage in the very field I could have reached in ten minutes had I gone from Judy's house by the way I came.

But I *was* there—and the air was like golden wine—and the sky blue—and I soon regained my peace of mind and had a walk home that was as sweet a pleasure as anything that came later on.

The next thing was to go to town. I had planned to go by train but, getting a chance in with "Jim Robert" Stewart, took it and we drove in the following Thursday, Oct. 31. It was a beautiful day and with anything of a companion I would have enjoyed the drive enormously. But with "Jim Robert"—well, silence is sometimes more expressive than words!

I had a bad tooth attended to, then met Bertie and did some shopping. The only important purchase I made was a fine set of mink furs. I have always loved good furs but never could afford them before. I got a beautiful collar and muff which were afterwards much admired in "The States."

At five we started home. The day was beautiful no longer. It had turned bitterly cold and a northeast hurricane was blowing in our faces. This was bad enough but might have been endured. What *couldn't* be endured was that four miles out it began to rain heavily and from that to the end of that twenty-four mile drive it *poured*. It was unendurable and we didn't endure it—we just tore through it and cussed—at least J.R.S. "cussed" and my *thoughts* were profane. I had a bad cold and neuralgia in my shoulder. It took us both to hold up one umbrella against the wind, and then our arms ached woefully. I don't think I should have thought it worth while to live through such a nightmare had it not been for the thought of some sausages I was carrying home with me. I have quite a weakness for sausages and the picture of myself at home, eating sausages for supper, gave me enough grit to worry through that fearful drive. I thought it was worth while to keep on living until I had eaten those sausages!

Seriously, we had a dreadful drive and I shall not soon forget the unpleasantness of it. I paid the price of my Boston pleasures in that expedition.

But I finally got home, got dried, and fried my sausages for supper!!

Having made all my arrangements I screwed my courage to the sticking point and told grandmother my plans. I had dreaded to do so, for I did not know how she would take it. Had I been going off on a mere "pleasure exertion" I fear she would not have taken it very well. But the word "business" had a magic sound and reconciled her to a great extent. Moreover, she knew Judy well and liked her.

From that until Nov. 5, the date fixed for going, I was exceedingly busy. But I enjoyed my "busyness" and found myself looking forward to my trip with a zest and keenness of anticipation such as I could not have believed possible a few weeks earlier. Friday, Nov. 4, was damp and foggy with frequent showers of rain. I completed my preparations, put the house in apple pie order, and packed. Then in the evening I borrowed Pierce's antiquated old "rig" and started to get Judy. No short cut was possible this time. I had to go by the road and a vile road it was, mud and water in equal proportions. Besides, it was drizzling and I could not hold up an umbrella and drive. Verily, for the moment my heart failed me and I thought pessimistically, "Is it worth while going through all this for the sake of a brief trip away among people I don't know and scenes I have no love for?"

However, I found Judy's place eventually, got her and started back. It was now dark and raining heavily. Old "Tom" was so slow I thought we'd never get home. But we did, and I went to bed with a conscience void of offence towards all men.

At 4.30 I was up. It was still raining—a nice prospect for an eleven mile ride. Was this to be an omen of my weather while away? I dressed, got breakfast, gave Judy sundry and diverse directions, including what to do in case of fire, and bestowed a farewell hug upon indifferent Daffy. At six Mr. Laird, who had kindly offered to drive me to the station, came. The rain had ceased but it continued foggy and we had several drizzles on the way up. The roads also were very bad. I wondered if Stella were likewise bowling along the Kensington road, and wondered dismally what I should do if anything prevented her coming.

At eight we arrived at Hunter River; and from that moment until I got off the train at Kensington on my return everything was as pleasant, easy, and delightful as it could possibly be. For a whole fortnight I sojourned in Fairyland.

When I reached Kensington I peered eagerly over the crowd and my heart gave a throb of relief when I saw Stella. We laughed almost incessantly from that until we reached Boston. Stella has some failings which render her a not altogether agreeable person to *live* with continually. But for a travelling companion she is almost as good as can be wished—full of fun, resourceful, seeing the humorous side of everything, even of discomforts. As for me, I enjoyed *everything*, as a *child* might. The most trifling thing had pleasure for me. For the first time in twelve years I had left home without having to carry a burden of worry with me. No wonder everything seemed like a dream!

We had a beautiful crossing from S'side to Pointe du Chene. The strait was as calm as a mill pond but the fog was too thick to see the scenery. Stella and I sat on deck until driven in by the drizzle becoming heavier. Then we went and had dinner. Hitherto, when I travelled I have always had to be as economical as possible and consider ways and means very carefully. This never increased the pleasure at all. I am candidly thankful that the day for this has gone by. Whatever worries life may still hold for me—and I have no hope that it will ever be very free from them—it does not seem likely that lack of money will hereafter be among them.

We had a good dinner on the boat and I ate with an appetite such as I have not known for years. All the time I was away I was wholesomely hungry and everything "tasted good."

When we reached the Pointe it was pouring rain but the train was waiting and we steamed away to St. John. The scenery from the Pointe to St. John must be very pretty in summer. Indeed, I know it is from my recollections of it when I went out west. But at this time of year there is little beauty and that little was effectually blotted out by fog and rain. However, Stella and I entertained each other excellently and did not find the journey monotonous. When we reached St. John station at 5.30 it was dark and we had an hour to wait. We put this in getting a dandy supper in a nice little restaurant in the station and writing post cards to friends. I thought of the last time I had been in that

St. John station—twenty years ago when I went west with dear old Grandfather Montgomery. Well, I have lived a lifetime since then; but that night I felt as if I were a girl of fifteen again. Life seemed to have suddenly started on from where it stopped with me thirteen years ago. It was all a dream, of course—I expected to waken from it at any moment—but while it lasted I meant to enjoy it to the utmost.

We left St. John at 6.40. Owing to the fact that I had delayed writing to engage a sleeper until too late we could not get one, so had to sit up all night. It was a very wearisome night, spaced by unrefreshing cat-naps, but we did extract a lot of fun out of our tribulations. We could see nothing of the scenery of course until sunrise. Then we rode for two daylight hours through a country which must be very pretty in summer.

When we had left Vanceboro we had put our watches back, thus gaining an hour. Of course when I returned to Vanceboro the process was reversed and the hour was lost again. To me there seemed a symbolism in this. I had found a new hour—and it was a fairy hour which held a lifetime in fairyland—it was *my* hour, which had struck at last, after a lifetime of toil and endeavor and waiting. It was mine and I lived it to the full, draining it like a cup of enchantment—and then I came back and had to yield it up again. But its memory is left to me—and the memory of an hour in fairyland is worth many years on upper earth.

We reached Boston at 8.30 Sunday morning. It was a beautiful morning—as all my mornings were while away. Every day was fine. We expected to be met by Lucy Ritchie—Aunt Emily's second daughter who is married to George Ritchie and lives in Roslindale, one of the Boston suburbs—and also by Mr. Nernay, one of Mr. Page's salesmen. Mr. Page himself, being a suburbanite, could not get in so early but Mr. N. was to wear a white carnation as a means of identification. Accordingly, when we got out in the big North Station I scanned the crowd anxiously and in a moment caught sight of a young man adorned with a white carnation pacing along. We pounced on him at once. Then Lucy Ritchie appeared also.

Stella and I had expected to go out to Roslindale with Lucy R. by the unpretentious and cheap electrics. You pay five cents and take a seat if you can get one or hang on by a strap if you can't—and in due time you get to your destination. But Mr. Nernay had a taxi all ready to take us out to Roslindale and in a few minutes we were all bowling along through beautiful streets to Roslindale. I had never been in an automobile before but I must say it is a very delightful way of getting about. Fifteen cents would have taken us to Roslindale; I suppose it took about fifteen dollars to get us there in a taxi.

Hitherto my literary success has brought me some money, some pleasant letters and an increase of worries and secret mortifications. I had experienced only the seamy side of fame. But now I was to see the other side. I was to find everything made easy and pleasant for me. It was very delightful—but of course it was only a dream!

Reason told me that it was no wonder that my publishers, who have made a fortune out of my books, should take some pains to please me. But my subjective mind, long inured, even from the earliest dawn of memory, to believing that I was an insignificant person, of no importance to anybody, refused to be convinced and went on telling me that the good people who made a fuss over me must be taking me for somebody else—or were making fun of me!

The Ritchies have a cosy little home. I had never met George Ritchie since we were children and then only once for a day. He is a very nice little chap, very intelligent and kind, but afflicted with congenital hip trouble which makes him very lame. Lucy R. was always a nice sensible girl but a bit of a "stick." They have two children—Kenneth, aged four, and Jean, aged two.

In regard to Kenneth Ritchie I had a rather strange experience. I have never, as to speak frankly, been a lover of children *as* children. I have always felt that if I were married I would strongly desire to have children of my own. If a friend I loved had children I felt interested in and attached to her children for her sake. Occasionally also I have met with children who were so sweet and attractive that I became very fond of them. Little Marian Webb, for example, here in C. is a dear kiddy and has always been a pet of mine. When people ask me that absurd question "Do you like children?" I always feel like retorting— and sometimes do, if I think the questioner has brains enough to understand the retort—"Why don't you ask me if I like grown-up people? I like some very much, detest others, and am indifferent to the vast majority."

Hitherto, even with the nicest children it has been a mere matter of *liking*. Never, until I met Kenneth Ritchie, have I seen a child I really *loved*. And I love Kenneth so much that I don't see how I could love him any more if he were my own child. If there was the slightest use in asking his parents to give him to me I would adopt him. I cried with loneliness when I left him and I long for him every day. He is the child of a woman who always bored me and a man who is virtually a stranger to me. I had not expected to care a pin for him—and I loved him. He is a beautiful child with a beautiful disposition. Yet I have seen as beautiful and as good children before and did not love them as I loved Kenneth Ritchie. To me this love is one of the sweetest things that have ever entered my life. If my visit to Boston has held nothing but my discovery of Kenneth I should think it well worth while.

Soon after we arrived at the house, while I was desperately trying to erase the too visible marks of a sleepless night from my face, the bell rang and a boy handed in a box containing a dozen magnificent roses for me, with the Page Co.'s card. They were so lovely that I haven't got over their beauty yet.

Stella and I wanted to go right to bed, but couldn't. Jim Montgomery—a second cousin of mine—and his bride had been invited to dinner to meet me. They came and we put in a dull afternoon. I was too sleepy and stupid to talk. Mrs. Jim was a pretty, sweet-faced, charmingly gowned little doll, and Mr. Jim was a rather patronizing and uninteresting individual. We felt devoutly thankful when they went.

After tea we decided to go into town to Tremont Temple and hear Cortland Myers. But when we got there there was not even standing room and we had to go to Park St. church instead where Dr. Conrad preached a rather prosy sermon. The music was good, however, and I liked the atmosphere of the service.

When I got into bed that night I thought it was the best place in the world!

At nine o'clock Monday morning Mr. Nernay was out with a taxi to take me into town. We first went to the Page Co.'s new office on Beacon St. where I met Mr. Lewis C. Page, the head of the firm, and his brother George Page. This is as good a place as any to record my impressions of them.

George Page is a short, stout, round-faced man, quite commonplace in appearance—quite likeable but without any special charm or distinction. He does not resemble his brother in the least. Lewis Page is a man about forty and is, to be frank, one of the most fascinating men I have ever met. He is handsome, has a most distinguished appearance and a charming manner—easy, polished, patrician. He has green eyes, long curling lashes and a delightful voice. He belongs to a fine old family and has generations of birth and breeding behind him, combined with all the advantages of wealth. The result is one of those personalities which must be "born" and can never be achieved. He was, in the main, very much like the mental picture I had formed of him from his letters.

Am I then perfectly satisfied with my publisher?

No—o—o!

Why not?

I cannot say definitely. But the fact is that I do not trust him.

Mr. Page was exceedingly kind to me during my visit and left nothing undone that might give me pleasure. This, combined with his personal charm, makes me feel very ungrateful and foolish in mistrusting him. Yet the feeling is instinctive and will not down.

Mr. Page seemed very anxious that I should come up to Boston to clear away the last shreds of misunderstanding re the Musson affair. Yet all the time I was there he never referred to it. Nor did I. I was bound I wouldn't until he did, for it was in his place to do so. Yet he never remotely hinted at it. Did he forget it? Or deem it of no importance? Or was he only too glad to steer clear of it since I did not bring it up?

Again, before I went to Boston I wrote Mr. Page that I did not intend to sign any more contracts containing the binding clause. It is not fair that I should be held indefinitely to such poor terms as he gave me for *Green Gables*. The clause was renewed with *Avonlea* and *Kilmeny* but I was resolved it should not be so again.

Mr. Page never referred to this part of my letter in his reply and later on invited me to Boston. I did not expect to receive or sign the contract for the *Story Girl* until I had sent the MS which would not be until my return home. Consequently I was surprised when, on the last morning of my visit, Mr. Page asked me if I would sign it if he brought it home that night. I wondered that he should want to commit himself to the publication of a story he had never seen but I said "yes" and at night took it up to my room. To my disgust, the binding clause was in it.

Now, did Mr. Page forget what I had written him two months before? Or did he reason thus:—"She has been my guest; I have been exceedingly good and agreeable to her; in my house and as my guest she won't want to start a discussion which might end in a wrangle and stiffness; so she will sign it without question."

If he did I justified his craft for I decided to sign for just those reasons, though I vowed it would be for the last time.

These two little things are slight matters to cause distrust and would not have done so if some instinct in me had not whispered a protest. Anyhow, I can do nothing just now. Even if I had more justification for my distrust I am bound hard and fast to him for five more years and must get on as agreeably as possible during that time.

After my call at the office Lu, Stella and I went shopping. Some of the big dep't stores up there are very fine. At first I found them bewildering places but in a few days I "got the hang" of them and began to feel quite at home in them.

That day I got a brown broadcloth suit and an exquisite afternoon dress of old rose cloth, hand embroidered in pink silk. This last garment cost eighty dollars. My old ingrained, economical instincts gave a wild squawk of protest as I said "I'll take it," but I heeded them not. There was no reason why I should. Yet I don't think I shall ever be able to spend money like this without an effort. I shall always have to remind myself that I can afford it—always have to appease my conscience by telling it that eighty dollars means no more to me now than eight once did. There have been very few years in my life when eighty dollars would not have covered the cost of all the clothes I got in that year.

In the late afternoon we went home and I had just time to dress when the ever useful Mr. Nernay again arrived with the customary taxi to take me out

"Front view, Page home"
[*Boston, Mass.*]

to Brookline. We had a delightful drive there through the crisp autumn dusk gemmed with its countless lights. Brookline is a beautiful suburb and Mr. Page has a beautiful home. I was met at the door by a maid and taken straight to my room. It was a nice one—well-furnished, rather stiff, but with every convenience. I think the convenience I found "convenientest" was the mirror door of the closet. It really was scrumptious—to see yourself from top to toe in full regalia—to know just how your skirt hung and how the different parts of you harmonized.

When I had got my wraps off the maid came up with a message from Mrs. Page—would I have some tea in the library. I went down over a polished hardwood staircase, the side of which was lined with a fine collection of prints of Mr. Page's ancestors. The library is the most beautiful room I was ever in. The furnishings were in perfect taste and nothing made any inharmonious

"Corner of Page Library"

note. Built-in shelves, beautiful windows, splendid books, delightful easy chairs, big fireplace. A large picture of *Anne*—the original painting of the cover design—occupied a prominent position on the wall.

Mrs. Page is a woman of about 35 and fairly good looking but utterly without "charm". She was so very nice to me—instructed to be so by Lewis P. no doubt—that I couldn't help liking her; but I

"Mildred Page"
[*Wife of L.C. Page*]

*"Mrs. Paul Marcone
in her wedding dress"*
[*Boston*]

found nothing of the race-of-Joseph in her. We do not talk the same language.

I was not the only guest in the Page household. Mr. and Mrs. Paul Marcone of New York were there on their honeymoon. He is an Italian, his father a New York Banker, his grandfather a Sicilian count. Anita Marcone is a niece of the notable Senator Hanna and is a Philadelphian. In evening dress she is the most beautiful girl I ever saw. When she is forty she will not be beautiful— she will be fat and coarse. But just at present, in full toilette, she is something I could not keep my eyes off. She is very nice; well educated, witty, superficially clever. I really liked her. Paul was a nice little boy, likable but not in the least clever or brilliant. I can't just make out why Anita ever married him. I am rather of the opinion that their marriage was something of a runaway, so she must have been in love with him; but he seems like a schoolboy to her woman of the world.

After tea I went to my room and dressed for dinner. I like dinner in the evening. I like the soft lights gleaming on pretty faces and white necks and jewels and beautiful gowns. And I must candidly say that I liked the life of the Page menage and that it fitted me like a glove. I suspect I should grow tired of it in time and long for the old simplicity. But for a change it was very rose at the side. That night there was a notice in the *Herald* that I was in Boston and thenceforth I was besieged with invitations and telephone calls. Wednesday Mrs. Page, the Marcones and I spent the day in the new Museum of Fine Arts. It was a wonderful day—but it should have been a week instead of a day. I had

no time to *study* anything—I could only look and pass on. And there was so much to look at—I wanted to stand for an hour before everything and absorb it. The collection of Japanese pottery was marvellous—the amber room was a delight beyond words; the Egyptian department was wonderful and the Greek Statues were—Greek statues. And as for the paintings—but I cannot write about them. I had seen engravings of most of them but to see the pictures themselves was a revelation.

We must have walked unconscious miles in our peregrinations about the Museum. When we got home I was woefully tired but so full of what I had seen that I couldn't remember I was tired. In the evening we all went to see "The Chocolate Soldier." It was

L.M. Montgomery in Page garden

a musical farce and I didn't care for it. The whole thing seemed deafening and dazzling—eye, ear, and senses ached. It was considered good of its kind by the others but I didn't enjoy it at all.

The Americans are a noisy nation. I had heard and read this and now I found it out for myself. They do not seem able to enjoy themselves unless there is a tremendous noise going on about them all the time. Even in the restaurants there is such a crash of music that you have to shriek to be heard. No wonder "The American Voice" is notorious. I cannot but think such a constant racket most injurious. One may "get used to it" but the bad effect on nerves must remain.

Thursday morning I went out to Wakefield where I had promised to lunch with Lucy Lincoln Montgomery, my unseen literary correspondent. As soon as I left the train I saw her, recognizing her from her photograph. She seems to be a very sweet woman, of about 60 years of age. Her sister and brother-in-law, General and Mrs. Goodale, live with her and they have a nice home called "Gladhill." Another sister of hers, Mrs. Slocum, the wife of a college president, was also there. I spent a very delightful day. They were nice, refined, cultured people, not so aggressively "smart" as the Page set and consequently much more restful. In the evening I returned to Brookline. A Mr. and Mrs. Jones dined with the Pages that night and we had a pleasant evening. Friday morning I spent in

Lucy Lincoln Montgomery of Wakefield, Mass.

Mr. Page's office—met all the staff, was shown over the establishment and was interviewed by Mr. Alexander of the *Herald*, a canny delightful old Scotchman. Then I went home and dressed for the luncheon which Mrs. George Page gave for me that afternoon. I wore my old rose dress and carried a big bouquet of double violets which Mrs. George Page had sent. The George Pages have a beautiful home at Chestnut Hill. Mrs. George is a "sweet" little woman—very much sweeter than Mrs. L.C. but not such good company. A number of her friends were at the luncheon. It was the "smartest" function I attended in Boston. The menu was quite elaborate. Here it is—in memory of the first society function at which I was "guest of honor". Oyster cocktail, green turtle consomme, mushrooms under glass, devilled squab on toast, cucumber and tomato salad, with cheese balls, and ice cream.

To tell the dreadful truth the only thing I really liked was the ice-cream. The other courses were very pretty but I wouldn't give a fig for them compared to a good P.E.I. "duck supper" with accoutrements.

From the luncheon we went into Boston to a reception which the Boston Authors' Club gave me at their rooms in the Kensington. Arriving there I was given another box of roses with Mr. P's card. I had a most enjoyable evening, meeting so many authors whose writings I had read—Nathan Haskell Dole, Charles Follen Adams, J.L. Harbour, Helen Winslow, Abbie Farwell Brown, Ellen Douglas Deland etc. A reporter from the *Post* also came to interview me. In the article which came out next day he described me as wearing a gown which "shimmered and dazzled." And me in that quiet little old-rose frock!!

I was tired when I got home but I sat up to an unholy hour reading the MS of a novel on which Mr. Page wanted me to pass an opinion.

Saturday morning I had to hie me into town to get an evening dress for a big reception at Basil King's, to which I was invited. I got a sweet little dress of apricot chiffon over silk, with all the appurtenances thereof. Then I went to the Hotel Touraine to meet and be interviewed by a *Traveller* reporter—a girlish little creature who looked too young to be a journalist but who was quite an expert in her line, as her consequent write-up showed. When she had finished asking me questions she took me out on the Common and had a photographer "snap" me. In her write-up she said I was "petite, with the fine, delicate features of an imaginative woman."

Anita Marcone then joined me and we went to the matinee to see the "Summer Widowers." It was another musical comedy but I enjoyed it considerably because of some very beautiful scenic effects and dances in it. When it was over Mr. and Mrs. Page, Mrs. Jones, and Paul joined us and we had a table-d'hote dinner in the Rathskellar of the American House where everybody—more or less—was celebrating the big Harvard-Yale football match. I enjoyed this immensely. The bill of fare was delicious, the "sights" most interesting. I revelled in enjoyment of it all. A certain requirement of my nature, which has been starved for years seemed to be having full satisfaction at last. There are things I love better and which are far more essential to me than gay, witty companionship and conversation, delicious food, and dazzling sights—*and Chateau Yquem*. But I *do* like them very well, too, and I believe that it is necessary for my normal well-being that I should have them occasionally.

As for the Chateau Yquem—well, I didn't drink as much of it as the others did. But I had to walk *fearfully straight* when I left the table!

When all was over I was woefully tired. So Sunday morning I went out to Roslindale and just rested and loved Kenneth.

In the evening I went back to Brookline for dinner. After dinner Miss Conway of the *Republic*, called to see me—a most charming woman. I liked her "write-up" better than any of the others. It was written seriously and not in the "smart", flippant style which the younger generation of journalists seem to affect. Some of the paragraphs ran as follows:—

"As the young author entered the Pages' beautiful library one thought came to us, 'It is a repetition of history—Charlotte Bronte coming up to London'— Miss Montgomery is slight and short—indeed of a form almost childishly small, though graceful and symmetrical. She has an oval face, with delicate aquiline features, bluish-gray eyes and an abundance of dark brown hair. Her pretty pink evening gown somewhat accentuated her frail and youthful aspect. It would not be easy to exaggerate the retiring manner and untouched simplicity of this already famous woman—more and more her individuality came out, until we remembered the word of the first eminent literary man of our acquaintance who was wont to declare that the strong original characters usually develop in the small, secluded places till the unconscious shining of their light attracts attention—For all her gentleness and marked femininity of aspect she

impressed the writer as of a determined character with positive convictions—
we could not imagine her as a 'woman of affairs' or aught but the modest,
quiet little gentle woman of the warm heart and vigorous, creative brain that
she is. Bostonions are charmed with her unique personality not less than with
her books".

Have I really a "unique personality," I wonder!

When Miss Conway had gone Mrs. Mountain of the Canadian Club and
Mrs. Morrison of the Intercolonial Club came to invite me to a combined
reception of the two clubs the next evening. When bedtime came I went to my
room and finished reading that MS. If it had been any good, or had shown any
sign of promise I wouldn't have grudged the time spent on it. But it was
absolute trash. "The Flight of Virginia" received a very unfavorable report
from me—a report which, I understand, settled its fate without any further
reading.

Monday morning I went into town—by this time I had become quite accustomed to the noise and bustle, to sprinting after cars and hanging to straps—
and met Lu Ritchie and Stella and that darling Kenneth. I gave them lunch at
the *Exeter* and then I went out to Worcester to attend a reception given me by
the Maritime Association of that burg. A deputation of the folks met me at the
station and took me for an automobile drive to see the city. Then we went to
the parlors of the Presbyterian church where the reception was held. After the
reception there was a short program. I had to sit on a chair on the platform
while the Rev. MacLeod Harvey sat on the other. Then he made a speech
referring to me and my books very nicely. To me, it seemed that my dream
was growing so ridiculous that I *must* waken soon. It could not be *I* who was
sitting there on that platform, honored by "potent, wise, and reverend seig-
niors" in that fashion while the audience gazed at me as if it did really suppose
I was a celebrity! Of course it was not I. I think I really wanted to laugh—it
all seemed so absurd that they should think my presence a matter of such
moment. I never felt so utterly insignificant in all my life as I did while I was
perched there on that platform and bepraised!

I left at 5 and got to the Back Bay station at 6.30. Mrs. Morrison met me
and whisked me out to Roxbury where the Canadian Club reception was held
at Mrs. Mountain's house. I would have enjoyed it if I hadn't been very tired.
But I was "dead" tired. It seemed to me that I must have been shaking hands
and smiling and saying, "I'm glad you enjoyed it" for a year. I met a great
many Island people there and they were all lovely to me and I did feel pleased
and proud. But under it all I was thinking, "Oh, if I could just get to bed!"

I didn't get to bed until twelve, and then I was too tired to sleep. I was
taking a cold, too, and altogether I didn't spend a very pleasant night.

Tuesday afternoon I went in to town, met Stella and took her out to Brookline. Then she, the Marcones and I, started out on an expedition which filled
in the most delightful day of my whole trip. First we went to Cambridge to the
Agassiz Museum to see the "Ware Collection of Glass Flowers". I wasn't
feeling very anxious to see them for the sound of "glass flowers" didn't please
me. But I am glad I didn't miss that wonderful collection. Yes, they are indeed

wonderful—so wonderful that they don't seem wonderful at all—they seem to be absolutely real flowers and you have to keep reminding yourself that they are made of glass—of *glass*—to realize how wonderful they are.

Then we went to Lexington which of course teems with relics of the war of '76. The most interesting of them was the old Hancock-Clarke house which is kept just as it was then and contains besides a great number of relics collected from all over New England. We had lunch at the Russell House and then went to Concord. Concord is the only place I saw when I was away where I would like to live. It is a most charming spot and I shall never forget the delightful drive we had around it. We saw the "Old Manse" where Hawthorne lived during his honeymoon and where he wrote "Mosses from an Old Manse", the "Wayside" where he also lived, the "Orchard

L.M. Montgomery, Anita Marcone, Stella Campbell

House" where Louisa Alcott wrote, and Emerson's house. It gave a strange reality to the books of theirs which I have read to see those places where they once lived and labored. We were very sorry that we could not go to the Sleepy Hollow cemetery and see their graves but we had not time.

Stella stayed all night with me. Wednesday was the most strenuous day I put in up there. In the forenoon, Mr. Page's mother, Mrs. Dana Estes (she was married twice) called on me—a very stately and imposing old dame. She took me for a pleasant drive around Brookline in her limousine and then drove me to the Hotel Touraine where the three girls from Mr. Page's office, Miss Lacey, Miss Chapman, and Miss Lebert gave me a luncheon. It was very sweet of them, but, beyond the by no means insignificant pleasure of tasting good food, there was no especial enjoyment in it for me. The girls seemed rather in awe of me and I consequently couldn't feel especially at ease with them. Besides, I was really so tired that it was an effort to talk at all. From there Mrs. Page and I went to a celebration of the N.E. Women's Press Association's 25th Anniversary in the Hotel Vendome. This was a big affair and the only thing I didn't enjoy in Boston at all. I was bored. The program didn't interest me at all. Then I had been asked to stand on the receiving line and I stood for two weary hours and shook hands with hundreds of women, who all said pretty much the same thing and had to receive pretty much the same answer. When Mrs. Page and I finally left I told her I was sure a smile must be glued on my face and that I doubted if I could say anything for the rest of my life but the parrot cry of "I'm glad you liked it." Anne, Anne, you little red-headed monkey, you are responsible for much!

We got home at half past six. I was dreadfully tired—so tired that I shrank from the thought of going to another reception that night. But a good dinner, a half hour's rest and the excitement of dressing toned me up again. My chiffon dress looked very pretty. It was the first time I had ever worn a low-necked dress and at first I felt as if I wasn't clothed at all. I had had my hair done in town and wore little pink satin roses in it, and I had a lovely white chiffon beaded scarf and the dearest little black velvet slippers. At least, I thought they were dear when I put them on; but there is a sequel to that.

"In evening dress for the first time" [LMM, c. 1910]

When we got out of the cab at the King house I happened to look up, while Mrs. Page was making some arrangements with the chauffeur, and I saw that the moon was in eclipse! Instantly I thought of home—I could see the dark hills, the old fields, the distant woods. If I had been home I would have been watching that eclipse—and it would have given me a keener delight and a more real pleasure than even the Basil King reception.

But the latter was very enjoyable. The Kings have a beautiful home and are very nice people. He is a noted author—a very peculiar-looking man, his peculiarity enhanced by green goggles, but he has a delightful voice and manner. The rooms swarmed with celebrities. One was Colonel Thomas Wentworth Higginson, a very old man, the sole survivor of the Longfellow-Whittier-Emerson set. I, myself, seemed not altogether uncelebrated. When I came away Mrs. King said, "You have been our 'great gun' this evening." Altogether, I had a really lovely time. But still, I did regret missing that eclipse!

I enjoyed that reception; and yet through it all I endured "agony untold." Those wretched slippers! They "drew" my feet until I could have shrieked. The minute I got into our homeward cab I kicked them off, thanking "whatever gods there be" for the relief.

Next morning I had to go into town and be photographed for the Press Bureau. That done I visited the State library—a very beautiful building; but I was too tired to enjoy it. After lunch I packed up; and that evening on the 7.30 train I left Boston. Mr. Page went to the station with me. A deputation from the Canadian and Intercolonial clubs were there to see me off. The ladies of the clubs gave me a bouquet of violets, the gentlemen gave me a box of big yellow chrysanthemums, and Mr. Page had another box of violets sent up. Then the train pulled out and I went to bed. In the morning I reached St. John. Aunt Mary met me and I stayed with them until Saturday. In the afternoon I went to a tea and spent the evening with a Mrs. Smith—a very clever woman, not quite clever enough to conceal her cleverness and consequently something of a bore now and then—but very kind and jolly.

I left next noon and arrived in Kensington at 8.30. I stepped off the train into a black, snowy night. My easy, pleasant times were over.

George Campbell met me but gave his place to Bruce Howatt who was looking for a chance down. We had a horrible drive. The roads were so bad the horse could only walk and the sleet blew in our faces the whole way—quite a change from the drives I had been having. Somehow, the whole thing seemed symbolical. I was going back to the worries and discomforts of my usual life. That drive was typical.

But we got to Park Corner eventually. I stayed there until Monday. It was very lonely without the girls. George brought me home on Monday. I found everything as usual and all well. Since then I have been very busy, trying to catch up with the accumulated work and correspondence. We have had a great deal of rain and it has made things very dull. I have also had a bad cold and am only now getting over it.

Sunday, Dec. 11, 1910
Cavendish, P.E.I.
This was a fine day and this evening I had a most beautiful and soul satisfying walk in Lover's Lane. Since coming home I have been so busy and the weather

"Lover's Lane"
[Cavendish, PEI]

and walking so bad that I had no opportunity to go before.

I have never found the lane so exquisite as it was tonight. It was not the Lover's Lane of June, blossom-misted, tender in young green; nor yet the Lover's Lane of September, splendid in crimson and gold. It was the Lover's Lane of a still, snowy winter twilight—a white, mysterious silent place, full of wizardry. I walked softly through it and, as ever, all things of life fell into their relative places of importance. The pleasures of my Boston trip seemed, after all, quite tawdry and insignificant and unsatisfying compared to the spirit delight of that dream-haunted solitude. That wood lane caters to the highest in my soul. *Its* pleasures never cloy—*its* remote charm never palls. How shall I ever be able to live without it?

Monday, Dec. 26, 1910
Cavendish, P.E.I.
Yesterday was Christmas—a very dreary day. It rained heavily from dawn to dark. This past fortnight has been dreary all through—bad weather, bad walk-

ing and a great many worries, especially over Aunt Annie's recent illness, a bad attack of congestion of the lungs. I have felt very dull and dispirited and, worst of all, there has been a return of that terrible feeling of inability and lack of strength to cope with life. Oh, I hope I shall not be as ill this winter as I was last. I shall never forget the horror of it. I would rather die than go through such a time again. But I hope I shall not be so bad. I feel much better physically than I did this time last year. And then I have Margaret near by to go to when I feel a "blue" spell coming on. An hour of cheery chat with her generally averts or at least lessens the nervous attack. So far, too, I am sleeping well.

I have been revelling for a week in Mrs. Gaskell's novels, Mr. Macdonald having given me a complete set of her works at Christmas. They are delightful. And I have read "Romola" again. Oh, truly, there were giants in those days in literature. We haven't a writer today of either sex who can compete with them. While reading those books I felt ashamed to think I had written things I called books at all. Mine seemed so trivial and petty compared to those masterpieces.

Saturday, Dec. 31, 1910
Cavendish, P.E.I.
Have been reading Bliss Carman's "Pipes of Pan." I enjoyed them, too. Carman is the foremost American poet of the present. That, to be sure, is not a dizzy elevation. There are no master singers nowadays. Some of Carman's work is very charming—yes, that's just the word for it—charming. A large dose of it palls. He has only one or two notes and the constant repetition of these becomes monotonous, no matter how much they pleased at first. Then, he deals only with the *joy* of life. And no poet can be great who does not take the *pain* of life also into his poetry.

1911

Tuesday, Jan. 17, 1911
Cavendish, P.E.I.
....I tried to do a little at revising a short story this evening. Mr. Page wants to bring out a volume of short stories sometime and I am re-writing such of them as are worth including in such a volume. I think very few of them are. Most of my short stories were written as "pot-boilers." I should like to write some good short stories. I consider it a very high form of art. It is easier to write a good novel than a good short story....

Sunday, Jan. 22, 1911
Cavendish, P.E.I.
....Last night at twilight I heard a sound of something falling upstairs. I dragged myself up to see what it was and could have cried—*did* cry—when I saw a lot of plaster fallen from the ceiling in my room. Plaster has fallen from nearly every ceiling in the house as a result of old leaks and I have had many trying times endeavoring to patch up the breaks with white cotton. But hitherto my own dear little room has escaped. And now such a sight! A great, ugly stretch of bare lathes over my bookcase, all the pretty paper torn and hanging in shreds. Somehow, it hurt me terribly. It seemed to have an evil symbolism. All my old world is falling into ruins. And oh, what will the new be like, even if I have strength to fashion it? Well, I suppose I can repair the damage in my room in some fashion but it will never look the same again.

I have been re-reading the life of Charlotte Bronte by Mrs. Gaskell this week. It is a wonderful book. It is hard to decide whether its charm is due to Mrs. Gaskell's style or to the real life of Charlotte Bronte—that woman genius whose outward life was so hard and bitter and tragic. It is a dear wish of my heart to make some day a pilgrimage to Haworth and see the old house she lived in and wrote her wonderful books in....

Something I read to-day set me thinking about trees—especially the old trees that are, or used to be, around this old house. Some of them are very dear to me. I have always loved them; and when I have "lived with" a tree for a long time it seems to me like a beloved human companion....

In the south-east corner was a spot I liked—"No Man's Land"—a comparatively open space with some fine maples and a beautiful birch in it. Close to the fence grew a pair I called "The Lovers"—a spruce and a maple so closely intertwined that the boughs of the maple were literally interlaced with those of the spruce. I remember I wrote a poem about them—"The Tree Lovers." They really did seem fond of each other and they lived in happy union for many

36

years. They are dead now. The little maple died first and the spruce held her dead form in his green faithful arms for two more years. But his heart was broken and he died too. They were beautiful in their lives, and in death not long divided; and they nourished a child's heart with a grace-giving fancy....

Just inside the south-west corner of the dyke grew a most beautiful little birch tree. I always called it "The Lady" and had a fancy about it to the effect that it was the beloved of all the dark spruces near and that they were all rivals for its love. It was the whitest, straightest thing ever seen. A few years ago Uncle John cut it down. He has been cutting the trees down recklessly for firewood ever since grandfather's death but I notice he never plants any. I notice, too, that it is always some favorite tree of mine that is cut down—a petty spite which is very characteristic of the man. It went to my heart that "The Lady" should be cut down. And yet I think I would rather that than know it was here after I had gone, neglected and unloved, growing old and ragged and unshapely. In my memory it will live as long as I do, young and fair and maiden like....

Of course, the apple trees were dear friends of mine too. The "front" orchard was the oldest one having been planted by grandfather's father, old "Speaker Macneill". We always called it "the front garden", although there was no garden in it. But there had been once and the name clung. The only traces of it left were in a blue-flowered, ivy-like plant, which grew lavishly in all the open spaces, and the caraway that spread wildly. The trees were nearly all "sweet" and we children were about the only ones who cared for the apples. The tree I loved best there was a very old one, near the spruce bush, leaning wholly over to the south like a bent broken old crone.

The "back" orchard was the one grandfather and grandmother had planted. Every tree in it had some humble, homely name. Just inside the gate on the left was a square of four large trees—"Uncle John's tree", "Aunt Emily's tree", "Aunt Clara's tree", (my mother's) and "Uncle Leander's tree". "Aunt Annie's tree" and "Uncle Chester's tree" had died. These four trees all bore large sweet apples. I called the space they overshadowed "The Bower". It was fit for a queen's bower in blossom time. Just behind Aunt Emily's tree was a smaller sweet tree called "Russell's tree" for the excellent reason that every fall we gave the apples to Russell Macneill who came up and picked them....

Since grandfather's death the orchard has been neglected and is a poor place now. It blooms and bears scantly. Today, in the graceless nakedness of a snowless winter, it is a sorry place. Only sometimes of a summer night in blossom time the moon makes a spell of wizardry, and youth returns for a space to the old orchard....

God be thanked for trees. I shall always be grateful that my childhood was passed in a spot where there were many trees—"old ancestral trees", planted and tended by hands long dead, bound up with everything of joy and sorrow that visited the lives in their shadow.

Dear old trees! I hope you all have souls and will grow again for me on the hills of heaven....

Friday, Jan. 27, 1911
Cavendish, P.E.I.

Margaret and I had a delightful walk down the road this evening in the twilight. It was a very still, breathless evening—a storm evidently brewing. The world was white and dim and windless.

I cannot get used to the pleasantness of having a congenial friend near me. It seems rather unnatural. I have never had living near me a friend with whom I could talk freely on subjects near to my heart. Even long ago, when I regarded Amanda and Lucy as friends, there was never any real communion of spirit or mind between us. Lucy could talk of nothing but dress and petty gossip and Amanda was little better. And of late years there has been no one near me with whom I could, or cared to, go any deeper than the surface. But now I have Margaret with whom I can discuss many—not all—subjects, understanding and understood. It means much to me. A little congenial companionship goes a long way to sweeten life.

After Margaret went in I prowled about a bit by myself. There were no stars out but there were shadowy woods and white spaces and dim tree-lands. I looked on them and loved them. How I love Cavendish! I love it for its beauty—I love it for its old associations, as I will never love any other spot on earth.

To-day I was again annoyed and amused—with the annoyance distinctly uppermost—to be asked, as I so constantly am, "Was So—and—So the original of This—or—That in your books"?

This annoys me because I have *never* drawn any of the characters in my books "from life", although I may have taken a quality here and an incident there. I have used real places and speeches freely but I have never put any person I knew into my books. I may do so some day but hitherto I have depended wholly on the creative power of my own imagination for my book folk.

Nevertheless I have woven a good deal of reality into my books. Cavendish is to a large extent *Avonlea*. Mrs. *Rachel Lynde's* house, with the brook below, was drawn from Pierce Macneill's house. I also gave Mrs. Pierce's name to Mrs. *Lynde* but beyond that there was no connection whatever between them. *Green Gables* was drawn from David Macneill's house, now Mr. Webb's—though not so much the house itself as the situation and scenery, and the truth of my description of it is attested by the fact that everybody has recognized it. Had they stopped there it would be well, but they went further and insist that David and Margaret Macneill figure as *Matthew* and *Marilla*. They do not. The *Matthew* and *Marilla* I had in mind were entirely different people from David and Margaret. I suppose the fact that David is a notoriously shy and silent man makes people think I drew Matthew from him. But I made Matthew shy and silent simply because I wished to have all the people around *Anne* as pointedly in contrast with her as possible.

In connection with this there was one odd coincidence which probably helped to establish the conviction that David was *Matthew*. *Green Gables* was illustrated by an artist unknown to me and to whom Cavendish and David were

"Ernest Webb's House from Back"
[*Cavendish*]

alike unknown. Nevertheless, it cannot be denied that the picture of Matthew when he brings *Anne* home, has a very strong resemblance to David Macneill.

The brook that runs below the *Cuthbert* place and through *Lynde's Hollow* is, of course, my own dear brook of the woods which runs below Webb's and through "Pierce's Hollow".

Although I had the Webb place in mind I did not confine myself to facts at all. There are, I think, willows in the yard but there are no "Lombardies", such as *Anne* heard talking in their sleep. Those were transplanted from the estates of my castle in Spain. And it was by no means as tidy as I pictured *Green Gables*—at least, before the Webbs came there. Quite the reverse in fact, David's yard was notoriously *untidy*. It was a local saying that if you wanted to see what the world looked like on the morning after the flood you should go into David's barnyard on a rainy day!

They had a good cherry orchard but no apple orchard. However, I can easily create an apple orchard when I need one!

Marilla is generally accredited to Margaret. This is absurd. Whatever accidental resemblance there may be between David and *Matthew* there is none whatever between Margaret and *Marilla*. The former is a very intelligent, broad-minded woman, which poor *Marilla* certainly was not. Others imagine *Marilla* was drawn from grandmother. This is also false. There are certain qualities common to Marilla and grandmother—and to many others—but those qualities I put into *Marilla* for the same reason I made *Matthew* silent and shy—to furnish a background for *Anne*.

When I am asked if *Anne* herself is a "real person" I always answer "no" with an odd reluctance and an uncomfortable feeling of not telling the truth. For she is and always has been, from the moment I first thought of her, so real to me that I feel I am doing violence to something when I deny her an existence anywhere save in Dreamland. Does she not stand at my elbow even now—if I turned my head quickly should I not see her—with her eager, starry eyes and her long braids of red hair and her little pointed chin? To tell that haunting elf that she is not *real*, because, forsooth, I never met her in the flesh! No, I cannot do it! She *is* so real that, although I've never met her, I feel quite sure I shall do so some day—perhaps in a stroll through Lover's Lane in the twilight—or in the moonlit Birch Path—I shall lift my eyes and find her, child or maiden, by my side. And I shall not be in the least surprised because I have always known she was *somewhere*.

The idea of getting a child from an orphan asylum was suggested to me years ago as a possible germ for a story by the fact that Pierce Macneill got a little girl from one, and I jotted it down in my note book. There is no resemblance of any kind between *Anne* and Ellen Macneill who is one of the most hopelessly commonplace and uninteresting girls imaginable. But I may mention here another odd co-incidence. Although Ellen Macneill never crossed my mind while I was writing the book, yet a stranger who was in Cavendish two years ago, boarding at Pierce's, told Ellen that her profile was exactly like the *Anne* profile on the cover of *Green Gables*! And when I heard this I agreed that it was, although the profile on the book has distinction while Ellen's is hopelessly common. This picture was also drawn by an artist who had never seen Cavendish or Ellen!

Bright River is Hunter River. *Anne's* dislike of being laughed at because she used big words is a bitter remembrance of my own childhood. *The White Way of Delight* is practically pure imagination. Yet the idea was suggested to me by a short stretch of road between Kensington and Clinton, which I always thought very beautiful. The trees meet overhead for a short distance but they are beech trees, not apple trees.

Anne's habit of naming places was an old one of my own. The *Lake of Shining Waters* is generally supposed to be the Cavendish Pond. This is not so.

The pond at Park Corner is the one I had in mind. But I suppose that a good many of the effects of light and shadow I have seen on the Cavendish pond figured unconsciously in my descriptions; and certainly the hill from which *Anne* caught her first glimpse of it was "Laird's Hill", where I have often stood at sunset, enraptured with the beautiful view of shining pond and crimson-brimmed harbor and dark blue sea.

"Corner of Lake of Shining Waters"

White Sands was Rustico and the "shore road" has a real existence, and is a very beautiful drive. I remember one moonlight drive I had around that road. I shall never forget the starry, sparkling, shimmering beauty of sky and sea.

The house in which *Anne* was born was drawn from my own little birthplace at Clifton. The *Katie Maurice* of Anne was *my* Katie Maurice—that imaginary playmate of the glass bookcase door in our sitting room. The idea of the *Haunted Wood* was of course taken from the old Haunted Wood of the Nelson boys and myself. But the wood I had in mind as far as description went was the spruce-clad hill across the brook hollow from Webb's. The *Dryad's Bubble* was purely imaginary but the "old log bridge" was a real thing. It was formed by a single large tree that had blown down and lay across the brook. As far back as I can remember it lay there and must have served as a bridge for a generation before that for it was hollowed out like a shell from the tread of hundreds of passing feet. Earth had blown into its crevices and ferns and grasses had found root in it and fringed it luxuriantly. Velvet moss covered its sides. Below was a clear, sun-flecked stream.

A year or two ago the old log-bridge became so worn and slender that it was quite unsafe. So Mr. Webb put a little bridge of longers across the brook and we use that now.

Anne's tribulations over puffed sleeves were an echo of my old childish longing after "bangs". "Bangs" came in when I was about ten. In the beginning they figured as a straight, heavy fringe of hair cut squarely across the forehead. A picture of "banged" hair of course looks absurd enough now; but, like all fashions, "bangs" looked all right when they were "in". And to anybody with a high forehead they were very becoming.

Well, bangs were "all the rage". All the girls in school had them. I wanted a "bang" terribly. But grandfather and grandmother would never hear of it. This was unwise and unjust on their part. Whatever the present day taste may think of "bangs" it would not have done me or anyone any harm to have allowed me to have one and it would have saved me many a bitter pang. How I did long for "bangs"! Father wanted me to have them—he always wanted me to have any innocent thing I desired. Oh, how well he understood a child's heart! I often pleaded with him when he came to see me (that was the winter he was home from the west) to cut a "bang" for me, but he never would because he knew it would offend grandmother. I was often tempted to cut one myself but I dreaded their anger too much. I knew that if I did I would be railed at as if I had disgraced myself forever and that I would never set down to the table that grandfather would not sneer at them.

"Bangs" remained in a long time—nearly twenty years. When I was fifteen and went out west I got my long-wished for "bang" at last. Grandfather sneered at it when I went home, of course, but the thing was done and he had to reconcile himself to it. Besides, the "bang" had changed a good deal in that time. The heavy straight bang was gone and the accepted fashion was an upward curling fluff, not unlike the pompadour of today in general effect, with only a loose curl or two downwards. How I did envy girls with naturally curly hair! My hair was very straight. I had to curl my poor fringe constantly and even then the least dampness would reduce it to stringy dismalness. It is only about six years since bangs went hopelessly out. It is not likely they will ever come in again—in my time at least. But I shall never forget them. I longed for them and how humiliated I felt when I could not have them.

I had beautiful hair when I was a child—very long, thick, and a golden brown. It turned very dark when I grew up—much to my disappointment. I love fair hair.

The *Spectator*, in reviewing *Green Gables*—*very* favorably, I might say—said that possibly *Anne's* precocity was slightly overdrawn in the statement that a child of eleven would appreciate the dramatic effect of the lines,

> "Quick as the slaughtered squadrons fell
> In Midian's evil day."

But I was only nine years old when those lines thrilled my very soul as I recited them in Sunday School. All through the following sermon I kept repeating them to myself. To this day they give me a mysterious pleasure.

I remember that Maggie Abbott and I swore eternal friendship as *Anne* and *Diana* did. Only we did not do it in a garden but standing on a high loft beam in Uncle John Montgomery's barn at Malpeque. Amanda and I also once wrote out two "Notes of Promise", vowing everlasting faith, had them witnessed by two of the schoolgirls, and finished them up with a red seal. I have mine yet somewhere. I think I was true to *my* vow. But if Amanda thinks she was, her ideal of friendship must be very different from mine. Still, she *was* my friend once in childhood and early girlhood. Perhaps she could not help—or did not know how to help—the strange temperamental change which came over her at the threshold of womanhood. These things are bound up with physiological mysteries beyond our penetration. In early life Amanda was her mother's child. When she grew up her dormant inheritance from her father developed and she changed into an altogether different being. To me, the Amanda who was my girlhood friend is as one dead. I think of her lovingly and regretfully. I can never feel that the Amanda of to-day is the same person as my friend of long ago....

Anne's idea that diamonds looked like amethysts was once mine. I did not know there were such stones as amethysts but I had read of diamonds. I had never seen one nor heard one described, and I pictured to myself a beautiful stone of living purple. When Uncle Chester brought Aunt Hattie to see us after their marriage I saw the little diamond in her ring and I was much disappointed. "It wasn't my idea of a diamond"—well, many things in life and in the world have not been like my idea of them! I love diamonds now—I love their pure, cold, dewlike sheen and glitter. But once they were a bitter disillusion to me.

Lover's Lane was of course *my* Lover's Lane. *Willowmere* and *Violet Vale* were compact of imagination. But the Birch Path exists somewhere, I know not where. I have a picture of it—the reproduction of a photo which was published in the *Outing* magazine one year. Somewhere in America that lane of birches is. *Avonlea* school was the Cavendish school, but the teachers were mythical. *Miss Stacey* resembled Miss Gordon in some respects but I cannot say she was drawn from her. The episode of the mouse falling into the pudding sauce once happened to a friend of mine—Mrs. George Matheson; old Literary concerts furnished forth the description of the concert in *Avonlea Hall*. The scene where *Anne* and *Diana*, jump into bed on poor *Miss Barry* was suggested to me by a story father told me of how he and two other boys had jumped into bed on an old minister in the spare room at Uncle John Montgomery's long ago. I worked it up into a short story, published early in my career in *Golden Days*; then used the idea later on in my book. The old "Mayflower" picnics of Miss Gordon's devising were used. The affecting farewell speech of James MacLeod was used also although, to do Jim justice, he was not in any respect like *Teddy Phillips*, being a very fair teacher. We used to make balsam Rainbows in the school spring, just as *Anne* and *Diana* made them in *the Dryad's Bubble*.

"The Birch Path"
[*From* Outing *magazine*]

As for the notable incident of the liniment cake—when I was teaching in Bideford Mrs. Estey flavored a layer cake with anodyne liniment just as it happened in the story. Never shall I forget the taste of that cake. What fun we had over it! A strange minister was there to tea that night—a Mr. Kirby—and *he* ate all his piece of cake. What he thought of it we never knew. Possibly he imagined it was simply some new-fangled kind of flavoring. The dialogues which the girls had in their concerts "The Society for The Suppression of Gossip" and "The Fairy Queen" were old stand-bys of schooldays. We had the former at our first school concert in which I personated the amiable "Miss Wise", and the latter at a school examination. I was the *Fairy Queen*, being thought fitted for the part by reason of my long hair which I wore crimped and floating over my shoulders from a wreath of pink tissue roses. I "appeared" suddenly through the school door, in answer to an incantation, in all the glory of white dress, roses, hair, kid slippers and wand—and I enjoyed my own dramatic appearance quite as much as anybody! That really was one of the most *satisfying* moments of my life.

The Story Club was suggested by a little incident of one summer long ago when Jamie Simpson, Amanda Macneill, and I all wrote a story on the same plot. I furnished the plot and I remembered only that it was a very tragic one and the heroine was drowned. I haven't the stories now—I wish I had—but they were very sad. It was the first, and probably the last, time that Jamie and Amanda attempted fiction but I had already quite a little library of stories—in which almost everybody died! I do wish I had kept them. I burned them in exasperation on the day I realized what trash they were. They *were* trash—but they would have been quite valuable trash to me now, because they were so enormously funny. One was entitled "My Graves" and was a long tale of the various peregrinations of a minister's wife. I made her a Methodist minister's wife so that she would have to peregrinate frequently. She buried a child in every place she lived in! All Canada, from Newfoundland to Vancouver, was peppered with "her" graves. I wrote the story in the first person, described the children, pictured out their death-beds and described their tombstones and epitaphs! That story was never finished. After having killed off about seven children—she was to have thirteen altogether—I wearied of so much infanticide and ceased from my slaughter of the innocents.

Then there was "The History of Flossie Brighteyes"—the autobiography of a doll. I couldn't kill a doll but I dragged her through every other tribulation. However, I allowed her to have a happy end with a good little girl who loved her for the dangers she had passed and did not mind a few legs and eyes missing.

But what dazzlingly lovely heroines I had! And how I dressed them! Silks—satins—velvets—laces—they never wore anything else! And I literally poured diamonds and rubies and pearls over them. But what booted beauty and rich attire? "The paths of glory lead but to the grave". They must either be murdered or die of a broken heart. There was no escape for them.

The incident of *Anne's* dyeing her hair was purely imaginary. Oddly enough, however, after *Green Gables* was written, but before it was published, Sadie Macneill, a Cavendish girl who had fiery tresses died her hair black. I was appalled when I heard of it for I felt sure that everyone, when the book came out, would think that I had made use of this fact. And they did! And probably always will! And her family are furious with me! Yet am I innocent.

The entrance examination of *Queen's* was "drawn from life" as well as the weeks of suspense that followed. *Matthew's* death was not, as some have supposed, suggested by grandfather's. Poor Matthew must die so that there might arise the necessity for self-sacrifice on Anne's part. So he joined the long procession of ghosts that haunt my literary past.

There was less of "real life" in *Avonlea* than in *Green Gables*, and much more of invention. Some of my own experiences in school-teaching were reflected in it, but in the atmosphere only, not in the incidents. I felt exactly as *Anne* felt when she opened school the first day—and I was as woefully tired and discouraged at night. My Bideford pupils used to drive crickets. A Bideford pupil gave the same definition of "freckles" as *Jimmy Andrews* did—"George Howell's face, ma'am", and several other answers were genuine.

The scene of the walk in the *Golden Picnic* was laid through the woods and fields back of Lover's Lane but Hester's garden is purely imaginary. *Davy's* idea that heaven was in *"Simon Fletcher's* garret" was suggested by a belief of my own childhood. One Sunday when I was very small—I could not, I think have been more than four—I was with Aunt Emily in Clifton church—the old church with its square box pews. I heard the minister say something about heaven. "Where is heaven?" I whispered to Aunt Emily. She simply pointed upward. With childhood's literal and implicit belief I took it for granted that this meant the attic of Clifton church. For a long time I firmly believed that heaven was there! As mother was "in heaven" she must be there, too. Now, why could we not get up there and see her? There was a square hole in the ceiling. Surely it was quite possible. It was a great puzzle to me that nobody ever seemed to think of doing it. I resolved that when I grew older *I* would find some way of getting to Clifton and getting up into heaven anyhow. Alas! Hood wrote in his delightful "I Remember" that he was further off from heaven then when he was a boy. I can echo that. When I was a child heaven was only seven miles away. But now! Is it not beyond the furthest star?

Kilmeny reflects very little out of my own experience. *Jack Reid's* sentence, "Courting is a very pleasant thing which a great many people go too far with" was the *bona fide* opening sentence Jack Millar wrote in a composition in Bideford school. The view of *Lindsay Harbor* and the gulf, with the revolving light, is drawn from the view I have so often gazed on over New London Harbor. "Old Charlie's" Latin prayer was really delivered by old Professor Macdonald at a Dalhousie convocation. James Laird's place up on the hill was my model of the *Williamson* place—but James and Mrs. Laird are most decidedly *not* the *Williamsons*. The woods through which *Eric* walked to meet his fate are the woods beyond Lover's Lane.

Sunday, Feb. 5, 1911
Cavendish, P.E.I.
....This week in a book of Barrie's I came across the following pertinent little sentence:—

"This is indeed a sad truth that we seldom give our love to what is worthiest in its object."

I shut the book and leaned back to think it over. Yes, it *is* a truth—and a sad one. We do not love people for what is worthiest in them. We *admire* them for their good qualities, but we do not *love* them for them. Nay, worse, we often love them for what is positively unworthy. I do not mean "love" as merely between man and woman—I refer to all kinds of love. It is very hard—nay, it is impossible to explain why we love some people and have no love for others. I know many people who, I feel sure, are good and admirable. Yet I find no pleasure in their society and in some cases dislike them. Again, they are people who are far from being perfect whom I do love and in whose society I find delight and satisfaction. Now, why is this? "Oh," says someone, "it is because you are very far from being good yourself that you dislike good people and find your kindred spirits among those not so good."

Well, this would be a very simple explanation if I disliked *all* good people and liked only bad ones! But I do not. There are many good people whom I fondly love and there are many not good whom I cannot tolerate at all. So that can't be how it is. George Eliot says, "In that curious compound, the feminine character, it may easily happen that the flavor is unpleasant in spite of excellent ingredients." Had she said "human" in place of feminine she would have struck the mark even more fairly, for I know many men of whom the same can be said. "Excellent ingredients"—yes; but they are not mixed well—baked well—the flavoring is left out—or, as with Mrs. Estey and the anodyne liniment, a distasteful flavor has been chosen. Yes, I believe *that* is the secret. *Sam Weller* says "It's all in the seasoning"—kitten or veal, it doesn't matter so long as it is properly flavored. Yes, it's "all in the seasoning". But for all that it is, as Barrie says, a sad thing that we do not and cannot love people for their good qualities alone, regardless of what may be lacking.

Tennyson says,

"We needs must love the highest when we see it."

But that is false—utterly false! There is no such compulsion—more's the pity. We must *admire* the highest when we see it—but it does *not* command our *love*. *Guinevere* was right when she said "The low sun makes the color."

I re-read *Adam Bede* this week. It is a great novel in spite of its inartistic ending. I could have pardoned the marriage of *Adam* and *Dinah*, however, if it had not been brought about in such a hurried and artificial manner. *Mrs. Poyser* is a delightful creature in a book. Out of it she might not be so agreeable. The character of *Hetty Sorrel* is wonderfully analyzed. *Dinah* is just a little bit too good for "human nature's daily food". Yet there are such people—and the rest of us are not fit to untie their shoe latchets. Nevertheless, *Dinah* does not enlist our sympathy or interest. We don't care a hoot whether she ever gets a husband or not. But our hearts go out to poor, pretty, vain, sinning, suffering Hetty. After all, it is the sinners we love and pity—perhaps because they are nearer to ourselves and we recognize so many of our own hidden weaknesses in them. So perhaps it is a kind of self-pity or self-excuse which leads us to pity and excuse them. "To understand is to forgive."

February 6, 1911
Cavendish, P.E.I.
Last night, when coming out of church, I saw one of the young bloods of Cavendish step up rather bashfully to a miss of fifteen and ask in the time honored formula "May I see you home?" I do not know if it was the first time she had been thus accosted but, judging from her expression, as they went past the lighted window arm in arm, I am inclined to think it was. Hers was the face of one upon whom the cachet of young ladyhood has been conferred. She was "grown up". She had "an escort home"!!

I smiled—and continued to smile as I took my escortless way across the field home. I thought of olden things and of the wonderful night, so amazingly long ago, when I, too, had an "escort home" for the first time—both of us secretly and desperately elated—he, in "seeing home", I, in being seen home....

Thursday, Feb. 9, 1911
Cavendish, P.E.I.
Stella came down Tuesday to spend a few days and we have been putting in a jolly time. This morning we went down to Will Houston's and spent the day. As usual there we had a delightful time. And as Stella was with me I could

enjoy it without being haunted by the secret fear that I might have to drive home alone with Will!

There are few—if any—things in life without a flaw. The "trail of the serpent" *must* reveal itself—some little mis-weaving or mischance *must* mar the perfect pattern. For several years my friendship with Tillie Houston has been one of the pleasantest things in my life. Yet it has been shadowed for me by my knowledge that her husband was in love with me and made no scruple of avowing it to me.

Tillie Houston was formerly Tillie McKenzie, my mother's first cousin. In her youth she was *not* the charming and lovable woman into which she developed later in life. She was remarkably beautiful and her beauty was not a blessing to her. It attracted around her a crowd of not always worthy admirers and "beaux"; and it seemed, in her own estimation, to absolve her from the necessity of making any effort to please apart from her beauty. In brief, I think, from what I recall hearing others say, that she presumed on her beauty. As a result, she was not well liked by her own sex; and, in spite of her numerous lovers, she did not marry and several broken engagements left her with something of a "shopworn" savor.

When I was a child of ten father was home from the west for a visit. Tillie, then 26 years old and still very pretty, attracted him. She liked him in return and their marriage would probably have been the result if it had not been for grandmother's interference. Somehow or other—I do not rightly know how— she succeeded in turning father against Tillie and the affair was broken off. It was long before Tillie forgave her for that. She and grandma had a bitter quarrel over it and for many years she never spoke to grandma or came here, though she was always friendly to me when we met elsewhere. I do not blame her for her resentment. Grandmother should certainly not have meddled in the matter at all. In view of the fine woman which Tillie eventually became it certainly was a great mistake. Father married a woman whose evil temper and hateful disposition made his life miserable, whereas with Tillie he would have been happy. But, as I have said, Tillie was at this time a rather frivolous beauty and grandmother cannot be altogether blamed for thinking none too highly of her. What *was* blameworthy was her meddling in the matter—and her *motive*, which was not any wish to serve father's interests or promote his happiness but a determination that Tillie McKenzie should not occupy her daughter's vacant place.

Well, father went away again and Tillie drifted more and more into an old maidenhood which I think was especially bitter to her. She had to occupy a home where a married brother and his family lived. She had no recognized place in society. Her beauty faded to a marked degree. She always remained a nice looking woman but nothing compared to what she had been.

Finally, at the age of 39, she married Will Houston of North Rustico.

Will was a remarkably handsome man, with an agreeable personality. He was also very well off. But he did not belong to Tillie's class. He was—a Houston! Moreover, his associates were of an inferior caste and he had a somewhat rank reputation where "wine and women" were concerned.

But Tillie, to use the country phrase, "made a man of him". Too often, when a woman marries beneath her, she sinks to the level of her husband's caste. Tillie was an exception to this rule. She lifted her husband to hers. He went with her into the society of her class; in a few years his old reputation was

"*Mr. & Mrs. Wm. Houston*"
[*Tillie McKenzie Houston*]

forgotten and he had acquired a new one, that of being a charming fellow. As for Tillie, she also seemed a changed being. She had a nice home and a certain prestige in society as the result of being the mistress of it. She loved her husband and believed herself loved in return. In this congenial soil of happiness all the better qualities of her character, hitherto shadowed and dwarfed, first by vanity and frivolity, and then by discontent and disappointment, began to grow and flourish. She became a staunch, loyal, sympathetic woman, with enough love of him and mirth to render her a very pleasant comrade and enough tact and tenderness to make her a true friend. In a very few years people had forgotten that she was ever anything else. She became beloved by everyone.

She and Will live in an old-fashioned cosy house in North Rustico. Tillie's taste has made of it a pretty, dainty place. She is a pattern housekeeper and a queen of cooks. Out of doors she has a lovely garden and orchard. Altogether, it is a charming spot. She and Will seem—and indeed are—a very harmonious pair. They entertain their friends royally and they visit a great deal—a smiling, good-looking, prosperous middle-aged couple.

All this would appear happiness. And it *is* happiness for both of them—a very real, substantial, work-a-day happiness, by no means to be despised. But, on Will's side at least, it is not perfect happiness. The flaw—the fatal flaw—to him is that he does not love Tillie—never has loved her. He liked her and he married her simply because he was badly in need of a housekeeper. He is fond of her and is a good and kind husband to her. But she does not hold his fancy and his heart.

Up to the time of Tillie's marriage she and I were little more than indifferent, superficial acquaintances. I belonged to the younger generation; and the relations between her and grandma were not at all cordial, although for a few years before her marriage the old bitterness had died away to such an extent that they "spoke" when they met and Tillie occasionally called here for the mail.

Grandfather's death took place soon after Tillie's marriage. I came home to stay and our friendship dated from that. I went often to see her in her new home. She and Will returned my visits; and we grew to be very good friends all round.

It was rather strange that she and grandmother became as fond of each other as they have been for the past ten years. The old quarrel and anger seem utterly blotted out. Grandmother really loves Tillie now more than she loves either of her own daughters; and certainly Tillie is more of a daughter to her than either Aunt Annie or Aunt Emily.

I liked Will Houston very much. For that matter I like him still, just as well as ever, when he behaves himself. I have always been frank and cordial with him. Although I am not a young girl Will Houston is old enough to be my father and it never occurred to me that there was any reason why I should not be as free and friendly with him as with Tillie.

Then, about five years ago, I discovered that he loved me. The knowledge dawned on me rather slowly from various significant speeches and looks on his part. It was long before I could believe it. At first I thought I must be mistaken. Then I thought Will was merely joking. Finally, I was compelled to believe it. He lost his head one night when we were alone in their living room for a few minutes and I realized what I had to combat.

I was appalled. For my own part, I knew there was not the slightest danger. Will Houston has no power whatever over me. He is not of the type that attracts me and I could never care a straw for him in any way, even if he were as free as air. But I was placed in a very difficult position and he knew it and took full advantage of it. I could not withdraw my friendship from him. To have done so would have offended Tillie, if she did not suspect my reason—or, if she did, would have destroyed her happiness. I could not do this and Will knew I would not unless he drove me to extremes. As long as he confined his love-making to words he knew I would be obliged to tolerate him for Tillie's sake. I could laugh at his utterances, snub his presumptuous remarks, and generally keep him in order; and he knew that if he persisted in attempting or asking for caresses, an open rupture would come. So, apart from speech, he has had to behave himself, and this is the basis on which we have been meeting for five years.

During these five years I have enjoyed many pleasant visits at Tillie's home. But over them all was this shadow of his unwelcome love. Sometimes my fears would prove quite groundless. Tillie would come with us when he drove me home—and I always coaxed her to do so most fervently—or Will, perhaps mindful of my previous mockery, would say nothing out of the way. But again an evening would come when nothing availed to keep his tongue in check. I could never understand why he persisted in talking so, when I say such merciless things to him. He knows I care nothing for him and never could care, under any circumstances. But this seems to make no difference. Talk and rave he will. He has a tolerable opinion of his own fascinations, this same W.H., and I really believe he has deluded himself into believing that it is only because he is married that I will have nothing to do with him and that if he were only a free man I would fall promptly into his arms. He thinks, I imagine, that any statements I may make to the contrary are only to save my pride and protect myself from his pursuit, since he *is* married.

I hate to be alone with him. And I always have the feeling that I am walking over a powder-mine. The last night I was down there, when he was driving me home and talking absurdly I said sharply, "You ought to have learned by this time that I don't flirt with married men". He said, "*And what if I am not always married? What then?*" It made my blood run cold. Heaven knows what mad thing that man might do if he fancied it would open a path to me.

The worst of the whole business is that it gives me such a degrading feeling of disloyalty to Tillie, who is a true friend of mine. This feeling is, of course, absurd. I am not disloyal to Tillie. I have never tried to attract, or desired to attract, her husband. I hate his insulting love and I would not even keep on civil terms with him were it not for her. But I suffer from the feeling nevertheless.

To-day, however, I had no secret dread of the drive home to cloud my pleasure. We had a lovely day—laughter and jest, a dinner and tea such as only Tillie can set up, and a merry drive home through a clear moonlight night over satin smooth roads.

Friday, February 24, 1911
Cavendish, P.E.I.
Wednesday morning I went to town to get a bad tooth treated. McGuigan's team came down for me and I left at daylight. Just as I was leaving it struck me how very frail and old grandmother looked. She had dressed hurriedly and was consequently rather untidy and her gray hair was hanging in wisps about her face. This always makes an old person look older. But apart from that there was a look in her face that sent a chill to my heart. For a moment I thought I could not go to town and leave her. True, I had Judy to stay with her; she was seemingly as well as usual; and it was really necessary that I should go. Yet I was on the point of sending back the team and staying home. I carried a sad, worried heart to town with me. I went to an afternoon tea at Mrs. Fitzgerald's that day and in the evening the Ch'town Women's Club gave me a reception. I should have enjoyed myself but I didn't. All the time I was haunted by the remembrance of the look on grandmother's face as I had seen it in the gray morning light. I laughed and talked and smiled—but my thoughts were elsewhere all the time. I came home Thursday evening over wild, "slewy" roads. As I drove up the old lane I felt a dread of what I might find on getting home. But what I found was a snug kitchen, Daffy purring on his cushion, and grandmother quite well and smiling. I laughed at my fears. But I shall not soon forget those two miserable days of absence.

Saturday, Mar. 4, 1911
Cavendish, P.E.I.
Both grandmother and I have been sick since I wrote last. A week ago I took grippe very badly. There has been an epidemic of it here. Last Saturday, Sunday, and Monday I was as ill as I could be. Since then I have been able to drag around, which was fortunate, since grandma took it on Wednesday and was very sick until yesterday. Since then she has been improving. But she will

not stay in bed and I feel so worried and anxious about her lest she get more cold. I feel very miserable yet. The worst of grippe is the langor and depression it leaves behind it for so long. I feel good for nothing—and don't want to feel good for anything! I just want to lie still and not talk or be talked to. However, we are both a great deal better tonight and I hope the worst is over.

Will and Tillie were up last night and cheered us up considerably. It's a good thing to have friends!

It is not often that I read a magazine story nowadays which takes any hold on me. Indeed, I read few magazine stories of any sort, for the majority of them are not worth the waste of time involved in reading them. There are a few writers, however, whose name is a tolerable guarantee of something worth while and when I met a story "Man and Dog" by Lawrence Housman in *Harper's* this week I read it—and re-read it—and read it again—and then cut it out to preserve and read at intervals all my life. I cannot recall reading any other story that gripped me so hard. The only thing I can compare it to is Poe's "Black Cat" and in some respects it is superior to that. It is as strong and vivid and weird as Poe's tale; and it has, besides, a bitter pathos which Poe's does not possess. Last night after I went to bed I cried myself to sleep over it. Of course, I am depressed and sad and sick at heart to an unusual degree, as a result of illness, and so the tale affected me more deeply and haunted me more insistently than it might have done in my normal state. I could not shake off its influence. One sentence in especial clung to my memory, reiterating itself over and over. "At nightfall the tired body and dull brain went back to their rest." I do not know why but the thought of grandmother seems strangely bound up with those words—perhaps because she has been so weak and feeble this past week and it seems so hard for her to move about as she insists on doing.

Oh, I am very tired and lonely and sad. I feel as if I could hardly drag myself upstairs to bed. But I really am much better than I was the first of the week and so is grandmother. It is just that we are both weak and dull as the grippe always leaves people. I know this; but all the "pep" seems to have gone out of me and I cannot look life in the face at all. How I wish the winter were over!

1912

January 28, 1912
The Manse, Leaskdale, Ont.

I look at the above entry rather stupidly, since I have written it down. It seems unreal. I cannot quite believe that it should be so written—that anything save "Cavendish" should be the correct heading for any entry in this journal. And when I force myself to realize it there are elements of bitter heartbreak and homesickness in its realization. In one way, I am well content—even glad—that it should be "The Manse, Leaskdale"; but I cannot, *cannot* forget "that far shore / Beloved and deplored" and it seems to me that I never shall be able to forget it, or the secret, ceaseless longing for it.

It is nearly a year since I last wrote in this journal—nearly a year since I laid down my pen that cold, wintry March night, never doubting that I should take it up again shortly to write another entry of my Cavendish life. But almost a year has passed—a year most strangely compounded of bitter heartbreak, of bereavement, of the agony of separation and parting, and of a certain joy and sweetness in the realization of long-cherished dreams. But the pain is more vividly remembered, as one day of storm and tempest stands out in memory more insistently than many days of quiet sunshine and peace.

Can I now, after a season of calm and leisure has again come to me after many months of ceaseless change, write out the story of this past strange year? I shall try. In part I may write it. But the poignancy of it can never be written.

I recall distinctly that night of March 4th—the last night I was ever to sleep in my dear old room! But I did not know that as I went drearily up the stairs to it—and it was well that I did not. I loved that little room more than I ever loved another place on earth—and more than I shall ever love any place. And I had often wondered how, when my last night in it should come, I should ever endure the anguish of it. But the last night came and I knew it not. Yet I was very sad and sick at heart—weak, ill, dispirited. There was on mind and soul, as well as on body, a weight I could not shake off. I cried myself to sleep in the cold darkness—and thus was passed my last night in that old beloved white room, where I had dreamed my dreams of girlhood and suffered the heartaches of lonely womanhood, where I had written my best, where I had endured my defeats, and exulted in my victories. Never again was I to lay my head on its pillow there—never again waken to see the morning sunshine gleaming in at the little, muslin-curtained window where I had knelt so many nights since early childhood to pray beneath the stars. I had looked from it on spring blossom and summer greenness and autumnal harvest fields and winter snows. I had seen starshine and moonrise and sunset from it. I had known there great happiness and greater sorrow. And now that was all finished and the Angel of the Years turned the page of life whereon it was writ. Thank God, I did not know it!

Sunday, March the 5th came. It was a bitter cold day, with a furious wind blowing and whirling the light snow wildly. There was no service in Cavendish that day and I did not go out and saw no one all day. I still felt very weak and languid. Grandmother seemed better than she had been. Her appetite was improved and she ate some dinner. All through the forenoon and afternoon she seemed fairly well, but she sat in her armchair and did not even read. I lay on the sofa most of the time. It seemed a long day. But it wore to its end, as even the longest day will.

We had our tea at five o'clock. We had sat so together at the old kitchen table for many meals, just the two of us. I did not know that we were sitting so for the last time. After tea grandmother washed the dishes. I had generally done this. But after tea I had gone upstairs for a few minutes and when I came down grandmother had most of the few dishes we had used washed. I let her finish them, as she seemed to wish to do so, and said she felt stronger. The little task done, she sat down in her chair and folded her hands—folded them forever after the work of almost eighty seven years. Her work at last was done.

The evening closed down—wild, dark, stormy. Just at dark I noticed that grandmother suddenly began to cough quite continuously. She had had a cough earlier in the week but it had almost gone. All at once, however, it returned. It was hard and tight and seemed to distress her. I applied what simple remedies were accessible and suggested to her that, since her room was very cold, she let me make her bed up in the kitchen where it would be warm. Grandmother assented with an indifferent willingness that surprised me. She was usually so strongly averse to making any change in the routine of her life that I had expected that she would refuse or yield very reluctantly. I moved her bed to the kitchen and we spent the night there. I did not sleep. Every little while I got up to replenish the fire, or prepare a hot drink for grandmother, whose cough continued troublesome, preventing her from sleeping. But about five o'clock she fell into a deep slumber, unbroken by any coughing. In my inexperience with illness I took this to be a good sign; but I knew she was feverish, and, thinking she was taking a relapse of grippe, I resolved to send for the doctor as soon as it was possible to venture out. As soon as daylight came I slipped out, leaving grandmother still sleeping, and made my way through the drifts down to Geo. R's to ask him to go for the doctor and also to send a telephone message from Stanley to Aunt Annie.

The news soon spread that grandmother was ill and in a short time I had plenty of kind and symphathizing neighbors to help me. We put up a bed in the sitting room and removed grandmother to it. She was very weak when she wakened up but said she felt better and did not like it when she found I had sent for the doctor. But very soon after she drifted into a sort of drowsy stupor from which she seldom again roused. The doctor came. He said grandmother had pneumonia. When that was said all was said. We knew that at her age such an illness could have but one ending.

I could not believe it. It did not seem credible or possible to me that grandmother should die—grandmother, who had always been there! The rest of that week seemed like a dream through which I moved and worked like an automaton—a dream? Nay, a nightmare, of people coming and going ceaselessly, day and night, of long vigils through the hours of darkness when poor grandmother moaned in distress. She had no pain, but the deadly weakness and difficulty of breathing were even worse. It was terrible to watch her. Tillie Houston came up Monday night and stayed till all was over—poor, poor Tillie, then so strong, cheerful, sympathetic—a tower of strength for us all in our weakness and dismay. The thought of her in that week wrings my heart now. For, strong, brave, cheery as she was, for her, too, the end was near. Before the mayflowers bloomed in the April barrens Tillie was to sleep near grandmother in Cavendish graveyard.

Aunt Annie and Aunt Emily came down Tuesday morning. And, for the first time in five years, Uncle John came over to see his mother. I think his conscience, if he possessed such a thing, must have been wrung as he looked down upon her and remembered how he had used her. I would not like to have had his memories at that moment. Nor did I pity him. Ever since his father's death he had behaved to his mother with the utmost selfishness, greed, and indifference, and for the past five years his conduct towards her had been heartless in the extreme. I watched him as he went away, walking with laggard step and bowed head like an old man. I think in that hour his punishment came upon him.

Dr. Simpson had said on Monday that he hardly thought grandmother would live through the night. Yet she lived until a little after noon on Friday. It was a bitter, anxious time, seeming in retrospection as long as a year. Grandmother suffered much distress part of the time; the rest she lay in a sort of stupor from which she seldom roused. She took no interest in anything; for her, the world and the things of the world had gone by and were as a tale that is told. She never asked after anyone or left any message for anyone, not even her first-born. The only living creature she remembered or spoke of was *Daffy*, the little gray animal she had petted and which had been her constant company when I had to be away. Wednesday evening, as I sat by her bed, holding her poor, nerveless old hand, she suddenly opened her eyes and said, clearly and distinctly "Where's Daffy?"

"He is out", I said. "Would you like to see him?"

"Yes, when he comes in," she said.

I went out, hunted him up, and brought him to her bedside. She put out her hand and feebly stroked his

"Daffy"

back several times. "Poor little Daffy! Poor little Daffy," she said gently. Not again did she rouse herself, or display interest in anything.

On Friday she died, after an hour of great distress and that moment, in which a lifelong tie was broken, was very dreadful to me.

At dusk grandmother lay in her casket in the same room—the old parlor— where I had seen my mother and grandfather lie. I went in alone to look at her.

Grandmother had always been a pretty woman and she retained much of her beauty to the end of life. She was tall, very slender, delicate featured with large gray eyes and cheeks that were pink to the last. In her coffin she looked so young. All the lines went out of her face and she looked no more than fifty-five or sixty—just as I remember her when I was a little girl. Her hair was quite dark under the little black "net" she had always worn. She was dressed in her black satin dress. She had that dress made twenty five years ago and wore it always on any special occasion. It always became her and never looked "out of fashion". She always looked stately in it—"like a queen", as poor old Aunt Jane said. And it had never become her better than it did in her coffin, with her black lace scarf over her shoulders and breast.

The most wonderful transformation was in her hands. Grandmother's hands, as long as I can remember, at least, had been her most unbeautiful feature. They were very thin and a lifetime of hard work and some rheumatism in her later years had twisted and distorted and discoloured them out of all proportion and grace. Yet Death, amid many other miracles, had transfigured them. Folded over her still breast they were waxen white and shapely as in youth. To me, nothing about grandmother was as touching as those hands, made beautiful again in the consecration of death.

Oh, what a wonder worker is that same death! How he blots out, for the time being at least, all remembrance of any human imperfection in our beloved dead! We can think of nothing then but their good and lovable qualities. As I stood there by grandmother's coffin and looked down at her I thought only of her much kindness, her faithfulness, her patience in earlier years, her love— ah, yes, her love! For she loved her own deeply and was very loyal to them. And, as Uncle Leander said to me in his letter later on, we of the younger generation had not known grandmother before age and infirmity had stolen most of the brightness from her life—we could not remember her as young, gay, happy and lovable.

I had often read of the "mysteriously wise" smile that is sometimes seen on the faces of the dead. I have looked on many dead faces and on none had I ever beheld it. But I saw it on grandmother's—the strangest little smile— "mysteriously wise" indeed, a smile such as I had never seen on her lips in life and which was quite out of keeping with her simple, non-subtle personality—a smile knowing and remote, with just a tinge of kindly mockery in it, as if she were smiling at our grief and at the importance we were so mistakenly attaching to earthly things. It was the smile of *one who knew* and, so knowing, thought us all little children, chasing bubbles, and grieving and rejoicing over things that mattered not a whit—"even as I myself did before I *knew*," said the smile.

Grandmother's maiden name was Lucy Ann Woolner. Her father was Robert Woolner and her mother's name was Sarah Kemp. Grandmother was born in Dunwich, England, on August 28, 1824. When she was twelve years old her parents emigrated from England and came to Prince Edward Island, where they settled at Rustico. She was married when only nineteen to Alexander Marquis Macneill, then aged twenty three.

To me, it seems difficult to think of grandfather and grandmother as a young couple of that age—mere boy and girl. They always seemed so icy and austere where youth was concerned....

For some time after their marriage—I do not know how long but not less than three years or more than four grandfather and grandmother lived on a farm at South Rustico, near the Catholic chapel there. Then they moved up to Cavendish to live with "Speaker Macneill" and his wife in the old Macneill homestead. They had six children—Uncle Leander, Aunt Annie, Uncle John, my mother, Aunt Emily and Uncle Chester. They were very happy together. They suited each other in temperament. Grandfather was a man who never interfered in minor household affairs, giving grandmother full liberty there, while she never interfered in his departments.

Grandmother's life up to the time of grandfather's death was a very happy one, I think. The happiness went out of it then, but seventy four happy years are more than fall to the lot of most people. My mother's death was the only bitter sorrow in it and even that, I think, was much blurred by the fact that before it and after it grandmother herself was very ill with a complication of ailments which threatened her life and rendered her so weak that what otherwise might have been keener feelings were blunted and softened. At times her death was hourly expected and one time they thought she *had* died—Mrs. Murray, the minister's wife of the time, always laughingly referred to the date as "the year Aunt Lucy died". But she recovered completely and became a remarkably healthy woman, never having another serious illness until the one that caused her death. Yes, on the whole grandmother had a happy life and at the last she died as she had wished to die—in her own old home, surrounded by familiar and loving faces, tended by affectionate hands, and with as little suffering as is generally found in death.

Saturday was a hard busy day. There was much to be done by way of putting the house in order for the funeral. All through the time I was haunted by a strange feeling of *disloyalty*. So many things had to be done which grandmother would have disapproved of had she been living. To me, it seemed dreadful that we should do them when she could no longer prevent us—as if we were, some how, taking an unfair advantage of her. This feeling was foolish and illogical, to be sure, but it existed and made me most miserable as long as I remained in the old house.

It was particularly strong during the sorting out of the contents of grand-mother's room. Aunt Emily, Aunt Annie and I did this ourselves, not choosing that the hands and eyes of any strangers should desecrate her personal belongings. The task was a hard one, indeed—one of heartbreak; and yet mingled with a ludicrous element, too. Many a time we had to laugh while the tears glistened on our faces. For we found the most curious things in that room.

As grandmother grew older she developed a tendency often found in old people. She hated to discard or throw away *anything*, no matter how completely its use was gone or its glory departed. Everything must be kept—"it might come in handy sometime". When I grew up and began to take a hand in housecleaning every room and receptacle in the house was crammed with odds and ends, most of them absolutely useless and serving only to accumulate dust. I soon found it was time and energy wasted trying to induce grandmother to discard any of them. So I said nothing but every spring I contrived to weed out and burn a few without her ever suspecting it. So, at her death, there was hardly anything superfluous in the house—except in her room. With this, and its boxes, drawers and chests, I had never meddled at all, and we had to ransack the hoards of years as we examined the contents thereof. And *such* a mixture! Old rags, cast-off clothing, old letters, boxes, clippings, odds and ends of every conceivable kind were mixed together with nice things, such as scarfs and shawls of lace, silk waists, handkerchiefs, sachets, etc. which had been given to her as Christmas presents by children and grandchildren and never used. Indeed, I think she had quite forgotten that they were there. As I have said, the exploration of that room was a mixture of comedy and pathos. For example:—in her old black trunk we found a pair of very nice new blankets. To them was carefully stitched a bit of paper on which was written, in grandmother's tremulous hand, "For L.M. Montgomery". She was afraid, I suppose, that they might fall into other hands and so safeguarded against it. It seemed as if she had come back from the grave to do me this little material kindness and the tears rushed to my eyes. And yet, when we opened two carefully wrapped up parcels under the blankets I had to laugh. In one, we found a faded, matted "false front" worn by her own mother over fifty years ago; the contents of the other parcel were still more ludicrous. A few years ago I had a small hand mirror with a white celluloid back. An accident happened to it by which the glass of the mirror was broken into fragments and the celluloid frame bent almost double. The thing was of no further conceivable use; and, as I could not burn it, I threw it away out in the underbrush behind the hen house. Grandmother, who often wandered through this brush, looking for hen's nests, must have found it and brought it in; for there it was, carefully wrapped up in that parcel!

The task, for all its pain, was finally finished. All the useless odds and ends were burned and the rest apportioned out among friends who would appreciate them. By night all was in order and a hush fell over the old house. For the first time in a week it was very quiet again; and in the darkening parlor grandmother lay at rest, with that strange little smile on her face, and all about her the whiteness and sweetness of the flowers I had sent for. For grandmother was fond of flowers. She seldom went out in summer without bringing a spray of blossom when she came back; and my culture of flowers was one of the very few of my pursuits with which she sympathized and to which she had never objected. And so I was determined that she should have them about her in death and that they should be laid close around her face in the grave.

Sunday was a quiet day—the last of many quiet Sundays in the old home. There was a very beautiful sunset that night which made the snowy front orchard a thing of wonder. On Monday afternoon grandmother was buried. There was a large funeral. Before anyone came I went in alone to say good-bye to her. It seemed to me an impossible—an *outrageous* thing that I should never see "Grandma Macneill" again. She had *always* been there. Even all through the preceding week it had seemed to me that she *must* be somewhere about—that at any moment the door might open and she enter, with her accustomed quick, noiseless footstep. But *now* I realized that the door between us would open no more. Grandmother, who for so many years had never left her home, was *gone*. She had fared forth on a long journey.

I said good-bye to her and went out and shut the door—shut it on the old life with all its sweet and all its bitter.

It was all over. Grandmother had been carried to her rest beside the bride-groom of her youth in Cavendish graveyard. To us, in the deserted home, all that remained was to strip and dismantle it—and go.

For my part, I felt that since the time had come to go I must get away as soon as I could. I wished to have the pang of parting over. Stella and Aunt Emily stayed down to help me, and Tillie Houston came up every day. The next morning we began.

It was a heart breaking—a hideous task. Every picture I took down from the walls, every article I packed away, seemed to wrench my very soul. It seemed sinful to *divorce* the old articles of furniture one from the other, to be given to this one or that. They had been together for so long that they seemed to have grown together—to belong to one another. But the work had to be done. We toiled unceasingly and by Wednesday night it was completed. That was the last night in the old home. For years I had slept under its roof—as child, as girl, as woman. And now I had to leave it!

Thursday morning the neighbors came with teams and took all that was to go over to Park Corner. Aunt Emily also went home. Stella and I spent the day in the old house, putting it in order and burning everything that was of no value to anyone. To me, the whole thing seemed like a dream—and I, moving in the midst of it, a dream.

When all was done we locked the house and went over to the manse. The Cavendish people gave me a farewell reception that night and presented me with an address and a silver tea-service. They were all very nice and I felt that I was leaving many kind and sincere friends behind me. That night I could not sleep. The fine weather had broken and a wild wind howled around the manse. I lay and thought of the old house beyond the spruce grove—stripped, deserted, its homelight quenched forever. For the first time perhaps since it was built, certainly for the first time in my recollection, no light shone out from its windows through the old trees. The soul of the home was gone. It was henceforth to be but an empty shell, the mockery of wind and storm. I knew this—I knew that no living creature was in it, save a little gray cat, crying his heart out with loneliness in one of the upstairs rooms; and yet I was haunted all night by a weird fancy that *grandmother* was there, wandering from room to room with her candle in her hand, muttering to herself over the desecration, complaining of those who had dismantled her home. It was a horrible fancy but I was nervous and worn-out and I could not dispel it. I was thankful when morning came. It was a very bitter day with a furious west wind blowing. George Campbell and Bruce Howatt came down for us. We went "over home" and got our wraps and valises. Poor Daffy was rescued from his solitary confinement in the "lookout" room and at once condemned to a still more ignominious incarceration in a market basket. Then I went out and closed the door of the old home behind me. Never again would I re-enter it. Whatever feet would cross its threshold in the future mine would not be among them. All the bitterness of death was in that moment—and it was repeated as we drove up through Cavendish and familiar scenes and beloved haunts disappeared one by one from view—the manse, the old trees that encircled home, the graveyard on the hill with its new red mound, the woods in which was Lover's Lane—beautiful, unforgotten, unforgettable Lover's Lane—the sea-shore, the pond, the houses of friends—all drifted finally out of sight. I had left Cavendish forever, save as a fitful visitor; and in leaving it felt that I was leaving the only place on earth my heart would ever truly love. The world might have a home for me somewhere; but the only home my inmost soul would ever acknowledge would be that little country settlement by the gulf shore....

We arrived at Park Corner after a cold drive. That afternoon, pursued by a spirit of restlessness, I began to unpack my personal belongings. But I was unequal to the task. Everything I took out of my trunk wrung my heart for I would see, as I touched it, the very spot it had occupied in my old room. I broke down utterly and spent the rest of the day lying on my bed in tears, aching with bitter homesickness, stripped of all courage for the future.

"Uncle John Campbell's house. X is my room there"
[Park Corner]

Next morning, however, I was calmer and though the task was a painful one I got all my things unpacked and arranged in the room I was to occupy while I remained at Park Corner. I do not know what I should have done if I had not had Park Corner to go to in the interval between leaving Cavendish and my marriage. Hard as it was, the wrench was somewhat alleviated by going to a place which had always been a second home to me. And though I could not

"View 1 of my Park Corner Room"

"View 2 of my Park Corner Room"

have stayed there long contentedly, owing to the discord prevailing between the two families, for a short sojourn that did not matter seriously and, save for the many inevitable hours of homesickness and heart hunger, I passed some very pleasant weeks at Park Corner last spring. All were very kind to me and Stella was a jolly companion.

But the first few days were hard—hard. In the day I could bear up but when nightfall came my spirit fainted within me. Few were the nights upon which I did not cry myself to sleep. The only comfort I had was to go to bed, shut my eyes, and imagine myself back in my old room at home, with all the old things in their places around me. This was an illusory peace but while it lasted it was very potent.

That little gray creature of a Daff was a real comfort to me. He seemed like a living link between me and the old life. Besides, his antics and our anxiety over them furnished us with a little comedy during those spring weeks. He was bitterly discontented at first and as wild and frightened as a hare. When he disappeared, as he frequently did, we were sure he had started for Cavendish. But he always turned up and eventually became reconciled to his new abode. At least, he loved the big barn with its mousy straw-loft and the woods around. But all the time I was at Park Corner he never became really domesticated in the house. He seldom was willing to stay in it and never seemed to get over his fear of strangers, of whom there were generally some about. The whole household made a pet of him and were as much interested in him as I was myself. Even George seemed to have a warm spot in his heart for "old Daff", and five-year-old Danny, who called him "a Newfoundland cat", because he was so big, was quite jealous of his affection and declared that "Daffy loves me more than he loves Aunt Maud." Daff was really wonderfully tolerant of Danny. He had always been so impatient of any handling save by me that I was seriously afraid if Danny began hauling him about as children generally do with cats Daff would injure the child. Instead, he submitted to be lugged around, half the time upside down, without a protest and with the most comically resigned expression on his face which seemed to say, "Danny is only a little boy so I am enduring this patiently, though I would rend in pieces any grown-up person who offered me such indignities."

Now that poor grandmother had gone there was no longer any reason for delaying my already long-deferred marriage and it was arranged that Ewan and

I should be married early in July. A little over a year previously he had left P.E. Island and taken a congregation in Leaskdale, Ont. I felt badly over the prospect of leaving the Island. But since I had left Cavendish it did not matter so much....

I had a very busy spring, preparing for my marriage and new home—so busy that most of my ordinary pursuits were dropped for the time being. During my first four weeks at Park Corner I was quite miserable physically. I suppose I felt the effects of the nervous strain and hard work of those last two weeks in Cavendish. I took a second attack of grippe and then had a siege of that most unromantic and painful complaint, *boils*. When this was over, however, I was very well the rest of the spring and, in spite of my frequently recurring agonies of homesick

"Danny" [Campbell]

longing, I could not but feel, as well, the relief from those thirteen long years of petty carking worries and anxieties.

I was so busy that I could not keep this journal up in any regular fashion. Besides, I long shrank from the pain I knew would be attendant upon the writing of grandmother's death and leaving Cavendish. But occasionally through the spring, when I had a little spare time, or when pain demanded some outward expression, I wrote some stray entries in a notebook....

†*"April 12, 1911*
Today was cold but fine. The snow is almost all gone and as it froze tonight the walking was good. This evening Stella and I went up to McKays on an errand. Coming back through the clear moonlight night I saw the row of silver birches at the back of the grove behind the house. They recalled the birches around the old front garden at home. A very anguish of homesickness overwhelmed my soul. It seemed to me that I must *die* if I could not get back to Cavendish. For the time, I did not believe that I could go on living away from it. Oh, if I could find myself in the cold spring moonshine walking up the old lane at home, seeing the kitchen light gleam yellowly through the trees, turning the curve by the cherry trees, opening the old kitchen door, and finding grandmother reading in her armchair by the fire and Daffy curled up on his prescriptive cushion on the sofa!..."

*On April 17th, I got a telephone message from William Houston, telling me that Tillie was dead!

†LMM quotes from her notebook.
*LMM continues the journal entry which began January 28, 1912.

When Tillie left our place it was to go to Hammond's to nurse her mother, who was very ill with grippe so ill, indeed, that it was not thought she could recover. While there Tillie took measles. I had known she was ill and very ill with them; but a letter from Margaret two days before had said she was over the worst and was recovering. Therefore this message was a horrible shock.

To this day I am not any more reconciled to Tillie's death than I was then, and I *cannot* become reconciled to it. Grandmother was very old and life had ceased to hold much happiness for her so that, although the rending of lifelong ties caused anguish at the time, my mind accepted it as what, after all, was best for her and what was inevitable in any case. But Tillie was in the prime of life, happy, useful, beloved by all. Her death has made in my life a blank which can never be filled. She was one of the few Cavendish people who really mattered to me, one of the few people in the world whom I deeply and intimately love. The bitterness in the thought of re-visiting Cavendish after the great change had been alleviated by the thought that Tillie was there, and that in her home I should always be a welcome guest. And now she was gone and when I went back I must always miss her. The pang in that thought, as I write, is just as keen as it was the day I first heard of her death.

The next day George drove me down to Cavendish. It was just when the roads were breaking up and they were in dreadful condition. I had dreaded going back to Cavendish the first time, fearing that it would be all pain. But it was not. Instead, it was a joy to see all the old places again, even though they were in the unbeautiful dinginess of earliest spring. But ah, the pang came when I had to go to the manse—and *not* home! Never before had I returned to Cavendish without a home there to go to.

That evening Mrs. Wm. Laird drove me down to Hammonds and I saw my dear friend—for the first time without a smile or greeting for me. She did not even look very nice—she who was so pretty in life. Her face looked as if she had suffered much.

That night in the manse I suffered from my old obsession that I should be home—that grandmother must be waiting for me in the old house through the spruce wood, and wondering why I did not come. My heart seemed steeped in the misery of it. And when I slept I dreamed I saw her there, sitting a-cold by her fireless hearth, weeping for my not coming.

I have dreamed hundreds of times since I left home, of being back there, and never once has the dream been a pleasant one. The first few months those dreams were absolute torture to me. It was always the same dream—I was back home and grandmother was there, too. But all was confusion and desolation, and grandmother was invariably reproaching me for having destroyed her home and deserted her while she was yet living. What a relief it was to waken from such a dream! Of late, the character of the dream has changed. Home is as it used to be and grandmother is in it; part of the time she is alone, in other dreams grandfather is there also. This is strange, because, in all the years after grandfather's death, I never dreamed, save once, that he was alive again. But now I dream it frequently. When I dream that grandmother is there alone I am in agony as to how I can be married and living far away while she is there and worried as to how I can leave her and return to my own home. These dreams are distressing. And, much as I have desired to, I have never once dreamed of being in Lover's Lane. Not a day passes that I do not think of it, but never in the land of sleep do I see it. Perhaps it is as well—for it might be with my dreams of it as my dreams of home—changed and desolate, and that I would not wish.

I found Cavendish in a flame of gossip over tales of Will Houston's indifference towards his wife during her illness. Knowing what I did of him, I found it hard *not* to believe them—though I did not say so to the gossippers! And yet, in another way, I found it hard *to* believe them. Will had always been very good to Tillie during her lifetime. He might cherish a crazy passion for me but even he could not have deluded himself into believing that I would ever marry him, even if he were free, and, apart from that, there could be no motive for any secret, horrible wish on his part for Tillie's death. I would hate him if I suspected him of it. But I do not. I believe he simply did not realize that Tillie was dangerously ill until she was gone. Nobody else did, so why should he? Even her own family—nay, her very doctor, had never felt the slightest fear that she might not recover. I saw Will for only a few minutes the day of the funeral but he seemed to me a grief-stricken man. He had lost such a home-maker as he would never find again and I think he had enough sense and perception to realize it, no matter how his inclinations might have wandered during her life.

And yet—it is hard to say what dark thought may have lurked in the recesses of his heart. God help us all. Life is a tangled thing. It is hard to know where truth ends and falsehood begins in a nature where both are entwined as they are in Will Houston's. At all events, he made Tillie happy while she was alive and the rest must be between him and his judge.

Tillie was buried in Cavendish graveyard, not far from where grandmother lay. George and I went back to Park Corner that same evening over dreadful roads, in the teeth of a bitter wind. I was almost played out when I reached there.

Poor Tillie! I think of her every day. It seems to me that I should be getting letters from her. I cannot think of her as dead—I cannot think of the little home, made beautiful by her taste and labor, without her presence....

On May 8 I went to town to attend to shopping and dressmaking. I stayed in ten days. Bertie and I had never had such a good visit together and we enjoyed it hugely although it was clouded for us both by the shadow of coming change. Bertie and I felt very badly over my leaving the Island and I felt wretched over the thought of being far separated from her and seeing her so seldom. We have been such congenial friends. There seems to be a perfect harmony between us and a perfect understanding. And in the future we may see but little of each other and have to find our associates among people whose companionship cannot give us one tenth the pleasure we can give each other.

I had a busy and fatiguing time in town, for in addition to a great deal of business I was asked out to tea almost every evening. Sometimes I enjoyed

"Bertie and I take a drive in park"
[Bertie McIntyre]

myself, but more often I was bored and wished myself in Bertie's room discussing "life and literature" with her. In younger days, when I would have enjoyed this social life and the opportunities of improvement it brings, it was not mine. And now that it has come to me I no longer care greatly for it or desire it....

†*"Tuesday, May 23, 1911*
Park Corner, P.E. Island
Today *The Story Girl* came—and with it a heartache. For I thought there were two dear ones who would have read it proudly but could never read it now. When I wrote it they were with me—and now they are gone. I wrote it in my dear old room where I shall never sit and hold pen more.

I have been haunted, ever since leaving home, with a nasty obsession that I can never write again. This I know, is foolish, but I cannot shake it off. The very idea of taking up my pen again is distasteful to me. No doubt, when the time comes that I can do so, I will find again the old joy in creation and fancy, but I cannot feel this way now...."

*....Frede came home from Macdonald College on June 17th. Stella and I went as far as St. John to meet her and had a jolly trip. From that out we were intensely busy, planning and working. My trousseau, which I had made mainly in Toronto and Montreal, began to arrive and we were all interested in that. My things were pretty. I had worn black for grandmother all the spring but I laid it aside when I was married. My wedding dress was of white-silk crepe de soie with tunic of chiffon and pearl bead trimming—and of course the tulle veil and orange blossom wreath.

These are snaps the girls took of some of my dresses. My suit was of steel gray cloth, with gray chiffon blouse and gray hat trimmed with a wreath of

---

†LMM quotes from her notebook.
*LMM continues the journal entry which began January 28, 1912.

L.M. Montgomery, wedding trousseau dresses

tiny rosebuds. My long wrap was of gray broadcloth. Besides the dresses 'illustrated' I had a linen dress, a pink muslin, one of white embroidery, and several odd waists.

On Friday, June 23rd Frede and I drove down to Cavendish and stayed until Saturday evening at the manse. I had been dreading this trip. It seemed to me that going back thus to Cavendish must be acute pain. But it was not. On the contrary it was all a sweet pleasure to be there again in that June beauty. The centre of interest at the manse was Margaret's baby—a little daughter, born in May. I felt a double interest in this little lady, because she was Margaret's child and because I had known of her expected coming almost as soon as Margaret herself and had talked matters over with Margaret all along the mysterious way of approaching motherhood.

Saturday afternoon I slipped away by myself. I went first to the graveyard and saw Tillie's and grandmother's graves. Then I went to Lover's Lane. I had expected to feel sad but I did not. Sorrow seems to have no place in Lover's Lane. Its beauty charmed soul and sense, its fairy voices called to me, its fair memories walked hand in hand with me. It was after I had left it that sadness came. I might never walk there again—and it must certainly be long ere I would. And I love that spot so! I do not believe that a day passes on which I do not think of it and long for it.

We had a long-to-be-remembered drive to Park Corner that evening. We went around by the Campbeltown road—a much longer way but very beautiful. I enjoyed every moment of that drive.

On Tuesday, June 27, I went to town to say good-bye to Bertie, who was going west for her vacation. We spent a rather sorrowful night together—the last for a long while of all our many pleasant nights and talks. It seemed to me that I could *not* endure any further rending of old ties. Could all that a new life had to offer me compensate for the things the old life took in its going?....

The last fortnight before my marriage was an intensely busy one. There were a thousand and one things to do and every day seemed hotter than the last.

Ewan came Tuesday night. The marriage was to take place next day, Wednesday, July 5th, at noon. That night I did two things I had never exactly pictured myself as doing the night before my wedding day. I cried for a little while after I went to bed—and then I slept soundly the rest of the night!

I hardly know why I cried. I was not unhappy. I was quite contented. I think I wept a lost dream—a dream that could never be fulfilled—a girl's dream of the lover who should be her perfect mate, to whom she might splendidly give herself with no reservations. We all dream that dream. And when we surrender it unfulfilled we feel that something wild and sweet and unutterable has gone out of life!

As for the sound sleep—well, I once thought I'd never sleep a wink on the night before my wedding day. I expected I would be too tremendously excited—too tremulously happy. But that went with the dream. I was just contented. Contentment doesn't keep you awake—but it isn't such a bad bed fellow! It was much better than the bitter loneliness and unhappiness which had often shared my pillow.

Yes, I was content.

The morning of July 5th was cool and gray, threatening rain. But it did not rain and in the evening it cleared up beautifully. Mr. Stirling came over to marry us. I was very sorry that Margaret could not come also. I had not many guests—just Aunt Emily, her son Jimmy and daughter Charlotte, Aunt Mary Montgomery and Cuthbert, Mr. and Mrs. Wm. Ramsay (Uncle John Campbell's next-door neighbors and great friends), Aunt Margaret Sutherland, Marian and Leigh, Bruce and Vivian Howatt. As I stood dressed in my room and heard the guests arriving I thought sadly of one guest who should have been there—whom I had always dreamed of having with me when I was married—who would have been so glad to be there but who, instead of helping to robe me for my bridal, was sleeping in Cavendish graveyard, her once so-busy, helpful hands folded on her breast. Poor Tillie! If she could only have been at my wedding.

"Room where I was married, standing before the mantel"

I wore my white dress and veil and Ewan's present—a necklace of amethysts and pearls. My bouquet was of white roses and lilies of the valley. At twelve Uncle John took me down, while Stella and the Howatts sang 'The Voice that Breathed o'er Eden.' In a few minutes the ceremony was over and they were calling me 'Mrs. Macdonald'—something I haven't quite got used to even yet, by the way. It always gives me an odd feeling to be called 'Mrs. Macdonald'. I have to remind myself mentally that it is I that is being spoken to. Somehow, I felt sorry at giving up my old name—the name of my father, the name linked with the experiences of a lifetime, the name under which I have won my success. To be sure, I shall always keep it in literature. But there will be a difference....

I was named Lucy after Grandmother and Maud after Queen Victoria's daughter, the Princess of Hesse, who died about that time I think. I never liked Lucy as a name. I always liked Maud—spelled *not* 'with an e' if you please—but I do *not* like it in connection with Montgomery. 'Maud Montgomery' has always seemed to me a disagreeable combination—why, I can't explain. I like 'Maud Macdonald' much better.

After the ceremony we had dinner. That dinner made history in Park Corner I believe. 'Gad, they never had the like of this at Government House', gasped old William Ramsay to Stell. It was certainly a memorable repast. Frede was just home from Household Science at Macdonald and she 'did herself proud' to produce a menu that should reflect lustre on her college, and training. Not that the Park Corner *cuisine* could not stand on its own merits. But Frede had all the latest frills of decoration and serving and it was the smartest repast I have seen anywhere.

And I shall always think mournfully of that dinner—for I could not eat a morsel of it. In vain I tried to choke down a few mouthfuls. I could not.

I had been feeling contented all the morning. I had gone through the ceremony and the congratulations unflustered and unregretful. And now, when it was all over and I found myself sitting there by my husband's side—*my husband!*—I felt a sudden horrible inrush of *rebellion* and *despair*. I *wanted to be free!* I felt like a prisoner—a hopeless prisoner. Something in me—something wild and free and untamed—something that Ewan had not tamed—could never tame—something that did not acknowledge him as master—rose up in one frantic protest against the fetters which bound me. At that moment if I could have torn the wedding ring from my finger and so freed myself I would have done it! But it was too late—and the realization that it was too late fell over me like a black cloud of wretchedness. I sat at that gay bridal feast, in my white veil and orange blossoms, beside the man I had married—and I was as unhappy as I had ever been in my life.

That mood passed. By the time I was ready for going-away it had vanished completely and I was again my contented self. We left at four o'clock for Kensington. The sun came out gloriously and we had a very pleasant drive. Frede, Stella, Mrs. Stirling, Marian and one or two of the others went to Kensington with us. We stayed all night at the Clifton House in Summerside and crossed on the boat the next morning to Pointe du Chene, where we took the train to Montreal. The day was very hot and fatiguing. By evening I was dreadfully tired—and once again that mood of the dinner table returned. Once again I felt fettered, rebellious, wretched—once again that untamed part of me flamed up in protest—and then subsided—forever. I never had any return of that mood, thank God. If it had lasted I would have killed myself. It was a curious psychological experience which I shudder to recall. Never did I reach a blacker depth of despair and futile rebellion than in those two moods. It was so dreadful that it *could not* last. Either I must conquer it or die. I conquered it—thrust it down—smothered it—buried it. Whether dead or quiescent it has not troubled me since.

"*On the deck of the Megantic*"
[*Ewan is standing in the foreground*]

We reached Montreal on Friday morning and that evening went on board the *Megantic*—a White Star liner and a very nice boat. When we wakened the next morning we were sailing up the St. Lawrence.

I had been dreading seasickness but we had a very fine voyage. I was never seasick for a moment and I enjoyed the trip over very much. The novelty of life on a big ocean liner was very pleasant. The scenery up the St. Lawrence is beautiful. We did not get out into the gulf until Sunday. The days were all fine and bright, the sea calm and blue. On Monday we saw several ice bergs but were not near enough to them to get a really good view....

Saturday morning we saw and sailed by the 'Calf of Man'—at which I gazed with considerable interest because of Caine's 'Manxman'. From one until three Saturday afternoon we were sailing up the Mersey between the famous Liverpool docks. They were interesting but not at all beautiful. We had hoped to get in in time to catch the train to Glasgow but we could not get through the turmoil of the Customs in time so had to stay until Monday in Liverpool. We went to a hotel and when I got to my room I suddenly realized how tired I was. A very wave of utter weariness submerged me. The preceding sleepless night, the excitement of the day, the worry and confusion of the Custom House, all took effect at once. And I was homesick—suddenly, wretchedly, unmitigatedly homesick!...

The next day was Sunday. As there was nothing very interesting about Liverpool, which is merely a commercial city, we went to Chester and spent most of the day there. Chester is a quaint old town, dating back to Roman days and still surrounded by its old wall. We enjoyed our ramble around it hugely. The appended photo is the first one I took on the old sod. As my first ruin St. John's chapel stands out in memory, although it was not to be compared to those we saw later on.

On Monday, July 17, we went to Glasgow and made it our headquarters for eleven days, while we 'did' various points of interest. We stayed at St. Enoch's hotel. I like the British hotels very well, but I detest the tipping system which infects them. It is not that I grudge the money. It is the wretched uncertainty of it. You never know whether you have given enough, too much, or too little. The whole thing is a constant worry and vexation—one of the worst of the annoyances which detract from the pleasure of travelling in Britain.

As soon as we arrived in Glasgow I began using my notebook again. The first entry was as follows:—

†"*Tuesday, July 18, 1911*
St. Enoch's Hotel, Glasgow, Scotland
This morning we went out shopping. Glasgow is a big, prosperous-looking city but there is very little about it that is interesting in any way. The names on the shops gave me a nice 'at home' feeling, though—McKenzie's, McLeods, Simpsons, Macneills, and so on, just like an Island street. I like shopping here—the clerks are so deferential and attentive.

In the afternoon we went to the Cathedral—St. Mungo's. This is one of the few interesting places in Glasgow. Moreover, the crypt was the scene of one of *Francis Osbaldistone's* adventures in *Rob Roy*. We saw the pillar by which he is supposed to have stood when warned of his danger by the mysterious voice.

From there we went to the Fine Arts Museum. I cannot say, however, that I enjoy visiting picture galleries, much as I love pictures. I get horribly tired, walking on stone floors and gazing at miles of canvasses. If one had unlimited time and could give an afternoon of leisurely survey and study to each room it

---

†LMM quotes from her notebook.

would be very different of course. But even then the eye becomes glutted with so many pictures and ceases to take pleasure in any."

†*"Glasgow, Scotland*
Wednesday, July 19, 1911
....The most interesting part of the afternoon was that we met Mr. MacMillan—my Scottish correspondent—by tryst at the fountain in the fairy court. We were on the lookout for each other but, although I thought I would know Mr. MacMillan from his photograph I did not recognize him until he accosted Ewan—having met the latter when he was in Scotland before. He is a slight, fair, nice-looking chap and one of the best conversationalists I have ever met. He dined with us this evening at St. Enoch's and we are to visit him in Alloa later on."

"Mr. Geo. B. MacMillan"

†*"St. Enoch's Hotel, Glasgow*
July 22, 1911, Saturday
Thursday afternoon we left on an excursion to Oban, Staffa and Iona. We went by rail to Oban and the scenery was certainly beautiful, especially along Loch Awe, with its ruined castle. Beautiful—yes. And yet neither there nor elsewhere in England or Scotland did I see a scene more beautiful than can be seen any fine summer evening in Cavendish standing on the 'old church hill' and looking afar over the ponds to New London Harbor. But then we have no ruined castles—nor the centuries of romance they stand for!..."

"Climbing over the Staffa rocks
to Fingal's Cave"

†*"Sunday, July 30, 1911*
Royal Hotel, Princes Street,
Edinburgh
If we 'count time by heart throbs'—by our experience for delight and suffering—it is much moie than a week since my last entry. This week has been a mixture of pleasure and misery.

Last Monday we went out to Ayr with a 'Cook' guide...; to the Trossachs...Wednesday....This was one of the expeditions I have looked forward to all my life—ever since I read 'The Lady of the Lake' in schooldays....

Friday we came to Edinburgh and are at a very nice hotel in Princes Street. Princes Street is another disappointment to me. It *is* a fine street—and the more I see of it the more I realize how fine it really is. But it isn't the Princes St. of my dreams—the fairy avenue of gardens and statuary and palaces. Probably no such street exists in the world—but I can't quite forgive it for that.

Saturday was a nightmare of a day. We went with a Cook's Excursion around Edinburgh. It poured rain the whole time and I was the victim of a peculiarly annoying and misery-producing ailment—to wit, cystitis, of which I had an attack several years ago in Halifax. It completely robbed the day of all pleasure for me. I went through Edinburgh castle and Holyrood Palace like one in a bad dream. Even the famous cabinet where Rizzio was murdered left me indifferent. I only wished to get back to the hotel and go to bed—hide myself away from every eye. Besides my physical discomfort my trouble produced a singular nervous effect. I shrank from being seen by anyone—to be looked at by anyone was absolute torture—to be compelled to speak to anyone, or have a remark addressed to me was agony.

"Coaching" in Scotland

I feel quite well to-day. I do hope I shall not have as long an attack of this as I had in Halifax. If I do my trip will be completely spoiled."

†*"Sunday, Aug. 6, 1911*
Royal Hotel, Princes St.
Edinburgh, Scotland

Sightseeing is really horribly hard work. I'm fagged out—though I suppose it was more the physical and nervous misery of parts of the week than the knocking about that has wearied me. Last Monday we went by train to Melrose and coached over six miles of most beautiful road to Abbotsford.... Abbotsford is most interesting and crowded with relics. I should have loved to dream over them in solitude. But that might not be. The rooms were filled by a chattering crowd, harangued by a glib guide. I wondered if Scott would have liked this—to see his home overrun by a horde of curious sight seers. I am sure I would not.

....On Wednesday we started on an expedition to Inverness, but stopped off during the afternoon to visit Kirriemuir, the 'Thrums' of J.M. Barrie's delightful stories....one of the few places in Britain to which I look back with a longing to see it again. It is not yet famous enough to be spoiled...."

72

"Abbotsford"

[*Postcard of Sir Walter Scott's home*]

†*"Sunday, Aug. 13, 1911*
Berwick on Tweed
....Wednesday afternoon we left Edinburgh and went to Alloa, Mr. MacMillan's town. We had been invited to spend a few days with the family of his *fiancee*, Miss Jean Allan. When we started I was so miserable I did not see how I was going to endure it at all. But. fortunately by the time we reached Alloa I was so much better that I could hide my indisposition from others, though not feeling well enough to enjoy myself really.

Miss Allan is a very pretty girl, owing most of her beauty however to her bright golden hair and to her complexion which is simply exquisite. I have read of 'dazzling' complexions but I never saw one before. 'Dazzling', however, is exactly the word to apply to Miss Allan's. Her skin is snow-white, with a most delicious wild-rose pink in her cheeks. *I* have always been reputed to have a good complexion, as complexions go, but Miss Allan positively makes me look brown and sallow. It is a wholesome corrective of vanity to look into a mirror when she is before it, too, but I don't do it when I can help it, for all that!

After dinner Mr. MacMillan came and we all walked out to Gartmorn Dam, by way of a lovely wood-road, companioned by a beautiful brook. I was not well enough to enjoy it, lovely as it all was. But in the evening I felt quite well and really enjoyed the long walk we took out to Tullibody. (Isn't that just such a name as a Scotchman could invent?) It must have been nearly five miles out there but the night was moonlight and Mr. MacMillan is a delightful companion for such an expedition. He knows all the legends and traditions of the surrounding country and is a most congenial conversationalist.

I doubt if poor Ewan, walking behind us with Miss Allan enjoyed the walk as much as I did. Miss A's stock in trade is her twenty-year-old freshness and her charming complexion. She has little else—no intellect, and certainly no conversational powers....

Yesterday we came to Berwick. Mr. MacMillan had planned to spend his vacation here with us and we asked Miss Allan to come too, as our guest, for his sake. Berwick is in the heart of the *Marmion* country. We have lodgings at a certain Mrs. Pringle's in a suburb known as Spittal. They differ somewhat from the hotel in Princes St. but we can put up with them for a week. It is difficult to get good lodgings here unless spoken for far in advance, as it is a popular seaside resort. Berwick is a most quaint antiquated old town. As we 'live' on the Spittal side when we want to go anywhere we have to be rowed over the river mouth by one of the half dozen quaint old ferrymen who have boats for hire.

Last night we all went for a walk along the shore in the moonlight. It was beautiful but so like the Cavendish shore that it made me bitterly homesick."

†*"Carlisle, August 20, 1911*

We are spending Sunday in Carlisle perforce, since we could not get any further last night, owing to the big railway strike which has been paralyzing England this past week. We, in our seaside seclusion at Berwick, did not suffer from it or heed it. We let the outer world go by and lived in realms of romance....

We had an enjoyable sail down to Holy Island but the return home was sadly different....Luckily seasickness is never fatal and we were all right next day and ready for another excursion to Norham Castle....Growing all over the grounds was a little blue flower which I never saw anywhere else save in the old front orchard at home in Cavendish. Grandmother Woolner had brought it out from England with her. It gave me an odd feeling of pain and pleasure mingled to find it growing there around that old ruined mediaeval castle which seemed to belong so utterly to another time and another order of things.

We walked from Norham to Ladykirk, a very interesting old church, and then back by the Tweed. When we grew tired we sat down on its twilight banks and rested—and dreamed dreams. What the others thought of I do not know. *I* was arranging furniture in Leaskdale Manse.

Next day we went to Flodden Field. We had to walk three miles from the station and as the day was fine and the scenery beautiful this agreed with all of us except Miss Allan, who didn't seem to like walking and sulked the whole way. That same young lady, in spite of her angelic appearance, has a temper which promises ill for Mr. Mac-Millan's future felicity. She contrived to spoil our Flodden expedition to a certain extent, for she gave a certain thunderstormy feeling to our mental atmosphere. Ewan had previously remarked to me that he thought Miss A. felt rather 'out of it' while Mr. M. and I were absorbed in long literary discussions. So on this day I was at pains to walk and talk with Miss Allan or Ewan. But this did not seem to agree with her either, so that my painstaking self-effacement was quite thrown away....

That evening we had a delightful moonlight walk along the shore. It was the best part of the day.

Thursday morning Ewan and I took Mr. M. and Miss A. for a motor ride. In the afternoon we had a delightful little expedition. We went out to Cold-stream Station and walked through a

"Ewan, Miss Allan and Mr. MacMillan"

pretty by-path along a ravine to a romantic old deserted mill in Horncliffe Glen. It might have served as a model for a ghost story. But the dearest part of it was that in the midst of the ravine we came upon a clump of spruce trees literally loaded with gum—the first of the kind I had seen since leaving home. Spruce gum and the delights of picking it seem quite unknown in Scotland. Ewan and I had a lovely half hour then and there picking it and fancying ourselves in the homeland. To me, the gum tasted delicious but neither Mr. M. nor Miss A. liked the flavor, declaring it was 'bitter'. When I come to think of it—which I never did before—spruce gum *is* bitter. But it's a nice bitterness.

From the old mill we walked on to the Union Bridge, which crosses the Tweed where the latter forms the boundary between England and Scotland. We had tea in a little house on the Scottish side—'tea' by the way, doesn't mean here what it means at home!—and then we went for a boat row on the Tweed. This would have been the most enjoyable part of the day if Miss Allan, who had behaved very well up to then, had not chosen to make another exhibition of her temper. When Mr. MacMillan first proposed the row she seemed quite pleased, while Ewan and I expressed ourselves enthusiastically. But when we got into the boat Miss A. suddenly discovered that Mr. MacMillan was himself to be the oarsman, instead of the proprietor. She at once declared she was frightened to go on the water with him and demanded that he give up the expedition. Mr. MacMillan replied by pushing out. I think he wanted to give Mr. Macdonald and me the pleasure we had expressed ourselves as so eager for and I think he was a little nettled at Miss Allan's tone and manner. I had opened my mouth to say we would not go since Miss A. objected but I shut it again without saying anything. I had looked into her face and had seen that, if she had been frightened when she first spoke, she was no longer so. She was simply and solely furious. Really, I never saw anyone behave much worse. It all made me uncomfortable and yet I was hugely amused. She was so ridiculous in her futile rage. Mr. MacMillan, I verily believe, kept us out all the longer for the occasional sarcastic sentences she threw at him, as if she had bitten them off with a snap from some bitter cud, and she was quite beside herself in a white fury when we got back to land. We had to walk two miles to the station and Miss Allan tore off up the road the minute she sprang on shore. I felt that it would not do for me to linger behind with the men so I hurried off with her! 'Twas a pleasant walk! Miss Allan would not talk and finally I, exasperated at her unreasonable and ungrateful behavior, gave up trying to talk to her and we strode over the last mile in complete silence. Poor MacMillan got a dressing-down later on. At least, the sole remark she vouchsafed to me was that she meant to give him one. He must be pretty deeply in love with her to tolerate her behavior. And he *must* have felt rotten over it. But he behaved irreproachably.

Friday morning Miss A. had recovered her temper and we spent the day prowling about the shore and talking—and I think it was the most enjoyable day of all. Saturday we packed up and left. We were not sorry to depart from the Pringle establishment, since it was the reverse of convenient or agreeable. Nor did we deeply lament leaving Miss Allan; but we were genuinely sorry to see the last of Mr. MacMillan who is a very fine fellow and the best of company.

We had hoped to reach Keswick last night but could get no further than here, owing to the strike. Our journey here from Berwick was most uncomfortable, for ours was the only train that got through and it was crowded. Our compartment was only seated for eight but thirteen were in it and it was a very warm day. We had nothing to eat or drink from breakfast time till six last evening. I was so tired and worn out that I spent most of today in bed.

I find railway travel here even more fatiguing than at home in any case. I do not like the compartment system at all.

We heard tonight that the strike is over and we shall be able to go on tomorrow."

†*"Sunday, August 27, 1911*
York, England
....Tuesday was, I am sure, the most delightful day we have yet spent. We took the coach drive to Buttermere Lake and back. The road is beautiful, grand, awe-inspiring—and wild enough in places. We enjoyed the whole day. And I may as well admit that after all the best part of it was the two hours after lunch at Buttermere when we sat alone together on a little wooded eminence overhanging the lake and forgot all the rest of the world in a little bit of 'honeymooning' in our green seclusion.

Wednesday morning we took a motor drive of 80 miles around Lake Windermere, calling at Wordsworth's grave and the quaint little cottage where he lived for twenty years after his marriage and where we talked with an old lady who in her girlhood had been a maid of Wordsworth's and his wife....

Thursday afternoon we went to Leeds and next morning motored twenty miles through a very ugly country to Haworth to visit the home and burial place of Charlotte Bronte. We could not see the interior of the old Parsonage where she lived her strange life and wrote her compelling books, but it was something to see it from the outside....

Yesterday we intended to go on to London but I was too miserable to travel. Since leaving Alloa I have been perfectly well but yesterday another attack of that wretched little trouble overtook me. I was most miserable in the morning but felt quite well in the afternoon and went out for a walk around York; in the course

Grasmere and Helm Crag
[*Postcard*]

of which I became the proud and happy possessor of two pairs of china dogs!

I have been pursuing China dogs all over England and Scotland! When I was a little girl, visiting at Grandfather Montgomery's, I think the thing that most

"The Parlor"
[in Leaskdale, with china dogs]

enthralled me was a pair of China dogs which always sat on the sitting room mantel piece....

I have always hankered to possess a pair of similar dogs and as those had been purchased in London I hoped when I came over I would find something like them. Accordingly, I have haunted the antique shops in every place I have been, but, until yesterday, without success. Dogs to be sure there were in plenty, but not the dogs of my quest. There was an abundance of dogs with black spots and some few dogs with red spots, but nowhere the aristocratic dogs with green spots. I had about given up in despair. But yesterday in a little antique shop near the Minster I found two pairs of lovely dogs—and bought them on the spot, lest they be enchanted dogs which would vanish forever if I made them not mine immediately. To be sure, they had no green spots. The race of dogs with green spots seems to have become extinct. But one pair of them had lovely *gold* spots and were much larger than the Park Corner dogs. The others were white ones, cutely got up as half shaved poodles. They are over a hundred years old and in that Leaskdale manse, which is as yet only a dream to me, I hope they will preside over my hearth with due dignity and aplomb."

†"*Sunday, September 3, 1911*
Russell Hotel, London, England
This has been, for the most part, a really wretched week for me. Last Monday morning we left York for London. Just as the train started I was attacked by another fit of my malady and that ride to London was a nightmare to me. I never suffered such misery in my life. I had looked forward to the journey through that historic country—but I do not now remember a single feature of it. It is all a blank of suffering to me. When we reached London we came to the Russell Hotel and have been here ever since. It is in Russell Square—the haunt of so many of the characters in *Vanity Fair*. One expects to see *Amelia* peering out of a window, looking for George, or perhaps *Becky* watching for *Jos*.

But when I reached the Russell I was in no mood for literary reminiscences—though I would most devoutly have agreed with anyone who stated that all was vanity indeed. What mattered it to me that I was in London, where great kings and queens had walked and great writers lived. All *I* wanted was to get to bed, out of sight of anyone, and to bed I went. Tuesday morning I continued to feel badly; but I felt better in the afternoon and we went to the British Museum, which is quite near the Russell. I had just began to feel the charm of its wonderful galleries when I became so miserable that we had to return to the hotel, where I went to bed and had a doctor in again—who looked even wiser than the Edinburgh one and did me just as much—or as little—good...."

†*"Sunday, Sept. 10, 1911*
Russell Hotel, London, England
....Yesterday morning we went by 'bus to Warwick and visited the castle there—not a ruin but a very beautiful and interesting place—a good example of 'the stately homes of England'. Then we took a taxi to Stratford to see Shakespeare's birthplace. The road lies through one of the loveliest parts of England—rural England at its best. On our way our driver pointed out the Lucy place—the residence of Sir Thomas Lucy, who earned a dubious fame for himself by fining Shakespeare for poaching. I really think poor old Sir Thomas has been hardly dealt with. His was no prophet's eye to pierce futurity and see what this stripling was ultimately to become. To him, Shakespeare seemed merely and quite naturally, to be a young scapegrace who richly deserved the lecture and fine bestowed on him lest he come to worse things. Perhaps, too, he *would* have come to worse things had not his deer-stalking escapade resulted in his being caught up thus sharply. It may be that the world owes a large and unacknowledged debt to poor pompous Sir Thomas. If he had let Shakespeare off the lad might have gone on sowing his wild oats until something really serious came of it and the poaching developed into some more reckless offence severely punishable by the drastic laws of the time. Shakespeare might have adorned a gallows instead of a stage and gone down to death 'unwept, unhonored, and unsung' as a wild ne'er-do-well who had come to the end meet for him...."

†*"Monday, Sept. 18, 1911*
Russell Hotel, London, England
This past week has been packed full—too full. I really can't enjoy things in such wholesale quantities. But when time is limited and 'sights' unlimited what are harassed travellers to do? For one thing at least I have been most devoutly thankful—I have felt very well, having had no return of that most distressing ailment....

We went to lunch in a noted Strand restaurant with Mr. Hynes, the business manager of the Pitman firm who publish my books in England. He was a very nice man and we enjoyed our lunch with him muchly. That over we rushed to a station and went down to Windsor to see the castle and palace there. When we came out we saw the crowd looking excitedly upward. Following their glances we beheld a flying machine soaring across the sunset sky like some huge bird. This was the first time we had seen one and I was quite excited over it.

When we got back to London we went to see 'Macbeth'. Beerbohm Tree played the name part. He was excellent and the staging was good. *Lady Macbeth*, however, was poor and they 'played to the gallery' in the supernatural parts, which were just vulgarly 'spooky' and entirely lacking in the real weirdness and mystery and subtlety which should characterize the scenes. Still, on the whole, it was exceedingly enjoyable.

Friday we went to Oxford and saw as many of its interesting old colleges as we had time for. This involved a great deal of walking and I was dreadfully tired when we got back to London. I am beginning to feel that I have had enough of sight seeing and knocking about, for one time. I am tired of living in a trunk—and I am tired of hotel cookery. And I want a *home* again. I am tired of living under stranger roofs. We sail for home next Thursday on the *Adriatic* and I feel heart glad at the thought. I want to get back to Canada, to build my nest and gather my scattered household gods all about me for a new consecration.

However, 'to resume and to continue':—

Saturday morning we visited the Houses of Parliament and in the afternoon we started on what was, to me, the most interesting of all our expeditions. We went down to Dunwich, the little seashore village on the coast of Suffolk where grandmother was born and lived until she was twelve.

I had always been determined to hunt this place up if ever I came over to England. My fancy had always clung around the idea of it. Grandmother, with the reserve that always characterized her, very seldom spoke of her old home; but she did so occasionally and her remarks always lingered in my mind. I learned more of it from grandfather, though, who often repeated what he had heard of it from Great grandfather Woolner. From one hint or another I had built up a well-defined picture of it—which, I need not say, proved to be quite unlike the reality.

We reached Darsham station in the afternoon and got a cab to take us over to Dunwich, a distance of six miles. I looked at everything as we drove along with keen interest and eagerness. Very likely grandma and Aunt Margaret, when they were little girls, had looked on those very scenes and may have driven over that very road. Half way to Dunwich we crossed a belt of waste land or 'commons' which was very bleak and uninviting. But beyond that it was pastoral England again and presently we found ourselves in Dunwich—the quaintest, sleepiest, most out of the world little village imaginable, right down on the crumbling Suffolk coast. We went to the 'Ship Inn' and got quarters with difficulty for they were full and we had to take an attic room of few conveniences. Then, after tea, we started out to try to find some trace of the whereabouts of the old Woolner farm. At first I was in despair. It seemed as if the race that knew Joseph had utterly passed away. Nobody had ever heard of the name of Woolner or had any idea where his home had been—or any other idea, apparently, for the natives of Dunwich seemed the most hopelessly stupid folks I have ever tried to extract information from. But at last, after persistent inquiry I located an old man of 86, named Samuel Scarlett, who gave me all the information I required. He said he remembered perfectly being at the Woolner auction when he was a boy of twelve. The farm where they had lived was about ten minutes walk from the village and he said the buildings were all in good preservation and exactly as the Woolners had left them. Much excited over this, I rewarded old Mr. Scarlett with a half sovereign and we started off, soon reaching the long lane with its hawthorn hedges, leading up to the old place. The house is a building of red brick surrounded by beautiful trees, with an old garden in front, hedged in by hawthorn. It is not occupied at present. By good fortune the man of the next farm, who had the key, was at the barn when we got there, and he unlocked the house and let us go all over it.

I cannot describe my feelings—nor account for them. I had expected to feel an interest in the place, naturally; but I had the strangest sensation of *coming home.* My emotion almost overpowered me. It seemed to me that grandmother and Aunt Margaret *must* be somewhere around, little laughing girls of twelve and fourteen—such as I had never been able to picture them before. Their bright eyes seemed to me to peep around the corners—I seemed to hear the patter of their flying footsteps, the

"Old Woolner house"
[*Dunwich, England*]

rustle of their whispers and laughter. I was homesick—and yet I felt as if I had come home. It seemed to me that the Woolner auction must have been a thing of yesterday—as if the family had just moved out of the house, leaving it still warm from their presence. If the house had been occupied I might not have felt like this. But as it was, it seemed as if the Woolners had just gone.

We left it in the twilight and walked back to the inn. Then we went to the shore and sat there for a long time, watching the peculiar and beautiful phenomena of phosphorescent waves—such as I had never seen before. My heart was full. It seemed to me that back there, behind that village, was a home—a home empty and deserted, with no light gleaming from its windows, just as another home, thousands of miles to the sunsetting was also blank and empty and fireless. I thought of grandmother and how interested she would have been in hearing from her old home. It was a bitter thought that I could never tell her. I cried myself to sleep that night—tears of longing and homesickness that seemed partly my own and partly some long-dead emotion of the vanished years.

The next morning we went again to the old place and I took several photos of it for Aunt Margaret. Then we went into the field behind the house and sat down for a couple of hours talking and eating bramble-berries from the hedge. I loved to be there and when we had to go I felt as I had felt when I left the old home of Cavendish.

We walked back to the village by way of the shore, seeing on our way the ruined tower, right on the very brink of the crumbling cliff, of the old church built hundreds of years before.

After dinner we hired a pony and trap—and oh, how slow that pony was! Slow!!!—and started out to hunt up a place called Knodishall, seven miles away, where lived a certain Mrs. Robert Collins of whom Mr. Scarlett had told me. Great grandfather Woolner was married twice. His first wife, Margaret Tuthill, died, leaving a daughter Caroline. This Caroline was grown up and married to one James Rous, when the Woolners 'went foreign', as the saying is in Dunwich. The aforesaid Mrs. Collins was one of Caroline Woolner's children and therefore a cousin of sorts. We found her home eventually. Mr. Scarlett had told us that she had married beneath her and that her father never forgave her. So I was not surprised to find her living in a rather humble way, though quite comfortable. She was very glad and interested when she found out who I was and she showed me her mother's picture and gave me a good deal of information about her family.

On our way back to Dunwich we stopped at Westleton churchyard, where we found several Woolner graves, including that of Margaret Tuthill and a certain 'Lucy Ann Woolner' who died in 1812—a hundred years ago almost— aged sixteen. I think she must have been a sister of grandfather Woolner's and that grandmother must have been called after her. *He* sleeps far from the wife of his youth. He is buried in the graveyard of the old English church at South Rustico and she sleeps alone in that quaint old English burying ground.

This morning we came back to London. We had planned to pack up this afternoon and go over to Ireland in the morning, to see the Lakes of Killarney and join our boat at Queenstown. But on arriving here we found that a big railway strike was on in Ireland and that it would be too 'risky' to go. I daresay when I am home and thoroughly rested I shall feel sorry that I did not get a glimpse of Ireland also. But at present my feeling is one of unmitigated satisfaction. I am horribly tired. I am sated with sight seeing. I had dreaded the task of packing up this afternoon and starting off again in the morning. Now I shall have a good rest before we start for home."

† *"Sunday, Sept. 24, 1911*
Deck of the Adriatic
Mid-Atlantic
Homeward bound! Leagues of tossing ocean behind us, leagues of tossing ocean before us! And beyond it our ain countree and the 'old familiar faces'. Though, for me, there will be no familiar faces in the new home to which I am going. The thought is a little bitter.

Tuesday and Wednesday we put in packing up and visiting one or two places we had not been able to see before. Thursday afternoon we did our duty in the way of tips and after lunch took the boat train for Liverpool, which we reached at seven, and went on board the *Adriatic*.

We had had a beautiful summer but we were both heart-glad to be going home. As I stood on deck and watched the splendid scene made by the lights of Liverpool and the docks as we steamed down the Mersey in the darkness I said good-bye to the wonderful old land and turned my thoughts joyfully westward."

*....It continued cold and damp and rough but I was not again seasick. We got into New York on Friday morning in such a driving downpour of rain that we could not see anything. Although our boxes went through in bond we had to wait a long while in the Custom House, and the horrible hurly-burly made my head ache. Then we waited in N.Y. station for our train. We travelled all night, getting to Toronto in the morning. Marjorie MacMurchy met us and we had lunch with her and her sister. At five we took the train for Uxbridge, our home station, and reached it at dark. Two or three of Mr. Macdonald's friends met us and it was nice to be welcomed. But I was dreadfully tired; it was a damp, murky autumn night, and when we started on our muddy seven mile drive I felt discouraged, heartsick and homesick.

"Uxbridge Station"
[*Ontario*]

The next time I went over that road it was glorious with October sunshine and crimson maples, with snug, prosperous farmsteads along it, and I thought it a very pretty road indeed. But that night in the starless darkness it was merely one long *blot* of wet shadow and seemed hopelessly dismal.

When we arrived at Ewan's boarding house—where we were to live until we could get the manse furnished—we found that our telegram had never reached them and we were not expected. "They" are two old maids, Mary and Lizzie Oxtoby, who would have delighted Dickens. No pen but his could do them justice. And oh, they are queer—at

"Ewan's boarding house, Leaskdale"

least, it was only their queerness I saw that first night. And I have never liked Lizzie who is a narrow minded gossip, but there is a sort of innocent sweetness—without a grain of flavor—about Mary, which makes me like her now as I would like a child. But that night I thought "Is *this* the kind of people I must live among?" And when we went up to the tiny little bedroom, more inconvenient than any place I have ever been in since I boarded at Fraser's in "Sixteen", I was homesick and tearful and blue. I felt that I would *never* like Ontario and that existence here would be impossible.

Next morning was very wet, but there was a fair turn-out at church. Curiosity, I suppose, was strong to see the "new minister's wife". I passed through

---

*LMM continues the journal entry which began January 28, 1912.

82

an ordeal of handshaking and good wishes. How I would be talked over at the dinner tables of the congregation that day!

Leaskdale Presbyterian Church Outside

Leaskdale Presbyterian Church Inside

Ewan's congregation has two sections—Leaskdale and Zephyr. The Leaskdale church is new and is a nice little one of white brick. The Leaskdale people are all quite nice, being for the most part well-to-do farmers. It is not quite so in Zephyr. The church is old and unattractive, with windows whose panes are—or were—of "frosted" glass; half of the "frosting" has worn off each pane, producing the effect of a dull day in winter time, no matter what the season of the year. Some of the people are nice; but there are many who are not attractive in any way and, taken as a whole, I do not like the Zephyr section. Ewan finds it unsatisfactory—lacking in "church spirit" and incapable of taking leadership.

The manse is quite prettily situated. It is not an ideal house by any means, but it will do, and it is certainly much more comfortable and convenient than my old home. It is built of white brick in the ugly "L" design so common among country houses. My greatest disappointment in connection with it is that it has no bathroom or toilet. I *had* hoped that I might have a home with these at least. But what is to be will be! It is Allah! We must submit.

Leaskdale proper is a small—a *very* small—village, called after the Leasks who originally settled here. I have always hated the idea of living in a small village. But Leaskdale is *so* small—only about ten or twelve houses—that it is almost as good as the pure country. It is quite a pretty little place. There are no young people in it—absolutely none. The residents are all oldish—or else mere children. There isn't one interesting or really intelligent person in it.

The first Sunday evening we slipped down in the dusk to see the manse—for I was eager to see my new home. As I have said, it is quite prettily situated—though a tumble-down old building on either side of it—the crumbling remains of old shops—detract terribly from the appearance of the place. We are much too close to the road for my liking—I love solitude and remoteness. We have a rather pretty little lawn. I wish it were eight times as large but we must make the best of it. It has some pretty trees in it and I plan to have some flower-beds in the spring. There is enough ground at the back for a fair sized kitchen garden.

When we came in that first night and surveyed the place by lantern light it didn't look very home-like! Boxes of goods and chattels were scattered about and torn paper was hanging in strips from ceilings and walls. But I had a mental vision of what it would be when we got it all in order and I ran over the house like a pleased child. It was *our* home and I was its mistress. No woman ever forgets that delightful sensation—especially if, like me, she has never lived in any house before where she had any rights or privileges beyond those of a dependent child. I was sorry to leave it and go back to the Oxtoby domicile. *En deshabille* as it was it was more like home to me than the latter place. The Misses Oxtoby had been very kind to me, but I did not like living there. The table was poor and our room terribly inconvenient. I longed to get into my own home. But before that devoutly wished consummation could come to pass there was some work to be done!

View of front lawn
[Leaskdale Manse]

I spent Monday in the manse unpacking some of my boxes and occasionally suffering agonies of homesickness over some of their contents. But it was nice to see my own little household gods once more.

†*"Tuesday, Oct. 3, 1911*
Leaskdale, Ont.
To-night the congregation gave us a reception in the church. We had a rather nice time, though I was dreadfully tired when it was over; meeting and talking to so many strangers. One of the names, however, was not unknown to me. Two of the men I met were Hugh and James *Mustard*. By the oddest of coincidences I have come to live in *John Mustard's* old home. These men are his brothers. They are nice, intelligent men, much superior to John. The Rev. John himself is now in charge of a small mission church in Toronto. He has married and has one son. He is coming out to see his relatives before long and we are to meet him. I really never expected that life would thus double back on itself and bring me into touch with John Mustard again."

---

†LMM quotes from her notebook.

*The next day we drove to Uxbridge—where, by the way, my stepmother attended High School—and went up to Toronto where we stayed until Friday, getting paper and furniture for our house. The two months that followed were months of hard work—work that was made harder by well-meant invitations to tea from the families of the congregation. To work hard all day, trying to get the manse in order and then in the evening, aching with fatigue, to dress and go out to tea spending the evening "making small talk" or looking at photographs of people I hadn't the slightest interest in, was something of a weariness to the flesh. Sometimes I would be so wretchedly tired that in spite of the most determined efforts, I could hardly keep my eyes open.

The manse had to be papered all over from top to bottom and while the man we got to do it was on the job we could not make much headway in getting settled, especially as we had the most aggravating delays in getting our stuff out from Toronto. However, I got my boxes unpacked and the contents ready to be put in place when place was made for them.

"Leaskdale Manse"

†*"Friday, October 13, 1911*
Leaskdale, Ont.
I had quite a surprise to-day. My half-sister Kate suddenly appeared at my boarding house!

It seems that she and Ila are in Toronto on their way to spend a year in Europe. Kate had come out to Beaverton to visit cousins of hers there and her

---

*LMM continues the journal entry which began January 28, 1912.
†LMM quotes from her notebook.

cousin had motored her over to see me. They had only a short time to stay.

When I last saw Kate she was a child of three and beyond doubt the most beautiful child I have ever seen, with golden curls and wonderful eyes of violet blue. She is now twenty three and has no trace of her childish loveliness. She is merely average in appearance—very short, dark haired and insignificant, but with a rather pleasant smile. Her eyes are pretty still but are her only good feature. She looks more like her mother than any of father's people but is better looking than her mother, who was a very plain woman.

From her letters and the reports of my P.A. correspondents I had formed a pretty clear idea of her personality and my idea approximated pretty closely to the reality. She seems a rather frivolous little creature whose sole aim in life seems to be to 'have a good time'. This is natural and excusable enough in a girl of fifteen or sixteen but from twenty-three one expects some real development of character, if there is ever going to be any. I found nothing congenial in Kate. We had nothing in common and her call could not have been any more a pleasure to her than it was to me."

†*"Wednesday, October 18, 1911*
Leaskdale, Ont.
Tonight we had our first meal in the manse under somewhat ludicrous circumstances—certainly not quite as I had fondly imagined would attend our first meal in our new home. The cookery of the Misses O. is not the highest expression of culinary skill. So, though I have a capital appetite, I cannot eat very heartily thereof, and am generally in a state of chronic hunger, especially at bedtime. To-day the table was particularly poor and I was uncommonly hungry, having been employed most of the day in scrubbing manse floors and getting my kitchen into order. In the evening we went to prayer-meeting and when we came out I was really ravenous. I knew that if I asked the Miss O's for anything to eat some 'sweet stuff' would be forthcoming and *that* I could not eat. But I remembered that in the manse pantry was a box of eggs which Mrs. Hugh Mustard gave me the night we were there to tea. So Ewan went down to the store and got a box of crackers. We went down to the manse, lighted the oil stove, boiled a couple of eggs, broke them into cups, as we had not egg cups, and with the aid of salt and the dry crackers ate what was quite as delicious and satisfying a meal as I have ever enjoyed! Truly, there is no sauce like hunger!

It was an exciting time. Every day something arrived—wedding presents, things we had bought, belongings of mine left at various places until sent for. We had no place ready for them and had to move about in terrible confusion. The kitchen was the only solace I had, for it was in order and things in their place. We worked from early morning until late at night. The work was delightful and interesting because we were home-making but it was none the less physically fatiguing."

†*"Saturday, Oct. 21, 1911*
Leaskdale, Ont.

There is the prettiest 'side road', running down from the manse, through trees and woods. Every time I pass it on my way back and forth between here and the Oxtoby domicile it holds out to me an almost irresistible lure. It beckons me—'Come, I have trees and solitude and the woodland beauty you love'. But I have to resist it, because I have no time to spare for it just now. Yet it tugs at my heart strings. Oh, how I miss Lover's Lane and my old woodland haunts! Can I ever really *live* without them?"

†*"Sunday, Oct. 22, 1911*
Leaskdale, Ont.

When we go out to tea I *wish* people wouldn't ask us to play 'Croquinole' or insist on showing me all the photographs they have! They don't seem to have any other way of entertaining. I loathe 'croquinole' with a deadly hatred. As for the photos—well if they would just give me the photos and let me look over them in peace, it wouldn't be so bad because human faces have always a certain interest. But somebody must sit beside you and explain them all—'That is my Uncle Richard'—'that is my grandfather'—'that is my cousin in Chicago'—'that is a hired boy who worked for us'. And you feel as if you were called upon to make some comment upon Uncle Richard and the hired boy and the Chicago cousin and you wonder miserably what in the world you can say, not knowing or caring anything about them and rarely finding any inspiration in their commonplace phiz's."

†*"Tuesday, Oct. 24, 1911*
Leaskdale, Ont.

Yes, we have really 'moved in'—set up our own Lares and Penates. The great event happened yesterday. I really couldn't endure the Oxtoby *menage* any longer, not to speak of the inconvenience of our double existence. We had planned to move in last Friday, the papering being done and the floors all scrubbed. But, although some of our furniture had come no bedstead had made its appearance. We hoped one would come yesterday. None did. But I declared desperately that I wasn't going to wait any longer. So after tea last night down we came. I have twenty right good fat feather cushions. I put them on the floor of a bedroom, made them up with sheets and quilts and pillows, and there we slept! It was somewhat hilly and hollowy, but I have slept on many a worse couch!

We did not seek it early however. We stayed up and worked till one o'clock, Ewan painting the border of the library floor and I getting various 'jobs' done. We were so tired when we went to bed that we could have slept soundly on a bare floor. But we were 'at home' and in spite of the wild confusion of every apartment save kitchen and pantry, it really is home-like."

*The next fortnight we worked slavishly. Most nights we worked till one, two and even three o'clock. But by November 2nd we had things pretty well in order at last, and I was ready to "receive". Much still remained to be done for our furniture came out from Toronto in driblets and delayed us terribly. But eventually we got all done. Room after room was rescued from chaos, and at last my longed-for home was an accomplished fact—no longer a dream but a reality.

I am pleased with my home. I think it is furnished as comfortably as its limitations permit and in good taste, with things we will not tire of. At first, all our new possessions seemed to me to be a little strange to each other. But now they have got acquainted. Up to New Year's I was so busy all the time that I really had no time to *enjoy* my home—to *realize* it. But now I have more leisure and am beginning to re-alize the delight and comfort of many things that have been long absent from my life—or were never in it.

This doesn't mean that I do not even yet have agonizing hours of homesickness—hours where nothing seems to me able to make up for the loss of my old beloved haunts and the wild sweetness of solitary dreaming therein. Such hours come very often when I am alone. But they are not continuous. I am contented—I may say happy. There is an absolute hap-piness and comparative happiness. Mine is the latter. After the unhappi-ness and worry of the past thirteen years this existence of mine seems to me a very happy one. I am—for the most part—content.

"Corner of Parlor"
[*Leaskdale Manse*]

Three rooms open off our entrance hall—parlor, library and dining room. The parlor is a large, square, bright room but not one which lends itself to decoration. It consists of nothing but a floor, a ceiling and four walls broken only by two doors and four high, narrow windows. Neverthe-less, I think I have made a rather pleasant room of it. The wall paper

"Parlor View showing dogs and jug"

---

*LMM continues the journal entry which began January 28, 1912.

is creamy yellow, my curtains are of lace, with straight green brocade over-curtains, and I have a moss-green rug on the floor. The furniture is of Heppel-white design, in mahogany done in brocade. I have some pretty pictures in it, and my big China dogs sit in state, one on either side of the little bookcase—for alas, I have no fireplace in my home. I want one too much ever to have it, I suppose. Great-Grandmother Woolner's old jug, filled with pot-pourri, stands on the table. This old jug has quite a family history. Great-grandmother Wool-ner had a sister named Harriet Kemp. This Harriet had a sailor lover who, on one of his voyages—to Amsterdam I think—had this jug made expressly for his lady-love. Her name and the date—1826—were engraved on it, along with several verses of poetry. On his voyage home he was drowned but the jug was sent to Harriet. Instead of prizing it, as one would rather expect her to do, she

"Library view—my secretary in Corner"

could not endure the sight of it, so gave it to her sister, Great-grand-mother Woolner, who brought it out to Canada filled with black currant jam from her English garden—per-haps the same garden we saw when we were there last summer. For many years thereafter she used it in her dairy to hold her cream—for 'tis a jug of no mean proportions! Once it met with an accident and was badly fractured. Great-grandmother Woolner mended it with white lead and, though the mending is not very artistically done, being all too evident, it was at least done thoroughly and holds good to this day. At her death it passed to grand-mother who, as far back as I can remember, kept it on the top shelf of the old china cabinet in our sitting room. It had by then attained to the dignity of heirloom and was never used for anything, but was generally brought out and displayed to visitors, while grandfather told the story. When we broke up the old home last winter I packed the jug most carefully and it came safely up to Ontario. I prize it beyond all similar possessions.

Our library is a large room similar to the parlor, but with only two windows. It is papered with golden brown paper, has a brown rug and is furnished with Early English oak. I have at last bookcases for all my books and a desk where

"Dining room showing China Cabinet"

I can keep all the notebooks and "utensils" of my trade together. At home I had to keep them in different places. But I did as good work there as I will ever do at my spandy new desk with all its shelves and pigeon holes. Nevertheless, they *are* conve-nient. On the library walls I have several enlarged photos of Lover's Lane and several other Cavendish views. I don't know whether they

"Dining room showing sideboard"

"Spare room"

"My Dressing Table"

"Corner of our room"

delight or pain me most. Over my own desk I have the framed pictures of *Anne*, *Kilmeny* and the *Story Girl*.

The dining room is my most unsatisfactory room, having almost every vice a room can have. It is too small; it is the only way of getting from the kitchen to the other part of the house and so cannot be kept clean easily. It opens into the kitchen and so gets too warm and too smelly. The furnace pipe goes up through it and is *not* decorative. It has five doors and only one window which gives a view of several ugly back yards including our own. Fortunately these things do not affect the flavor of our food!

Upstairs there are five rooms. Ours is a large, pleasant one, with two windows looking south but no closet. I have a pretty set of pearl-gray furniture in it, a crimson rug, and intimate home pictures on the walls. I do not think it possible that I can ever love it as I loved my little room at home. It can never mean to me what that room did. But I like it very much—*especially* after that awful room at Oxtoby's.

The "landing" is quite a nice size and I have furnished it as a sewing room. The other four rooms are small. One which I call the "rosebud room" is done in tones of pink, with a set of white furniture and the other is in blue with Circassian walnut. This one is to be my spare room. One of the others we use to keep trunks and "junk" in and the remaining one is to be furnished later on for a maid.

On November second and third I went through the farce known as "receiving". I had many callers, who came, drank a cup of tea and ate a piece of cake, left oblongs of pasteboard and went away, believing themselves acquainted with me. Later on I returned the calls and left oblongs in my turn—at least, in Uxbridge. Zella Cook, one of the Leaskdale girls helped me "receive". She was Hobson's choice. I do not care for her greatly; I have not found nor did I expect to find any really "kindred spirit" here. Of course, a minister's wife is, or in the interests of discretion should be, barred from making an intimate of any one person among her husband's people. But even if that were not the case there is no one here whom I could admit into my inner circle. To all I try to be courteous, tactful and considerate, and most of them I like superficially. But the gates of my soul are barred against them. They do not have the key.

Early in November I began to suspect that what I had intensely longed for was to be mine and now I know it. I am to be a mother. I cannot realize it. It seems to me so incredible—so wonderful—so utterly impossible as happening to *me*!

But I am glad—so glad. It has always seemed to me that a childless marriage is a tragedy—especially in such a marriage as mine. I realize that maternity is a serious thing and all the more serious to a woman of my age. But not for that would I wish to avoid it. I want to have a child—something to link me with the future of my race. I want to give a human soul a chance to live this wonderful life of ours. I want something of my very own—bone of my bone, flesh of my flesh, to love and cherish. This desire, and the joy in its now probable fulfillment, overpowers all the fears and anxieties that sometimes creep in to disturb me. And above all is the *wonder* of it. I cannot get used to it. The thought that within me I carry *life*—a *soul*—a human being who will live and love and suffer and enjoy and struggle—is so amazing that I am lost before the marvel of it.

But, though thus mentally and emotionally uplifted by it, *physically* I don't seem to be taking to it quite so kindly. While so far my discomfort has not been so great as many women have to undergo, still it has been pronounced enough. I generally feel very miserable in the mornings and very little exertion tires me out completely.

As soon as my house was "set in order" we had to begin a series of "pastoral visitations" which are not yet concluded. I detest this "visiting" since nine out of ten of the visits are wearisome beyond description, both mentally and physically. I have never thought it a very enviable lot to marry a minister but when I did it I made up my mind to perform as best I could such duties as are commonly expected of a minister's wife. Of these, "visiting" is one. Then there are three Missionary Societies here—the Foreign Missions, The Home Missions, and the Mission Band. I am expected to attend all these, of course, and I do it—but!!!

I believe in Missions, especially in Medical Missions—and in giving as one can afford to them. And it may be necessary to the success of Missions—at least from the financial aspect—that these societies exist. But they are most deadly dull affairs. At least, I find them so, and I feel sure I shall never find them anything else. Some women have a natural leaning to them—a sort of *flair* for them, so to speak—and I believe they really enjoy it. I have not, and never will find such meetings anything but unpleasant duties. We meet—the President, Mrs. Geo. Leask—a hopelessly dull and uninteresting woman— opens with a hymn and follows it with a stereotyped prayer. After a little business someone reads a dull chapter out of some book on missions, we sing another hymn, take up a collection and go home. The only part I enjoy is the collection. I like to give the money—and it comes near the last!

During the first three months after coming here I was pestered by letters from women all over the country asking me to "give an address" before some Missionary Meeting or convention of some kind. Really, such women must be geese. They could not, of course, be expected to know that I never give "addresses" on any topic, least of all on missions. But they might have had sufficient common sense to realize that, when I was just home from my wedding trip, with all the work of "getting settled" on my hands, I would certainly have no time or strength to career around the country giving "addresses".

To one and all I sent a polite refusal. I said that the claims of my own special work would take all my spare time and that *I* could not undertake any active mission work beyond the bounds of my husband's congregation. To this resolve they will find I shall firmly adhere. I am not going to waste my time and strength on work for which I have no aptitude, to the neglect of my own work which has been as truly "given" to me to do as any missionary's or minister's.

Besides these aforesaid Societies I teach a class in Sunday School and do a good deal of work for our Young People's Guild, which meets fortnightly. This

I rather like however. It is more in my line. We have a very good guild and the young fry take a great interest in it.

Thursday, November 23rd we spent visiting in Zephyr. I arrived home, very tired, late at night, to find a telegram from George Campbell—"Valuable box shipped today". I felt quite excited at once, despite my fatigue, for I knew that the "valuable box" contained—Daffy.

Of course I must have Daffy sent to me! I couldn't keep house without him. So they shipped him from Kensington by Express, in a box properly provided with air holes and food! Knowing what a nervous animal Daff is, I was really afraid the journey would terrify him to death and at any rate I expected he would make his entire journey vocal with shrieks. Thursday night I knew he must be travelling between Moncton and Montreal, probably half dead with terror, wondering in misery why he had thus been torn from his home again, consigned to the ignominy of such narrow imprisonment, and carried he knew not where. Such a picture of the wretchedness of his little cat mind did my imagination draw that I almost repented having sent for him at all. I felt sure he could never get here alive! He would be smothered or starved or frightened to death. I hoped he would get into Toronto Friday night in time to come out on the last train, so Ewan and I drove into Uxbridge to meet the "Flyer". But no Daff came, so we had to drive home again. Next morning, however, we phoned down to the station and learned that a box "containing a pet" had come for us on the morning train. Ewan could not go down for him then but a neighbour promised to bring him out. He arrived about five o'clock. When Ewan went out to get the box Mrs. Cleland said, "Your kitty is very quiet. There has never been a sound from him since we got him." I heard this and said to myself, "Daff is dead. Otherwise he would never be so quiet as that."

It had, however, probably been the silence of despair for when Ewan brought the box in I saw Daff's bright eyes peering wistfully through a slit in the top. In a few minutes he was free and I had my own gray pussy again. He knew me and seemed quite contented. He was not hungry but terribly thirsty. We kept him in the house and cellar till Monday night when we put him in the coach house loft. There was no Daff in the morning and I spent a most unhappy day and night. But next day Daff walked coolly in and has been perfectly at home ever since. It makes me feel "at home" to have him, too, for he is a living link with the old life, and Cavendish does not seem so far away when I see Daffy curled up on his cushion in perfect feline contentment.

On Tuesday, December 5, I went up to Toronto for a short visit with Marjorie MacMurchy, mainly to attend a reception given by the Canadian Women's Press Club to "Marian Keith" and me. On Tuesday evening Marjorie, Jane Wells Fraser and I went to see John Drew in "A Single Man". This was enjoyable although the play is a silly backboneless affair. On Wednesday "Marian Keith" and I lunched with Marjorie at their club rooms. The former is Mrs. Duncan MacGregor in private life and has written several novels. I have read only one "Duncan Polite" and cared little for it, so I felt very uncomfortable when she praised *my* books enthusiastically. I liked the lady herself very much though. She is a bright little soul, full of fun and humor. The reception

came off at the King Edward that afternoon and was pronounced by all a great success. In reality it was the wearisome, unsatisfying farce all such receptions are and, in their very nature, must be. Thursday I did enjoy myself at luncheon Mr. and Mrs. Beer gave for me at the National Club. But I was heartily glad to get back home that night. There is no place where I enjoy myself more than at home and the older I grow the less inclination I have to go away—at least, on other folk's invitations. Some outings I like. But they are such as I plan myself and are not of the conventional kind at all. Stella and Frede came to spend Xmas with me, Stella coming up from home and Frede from Macdonald College. It was good to see them.

Christmas day we spent at Hugh Mustard's and John Mustard and his wife and son were there. John has not changed much, except to get very gray—almost white. In personality he has not changed at all. He is just the same slow John Mustard, with the same old irritating habit of assuring you that he is "going to tell" you something "awfully funny" and then telling you some flat commonplace thing in which you cannot discern anything even to smile at. His wife, however, is a jolly soul and can talk enough for two. She has a rather pretty face with sparkling black eyes but is so very fat that her appearance isn't especially attractive.

"Marjorie MacMurchy"

On New Year's night I had a dinner party of "down-easters". Cuthbert MacIntyre came out from Toronto where he is in the bank of Nova Scotia.

"Hugh Mustard's House"

Rev. Mr. McKay of Wick and his wife came also. She was Mary James of Ch'town and a chum of Margaret Ross! Rev. Mr. Fraser of Uxbridge is a Nova Scotian and a friend of Ewan's. He is a widower and a clever, intellectual man.

"Cuthbert McIntyre"

"Mr. Fraser"

Win Ross was also here—Margaret's sister. She was visiting with the McKays. I think they all had a nice time and we had a splendid dinner— which I could not enjoy at all. I was just getting over an attack of grippe and felt very miserable and appetiteless. Frede and Cuthbert went away the next day but Stella decided to stay here for the winter. I had to have somebody so I offered her a good salary to help me out.

After New Year's I began my long neglected literary work again. I had been craving to get back to it but it was out of the question previously. I am now re-writing and revising several of my magazine stories. Mr. Page is going to bring out a volume of them in the spring under the somewhat delusive title "Chronicles of Avonlea". Short story volumes never amount to much, so this must just be regarded as a "filler". Nevertheless, I never like to put out work that is not the best I can do, so I have put just as much painstaking into these stories as into my more important books.

March 22nd, 1912
Leaskdale Manse, Ont.
The winter is wearing away—for which thanks be. It has been an unusually cold and stormy one. The roads have been dreadful and this has made our visiting very difficult. It seems to me that we have been doing nothing all winter but "visit". How I loathe these "visits". It seems to me that I waste time horribly thus which would be far better spent on other things. I get home from these calls tired out physically and mentally. The bad roads prevent any pleasure even in the drive.

To-day I finished re-writing the short stories for my new book. It has been hard to find time for it and it is a great relief that it is at last done.

Thursday, Mar. 28, 1912
The Manse, Leaskdale
This has been such a wretched sort of day that I must growl it off in my journal. Being Thursday we went to Zephyr in the afternoon. As Thursday is

Guild and Prayer meeting night there we generally go over that day to do our visiting. I think I hate Zephyr more every time I go to it. It has become inseparably associated in my mind with long wearisome drives over dreadful roads, mixed with calls on the most uninteresting and in many cases ignorant people. I should not have gone today for the roads were beginning to break up. But it was fine and mild and I had promised to go. We made several calls and as the roads were very "pitchy" I began to feel very miserable physically, with a return of cystitis. We had tea with a Mrs. Urquhart—who, by the way, is

"Winter View from front door"

a woman I dislike and distrust. After that came Guild; I was not fit to go—but anything was better than further endurance of Mrs. Urquhart. So I went and endured such misery all through the evening that when the meeting was out I was on the verge of collapse. Had I been near home I might have avoided it. But I had seven miles to drive over a dreadful road and my courage quailed at the prospect. I simply did not see *how* I could endure the drive home—nor did I endure it! I held up until I got away from the people. But as soon as we were alone on that horrible road, where our horse plunged to the bottom at almost every step I gave way and burst into a wild fit of crying—the culmination of my physical discomfort and nervous stress. I *couldn't* stop crying, try as I would. Every bit of courage and strength went out of me and left me limp as a rag. Poor Ewan was dismayed, not being used to "nerves" in women. But he was very patient, understanding what a fearful strain the day had been on a woman in my condition. But I shall never forget that horrible drive home. I suppose it is quite unfair to charge it to the account of Zephyr, but certainly the two will always be associated in my mind.

Still, I have never this winter suffered from any of those distressing nervous attacks which used to harass me in winter. My health is better than it has been for many a year and I am fatter than at any time since I taught in Bedeque. Tonight was simply the climax to a very trying day. One of the little ailments of pregnancy from which I suffer a good deal just now is one that is very trying to the nerves and when an attack of it comes on when I am away from home it almost wears me out, since I cannot yield and explain the trouble but must sit up and talk brightly, pretending that nothing is the matter.

Oh, how besottedly thankful I was to get home tonight! The peace and rest of my own room seemed like a haven of Paradise to a storm-tossed soul. And I am also thankful that "visiting" has come to an end for a time. The spring break-up is on and I shall have a vacation.

Thursday, April 4, 1912
The Manse
Leaskdale, Ont.

Have had such a lovely week of home life and work. I feel like a new creature. To shut the door of my soul on the curiosity and ignorance displayed by so many and retreat into a citadel of dear thoughts and beautiful imaginings—this it affords me peculiar satisfaction to do.

I am very busy just now sewing—making *tiny little dresses* and garments of materials very nice and soft. It is a very sweet and dear occupation—though it doesn't make it seem any more real to me that *my* baby is really coming. *That* continues to seem like a dream. I imagine dimpled little hands coming out of the lace-edged sleeves, dimpled little toes kicking beneath the flounces, laughing eyes gleaming over the frills. Eyes—what color will they be? Brown like its father's, or blue like mine? And will it be a little son or daughter? Of course I want a boy first. But I shall be satisfied with either if all goes well. I feel very nervous when I think of the ordeal before me. It cannot be easy at the best. But I try not to think of it. The pain will not be lessened by living it through a hundred times in anticipation.

The little basket which is to serve as a cradle came to-day and I fixed it all up with pillows and tiny sheets and blankets. How strange it all is—this life coming out of the silence—out of the unknown. My child at least will "come desired and welcomed into life".

Tuesday, April 30, 1912
The Manse, Leaskdale, Ont.

April—and spring! Spring comes a good three weeks earlier here than down home. The last fortnight it has been so delightful to get out and feel the good dry ground underneath my feet instead of wading through snow. April has been a good month. I did not have to go anywhere and I sewed and read and wrote, none daring to make me afraid. I have begun work on a second "Story Girl" volume, though I don't expect to get on very rapidly with it. However, if I can get the skeleton of it blocked out before my confinement I shall be content.

This last fortnight in April I have been miserable enough physically—at least in the afternoons and evenings. I don't suppose I shall be much better until it is all over. I do not mind it so much when no one is here and when I do not have to go anywhere. But when company comes or I have to go to meetings etc. I really suffer a martyrdom of misery, partly physical, partly nervous. This last week, too, we have been housecleaning and I find it doubly hard for a number of reasons. I always liked housecleaning before, but this spring I certainly did not like it.

May 31st, 1912
The Manse, Leaskdale, Ont.

May has been a most interesting month. We began our garden and it is flourishing. It is so delightful to have a garden again. It is so many years since I had one. In the backyard we have our vegetable array and on the lawn our flowers and shrubs. We have had a lot of work getting the place into tolerable shape—for it had been pretty well neglected for several years—but it was pleasant work. Our little "lot" looks so pretty now, when the trees are out and the grass is green. Every morning I make a pilgrimage over our domain to see what has come up during the night.

Oh, how I missed the mayflowers this year! They do not grow here—and spring does not seem wholly spring without them. To be sure, we have some lovely flowers in their place—delicate white and pink "spring beauties" looking very like mayflowers at a little distance, beautiful white and pink trilliums like hot house blossoms, and long-stemmed blue violets. The children hereabouts kept us supplied with bouquets and one delightful evening we had a still more delightful stroll—Ewan, Stella and I—along the side road and up through Mr. Leask's woods to gather trilliums ourselves. 'Twas in wild cherry time and the world was abloom. Memories of Lover's Lane in springtime tugged at my heart.

But all the loveliness of trillium and violet could not quite atone for the lack of mayflowers.

The first two weeks of May I continued subject to attacks of "misery". Since then, however, I have been very well. But I am beginning to feel the inconvenience of increasing size. It is difficult for me to move about. I am not nearly so ungainly as many women are. The "old women" say I "carry it well". Nevertheless, I am decidedly not the slight creature I was a year ago. I seem big all over now—not misshappen but just a big woman. I find it is becoming hard to get up and down, or change from one posture to another. All this however is very little. If it were not for the anguish of the final ordeal, these discomforts would be a small price to pay for the delight of a child. Perhaps, if all goes well and my baby comes to me safely, I shall think even the pain of birth not too large a price. But now, when the end is coming so near, I cannot avoid feeling dread and anxiety. I have never had to endure any intense physical pain. So I fear I shall not bear it well or be very brave and patient. And then— it may even mean my life. The thought is a strange one. To-day I found myself thinking, "Will I be here this day two months?—or shall I be lying in Cavendish churchyard?" And I sowed not a seed this spring without wondering if I should live to see it blossom and bear. I want to live—I have many things I want to do and accomplish and enjoy—and oh, I want to live for my child's sake, if it lives. It is my greatest dread that I may die and yet leave a living child to suffer and lose what I have suffered and lost by being motherless! If I am not to live I pray that my child may not live either.

I do not allow these thoughts to master me or make me morbid. But all contingencies must be faced calmly and provided for. I think I have made all such provision as fully as possible. My business affairs are all in order, my personal wishes written out clearly. If I have to go those who stay behind will know what to do.

But I hope all will go well, both with my child and me. If I were to live but lose my baby I think the disappointment would almost kill me.

Ewan went home for a flying visit of ten days in May. How I wished I could have gone with him! It is my only regret that I cannot go home this summer. And yet it is not so poignant as I would have expected. It is the *old* Cavendish that I long for in my homesick hours. And the changes there are so great that, in one way, I have a strange shrinking from going back. Home, as it was, I can never see again.

After Ewan came back Stella and I took a jaunt to Niagara, as Stella wished to see it before going home. The falls are, of course, magnificent though much spoiled by the power houses and buildings along the brink of the gorge. If one could see the falls in the midst of their green primeval wildness! But with all drawbacks their grandeur is indisputable and I could gaze upon them endlessly. Yet would I rather look out from Cavendish shore upon a gulf storm!

Sunday, June 30, 1912
Leaskdale, Ont.

June has been, on the whole, a very pleasant month of fine weather and interesting occupations. A busy month, too—gardening, sewing etc. I have

"A weird picture of Stella and myself at Niagara"

been remarkably well—much better than in May and am quite active and "spry" yet. But my time is drawing very, very near and—what will be the outcome?

My new book "Chronicles of Avonlea" came the other day. It is got up like the others. The reviews have been very kindly so far. There is less of "real life" in it than in any of the others—in fact, all the tales and personages are "compact of imagination" only and have no proto- types in actual existence. To me, from much re-writing they are very stale but to those to whom they come newly they may give pleasure.

But just now one thought domi- nates my mind. In a little over a fort- night comes "my hour". How shall I meet it? What will it bring me? Will I pass safely through the valley of the shadow and bring therefrom a new life? Or shall I remain among the shadows?

I shall not write in this journal again until all is over. Perhaps I may never write again. If not, Old Journal—greeting and farewell!

Sunday, Sept. 22, 1912
Leaskdale Manse, Ont.

This is the first time I have had a chance to "write" up my journal. The past three months have been packed so full of busy doings and wonderful experiences that journal writing has been out of the question. Now, however, on this quiet afternoon of the waning year, I find myself at liberty to take it up again. Ewan is away to afternoon service in Zephyr—Frede is asleep in her room upstairs—and down the hall in my room, in a white-lined basket with soft little blankets tucked around him, wide-awake, cooing to himself, and playing with his little hands is the dearest, sweetest, darlingest, loveliest little son—yes, he is!—whose coming ever made a mother glad and thankful.

I am indeed a most happy and thankful woman. Motherhood is *heaven*. It pays for all.

I laid down my pen that afternoon in June, not knowing if I should ever again take it up to write in this journal. I was expecting my confinement shortly. I was thirty seven years old and I was a slight woman, never very robust. All my life I had heard and read of the anguish of childbirth, its risk, its dangers. There were times when I could not believe that I would get safely through. In the dead, dim hours of night fears and gloomy dreads came to me. I put them resolutely away, but always they lurked in the background of my mind. Would I escape with my life? Would I, as some of my friends have done, suffer so dreadfully that the remembrance would always be a horror? Would my child live? Would it be "all right"? What if it were *not* right—if it were some monstrosity—or if it were blind or deaf, or crippled mentally or physically? These and a score of other fears haunted me. And not the least dreadful among them was the quiet, persistent, secret dread that I would not *love* my child when it came.

As I said once before, when writing of Kenneth Ritchie I do not, as a rule, love children merely *as* children. Some I *like* very much because I love their parents or because they are really attractive in themselves. One or two, like Kenneth, I have loved because they are lovable and beautiful. But would I love my own? My reason told me I would—that a child, according to the old saying "brings its love with it"—but I could not quite convince myself. And if I did not love it—how terrible! This nightmare dread haunted me like a spectre that refuses to be laid by any exorcism.

The first ten days in July were really dreadful. A "heat wave" struck Ontario, and earth and air were like a burning fiery furnace, day and night.

On July second Frede and my nurse, Miss Fergusson, arrived. Frede graduated in Household Science in June and came here for her vacation. Miss Fergusson was a Toronto nurse—originally belonging to the West Indies—who had been recommended to me by Dr. McMurchy. The first sight of her was quite a shock to me. She looked so young—and was young, being only 28. My idea of a confinement nurse was that of an old or middle aged woman, such as I had always seen in such cases. I *knew* perfectly well that trained nurses are as often young as not, and that it is experience that counts, not years. But unconsciously I had been expecting to see a motherly middle aged sort of person, and girlish, black-eyed, curly haired Miss Fergusson was a surprise to me that I couldn't get over.

It was *good* to see old Frede and have her by me in those critical, anxious days.

The schedule date for baby's arrival was July fifteenth but Miss Fergusson cheerfully assured me it couldn't be so near—I was "too spry". She thought I'd certainly be a week and possibly a fortnight later.

I *was* spry. Wednesday afternoon I attended a meeting of the W.F.M.A. in the church and that evening I went to the Guild and read a paper on *Paradise Lost*. Thursday and Friday passed. The heat was excessive and we all sweltered and groaned. Saturday came, hotter than any preceding day. I worked about at odd jobs all day until three in the afternoon, when I felt the heat so terribly that I went upstairs to lie down a little while. I did not come down again for nearly three weeks. Soon after I went upstairs I began to feel faint, transient little pains in my back. When I mentioned this to Miss Fergusson, she looked at me.

"I think labor has begun", she said.

The next day, Sunday, July 7, at 12.40 my little son was born.

I have heard much of the agony of the birth chamber. That such agony is the rule rather than the exception generations of suffering women have testified

"*Miss Ferguson, Frede and Daffy*"

since the dawn of time. But I know no more of it then I did before my child's birth. From first to last I had *no* severe pain. I have suffered more many a night with toothache. If I knew I was to have another baby tomorrow it would not worry me in the least, as far as the ordeal itself goes. I felt nothing but cramp-like aches in the back and had it not been for the dreadful stifling heat and several hard and exhaustive attacks of vomiting I would not have minded it much at all. Dr. Bascom said he could not understand it. He said it was perfectly marvellous, in a woman of my age, at a first birth, and with a child having such a large firm head.

Ever since I knew I was to have a child I persistently took, every day, a set of exercises recommended in a medical book for pregnant women. These exercises were said to affect all the muscles used in parturition, making them flexible and elastic. Perhaps it was because of this I suffered so little. Personally, I have another opinion but I do not tell it to all and sundry.

A few years ago I read Hudson's "Law of Psychic Phenomena". Ever since I have had a strong belief in the power which the subconscious mind can exert over physical functions. Every night, as I was dropping off to sleep, and frequently through the day I repeated over and over the command to my subconscious mind "Make my child strong and healthy in mind and body and make his birth safe and painless for me."

Well, his birth *was* safe and almost painless for me and whatever he may develop into he is certainly strong and healthy now. I believe it was the "psychic suggestion" which produced my "easy time". But it may have been the exercises—or *both*—or *neither*. It is one of the things that can't be *proved*, believe what we will.

I have said that I had been afraid that I would not *love* my child. And for a few hours after his birth I did *not* love him—or rather, I was not conscious of loving him! I heard his first cry with emotions of wonder and delight; but when the nurse brought him to me, bathed and dressed, and laid him on my arm, it was *not* the great moment I had dreamed of its being. I looked at him with interest and curiosity, as I would have looked at the child of a friend, but I felt nothing more than interest and curiosity, and I lay back on my pillow with a sickening sensation of disappointment and shame and dismay! I did not love my child! I did not feel like a mother. And how was I ever to care for and train that child with the requisite patience and tenderness when I did not love him? I was appalled at the prospect. The first few hours after my baby's birth held for me some of the keenest mental suffering I have ever experienced. That night I could not sleep. I lay alone in my room—Miss F. having taken baby to the spare room with her—and cried bitterly.

I understand now why it was so. The strain through which I had passed had robbed me temporarily of almost all power of sensation, physical and emotional. Although I had just given birth to a child I felt quite well and strong with no feeling of weakness or soreness. It seemed to me that I could get right up if it were allowed. But by next morning sensation had returned. I felt weak and bruised and every movement was an effort. And with the return of physical feeling came the power of emotion. When the nurse again laid my baby beside me my "great moment" came—the exquisite moment of the realization of motherhood. It seemed to me that my whole being was engulfed in a wave of love for that little blinking mite of humanity that lay cuddled to my breast. Love—such love! I never dreamed there could be such love. It seems blent and twined with the inmost fibres of my being—as if it could not be wrenched away without wrenching soul and body apart also. And, ever since, that love has grown and deepened. Oh, how I love him! At times I am terrified that I love him *too* much—that it is a defiance of God to love any created thing so much. *How* can a mother bear to lose her child! It must be possible, since mothers *do* bear it and live. But I cannot believe that I could go on living if anything happened to my darling. The mere thought of it sends a thrill of agony to my very soul. The love of motherhood, exquisite as it is, is full of anguish, too. I see and realize deeps of pain I never realized before. Motherhood is a revelation from God.

In reading tales of the martyrs I have shuddered with horror—and been lost in wonder. How, for instance, could any human being face the prospect of death at the stake for his religion? I knew I could never do it. I would recant anything in the face of such a hideous threat. *Nothing*, I thought, could fortify me to endure it. And now—I know that for the sake of my child I could and would undergo the most dreadful suffering which one human being could inflict on another. To save my child's life I would go to the stake a hundred times over.

Always when I read of a child being neglected or ill-used I would thrill with indignation and horror. But now I can scarcely endure to read such a thing because of the anguish it causes me—for in every child I see my own child—and I picture him undergoing that. I have cried aloud with the pain that came with such a picture.

Oh, my darling little son, you make up for everything I have suffered and missed in life. Everything led to you—and therefore I feel that all has been for the best.

I recovered strength with normal rapidity and never had any trouble of any sort. But it was unpleasant enough lying there in the extreme heat and having to have everything done for me by the nurse. I hate to be waited on in little personal offices. How glad I was when I was able to brush my own hair and wash my own face! Miss F. was a capital nurse, capable and efficient, but with the drawback common to most trained nurses—a Procrustean determination to fit every patient to the same set of rules, leaving all individuality out of the question. I suppose it is unavoidable, since not one nurse in a thousand could be trusted to discern clearly just how far any rule might be relaxed for a certain patient. But I suffered some as a result. For example, I craved for a bit of beef ham. But Miss F. decreed that I must not have any salt meat and no decree of Mede or Persian was ever more relentless than she. I lost my appetite completely. I could eat nothing and this continued until she became worried. Finally she became so alarmed that she let me have some ham as the lesser evil. Result—it not only did me no harm but my appetite for other things returned and thenceforth I had no trouble in that respect. Frede and I are alike in this. There are certain times when our digestive tracks seem to *demand* a bit of beef ham as a sort of tonic or stimulant and when we get it we are all right again.

Baby was—and is—so good. I had dreaded having a "cross" baby but from his birth the precious little soul has been as little trouble as any baby could possibly be. Miss Fergusson started him in good habits and I have kept them up. He sleeps, or lies and coos to himself. The only time he ever cried was when the nurse was bathing him. *Then* his shrieks of protest would ring through the house. I saw him bathed for the first time the second day I sat up. Never shall I forget it. I laughed and cried. The naked little body, trembling and cringing as the nurse put him in the water was both comical and pathetic. But after a time he learned it was not a fatal affair and he became reconciled to it; then he began to like it. Now he loves it and it is so delightful to sponge his dear, firm, plump little body and work with it, and see him splash in the water, crowing with delight. He has learned to smile and he has such a pretty smile.

His whole wee face lights up and his eyes gleam with mirth. Such a moment as it is when one catches "the earliest ray of intellectual fire". At first his eyes were the blank indifferent eyes of all babies. But one day he looked at me—*looked*, with an expression of intelligent wonder in his eyes. It passed quickly but I had caught it while it was there and I realized with a thrill that the little mind in that little body had begun to develop—and what would the full development be?

I gaze at my child often with an aching wonder as to what germs of thought and feeling and will and intellect are unfolding in that little soul. I can see what he is externally. I can see that he is plump and shapely and sturdy, with long-lashed dark blue eyes, chubby cheeks, lacking his father's dimples but with dear wee waxen fingers and toes. But I cannot peep into that baby brain and discover what is hidden there. He is my child—"bone of my bone and flesh of my flesh"—but his little individuality is distinct from mine. He is the captain of his own little soul and must live his own life as we all do from the very cradle.

It is heavenly to stand by his basket and watch him when he is asleep. I am sure there is nothing on earth so unutterably sweet as a sleeping baby. And then to waken up in the night and hear his soft regular little breathing—and to think with a thrill of pain, how awful it would be to waken and *not* hear it. As long as the nurse was here she kept the baby at night, and when she carried him out at bedtime I could hardly bear it. The room seemed so very lonely and empty.

Miss F. would not let me go down stairs until July 26th. How strange and nice it was to be down again. I felt as if I had been away a very long time. The garden looked so beautiful. The flowers were in their prime. We have literally revelled in flowers all summer, especially sweet peas.

In a month after baby's birth I was as well and strong as ever and Miss Fergusson left. I felt considerable trepidation at her departure, especially when I thought of giving baby his bath. But I got on all right. I daresay I was awkward enough at first but I am quite expert now and it is lovely to do everything for him myself. I really feel jealous of everyone who does anything for him!

We had him baptized on September 8th—Chester Cameron Macdonald. Chester was my choice—not "after" anyone but because I have always liked the name and Cameron after the family name of Ewan's mother. I really would have liked to call him "Sidney Cavendish", Sidney being my favourite masculine name, but I couldn't get Ewan to see it that way.

Rev. George Millar was up from the Island, visiting friends in Ontario, and as he is an old friend of both of us, we got him to come over and baptize our small son. I should have liked to have had Mr. Stirling christen him but that could not be, and Mr. Millar was next best. Baby behaved well and looked sweet. He wore a little dress I had made for the occasion. It was a very simple little gown but every stitch was set in it with a prayer and a blessing.

Well, I have my baby and none of my forebodings have been fulfilled. I can smile at them now—but they were nonetheless harrowing while they lasted. I

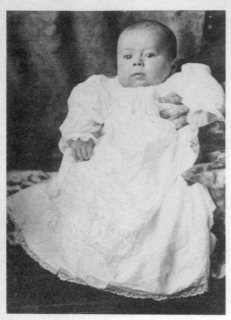

"Chester in his christening robes"

remember one dreadful dream I had in April; and I could not help feeling strangely over it for it is an undeniable fact that some of my dreams have been strangely fulfilled.

I dreamed that I wakened in the night, sat up, and looked over the footboard of the bed. On the floor between the box couch and the wardrobe lay a big empty black coffin, with a man standing at the foot and another at the head. As I fell back on the bed, overcome with the horror of the sight, the men lifted the coffin and laid it on my bed across my feet. The pressure of it wakened me, but for a few minutes I could hardly distinguish between the dream and reality. That dream haunted me. From that out I saw that hideous empty coffin waiting for me at the end of my months.

In the days that followed baby's birth I was surrounded by kindly living friends. But in the night the dead companioned me. I dreamed of almost everyone I ever knew who had passed on—my father, Mrs. Houston, Pensie Macneill, grandfather and grandmother, Herman Leard, Uncle John Montgomery and many more. I saw them as in life and heard them speak and laugh as in the olden years. When I wakened it was always with a curious sense of really having been with them again—especially when I dreamed of father.

How father would worship my baby if he were living! It would be his first grandchild and I know just how his eyes would shine over it! And poor Tillie, too—she would have been almost as much interested in it.

How strange I felt the first time I left the house and went to a neighbor's after baby's birth! It was the first time we had been separated—the first of the little tragedies of motherhood. When I came home I rushed to see him as if I had been away for a year.

And how fussy and anxious I was the first time I took him out driving. I nearly smothered the poor darling with clothes, lest he be cold. How besottedly pleased and proud I was when people told me I had a lovely baby! And how fiercely I hated the woman who remarked to me that he did not have much hair! I feel sure I can never forgive that woman either in this life or that which is to come!

Yes, I am just as big a goose over my baby as any mother ever was. But I shall try to hide my folly in the pages of this journal. I shall *not*—if it be humanly possible—bore my friends with my raptures.

On August 21st Stella went home. Poor Stella, I am afraid her departure caused very little real regret in the heart of anybody in Leaskdale manse.

Last fall I invited Stella to visit me at Xmas, when Frede would be here—and sent her the money for her ticket also. For a visit Stell is a good thing. She is full of fun when she likes, the jolliest of the jolly. But when she wrote back and asked me if she couldn't stay with me for the winter—well, I was honestly dismayed!

There was no way out of it. To refuse was out of the question. It would have turned Stell against me forever and I would not have a family row for anything, especially with one of Aunt Annie's girls. But I felt very dubious as to the outcome.

When a young girl Stella was "livable" enough, though always with a quick temper. But during the past fifteen years she has been developing along wrong lines. I had heard a good deal about the sort of person Stella was to live with and had seen enough in my Park Corner visits to verify it; and last spring during the four months I spent there I realized to the full just what a disposition the poor girl had.

We did not clash at all, because I did not interfere with her in any way. I was only going to be there for a short time and I had my own work to do. So I held my tongue and possessed my soul, though many a time my blood boiled over Stella's behavior to the rest of the people in the house, especially her brother's wife.

In the first place she is the most tyrannical creature who could be imagined. She must have her own way in *everything* or there is no living with her. Even to express an opinion on an indifferent subject which differs from hers is taken as an insult. Then she has an *infernal* temper—a temper which she never tries to govern and which explodes on the slightest provocation. She continually makes the rudest and most insulting remarks to everybody, and yet if anyone, driven to desperation, retorts with even the mildest rebuke or protest Stell is outraged—and sulks and bawls for hours as if she considered herself the most injured of mortals. All this is bad enough, yet I do not think it is as bad as her ceaseless endless complaining. Stell is the picture of health. She is as fat as a seal and as strong as a horse. Yet from the time she gets up in the morning until she goes to bed at night she complains ceaselessly of aches and pains. She has almost every ill known to human existence. She pores over patent medicine ads. and "doctor books" and discovers in herself every symptom recounted there. And she is furious if everyone does not take her agonies as seriously as she takes them herself. Her ceaseless complaints are farcical enough

"Stella"
[*in bathing suit*]

to outsiders but when you have to listen to it day after day it is really dreadful.

Therefore, I felt, as I have said, dismayed. But as I saw no way out of it without creating family bitterness I tried to look on the best side of it. I determined to offer Stella a salary to be my "assistant housekeeper", so that—as I fondly hoped—she could not presume too much, as she would undoubtedly do, if she just "helped around" as anyone living with me might; and I got Frede to give her a preachment on the difference between living in her own home and in a house where another woman was mistress. Stella is good company when she chooses to be, a capable though not a dainty housekeeper, and a good, though extravagant cook. I was not well and was dubious about my prospects of getting a good maid. Perhaps when Stella was away from George—who certainly was as hateful to her as she to him—she would not be so irritable and unreasonable. In short, I made a virtue of necessity and hoped against hope.

Stell is an odd compound. She would work her fingers to the bone for you, complaining bitterly of it all the time and furiously resentful if she is not allowed to do it. She insults and derides you to your face, but behind your back she is the most loyal of friends and would defend you against the world. But everyone who ever has to live with her will be miserable—there is no doubt of that.

Well, Stella came. For about a month or six weeks all went fairly well. And then the leopard showed that its spots were quite unchanged. From that out she got worse and worse until it is hardly believable what she was like.

She was "boss" here. I was nothing more than a cipher in my own house, existing on sufferance. I hardly dared venture into my own kitchen to concoct a cake. Stella was angry if I did. Everything had to be done her way and all the work planned in accordance with her convenience. If she were crossed in the slightest degree she was furious. To Ewan she was as impudent and insulting as to her own brother and father. And oh, her complaints—her ceaseless complaints! They were dreadful. I was not very well and sometimes it seemed to me that I *could not* bear them. She never stopped talking of "the untold agonies" she was enduring. But let anyone 'phone down asking her to go for a drive or some such outing and we heard no more of "the untold agonies" just then.

And nothing suited her! Everything about the house and place was inconvenient or useless. Nothing in Leaskdale pleased her, from the weather up. I shall certainly never forget last winter.

I endured it all in silence for two reasons. As aforesaid, I did not want a fight with her; and I was determined for my coming child's sake not to give way to anger and have any upsetting fuss that might affect it unfavorably. These considerations also restrained Ewan, whose patience was sorely tried. He never said anything to her, but he hated her and it could not be wondered at. The way she bullied him and insulted him, even at his own table, was absurd.

And her *noisiness*—oh, her noisiness! She could do nothing without racket and fuss. She seemed to live, move and have her being in the centre of a whirlwind. Everything banged and slammed and rattled and clattered when Stell was working.

Unpleasant as it was to be home with Stella it was almost as bad to be out in company with her. To be sure, she was on such occasions genial, witty, jolly. People congratulated me on having her—she was "such good company etc. etc." They did not notice the grim smile with which I responded to such remarks. But Stell could not remember her place any better abroad than at home. She was constantly humiliating me. For example;—one evening we were out calling. The lady of the house said to me, "When are you going to begin housecleaning, Mrs. Macdonald?"

Before I could reply Stella, as was her custom, spoke up "*I* am going to begin next week."

This was news to me. Housecleaning had not been mentioned between us. I was nettled and could not refrain from saying drily, "*I* am not going to begin until the need for furnace fires is past." And then poor Stella sulked for the rest of the evening.

Again, one evening when we had company to tea and I was pouring out the tea Stella rudely exclaimed to me, "Put more cream in the tea, Maud." I am *not* niggardly in regard to my rations of cream—do I not remember Oliver Wendell Holmes' dictum, "Big heart never loved little creampot"— but even if I had been it was not Stella's place to insult the mistress of the house like that. She really resent-

"*Stella*"
[*Campbell*]

ed the fact that *she* could not sit at the head of the table and pour the tea herself. I could hardly keep the tears of mortification out of my eyes. To be insulted like that in the presence of members of my husband's congregation was really too much!

And if I asked anyone here to tea without first getting her approval I was made to repent it. Oddly enough, I think this was what I found hardest of all— perhaps because it was what I had had to endure all my life with grandmother.

I was in terror lest Stell would just stay on until she was told to go. Rant as she might, at Leaskdale she was very well satisfied with the place and in no hurry to return home where George would give her as good as she sent and where she would have to work three times as hard as she did here without any fat dollars coming in every week. When she began throwing out hints about staying on I said nothing; but I wrote to Frede and begged her to get Stella to go home without a fuss if it could be managed. Frede accordingly convinced

Stella that she ought to go home because Aunt Annie was not well—as is really the case—and much to my relief Stella finally announced that she meant to go home after baby came.

She was very good to me when I was ill. She had everything her own way then, without any irksome shadow of authority over her. I do not deny that it was a comfort to know that someone I could depend on was running the house. But I consider that last winter was too high a price to pay for that comfort.

"A flashlight photo of our supper table"
[*LMM, Frede, Ewan, Chester*]

Stella liked baby, too, and was wondrously gentle and tender with him. When she went away I forgot temporarily how she had acted and thought only of our mutual jokes and laughter and the bonds of olden days and interests. And I cried sincerely, thereby leading poor Stella to suppose, I fear, that I was quite inconsolable over her departure. But my tears were soon dried; and since then peace and harmony have reigned in Leaskdale manse. Frede and I work together in beautiful concord and at last I have the home I had dreamed of having. Stella writes us the most doleful epistles of her aches and woes and crosses at home; but her shadow lies not on our threshold.

Thursday, Sept. 26, 1912
The Manse, Leaskdale

This morning, Frede and I, with fear and trembling, feeling as guilty as if we were committing murder in the first degree, chloroformed a cat!

Ever since coming here last fall I have been persecuted by starving cats. It has been a joke and a by-word with us. Last fall two hungry cats, a handsome gray "Tom" and a lean little Maltese, contracted the habit of coming here, because I, in the weakness of my heart, threw out some scraps to appease their ravening hunger. They came all winter and literally camped on the back veranda. We could not go out of the door without falling over a starving cat, with eyes of wolfish hunger and bones sticking through its skin. How poor Stell raged at them! We did not like to do away with them, because we knew they belonged to some near-by neighbors who might be annoyed if we disposed of them—though certainly they did not seem to prize them much! And they were such thieves—the cats, not the neighbors! We couldn't leave a door open but one of them darted in and decamped with something, or sneaked down cellar and stole the cream.

However, we bore with them all winter. But in the spring another cat adopted us—the most foresaken looking feline I ever saw—ragged-eared, and her two sides almost slapping together. She was worse than the others. The gray tom had lost an eye through the winter and "One-eyed Oxtoby", as we called him and the forlorn old spotted cat used to sit on our door mat and swear at each other by the hour. As for poor Daffy, he fought valiantly, but he was harried from home and mother. He would not stoop to fight with "The Dweller on the Threshold"—as we called the spotted cat—but she clawed him viciously whenever he passed near her. I have borne with her all summer but the other day my patience gave way. She got down cellar and drank up a whole pint of cream—all there was and poor me expecting "company to tea". I hied me to Uxbridge and got two ounces of chloroform. Even then it was in the house a fortnight before I could get up my courage to use it. But today we've been and gone and done it. We decoyed her in this morning, gave her a good meal and then—guiltily, for the poor old thing looked so confiding and trustful—we clapped a box down over her, slipped the uncorked bottle of chloroform under it, and put a weight on top. We heard two faint "mews"—then silence. We dared not lift the box till evening however, and then did it with set teeth. But the poor old Dweller On The Threshold had gone where good cats go—very painlessly and peacefully to judge from appearances. She was curled up as if asleep. We buried her in the back yard. May her rest be sweet! But alas, One-Eyed Oxtoby and the Maltese are still at large; and the latter has had two brisk kittens that are running about the yard. I foresee more expenditure for chloroform and more harrowing executions—for I cannot have these pests around here another winter, no matter who they belong to.

Friday, Sept. 27, 1912
The Manse, Leaskdale, Ont.
This evening was fine and crisp and I drove in to Uxbridge to meet Ewan who has been away all the week attending a conference in Toronto. We have a dear little mare "Queen", who is not afraid of motors or anything of that kind and I can drive her without fear. We had a pleasant drive home through the moonlight and a delight-

"Queen"
[*the Macdonalds' horse*]

ful home-coming, with Frede and Sonny Punch, a bright fire and a good supper awaiting us. I am beginning to have a very nice "home" feeling in connection with Leaskdale manse. I like to get into it and shut the door behind me in the world's face.

Wednesday, October 2, 1912
Leaskdale, Ont.
On Monday Punchkins had his first little journey into the "big World". Frede and I went up to Toronto to do some shopping and of course had to take him along. He was very good but it is a fatiguing thing to travel with so young a baby and I was pretty well tired out when I got to Uxbridge station last night. But the worst was to come. Ewan could not meet us because of a meeting with the Bible Society which was held that night, so Fred Leask, a stolid urchin of eleven or twelve met us. We stowed ourselves away in the buggy and started on a cold dark drive home. Punchie remained good for five miles. Then the

poor mite's patience gave out. He must have been desperately tired. He began to cry and for the remaining two miles he shrieked blue murder. I thought every inch of those two miles a league. Never was I more thankful than when

"Punch au naturel*"*

we got home. I was so tired I could hardly stand and my arms ached as if they would drop off at the shoulder. But we got in, got a fire on, and got poor baby undressed and fed. When I put the dear mite down in his basket he looked up at me and laughed as if he appreciated his nest. Then Frede and I had to fly round and get the house in order, for the Bible society man was coming to stay all night and Ewan had been keeping bachelor's hall for two days!!

McKenzie-Naughton was his name. He was here all night and half to-day and is about as conceited, self-assured a young snip as I have ever encountered. He was quite clever and good-looking and Lord, but he knew it! And oh, how seriously he took himself and his hyphenated name and his pet theory that the English people are the descendants of the lost ten tribes! He was really furious, I think, because I would not discuss it seriously. As for Frede, she shocked him so badly with some of her heretical remarks that I fear he will never get over it.

But I'm glad to get home. Wow! (As Punch would say, it being the sole extent of his vocabulary at present.) No more of Toronto for me until Punch is able to stand on his feet and play the game!

Monday, Oct. 7, 1912
Leaskdale, Ont.

To-day there was a tragedy in Leaskdale Manse. We "shortened" our baby!

Joking apart, I could have wept. It made such a change in him. My little baby disappeared and in his place was just a big fat chubby-legged "bouncing boy". I felt as if he were dead as I folded up his dear little long dresses and put them away in a trunk—little dresses I made last winter when I hoped for him. His short ones I bought and they have nothing of the sacredness that pertains to the others.

Frede and I have such fun in the mornings when I bathe and dress him in the kitchen while she is washing the breakfast dishes. We talk the most delicious nonsense to him, make all the funny impromptu rhymes we can about him, and act the fool generally, none daring to make us afraid. Here for example is this morning's classic on "The Pirate Wag"—which is one of Frede's nicknames for him.

> "There was a pirate known as Wag
> Whose Sunday name was Punch
> He sailed upon the raging main
> And ate his aunts for lunch.

He liked them fricasseed and stewed
But sometimes for a change
He broiled them nice and tenderly
Upon his kitchen range....

And when an aunt was saucier
Than usual Waggy said,
"I'll have you made into a hash
You gristly old Aunt Frede."

But when Aunt Stella was served up
Wag wouldn't touch a bite,
He said, "If I et her I'd have
Most awful dreams tonight"....

It's all pure foolery but we get heaps of fun out of it all. Frede felt as badly as I did over the "shortening". But tonight when I put him in his long nighty, lo, there was my ownest little baby again. And I cuddled him in my arms and tucked him away in his basket and cosied the blankets and down puff about him. It is so lovely to make him warm and comfortable and happy. The very hardest thing I have to do is sometimes to steel my heart against him when he cries to be taken up at some hour when, per schedule, he is fed, warmed and should be asleep. I just have to hold on to myself to keep from rushing to him. And I sit there in misery and harrow my soul by thinking, "What—if—he were to—if anything should happen to him ever—I would be haunted to my death by the agonizing thought that I had let him cry his poor wee heart out without consoling him." And I see myself lying alone at night thinking of the little creature far away from me in his grave and his little basket empty—and the horror is often so great that I fly to him, rules and regulations to the contrary not withstanding, and catch him up and cuddle him against my breast, with his darling head nestled on my shoulder. And then the sweet baby smiles and the blue eyes laughing through the tears!

Thursday, Oct. 10, 1912
Leaskdale, Ont.
To-day I received a letter containing the sad news of the death of Aunt Mary Lawson. It was not unexpected for she has been ill for three or four weeks but it gave me a bitter sense of loss and sorrow. I do not grieve for Aunt Mary. She was almost 89. She was very lonely. All her dearest had gone and she had no home of her own. Life, to that high-spirited, sensitive woman had been a bitter thing for many years. For her sake I was thankful that she was at rest. But I am the poorer by another loss of a rich-souled, beloved friend. Aunt Mary was one of the "ancient landmarks" of my life. It seems strange to picture a world without her—hard to realize that I can never see her again. Somehow, when we last parted, although she was in good health and seemed

as strong and bright as usual I had a feeling that I had looked my last on her strong, gentle, intelligent old face. She is gone and I shall not look upon her like again. Women of Aunt Mary's type are rare indeed. I wish she could have lived to have seen my baby. How she would have loved him! But for that matter how many friends have gone who would have loved him—father, Tillie, grandmother and my own young mother. In certain lights my baby's eyes and brows are strangely like my mother's in a little old picture I have of her, taken when she was a young girl. It gives me a strange ghostly feeling when I see it, as if something of mother were living again in my child. My mother! How near I feel to her now in my own motherhood. I know how she must have loved me. I know what her agony must have been in the long weeks of her illness when she was facing the bitter knowledge that she must leave me. My dear, beautiful young mother whose sun went down while it was yet day! I am glad my child has a resemblance to you and I hope it will be a permanent one.

Sunday, Dec. 1, 1912
Leaskdale, Ont.
....I have had a very busy fall—too busy in some respects. I haven't had time to *be*, because I have so much to *do*. I have had a good many visitors. Not many of them were very interesting. But I don't mind seeing them come. Never shall I forget how I hated to see anyone coming to the house those last few years in Cavendish—the humiliation of not having fit accommodation for their horses, of them seeing the general tumbledown appearance of the place, and of the display of grandmother's peculiarities of age. Nor, at any time in my life could I welcome anyone very freely, for I never knew how grandfather and grandmother would regard their advent. All this is changed now. I can invite what guests I please and treat them properly. This is a great relief; but in my position as "minister's wife" I have to entertain, and waste my time and soul on, some awful bores!

But we have some interesting visitors once in a while. Mr. Fraser, the Presbyterian minister in Uxbridge, comes out occasionally and is a clever fellow. He is a widower and it has been rather plain of late that he has cast a tentative eye Fredeward. It has been great fun for us all—that wicked Frede included. Mr. Fraser stands no chance with her of course but she is quite willing to amuse herself and us with him.

I think these missionary society meetings will be the death of me. We have three societies here—Woman's Foreign, Home Missions and Mission Band. And I have to attend all three every month. I grudge the time—for they are so deadly dull. And I have "to lead in prayer".

This is truly one of my greatest "crosses". I dreaded it more than anything else before I married and it is fully as dreadful as I feared. To me it seems a mockery. I am so nervous that I seem to be merely reciting—and reciting badly—the form of words I have "thought out" beforehand. There is no real "prayer" about it. Perhaps through time I may get so accustomed to it that the nervousness will cease, but I will *never* be able to pray a *real* prayer before others. To me prayer has always seemed something very sacred—the intimate communion between the soul and its Great Source, hardly to be breathed into words, much less uttered before others. *I* cannot *pray* in any other fashion and therefore any public prayer on my part must forever be a sacrilege and a mockery. To me, a petition asking for various "blessings" of one sort or another is merely rather ridiculous. I do not believe that God is "a changeable Being whom our prayers can alter"—who will give or withhold according as we do or do not ask, and therefore I see no use at all in such prayers as are commonly "offered". To me, ten minutes alone in a great forest, or beside the sea, or under the stars would be filled with more of the essence of prayer than could be contained in a lifetime of "asking for blessings". Prayer to me is an aspiration and an up-reaching not a string of more or less selfish and material requests.

Sonny Punch keeps well and good and sunshiny and happy. He is growing so fast. His dear little body is so firm and plump and shapely and comical. I love to handle it. And he has such darling funny smiles and chuckles, and the most enviable knack of always laughing at exactly the right place in your remarks!

But happy and sheltered as he is he cannot escape the common foes of humanity. From the beginning he was acquainted with pain—yea, at his first breath he met that grisly enemy. And the other day the second greatest woe of our race came upon him—*Fear* entered into his little experience. I never saw him afraid before. But one morning I was nursing him in the dining room. Frede opened the kitchen door. Daff was just inside and on the threshold was a stray Tommy whom the soul of Daff hated. Both cats split the air with that fiendish shriek of conflict which only cats can give. Poor little Punchkins shrank away from my breast with a cry of terror—the pitiful, agonized cry I have heard him give when a spasm of pain shook his wee body. Into his little eyes came a questioning hunted look of dread. His darling face blanched and quivered. I caught him close to me and comforted him until he forgot about it. But ah, little son, some day there may come a Fear into your life such as not even your mother can charm away. The "twin Eumenides—Fear and Pain"— they cannot be escaped by mortals.

As I hold little Punch's dear body in my arms I am lost in wonder—and awe—and terror—when I *realize* that *everybody* was once a baby just like this. All the great men, all the good men, all the wicked men of history. Napoleon was once a chubby baby, kicking on his nurse's lap—Caesar once smacked his lips over his mother's milk as does my mannie—Milton once squirmed with colic—Shakespeare cried in the night when he grew hungry. Yes, and—horrible thought—Nero once looked up with just such dear, star-like innocent eyes and Judas cooed to himself with the same sweet noises and vocables. Nay, even that wondrous Person—so grand and wonderful and amazing that it seems almost sacrilege to call him man, even to those of us who can no longer believe him anything but the consummate flower of humanity at its best—even He was once a white, dimple-fisted, waxen-faced little creature like this, cuddled in his mother's arms and drawing his life from her breast. What a terrible thing it is to be a mother—almost as terrible as it is beautiful! Oh, mothers of Caesar and

Judas and Jesus, what did you dream of when you held your babies against your beating heart. Of nothing but sweetness and goodness and holiness perhaps. Yet one of the children was a Caesar—and one was a Judas—and one a Messiah!

Thursday, Dec. 12, 1912
Leaskdale, Ont.

Last night we had a "Kipling Night" in Guild and I read an old paper on "Kipling's Verse" which I wrote and read many years ago to the Literary Society in Cavendish. It made me homesick and my soul ached when I lay awake in the darkness afterwards and thought over the old days.

Letters from Cavendish tell me that the old Literary Society has finally died. It struggled poorly through last winter but this year no effort was made to revive it. The old set who organized it and the younger set who carried it on for so long have nearly all died or gone away. And it is a sad fact that there is not among the present young set in Cavendish enough of either ability or interest to carry it on. I am sorry. I hate to see that dear old spot degenerating in any way. Yet degenerating intellectually it certainly is. Most of the old "brainy" stock of Simpsons and Macneills have gone. Such of their descendants as still live there are indeed "degenerate sons of noble sires". The old Simpsons and Macneills, whatever their faults, were intellectual people with a keen interest in intellectual things. But the young folk in Cavendish now decidedly are not.

It must be twenty-five years since that Literary Society was first organized—soon after the hall was built. Walter Simpson and George Simpson, Arthur Simpson, "Will Effie" Simpson, George R. Macneill, John C. Clark and Rev. Mr. Archibald were its main supports then. It was a flourishing institution, beguiling the winter months with debates, lectures, and concerts. A good library was started in connection with it and grew to generous proportions. That society was a boon to us young people. It was the greatest social factor in our lives. For the first few years I was very rarely allowed to go and I was not allowed to join the society. After that I attended regularly and always enjoyed the meetings. The fortunes of "The Literary" ebbed and flowed, some winters being highly successful, others, for various reasons, being less so. But on the whole it flourished and was an excellent educational factor in our simple country life. As the older members grew too old or indifferent to run it younger ones came up to fill their place. But there is an end to all things under the sun and I fear the end of the old Literary has come at last. Nor do I think it will ever be resuscitated. The spirit is gone.

So tonight I read the Kipling paper to an Ontario guild. But I do not think it was as much appreciated as when I read it to "the Simpsons, Macneills and Clarks" on the old Cavendish benches.

Monday, Dec. 16, 1912
Leaskdale, Ont.

I feel sad—lonely—sick at heart tonight. Frede went away this morning.

She goes to Alberta to take a position in the new "Ladies College" in Red Deer. It seems so horribly far away. We have never been so far separated before. It makes me wretched to think of it. I shall miss her so horribly—our little chats, our mutual jokes, our delightful eye-to-eye vision of everything, our sympathy with and understanding of one another. Frede has a pet expression by which she denotes congenial souls—"the race that knows Joseph". People, in her classification, either belong or do not belong to the race that knows Joseph. And oh, how few and rare and precious are those who do! And how miserable it is when they are separated.

"Frede"

Now that Frede has gone I have absolutely no real friend near me—and that is a hard position for any woman. It seems just now as if I *couldn't* live without Frede. I'll get over this in a few days and life will be pleasant again, but something will always be gone from it. We have had such a happy, delightful summer since Frede came from Macdonald—so full of jokes and laughter and sweet simple little pleasures. And now Frede has gone—and it is winter.

I have got a very good maid—a Mrs. Reid who has been here since the first of the month. She is a young widow, neat and efficient and as her home is near here everything fits in very nicely. I am very fortunate in having secured her, but of course, she is no real companion for me in any way. No one can take Frede's place in that. Poor Frede! I hope life will be easier for her in the future than it has been in the past. She has had a hard struggle and many bitter experiences. Perhaps it will be made up to her yet as it has been to a great extent, made up to me.

But oh, I miss her—I miss her! The house seems so vacant and still without her—her room so lonely and deserted. A pang goes through my heart as I pass the door—and glance into the empty darkness....

Tuesday, Dec. 31st, 1912
The Manse
Leaskdale, Ont.

To-day I had a letter from Mr. MacMillan in which he told me that his engagement to Miss Allan was at an end. It seems that young lady went back to Berwick again last summer—having been so pleased with it during her first visit—for her vacation. There she met someone who pleased her fancy better, it seems, than Mr. MacMillan—or perhaps one who had more money! At any rate she coolly wrote the poor fellow that all was over between them. Mr.

MacMillan seems to feel very badly over it. This is natural; but I must say that in view of the disposition Miss Allan betrayed more than once during that fortnight in Berwick I think it is really the best thing that ever happened him and that he will realize this when the first sting is over.

"Lily Reid"

"Aunt Jane of Kentucky" says, "There are mighty few things that ain't little until you foller them up and see what comes of them." It seemed a little little thing that we should have invited Miss Allan to be our guest at Berwick for that fortnight. Yet it probably has had and will continue to have tremendous effects on three lives. If we had not taken Miss Allan to Berwick she would have had no chance to be so charmed with it; it would never have occurred to her to go there this last summer. She would thus never have met the unknown and her engagement to Mr. MacMillan would be still unbroken. Though, if it comes to that and to go back further still, if Mr. MacMillan himself had not gone to Berwick a few years ago to spend his vacation and written me from it such a charming descriptive letter we, in turn, would never have thought of visiting Berwick. It's all like the old nursery rhyme of the stick that began to beat the dog and the dog that began to bite the pig.

This is the end of 1912. It has been the greatest year of my life—the year that brought me motherhood. I faced death in it—and came off conqueror, bearing as my guerdon a new and unspeakably precious life. So it to me must always be the *annus mirabilis*—the wonderful year.

1913

Friday, Feb. 7, 1913

Punch was seven months old today—and signalized the date by getting up on his own wee feet in the basket holding on by a chair—and then alas, pitching out on the floor on his dear head. This means that he has outgrown his basket as an abode by day; the old "Jolly Roger" is done with, save as a pirate bark o'night, and we must get a high chair for him, the dear wee adventurer. Every week brings him some addition of strength and knowledge.

But for me another of the little tragedies of motherhood took place today. I gave my little son his first meal of milk—the beginning of his weaning. I felt it bitterly. From his birth he has been wholly dependent on me. He has drawn all the sustenance his darling wee body demanded from me—he has been mine, wholly mine. But henceforth this is not to be so. He is beginning to owe his nourishment to an outside source and must continue to do so more and more. In one way it will be, I suppose, a relief. Certainly there are some aspects in which nursing is a nuisance, especially when one lives in an epoch of fashion which ordains dresses hooked in the back. But I hate to give it up. I am so thankful I have been able to nurse my baby and I cannot understand how any mother can refuse to do so if she is able. Yes, today it gave me a pang when I gave my wee man his cup of milk.

Saturday, Feb. 22, 1913
Leaskdale, Ont.

This has been that most delightful and rather rare thing—a quiet home day; and it was doubly delightful coming after a very strenuous week.

The Hypatia Club has been getting up "The Temple of Fame" in aid of the Uxbridge Library and I had promised to take part in it in my own character as the author of "Anne". So I had to drive in last Monday night to a practice. It was a crisp, frosty moonlight night with excellent roads and I enjoyed the drive. But next morning I had to go over it again on a shopping expedition. Then Wednesday the Home Mission Society met in the afternoon and the Guild in the evening. Thursday I had two ladies here to tea and last night the concert came off in Uxbridge. It was capital but I had to take Chester and we did not get home, over bad roads, till two o'clock. Consequently my "quiet home day" has been a boon and a blessing. I certainly want badly to get a good rest. But my life is very busy—almost too much so. There is always some duty waiting to be done—and all too often something unexpected turning up to interfere with the doing of it. But motherhood pays for all. I don't complain—

117

that is, I don't complain of all I have to do in connection with my home and dear ones. But I do grudge the time I have to give to outsiders for whom I don't care a straw.

Saturday, Apr. 26, 1913
Leaskdale, Ont.
We have had the most beautiful April. One thing I do like about Ontario and that is its early springs. They are fully three weeks earlier than down home and so mild and ungrudging. And yet—after all, there is an indefinable sweetness about an Island spring that is lacking here. What it is I cannot tell but I feel it and miss it. Perhaps it is in the very austerity of an Eastern spring that its charm consists.

We have been housecleaning furiously all April. We have finished all but the kitchen and I am not sorry. I used to love housecleaning down home. But it was a much easier affair there where all the furniture and appointments were so much simpler and plainer. The price one has to pay for having many nice things is the much harder work which it is to clean and care for them. Of course, I do not object to this for I love nice furnishings and always longed for them. I am quite willing to pay the price, but I may be permitted to state the fact that housecleaning here is hard work and that I am glad it is over. Hard as it was, however, it was easy compared to last spring's, with Stella's bad-temper, complaining and "driving" ways. This spring the housecleaning was done as *I* wished it and in accordance with my convenience and plans. The difference is a huge one.

Thursday, May 1, 1913
Leaskdale, Ont.
To-day I got a box of Mayflowers from home! They were somewhat faded— but oh, they were Mayflowers; with all the old haunting woodsy sweetness. I buried my face in them and shut my eyes—and in fancy I was back again in those old barrens a thousand miles away, with the blue harbor gleaming westward and the spring winds tossing the fir trees. I don't know whether those mayflowers gave me more of pain or pleasure. But even the pain was very sweet.

Lily and I papered the kitchen today and I got a young girl to come and look after Chester, so that I could work uninterruptedly....

Tuesday, May 6, 1913
Leaskdale, Ont.
I weaned Chester finally today. How I hated to do it! It seems to me that the dearest bond between us has been broken. He is a little less my own now. And he is wearing creepers and looks so much the big sturdy man-child in them. I sometimes wonder if he can really be the wee white thing that nestled by me last summer. My moments of greatest happiness come when I stand by his little crib and look down upon him sleeping—the little, relaxed, perfect body, the bare, chubby limbs, the wee dimpled fists flung up by his head, the rosy

cheeks, the shut, long-lashed eyes. I think he is going to be a handsome little lad. He has a fine complexion, starry, dark blue eyes, and dimpled cheeks. His hair is beginning to grow nicely and promises to be a golden-brown. My own dear little son! What a blessing you are to me! Will you always be so?

Sunday, May 18, 1913
The Manse
Leaskdale, Ont.

We have been gardening furiously since housecleaning was finished and I am besottedly happy in it. My tulips and daffodils are out most beautifully. Tulips are really rather a barbarous sort of blossom and seem as if they could not really belong to a spring, the season of delicacy and evasive charm. But they certainly make vivid patches of color on the lawn and "look well from the road". But it is the daffodils I love—especially the sweet "poet's narcissus" and the little starry jonquils. My garden is such a joy to me. I had to go without one for so many years and now I'm quite drunk with the joy of having one again.

Wednesday, May 21, 1913

To-day I finished my new book "The Golden Road"—a second *Story Girl* volume. I have not enjoyed writing it. I have been too hurried and stinted for time. I have had to write it at high pressure, all the time nervously expecting some interruption—which all too surely came nine times out of ten. Under such circumstances there is very little pleasure in writing. I often think wistfully of the quiet hours by my old window "down home", where I thought and wrote "without haste and without rest". But those days are gone and cannot return as long as wee Chester is a small make-trouble. I do not wish them back—but I *would* like some undisturbed hours for writing.

Nevertheless, the book is done and may be quite as good as those written more pleasantly. I am too *near* it yet to judge and having written it under stress and strain I have not that intimate sense of having *lived* it which made my other books seem so *real* to me.

Tuesday, June 10, 1913
Leaskdale, Ont.

....I am going home in July! I can hardly believe it. It seems so long since I left—so much has happened since then.

I cannot help looking forward to being in Cavendish again. The thought of walking once more in Lover's Lane and by the shore thrills me with a delight not felt since I left them. And yet I fear it will seem very sad and bitter to be in Cavendish and not be *home*. Moreover, cold reason steps in and tells me that it will be a very fatiguing thing to visit about for weeks with an active, restless, ever-moving piece of mischief like young Chester.

Then I shall have to go to see dozens of people I don't really care much for. Of course in a way I shall enjoy seeing them but—oh! If I could only go to Cavendish and spend my time wholly in the woods and by the shore, visiting only a few choice spirits. That cannot be; even if certain folk did not have to be visited I could not have my dear old solitary rambles because I could neither take nor leave Chester.

Still, there will surely be some pleasure in my trip—and I have the pleasure of looking forward to it. And glory be, I will be free for five or six blissful weeks from the boredom of missionary societies and "pastoral visitations". That alone will be a great deal to be glad of.

Wednesday, June 11, 1913
The Manse, Leaskdale, Ont.
....I get almost no time for reading now. I miss it horribly; but then I have lots of other things worthwhile and my little man-child is far more interesting than any book. He stood alone the other day; but he is so expert at galloping about on all fours that he is not at all keen about walking. It is too funny to see him scuttling about in his "creepers". He runs like a little dog.

Sunday, June 29, 1913
Leaskdale, Ont.
I felt so tired to-night that I'm about "all in", to use a slang phrase. This past week has been one wild scramble to overtake a hundred "must be dones". Tomorrow we leave for home.

Monday we had to go out to tea. Yes, there was no escaping it. It was a "pastoral duty"—and hopeless boredom. Tuesday a heat-wave struck Ontario and we have been sweltering ever since, night and day. I had to go to Uxbridge, do a lot of shopping and then go out to tea again. Wednesday I had to go to a Home Mission Sewing Bee over on the 6th. Thursday I had company—more bores—to tea. But there was one very sweet thing about that evening to me. At dusk I was alone for a moment outside with Chester. I was standing on the walk and he was scuttling up and down the veranda on all fours. On the stand on the veranda was a large potted geranium brilliant with clusters of red

blossoms. Chester came to a stop before it, put his wee face close to a scarlet cluster and smiled at it—the dearest little *companionable* smile, such as he might give a beloved playmate. I never saw anything sweeter or more spontaneous.

Friday I was busy packing and getting the house in order for leaving Saturday. I finished this and then went out to another tea-martyrdom. Oh, the precious time I have to waste utterly, going out to tea! It makes me

"The Veranda"
[Leaskdale Manse]

wild to think of it. And if I even enjoyed it I wouldn't grudge it so bitterly. I would then have the pleasure at least. But as it is I find these visits insufferably dull. I force myself to chat and smile and make suitable comments when I am shown the family photographs. But I detest it all.

To-day brought little respite. I went to service in Leaskdale in the forenoon and then in the afternoon drove over to Zephyr service. I have to show myself there once in so long or the jealous Zephyrites would think they were not getting their share of my attention. This evening callers came in and stayed late. I am very tired and the heat is stifling. What will it be travelling? But it can't be any worse than going out to tea in the congregation!

Why do I go? Because the people expect it. If I did not go they would resent it and my husband's work would suffer in consequence. It is for his sake alone I go. Otherwise I would say—in effect—to those people, "Begone! I refuse to waste my precious time catering to your petty vanity—a vanity which makes you want to have the minister and his wife to tea so that you can say they visit you as often as they visit your neighbor. I have other and more important work to do. You have no right to expect me to sacrifice that work to your trivial round and common thought. I will not do it. I will live my own life—and the devil take you all!!!!"

But I can't and don't say it. What would happen to "Society as she is" if the truth were told always? It's an amusing speculation.

What a grand saying it is—"Ye shall know the truth and the truth shall make you free." It is the greatest of the great Teacher's sayings. Were I a minister I would preach one sermon on that—only one for I would certainly not be permitted to preach any more! It would reek with heresy. The truth *does* make us free—but only when we have the honesty to accept it and the courage to tell it. I think I have the former but I have not the latter. I am a coward and dare not tell the truth as I see it and consequently I am not free—I am a slave to old customs and old conventions and old rules. But that is not the fault of the truth. It *would* make me free if I told it. But even freedom may be too costly a thing—for us weak ones at least.

Jesus told the truth—and he was free, as no man ever had or has been free. But his society cast him out—and his world crucified him for it. The world always has crucified those who tell it the truth. *That* is the price to pay for freedom on this planet.

Thanks be, I'll have a taste of freedom the next few weeks.

Thursday, July 3, 1913
Bellevue, P.E. Island.
As I write I breathe P.E. Island air—P.E. Island's blue skies are over me—P.E. Island's greenness is around me. It's almost "too good to be true".

Last Monday afternoon we left Leaskdale in a wave of blistering heat, spent the night in Toronto and left Tuesday morning for Montreal.

I am sure that that Tuesday was the most uncomfortable day, in regard to purely external discomfort that I ever endured. It was incredibly hot and vilely dirty. Clouds of black cinders blew in at the windows and in a short time we were so dirty that I longed to hide me from the face of man. Anything like my face when we got to Montreal I never saw before surmounting my body. As for Chester's white dress and my white blouse—did I say *white*? Nay, like our faces they were inky black. To make matters worse it was Dominion Day and the trains were crowded. At every station new arrivals got on, all fresh and spick and span. And we hated them fiercely for half an hour and then forgave them because they were as dirty as ourselves.

"Chester at one year old"

At Montreal we struck a glorious cool wave and by the time we reached the Point next day it was positively cold and raining. It was dark before we reached "the Island"—but wasn't the tang of the salt air good! It is so different from Ontario's languid air.

We went right down to Ch'town, getting there at eleven o'clock in a pouring rain. But next morning was glorious—clear, sunny, bracing. Ewan got a team and we drove out here to his old home, a distance of 24 miles. It was delightful to roll over the soft, easy red Island roads again. In Ontario the jar and rattle of the gravelled roads tires me out when I go driving.

We caught our first real glimpse of the sea from Tea Hill. There is a very famous view, about which I have heard much all my life but had never seen before. It is certainly magnificent. I was not prepared for the flood of emotion which swept over me suddenly when I saw the sea. I was stirred to the very deeps of my being. Tears poured into my eyes—I trembled! For a moment it seemed passionately to me that I could *never* leave it again. I *belonged* here. No other land could ever claim me—in no other land can I ever feel satisfyingly at home. Somehow, I have always had a queer instinctive feeling that I shall yet come back to the Island to live.

Saturday, July 5, 1913
Bellevue, P.E.I.

Ewan and I had a drive this evening—one of the most delightful drives I ever had in my life. We went along what is called "the county line road". For over three miles it winds through glorious maple woods where the trees met overhead and the green carpet of ferns comes out to the very edge of the red road. The evening was perfect besides. I shall remember that drive and the beauty of that road all my life. There are no such roads in Ontario. There are beautiful roads there, and beautiful landscapes. But they lack the indescribable charm which haunts the roads and landscapes of the Island. I have often tried to define the difference but I have not succeeded. It is too elusive—too subtle. Is it the touch of austerity in the Island landscape that gives it its distinctive beauty? And whence comes the austerity? Is it from the fir and the spruce? Or the glimpses of the sea? Or does it go deeper to the very soul of the land? For lands have personalities as human beings have.

Park Corner, P.E. Island,
Wednesday, July 9, 1913
Again at Park Corner. We came up to Kensington yesterday evening and drove down here. It was a beautiful evening and our drive was delightful. Besides, for me it had the charm of old scenes revisited. And when we came over the Irishtown hills and saw the blue gulf again and heard its low distant murmur! I thought of another evening long ago—over twenty years ago—when I came home from my western exile over that very road. I recalled the rapture and ecstasy that filled my heart when from that same hill the same glimpse of the purple evening sea flashed on my eyes. That same view always brings a resurrection of that old thrill and rapture.

Then we turned at the corner—and down before us ran the long, hilly red road—and a little further on we saw the pond—the "Lake of Shining Waters" and the trees that shut Uncle John's place in from the world. And then we were driving through the spruces by the gate and up the slope by the orchard. The big white house was before us, and I thought of the last time I had seen it when we had driven away from it on that dream-like afternoon of our wedding day. It seemed as if it must be much longer than two years. And now I was coming back to it with my little blue-eyed man on my knee. I had often dreamed of this very thing—and now the dream had come true. Not all my dreams have come true—not many of them indeed—but this one had.

As we rounded the maple curve Aunt Annie and Stell came running to meet us—and there was the old welcome and laughter and jests and chatter. And then in to one of Stell's famous suppers, to which we hungry travellers did full justice. Was there ever such a house as Uncle John Campbell's for "spreads"? Aunt Annie and her girls were all resplendent cooks and Uncle John C. had always the old Montgomery traditions of lavish hospitality.

This evening Stell took Ewan and myself for a drive around the harbor. Of course it was lovely. It *is* a delight to be back here in this old spot again. And yet amid all the pleasure there is a constantly recurring note of sadness—which must, I suppose, sound through most of the symphonies of life when we have left the golden road behind. For 'tis only on the golden road that music knows no minor key.

I can see poor Uncle John C. sadly failed. One cannot wonder that it is so—he is over eighty. But I cannot realize that Uncle John Campbell is eighty—or anywhere near it. My mind stubbornly refuses to conceive of him as being older than forty or fifty—the age at which I first knew him. It is as hard for me to realize that he is eighty as it is for me to realize that *my* next birthday but one will be my fortieth! Uncle John has failed in mind and body and I fear it cannot be long before he will be gone from the old home amid the orchards.

Another thing that hurts me here is this:—everywhere I turn I see something from the old home in Cavendish. And the sight of these things, divorced from the old surroundings of which they seemed a part, is painful to me. In the dining room is the old oval table which was in the sitting room at home, around which so many sat in the old days. In the hall is the bookcase which held our china at home and which was the habitation of "Katie Maurice" and "Lucy Gray". It is now used more legitimately as a bookcase. Upstairs in the hall is the carpet we had in the parlor at home and the horse-hair rocker with the black and red cushion and the knitted red and white woollen tidy I thought so very wonderful in childhood. In the room I sleep in is the bedstead from the downstairs bedroom I used to occupy in childhood; and the feather bed on it is the very one I slept on always to the last.

I used to think it a most comfortable bed. But truly last night I didn't find it so. I have become used to a spring mattress and alas, I found the old bed I used to think so soft and cosy very stuffy and smothery. So much depends on what we are used to!

Thursday, July 10, 1913
Park Corner, P.E.I.
This morning Ewan and Chester and I drove up to Malpeque to see Aunt Emily. We had a pleasant drive both ways. But a queer little disappointment was my portion. I knew Lucy Ritchie was home with her two children and I was looking forward to seeing Kenneth. Three years have passed since I saw him, a child of four. I *knew* he must have changed somewhat but I could not grasp it. Subconsciously, I suppose, I was really expecting to see the beautiful child I saw in Boston three years ago. I was utterly taken aback when Kenneth presented himself. I felt as if he were a total stranger. His hair was clipped to the bone. He wore a shapeless overall suit, the trousers reaching to his feet and making him look like a grown-up dwarf so to speak. The only thing I recognized about him were his beautiful brown eyes. Yes, I *was* disappointed. I daresay if I had stayed long enough to get acquainted with him all over again I would have found him lovable and charming enough in his new incarnation. But as it is I've lost the little dream boy I loved. The present Kenneth Ritchie seems as nothing to me.

Monday, July 14, 1913
Park Corner, P.E. Island
I had to-night one of those little psychological experiences which make an otherwise commonplace day stand out in memory as a beacon through the years. I had a walk over the pond tonight which I shall always remember.

To-day was showery but tonight the rain ceased to fall. It was a dull, damp brooding night. At nine o'clock, Chester being asleep, I slipped away for what is my rarest pleasure nowadays—as it used to be my commonest and almost my only one—a solitary ramble in the twilight.

As I went down the lane my very soul became penetrated with and steeped in the mystic, sinister, uncanny charm of the night. It was close and shadowy and breathless and still—like the night of a forsaken world. Thickly in orchard and wood glimmered the goblin firefly lanterns. I walked through the dark belt of spruces and across the pond, lying silent and shadowy and deadly still beneath me. I lingered long by the railing—"doubting, dreaming dreams no mortal have dared to dream before", as I peered through that strange baffling twilight. And then fancy began to summon up from the vasty deeps of the old years many by-gone memories of mirth and frolic—and the imagined laughter of those memories seemed to echo alienly through the deserted haunts of those who had so laughed. Back they all came trooping—those I had walked over that bridge with years ago—in their merry youth they came, their forms were around me, their voices whispered half-mockingly, half tenderly through the gloom, their viewless hands plucked at me, drawing me into their charmed circle once more. They were all there—Clara, Stella, Frede, in their youth, Lem and Ed and Howe and Ev and Irv and Jack—all the boys and girls who formed our "set" that gay winter at Park Corner. They seemed so oddly *near* to me—I felt that if I could only tear aside that thick curtain of twilight I could see them all with the body's eye. But I could not tear it aside—and presently my ghostly company left me sorrowfully—and I walked back to the house alone, save for an impish black kitten that frisked along before me, looking like the very incarnation of some witch's work. And those who saw me come in knew not that I had just come from that strange, weird borderland which parts the present from the past and where we can only wonder when dark meets light on a summer eve.

Thursday, July 17, 1913
Park Corner, P.E. Island
After dinner this lovely day Stella and I got the hired man to row us down the pond to the shore. It was delightful. Oddly enough, in all the times I have been at Park Corner I have never once been on that pond in a boat. The views as one rows down it are charming. I took my bathing suit along with me but I really hadn't the least interest of going in. I was sure the water would be too cold. But when I got down there and saw the little white ripples crisping over the sands the old water lust awoke in me and would not be denied. I *must* go in—yea, though the water were as cold as ice. It *was* cold enough at first but soon that was over and I had a glorious dip.

Then the pleasure of the day was over. I had to come home and dress for a visit to Aunt Mary Cuthbert's.

I have always liked Aunt Mary and have always liked to go there. But Aunt Mary, though the soul of kindness, has always been *fussy*. At first it was not so bad; but as the years went on it intensified. To-day she completely spoiled my visit for me. Not one moment could she leave me in peace. Did I feel a draft?—she asked me that half a dozen times and in spite of my desperate assurance that I hadn't even noticed that the window was open she finally shut it down. Wouldn't I like a shawl?—did I find that chair comfortable—try this other chair, yes, I must—and so on and so on. At tea time it was still more awful. She urged and entreated me to eat—she *pestered* me to eat—she lamented that she had nothing nice for me—nothing that I cared to eat. And poor me eating furiously until I was ready to burst. I was so thankful when my visit came to an end. My nerves were almost frayed out and I was deadly tired when I got home. Why can't people have a little sense?

The Manse, Leaskdale, Ont.
Saturday, Sept. 27, 1913
I had to give up "journalizing" since the foregoing record, save for an occasional hurried entry in a notebook. I hadn't the time for it; and since coming home I have been so busy I had no opportunity to write it up.

I left Park Corner on Monday, July 21st—left it sadly and regretfully. I felt that it was all too likely that sad changes would have taken place before I could ever visit it again. And I had had a delightful sojourn there. Stella could always act the hostess' part very well and she did everything to make my visit pleasant. Chester was good all the time and Aunt Annie looked after him a good bit, thereby giving me a rest.

George took me down to Cavendish Monday forenoon....The rest of the day Chester kept me pretty closely at home. By half past eight that night he was asleep. I was rather tired; outside it was damp and dark; common sense said I should go to bed myself. But a stronger emotion than common sense was drawing me. I *had* to yield to it. I had to go. Voices were calling to me that could not be resisted—voices of the past, fraught with all the past's enchantment. They summoned me imperiously and I obeyed the summons. I slipped out into the darkness of the summer evening and went to find the lost years.

In one way it was a bad evening for such a stroll. It was dark, damp, misty, brooding—a sorrowful evening such as might turn mirth into joy and weigh down the gayest heart with nameless foreboding and regret. Yet, in another way, it was the very evening of such a pilgrimage to shrines forsaken and altars overthrown. There was nothing to detract from the sway of memory—nothing to clash with the dreams of old days. Something about the night itself filled me with longing and pain—nearly broke my heart—but it was in keeping with my mood and my object. The result was an hour I can never forget—an hour whose pain was sweeter than joy, whose loneliness was dearer than delight.

In the dim, still, eerie twilight I slipped down the hill, over the bridge across the brook and up the dark path under the spruces. It was the old way home. I found the little gate in the fence and went through. Then I stopped in dismay, my soul rent with a pang of grief and indignation.

I was in Pierce Macneill's hill field. As long as I can remember the north western corner of that field was occupied by a grove of spruce and maple. It was always one of my beloved haunts. The maples in the jutting corner were among my dearest tree friends. What then were my feelings to see that the grove was—gone. Only a desolation of stumps remained. That soulless Pierce Macneill had cut it down—may jackals sit on his grandmother's grave!

Really it hurt me horribly. I felt lacerated and rent as I walked across the field to the main road. Arriving there I turned and walked up Laird's hill. How many times I had walked up that hill in the old evenings. At the top I turned to the gate in the hill field—and from there I looked down on home.

Yes, there it was. In the fading gray light I could see the old gray house hooded in shadows—I could see the little window of my old ⌐oom—I could see the blot of dimness beyond that was the orchard.

"Home as it was long years ago"

I stood there long—and never have I felt keener pangs—never did my heart ache more bitterly with longing and sense of loss. And as I stood there I thought—not of home empty and forsaken—not of home as it was in the years before I left it—but of home as it was long years ago. It seemed to me that if I could only put out my hand and draw aside that gray veil of twilight that hung over it I should see it again as it was then—steeped in summer sunshine, surrounded by green, apple-bearing trees, filled with laughter and light steps and mirthful hearts with the homelight shining from its windows at night. Yes—yes, it was all there—only those cruel shadows hid it from me. They barred me out in the darkness—I could not pierce through them to my own—I could only hover longingly on the outside.

I wept bitterly. It seemed to me that my heart was broken with realization. I found no comfort in any thought. I thought of my husband down at Bellevue— thought of my little son asleep in the house behind the spruces. But they seemed unreal and far away. I had strayed back into a past which knew them not and where I could not find them but only the ghosts of old friends and companions. It was horrible—it was heartbreaking—but withal there was a certain luxury in it to which I abandoned myself until I knew that I must tear myself away from that gray kingdom of shadows.

As I walked down the hills I pleased and tortured myself with a bit of pretence. It was four years back. All was as it used to be. I had slipped away in the dusk, as was my custom, for a solitary ramble. Now I was going home again. I would go down the hill and up the "school hill". I would turn into the old lane. As I walked up it I would see the kitchen light shining through the trees. I would pass under the birches and then under the cherry trees and then around the curve. The old house would be before me; Daffy would come frisking across the yard and bound before me to the old red door. I would lift the latch and walk in, a little tired, and glad to be home again. Grandmother would be sitting in her old arm-chair by the table, reading, with her gray shawl about her shoulders.

It was very real to me. My vivid imagination can always deceive me—for a little while. When I reached the top of the school hill I thought I would go up the bank and look up the old lane once more, over the bars that were now across it. I had no thought of going further, but I would just look up the lane and spin out the thread of my fancy.

I went up to the bars and looked over. The shock of what I saw turned me quite faint. *There was no lane*—it was gone! All I saw were the rows of potatoes with which the field was planted.

Somehow, I had never once thought of such a thing. I had often thought of things that might and probably would happen to the old house. I had pictured it as torn down—I had pictured another house built there. But it had never occurred to me to think of the old lane being done away with. It seemed to me as much a part of the landscape as the hills or woods. Some men, indeed, would have hesitated before doing away with it—the old homestead lane their feet had trod in childhood, in farings forth and in returnings home. But such sentiment could, of course, have no power with a man of Uncle John's type—especially when weighed against the few bushels of potatoes the soil of the lane would grow!

I turned away. I pretended no longer that I was going home. To me, the disappearance of that old lane had a symbolism all its own. It was not only that the way to the past was closed—it was altogether gone. Only on the wings of imagination could I revisit it—could I cross the gulf of time and change that yawned between me and the spot I loved.

I walked on to the graveyard. I met no one. I seemed alone in a dark world upon which the sun would never more rise. I went into the graveyard. I stood by the graves of grandfather and grandmother, of mother and Tillie. And then I left them and wandered down the old church hill, choking with sobs. The tears poured down my cheeks in the darkness. I wished wretchedly that I had never come back to Cavendish—the pain of it was unbearable. I would not enjoy a minute of my stay. I only wanted to get away—far away from those haunting memories. On the hill there had been a strange, mysterious pleasure mingled with the pain—but now it was all pain.

Not until I found myself back beside my little son and felt his dear warm chubby arms go round my neck clingingly did my heart stop aching. And even then I cried myself to sleep.

But next day all was magically changed. It was bright and sunny; with the darkness had fled the eerie unwholesome charm the night had woven over my soul and my senses. I drove myself up to Bay View post-office and I did not hurry, either going or coming for it was delightful to be on that pretty road once more and see the blue sea sparkling beyond in every break of tree and hill. In the afternoon was another dear walk up Lover's Lane and through the woods to "the devil's punch-bowl" and beyond it out through the wood-path to the fields again. Then a merry call from Margaret—and finally a blissful evening of berry-picking in the grove of maple and apple trees they call "the old orchard" closed a flawless day.

I had been craving wild strawberries. Never since I left the Island had I so much as seen one. And all the time I was there I revelled in them. It was a banner year for wild berries there. The very roadsides were red with them. Almost better than eating them was the picking them. Every evening that I was home Myrtle and I would take the children and hie us to the Old Orchard. The kiddies enjoyed it as much as we did. Chester tumbled and crept among the fragrant grasses, laughed and crowed, picked and ate his first wild strawberries, "tops and all". Below us we could see the pond and the sea—and away to the west glorious summer sunsets. After the first day it seemed quite natural to be at Myrtle's and I had no more visitations such as I had that first night. I was in Cavendish—that was enough.

Wednesday afternoon I went down and had tea with Tillie Macneill—who is now Tillie Macneill no longer. She was married the next week to a widower, Mr. Bentley by name, and departed for Calgary with him. Cavendish was tremendously excited over her courtship. It really was all very funny. Poor Tillie is a good soul but she has always had a quite frantic desire to be married—it did not really matter much to whom, I think, so long as he was respectable. Tillie has had two or three affairs which came to nothing; and now in her 48th year

"Mr. and Mrs. E. Webb and the oldest children"

she has achieved matrimony at last. I am glad she has because she would never be happy otherwise; but really it was all very comical and Tillie did make a goose of herself and her elderly lover.

I can't say I enjoyed the afternoon very much for it was a constant effort to keep Chester out of mischief. That house was never meant for children. Tillie has no idea what to do to amuse them; and I cannot picture her poorly-concealed anguish when Chester strewed crumbs from his cookie over the sacred parlor floor! But after tea came a lull when I took Chester outside and let him tumble harmlessly about on the grass, while I sat on the front doorstep. That was a favorite seat of mine in old days. How often had I sat there in summer evenings gazing on that self-same scene bathed in the golden after light. It was still the same—the pond between the gnarled old apple trees—Pierce Macneill's place—the red hill—the graveyard with its white stones—the trees beyond that shut in my old home. I had a happy half hour; but when I went back to Mr. Webb's I was horribly tired. That was the drawback to my vacation. I had to visit so much and it tired me so, looking after Chester-boy and keeping him out of mischief. But no afternoon was quite so hard as that one at Tillie's.

Ewan came that evening and left early the next morning for home. I must say I felt as lonely and forlorn over his departure as if I did not expect to see him again for years. I went with him as far as the top of Laird's Hill and waved him out of sight. Then I went to the gate in the hill field and looked down upon home again.

I could see it plainly then, in the fresh morning sunshine. But, although I gazed on it sadly, I felt none of the strange agony and desolation I had felt that first evening. Then I went across the fields to Lover's Lane and walked home by way of it.

In all the many walks of long years I had never been in Lover's Lane in the early morning. I had been in it in forenoons and afternoons, in evenings and twilights, even late o'nights. But never till that day had I seen it in the first morning sunshine. And it was very lovely; and I discovered a woodland secret I had never known before. The sunshine, striking down through the woods revealed across the brook a charming woodland hill nook that had never been visible before. I explored it later on and found it lovely. And I had passed it a thousand times and never dreamed of it, though I thought I knew those old woods so well.

In my notebook I find written:

†*"The Manse, Cavendish, P.E. Island*
Sunday, Aug. 3, 1913
....This evening I went again to church and saw Jack Laird and his wife who are visiting in C. at present. I was glad to see Jack again. He hasn't changed much—except to grow stout and broad-shouldered—and there is a good deal of gray in his hair. Well, for that matter I have a good many gray hairs myself, scattered through my tresses, although as yet they show only on close inspection. We of that old class are all getting on. It seems quite unbelievable that we should have gray hair. Once gray hairs seemed so very very far away from us.

I remember acutely the anguish the discovery of my first gray hair brought me. It was ten years ago. One spring day I had washed my hair and in the twilight I went to the window of my room to examine the scalp to see if it was perfectly clean. I drew the comb through my hair, parting it midway. And there, cruelly distinct in the harsh light of the gray spring evening, was a white hair—snow-white. I gazed at it with incredulous eyes. It could *not* be. But it *was*. With shaking fingers I searched through my hair and found a second white one. Well, it seemed to me that I finally turned my back on youth that night. I cried myself to sleep and for days the thought of those gray hairs haunted me. Then I accepted them and became resigned. I found that life went on pretty much the same as ever in spite of those gray hairs. They have gradually increased since then but not so rapidly as I once feared; and they do not worry me much now—nothing ever does worry you much once you accept it. I admire gray hair—on other people; and when my own is all gray I daresay it will be very becoming. When I was a child my hair was very thick and long

---

†LMM quotes from her notebook.

and of a very pretty shade of golden brown. When I began to grow up it began to darken and soon became a much less beautiful shade of dark brown. It was never curly, alas! I have always envied people who have naturally curly hair. When I had typhoid fever at the age of five or six the doctor wanted to cut my hair. Grandmother would not allow him to do so. She meant well but I have always wished she had not refused. If it had been cut it might have come in curly. But what matter? I don't suppose it would have made any great difference if it had—only it would have saved me much time and trouble curling and waving my hair."

†*"Wednesday, Aug. 6, 1913*
Cavendish, P.E. Island
This morning I drove in and spent the day with Amanda. She was very nice—more like her old self than I have seen her for years. I quite enjoyed the day. She talked much of old schooldays and frolics—something she would never do for years before I left home. I often used to try, in desperation for something to talk about, but she always avoided the subject. I think perhaps since I passed finally out of her life, she has realized the worth of the friendship she threw away and now would fain regain it. Alas, she cannot! Not because I would be unforgiving but sheerly because of the change in herself—the lack of all development, the dwarfed, stunted nature. Poor Amanda, she cannot be happy, with such a husband and such a home. Yet her young girlhood promised fair—and this thwarted, unlovely womanhood is the result. It is a pity she has not had a child. It might have made up to her for all. And yet, looking at her and at George Henry, we cannot but feel thankful for the child's sake that it was never born!"

*....I hated the thought of leaving Cavendish. It was so lovely to be there again, among all my own old friends. Somehow, I could not feel a bit glad to be going back to Leaskdale. I knew that by the time I got here the discomforts of travel would have made me heartily glad to be here, but as long as I was in Cavendish I didn't want to leave it. My heart clung to it and ached at the thought of leaving it again.

I packed up Thursday and made some farewell calls. Friday morning Mr. Stirling drove me to Hunter River, Alec taking my trunks. It was a lovely morning. Cavendish looked so beautiful as we drove through it—so green, for the season was late and the grain had not begun to ripen. I knew the harvest was on in Ontario and that it would seem like stepping from spring to autumn when I went back. We had a lovely drive to Hunter River. I went from there to O'Leary to see Mary Beaton. I had not seen her for nine years. She has failed a good deal—is very thin and I do not think she is very happy. My namesake, Maud, who was a tot of two when I last saw her is now a big girl of eleven and quite nice-looking.

From O'Leary I went on Saturday to Elmsdale and stayed over Sunday with the William Macneills. I wanted to hear all about poor Aunt Mary's last days. How I missed her! How she would have loved to have seen my boy! But alas, how many others would have loved to see him, too, had they been there to welcome me. And Tillie most of all. Poor Tillie! It almost broke my heart to drive past her little home the first time I went to Rustico and recall all the happy hours I had spent there with her. I did not go there at all, though Will invited me the Sunday I saw him in church. It would have been too painful; and anyway I could not go. Will was very gushing that day and had been at Webb's the night before to see me but I had been away. I was furious with him, for I had been hearing things. It seems he acted insanely when he heard about my marriage and went about talking promiscuously in the most idiotic fashion—raving against Ewan, whose friend he had always professed to be. He has said unpardonable things and betrayed to everybody that he was mad with jealousy, thus opening their eyes to facts that otherwise would never have been suspected. He even went to Park Corner after I was married and made an absurd scene there. Aunt Annie thought he must be out of his mind. I was furious when I heard it all and resolved that I would never make any pretence of friendship for Will again. He has made it impossible. And yet I feel sorry. I liked Will in olden days and he was always so kind to grandmother. For Tillie's sake I would have forgotten his folly in the past and remained his friend. But that cannot be now. He seems to have sunk back to his old level since Tillie's death. Hilda McKenzie, a cousin of Tillie's whom she had with her a couple of years before her death, keeps house for him. He must have a lonely life. I would feel sorry for him if he had not behaved so outrageously.

On Monday, Aug. 18th, I went down to S'side and crossed in the boat. Stella came as far as Moncton with me to help me through the turmoil of changing cars there. From Moncton to Montreal I got on beautifully as I had a drawing-room compartment where Chester could range at will. Tuesday morning my troubles began again. The train was an hour late when we reached Montreal. Result—the train was gone which would have reached Toronto in time to catch the Uxbridge train and I could not get home that night. I had to come on in a slow train. Chester was a huge trouble owing to his roving tendencies. I was tired out when we reached Toronto at nine. There was no one to meet me, Ewan, as I learned later, having returned home thinking that I would not be along till next day. I stayed all night at the Walker House and Ewan came next morning. We reached home at 8 o'clock that night.

Up to the very moment of getting here I was not reconciled to coming back. The drive from Uxbridge home depressed me. The road was dusty and dry and white. The dim slopes on either hand were sere and harvested. The air seemed dull and languid after the tang of the gulf breezes. There seemed a smouldering revolt in my heart at coming back. But when our gate shut behind us it vanished. I was suddenly glad to be back—to be home! Glad to see again my garden, grown out of all recognition in my absence, glad to see my flowers, gray Daffy, my books and pictures, my own comfortable room. My house looked pretty nice to me. I saw it with a stranger's eye after my long absence and when my impression of it was not blurred by familiarity. I liked it! Yes, it was good to be home again among my own household gods.

For a day or two it seemed odd to me to take up the reins of household government again after being a guest in other people's homes so long. And it was *not* pleasant to have to take up again the burden of boring congregational visits and missionary societies.

On the Friday night after my return I got a card from Frede Campbell saying that she would be at Uxbridge on the seven o'clock train that evening. I had been expecting her, as I knew she did not intend staying in the West another year. As Ewan was busy I drove down to meet her. In the excitement of our meeting we were only vaguely aware that a very heavy thunderstorm was coming up and that rain was already falling. For the first two miles of our homeward drive our excitement continued to burn so red-hotly and our tongues to fly so vehemently over the much matter we had to discuss that we did not realize our plight—and then suddenly we realized it with a vengeance! It was pouring rain; it was inky black, relieved by blinding flashes of lightning; we had no idea just where we were; we could not see our hands before our faces.

I have always had a dislike for afternight driving. And here I had to drive home from Uxbridge on a night like this!

Well, needs must when the devil drives! We had to keep on. We could not see any gate or place to turn in, or we would have gone to some house. The road was straight so we could not lose it. So perforce we kept on. Queen could only walk for the rain drove in her face and if she trotted she could not keep the road but diverged towards the gutter. I am sure neither Frede nor I will ever forget that nightmare drive home. Our greatest dread was that we might meet teams and have to pass. We welcomed the lightning flashes that at least served to show the road ahead clear. It seemed as if we would *never* get home. And yet we talked and jested through it all and by the time we did get home we had emptied our souls of all the accumulations of the past months. But heaven send I may never have another such drive!

I have been exceedingly busy ever since coming back—preserving, canning, sewing and visiting. That never-ending visiting! What precious moments it eats up!

On September first I began work on a third "Anne" book. I did not want to do it—I have fought against it. But Page gave me no peace and every week brought a letter from some reader pleading for "another Anne book". So I have yielded for peace sake. It's like marrying a man to get rid of him!

I don't see how I can possibly do anything worth while with it. *Anne* is grown-up and can't be made as interesting as when a child. My forte is in writing humor. Only childhood and elderly people can be treated humorously in books. Young women in the bloom of youth and romance should be sacred from humor. It is the time of sentiment and I am not good at depicting sentiment—I can't do it well. Yet there *must* be sentiment in this book. I must at least engage Anne for I'll never be given any rest until I do. So it's rather a hopeless prospect and I feel as if I were going to waste all the time I shall put on the book. I might be doing something so much more worthwhile. Perhaps when I get fairly underway I shall warm up to the task but at present I feel very coldly towards it.

"The Golden Road" came out on September first—in appearance just like the preceding five. It is getting monotonous. I wish Page would make a change. It is my sixth book. Can I really have published six books! Some readers and critics think *"The Golden Road"* is the best since *Anne*. I rather like it myself now that I have got far enough away from the turmoil of writing it—the odor of its brewing. It is simply a continuation of the *Story Girl* and ends that series. There is not a great deal of "real life" in it....

Lily was away for her vacation of seventeen days in October and I had few spare moments those days. And yet it was very nice to be alone. There was a sweetness in our home life then that cannot be present when a servant shares it—especially when said servant has to be treated as a member of the family, as is necessary here. Lily is an excellent maid and I am well satisfied with her. Still, any outsider is an alien. I wish I could do without a maid but it is impossible.

Not long ago I had a letter from May Macneill in which she informed me that Cavendish post-office had been closed.

I felt sorry—and a little indignant. It was a shame to close that historic old office. Of course the recent introduction of rural mail delivery all over the Island has done away with the need for many of the small offices. But they should not have closed an old one like Cavendish. It must have been one of the oldest country offices on the Island. Grandfather and grandmother kept it for forty years. Well, I am glad the change did not come there in my day. Up to about fourteen years ago we had mail only three days in the week—Tuesday, Thursday and Saturdays. It seemed quite wonderful when we got the daily mail; but soon it seemed as if we must always have had it. And now the old Cavendish office is closed. *Sic transit gloria mundi*. It is another one of the little changes that make the big sum total of all change. Dear heart, how homesick it makes me to write anything about Cavendish!

Last Monday Frede left, going to Montreal to take a position in Macdonald College. Again I missed her horribly but I am thankful she is comparatively near me.

Saturday, October 18, 1913
The Manse, Leaskdale, Ont.
Ever since my last entry I have been, so it seems to me, scrambling through the days striving to do a thousand things in the time that might comfortably suffice for a hundred—doing household duties, tending Chester, sewing, writing novels, and letters and "Guild" papers and lectures, visiting and being visited, attending missionary societies, running Mission Bands—and ending up most of the days by being woefully tired and rather disgruntled. But it is my "kismet"—therefore I must submit!

To-day in the Charlottetown *Guardian* there was an announcement of Uncle Leander's death. It is not to be regretted by anyone for the past ten years have been to him death in life and he longed for release. I have never had any especial reason to be very fond of Uncle Leander but nevertheless I felt sad over his death. He was so largely a part of the old life that I feel as if something had been wrenched away in his going—a something not wholly pleasant perhaps but still a something so interwoven with the fibres of my life that tearing it from them meant pain, keen though transient.

Uncle Leander was the first-born of grandfather and grandmother. Great-grandfather Macneill gave him the name of Leander "after him who swam the Hellespont". He was never over-grateful to Great-grandfather for this—nor do I wonder at it! He was a clever and ambitious boy, noted for always getting his own way in everything and carrying out his plans, quite regardless, I have been given to understand, of anyone else's feelings in the matter. He went to Prince of Wales College and from there to Edinburgh University. When he graduated from it he took a position as teacher—of mathematics I think, although I am not sure—in Prince of Wales College, and soon after he was married to Janie Perkins of Charlottetown. I have no memory of "Aunt Janie" but I have been told that she was a very sweet woman. And now Uncle L.G. discovered that teaching was not his vocation. He hated it and he was so unreasonably severe with his pupils that many of them refused to go to school to him. He could not keep order without thrashing several of them every day which, as they were all nearly as old as himself, was rather too strenuous. So he resigned his position and went to Princeton to study theology. I do not think I do Uncle Leander any grievous wrong in saying that he had no over-loud "call" to enter the ministry. He had a wife and child to support, so he must choose a profession that would promise subsistence from the start. There was certainly nothing "spiritual" about Uncle Leander. He was an intensely selfish man, keenly ambitious of place and supremacy, and neither in his life nor his ideals did he have much in common with the teachings of "the meek and lowly Jesus". But during my two years sojourn in the manse and consequent close association with many ministers I have been driven to conclude that this is not so uncommon as it should be. He was strong and brilliant, with a charming society manner and so, from a worldly point of view, he succeeded. He had wealthy city churches and an unquestioned standing in the councils of "the cloth".

His first charge was in Maitland, N.S. Then he went to St. John's, Newfoundland. Here Aunt Janie died of consumption. Later, he married Annie Putman of Maitland. In my first recollection of him he was in Newfoundland, coming home every summer for his vacation. Uncle Leander was always very fond of his home and his "folks". He had the Macneill "clannishness". Unlike Uncle Chester, who never seemed to care for his home after he had left it, Uncle Leander never grew away from it. This was not only because it was a good and economical place to spend vacations in and send his boys for the summer. He really loved it.

I never was very fond of Uncle L.G. In society he could be very agreeable. In private life he was a domineering, selfish man and rode rough-shod over everyone's feelings. Aunt Annie was a very sweet woman and I always liked her. She was an excellent mother to her stepsons and fostered her husband's selfishness by adoring him and submitting to him in everything.

In course of time Uncle Leander was called to St. John, N.B. Here his only living daughter—three other daughters had died in babyhood—Edith died of consumption at the age of eighteen. This was a sad blow to him. In a few years it was followed by Aunt Annie's death. In three or four years time he married his third wife, Mary Kennedy. This was his fatal mistake. He lost his hold on his congregation by such a step. She was a very inferior, illiterate person, a jolly good soul enough, suited for some laboring man's wife but wholly unfitted for his position. His own family resented it bitterly also. Uncle Leander's decline dated from then. He saw his church going down and worried about it. Before long the first symptoms of *"paralysis agitans"* became apparent and for the next fourteen or fifteen years he grew worse and worse until he was a hopeless wreck—a sad ending to a brilliant career.

In my childhood and young girlhood Uncle Leander took very little notice of me, except to hector and snub me, in season and out of season. Grandfather and grandmother, who idolized him, never attempted to check him in the slightest degree. He would never have dared to use me so if my parents had been there to protect me. He never meddled with Uncle John's children or Aunt Annie's. Having no one to defend me I was sometimes goaded to defend myself and so was considered "saucy and impertinent" by Uncle L.—whose own children often "answered back", precisely as I did, but were never so condemned for it!

For twenty years Uncle Leander and some or all of his family came to Cavendish to spend the summer. Yet he never once asked me to visit them. If he had asked me, now and then, to spend two or three weeks with them in the winter the advantages of such a visit would have been incalculable to me, especially from a social point of view. But no such invitation was ever given. I was only an insignificant "country cousin" whose mission in life was, or should be, to wait humbly upon Uncle L's family during the hot weather of July and August and feel myself honored! That sounds bitter. But I *did* feel bitter about it in those days.

But there was in Uncle Leander a rather decided disposition to worship the rising sun. It was not very long after the success of "Anne" until I was aware of a very pronounced change in his manner to me. He ceased to snub or patronize. He seemed to accept me as an equal—deigned to converse quite seriously with me and was really quite agreeable. But it was a little too late. Had he been one half as nice to me when I was a child or a young struggling girl I would have worshipped him. As it was, he could not quite blot out the old memories of him.

Yet those memories of Uncle Leander are not all bitter or unpleasant. He was not always disagreeable, even to me. On the contrary, there were occasional times when he was quite kind and companionable, and it was always a pleasure to me to listen to his conversation with others—he was so witty and polished and pointed. When I visited him on my return from Boston he was delighted. Nobody could have been kinder—nobody more the hospitable host.

Uncle Leander had many fine qualities. Had it not been for his domineering habit he would have been a delightful and lovable person all the time, instead of only at intervals. And had he remembered that a child had feelings and rights as well as an adult he would have left a kindlier memory behind him in my heart.

But he is gone—not quite three years after the mother who so idolized him and whom, to do him justice, he loved most tenderly and faithfully. After her death he wrote a letter to Aunt Annie in which he said that, as head of the family, he felt that he ought to convey to me his thanks for the faithfulness with which I had stayed by grandmother to the last. It was a fair and just thing of him and I appreciated it—but what a pity the justice and fairness couldn't have been sprinkled along the way and not all reserved for a parting bouquet.

I am glad grandmother went before him. It would have been very bitter for her had he gone first. I understand now her love for him in the light of my own love for Chester.

Saturday, November 1, 1913
St. Paul's Manse, Leaskdale, Ont.
I have been rushing madly through the days since writing last. On Thursday, Oct. 23rd I went up to Toronto. Last spring the Women's Canadian Club of Toronto asked me to address them at their opening meeting this fall, taking as my subject, Prince Edward Island. I had never made a speech in public, had no wish to do so, was in a blue funk at the idea—and yet I consented. I do not know why I consented. It seemed as if I were compelled to do so by some psychic impulse, such as led to my going to Boston three years ago. In evangelistic jargon I was "led". At any rate I agreed to go. All through October I was getting my address ready and as aforesaid I went to town on the 23rd. I stayed with Marjorie MacMurchy while I was in and had a very delightful time. I do like Toronto. I almost think I would like to live there. I have always said and believed that I could never wish to live anywhere save in the country. But I now begin to suspect that what I meant by "country" was really "Cavendish". I would rather live in Cavendish than anywhere else in the world. But apart from it, I really believe I would like very much to live in a place like Toronto—where I could have some intellectual companionship, have access to good music, drama and art, and some little real social life. I have *no* social life here—none at all, not even as much as I had in Cavendish, for there at least I had a few "chums" whose society I really enjoyed. But here, though I am "visiting" and being visited half the time, there is no pleasure whatever for me. As "the minister's wife" I dare not talk gossip. It would be fatal. But there is nothing else the women here, even the nicest of them, can talk about—except market prices and crops—so conversation on these occasions is a dreary desert. Of course I can rattle on in "small talk" but in my inmost soul I am "cussing" the waste of time. Real enjoyment is never a waste of time; but these horrible "pastoral visits" are, I really believe, an invention of the devil himself.

But I had a good forty-eight hours in Toronto. I had no cares, no worries. I didn't have to watch over everything I said, lest it might be reported to my own or my husband's discredit. I could just "talk". And I had left Chester-boy home, so I wasn't obliged to watch him out of mischief every minute. I felt quite girlish again.

The first evening the MacMurchy girls had some friends in to dinner and after dinner we went to see an amusing little musical comedy at one of the theatres. It was silly and superficial enough but the music and costumes were pretty and it was certainly more interesting than the dreary "inanities" of the Zephyr "guild", where I would have had to be if I had been home. Friday afternoon the MacMurchy girls gave an afternoon tea for me, which was very pleasant. Saturday afternoon I addressed 800 women in the Forresters' Hall. Mrs. Dickson, the president of the club, is a woman of notable distinction and charm. I have met few women who impressed me so favorably.

"Mrs. George Dickson, of Toronto"

I was not at all nervous. My address lasted an hour and nobody seemed bored. Judging by the newspaper reports it was quite a success.

One paper said, "Her address lasted for over an hour during which she held the interest of her listeners without a moment of boredom intervening and her clear enunciation carried her every word to the far end of the hall, a feat seldom attained by women speakers unless they have had considerable training in delivery."

One paper described me as follows:—

"In appearance Mrs. Macdonald is slight, of medium height, with dark hair and eyes and a fair complexion. She wears her hair waved and drawn down over her ears. There is something quaint and taking in her whole personality. She is quiet, with a great deal of reserve force and strength. Few writers impress one to the same degree with the conviction that she lives in a mental world of her own....She has a voice of admirable carrying quality."

The *Courier* said:—"It was very delightful to find that this entertaining author is also an entertaining speaker.—L.M. Montgomery is a vari-talented woman who did not quite all go between the covers of 'Anne of Green Gables'".

I have no intention however of rushing into a career of platform speaking.

After my address the Club had an afternoon tea and I had to shake hands with and say something amiable to nearly all those women. So I was very tired when I got on the seven o'clock train for home. Rev. Dr. Gandier of Knox College came out with me. He preached the next day and was with us two days canvassing the congregation. Lily and I have been trying to get some house-cleaning done this week and everything has been rushed.

Wednesday, Nov. 5, 1913
Leaskdale, Ont.
A beautiful wasted day. Wasted because I had to spend it attending a Home Missionary Convention in Uxbridge. It was deadly dull. All the good I got from it was learning how to pronounce "Heimweh" correctly—that is if the anemic-looking lady who used it in her speech knew herself! I brought Mrs. Horne of Lindsay home with me. She is to speak before our Auxiliary tomorrow and we are going to have afternoon tea. Mrs. H. is hopelessly uninteresting and seems to have resolved to know nothing but Foreign Missions and them only. What a pity it is so hard to be both good and interesting.

I am not good—but I *am* interesting!

Thursday, Nov. 27, 1913
The Manse, Leaskdale, Ont.
This being "black Thursday" again meant that I must visit in Zephyr. I loathe Thursday as much as I loathe Zephyr. This afternoon, too, I felt very miserable. I suppose I can expect nothing else for some weeks now. Chester's little sister—let us hope!—has, I think, started on her journey from "the kingdom of the future". I am very glad of this but that fact will not prevent physical discomfort. And it is a discomfort which one must hide, pretending to feel quite well. This afternoon was hateful to me. We were visiting an ignorant, bigoted family. I found it wretchedly hard to "make talk". And for tea we had cold roast pork and fried potatoes.

Normally, I am, I admit, very fond of pork and fried potatoes. This may be a very plebeian taste but it is undoubtedly mine and praise be that it is—for almost *everywhere* we go to tea—absolutely everywhere in Zephyr—we have cold pork and fried potatoes. What my fate would be if I did *not* like them I tremble to think. But lately I have turned against many things that I like and the mere thought of eating pork or fried potatoes nauseates me. Yet there was hardly anything else on the table tonight that I cared for. I made a miserable meal and my hostess watched me with an unfavorable eye. Doubtless she resented my not doing better justice to her viands.

After tea we drove to the village and I put in the evening talking to two deaf old ladies while E. went to prayer-meeting. We had a cold drive home, I felt sick all the way and very tired holding Chester. There, I've written a whole page of grumbles. Great is the relief!

Tuesday, Dec. 16, 1913
The Manse, Leaskale, Ont.
Ever since my last entry I have been deathly sick with almost no intermission. "Deathly"—yes, that is the very word to express my feeling. I have been ten times worse than during the same period with Chester. The last three weeks have seemed like a nightmare to me. I have been sick with nausea almost unceasingly—I have the most horrible taste in my mouth—I loathe the thought of food—any food—*all* food—I have headache—I am miserably tired all the time and—hardest of all—I have not a spark of energy or interest in anything. Everything I have done in those three weeks I had to *drive* myself to do. I have done nothing except what had to be done. The rest of the time I have had to lie around like a log. Finally today I sent in desperation for Dr. Shier. If I do not get better soon I don't know what I'll do.

Saturday, Dec. 27, 1913
Leaskdale, Ont.
I have been no better—worse if anything. Really, it has been horrible. I am absolutely useless. Thanks be, Christmas is over. It was a hard one. I had to go to Uxbridge Monday morning to do some Christmas shopping. This tired me out; and then in the evening we had to go out to tea and have a family baptism. I was worn out when I got home and sick all the next day. In the evening I had to go out and take part in the Sunday School Concert. Wednesday I spent in bed.

Thursday was Christmas—the most doleful one I ever put in. Lily went home so I had to cook the dinner. When I'm well I love cooking. But just now the sight and odor of food is nauseous to me. Sick as any dog, I cooked that dinner and choked some of it down. Turkey—cranberry sauce—pudding—what booted it? One and all were vanity. Friday I had to cook all day again, preparing refreshments for the Guild executive which met here in the evening. To-day I've been doubly miserable. I cannot describe how miserable I do feel—*all* the time, day and night. I had not expected this for I had not a great deal of trouble before. As it is, I look forward to the months of winter with dread. When I waken in the morning, I think, "Oh, how can I drag through the day?" At night I think "Oh, Thank God this day is ended."

1914

Saturday, Jan. 3rd, 1914
Leaskdale, Ont.
This week I have had a visitation of Zephyr people—two days of them. In all the time I have been here hardly any of them have ever come—not that I lamented that, though I religiously invited them! But of course, now that I am sick, they will come. To talk to Zephyr folk when I am well is something by way of penance. When I am as sick as I have been all this week it is martyrdom. One family came and brought three children, two of them "enfants terribles". The mother seems to have fashioned her views and conversation on the "Pansy" books. She talks a sort of cant I never heard outside of those fairy tales. Evidently she expected me, as a minister's wife, to appreciate it and respond in like manner. But alas, I cannot talk Pansyese. I was indeed put to it to hide my amusement over her speeches. Had I not been so miserable physically I fear I could not have succeeded and the result would have been dire, for her husband is an elder and quite the most influential personage in Zephyr church, therefore has power to make it unpleasant for Ewan if he choose. So I tried to steer between Scylla and Charybdis and think I succeeded tolerably well.

Saturday, Jan. 10, 1914
The Manse Leaskdale.
....These past six weeks I have done more reading than in the preceding two years. I am good for nothing else, so when I finish what has to be done I lie on my bed and read—when I *can* read. Sometimes I am too sick even to do that; and at the best I don't enjoy it as I would if well. Still, it passes the time and I have got through with quite a number of books. Among the rest I have read the twelve volumes of Grote's History of Greece. I have never read a continuous history of Greece before. Grote's scholarship is quite marvellous and there are many "purple patches" in his work. But much of it is dry enough. Still, I am glad to have managed to read it. My knowledge of a very important part of ancient history has been much enlarged.

To employ a trite and bromidic remark, "dreams are curious things". I had one last night which illustrates this remark.

Long years ago, when I was about ten years old, grandmother took a monthly magazine called "Godey's Lady's Book". She took it for several years. I do not know that I should think a great deal of that magazine now, but then I thought it very wonderful and its monthly advents were "epochs in my life". It was, of course, a fashion magazine. The first pages were full of fashion plates of the day and were as delightful to me as any other part. I hung over them with rapture and whiled away many an hour "picking" what ones I would have, had I but to choose. Those were the days of bangs, bustles, and high-crowned hats—all of which I considered wondrously beautiful. Past the fashion pages came the literary pabulum—short stories and serials. In those blissful days I read serials. I never read them now—I haven't the patience to wait from month to month. But I devoured everything then. One of those serials was "The Dreeing of the Weird" by *Helen Mathers*, and a most exciting thing it was. I hadn't any idea what the title meant and nothing in the story explained it. But the story was easily understood—and I think it was of higher literary excellence than most of the stuff in the "Lady's Book". I enjoyed it immensely, re-read it many times—and then as years passed forgot it—forgot it absolutely. It was as if I had never read such a story. Not since I was fifteen have I thought of or recalled that story. But last night I dreamed I was reading it again and every incident, every name returned to my memory as clearly as if I had read the story yesterday. Nor did it flee with the visions of the night. Waking, I recalled it all from beginning to end.

Do we ever really forget *anything* in our lives? I do not think we do. The record is always there in our subconscious minds, to be suddenly remembered when something brings it to our recollection—perhaps never to be remembered, but always there.

One night, when I was about ten years old, I dreamed a curious and rather horrible little dream. I dreamed that there had been a terrific snowstorm and that I was walking to school through a low and narrow tunnel that had been cut through the enormous drifts from our house to the school.

This tunnel had many curves and turns in it. I turned around one sharp angle to find my path completely blocked up by a huge, hideous *face* which filled the tunnel before me. The horror of the face wakened me. I recalled the dream when I woke. Perhaps I remembered it for a few days. Then it passed complete-ly out of my memory. For twenty years I never recalled it. Then one day I was reading *Undine*. While the hero was riding through the Enchanted Forest his path was suddenly blocked by a hideous head and face. Like a lightning flash came back to me that old forgotten dream. As vividly as if it were of yester-night I saw the white walls of my snow tunnel and the huge face that barred my way. Last night the process was reversed and the dream recalled the tale.

Tuesday, Jan. 27, 1914
The Manse, Leaskdale, Ont.
Have been most miserable ever since last writing. I am beginning to feel discouraged. I have never felt well for a moment and most of the time wretched in the extreme. But it boots not to enlarge on the theme. If I did it would seem like a page from a patent medicine almanac.

To-day *I began to knit a quilt*. That sounds like an arrant folly in a woman who is as busy as I am. Yet there is a method in my madness. There have been so many days lately that I could do absolutely nothing, not even read, because my nerves got in such a state. Now, *knitting* has always had a good effect on me when I am nervous. I was always very fond of knitting and I find that it helps me greatly these bad days. So I began the quilt. It doesn't matter if I never finish it.

Quilt knitting, in this particular pattern especially always makes me think of Malpeque. I spent a winter there once with Aunt Emily. Every girl and woman in Malpeque had knitted, was knitting, or intended to knit a quilt—some of them several quilts. They possessed many patterns and considerable rivalry went on. Lace knitting was very popular also. I caught the fever and began a quilt. I think I was three years knitting it. It was very pretty but was worn out long ago. Ten years ago I knitted a second which I still have. Shall I ever finish a third? I feel so blue and wretched just now that it does not seem to me as if I would ever be able to accomplish anything again.

Friday, Jan. 30, 1914
The Manse Leaskdale, Ont.
Yesterday we went to Zephyr. A thaw was on and the roads were dreadful. We visited another rough, ignorant family living in a little log house at the back of beyond. At night we went to Guild. When we came out I thought of the drive home with dismay. The roads were so bad—and I was so tired and sick. How could I endure those endless seven miles of half bare hills and swamps? But lo, that drive home proved to be one of those peculiar psychological experiences I have by times. As we left the church something suggested to my mind a verse from "The Lady of the Lake". I began recalling the poem, which I have known by heart since childhood—and not only recalling it but *living* it. I roamed through its vivid scenery. I talked with its people. Other poems followed and them I also lived. The physical discomforts of the drive were quite unnoticed. I was snatched far away from them and in spirit lived "one crowded hour of glorious life" oblivious of all my surroundings, save only the stars shining over me. That drive home, instead of being the nightmare I dreaded was a strange, scintillating, vivid dream of unearthly delight.

Nevertheless, the aforesaid physical discomforts were present, though for the time unfelt; and to-day I felt their effects. I have been exhausted and ill all day.

Wednesday, Feb. 25, 1914
The Manse, Leaskdale, Ont.
I have had another bad cold for four days. It seems that I cannot throw off colds this winter. They cling to me closer than a brother. My other discomforts are, however, slowly lessening. I never feel *quite* well but the insufferable misery of the past three months seems to have passed and I do not know how to be sufficiently thankful.

To-day I finished re-reading Anthony Trollope's inimitable "Barset" series of novels. I read them last six years ago down home. They *are* delicious. The glorious scene where "*Mr. Crawley*" turns upon "*Mrs. Proudie*" with his splendid, "Peace, woman!" is finer than anything in Dickens or Thackeray. As I am beginning to be able to work again I have scant time for reading now—

a half hour or so after I am ready for bed. I ought to be asleep for I need all the sleep I can get. But man cannot live by bread alone. I *must* have a little sustenance for soul and mind and where can I get it here save in books. That half hour is well spent, sleep to the contrary notwithstanding. And as I am a fast reader I get through a good deal in it.

Friday, Feb. 27, 1914
The Manse, Leaskdale, Ont.
A case of "stolen goods" came to my knowledge today. In a current magazine I found some verses entitled "Come Back" purporting to be by one "Margaret Gibson", of Plainfield, New Jersey. The poem was written by me six years ago and published in the *Youth's Companion* in 1909, under the original title "The Old Home Calls". I must see to the matter, as I intend to include this poem in a published collection someday and can't permit its publication under another author's name to pass unchallenged. It was a bare-faced trick of "Margaret Gibson" and absurd as well. She must have known she ran a risk of being found out. "I can stand *wickedness* but I can't stand *foolishness*."

Sunday, March 22, 1914
The Manse, Leaskdale, Ont.
I have been much better this month—but much of the time feel very weary and useless. I had a nice little time this week—I went in to Toronto Thursday morning and stayed till last night. I stayed with Mrs. Norman Beal who lived in Uxbridge until recently and who is a nice jolly soul of the race that knows Joseph. I was glad of a short jaunt away from the cares and responsibilities of my daily routine—cares and responsibilities which are pleasures when I feel well but have been a heavy burden this winter. Mary and Norman and I went to the theatre Thursday night and saw "Peg O' My Heart"—one of the most charming little comedies I've ever seen. I enjoyed it so much. But some wretched newspaper reporter saw me there and put it in the society column of Friday's *Globe*—bad 'cess to him! All "the parish" will see it and what will the Zephyrites think!! Verily, that I am a brand, not yet plucked from the burning!

Mary gave an afternoon tea for me Friday. I suppose she wanted to show off a real live though small lion as her guest! Afternoon teas are such senseless things—satisfying neither to mind, soul, or stomach. I shopped a good deal, finding it very hard under existing conditions. But I had two glorious nights of unbroken sleep! Such are very rare with me now—and must continue to be rare for some time I suppose! "The gods don't allow us to be in their debt." That they do not!

Wednesday, April 15, 1914
The Manse, Leaskdale, Ont.
Verily these last few days have been to me as manna to a hungry soul. Frede came on Friday for Easter and stayed till yesterday. We emptied out our souls

and rinsed them. I feel that I can go on again for awhile. I had bottled up various things so long that I was dangerously near exploding point.

We are into housecleaning and I am finding it desperately hard this year. I am very short of breath and if I am much on my feet my back aches woefully. I just drag through the days and am always very thankful when night comes. Yet people seem to expect me to do just as much visiting and attend just as many meetings as usual. At times my soul is sick within me. I remember in an old reading I used to give years ago there was one sentence "The life of a minister's wife is a sort of refined slavery". Bitter truth! Well, I always knew it and expected it; but when I am not well parish fetters are a little hard to bear.

This evening I read a rather entertaining article in the *Bookman*, dealing with "Confessions in an Album". Such were in vogue years ago. You had to answer a series of questions on your preferences and dislikes. The article in question dealt with the answers of several noted people of bygone days. I amused myself mentally answering, or trying to answer, the queries myself.

No. 1. What is your favorite flower? Well, I love all flowers so much it is hard to choose. But of wild flowers I love best the shy sweet wild "June Bell"—the *Linnea Borealis*—of Prince Edward Island spruce woods; and of garden flowers the white narcissus—the old "June lilies" of girlhood days. We did not have them but they grew in the grassy nooks of many old Cavendish gardens.

No. 2. "Your favorite tree?" Most certainly the pine—though the fir runs it hard. There were few pines in Cavendish—an odd one or two back in the woods. Indeed, there are not many anywhere on the Island. It is the habitat of spruce and fir. I first got well acquainted with pines in Halifax Park.

We have a good many pines in Scott township but none very near the manse. Spruces are scarce. There is an abundance of scrubby cedar—a tree I despise. They seem like a wretched imitation of spruce when seen in the twilight. And they are generally so shabby and faded and draggled. There are many lovely elms, which are great favorites of mine, and some nice maples. White birch, which comes next to pine and fir in my affection, is rather scarce.

No. 3. "Your favorite object in Nature?" Rather an obscure question. Many of the noted people aforesaid answered "the sea" and I am half inclined to also. But it seems incongruous to call that blue lone entity an "object in nature". After all, I think my answer to that must be "A Prince Edward Island wood of fir and maple, where the ground is carpeted thick with ferns". Specifically, my favorite object in Nature is *Lover's Lane*.

No. 4. "Your favorite hour of the day?" —day presumably meaning the twenty-four hours. Sunset and the hour following for me. That time used to be my happiest at home—I hovered then between two worlds, forgetting all the cark and care of this one. Nowadays I have seldom a chance to enjoy the twilight; the sunset is generally swallowed up by Mr. Leask's woods. Once in a while though, I can enjoy the afterglow, sitting out on the lawn in the dusk.

No. 5. "Your favorite season of the year?" Spring—spring—spring! The last two weeks of May in Ontario, the first two of June in P.E. Island. Who could love any season better than spring? And yet several in the aforesaid article answered "Autumn". Well, autumn is love-deserving, too. But it advances to decay while spring flies on to abundance of life.

No. 6. "Your favorite perfume?" The fragrance of freesias.

No. 7. "Your favorite gem?" The diamond, when all is said and done. But I love gems of all descriptions—all except turquoises. Them I loathe—the shallow, soulless, insipid things. The gloss of pearl, the frosty glitter of diamond, the glow of ruby, the tenderness of sapphire, the melting violet of amethyst, the moonlit glimmer of aquamarines—I love them all.

No. 8. "Your favorite poets?" Byron and Scott.

No. 9. "Your favorite poetess?" Jean Ingelow.

No. 10. "Your favorite prose authors?" Nay, nay, there are too many of them—Scott, Dickens, Thackeray, Collins, Trollope and fifty others. I love them equally well, one for one mood, one for another. When I was fifteen I should have answered unhesitatingly, "Lytton, first and last, and the rest nowhere." Now he would not be on my list at all. *Sic transit gloria mundi.*

No. 11. "Where would you like to live?" Cavendish, Prince Edward Island.

No. 12. "Your favorite amusement?" Reading and walking in the woods are ties.

No. 13. "What trait of character do you most admire in a man?" Justice.

No. 14. "In a woman?" A sense of humor. I would also admire justice in a woman if I ever saw it.

No. 15. "What do you most detest in each?" Deceit and love of meddling.

No. 16. "If not yourself, who would you rather be?" Humph! When all is said and done I don't know. I can't just now recall one person I would really like to be—though there are some *in whose place* I would like to be.

No. 17. "Your idea of happiness?" A good novel and a plate of russet apples! Well, that is a flippant definition. But to give a faithful account would require pages. And yet—and yet—no! Holding my little son in my arms or feeling his chubby arms around my neck is happiness. Once I might have answered "To be in Herman Leard's arms". I would not so answer now. But to be in the arms of a man whom I loved with all my heart and to whom I could willingly look up as *my master* is, after all, every woman's real idea of happiness, if she would be honest enough to admit it. There are dear and sweet minor happinesses. But that is the only perfect one.

No. 18. "Your favorite dream?" To write a book that will live. I can never do it—but dreams don't have to come true.

No. 19. "What do you most dread?" Dying of cancer.

No. 20. "What is your motto?" What is worth doing is worth doing *well*. It doesn't make for an easy life, though. The ability to *shirk* is really a desirable one, I believe—at least I think so when I am all tired out.

Saturday, April 18, 1914
The Manse, Leaskdale, Ont.

Having been, thanks to my ill health, ever since last September getting together material for "Anne III" and blocking out the chapters I really began to write it today. *Beginning* a story is always a hard thing for me to do. I feel as if it were half done once it is really begun. And I *never* feel satisfied with my beginnings. In especial my beginning today seemed horribly flat. My pen dragged. I find it very hard nowadays, with all my manifold duties and interruptions to get into the mood for writing. I seem to feel an undercurrent of hurry that spoils my work and my pleasure in it. I can't believe this third Anne book will be any good. I have no faith in it. It seems *going backward* to try to write it. I feel as if *Anne* and all pertaining to her had been long left behind.

I remember well the very evening I wrote the opening paragraph of *Green Gables*. It was a moist, showery, sweet-scented evening in June ten years ago. I was sitting *on the end of the table*, in the old kitchen, my feet on the sofa, beside the west window, because I wanted to get the last gleams of daylight on my portfolio. I did not for a moment dream that the book I had just begun was to bring me the fame and success I had long dreamed of. So I wrote, the opening paragraphs quite easily, not feeling obliged to "write up" to any particular reputation or style. Just as I had finished my description of *Mrs. Lynde* and her home *Ewan* walked in. He had just moved to Cavendish from Stanley, where he had previously been boarding and this was his first call since moving. He stayed and chatted most of the evening, so no more of *Green Gables* was written that night. And now today I began my seventh book, a thousand miles from that twilight window looking out into the rain-wet apple trees of the front orchard. The window by which I wrote today looked out on several unlovely, spring-naked back yards—for the only chance I have to write is to shut myself in my room where young Chester cannot prowl. But then he is worth all the books in the world.

Sunday, May 24, 1914
Leaskdale, Ont.

We are in mid-spring now and everything is very lovely. Yesterday Lily and I took her two children, Archie and Edith, Jessie and Cameron Leask, and Chester back to Mrs. Leask's woods for a picnic. It was the first time I had been back to the woods this spring. It is lovely back there now—so green and cool and remote. The path under the trees along the old mill race is very pretty and the open glade where we had our lunch is beautiful with its big elms and its carpet of white and pale purple violets. My present physical clumsiness rather spoiled my enjoyment; but it was beautiful to sit there on the flower-starred grass and look up into the green arches above us, with Chester-boy, looking like a wee man in his red cap and blue sweater beside me. There is nothing of the baby about him now. I'm sorry, for he *was* an adorable little baby. Now he is just a big boyish boy. He has begun to talk at last. I don't think he has been very precocious about it all. But it is so interesting to watch his little mind developing and broadening as he adds new words to his vocabulary. So far he deals only in single words and hasn't attempted to join them together. He makes one word in its time play many parts. "Door" means *anything* that opens—door, window, drawer, lid, box-cover. He pronounces

Chester at the pump

such words as he has acquired very well and plainly.

I suppose in about two months more he will have a wee sister or brother—if all goes well. I *do* hope it will be a sister. I want a little daughter so much and I will be bitterly disappointed if the baby is not a girl—for at my age I cannot confidently count on having any more children, though I hope I will. And will all go well? Somehow, I look forward to this second birth with more anxiety than I did to Chester's coming—perhaps because I realize more clearly how many things *might* go wrong. Somehow, too, I can't believe that I shall have as easy a time as I had when Chester was born. And it will be so lonely. Neither of the girls will be here and I have to have both a new doctor and a new nurse. I wish it were all well over, for at the best, it is not a pleasant experience, especially in hot weather.

I have all my housecleaning and gardening done, for which praise be. I found both very hard this spring. Ewan leaves for P.E. Island tomorrow for a short vacation. It makes me lonely to think of his going without me. But I can't visit the dear old spot this summer, alas!

Sunday, June 28, 1914
St. Paul's Manse, Leaskdale, Ont.
This has been for once a real "day of rest". And I needed it sadly, for the past fortnight has been a decidedly strenuous one. Ewan returned from his holiday on June 9, and the next week the rush was on.

Last fall Ewan began to carry out his long-cherished project—getting the congregation to support a foreign missionary of its own. It was rather a big undertaking to engineer in a country congregation. I do not think there is another country congregation in Canada doing it. I did not think it a wise thing for him to attempt—and I don't think it a wise thing now. As soon as the initial enthusiasm wears off I fear it will mean a lot of extra work and worry for him if it is kept up or a certain humiliation if it fails. But at anyrate he has accomplished it and the salary is pledged for five years.

"Our missionary" came on June 15 to spend a week in the parish. His name is Stewart Forbes and he is a young Knox graduate of boyish appearance and with just a tinge of the new-fledged collegian's comfortable assurance that he knows it all and a cheerful ignorance of human nature. But he is nice and sincere, and improves on acquaintance. I found him an agreeable variant from the type of most foreign missionaries I have known. He is free from cant and narrow-mindedness and does *not* appear to think that foreign missions are the one thing needful and foreign missionaries the only people who are doing God's work in the world. On the other hand, he has no magnetism or enthusiasm and I don't think he is just the man for a "special missionary". He will not inspire zeal and interest in the congregation supporting him and that will be very necessary in this case.

He and Ewan plunged into an orgy of visiting. Then on Tuesday came the ordination and designation service. Monday Lily and I were very busy all day for we were to have three or four ministers to dinner Tuesday and had also to help prepare the supper which was served in the basement after the service. All Monday and Tuesday I was on my feet much more than I should have been. Result—utter weariness of soul and body on Wednesday and Thursday. But company came to tea on Thursday. Then on Friday we had to prepare for the S.S. picnic; that came off yesterday—the unholy thing! I believe S.S. picnics are necessary evils because the children enjoy them. I used to enjoy them when I was a child. Now they are an abomination unto me. I started late after all the rest had gone. It was a cool pleasant day and I was all alone—something that happens so rarely nowadays that it is by way of a treat. I decided to walk as slowly as I could to prolong the enjoyment, going by the pretty mill-race path. It was the only pleasure the day offered me. Alas for my anticipations! Just as I turned into the side road I saw Mary and Lizzie Oxtoby. I walked still more slowly, praying that they might keep ahead. Not they! They stopped and waited—and I had to walk to the picnic grounds with them. I said it looked a little like rain—and Lizzie Oxtoby laughed. I said the path along the race was very pretty—and Lizzie Oxtoby laughed. I said there still seemed to be plenty of mosquitoes—and Lizzie Oxtoby laughed. If I were to say to Lizzie Oxtoby "My father has hanged himself, my husband has gone out of his mind, my children have been burned to death and I am suffering from an incurable cancer"—Lizzie Oxtoby would laugh. She can't help it—she was born so—but it is very awful!

Arriving at the picnic ground I picked out a soft stump and sat upon it. Moving about much or standing is a physical impossibility with me now. A lady sat beside me who will probably go into the kingdom before me, but who offers a horrible example of how not to converse. She passed a whole hour detailing to me the sayings of her three-year-old son—and all the sayings were commonplace to a sinful degree. Yet she seemed to expect me to laugh over them. I couldn't and didn't—I had no desire to rival Lizzie Oxtoby. But I groaned in soul. If I could only have been there alone with winds and trees and clouds. Or if I could just have been at home reading a book or lying down to ease my aching back and tired muscles!

Then came the repast. I sat sideways on the ground and ate several sandwiches and a piece of lemon pie and one of gooseberry. I think I also ate several crickets who had got tangled up with the meringue of the pie. After that I concluded I might go home. I got Chester-boy and we went. Thank heaven, there was no Lizzie Oxtoby this time. Chester-boy toddled by my side, clinging to me with his dear sun-burned hand and chattering about "orses" and "geesies" and all other objects he saw and if I had not been so horribly tired I would have enjoyed the walk.

To-day, therefore, my rest was as manna to a hungry soul.

August 5, 1914
The Manse, Leaskdale, Ont.
England has declared war on Germany!

Good God, I cannot believe it! It *must* be a horrible dream. It has come up like a thundercloud.

Sometime in June I picked up a *Globe* and read that a Serbian had shot the Archduke of Austria and his duchess. The news was of little interest to me—as to most people on this continent. We dreamed not what was to come of it. But verily *that* was "the shot heard round the world"—to be echoed and re-echoed by the death shriek of millions and the wails of heart-broken women.

Seemingly nothing much did come of it as far as we were concerned. A short time ago we read that Austria had demanded certain things of Serbia. Serbia refused to comply. Austria declared war on Serbia. Russia told Austria she would not allow Serbia to be attacked without coming to her assistance. So far, who in this hemisphere cared? There is always war somewhere among the Balkan States. It seems to be their normal condition.

But—Germany declared that if Russia mobilized she would back up Austria. When that news was flashed around the world the world suddenly held its breath and began to tremble. What did it mean? It meant that France, according to treaty obligations must stand by Russia—it *might* mean that England must fight, too.

For a few days we have hoped desperately that England's diplomats might succeed in averting the peril. Germany's wanton and utterly indefensible violation of Belgium destroyed that hope. England's honor was pledged to Belgium and to France. And yesterday she declared war.

The *Globe* came as we went to dinner. I sat down weak and unnerved. I could not eat. I could only sit there dumbly trying to realize it—to realize that our Empire was at war. And such a war! No paltry struggle in an out-of-the-way corner—no Boer conflict which we all thought so terrible at the time—but a death grapple. For Germany comes to conquer or to die.

Germany provoked this war because she wanted it and was ready for it. For the last twenty years she has been preparing for it. That fact has been open and notorious. Four years ago Earl Grey told me that war between England and Germany was surely coming in a few years. I said, "Don't you think that is one of the things that are expected so long they never come to pass? It is generally some other thing—the unexpected thing that happens." But he said gravely, "No. This is coming. We must get ready for it."

It has come. Britain or Germany must fall. But the death-grapple will be awful beyond anything ever known in the world before. Oh, if I could but waken up and find it all a dream! These last four days have seemed like a nightmare. Already Canada is ablaze. Volunteers are being called for Red Cross and patriotic funds are being started. The bottom has fallen out of the world's markets. Civilization stands aghast at the horror that is coming upon it.

The worst of it is that Germany is so fully prepared. England is totally unprepared as far as an army goes. Thank God, her navy is ready. That may save her—may save us all. If Germany wins Canada will become a German colony—there is no doubt of that. God save us!

As for me—I had expected that by this time I would have had my baby. But my hour has not yet come. I have been feeling very miserable and the days are long and trying. My nurse, Mrs. Aubin, has been here ever since July 17th. When she first came I did not like her. She was a voluble Irishwoman—by ancestry—knowing not the meaning of reserve, with an irritating habit of laughing nervously at the end of every sentence. I recoiled from the thought of having *her* wait upon me in the intimacies of childbirth. But that is past. I begin to like her very much. She is very kind and sympathetic and now that the edge of her is off I don't mind her chatter. She is the utter antithesis of Miss Fergusson in every way as far as personality goes.

I wish greatly that it was all over. I am full of forebodings. And now this war will make everything harder.

Sunday, Aug. 30, 1914
The Manse, Leaskdale, Ont.
Have the past three weeks been a dream of horror? No, they are a fearful reality. My heart seems broken. On August 13th a darling little son was born to me—dead.

Oh God, it almost killed me. At first I thought I could not live! All the agony and pain I have endured in my whole life heaped together could not equal what I felt when I realized that my baby was dead—my bonny sweet boy, so beautiful and perfect.

The cause of his death was a knot in the cord—an accident that could not be foreseen or prevented. It very rarely happens but when it does it is always fatal. Oh, I had never thought of this—strangely enough I had never once thought of it. I had thought of it in Chester's case but never in this. I had had dread forebodings—but they had been for myself—not for my child. Oh, will the pain ever grow less? My heart is wrung with the agony of it while I write. Oh, it was cruel—cruel—cruel!

Never shall I forget the misery of that afternoon, after I came out of the valley of the shadow to find that my darling was dead—that the reward for which I had suffered through long months and faced death had been denied me. I lay there—weak, broken in body and heart. And beside me lay that tiny waxen form clad in the little dress that had been Chester's christening robe. Oh, when I made it with happy dreams and hopes for my first born I little thought it would one day be a shroud. And he was such a lovely baby—so plump and sweet and dimpled. His dear eyes, that would never lighten with intelligence, were large and blue as violets, and so bright. His dear little feet that would never toddle to me—his dear little hands that would never reach out to cling to mine. Oh, it *was* cruel! I can never forget the horror of the night that followed. They had taken my baby away and laid him in a little white casket in the parlor. I was alone. I could not sleep. I could not cry. I thought my heart would burst.

My convalescence was a dreary time. If my baby had lived I would have been so happy, contented to take the days as they came and grow strong gradually. But to lie weakly there, enduring all the discomforts of my condition and nothing—nothing—to recompense me for it. It seemed as if the days crept by on leaden feet. Mrs. Aubin was a good nurse, skilful, tender, sympathetic. I was thankful I did not have Miss Fergusson who, with all her skill, was hard. But nothing could heal my deadly hurt. I fought my sorrow during the day but night betrayed me. I always broke down when twilight came and cried through the terrible hours until exhaustion brought sleep.

Oh, it is not fair—it is not fair! Children are born and live when they are not wanted—where they will be neglected—where they will have no chance. I would have loved my baby so, and cared for him so tenderly and tried to give him every chance for good. Yet I was not allowed to have him.

And while I was lying helpless bad war news began to come, too—news of the British defeat at Mons and the resulting long dreary retreat of the Allies which is still going on before the victorious rush of Germany's ready millions. Everything seems dark and hopeless.

I was so thankful when I was able to sit up. Yet I dreaded with a sick dread going back to the routine of everyday life. I could not have faced it but for Chester. Oh, what a comfort that little creature has been to me!

I came downstairs today. And this evening Mrs. Aubin left unexpectedly. Dr. Shier wanted her for a typhoid case in Uxbridge. I miss her so much. The loneliness is terrible.

Monday, Aug. 31, 1914
The Manse, Leaskdale

I tried to take up life again to-day and began work on my new book. It was very hard to go back to it but work and duty must be done. Perhaps they will help me to forget. To-day I put away the little muslin-lined basket and the little garments I had ready for my darling. His tiny limbs never rested in the nest I had prepared for them. They found a narrower, colder bed. "Little Hugh". That is what we call him to each other. If he had lived we would have called him Hugh after my father. He shall have his name at least. We can give him nothing else.

I wrote in this journal before his birth that I would be much disappointed if my baby were not a girl. It seems to me now that it was wicked to write or think such a thing. But I was *not* disappointed. In that brief moment when I knew my child was a boy and did not know that it was dead, I felt no disappointment—only gladness that I had another son. There must be some-thing—some deep instinct in us women that makes us rejoice when we have brought a man child into the world, no matter what we have hoped for. Oh, what a proud, happy mother I would have been with my two boys! Too proud—too happy. The gods were jealous!

And Chester would have had a little brother. I suppose he never will have one now. If I were a younger woman I might not feel so terribly over it all. But I hardly dare hope for another child. And if God were pitiful and gave me again the chance of being a mother I tremble to think of the months of dread I would have to undergo for fear that the same hideous thing would happen again. Almost I would rather not run the risk. And yet—I *must* hope.

Thursday, Sept. 3, 1914
Leaskdale, Ont.
Today Ewan got a telegram announcing the serious illness of his father. He left for the Island at once. I am not at all strong yet and the excitement and worry of helping him to get away at an hour's notice has rather upset me. I feel very lonely and nervous tonight—as if he would never come back to me. This is foolishness. But physical weakness makes cowards of us all. Oh, if my darling baby had only lived! When I am alone now at night I am haunted by the thought of him, lying lonely in his little grave down the Seventh. My little, little son, how my heart yearns for you! You had no chance—not even a fighting chance for your little life. Oh, it was cruel—cruel!

Friday, Sept. 4, 1914
Another of those horrible "letters of condolence" came to-day. I have received so many. Two or three, written by friends who understand me and who think as I do in regard to the great mysteries, were helpful—or at least soothing. But the rest only opened the wound afresh and jarred every sensibility I possess. The writers meant kindly. But they hurt me as keenly as an enemy could have done—their blundering attempts to console, their trite, threadbare assurances only wounded me. Platitudes can never cover the nakedness of bereavement. One of the most common and most painful was, "the baby is better off". I do not believe it! Why should it be born at all—why should anyone be born?—if it is better off dead? I do *not* believe that it is better for a child to die at birth than to live its life out, and love and be loved, and enjoy and suffer, and do good work, and shape a character that would give it a personality in Eternity. And I do not believe that it was "God's will" either. Why blame every sorrow on God's will? I believe it is God's will that every human being born into the world should live and do its work; and if it does not it is not God's will but a crossing of His purpose by the mysterious Power of Evil that is manifest in the universe. I do *not* believe that we are called upon to be resigned to *that*. I believe we have a right to grieve when It accomplishes Its malignant purposes. And it is no comfort to me to be told that I shall meet my little son "some day". I cannot wholly believe that; and if I could it would still be little comfort. For it would not be my little blue-eyed baby but a personality that had developed and grown apart from me and so would be to me a stranger. Oh, "Not all the preaching since Adam / Hath made death other than death"—nor ever will!

Saturday, Sept. 5, 1914
The Manse, Leaskdale, Ont.

The war news has continued steadily depressing. Every day brings the news of the steady advance of the Germans towards Paris. They are little more than thirty miles away now. They are steadily pressing back the British and French armies. It seems as if they were sweeping irresistibly to their goal. Oh, will they reach it? Will not some mighty arm even yet interpose? Will not God's finger touch them and say, "Here—but—no further?" If Paris falls France will be crushed. She will have no heart to struggle further.

Tuesday, Sept. 8, 1914
The Manse, Leaskdale, Ont.

Oh, God's finger *has* touched them! The German Army, almost at the gates of Paris, has been foiled—driven back—forced to retreat!

This morning was a delightful one. Lily and I drove to Uxbridge. It was the first time I had been out for a drive since my illness and I enjoyed it as a child might. It was delightful to be a part of the sunshine and fresh air once more. And yet at one part of the drive my heart was wrung with agony. And through it all there was an underache of ceaseless worry—the thought "What will the war news be when we get to Uxbridge? Will it be that the Germans have hacked through to Paris?

Down the Seventh, about half way from here to Uxbridge is a little country graveyard, rather grassy and overgrown, with elms around its borders. It is called"Zion". Long ago there was a Methodist church near it but it is no longer there. Many of our Presbyterian families bury there, as there is no Presbyterian graveyard close at hand.

I have driven past this little graveyard many times, carelessly and indifferently. It never occurred to me that it was to become the saddest and most sacred spot on earth to me. But our wee darling lies there in a little green corner under the elms.

How my heart ached as we drove past it today! It seemed so cruel and bitter to go by without stopping. It seemed to me that Little Hugh was calling to me from his grave—"Mother, won't you come to me?" It was anguish not to respond. But I could not make my first pilgrimage to that little grave with anyone but Ewan. So I went on, my eyes burning with tears.

When we reached town I went to see Mrs. Aubin. She had just opened the morning's papers. And there was the headline—"General French Inflicts Great Defeat on the Enemy." Oh, the relief was almost painful, coming after all these weeks of strain and growing dismay. I hardly dared believe it. But it is true. The Germans have been hurled back from the Marne. God be thanked! Oh, we all come back to God in these times of soul-sifting—humbly, starkly, unconditionally. Perhaps this is why this awful war has come. The world was forgetting God. It had to be reminded of Him.

Thursday, Sept. 10, 1914
Leaskdale, Ont.
The war news continues good. Every day since Monday I have opened the paper with fear and trembling; but each day brought the blessed news that the Germans were still retreating. There is but little fear of Paris ever being captured now.

But I have been so lonely to-night—so heart-broken. I wish Ewan were back. He seems so far away. I seem alone among aliens save for darling Chester. Last night I had the sweetest experience—one of those brief, fleeting joys that transform life and illuminate the meaning of motherhood.

It was a cold night with a touch of frost. When I went to bed I thought of taking Chester in with me but decided not to, as he seemed so warm and cosy in his own little crib. But in the night I wakened. Chester was whimpering softly and pitifully in the darkness. I rose and bent over him. The poor mite had thrown off his blankets and was curled up on his bed, a little round, cold, forlorn ball. I lifted him quickly into my own warm nest and snuggled down beside him. I thought he had dropped asleep but suddenly I felt the little head move near me in the darkness and the next moment his little lips were pressing the softest, sweetest little kiss on the back of my hand which I had up to my cheek. That little kiss thrilled my soul with its sweetness. I shall feel it on my hand forever.

Saturday, Sept. 12, 1914
The Manse, Leaskdale, Ont.
Ewan came back tonight. How glad I was!

The war news still continues encouraging. The Germans are still retreating. But oh, there have been such hideous stories in the papers lately of their cutting off the hands of little children in Belgium. Can they be true? They have committed terrible outrages and crimes, that is too surely true, but I hope desperately that these stories of the mutilation of children are false. They harrow my soul. I walk the floor in my agony over them. I cry myself to sleep about them and wake again in the darkness to cringe with the horror of it. If it were Chester! Oh God, why do you permit such things?

Monday, Sept. 21, 1914
Leaskdale, Ont.
Last Friday Mrs. Alex Leask and I drove to Whitby to visit friends of hers and stayed until Sunday evening. It was a long and tiring drive for me, as I am not strong yet. But we met some nice people and I enjoyed it very much. Today Ewan and I went to Uxbridge and we went together to our darling boy's grave. I cannot write about it.

Tuesday, Oct. 13, 1914
Leaskdale, Ont.
Yesterday came news of the fall of Antwerp. For a week it has been expected though we hoped against hope. The news seemed as bad as if it were entirely

unexpected. I was all alone. Lily was away on her vacation and Ewan went to Toronto yesterday. When I went down for the mail I dared not open the paper until I got back home. Then I saw the head-line, "Antwerp has fallen".

I went all to pieces. I could eat no dinner. I walked the floor in nervous agony. When night came I could not sleep until nearly morning. The word "Antwerp" reiterated itself over and over in my brain until I thought it would drive me mad.

Friday, Oct. 30, 1914
Turkey has plunged into the war on the side of Germany. Ultimately this can only mean that she has committed suicide. But it will prolong the war and harass the Allies—and so means more and longer strain and anxiety for us all. England is now reaping the fruit of her mistaken policy in always posing before Europe as Turkey's defender. She would not intervene to prevent the hideous Armenian massacres and now she must pay for that with the lives of her best. Truly, the mills of the gods do grind small though slowly. National as well as individual sins are punished in the long run.

Tuesday, Nov. 10, 1914
'Tis a dark dreary night and snow is falling for the first. On such an evening I think always of the old home in Cavendish—that old deserted house I love so much. I have been haunting it in spirit all the evening. I could see it, gray and dark, through the falling whiteness. I wandered through its empty, cheerless rooms where the flakes spotted against the bare windows. Its desolation and loneliness pierced my soul. I wish it were torn down. It would not hurt me then to think of it, for then it would exist only in the land of dreams and there is no loneliness there. Old home, once warm and bright, now the November twilights are never starred by your out-glowing light.

The Manse, Leaskdale, Ont.
Nov. 19, 1914
A week of anxiety! But better news has come. The Germans could not advance beyond Dixmude and now they have been driven back across the Yser. The drive on Calais has failed! But oh, this constant strain is horrible!

Friday, Nov. 20, 1914
I finished "Anne of Redmond" to-day. And I am very glad. Never did I write a book under greater stress. All last winter and spring I was physically wretched and all this fall I have been racked with worry over the war and tortured with grief over the loss of my baby. From a literary point of view I don't think much of it. Yet there is some fairly good material in it. But I cannot write of sentimental college girls. Anyhow, it is done, praise the nine gods!

Monday, Nov. 30, 1914
Leaskdale, Ont.
My fortieth birthday? Once I thought forty must be the end of everything. But it isn't! I don't *feel* any older today than yesterday—when I was only 39! Or

the day before yesterday when I was—19! Thank God we don't *feel* old. Life is much richer, fuller, happier, *more comfortable* for me now than it was when I was twenty. I have won the success I resolved to win twenty years ago. It is worth the struggle—but I would not wish to be twenty again with the struggle still before me. No, I am quite content to be forty—though it does sound so impossible. And I suppose the next twenty years will fly even more swiftly. Then I shall, if living, be sixty. That sounds grandmotherly.

To-night brought me a bitter pang, though not on account of the vanished years. On our way home from Uxbridge Ewan and I stopped at Zion to see the tiny tablet we have had put down to mark the spot where "Little Hugh" sleeps. Oh, as I stood by that wee grave in the dim, dull November twilight, with the cheerless autumn landscape all around my heart ached agonizingly. Why, oh why must it be? My bonnie, blue-eyed darling. He would just have been beginning to be so bright and interesting.

Monday, Dec. 7, 1914
Leaskdale, Ont.
A *Globe* headline to-day was "The Germans Capture Lodz."

This war is at least extending my knowledge of geography. Six months ago I did not know there was such a place in the world as Lodz. Had I heard it mentioned I would have known nothing about it and cared as little. To-day, the news that the Germans have captured it in their second drive for Warsaw made my heart sink into my boots. I know all about it now—its size, its standing, its military significance. And so of scores of other places whose names have been lettered on my memory in blood since that fateful 4th of August—Mlawa, Bzura, Jarolsav, Tomaskoff, Yser, Lys, Aisne, Marne, Prysmysl. At the last mentioned the newspaper wits have been poking fun since the siege of it began. Nobody seems to know how it is pronounced. I daresay the Austrians would think that Saskatchewan and Musquodoboit were about as bad.

The Manse, Leaskdale, Ont.
Thursday, Dec. 10, 1914
To-day at noon Ewan came in jubilantly. "Good news!" he said. I snatched the paper and read that a German squadron had been totally destroyed by a British one off the Falkland Isles. Coming after the long strain of the recent series of Russian reverses I rather went off my head. I waved the paper wildly in air as I danced around the dining room table and hurrahed. Yet hundreds of men were killed in the fight and hundreds of women's hearts will break because of it. Is that a cause for dancing and hurrahing? Oh, war makes us all very crude and selfish and primitive!

Saturday, Dec. 12, 1914
To-day's war news was better than it has been for some time—the second German invasion of Poland seems to have been definitely checked. Ever since it began—a fortnight or so ago—I have been racked with dread. If Germany should smash Russia and then hurl her victorious army back against the French

and British lines! That thought was the Dweller on my Threshold. All through the forenoons I could manage to work and hold my dread at bay. But when at twelve I saw Ewan going out for the mail my nerve invariably collapsed. I could not do anything—it was of no use to try. I could not even read. I could only pace the floor like a caged tiger, nerving myself to meet the worst. Then when he came back I would snatch the *Globe* and desperately tear over the headlines. It has been agonizing.

Saturday, Dec. 19, 1914
The Manse, Leaskdale, Ont.
To-day I began re-reading Mrs. Hemans' poems. I read them *all* through once before. In my childhood those sweet and tender lyrics of hers, many of which were in the old *Royal Readers*, were a source of great pleasure to me. I admit that I love them yet, partly for their own sake, partly because of the old associations connected with them. I think Mrs. Hemans has been hardly dealt with by our hurrying, feverish, get-rich-quick age. Surely sweetness and charm of sentiment have their place in literature as well as strength and grandeur. A violet is a dear thing though it is not a star and a ferny dell is delightful though it is not "a heaven-kissing hill". In one mood Mrs. Hemans gives me quite as much pleasure as Kipling does in another.

1915

When has a New Year dawned, freighted with such awful possibilities? Never did I ask with as great a dread of the answer, "What will the New Year bring"? Nineteen-fourteen has gone. Its sun which rose fairly has set in blood. It brought to me the greatest anguish of my life. Never shall I recall 1914 without a shiver of pain.

I am very lonely tonight. Frede left to-day on her return to Macdonald. She came on December 22nd. I had been counting the days till she should come—looking forward to her visit for months. And now it is over. But we *did* make the most of it. I have emptied and rinsed my soul and taken fresh courage.

In especial it was a great thing to have someone to talk over the war news with as it came each day. Hitherto I have had no one. Ewan refuses to talk about it. He claims that it unsettles him and he cannot do his work properly. No doubt this is so; but it is rather hard on me, for I have no one else with whom to discuss it. There is absolutely *no* one around here who seems to *realize* the war. I believe it is well they do not. If all felt as I do over it the work of the country would certainly suffer. But I feel as if I were stranded on a coast where nobody talked my language. While Frede was here I had the relief of thrashing everything out with her. We flayed the Kaiser every day and told Kitchener what he ought to do. Not but that we both have absolute confidence in K. of K.—which is doubtless a great consolation to him! It seems to me that he has been predestined to the present crisis in the Councils of Eternity. My greatest faith in the ultimate success of the Allies consists in the fact that Kitchener is at the helm. I feel sure that Fate would never have wasted him on the losing side.

We had a quiet "homey" Xmas. Lily went home so we had no aliens. We had a good dinner and a satisfying afternoon of talk—*real* talk which is the best amusement in the world.

The day after Xmas I had a letter from Kate saying that my youngest half-brother, Carl, was going with the Second Contingent. Kate announced the fact as airily and indifferently as if she were saying that he was going to a concert. Is she really as heartless and devoid of all feeling as her letters indicate? Her mother's daughter might very well be, 'tis true but how could her father's child be? As for Carl, I have never even seen him, poor little chap. But as I read Kate's careless lines my eyes suddenly filled with tears. My father's son was going to do what he could for our Empire. "He goes to do what *I* had done / Had Douglas' daughter been his son."

I wrote him at once a letter in which I spoke from my heart. If there is anything of father in him it will appeal to him. If he is solely of the mother and is going into this war from a mere hankering for change and adventure—which God forbid—it will mean nothing to him.

I remember, long ago, when I was a little girl, the Metis Rebellion broke out in "the North-West" as it was then called. Prince Albert was in the fighting zone and all communication between it and the outside world was cut for months. During all that time I had no word from father and it was not known if he were living or dead. I was too young to fully realize the situation but oh, how glad I was when at last a letter came from father. A courier had crept into P.A. contriving to elude the rebels and when he crept out again father sent a letter with him. Father was present at the battle of Batoche as a volunteer, though not actually in the fighting line. I have not thought of all this for years until tonight. And now father's son is going to a war compared to which the Riel Rebellion was as a match-flare to Vesuvius.

I thank God that Chester is not old enough to go—and as I thank Him I shrink back in shame, the words dying on my lips. For is it not the same thing as thanking Him that some other woman's son must go in my son's place? "Without shedding of blood there is no remission of sins." Without shedding of blood there is no *anything*! Everything, it seems to me, must be bought by sacrifice. The race has marked every footstep of its painful ascent by blood. And now torrents of it must flow! Stella recently wrote me that somebody she had met had said to her, "This war is the greatest tragedy since the crucifixion." Will some great blessing, great enough for the price, be the meed of it? Is the agony in which the world is shuddering the birth pang of some wondrous new era? Or is it all merely a futile "struggle of ants / In the gleam of a million million of suns?"

We would think lightly of a calamity which would destroy an anthill and half its inhabitants. Does the Power that runs the Universe think *us* of more importance? We *must* believe that it does or we could not live.

"Nothing can ever be quite the same again for any of us." I read the other day in a London paper. Oh, horribly true! The old order has passed away forever. Life can never again be for us what it was before that fatal day in August.

Last Wednesday Frede and I drove down to Uxbridge and spent a very enjoyable day at Harvey Gould's. On New Year's eve I gave a little dinner for Frede—had Fraser and the McKays, Rev. John Mustard and Mr. and Mrs. Hugh. We had a nice, nice time. I do enjoy entertaining a little like this. It is such a contrast with my past life for *never*, before I was married, could I ask my friends to my home and have things nice for them. To be sure I do *not* care much for the teas to which I must invite the newly-weds of the parish or the prosy old elders and their dames. Those are painful duties which I perform as gracefully as may be. I *can't* talk eggs and butter with the female of the species—and that is almost all the most of them can talk, apart from gossip with which I dare not meddle. However, "a reasonable amount of fleas is good for a dog".

But Frede had to go this morning. I watched her drive away drearily. Under what circumstances shall we meet again?

The Manse, Leaskdale
Wednesday, Jan. 6, 1915
The war news to-day was good in its way—the Russians have won a big victory over the Turks. If England were not an ally of Russia in this war the news of this victory would but faintly interest me. Yet the death and agony and horror of it would have been just the same. Oh, we are very selfish. There was one horrible account of a regiment of 900 Turks who were found frozen to death. The sufferings of the men everywhere in the trenches this winter must be dreadful. I never go out on these cold dark nights without thinking of them miserably. I am ashamed that I am warmly clad and housed. When I snuggle down in my comfortable bed I feel ashamed of being comfortable. It seems as if I should be miserable, too, when so many others are.

The Manse Leaskdale, Ont.
Sunday, Jan. 17, 1915
This has been a lonely afternoon. Ewan, of course, was away, wasting a good logical hard-hitting discourse on the stolid unappreciative Zephyrites who would no doubt infinitely prefer a Billy Sunday rant on hell-fire and brimstone. Lily took Chester home with her. These pilgrimages to "the farm" are a delight to his small soul. Poor baby-man, I am sorry that he can't be brought up on a farm and have the birthright of green old orchards and clover meadows and big, dusky, sweet smelling barns to romp and frolic in. Well, we shall have to make it up to him in other ways. I am very anxious that Chester should have a happy, *normal* childhood, with all the simple world-old pleasures that are the right of children. I do not want him to be spoiled by over-indulgence but I do want him to have a childhood which will fit him, mentally and physically for life and which will be a delightful memory to him. He is learning to talk rapidly now—and puts sentences together, with such a funny, triumphant note in his voice when he arrives at the end of one. So far all is concrete—no appearance of abstract thought yet, no attempt at reasoning or reflection. He has an affectionate little heart and very dear little ways. When he creeps into my lap, pats my cheek so softly with his chubby hands, and says in the softest and sweetest of voices, "Dear mo'er—poor mo'er, I mo'er's dear *son*"—why, the delight that sweeps over my soul is the last revelation of the sweetness of motherhood. When a woman hears her own son call her "mother" she thanks God that she *is* a woman.

Oh, do I love my wee mannie too much? Sometimes, especially since that hideous 13th of August I fear that I do—that I will be punished for it. "Thou shalt have no other gods before me." It seems an almost instinctive fear. I am near kin to the heathen who call their children evil names that the listening spirits may hear and, supposing them unloved, work them no evil and afflict them not with disease. But I could not pretend, even to a God, that I did not love Chester. When I look at him lying asleep, dimpled and flushed, my love for him is almost agony, so intense is it. And yet children as sweet and dear as he have been cruelly murdered or have died from neglect in Belgium. Oh, motherhood is awful—motherhood is awful! I re-read Tennyson's *Rizpah* lately. How could a *man* have written it? All the agony and tragedy of motherhood is in it. I said once that Tennyson never hurt me. That was before I was a mother. To read *Rizpah* now tortures me. After I had read it the other night I walked the floor and wept wildly. It was as if *I* was that mother who collected the bones of her baby and buried them by the churchyard wall. Her soul, her sorrow entered into me and possessed me and wrung me.

I have wandered far from my subject. I began by saying I was lonely because I was alone this afternoon. It was dull and gray in the outer world, too, and the shadow of the war was over me. I felt dreary—as if life were all "gray rocks and grayer sea."

I wrote to Stella. Writing to Stella was once a pleasure. Now it has become a painful duty. I have not for two years received a letter from Stella which I did not shrink from opening. There is no disguising the fact that Stella has become a very serious problem to those of us who are unfortunate enough to be closely connected with her.

Stella spent most of the winter of 1912-1913 in the hospital at Ch'town where she underwent several "operations", spent a great deal of money and drove doctors and nurses frantic. She came home no better and in every letter poured out her old complaints of "untold agonies". I grew sick to death of the phrase. There is really, so all her doctors have told me, very little the matter with her. But unbridled indulgence in bad temper seems to have unsettled her mind and she is really insane with "hallucination of disease". A year ago she took it into her head to go to California and spend the winter with Clara. She has been there ever since and poor Clara is almost wild. She has had a dreadful time. Stella has been absolutely outrageous. Ever since she went to Los Angeles she has poured out to me in her epistles unceasing floods of complaints. She had hardly arrived there before she wrote me that she hated it, would not stay, and would likely come to Leaskdale before the winter ended.

Well, I could not and would not have her here. So I never once, in any letter to her, mentioned her coming. I was impervious to her broadest hints. But I go in mortal terror that, finding I will not "rise" to them, she will simply come without an invitation. If she does I really do not know what I will do. Stella has got to such a stage that *no one* can live with her. She is violently discontented everywhere. I really fear she will go quite insane before long. Clara is afraid she will commit suicide but Stella's threats along that line do not worry me much. It is one of her Satanic devices for getting her own way. But she obsesses us all like a nightmare. It is piteous and terrible.

The Manse, Leaskdale, Ont.
Friday, March 19, 1915
Have been very busy of late and very miserable physically. I do not complain of this latter fact, however. Nay, in one sense I rejoice in it. It means that I may hope to have another wee baby yet and I am so thankful and glad—and so

frightened that I will lose it again. That dread companions me night and day.

But, though I bear the ceaseless nausea that seems my daily portion thankfully, that does not prevent it from making my existence rather difficult. I have so much to do—so many things to attend to—and I have to force myself to do them all without betraying my wretchedness. I am just as sick as I was last winter and I suppose will continue to be for many weeks yet. Before I suspected my condition I had embarked on the enterprise of training several of the Guild members in a little play for a Social night. I have to go through with it now as I have no excuse I can offer for backing out but I have to set my teeth every practice night.

The war drags on. The Allies are now trying to force the Dardenelles. I cannot believe that they will succeed. It would be a great thing if they should. On the west and east the ceaseless trench warfare goes on—on—on. What will the spring bring? I dread it as I never dreaded a spring before.

Sunday, April 11, 1915
Leaskdale, Ont.
In my new book "Anne of The Island"—as Page insists on calling it, much against my will—I used an expression—"She tasted the poignant sweetness of life when some great dread has been removed from it." That expresses my condition at present. I am tasting most thankfully the sweetness of life from which has been lifted a hideous dread.

On Saturday afternoon, March 20th, I was lying on my bed when I heard the telephone ring. I was physically most wretched, having had an attack of grippe the day before and suffering in addition the nausea of pregnancy. I got up and went down to the 'phone. The Uxbridge central was calling saying that a telegram had come for me. This it was:—Kensington, P.E. Island. Boat stuck. Go at once to Frede in General Hospital, Montreal. Aunt Annie.

In half an hour I was on the road to Uxbridge, with my agonized fancy imagining all possible illnesses for Frede. I had not heard from her for some weeks. She had just been recovering from a very severe attack of jaundice when she had written. I knew she must be seriously ill or Aunt Annie would never have sent such an urgent message. I caught the seven o'clock train to Toronto and arrived there in time to get the 11 o'clock to Montreal. I spent a wretched, sleepless night, physical misery and mental agony overcoming me in turn. I reached Montreal at 8 in the morning and drove through a snowstorm to the hospital where I found Frede's nurse. She told me that Frede had typhoid, had had two hemorrhages, and that there was very little chance of her recovery!

She would not allow me to see Frede until the doctor came. Besides she said Frede was delirious and would not know me. I doubted the latter statement but said nothing. I got a room, shut myself in, and tried to face the thought of a world without Frede!

I could not do it. With clenched hands I strode up and down the room wrestling with my agony. *Frede dying*! Frede, my more than sister, the woman who was nearest and dearest to me in the world! My mind refused to accept the decree. It pushed it away and mocked at it with such intensity that I became calm and met the doctor at two o'clock with outward composure.

Dr. Gordon was most sympathetic and confidence-inspiring. But he shook his head over Frede's case. He told me I might go in and see her but not to be surprised if she did not know me. She had been in the hospital a week and had at first refused to let her friends be told of her illness. But on Friday night, when the first hemorrhage occurred, Dr. Gordon had decided that he must send word to her parents.

I went across the hall and entered Frede's room. When I had watched her drive out of the manse gate at New Year's I had had a dreary presentiment that our next meeting would not be a happy one, and I had wondered when and where it would be. The question was answered.

Frede was lying on the cot. I can never forget the sight of her. Her face and eyes were as yellow as gold with jaundice, her cheeks were glazed and purple with the fever flush, and her mouth was surrounded with fever sores. For a moment my stricken consciousness re-echoed the dictum of doctor and nurse, "she cannot recover".

Frede opened her eyes, "Maud!" she said, in a tone which she might have used had she seen an angel from heaven. Afterwards she said that my face was the only one she had been able to see clearly since she had come to the hospital—all the others were clouds and blurs; and that no heavenly visitant could have been as welcome. She would not now die alone among strangers. She knew I would stay by her.

That night as I knelt to pray desperately for Frede's recovery there suddenly came to my mind, clear and distinct, as if a voice had uttered them, the words, "Strength and honor are her clothing and she shall rejoice in days to come". From that moment I believed that Frede would live.

And she did. As Dr. Gordon said to me later on, "It is a strange thing, Mrs. Macdonald, but from the moment you came to this hospital Miss Campbell began to improve."

Well, perhaps that was only a coincidence. Or perhaps my coming did give Frede just the little impulse and stimulation she needed to start her on the road to recovery. At all events, she came up again from the valley of the Shadow.

But it was very slowly. Very slowly the fever ebbed. Again and again it came up and our hopes fell as it rose. I learned to watch in gnawing suspense when the nurse brought the basin of water to bathe Frede. If I heard the clink of ice rattling in it—I shall hate that sound forever—I knew that the fever had gone up again. If I heard it not—I knew that Frede was at least no worse. Finally the jaundice cleared away and the purple flush passed and Frede, worn and pallid, looked once more like herself. The day came when the doctor said, "If no set-back occurs she will recover".

For myself, I was also very miserable, if my anxiety about Frede had permitted me to think about myself. I had nausea night and day—I was always tired and drowsy—*and* I was in a chronic state of starvation. The hospital rations, which may have been ample enough for invalids seemed a mere bird's bite to me with the voracious appetite I always have in this condition. Frede, too, was beginning to be very hungry and of course could have nothing but liquid food. She and I whiled away many tedious hours planning out all the good old "down-east" dishes we would have as soon as she was strong enough to come to Leaskdale. The nurse must have thought us dreadful gourmands.

Frede's Macdonald friends kept her room a bower of flowers and came to inquire about her in shoals. At the end of a fortnight the doctor pronounced her out of ordinary danger and I decided that I must return to my forsaken family. Last Sunday night I left Montreal and got home the next evening a very weary but very thankful woman. Once more life is lovely to my eyes. My friend is spared to me.

To-night we all laughed over Chester's prayer. Last night for the first time I taught him a prayer ending up with the old petition, "make me a good boy". Tonight he insisted on saying it himself and ended up triumphantly, "Dear God, make me a good boy *in the hall closet*."

The hall closet is where he is sometimes imprisoned when he is naughty until he promises to be good. I suppose he thinks God will adopt the same method of reforming him!

Monday, April 26, 1915
The Manse, Leaskdale, Ont.
I said I dreaded the spring for what the war news might be. My dread has been justified. Terrible news came on Saturday of the awful battle of Langemarck, the fearful slaughter among our Canadian soldiers—who saved the situation at an awful cost—and the advance of the Germans by the aid of asphyxiating gases. Today the despatches claim that their thrust has been checked but the situation is still terribly critical.

Thursday, May 6, 1915
Truly "the woman pays". Well, if all goes right at the last I shall not grudge the payment. But certainly, I have found the last fortnight a hard one. I have suffered absolute agony with two ulcerating teeth. For a week I had no relief night or day. Then the abscess broke and left me five pounds lighter....

Sunday, May 30, 1915
The Manse, Leaskdale, Ont.
In one way May has been a pleasant month. It has not been the usual delightful May of Ontario—more like an Island May, coldish and grudging. But Frede has been here and we have had a month of delightful companionship.

I went to Toronto to meet Frede on the evening of May 7th—a date that must ever seem of hideous import to many heart-broken people. For it was the day the *Lusitania* was sunk by a German submarine and the whole world shrieked with horror and rage over the hellish deed—a deed that will brand the name of Germany with indelible infamy through generations yet unborn.

When I got to Uxbridge station I saw the announcement in the evening papers. But at that time it was supposed that nearly all on board had been saved. It was not until the next morning that the terrible truth was known. I shall never forget the scene as I walked up Yonge Street the next morning. As usual it was crowded and every man and woman on it held a morning paper and blundered along reading it, indifferent to everything but the news it contained. For myself, when I read of those scores of murdered babies and pictured their dear little dead bodies floating about in that pitiless ice-cold water I felt a hideous nausea of life. I wanted to get out of a world where such a thing could happen and shake its accursed dust from my soul. Can there be a God? Can there be a God?

For weeks the papers have been full of the details. Some of the things I have read have left an indelible brand on my heart. May Wilhelm of Germany go down to the deepest hell haunted by the cries of the babes he has murdered and the women whose hearts he has broken!

The war news of this month has been disquieting. On the Western front the German drive has failed but in the east they are driving the Russians back. I don't like the situation there.

To-morrow we leave for the Island and Frede returns to Macdonald. Somehow I do not look forward to my trip with much pleasure. I feel a conviction—probably born of my physical discomfort—that I shall not enjoy myself. And I feel loathe to leave my home. It is so beautiful just now—the fresh luxuriance of the young leaves, the garden coming up so nicely, the splendor of blossom and grass. I want to stay here and enjoy it. But if I do not go down home this summer I don't know when I may get again and I must go early because later on it would be out of the question. I think it is because of my hunger for the sea that I am going. I *must* look on it again.

Monday, June 7, 1915
Kinross, P.E. Island.
We left Leaskdale the evening of May 31st and went to Toronto, spending the evening at the Walker House. We met and had a chat with Uncle Leander's son Eric. I had not seen him for seventeen years. He was a little boy when I saw him last and now he is verging on baldness. He is very nice—always was the nicest of Uncle Leander's boys. He looks like his father and has his father's agreeable society manner. Looking at him I recalled with a pang of homesickness that long-ago day I saw him first, when Uncle L. and his family arrived to spend their vacation in that old farmhouse by the eastern sea. Eric was an adorable chubby youngster of about two then, with a round face, golden hair, and big brown eyes. Of that old group grandfather and grandmother and Uncle Leander and Aunt Annie have gone. And we who were children then are men and women now, with our own heartaches and struggles and cares. To-morrow our children will fill our places and our hands will be folded. Such a "scunner" of life has come over me since the outbreak of the war that such a consummation seems to me rather to be desired than dreaded. I am tired of this horrible rack of strained emotions. When every day brings a new horror or the dread of it the tortured consciousness grows very weary.

We reached Montreal the next evening where we had to part from Frede. I looked back as we hastened to our train and saw her standing, a lonely figure in the crowded station. It made me feel very lonely, too. If Frede and I could only see each other oftener it seems to me that I would ask nothing else of life.

We reached the Island Wednesday evening and stayed all night in Charlottetown. Our journey down had a peculiar feature. When we left home Ontario was in full mid-spring—the maples on our lawn were in summer luxuriance, the grass lush, and the day of the daffodils over. But Ontario springs are a full three weeks earlier than Island springs at any time and this year, as Ontario had an early spring and P.E. Island an abnormally late one the difference was fully six weeks. As we got further and further east spring seemed to recede from us. The leaves grew sparser until they ceased. When we arrived on the Island last Wednesday the trees were as bare as in mid winter, there was not a hint of green anywhere and only one or two brave dandelions were peering out. I never recall so late a spring here. Always by the first of June at the latest the leaves were out. Was it this that gave me such a sense of being an alien? Or was it simply the effect of change and absence?

On Thursday we came to Aunt Christie's at Kinross. Friday the *Guardian* contained the bad news that the Germans and Austrians had retaken Prysmysl from the Russians. It made me terribly nervous and depressed. Of course, in my present condition worries possess me abnormally and I cannot fight against them.

Saturday night we were at Annie's for tea. It was a cold gray night and as we walked back to Christie's in the darkness Ewan and I owned to each other that we were homesick for Leaskdale. *There* was our home—our interests now. Here, in this old Island, we had become as pilgrims and sojourners. It hurt me to acknowledge this—it seemed utterly disloyal to the land I have loved so well—that I still love so well. I think I might not have felt so if we had found the Island in the June loveliness it should have had by now. As it is, I have a sense of desolation and banishment.

Friday, June 18, 1915

....On Thursday Mrs. William Simpson was buried and I went over to the graveyard when the funeral came there. She was one of the Cavendish people until a few years ago and her sons and daughters were my schoolmates. Ella, a girl I always liked, had brought her mother home and I was glad to meet her again.

Mrs. Simpson died of internal cancer. I asked Ella how long she had been ill and Ella said that it was a certain week in March that she had just felt badly and had gone to a doctor about it. He had told Ella and Lottie that the trouble was cancer in a quite advanced stage and that there was no hope. It was the first time they had even suspected that their mother's symptoms betokened serious trouble.

I mention this because of a strange fact—too strange and marked to be a mere coincidence. One night of that very week in March—I could not recall the exact night but I distinctly remembered the week, because it was sandwiched in between two visits to Toronto—I had a very vivid dream. I dreamed that I was in Eaton's store in Toronto, watching the throngs of people go by.

Suddenly, I saw Lottie and Ella Simpson passing, I hurried up and accosted them. They responded civilly but walked on and seemed anxious to escape me, but I stuck to them, walking along by them and trying to engage them in conversation. They seemed troubled and disturbed and presently one of them said to the other, "We must tell her about mother or she will not leave us alone." At that I woke. The dream was so vivid that it haunted me and when I wrote Myrtle soon after I asked her if she had heard anything recently about the Wm. Simpson family. She wrote back and said that she had had a letter from Lottie a few weeks before and they were all well. I concluded my dream had meant nothing and did not think about it again. But when Ella told me that they had discovered the cause of their mother's illness that week in March I was struck by the co-incidence. I do not believe it was a co-incidence. I have had too many significant dreams to believe that. Somehow I received a tele-pathic message that night, sent out by the Simpson girls in their distress. Why *I* should receive it I don't know, since we were not anything in particular to each other. But come it did; and I feel sure that the night I dreamed it was the very night after their discovery....

Sunday, June 27, 1915
The Manse, Cavendish, P.E.I.
....Last night I had a very dear, very sad, very strange and unlooked for experience.

When I was on the Island before I shrank from the very thought of going near my old home. This year I felt the same until last night. I was on the manse veranda. The dew was falling. In the south-east a large, hazy, full moon was rising. To my left lay the dark trees that screened the old house from sight. Suddenly an irresistible longing took possession of me to go to it once more—in that pale enchantment of moonlight when one might chance to slip back through some magic loophole into the olden years. I could not withstand it. I slipped over to the church grounds and through the old gap in the fence through which I used to go to church. I walked along the meadow edge where the foot path used to be, past the grove of spruces, and on till the old house lay before me in a soft, silvery shadow. I turned aside for a moment to the old well and looked down it. The ferns that always lined its sides had grown completely across it.

I went on to the old kitchen door. Beside it, every summer a certain shoot of balsam poplar used to start up, to be trodden down under passing feet. Since the old house was closed it had been able to grow and so fast had it grown that the whole angle between the kitchen and the cook house was full of it. It was as high as the kitchen roof.

I went around to the end of the house and stood under my old window. The moon was floating over the valley below. I had looked on that very scene a thousand times on moonlit nights of long ago. My heart beat with mingled pain and pleasure until it almost choked me. Everything in that kind radiance seemed so much the same. For a space the years turned back their pages. The silent sleepers in the graveyard yonder wakened and filled their old places. Grandfather and grandmother read in the lighted kitchen. Old friends and comrades walked with me in the lane. Daffy frisked in the caraway. Above me my old white bed waited for me to press its pillow of dreams.

Most of the windows were boarded up but the south one in the parlor was not. Through it I could see the bare old room distinctly with the black colonial mantelpiece that was the admiration of my childhood. I went around and stood on the stone steps of the front door. The old "front orchard" and the grove beside it seemed more bowery and bosky than of yore but I think that was only because I have grown used to a thinner screen of trees on my Leaskdale lawn. How lovely and lonely it all was, and yet how unreal. I seemed to be in a dream—and yet it seemed the only waking. Oh, as long as that moonlit magic worked the past was mine once more—the *old* past, before the last sad years I had spent in the old home. Oh, beloved old place, that half hour I spent with you last night was worth the coming from a far land. You were glad, I think, to have me back—me, who loved you so. For there is not one living now but me who loves you—not one. As I stood there I seemed to feel a presence enfolding me as if it claimed me—as if something that had been forsaken and desolate were once more rejoicing in my affection. Have not old homesteads souls that cling to them until they crumble to dust?

I could hardly tear myself away from the spot. Perhaps the charm it had for me was not a wholesome one—not altogether one to which it was well to yield. Perhaps the dead past should bury its dead. It may not be well to linger too long among ghosts, lest they lay a cold grasp upon you and bind you too closely to their chill, sweet, unearthly companionship. Certainly all the pleasures and joys of my real life seemed to grow pale and fade into nothingness beside the strange enchantment of that shadowy tryst.

Park Corner, P.E.I.
Sunday, July 11, 1915

....Chester is having a glorious time. He seems to get on beautifully with the children here—I suppose because they are all of "the household of faith". He and Doris did not hit it off especially well and even among the Webb children he seemed rather alien. But with Amy and Jim he is among his own and they play happily in the old beech wood where Clara and Stella and I once played long ago—long ago.

The war news is mixed—one day fair, the next bad. But the Russians are being gradually forced back and now Warsaw, twice saved, is again in danger. My dread is that Germany will crush Russia and then hurl her victorious legions, flushed with success, against the western front.

Yesterday Frede and I spent a beautiful forenoon gathering flowers and ferns in the hayfield by the pond with the children. The most beautiful irises are blooming now all about the pond.

Park Corner
Sunday, July 18, 1915
To-morrow I leave Park Corner....To-night Frede and I planned to have a walk together over the bridge in the dusk—a last farewell walk, the last one we could have there for many years—perhaps forever. In the twilight we slipped away and had our hour. The western sky was full of the hues of a weird sunset. Before us the old pond lay in shadow and silver. The evening was very still, very calm, very clear. And through the stillness came the strangest, saddest, most unforgettable sound in nature—the soft, ceaseless wash on a distant shore of the breakers of a spent storm. It is a sound rarely heard and always to be remembered. It is more mournful than the rain wind of night—the heartbreak of all creation is in it.

Frede and I walked back and forth over the bridge many times, sometimes in silence, sometimes speaking lowly of the deepest thoughts in our hearts. We seemed a part of the night—of the dreaming water, of the dusk in the cloudy firs, of the far remote stars, of that haunting moan of the sea. And when the twilight suddenly was night and the shining new moon swung above the tree tops that bend over that old homestead, we walked away from the glamor in a silence that touched the lands of dream and tears.

The Manse, Leaskdale, Ont.
Saturday, July 24, 1915
Home again—the gods be praised therefore!....On the night when Frede and I walked on the bridge at Park Corner I had said to her, "Is it not strange, when you come to think of it, how very *very* few things in life are *flawless*—how very few pleasures have no sting—how very few "good times" are wholly unmarred by some little, untoward circumstance—the secret pinching of the shoe?"

That is true; but now and again some things seem to slip past the grim fate whose mission it is to distil one drop of poison into every draught—an occasional hour *is* unmarred by the grim deity. My home-coming...seemed one of them. It was perfect....

The Manse, Leaskdale, Ont.
Monday, July 26, 1915
The war news continues bad—still the Russians are retreating. What a horrible strain this long-drawn-out retreat of theirs has been ever since May!

I found "Anne of The Island" here when I got home—my seventh book. It is well-made, like all of Page's books. There is less of real life in it than in any of my other books. *Kingsport* is Halifax—more or less—but *Anne's* experiences there certainly are not a reflection of my own. I never liked Halifax—although I loved its park and "Old St. Paul's" cemetery. The afternoon spent there by *Anne* and *Priscilla* was sketched from an old ramble of my own in it and the chloroforming of "Rusty" was an echo of the time when Frede and I darkly did away with a homeless pussy cat which infested our back door. But all the rest of the story is "jest lies and nothing else".

With its publication my old contract with Page expires. It was a hard contract even for a first book—and when my books attained such marked success it became an increasingly unjust one. Page has made a fortune out of my books— and spent it in gambling, I am told. I certainly have not received a fair recompense. Lately I have been hearing many things that have filled me with distrust of Page. I hate to believe them; for ties of association are strong with me and the Page Co. is bound up with my memories of my "arrival" at the goal towards which I had struggled for so many hard, disappointing years. *Green Gables* was refused five times before I sent it to Page and I cannot forget that it was his house that accepted it and so gave me my chance. But I cannot sacrifice my interests and, what is more, my children's interests, to mere sentiment, if Page is not "straight". Matters will have to be cleared up and settled before I give him another book. There will, I know, be a fight, and I dread it, because if Page is not honorable I am no match for him.

When I signed the contract for the "Chronicles of Avonlea" I would not sign it unless he left out the clause binding me to give him all my books for five years on the same old terms. Page was very loathe to yield and made a veiled threat that he would not continue to "push" my books if I would not sign. I persisted and eventually he yielded, with a very bad grace. If he had offered me better terms—the ordinary terms offered to any successful author—15% on the retail price—I would have signed. But he never hinted at such a thing—and I knew it was of little use to ask it. He wanted me to go on binding myself forever to his beggarly 10% on the wholesale price. This means only 7 to 9 cents per book, when I should have about 19. But the worst feature of it is that when the royalty is on the "wholesale price" there is absolutely no way in which an author can "keep tabs" on her publishers in the matter of a fair accounting.

The Manse, Leaskdale, Ont.
Friday, Aug. 6, 1915
News came today of the fall of Warsaw. We have been expecting it for a week and knew it was bound to come but the announcement seemed as much of a blow as if it had been entirely unexpected. I have been so nervous and de-pressed since that I am "down and out". The weather, too, is horrible—almost constant rain and very close and hot.

The Manse, Leaskdale, Ont.
August 13, 1915
It is just a year to-day since little Hugh was born dead. Oh, that hideous day! Shall I ever be able to forget its agony? And will it be repeated in October? This thought is ever present with me. I have had some bad attacks of nervous depression lately—one last night that was almost unbearable. My condition— the war news—the weather—all combined to make me very miserable. Some-times I feel so unutterably disheartened that if it were not for Chester it seems to me that I would rather not go on living.

Friday, Sept. 10, 1915

I feel rather at the end of my endurance. I have been having a bad time with another ulcerating tooth. And I am so worried about Chester. He has been ill off and on ever since my last entry. He seems a little better now but the child has got so pale and thin that he frightens me. As for myself I am uncomfortable every moment. Will I ever feel well again! It seems to me quite impossible.

Friday, Sept. 24, 1915

Even yet in these woeful days we can sometimes have a laugh. Last night when Chester came to say his prayers he was in a very bad humor with Lily who had done something that displeased him. He always concludes his prayer with a petition to "bless father and mother and Lily and make me a good boy". But last night he omitted Lily's name. I supplied the omission—"and Lily". "No", said young Chester very decidedly, "make me a good boy *without Lily*, Amen." But my laugh did not bring me a good night. It was not exactly the war that kept me awake—rather my own discomfort. But since I could not sleep I *did* think continuously about the war. There is a gleam of brightness in the news that Greece is mobilizing on the side of the Allies. If she will only do so Serbia will yet be saved. But in this war one is sure of nothing until it has happened. Constantine of Greece has a German wife!

To think that I should have to care what kind of a wife Constantine of Greece has!

Wednesday, Oct. 6, 1915
The Manse, Leaskdale, Ont.

We cleaned the parlor today and so I am very tired—so tired that, as I sit here at my desk I dread the thought of climbing the stairs. Besides, I have been horribly worried over the war-news. Today came the announcement that Constantine of Greece has dismissed Venizelos, the Greek premier who was responsible for the mobilization. This means that Greece will *not* enter the war on the side of the Entente—*may* mean that she will declare for Germany. Not for nothing has Constantine a German wife! Will there ever be an end to these wretched thunderbolts? We were all so sure that Greece would join the Entente. Will peace *ever* come? Yes, yes, it will—but peace will not mean a return to "that ancient world of 1914." We can never go back to that. Nothing will ever be the same again.

Saturday, Oct. 23, 1915
The Manse, Leaskdale

I am able to sit up all day today. All is over and well over—and I have another dear wee son. He came on the afternoon of October 7th, ten days before he was expected. Perhaps Constantine of Greece was responsible for that—and perhaps not. As all went well I was glad that I was spared ten more weary days, though I was taken by surprise with no nurse on hand. But Dr. Shier brought out an Uxbridge nurse for the day and Miss Barnard got here at night.

Ewan Stuart Macdonald is another dear plump chubby little man of ten pounds. I had a very easy time and oh how glad I was when I heard the baby's lusty cry. I had rather hoped he would be a girl but now I would not exchange him for a thousand girls. And I *am* glad that Chester will have a brother. Babykins does not look at all like Chester. He is thought to "favor" my side of the house. His eyes are certainly very like my father's. He is as good as a baby can be and so bright. When he was no more than half an hour old the nurse picked him up and he suddenly *lifted up his head* and looked all round the room for a moment with bright wide-open eyes. I shall never forget the look of the ridiculous mite, with his seemingly black eyes in his tiny white face, thus challenging the strange world in which he found himself.

Ewan named him Stuart—after some Stuart he had known at college. I did not really care for the name. I wanted to call him Sidney. But Ewan seemed to think that as I had my choice in naming Chester he ought to have his this time, so I gave way. I added Ewan to the name because I thought one of the boys should bear his father's name, though it is a name I never liked and Ewan does not like it himself.

Yes, I was thankful and happy. And yet my convalescence was a somewhat dreary time. The war-news was bad all through. Serbia was overrun and every day the papers were full of depressing despatches. I did not care very much for my nurse. I didn't actually dislike her but she was woefully dull and cow-like. I almost ached with loneliness. It all seemed very different from that gay time after Chester's birth. But then it was blessedly different from that horrible time last year after dear little Hugh's coming—and going.

For the first time the ache has gone out of my heart. And yet this baby does not, as someone said, "fill little Hugh's place". None can ever do that. He will always have his own place—that dear little shadowy baby who will always be a baby to me—a little phantom companion, unseen and unheard, of his brothers. Wee Stuart is doubly precious for his life was purchased by "little Hugh's" death. But he has his own place; he does not fill that where a little cold waxen form is shrined.

Monday, Nov. 29, 1915
The Manse, Leaskdale, Ont.

A day of "chilling winds and gloomy skies". But November has been like this most of the way through. And the war-news has been bad. The Serbian campaign has gone against the Allies and the attitude of Greece and Rumania is very dubious. It is becoming more and more evident daily that the Gallipoli campaign from which we all hoped so much at one time is a fiasco. It is hard to keep up one's courage in the face of so many failures and reverses. Sometimes mine goes down below zero. If it were not for the British fleet I would give up hope. But to that I still anchor my storm-tossed soul.

Baby is doing fairly well but does not gain as steadily as I would like, though he is very good. I daresay my constant mental disturbance is bad for him.

But I feel real well physically and it is really a delightful sensation. To be able to move easily, enjoy my food, sleep well, and wear pretty dresses again seems all rather too good to be true. I survey my slim shape in the mirror with an odd conviction that it doesn't belong to me.

We organized a Red Cross Branch here this month. I am President. I could not refuse for the need is urgent; but I felt and still feel that I had neither the time nor the strength for this, in addition to all my church societies. Nevertheless it is a demand that must be met and I must not shrink from a little sacrifice. What is it compared to that which some women have to make? But I do *not* shrink from it. Only, I must not neglect other duties for it and I do not honestly know whether I have sufficient strength to do all that seems expected of me. Household, literary and family interests—missionary societies, Guilds and Red Cross, endless visits—all seem to pile up before me and every night I feel so tired that I can hardly drag myself upstairs.

A few days ago I read in the *Guardian* of Toff Mckenzie's death. I can't picture Cavendish without Toff. He was a central figure in our social life as long as I can remember—jovial, friendly Toff. He never seemed to grow old. And yet he was seventy. His mother is ninety three. He was her first born; he had lived out man's allotted years; and still she survives him.

The other day I resumed work on a short story called "The Schoolmaster's Bride". I say "resumed" work. Nearly five years ago a month or two before grandmother's death I began work on it. I got it blocked out and I got no further. Never since then have I been able to take it up again. But this fall I am not at work on a book and I want to write a few short stories if I can. It is difficult to get the time for writing at all. But it must be managed. As matters are, I cannot afford to give it up, even for a time.

1916

The Manse, Leaskdale, Ont.
Monday, Jan. 3, 1916

The New Year has opened amid bitter anxieties and worries. Chester was miserable all December with colds and sick stomach spells. About Christmas one of the glands in his neck swelled and we had the doctor last Friday. He looked grave and said it might possibly be a tubercular gland! I cannot believe it for the child has always been so strong and well until lately, but the worry is killing me. Neither Ewan nor I slept a moment Friday night.

But the thing to do is to *fight*—to build the child up so thoroughly and speedily that his vitality will kill the disease if it has got a hold upon him. Tuberculosis! The very thought of it makes my soul cringe with agony. Waking or sleeping, the thought is ever present with me. Dear, dear little Chester, the core of my heart since his birth—my first born.

On the first of December Lily, who had been with me for three years, left to be married to Rob Shier of Zephyr. I was sorry to lose Lily for she was a very good girl—neat, efficient, capable. But I was not quite as sorry as I would have been had she left a year ago. After her engagement to Shier she ceased to be as anxious to please as formerly and was not nearly so satisfactory in a great many ways. This reconciled me to her going. I have Edith Meyers, a Zephyr girl, in her place. In a good many ways I really like her better than Lily. Her worst fault is that she is very untidy; but she is better tempered, more obliging, and really saves me much more time. And she does not take the morose melancholic spells with which the latter was afflicted. On the whole I certainly would not change back.

All the month the war-news has been bad, especially in regard to the British retreat from Bagdad, when they seemed on the point of capturing it, and the overrunning of Serbia by the Teutons. It is hard to keep faith in the ultimate triumph of the Allies. It really seems that they are doomed to fail or bungle everywhere. And now a second New Year has come and the war seems no nearer an end than last year.

Frede came on December 23rd and left to-day—that has been the one bright spot so far this winter. Up to Friday night I took unmixed joy in her companionship and we had hours of old soul communion. Since Friday all has seemed a dream. I hardly felt regret when she went to-day. When one mighty emotion, be it joy or sorrow or anxiety, takes possession of the mind there is no room for any other.

Yesterday we had Will and Allan Mustard here to dinner. They leave in a short time for England to train in the artillery. They are such fine young fellows. Will they ever sit at my table again?

Friday, Feb. 4, 1916

To-day Ewan came in saying, "Bad news! The worst yet." I turned cold with terror. Had the Germans smashed through on the western front? Or invaded England? I seized the *Globe* and opened it with shaking hands. The headlines announced that the Parliament Buildings in Ottawa had been burned—presumably by a German incendiary. Bad enough news, indeed. But not what I had dreaded. New Parliament Buildings can be built; but if the British line were broken—well we might not need Parliament buildings in Canada! The Germans would see to that.

Monday, Feb. 7, 1916
The Manse, Leaskdale, Ont.

Had an attack of grippe Saturday. But as I had promised to read a paper for the Hypatia Club today I drove to Uxbridge in the teeth of a furious gale and drift. I deserved to catch my death of cold, of course, and perhaps I did.

My royalty reports came from Page to-day and were rather disappointing. *Anne of The Island* did not sell as well as I had a right to expect—only 32,000 copies. There is certainly something wrong somewhere. The booksellers and retailers complain terribly of Page. They say he is so "hard" they cannot deal with him. Some have told me that they would not deal with Page at all if it were not necessary to get my books because the public demands them.

Wednesday, Feb. 9, 1916

I should be in bed—but I feel as if I could not sleep. I am overtired, and worried and nervous into the bargain. Last night I got very little sleep. Ewan coughed incessantly. I fear he has bronchitis. He was so hoarse to-night that he could not go to the Guild, so I had to drag wearily over in his place and read his paper. It was cold and dreary and as I stumbled back home alone through the darkness and snow I almost let go of my "will to live" altogether. So I come to "growl it off" in my journal as of yore. Before the "congregation" I must wear a mask and assume a cheerfulness I am far from feeling.

Wednesday, Feb. 16, 1916

"Pray ye that your flight be not in the winter"—ay, verily. Everything is harder to endure in the winter. Ewan is no better yet. His cough has improved slightly but his hoarseness has grown worse. He cannot speak above a whisper. Everybody in the congregation has a different remedy which is a certain cure and everybody is somewhat offended if his or her pet remedy isn't tried. We have experimented with most of them to no visible benefit. Flaxseed tea seems to be the staple. I make it by the quart and poor Ewan obediently swallows it.

Saturday I felt very miserable with an attack of what I think must be inflammation of the breast. Nevertheless I had to go and preside at the Mission

Band and then help prepare for a Knox college student who was coming out to supply on Sunday. I kept up until I got him out of the way in the spare room. Then I went to bed but not to sleep. I spent the night going from icy chills to burning heats, followed by drenching perspirations. In the morning I could not get up so had to spend the day in bed. By Monday the attack seemed to have spent itself and I got up.

That night Cuthbert McIntyre came and stayed till Tuesday night. He has been in Edmonton the past two years and was paying a flying visit to Toronto. I was heart-glad to see him although in my wretched condition and with poor Ewan quite debarred from conversation I could not enjoy his visit as much as I would otherwise have done. How it brought old days back to see him!...

Tuesday, Feb. 22, 1916
The Manse, Leaskdale, Ont.
Last night I had a very strange dream. I cannot shake off the impression it made on me. It was so vivid, so real, so strangely broken and resumed.

I was in my room at noon, standing by my dressing table. Outside the sun was shining on a summer world. Suddenly—nay, instantaneously—the sky became overcast with inky blackness, torrents of rain fell, thunder rolled and lightning flashed incessantly. Though alarmed, I stood my ground for some time. Then came a crash and flash that seemed to rive the universe. I was sure the house was struck. In a frenzy of terror I ran shrieking downstairs and through the hall, calling for Ewan. He, at the same time, came running in from the stable, and we met in the dining room, clasping each other in dismay. As we passed back through the hall I saw a man running up the walk. I opened the door and he dashed into the hall, out of the rain—a soldier in khaki.

At this moment the cry of the baby awakened me. At the instant of awakening the curious conviction flashed into my mind that my dream had to do with events of the war about to happen and I felt deep regret that I had wakened before I finished it and knew how it ended.

I arose, attended to the baby's needs, and returned to bed. I fell asleep and did what I never did before—I resumed the broken dream and dreamed it out. The storm was just over; the sun was shining and the drops of rain were glistening on the young grass like diamonds. The whole world seemed joyous and springlike. I was walking down the hill beyond the church—nay, not walking but dancing, as a child might dance, and I wore a wreath of white blossoms on my hair. I danced the whole way home and I felt inexpressibly light-hearted and jubilant. Then I awakened again.

Curious? Well, if the dream "comes true" and the storm breaks, we are to be happy after the storm has passed. I must remember that for any comforting.

Monday, Feb. 28, 1916
Did that strange dream of mine have any real significance? It has been most strangely fulfilled. Two days after I dreamed it came the news of the great German offensive at Verdun and since then the strain has been hideous. Last Thursday the French line was broken. Every day since has brought tidings of

a German advance in spite of the desperate resistance of the French. The situation is horribly critical. If the Germans capture Verdun the spirit of France may be broken, or the way to Paris opened.

Apart from the horrible strain of the war news this has been a dreadful week. Last Wednesday night I came home from a Guild social and went to bed feeling fairly well. In the night I wakened with another attack of inflammation of the breast—dreadful pain, chills and sweats. I had to spend the next day in bed and the pain and sweats weakened me so dreadfully that I could hardly stand on the following day. Get up I had to, though, for there was to be a "pie social" in aid of the Red Cross at Webster Fawn's that night and as I had charge of the programme it was necessary that I should be there. It was a cold, raw blustery night. I went up in Alec Leask's big sleigh. There were about twelve in the sleigh, the rest being young folks full of jollity and laughter— harmless and natural enough but not much in accordance with my then mood. I felt inexpressibly miserable—weak, chilly, tired, discouraged. Ewan's voice was no better—the Germans were advancing—the baby had been failing for three weeks—I was wretchedly ill. I gazed over the stormy fields in the bitter wind of night and wondered if it were any use to keep up the struggle. I have seldom been more sick at heart than I was that night.

But nobody knew it. Of course, I looked quite ghastly—hollow-eyed and haggard from lack of sleep, with a racking cough. But I smiled and laughed and jested and engineered the programme; I gave a comic reading that brought down the house; I ate a third of a pie with the purchaser thereof—an awkward schoolboy who could say nothing and to whom I could say nothing. We ate that pie in silence and I felt as if every mouthful must choke me.

I got home at one so overtired and ill that I couldn't sleep. Saturday seemed like a nightmare. It was stormy and bitterly cold. Ewan's voice was no better. The war news was bad and the baby was ill. Worst of all, my illness, lack of appetite and loss of sleep had their inevitable effect. I had not enough nourishment for him and what little I had didn't agree with him—has not agreed with him ever since my first attack. He has simply been fading out of life for three weeks. It is breaking my heart. He never cries—never complains—just lies in his little basket and gives a sweet, piteous little smile when someone bends over him. He weighs less than he did two months ago. Something must be done. I hate the thought of weaning him so soon, but I am going down terribly myself and if there is not a change for the better in him soon I will lose my baby. I have been so blue and nervous and depressed these last three days—so weak and ill, too, yet I must be on my feet constantly. I cannot sleep at night, between worry and physical pain. If Ewan were only better! I get so worried lest he lose his voice altogether. In fact, I seem to be the prey of a score of worries just now—worry over the war, over Ewan, over the baby, over myself. Verily, this is the storm of my dream with a vengeance. Oh, for Frede or Bertie—for any "kindred spirit" to help me out a bit with a little encouragement or laughter.

Thursday, Mar. 2, 1916
Leaskdale, Ont.

I am seriously alarmed about Ewan's voice. There is no improvement—nay, he is really worse. I have slept hardly any this week and when I do I waken with a night sweat. It is probably the result of the trouble in my breasts but it is extremely weakening. I look like a ghost and feel like a lunatic. It seems to me that I *cannot* bear the suspense of that hideous struggle at Verdun, where men are being mowed down in indiscriminate butchery. "The snow around Verdun is no longer white" was the hideously suggestive sentence in a paper today.

I drag through the days like a doomed creature. There are times when I could scream aloud. It is dull and gray and cold. Chester goes about the house lustily singing that absurd old song, "Polly Wolly Doodle" which is his reigning favorite at present. The contrast between present conditions and that chorus is grim. Thanks be, *he* keeps well and rosy. Baby, too, has seemed better today. I began on Monday to give him some cow's milk. It is agreeing with him well and certain things have altered for the better with him.

Friday, March 10, 1916
Leaskdale Manse, Ont.

I have had a rather strange experience tonight. To-day was hard. I had another sweat last night and could not sleep after it or prevent myself from picturing everything in the gloomiest colors. One of my breasts was sore again and I felt as if I could *not* bear another attack of inflammation. To-day a wild snowstorm raged and no mail came. It is a torture every day to get the mail—but it is a worse torture *not* to get it. Ewan's voice was worse again—baby was not so well—everything seemed as bad as it could be. I had no physical strength to fight off worry and at dark my nerves suddenly went to pieces as they have not gone since that terrible winter of my nervous breakdown long ago at home. I could do nothing but walk the floor in agony of mind and travail of spirit. This continued for two hours. I looked forward to a night of sleepless horror. All my misery seemed to centre around Verdun where "the snow was no longer white". I seemed in my own soul to embrace all the anguish and strain of France. Not for one moment would I tear my tortured thoughts from it.

Suddenly the agony ceased—a great calm seemed to descend upon me and envelop me. I was *at peace*. All unrest passed away from me. I seemed to have emerged from some awful crisis. The conviction seized upon me that Verdun was safe—that the Germans would not pass the grim barrier of desperate France. I was as a woman from whom some evil spirit had been driven—or can it be as a priestess of old who, out of depths of agony wins some strange foresight of the future? I feel as if I had wrestled with principalities and powers, with things present and things to come, and come off victor. Is it so?—or is it merely the reaction of tortured nerves, agonized to their limit?

Saturday, March 11, 1916
Leaskdale, Ont.

I slept well and feel much better today. And that strange calm continues—that strange conviction that the Verdun crisis is past, no matter how much longer the struggle may continue. It was not disturbed when the mail came bringing bad news of the Germans again winning the Crow's Wood. Yesterday that news would have agonized me. Today it did not affect me at all.

Ewan's voice is certainly a little better and he means to try to preach tomorrow. I don't envy his listeners but he has lost four Sundays and is determined he will not lose another.

And so I finish this volume. It covers six years—a very full and happy six years, in spite of some dark hours. How I love my old journal and what a part of my life it has become. It satisfies some need in my nature. It seems like a personal confidant in whom I can repose absolute trust. I shall begin a fourth volume with my next entry and I wonder how many years it will embrace—what records of joy and sorrow, of success and failure it will contain.

> "The Moving Finger writes; and having writ
> Moves on; nor all thy piety and wit
> Can lure it back to cancel half a line
> Nor all thy tears wash out a word of it."

[THE END OF VOLUME 3]

Tuesday, March 21, 1916
Leaskdale Manse, Ont.

Last Monday I went to Toronto for a week. Ewan's voice, though not yet fully recovered, was considerably improved and I felt that I really needed a little change after the strain of the past four weeks. I had a good deal of shopping to do also, so I went, though not feeling very fit for it.

The war news of Monday was fair—the French lines still holding. Baby and I went to Toronto on the afternoon train and Norman Beal met us. I spent the week with the Beals. Mary is a dear jolly soul—"one of the race that knows Joseph"—and Norman is very nice. I should have had a good time that week but physical discomfort poisoned it all.

Tuesday the Press Club gave an afternoon tea for me and that evening Messrs. McClelland and Goodchild, of McClelland, Goodchild and Stewart, called to discuss the Canadian publication of my next book. I have decided that I shall give them the Canadian rights. Hitherto I have not had a Canadian publisher, Page holding the world rights—a very unsatisfactory arrangement. I told Mr. McC that I intended to give Page the U.S. rights. McC and G. looked at each other. They said nothing against Page but all through the interview I had a feeling that they *could* say a good deal if I gave them a chance. I did *not* give them the chance. Whatever Page may be I shall not give rival publishers the chance to vilify him unless he gives me greater reason to distrust him as a publisher than he yet has. As for the McClelland firm, they are well spoken of in quarters where I have confidence and I think I am safe in trusting them.

No definite arrangement was come to in regard to the new book but I have arranged with them to bring out my poems next fall. I have always wanted to do this—not that they are of any special merit but solely for my own satisfaction. Page practically refused to bring them out some years ago declaring that poetry would not pay. Considering the amount he has made out of my novels I thought he might have published the poems for me even if they did not "pay". So I felt that I did not need to consider him in this deal.

I had another attack of inflammation of the breast that week and of course it spoiled my visit—I had it all over again—the pain, the chills, the night sweats, the nervous restlessness. And I had to run around to afternoon teas and smile and talk. Of course, the sensible thing would have been to cut them out. But having promised beforehand to be present I felt that I could not disappoint hostesses whose guest of honor I was and who had invited their friends to meet me. Fame, as well as rank, imposes certain obligations!!

But I did feel disappointed that my little visit, to which I had been looking forward all winter, was completely spoiled.

Baby was in with me and was entirely good and adorable.

At one of the teas I received quite the most stupendous compliment that has ever been paid to me on account of my books. A lady came up to me and said, "Oh, Mrs. Macdonald, I want to tell you how much my little girl loves *Anne*. I found her with *Green Gables* the other day and I said, "Child, how often have you read that book." She said, "Oh, mother, I don't know. I *just keep it and my bible together and read a chapter of both every day.*"

In my salad days I may have dreamed of rivalling Bronte and Eliot. I certainly never in my wildest flights dreamed of competing with the Bible!!!

Seriously, though, I thought that incense of a child's adoration the sweetest that has ever been offered me.

I came home yesterday and have spent the day putting things to rights. I am very tired tonight and, worse than tired, I am nervous and depressed as a result of my breast trouble. Ewan's voice is much better, though not normal yet. The German attack on Verdun still rages but so far they have made no further progress. The struggle at present centres around "Dead Man's Hill"—so named surely by some prophet—and "Hill 304". The carnage is dreadful but the French watchword is "They shall not pass."

I read a horrible statement in a paper the other day. It haunts me. When I cannot sleep at nights it tears my soul. "No child under eight years of age is left alive in Poland. They have all perished from starvation or exposure".

And this is the year 1916 of the Christian era!

Thursday, March 23, 1916
Leaskdale Manse, Ont.
I have been having some bad night sweats and the breast trouble seems to have become chronic. I have lost so much sleep that I am getting terribly run down. I weigh only 109 pounds. I never weighed so little in my life. I have lost sixteen pounds in the last six weeks.

Ewan is not any too well either. Baby, though, is thriving like a weed.

"Gay"
[*Stuart*]

Wednesday, April 12, 1916
Mr. Noonan, of the Britton Publishing Company was here today, trying to get my new book for them. Well, there was a day when publishers did not hustle over one another to get my books! Mr. Noonan was one of Page's salesmen for seventeen years. I asked him candidly to tell me his opinion of Page and his methods. His revelations were rather ghastly. Perhaps too much credence should not be given them. Yet Noonan is highly spoken of by book sellers. He said he left Page because he could not tolerate his methods any longer. The offer the Britton Co. made seemed a good one. But I feel all at sea. I have not sufficient knowledge of the publishing business to protect my own interests. I don't know whom to trust. I am afraid of Page. There are times when I half regret my old free-lance days of magazine writing. I could steer my own bark then. Now it seems rather beyond me.

Monday, April 17, 1916
The Manse, Leaskdale, Ont.
Am in a condition of worry tonight caused by a telegram from Page. I foresee much trouble. He wires that he has had "a very unsatisfactory interview with McClelland" and asks me to do nothing further in the matter until I hear from him, adding that he will write fully on Monday—the wire was sent Saturday night. I have no doubt that the interview was unsatisfactory because Page could not get his own way in everything. He is, I understand, that kind of a man. Well, the battle is evidently on, this poem business being in the nature of a preliminary skirmish. God defend the right!

Thursday, Apr. 20, 1916
Yesterday the war news announced the capture of Trebizond by the Russians. This is good, though perhaps it will not affect the main campaigns. But we have not much to rejoice over these days so we ran up the flag for the fall of Trebizond.

I am dreadfully tired tonight and worried to boot. Mr. McClelland came out today and we spent the whole day thrashing out various matters. He and Page had a battle royal over the matter of the poems—which is their affair. It is very much my affair, however, that in the course of their stormy interview Page uttered the threat that "the courts would decide the matter" if I gave my new book to anyone but him. If Page were not merely "bluffing" to intimidate McClelland I do not know what he meant. We have had some correspondence about the literary contents of my next book but I feel sure that there was nothing in my letters to bind me. I wish I had kept copies of them. Anyhow, I have given McClelland the right of placing the book in the U.S. market. If Page has any unknown hold on me I must have good backing; and if he hasn't he must be taught not to make threats like that—and after making a fortune out of my books on his niggardly contract! McClelland confirmed what Noonan told me, as far as his own firm went. I have been making some inquiries about the Mac firm and find them very well spoken of. But Page has rather shaken my faith in everyone. I shall not sleep much tonight.

We begin housecleaning tomorrow. Now for a month of hard work, combined with worry over the war and over the Page affair. Nice cheerful prospect!

Wednesday, Apr. 26, 1916
The Manse, Leaskdale, Ont.
Every week we can confidently count on some new and startling and unexpected war news. This week it is the Sinn Fein rebellion in Ireland. The authorities claim to have it in hand but the situation is nasty. The Verdun struggle goes on without cessation while the world holds its breath.

Page has never written yet in spite of his promise to do so. I suspect the reason of his silence is that he hopes *I* will write and give away what McClelland said about their interview. Then Page would have the chance of denying everything he wanted to, whereas, if he writes first, he runs the chance of saying things that will incriminate him in my eyes. Well, I shall not write. If Page is playing a double game he will hang himself if he is given enough rope.

Mr. McClelland advises me to join the Author's League of America. He says it is a capital organization and a great help to authors. So I have applied for membership. I understand that Page has a wholesome respect for the League, having run up against it several times in his dealings with authors.

May 1, 1916, Monday
Kut-el-Amara has been compelled to surrender at last. We have expected it for some time but that did not prevent us from feeling very blue over it all. It is an encouragement to the Germans and a blow to Britain's prestige. I feel too depressed tonight to do anything.

Page has never written yet. His silence is getting on my nerves because I believe it means he is hatching some deviltry. I have got so that I cannot sleep at nights and really I think I'll end up in a hospital or sanatorium. I understand that Page worried another of his authors into an asylum not long ago—and she was his cousin, too. I wrote recently to Bertie McIntyre asking her to investigate Page's standing with the Vancouver booksellers. She has answered with some lurid disclosures. The booksellers, one and all, condemn Page's methods utterly; and one added the information that he was not "straight"—that he had repudiated his gambling debts etc. From another source I have recently learned that Mildred Page is his second wife, his first wife having divorced him, and that he is notorious for immorality. It is all very sickening. I suppose there is nothing to do but break completely with him. And if he is the man rumor paints him he will make all the trouble he can for me, there is no doubt of that.

Friday, May 19, 1916
The Manse, Leaskdale
This was quite a day in the annals of our little village. The 116th Battalion which has been training in Uxbridge all winter and to which many of "our boys" belong made a route march through the township and passed here at noon. We had several arches erected for them and treated them all to fruit and read them an address. Poor fellows. I wonder how many of them will ever return.

The 116th Battalion, trained in Uxbridge, passing under Leaskdale Arch

The Verdun carnage still goes on. The Germans have crept nearer the fortress but their losses are enormous. So are those of France. "Dead Man's Hill" must be soaked to the core with blood. And *still* England does not strike! God, *when* will this strain end?

Wednesday, May 24, 1916
The Manse, Leaskdale
On Monday the long-expected letter came from Mr. Page—a very lengthy epistle. He makes several statements in it that I happen to know are false and

"Chester under arch outside of our gate"

several more that I am almost sure are false. He asked me to give a personal interview to his salesman Mr. Mullen who was in Toronto. So I went in on Tuesday and conferred with Mac's first. They told me they were quite intimate with Mullen who was a very fine fellow and who intended to leave Page as soon as his contract was up, being unable to tolerate his methods. I met Mullen at the King Edward and had a long talk with him. The first question he asked me was, "Are you a member of the Author's League?" Evidently Page had told him to find this out. I said I was and declined to discuss the question of my new book, saying that I had appointed Mac my agent and he must apply to him. We had a long talk on various subjects and it was plain to be seen he had no good to say of Page, though he did not positively say evil of him. When we parted he said, "Have you any other questions you would like to ask me, Mrs. Macdonald?" I said, "Yes, but it would not be fair to ask them of Mr. Page's salesman." He then said, "Sometime in the future you may ask me those questions and I will answer them"—a remark which I would not have understood had it not been for what Mac had told me of Mullen's intention to leave Page as soon as his contract was out. It seems Page cannot keep his salesmen at all unless he binds them by contract. Of course, Mr. Mullen meant that his answers would not be favorable to Page, otherwise there could be no reason for his not answering the questions at once.

Well, the die is cast. The issue is on the knees of the gods.

Thursday, May 25, 1916
The Manse, Leaskdale
I have written to Mr. Page, telling him that I have appointed McClelland my literary agents and that he must negotiate with them for my new book. I told him he was to have the first chance for it. I had insisted on this, although Mac was not any too well inclined that way. But I shall be fair if Page is not. He shall have his chance, even though I would prefer, in the light of recent revelations, to break with him altogether.

The war news is very bad. At Verdun the French have again lost Douamont and in Italy the Austrians have begun a drive that bids fair to have disastrous results for the Italian army.

We are having the wettest spring on record. It has rained almost every day since the first of April and is also very cold. We have had none of the lovely spring weather we usually have here. It all makes the worry and strain and suspense harder to bear. Well, "he that endureth to the end shall be saved." But what about those who are not strong enough to endure to the end?

Saturday, June 10, 1916
It seems to me that *everything* has been crowded into the past eight days—as if every emotion possible has been experienced. It has been horrible beyond words. This war is slowly killing me. I am bleeding to death as France is being bled in the shambles of Verdun. On last Saturday came the first news of the battle of Jutland—and it was announced as a German Victory! I felt as if I had received a staggering blow in the face from a trusted friend. And the physical effects of that blow were not removed when on Monday the news came that the first reports were German lies and that instead it had been a British victory though a dear-bought one. Never shall I forget that intervening Sunday. If the British navy had failed in what were we to trust? On Monday morning I drove Ewan to the station on his way to the General Assembly in Winnipeg and the morning papers were a relief. On Tuesday Mrs. Oxtoby and I drove to Sunderland to attend a meeting of the W.F.M.S. Presbyterial. I went in good spirits, for the *Globe* had brought an encouraging report of a sudden blow and a big victory for Russia on the eastern front. But my elation was short lived. During the afternoon the word came of Lord Kitchener's death off the Orkneys!

I cannot describe the effect the news had on me. Since the Boer War Kitchener has seemed little less than a demi-god. He was the greatest man and the most dramatic figure in the British Empire. His death brought to me an agonizing sense of personal loss. I have felt as if I were in a bad dream ever since.

Well, perhaps Kitchener's death is the last sacrifice demanded by the god of battles and from now on the tide will turn....

Saturday, June 17, 1916

This has been a week of worry. I have neither eaten or slept much. I had a letter from Page on Tuesday threatening a lawsuit if I give the book to anyone but him. The letter reveals the scoundrel in the man and confirms all I have heard of him. I do not believe anything I have written can give him any hold on me, but I have not copies of my letters and it is of course possible that some incautious phrase, used innocently, may give him some ground for legal claim. On the other hand, he may be merely "bluffing". Anyhow, he shall not frighten me. I will fight him now to the last ditch. But my resolve cannot prevent his threats from worrying me and life has been nightmarish this week.

The war news has been good—the Russians continuing their advance and taking an immense number of prisoners.

The General Assembly has voted for church union. I expected they would but I feel bitterly on the subject. I have never been in favor of union, although Ewan is. But when the whole world is rent and torn what matter another rending and tearing? Our old world is passed away forever—and I fear that those of us who have lived half our span therein will never feel wholly at home in the new.

I have a nasty, queer, crampy feeling in my hand nowadays when I write. I am really terribly run down. Since the New Year I have been constantly either worried or ill and often both, and there seems to be no prospect of a respite.

I began to write my new book on Friday—"Anne's House of Dreams". I have been getting the material for it in shape all winter and spring. I am not likely to have much pleasure in the writing of it, with Page's threats hanging over my head. Oh, it all makes me heartsick.

Stuart is well and flourishing. He is known locally as "the baby who never cries".

Sunday Afternoon
July 30, 1916

I am sitting on the veranda, trying vainly to get a breath of cool air. The children are asleep beside me—Stuart in his basket and Chester in the hammock—both suffering from the heat. July has been a terrible month—not a drop of rain and the most intense burning heat, especially for the past eighteen days. I never recall anything like it in my life. I feel the heat all the more because of my ailment which has persisted now for six weeks. It makes life a burden to me and embitters everything. Yesterday was a nightmare of suffering from my trouble and the heat combined. To-day I feel fairly well, so suffer mainly from the heat. Ewan, too, has been miserable all the month with rheumatism or neuritis in arm and back. Fortunately, the children have kept well so far. Stuart is such a darling—just a big white dumpling with such large, lovely blue eyes. Chester is growing. His favorite post these days is perched on the gate post watching passing cars and teams. He sits there by the hour. It is well that with all this discomfort and suffering the war news is good. Were it like

"I feel pretty comfortable"
[*Stuart*]

last July I don't see how we could live. The British and French are still creeping on in the Somme Valley—nothing spectacular yet—nothing to fly the flag for, but steady progress which all the German counter attacks cannot check. Russia is doing marvellously—her resurgence seems like a miracle. The Verdun crisis *seems* past—but it has seemed past many times before.

On July 12th I had a very nasty letter from Page re-iterating his threats of a lawsuit. I did not reply to it but of course it worries me. The next day I went into Toronto to meet Mr. Jewett of Appleton's who had come up to bid for my book. He made me an offer which made me gasp, comparing it to Page's niggardly contracts. The Mac firm has been snowed under with offers. Humph! It was rather different when I was peddling *Anne* about from place to place!

In one of his letters Mr. Page referred to this and asked me to remember that *he* had accepted my book when other houses turned it down. Well, I *did* remember this—though he did not accept it out of pity or consideration for me but simply because he thought it would succeed. And his belief in its success was *not* due to his own superior insight in discovering its merit. I have recently found out just how *Anne* came to be accepted by the house of Page. Page himself was strongly opposed to accepting it—wanted to turn it down. But there were on his staff at that time two people. One was a Miss Arbuckle from Summerside, P.E. Island. *She* had been interested in the book because of its scene. She had read it with more care than most readers bestow on a manuscript from an unknown author and she had talked about it to the other readers and piqued their interest too. A young man—Hardress, or some such name, who was then on the staff, liked the book and insisted that it should be taken and Lewis Page yielded to their opinions and accepted the book. Lewis Page does not know that I know this and, as I was told it in confidence by one of his salesman, I cannot retort upon him with it but must accept his reproach of ingratitude to him in silence.

I liked Mr. Jewett and Appleton's is a good firm. I think probably I shall accept his offer but the matter is not definitely settled yet. I went in last week to meet Mr. Dominick of Stokes who also made a good offer; but I think I prefer the Appleton firm. I wish it were all settled. I do not want ever to have to change publishers again. I want to form "a partnership for life" as Mr. Jewett says.

Recently I had a letter from Annie Fellowes Johnston, the author of the "Little Colonel" series. She published with Page for twenty years and has recently left him, as has also another popular author, Mrs. Porter of *Pollyanna* fame. I wrote to Mrs. J. and asked her why she had left Page etc. She wrote fully in reply. He behaved as badly as possible to her—refused flatly to give her any better terms and then when she gave her last book to another firm bombarded her with insulting telegrams, letters and threats of lawsuits etc. She says she seriously doubts the man's sanity—he does so many things flatly opposed to his own interests. The same thought had crossed my mind before her letter came. It is a consoling prospect truly to reflect that my seven books, which properly handled ought to bring me in good returns for many years yet are hopelessly in the power of so unscrupulous and vindictive a man.

The queer, persistent, indefinable distrust I felt regarding Mr. Page during that visit in Boston has been justified.

The only thing I regret in changing publishers is that my books will never be quite so nicely gotten up again. The Page firm are the best bookmakers in America. Everybody admits that.

Tuesday, Aug. 1, 1916
The Manse, Leaskdale, Ont.
Verily, no wonder we found Sunday hot. It was 98 in the shade. Yesterday a delicious cool wave reached us and today was delightful. But I am still miserable and have a racking sick headache tonight also. Yesterday evening I felt fairly well and had a rare hour reading Rupert Brooke's poems. They are very wonderful. His "Song of the Pilgrims" is one of the most exquisite things I have ever read. One feels that a great poet died in Lemnos, a victim to that fatal Gallipoli error. One drop of his blood was worth an ocean of Hun gore. If he could do such in youth what might he not have done in maturity? But he sleeps well and the Kaiser and his six sons are all well and thriving. So the world is not left wholly desolate!

Wednesday, Aug. 2, 1916
Woke early this morning and as usual could not sleep again. I have slept miserably ever since the New Year. My nerves have never recovered from the shock of Chester's illness, the strain of the winter and the agony of Verdun. Finding I could not sleep I sat up and read a bundle of Mr. MacMillan's letters I had wanted to look over. They were all very delightful but seemed to belong to a world and a day gone by. I felt very miserable all day but had to "keep going" as raspberries and cherries had to be canned.

Tuesday, Aug. 8, 1916
....This evening I had a rather curious experience. I read the last chapter of a serial story, all the other chapters of which I read—thirty-three years ago!

When Well Nelson was in Cavendish his aunt sent him a magazine called "Wide Awake"—a capital juvenile. During the last year it came a serial by Harriet Prescott Spofford ran in it—"A Girl and a Jewel". I revelled in it. But alas, it was not quite concluded before the magazine ceased to come. And it stopped just at the most exciting, dramatic point! I never found out what happened and who "Lucia" really was. And now, more than 30 years after, I read the last chapter and solve the mystery. Recently, I had a chance to purchase four bound volumes of the old *Wide Awake* and I got them for the children. It is impossible to tell how much I have enjoyed re-reading them and what delight they gave me—a strange, eerie pleasure as of a journey back into the past. It was not only that their contents had still a literary relish even for my maturer taste; but as I read I seemed to be back again in the surroundings of the days in which I read them first. I was back in the old home in Cavendish. Grandfather and grandmother, and Dave and Well were there. The blue gulf sparkled beyond. The spruces and maples crowded about the old house. The orchards were fairy-haunted. Our little playhouse waited for us in the fir wood. I went again to the white washed school on the crest of the hill; the stars were in their right places in the heavens; the cherries were ripe on summer evenings; a world utterly passed away was my universe once more. I felt curiously homesick and strange, every time I shut the book and came back to this one.

Sunday, Aug. 13, 1916
The Manse, Leaskdale
This has been a busy week—the Red Cross lecture Monday, a trip to Uxbridge and the Missionary society Wednesday, the Red Cross Thursday and the Mission Band yesterday—and two hours writing every morning at "Anne's House of Dreams". But I growl not; for it has been cool, with one beautiful rain and—mercy of mercies!—I have been well. My cystitis has disappeared with the suddenness that always marks its going; I have been sleeping splendidly, as I have not done for a year and a half—nay, more, as I have not done since Chester was born. Oh, if I can only get really well and keep well!
....I often recall that curious experience of mine that terrible March night last winter—when after hours of agony the sudden great peace came to me. I believe and always shall believe that on that night the Genius of Victory left the German lines and passed over to the Entente powers. Since then the Central Empires have won no lasting successes and they have sustained some serious defeats. But the end is not yet.

Saturday, Aug. 19, 1916
The Manse, Leaskdale, Ont.
....I was in Toronto Tuesday over this interminable business of contracts. A question of possible serial publication has come up and I have to prepare a synopsis of the book. I have been working feverishly at it every evening since and writing all the forenoon at the book itself. I do my writing in the parlor now, as said parlor possesses the only door in the house which young Chester cannot open. Besides, it is a pleasant green, summer-like room and has an

agreeable effect on me. Wednesday and Thursday I was miserable with an attack of bowel trouble. Naturally, visitors took that day for appearing.

The Russians have captured Tarnapol heights and the British and French have renewed their offensive, which lately seemed to have been petering out. I am horribly tired. It is now 10.30 and I have been working at my synopsis for three hours.

Monday, Aug. 21, 1916

We have had two days of terrible heat—100 in the shade. Last night sleep was all but impossible from the heat.

I was intensely shocked on reading the *Guardian* today to find an account of the accidental drowning of Mrs. Bayfield Williams—Edith England—in Edmonton. In company with several friends she was out boating on a lake at a summer resort near Edmonton; a sudden squall came up; the boat went down and all on board were lost.

Edith and I lost touch with one another after she and Bayfield went west. But on seeing this notice of her tragic death the old girlhood affection revived in my heart. I was very fond of Edith once. She was a sweet, kind-hearted little girl. I remember our first meeting—that summer day twenty-two years ago when I alighted from the train at Ellerslie station and she and Bayfield met me. Edith and I were chums all that year. Many a night we spent together in her beautiful home and poured endless confidences into each other's ears, after the immemorial fashion of girlhood. And now one is taken and the other—as yet—is left. Poor little Edith! Her girlhood was very bright and happy, as the indulged and idolized only child of well-to-do parents. I used to envy her in some ways. But I do not think life was very rosy for her after her marriage. Bayfield was dissipated and more than once they were on the verge of financial ruin. I am sorry for her mother who is living alone in the old home at Bideford, husband and child both gone. "Why can't yesterday come back, mother?" Chester asked me the other day. Oh, my little laddie, you asked one of the saddest and most unanswerable questions in life.

Saturday, Sept. 2, 1916
Leaskdale, Ont.

This has been for me a dragging profitless week. I don't seem to pick up. I have no appetite and have "gone stale" on everything. Ewan, too, has been suffering severely from neuritis in his arm with a resultant loss of sleep for him and myself.

Thursday Jas. Mustard's received a telegram stating that Allan had been shot in the back. He had been at the front only for a few days. They do not know yet if the wound is serious or not. Poor Allan! He and Will were to dinner here when Frede was here Christmas week and I asked myself then what would be their fate.

I am tired and useless and don't care—at present—what happens to me.

Monday, Sept. 4, 1916
The Manse, Leaskdale

The war news was good today—the Russians have won an important victory on the Dneister, the French have captured Clery and the British have taken Guillemont. Good news? I wonder if the wives and mothers whose husbands and sons were killed for it will call it very good news.

Ewan and I spent the evening calling on an old couple in the village. The old lady is about as graceful as the proverbial feather bed with the string tied round the middle. She entertained me by showing me photographs and Christmas cards! Heaven save the mark! It was certainly an evening of boredom. And yet that same waddling, uninteresting old dame has two sons at the front. So I take off my hat to her. She may be prosy—but she has done her bit....

Saturday, Sept. 9, 1916
The Manse, Leaskdale, Ont.

....I've been especially busy this week, preparing for a short visit to Warsaw Ind. where Ewan's brother, Dr. Angus Macdonald lives. If I were not taking the children I would look forward to it with pleasure; but as it is I feel only dread of it and a wish that it were all over and I safe home again. I am tired already. What will I be after looking after two young children away from home for ten days? Chester hasn't been very well this week either—his stomach is unsettled and he has no appetite. He hasn't had a sick spell since last February, even in all the hot weather; but I always dread his taking one. When Angus wrote asking us, I would rather not have gone. But Ewan wished to go and would not go alone. So I agreed to go for his sake. Edith will take her vacation at the same time and we will lock up the house. Mrs. Warner will feed Daff and water my plants.

The Walker House, Toronto, Ont.
Tuesday, Sept. 12, 1916

We left home at one today. Mr. Warner—our next door neighbor—motored us to the station and we came in on the afternoon train and had dinner here. I like an occasional dinner at an hotel—I like the lights and guests and the change of viands. Stuart sat in his high chair, his great blue eyes like stars, his cheeks like roses, and attracted the attention of all in his vicinity. Everybody seems to love him at sight. Chester is at the hard age—it is difficult to get him to behave properly at the table. Not that he is bad—only heedless and mischievous, and very determined to have his own way! Now we are up in our room. Ewan is reading, Chester is asleep and Stuart is having a glorious romp all over the bed.

Friday, Sept. 15, 1916
Warsaw, Ind.

It seems so strange to be in a country that is not at war! I did not realize until I came here how deeply Canada *is* at war—how *normal* a condition war has come to be with us. It seems strange to go out—on the street or to some public place—and see no Khaki uniforms, no posters of appeal for recruits, no bulletin boards of war despatches. It all makes me feel that I ought to be back home in the thick of it. And we miss our Toronto papers so. The papers Angus takes are all Chicago papers. They give a few offical reports—nothing else.

"Dr Macdonald's house (x).
His private hospital (xx)"
[*Warsaw, Indiana*]

Chester hasn't been well today. He seems to have caught cold while out motoring with his father and uncle today. I did not know he was going and he did not have on his overcoat. They put him in the back seat alone and man-like, forgot all about him—went away out into the country where a very bitter wind was blowing. When they came back the child was crying with cold and his bare legs were simply blue, for they had not even wrapped a rug around them. I admit I was a little provoked with Ewan. He promised, when I consented to go to Warsaw, that he would look after Chester and take him entirely off my hands. And this was how he did it! Since then Chester is fretful and won't eat. He is so fussy at the table that I feel ashamed, for Angus and Edith know little about children and seemed to think the child is very finnicky, whereas he is half-sick. He is hearty enough when he is well. Stuart has been fussy today, too, because of cutting teeth, so that, between the two, I have had a harder day than if I were home working.

Angus is a very nice man—a really remarkable man in many ways. I like him immensely; but I find nothing congenial in Edith. She has been very kind in one way—takes us out in her car every day and spreads most elaborate meals for us. But she is one of those "pizen neat" housekeepers who turn pale at a fleck of dust. I know it is absolute agony for her when Stuart is eating a biscuit on the floor. She watches him with a fascinated eye and before he has jammed the last bit in his mouth she flies for broom and dust pan. As a result I am in constant misery, trying to keep the children from making a litter. This afternoon I had to smile to myself. Chester had gone to the window to look out at a passing train. When he turned away Edith sprang up, crossed the room,

"Photo of Ewan, taken in Warsaw".

picked up the corners of the curtains which he had—very slightly—pushed aside, and matched them with the most scrupulous care. Then she sat down again with a martyr-like expression. She has given me some rather nasty digs because the children don't always shut the screen door quickly enough to prevent an odd fly or two getting in. I suppose it is all such second nature with her that she is hardly conscious of it. She certainly has no idea how it makes me feel. I am never comfortable or easy one moment I am in the house. Stuart is creeping everywhere now and I follow him about and try to keep him out of mischief.

My Own Roof-Tree,
Sunday Evening,
Sept. 24, 1916
I *am* here—and besottedly thankful....

Thursday, Oct. 5, 1916
Today I finished "Anne's House of Dreams". I never wrote a book in so short a time and amid so much strain of mind and body. Yet I rather enjoyed writing it and I think it isn't too bad a piece of work. I am glad it is done however. It has taken a lot out of me. Mrs. Lapp came this afternoon and we made the boxes for Tag Day.

Tuesday, Oct. 17, 1916
Last Friday I had a bit of amazing news in a letter from McClelland—a clipping from a Boston paper stating that Mildred Page was suing for a divorce from her husband on the ground of cruelty and failure to support. I could hardly believe it. She seemed so happy when I was there six years ago in her beautiful home. I rather think Lewis Page has gone down rapidly these past six years. But of course, he was always a bad lot and Mildred herself as I have recently discovered was not an angel. Annie Fellowes Johnston and Marshall Saunders between them have given me the history of the Pages....

Thursday, Nov. 2, 1916
Lately the Roumanians have been doing pretty well—advancing in some passes—holding firm in others. One ventures to draw a long breath and hope fearfully that the crisis is past.

Our Red Cross met over on the Sixth today. I went, feeling dejected. I had a letter from Frede saying that she feared she could not come on Christmas—she felt she ought to go home and see her father. I dare not urge her—I recognize the condition of things. But I am inexpressibly disappointed. All that has helped me during this past hard year was the

"Red Cross Packers"
[Uxbridge]

consoling hope of "talking it all out" with Freddy when she came at Christmas. Some virtue seemed to go out of me today when I read her letter. I went to the Red Cross and sewed and planned and talked like an automaton. My soul seemed to be somewhere else in a dark little torture chamber of its own.

Saturday, Nov. 11, 1916
The Manse, Leaskdale, Ont.
To-day my volume of poems "The Watchman" came from my Canadian publishers. It is very nicely gotten up. I expect no great things of it.

Mackensen is still retreating in the Dobrudja and the Roumanians are doing well.

Thursday, Nov. 16, 1916
We had good news today of a big Serbian victory on the Macedonian front. But the Roumanian situation is very very bad. I can't sleep at nights for thinking about it. This past month has been the Verdun agony of last spring over again—not quite so dreadful, of course, but very nearly. I wonder if I shall ever be able again to await the coming of the mail with feelings of composure—never to speak of pleasure. For over two years I have dreaded the arrival of the paper every day. I am always so thankful when Sunday comes— it is free from that nightmare. But I pay for its ease on Monday mornings when the agony of suspense seems doubly dreadful—so much may have happened in the long interval between Saturday and Monday.

I was reading over Bertie MacIntyre's old letters to-day. It is five and a half years since I saw Bertie. That is terrible. She is one of the few women in the whole world who really matter to me, and something is wrong when we have to live so far apart and meet so seldom.

Friday, Nov. 24, 1916
This was a rough, doleful day of high winds and squalls of snow. I have finished correcting the four copies of the *House of Dreams*, glory be. The war news is scanty but it is said that Russian reinforcements have arrived in Roumania, so one feels a little more optimistic—which seems to be an ominous feeling in this war for I have noticed that whenever we have dared to feel optimistic something dreadful happened soon afterwards.

We had to drive over to the Sixth tonight in the teeth of that wind and have supper with one of "our families". It was really a very dreary performance.

Thursday, Nov. 30, 1916
What a day was Tuesday! I had had a sleepless night and passed a wretched forenoon trying to work but unable to fix my thoughts on anything. The mail was late, which prolonged the agony; and when it did come the news was bad. The Germans are drawing near to Bucharest. I shall never forget Tuesday afternoon and evening. I have suffered nothing like it in all the months of the war, not even in the dreadful Verdun struggle. I gave up all attempt to work. I did what *had* to be done and between times I shut myself in the parlor, walking

the floor unrestingly, muttering incoherent prayers—prayers that will not be answered. I feel that Bucharest must fall.

At bedtime I took a sleeping powder and so obtained a few hours of loggy sleep and forgetfulness. At five I wakened to sleep no more, so lighted a lamp and tried to read. We left before the mail came Wednesday to attend a wedding. I talked and laughed and did all the proper didoes, with the under-ache of dread and worry gnawing at my soul. Drove home ten miles through the dark, sloppy, wet night, forced myself to look at the papers—and found the news bad. The Roumanian Government had left Bucharest. Then I dressed both children and took them to the Guild Social. Came home worn out in mind and body and slept the sleep of exhaustion.

To-day as E. was away I ploughed down through the mud for the mail. Still bad—still bad! The Russians have begun a counter offensive in the Kirlzbaba pass but I feel that it will peter out. They do not seem to have the munitions.

After I read the papers I drove over to the Sixth to a meeting for the Red Cross, sewed all the afternoon, and have come home tired and blue.

Sunday, December 3, 1916
The Manse, Leaskdale
The war news continues bad. Friday evening Edith and I drove over to Zephyr because I had to recite at a Red Cross concert there. I was very miserable all the evening with an attack of cystitis. It was pitchy dark coming home and it was one o'clock when we got here. Then up at seven in the morning and hard at work. But I am always thankful when I *can* work—when I can compose my mind sufficiently to think and plan and do. But I lost my usual Sunday rest today, wherefrom I usually obtain enough strength and grit to face another week. I was asked to go to a certain place to spend the afternoon and have tea. There were circumstances which made it advisable for me to go, so I reluctantly went, taking the children. I spent a miserable afternoon of worry and headache and boredom. Came home, exceedingly tired, to find that a certain worthy old dame from Zephyr had invited herself here to spend a week. At another time I would not have minded it muchly but just now when I am so nervous and worried it really seemed to me almost "the last straw."

Sunday, December 10, 1916
The Manse, Leaskdale
The calendar says it is a week—viz. seven days—since last Sunday. My soul cries out that it is seven years—for seven years would not have aged me in mind and soul as this past week has done.

Last Monday I got up, wondering how I could get through the morning and face the mail when it came. I held myself down to work until I saw Ewan leaving for the office. Then, as usual, I went to pieces, fled to the parlor, shut myself in, and walked the floor. There should surely be a path worn from corner to corner across that parlor carpet from my peregrinations there since the war began.

Ewan came back with the *Globe*. With icy hands, pallid lips, shaking fingers, and fluttering heart I seized the paper and looked at it. The news was unbelievably good. Mackensen's army had been driven back south of Bucharest and badly defeated. The papers were jubilant. Bucharest, like Paris, was to be saved at the eleventh hour etc.

Weak from reaction I fled to my room and flung myself on my knees to thank God. The rest of the day I passed in comparative calm, but when I got up Tuesday morning I felt even worse than before. It was a very dull, dreary day. The agony of waiting for the mail had again to be gone through—an agony even greater than if the previous day's news had been bad. After that short respite from torture it was unbearable to fear being stretched on the rack again. But "the Moving Finger writes"—and turns not back or falters for human agony. The paper came—the news was as bad as could be—the Germans were again closing in on Bucharest. Constantine of Greece had played the Allies false and in England a cabinet crisis had at last been precipitated by the war situation and the Asquith government had fallen.

I passed a horrible afternoon and evening. And I could not even show my suffering. I had to repress every sign of it and go to a Missionary meeting, taking Mrs. Lockie along with me. I sat there while the women talked local gossip before the meeting began, as if they had never heard of the war, and I made no sign. I occupied "the chair" while the officers for the next year were elected and I put the business through with composure and despatch; I read a lengthy screed from the Mission Study Book and knew not one word I was reading; and I walked home afterwards with some of the village women and talked gossip, too—harmless gossip, of course, such as is permitted to ministers' wives, as to who was ill, and whose hens were laying and whose hens were not—and smiled and bowed and went through the motions. And inside of me my soul writhed and gibbered on its rack!

I got tea over and then settled down to keep the lid on for the evening. I sat and crocheted a medallion and talked to Mrs. L. and listened to her. She is a fluent talker and never, even by accident, says a word worth saying or hearing. She talked about people I never knew—told me who they married and where they were born and how many children they had. Ewan was away at a recruiting meeting and there was no one to take the edge off her. I smiled with the muscles of my face and compelled my tongue to utter sounds, while my mind spun round and round, impaled on one sharp point of torturing thought, unable to escape it. I thought over every possible chance of saving Bucharest, including a miracle, but I could see no hope. And Mrs. L. talked on!

The woman really amazed me. The war news seemed to have no more effect on her than if it were a conflict between the kingdoms of Mars. She asked what it was, agreed that it was very bad and very sad and then went placidly on with her fancy work and her biographies. If this had been the result of a fortunate strength of mind, such as I assuredly do not possess, which enabled her, after the first shock and pain, to go steadily on with the routine of life, suffering but calm, I should have admired and envied her. But it was nothing of the sort. It was simply the most inaudible insensibility and indifference. And if she had guessed what a turmoil of feeling I was concealing under my calm exterior she would have thought me crazy. Why, Bucharest was thousands of miles away! Why worry over what the Germans were doing there?

But bedtime came at last and I thankfully deposited Mrs. L. in the spareroom and fled to my own. Then the lid flew off. I had a nervous collapse, the result of my self-suppression all day. I had a wild fit of crying. When it was spent I felt calmer and finally fell asleep, but wakened up at two with a bad headache. I could not sleep again but lay there and listened to the high wind banging the shutters and rattling the windows.

Wednesday—bad news again, from Roumania, and *no* news from Greece. I worked doggedly all day and in the evening went to a Red Cross lecture in the church—an illustrated lantern affair. I looked at the pictures with blank eyes that stared straight through them and saw only the Huns closing in on the doomed Roumanian capital. Several soldiers were present and after the lecture they made recruiting speeches. Captain Cockburn, a boyish-looking fellow, whose brother was killed "somewhere in France" last spring, made a speech in which he drew a very gloomy picture of the war situation. My reason told me that, despite the Roumanian reverse, it was *too* gloomy—probably deliberately so, with an eye to stirring up reluctant recruits who might be disposed to think the war could be won without their aid. But reason has small power to help me in my present condition of nerves, and I felt as if Cockburn's speech was more than I could endure.

However, I slept well that night, being so worn-out that I ceased to suffer actively. And on Thursday came the news that Bucharest had fallen!

I was calm that afternoon with the calm of despair. Even the certainty of the worst is more endurable than the horror of suspense.

And Lloyd George is Premier of England—the ruler of the British Empire. It took the Roumanian crisis to bring that about. Nothing less could have put the foot of the Welsh lawyer on the neck of the aristocrats of England. Perhaps that was why the Roumanian disaster was decreed in the Councils of Eternity— since the gods themselves, it seems, must work out their purposes by indirect means. I believe that Lloyd George is one of the greatest men Britain has ever produced and that he, if anyone, can yet snatch victory from the jaws of defeat. Well, it is something to live in such times as these in spite of the agony of them!

Thursday night I could not sleep for hours. Lay awake thrashing over the Balkan situation and wishing I could skin Constantine of Greece alive. I woke early, lighted a lamp, and read Wordsworth. The classic calm and repose and beauty of his lines seemed to belong to another planet and to have as little to do with this world-welter as an evening star.

There was little news of any kind on Friday. Had a letter from Ella Campbell, telling me of her new girl-baby which is named after me. I have six namesakes now.

Yesterday brought alarming rumors of Greece going in on the side of Germany. Still, I feel strangely calm now—as if the climax of the war were passed, for good or ill. Mrs. Lockie went home today. Poor old soul, she told me she had had a lovely time. I think she had. She got to see all her old friends and I tried to make her visit pleasant. It was not her fault that the week was such a dreadful one for me and I am glad I succeeded in hiding my unrest and worry from her. But I pray that if ever I have to live through such a week again I will not have to keep up appearances before a Mrs. L.

Wednesday, Dec. 13, 1916
The Manse, Leaskdale, Ont.
The date should be written in capitals! Today came the news that Germany has offered peace. This means that she realizes that she is nearing the end of her rope, despite her Roumanian campaign. In so far, it is good news. For the rest it means nothing. The Allies will not be fools enough to put their heads into the noose she dangles. I feel sure they cannot be so mad. Yet there is always a dark possibility where Russia is concerned, and so the news has upset me. It has also upset the world. Every stock-market on the planet quivered and rocked under the impact.

As for Mackensen, he is still advancing in Roumania, though more slowly and gruesome rumors still come through from Greece. Constantine is said to be mobilizing. But I think the Allied Blockade will hammer some gumption into his head.

Saturday, Dec. 16, 1916
To-day we had some splendid news to offset the usual bad—a pungent taste of victory to flavor the bitterness of our recent diet of disaster. The French have won another great victory at Verdun and captured 10,000 of the enemy. Douamont and Vaux are in their hands again. Oh, Verdun, surely some new Homer will arise to sing you! What was Troy compared to you? The British, too, have made an advance in Mesopotamia, where there has only been dreary silence since the disaster of Kut-el-Amara last spring! And Greece—'tis said— is consenting to all the Entente demands. But Mackensen has captured Buzeu— a victory of evil omen to Roumania.

Today I had a letter from McClelland. The Frederick Stokes Co. have got my book. This seemed best; but I feel slightly disappointed that the Appleton dicker fell through. They split on the terms between them and Mac for the Canadian edition. I did not feel that I could insist on giving them the book, when Mac had been so generous in his contracts, so I told him he could give Stokes the book. Of course the standing of Stokes is equal to Appletons and they gave me the same terms—twenty percent on list price and five thousand down advance royalty. Such terms rather frighten me. Can I continue to write up to them? I am always haunted by the fear that I shall find myself "written out."

Mac writes enthusiastically of *The House of Dreams* and says it is so good he feels sure we shall have a record sale.

Monday, Dec. 18, 1916
....Frede...is coming for Christmas. It sounds inadequate to say I am thankful. It has seemed to me that I couldn't endure it if she didn't come—though I suppose, as in the case of the war news, I would have found that I *could* when

I had to. But mercifully I am to be spared the test. She is coming; and I am not so sure as I was a few days ago that I have quite lost all my youth. Then tonight Ewan came home from Presbytery and brought an evening paper which said that the British were closing in on Kut again and that the Roumanian army was safe behind the Sereth. The latter is *very* good news if confirmed.

Wednesday, Dec. 20, 1916
Got up, very tired still, and Edith and I drove to Uxbridge. Lloyd George's first speech as Premier, for which the whole world has been breathlessly waiting, was in the papers today. Never before, in the history of the race, I feel sure, was any speech so awaited by every nation in the world. The speech itself is a satisfying thing. The Kaiser will assuredly make some wry faces over it. There was no other war news of any importance.

Thursday, Dec. 21, 1916
All the papers were in a white fume of indignation today because that colossal old idiot, Woodrow Wilson, has been ass enough to send a peace note to the warring powers! They might save their splutter. He is a man of straw and not worth taking notice of. The Entente will put him delightfully in his place in due time.

I re-read Kipling's "Kim" tonight—that is, I finished re-reading it, having had it out several weeks—for alas, I get so little time for reading now, and what I do get I steal from sleep. I read it many years ago when it first came out and cared little for it as contrasted with his short tales. But this time I found it charming. And yet how strangely *far away* everything written before the war seems now. I felt as if I were perusing some classic as ancient as the Iliad.

Sunday, Dec. 24, 1916
The Manse, Leaskdale, Ont.
There was no especial war-news Friday. We had our annual Xmas concert at night. As it was necessary to take the two children and look after them myself, since Edith was one of the performers, I anticipated a hard evening. But Stuart was exceedingly good as he always is and Chester was good also. He is beginning to "have sense" when he is out and realize that he must keep quiet while a programme is going on. So I got on very well. Yesterday the war news was scanty but the Russians are still retreating in the Dobrudja.

The outstanding event of the week however, was Frede's arrival yesterday. We talked till two o'clock at night—a very orgy of confidences. Of course, I've felt rather rotten today as a consequence but who would regret it for so good a reason? I am going to have a real holiday while Frede's here—do nothing that I do not absolutely have to do but just have a good time. I am thankful that the Roumanian agony was over before she came. Were it going on now, it would spoil our visit.

Monday, Dec. 25, 1916
The Manse, Leaskdale
This has been an ideal Christmas day as far as weather is concerned. We had a nice, homey time. A Christmas tree in the morning gave great delight to Chester and we had a good dinner and lots of good talk.

Sunday, Dec. 31st, 1916
Thursday Frede and I drove over to Zephyr and spent the day with Lily Shier. Friday we had Mr. Fraser up to tea and Saturday we drove over to Wick and spent the day agreeably at the manse. Frede has certainly had Queen's weather for her visit.

The war news from Roumania remains rather bad.

And so 1916 closes. Looking back over it I can say that I have never, in all my life spent a year so physically hard—or indeed I may say more torturing mentally. From beginning to end it has been a hard year. It dawned for me in the anguish of alarm over Chester's condition—an anguish that lasted through January. February brought Ewan's six weeks of bronchitis. March brought my dreadful attacks of mammitis, anxiety over Stuart, and the worst of the Verdun agony. Then followed my terrible worry over Page and over the Austrian offensive in the Trentino. The first reports of the battle of Jutland and Kitchener's death were followed by a summer of almost unrelieved misery with cystitis. Then in the autumn came the Roumanian disaster. Verily, 1916 has been a black year.

And what of 1917? This is the third year that has come in since hell broke loose upon earth. Surely—surely it will be the last New Year of war. I look forward to it with dread. Some things will certainly be dreadful. And the Page worry still haunts me. I had not received any communication from Page since his letter of June, threatening a lawsuit, until just before Christmas when one came. I turned very cold as I opened it. But to my amazement it was a most suave epistle, signed by George Page, but as I know from internal evidence, dictated by Lewis, and saying that they were enclosing an advance royalty check thinking "it might come in handy about this time." Now, in the days of my most cordial relations with the Pages, they never sent me a royalty advance unless I asked for it. I am quite sure I know just what is behind the manoeuvre. Page imagines, because my book has not yet been announced by any firm, that his threats have deterred me from offering it or that I have failed to find a publisher. He therefore reasons that if he sends this nice "peace note" I may revert to him and give him the book after all. My curt and business-like acknowledgement of the receipt of the check will not give him much encouragement—or enlightenment.

But, as aforesaid, his attitude worries me. Still, matters are much better than at the dawn of 1916. Chester is a big rosy fat sturdy fellow, the picture of health. Stuart, who is walking now, and amusingly proud of it, is ditto. I am feeling much better physically than I did all summer and fall. So I hope 1917 will not be quite as nerve-racking as its predecessor. Yet I dislike to be wished "a happy New Year." It seems like a tempting of the gods!

1917

The Manse, Leaskdale, Ont.
Friday, Jan. 5th, 1917
I had an amusing letter from the editor of *Everywoman's World* today. At least, it was amusing to me. I recently wrote the story of "My Literary Career" for them at their request—only I didn't call it *that*. I called it "The Alpine Path", taking as motto the little verse which I wrote in my port-folio over thirty years ago—one of the verses of a short poem "The Fringed Gentian" which was published in the old *Godey's Lady's Book*. I have forgotten if I ever knew the name of the author but I have never forgotten the poem. As literature it was *non est*; but as an expression to the restless dreams and desires in my own soul it seemed to me perfect; and I echoed the last verse to the core of my being.

> "Then whisper, blossom, in thy sleep
> How I may upward climb
> The Alpine path, so hard, so steep
> That leads to heights sublime.
> How I may reach that far-off goal
> Of true and honored fame
> And write upon its shining scroll
> A woman's humble name."

When I grew discouraged and down-hearted in those old early years of struggle I used to repeat that verse over to myself and always there was something in it that inspired me afresh—and lured me on again to that "far-off goal."

Let me return to my sheep.

I sent "The Alpine Path" to the editor and he writes, professing himself as delighted with the story, but laments that there is nothing in it "concerning my love affairs." He is sure I must have had some. Will I not write an additional thousand words and tell my "adoring Canadian girls" of my pangs and passions!!!!!

Ye Gods! Suppose I were to do it!

I smile when I imagine what the "parties of the second part" would think if they picked up a copy of *Everywoman's World* and read a cold-blooded account of their "affairs" with me in it. But I do *not* smile when I imagine what their wives would think!

The dear public must get along without this particular tid-bit. I have snubbed that editor very unmistakably, telling him that I am not one of those who throw open the portals of sacred shrines to the gaze of the crowd.

But for my own amusement I *am* going to write a full and frank—at least as frank as possible—account of all my "love affairs". Possibly my grand-children—or my great grandchildren—may read it and say, "Why, we remember grandma as a thin, wrinkled, little, gray-haired body, always sitting in a warm corner, with a hug-me-tight on, reading a book (If I ever am a grand-mother I am going to do nothing but read books and do filet crochet!). Surely she couldn't really have lived these love stories."

Yes, dear unborn grandchildren, I did. For I was not always old and gray-haired and hug-me-tighted, you know. I was once young and brown-tressed, and wore lace and georgette crepe and silk stockings—and was called a flirt by my enemies; while my friends said "It is only Maud's way."

Well:—

I was twelve or thirteen years old, I am not quite sure which, when I first fell in love. There was a musical concert in Cavendish Hall one night, given by three graduates of the Blind School in Halifax. One of these was a Mr. Chisholm—a tall, slender young man with little golden dabs of side-whiskers, a most angelic face, and a more than angelic voice. He sang several songs and I, small miss, gazing up at him from the audience lost my heart completely.

It is the truth that I felt, for the first time a very strange sensation—a romantic yearning of hitherto unknown and of almost terrifying sweetness. It mattered not at all that my hero was blind. He was perfection, that was all. When I went home it seemed to me quite intolerable that I should never see him again and the world was suddenly big and lonely. I thought about him for a week—and then forgot him.

Fifteen years afterwards in Halifax I met his widow. Her husband had recently died and she was heart-broken—for it seems that he had really been all my young fancy had painted. I told her with a smile that her husband had been the first man I had ever been in love with and she laughed sadly and said that everyone who knew him loved him. So I did not bestow my virgin passion unworthily.

It seems absurd to speak of that experience as *love*; but, save in intensity and duration, what I felt that evening, as I gazed at the young singer's pale, spiritual face—it really *was* spiritual in spite of the side-whiskers—and listened to his thrilling voice differed in nothing from the similar emotions of after years. There was no passion in it, save of the soul, but that night I crossed the threshold of life's temple, though I did not penetrate to the inner shrine.

When I was fifteen a boy of fifteen said to me "I love you." Nathan Lockhart and I had been good school friends for a year, finding in each other an intellectual congeniality which we could find nowhere else in Cavendish. I liked Nate as a friend—and I liked to have him dangling after me, and "seeing me home" from the hall, and setting certain other girls wild with jealousy—not so much because they wanted him themselves; but they were Baptists and I was a Presbyterian and they were furious because their "minister's son" singled *me*, of a rival church, out. It really was glorious fun—I was a minx, I am afraid. But I did not care in the least for Nate, save as a friend. I wanted to because I thought it would be romantic; I tried to—I even wrote him some love-letters in response to various ardent epistles of his, which he used to while away the tedium of Sunday afternoons in the decorous parsonage by writing. But the fact remained that he meant nothing to me—had no power over me, either of the senses or of the heart. His memory, personally, means nothing to me. But he was the first male creature who said to me "I love you"—and no woman ever forgets the man who first says that. As a man he may mean nothing to her: as a symbol, he means more than any other ever can.

When I went out west in 1890 I was beginning to wonder how I could get free from the cobweb entanglement which linked me to Nate. He had talked boyishly and shyly about "after years"—when he "would be through college"—and I would be his wife. I had never said "yes" or "no". I knew in my heart I could never marry him but I hated to hurt his feelings by telling him so. He felt, so gossip informed me, very badly when I went away. But he went to college. We corresponded for a time but as years passed our letters grew cooler and less frequent—it happened that we did not meet again for a few years—we had both forgotten. At least, Nate never made any effort to resume the tenuous relationship that had somehow grown-up between us. Whether he would have done so had I been less cool and deliberately friendly I cannot tell nor does it matter. Somehow, I never like to think of my affair with Nate. Why I don't exactly know. It was a very innocent and harmless thing; perhaps the faint physical repulsion,—so faint as to seem as much spiritual as physical—which I always felt more or less conscious of when we were alone together colored subconsciously my memory of our friendship and affects it now. When a third party—Amanda, for instance—was with us I felt perfectly at home with Nate and enjoyed laughing and talking with him immensely. But the minute we were alone together, even if it were only walking primly down a country road, I felt ill at ease and conscious of a longing to escape. It was not shyness; I was never shy with Nate. It was simply the dissonance of two natures which required a third to harmonize them. If by any fluke Nate and I had ever married we would have been wretchedly unhappy.

Nate was not good-looking. He was tall and had curly hair, a pale face somewhat freckled, greenish-gray eyes which were apt to twinkle teasingly. Yet sometimes—especially when he wore a certain cap I remember well—he had decided distinction of appearance and used to make the other C. boys, even the handsome ones, look rather commonplace and "bumpkin-y". He was very clever and had a fine voice for singing. There was no charm of any kind about him—he was singularly lacking in it. Yet he was a very agreeable companion intellectually. I have most of his letters still—tied with ribbon in my old trunk. Once in a while I take them out and read them. They always bring those old days back very vividly. I have no photograph of Nate—there were no kodaks in those days; more's the pity.

Nate is a lawyer in some Western town—Estevan, Sask. I think. He does not seem to have risen as high as he should, considering his undoubted talents. He married a Miss Saunders of Halifax. I never heard anything about her save her name. Sometimes I have thought Nate might have written me a line of congratulation on my literary success. I used to talk over my aspirations with him in those old days. But he has never done so (I always have felt that Nate felt a little resentful that I let him drift out of my life, even though he had ceased to care. His vanity suffered a little, I think.) I remember he once told me, a little condescendingly, that I had a "very fair intellect" and if I could have a college course I might attain to "some success" in the world of letters!

Well, I went out to Prince Albert. I was sixteen that winter—and still a minx. Poor John Mustard could testify to that. I laughed at him, jeered at him, flouted him, made him the laughing stock of Prince Albert. And yet—when a man persisted in dangling after a girl who used him so didn't he deserve to be minxed? I hold he did.

I never could understand why John Mustard endured it. I was a pretty girl, but I was never such a distracting beauty that a man would be involved in such an infatuation because of my face; and in no other way did I try to attract him. Yet he kept up the crazy pursuit until he had to be flatly refused. There have never been any pleasant memories in connection with this one of my lovers. I have always felt queerly ashamed of the whole incident—I suppose because Mustard was such an awkward shambling shamefaced sort of lover.

Meanwhile, I was hand in glove with Willie Pritchard. I *liked* Willie I am quite sure better than any man I ever had as a friend. He was not in the least intellectual; but he was an exceedingly congenial companion. I always felt perfectly at home with him—enjoyed every minute I spent in his company. But I was not in the slightest degree in love with him, even sentimentally. He was as deeply in love with me as a boy of eighteen could be. We corresponded for six years—at first enthusiastically—then more coldly, till finally in the year before his death our letters were few and far between though very friendly. I think Willie had ceased to care for me save as a friend, though I never heard of him going with any other girl.

But while Will was my cavalier all through my P.A. year I had a certain *tendresse*—sentimental and concealed—for a young Englishman named Barwell who was in P.A. that year. I never met him but I used to hear him sing frequently at the many concerts and there was something about his *eyelids* that intrigued me. It was the eyelids with which I was in love, I am quite sure. My unrequited and unsuspected affection never bothered me in the least or prevented me in the slightest degree from having a splendid time with Will and tormenting John Mustard to the verge of insanity. Thus are we fashioned.

The next winter I was in Park Corner. Lem MacLeod and Edwin Simpson were both aspirants for the privilege of walking home with me from "Literary." I snubbed Edwin till he left me alone and went around with Lem. But all the time I had a romantic passion for Irving Howatt, who was not in the least interested in me. It went a little deeper than any of my previous ones. I did a great deal of day-dreaming that winter, with Irv as central figure; but I was not in the least unhappy because he was not in love with me. I had a jolly good time every way. I soon forgot all about Irv after I left Park Corner and as the years passed on began to find him a bit of a bore in our chance meetings. Then Fate played one of the jokes she loves. She gave me the "colored box" I had once so ardently wished for—and the spools were gone! Irv Howatt was at Dalhousie the winter I was on the *Echo* staff. He began calling to see me and "seeing me home" from Fort Massey. He was very "soft"—yes, "soft" is exactly the word, horrible as it is. If I had wished I could have had him at my feet—have been engaged to him in short order. I did not wish it; he bored me to tears; I loathed his attentions; I could not imagine what in the world had ever attracted me to him ten years before. I snubbed him so pointedly that he took the hint and came near me no more. How relieved I was!

As for Lem I never cared for him in the least and liked him only moderately. He liked me about as well as he could like anyone and wanted to marry me but he was not capable of really *loving* anyone, I think.

As for Edwin Simpson—well, there is no need, nor any desire on my part to say much of him.

Alec Macneill drove me around for years during my Cavendish vacations. I haven't any idea whether he cared for me or not. I think he would have liked to marry me but had sense enough to know he never could and was too shrewd to make a fool of himself over a girl he couldn't get. Alec has always been an excellent friend of mine and is very fond of me in a harmless platonic fashion to this day.

During the winter I was at Prince of Wales I went around with Lem but it was John Sutherland I was in love with. John was my cousin, a tall homely fellow but with something very charming in his personality. I really cared a goodish bit for Jack, though still not enough to hurt at all. He liked me pretty well too—was a *little bit* in love with me I think but not enough to hurt either. But I *could* have cared for John quite deeply if I had "let myself go." But it wouldn't have lasted—I would have grown tired of him. He could not have held me.

In Bideford Lou Dystant cared terribly. He was a good sort who mattered nothing to me. In Belmont, Fulton and Alf Simpson made asses of themselves more or less. I loathed Fulton but I *had* a queer unaccountable attraction toward Alf. For a few months I let myself feel it, though I never showed it. It was quite safe to feel it—I knew I had it easily in hand and could stifle it whenever it seemed good to me. Alf was homely and uncouth—but it was there, for all that. Finally, when I decided to marry Ed I said, "Now, this nonsense about Alf must end"—and end it did. That was all it amounted to.

Then I went to Bedeque and—for the first time—*loved*. Loved with heart and soul and sense—with everything but *mind*. For the first time I experienced the overwhelming power of senses—of sheer physical passion. It had never touched me before. My infatuation for Herman Leard was undoubtedly, the *deepest strongest* feeling I have ever experienced. It lacked only mental subjugation to be all-conquering. But that it *did* lack—and so I escaped. But I left something behind in that fiery furnace of temptation—and I brought something out. Passion gives and takes away.

In the years after I gave up teaching to live with grandmother there were various men. Joe Stewart, a good-looking inanity, drove me around one summer and was quite madly in love and horribly cut up because he knew there was no chance for him. He never told me this but used to pour out his woes to Clara Campbell. Henry McLure was another. These two men meant nothing to me in any way—I did not feel even friendship—nothing but a tepid toleration. As for Will Houston—well, *that* was not one of *my* "love-affairs" certainly.

For Oliver Macneill I felt a certain mad infatuation of the senses—nothing else. I lived through a few hectic weeks on his account and then forgot him utterly.

I was never in love with Ewan—never have been in love with him. But I was—have been—and am, very fond of him. He came into my life at its darkest hour when I was utterly lonely and discouraged with no prospects of any kind, and no real friends near me. At first I thought I could never care at all for his type of man; but I did; and I married him—and I have not regretted that I did so. I have been contented in my marriage, and intensely happy in my motherhood. Life has not been—never can be—what I once hoped it would be in my girlhood dreams. But I think, taking one thing with another, that I am as happy as the majority of people in this odd world and happier than a great many of them.

But I write not of these things for the Editor of *Everywoman's*. My grandchildren may include what they like in my biography. But while I live these things are arcana.

There was a recruiting concert at Udora tonight. Ewan and I drove up in the teeth of a biting wind and stinging drift to speak and recite respectively. It was past one when we got home. I must cut this sort of thing out for I cannot stand it. I am willing to do my bit but I can serve neither my family nor country by wrecking my health.

Wednesday, Jan. 10, 1917
Got a check for $2,500 from Stokes to-day, being half of my royalty advance. Tonight I began work on a new book, that is, I began looking over my notebook for ideas, etc.

Saturday, Jan. 20, 1917
Another week ended, thanks be—for it is one week nearer spring, for which long ceaselessly.

I had a letter from Hattie Smith this week. Her youngest brother has been killed in France, and her son is in the U.S. army and has been on the Mexican border. Is there a heart in the world that does not ache today?...

Today I had a letter from Amanda so compact of envy, malice and uncharitableness that it made me sick at heart to read it. She seems to be living in there at Mayfield, literally stewing in her own venom and exhaling it in everything she says or writes. What a tragedy to befall a nature that once promised fair. I never can get over the pity of it.

Sunday, Jan. 21, 1917
The Manse, Leaskdale
Really, this has been a dreadful day. All day a bitter and furious north-east wind blew. This is the only wind that affects us here and when it blows the house is really not fit to live in. All day the kitchen and dining room were literally as cold as a barn and the rest of the house little better. I was all alone from noon until Ewan came home from Zephyr church at ten. Storm outside and gloom and cold within. I put the children to bed after supper to ensure their being warm and then tried to read the evening away but was so blue and lonely I could not fasten my thoughts on my book. It is very seldom I feel as I felt tonight—like some imprisoned soul. I was very thankful when Ewan got home safe for I had been afraid the roads would be blocked. I seemed haunted all the evening by some dismal presentiment of impending evil.

The Manse, Leaskdale
Monday, Jan. 22, 1917
My presentiment came true. This morning word was 'phoned over that Goldwin Lapp had been killed at the front. The news upset me for the day. I could not help crying all the time. The Lapps are especial friends of ours and Goldwin was the first Scott boy to go to the front. He has been in the trenches for a year and four months and went through the Somme offensive without a scratch. Poor boy! We drove over to Lapps' this afternoon. It was bitterly cold and the roads were dreadful. And it was a heart-breaking errand. But is not life a heart-break these days? It seems to me that the very soul of the universe must ache with anguish.

The Manse, Leaskdale, Ont.
Tuesday, Jan. 30, 1917
To-day was fine though cold. Ewan and I had to go over to a family on the 5th to tea. The lady of the house shouted at me as if I were deaf and the "old man" remarked feelingly, "You bet your boots," whenever I said anything he agreed with. So it may be inferred that our sojourn there was not exactly a feast of reason. But we had a most excellent supper—for which I pardoned all, as my long cold drive had given me a ravenous appetite. But oh, these "pastoral visitations"!

Saturday, Feb. 3, 1917
Ewan went to Toronto Wednesday morning for a three days visit to take in the Social Congress. We have had it frightfully cold ever since—everything way, way below zero. On Thursday came the terrible news that Germany had declared her intention to indulge in unrestricted submarine warfare. It *sounds* very alarming but can she really do much worse than she has been doing? I doubt it.

I got Kenneth Cruit's photo today. He is an English boy with whom I have corresponded for four years at occasional intervals. He first wrote me when he was fourteen to tell me that he was delighted with my books. Last summer he wrote to tell me he had enlisted and would like to send me his photo in uniform "if I would not think it presumptuous". Needless to say I wrote and told him that I would be delighted to have it. So it came today—two of "it". I shall have one framed and hung on my "khaki row." He has such a pure winsome boyish face. I never saw a more attractive countenance. And it is this boy and thousands like him who must be sent away for cannon fodder because a crowned madman has set the world on fire. Oh, it is iniquitous! Kenneth's photo made me cry.

Yesterday the house was uncomfortable all day because of the cold. The gloom of the weather was increased for me by the receipt of a letter from Stokes saying that Page had written them claiming to have a contract for my next book etc. Of course I had expected Page would do this as soon as he had found out that I had given the book to Stokes. But it upset me miserably. Mr. Dominick asked for a copy of all the correspondence between Page and me, so I spent the afternoon copying it out—in so far as I have it, for unfortunately I have only memoranda of the contents of my own letters. I was very tired when it was finished and between over-exhaustion and worry I passed a sleepless night.

To-day was very stormy. Ewan got home in the afternoon. Shortly after his arrival a telephone message came up from Uxbridge saying that the U.S. have severed diplomatic relations with Germany because of the submarine outrage. Edith and I made some candy to celebrate the event!

Tuesday, Feb. 6, 1917
The Manse, Leaskdale
Still very cold. Ewan's tooth aches constantly and keeps us all in misery. Besides, today he has developed German measles!

The war news was scanty but the reports from the Tigris are good. But oh, that wretched Page affair! What will be the outcome? I find life bitter because of it.

Wednesday, Feb. 7, 1917
When I went to the office today and found two letters, one from Stokes and one from McClelland I was much upset—for I dreaded what the contents might be. But I had to assume a calmness I did not feel and chat to Mrs. Cook and Zella Mustard. I walked home with the latter, trying to talk; but my legs were trembling beneath me. I did not dare open the letters till after dinner. Even so I could not eat. Then I put Stuart to bed and shut myself up in the parlor to face it alone. But there was no further bad news so I felt great relief for the time being. Mac does not think that Page will really carry the matter to the courts. But Page is not a reasonable man so there is really no knowing what he will do.

Saturday, Feb. 10, 1917
Bitter cold again. With mail came a letter from Page. I took it in my hand as if it were a snake. Did not dare open it until after I had been to Mission Band

for I did not want to be unfitted for my duties. When I came home I opened it. It was not about the new book which was a relief. But it is a most barefaced attempt to cheat me out of a thousand dollars due me on my 1916 royalties on the ground of an alleged discovery of a "mistake" in the royalty reports of three years ago. I have written to Mac about it, asking if he advises taking legal action in the matter. Page is certainly a most thoroughgoing scoundrel. I shall likely lose this money and I cannot afford to do that, especially at present.

I was reading the proof of *Anne's House of Dreams* tonight. It should have been a pleasant task but there was no pleasure in it as matters are.

Sunday, Feb. 18, 1917
The Manse, Leaskdale, Ont.
A hard, hard week. Last Sunday was exceedingly cold. I felt very draggy and listless the whole day but went to the church in the afternoon and superintended the decorations for the memorial service for Goldwin Lapp at night. In spite of the fearsome cold the church was crowded. The service was sad and impressive. Oh, God grant that we do not have to have another.

Monday was the coldest day this winter—22 below zero. I thought my feet would freeze while I was working in the kitchen.

I had a letter from Stokes. Dreaded to open it; but there was nothing in it to cause fresh alarm—on the contrary, it was encouraging, for they are in possession of all the facts and are evidently of the opinion that Page cannot do much except "bluff." Nevertheless the possibility hangs over me like a sword of Damocles. All week I lived in dread of the next letter from them, telling what happened when Page received their reply. Every day I dreaded the mail. Yesterday the letter did come, enclosing one from Page, uttering all sorts of threats and stating that he had put the matter into the hands of his lawyers. Whether this necessarily means that he is really going to take the affair into court I do not know and cannot find out for a few days. The suspense will nearly drive me wild I think. I can neither sleep nor eat. My face frightens me when I look in the glass—it is so pale and haggard and hollow-eyed. Page worried another of his authors into an asylum and I verily believe he will drive me there, too. At present I have nothing to distract my thoughts. I am cooped up here by cold and snow and even if I could get out Leaskdale society offers no attractions to me. Ordinarily this does not matter. My work and my books furnish me with plenty of interest and amusement. But in this state of mind I cannot read or do anything but necessary routine work and I find it very hard to get through the days. It is the *uncertainty* that is so terrible. If I knew that I *had* to fight and *what* I had to fight I think I could summon up enough "grit" to face the issue squarely. But I *know* nothing and I torture myself with a hundred conjectures and suppositions.

The war news yesterday was not good either. The Germans have scored a local win in Champagne. In itself it is not very alarming but it may be the opening of another terrible offensive. *That* is the dreadful thought. It was just about this time last year that they opened their Verdun offensive.

Life has been so full of terror and worry these past two years. I begin to feel a certain weariness I never felt before. And how I dread the coming week. What news will it bring? This afternoon I am alone with the children. They have to be amused, poor little souls, and I find it hard, for my heart is not "at leisure from itself"—it is eaten up with worry and dread.

Sunday, Feb. 25, 1917
The Manse, Leaskdale, Ont.
Have been nearly "visited" to death this week. The war news was good on Monday from both the Ancre and the Tigris. Went to Uxbridge and had another dental seance. Drove home over the wildest roads in a snowstorm. Tuesday I had a young bride and groom to tea and was busy all day preparing for them. Then sat and talked to them until eleven, while my soul yawned and my back ached and my mind whirled around on the Page matter.

Wednesday was a fine and pleasant day—a great rarity this winter. A reassuring letter from McClelland buoyed me up and relieved my mind to such an extent that I enjoyed our evening drive when we went out to tea. The enjoyment ended with the drive, however.

Thursday I went to the Red Cross at Jas. Mustard's and when Ewan came for me we stayed the evening. The Mustards are nice people and ordinarily I do not look on a visit there as an umpleasant duty. But I was too tired Thursday night to enjoy myself and only wished I was home in bed. Friday we again had to go out to tea and then to a Guild social in the evening with both children. Stuart, being made too much of, could not sleep and grew very cross and fretful. Edith was away so by the time I got them both home and to bed I was too tired to sleep. Yesterday we again had company to tea and were late in getting to bed. Today was Sunday and I have had a blessed rest. Fred Leask came down and took Chester up for the afternoon and Stuart was good. So I had a good "read"—to my great content, as dear Pepys says. I am at present reading *Pepys' Diary*. I never read it before though I have heard of it all my life. It is the most unique book. No one but an Englishman could have written it. It is a book without a spark of wit, without a gleam of conscious humor, without passion, imagination or insight. It is a book which deals almost wholly with commonplace people and incidents. And yet it is packed with interest from cover to cover and is irradiated on every page with unconscious humor. Its great charm is its sense of reality. It is impossible to believe that it is over two hundred years since Pepys lived. He must have been alive yesterday. The people he mentions—his neighbors and servants and sweethearts—are alive. We know them. Pepys himself is a most naive and engaging old sinner in his love of fine clothes, of "good eating" and of "gadding abroad looking for beauties." The book is delightful. I always come back to my own world after reading it with a jolt as if I really had been back in the 1660's.

Sunday, March 4, 1917
The Manse, Leaskdale, Ont.

The war news has been uncannily good all the week. The British have been advancing steadily on the Somme front and on the Tigris also. In the latter theatre they have recaptured Kut and wiped out the disgrace of last spring.

The children have both had a very severe cold all the week. Stuart took it Monday night with an attack of croup which gave me a bad scare. But he has had no return of it although his cold has been very bad.

Looking over this journal I find that I have written little of Stuart compared with what I wrote about Chester. This may be partly because he is not such a novelty but more, I think, because I about "wrote myself out" in that line and could only repeat myself if I went into raptures over Stuart. It is certainly not because I love him less, or find his development any less enthralling and delicious.

He is entirely different from Chester in every way—in personality as well as appearance. He seems to have less aggressiveness—he is a much quieter baby. He is what might be called "a sweet child." He looks like a big wax doll and has dear, appealing ways and delicious little gurgles of laughter and fun. He has remarkably beautiful eyes—large, soft, sky-blue, clear, full of vivacity and yet dreamy, crimson cheeks, and silky thick hair that curls in dear ringlets all over his head.

Stuart Macdonald

The Ontario government has given the suffrage to women. So I may vote yet ere I die! I wonder! Certainly I shall never vote along merely party lines. But I am glad it has come. Soon, I think, all the provinces will fall into line and then we will have Dominion suffrage. But I truly doubt whether it will make as much change in things as its advocates hope or its opponents fear.

Tuesday, March 13, 1917

Stokes had planned to issue the *House of Dreams* in August. But Mac writes me that they are going to bring out a small trial edition in June to test the reality of Page's threats. It will shorten the period of suspense. But how I shall dread June. The whole spring will be embittered for me by my anxiety and worry.

Friday, Mar. 16, 1917
The Manse, Leaskdale, Ont.

I did not think any development of the war could surprise me. But one has come. Today word came of a Revolution in Russia and the abdication of the Czar. The whole thing is so stupendous that I feel dazed. Internal conditions in Russia have been disquieting for some time but no hint of this was ever foreboded. What the outcome will be God knows. Most of the despatches take the view that it is a good thing for the Allies since the Russian court was infested with pro-Germans. It *will* be a good thing if it holds. But no one can tell what will come of such an overturn. It is not likely the reactionaries will give up without a struggle and if Russia is distracted by internal broils her power of assisting her allies will be lessened. But why worry? It is all part of the Great Plan. After the strange series of dreams I have had since the war began I have become a fatalist. I believe that all is planned out in the councils of Eternity—yea, in the words of the old theology, foreordained. Some day, when I have time, I shall write out those dreams in this journal. To say the least they have been curious.

Sunday, Mar. 18, 1917

To-day I read "A Hilltop on the Marne"—a quite delightful little thing, though lacking the charm of "My Home on the Field of Honor".

No sign of spring yet. To-day was bitter and wintery. These winter Sundays are dreary enough but not so dreary as they used to be at home in those few winters before I left it. How terrible they were! I have been glancing over some pages of my journal written then. Life is a very different thing now. I am often—very often—tired and worried. But I never have any of the terrible days or hours of nervous agony I suffered then. They seem like strange terrible dreams to me now. But—for nothing is perfect—there were some very sweet-things in my life then that are lacking now and which I often long for—walks of wood and shore, accompanied by invisible companions of dream and fancy— friends and lovers. I hanker oftentimes for their wild, elusive flavor.

But my two little sons—they fill life and heart and soul. When Chester puts his arms about my neck and says "*Dear* little mother" or when Stuart cuddles his curly little head against my breast I miss nothing, lack nothing of bliss. Life is full and perfect and complete at such moments.

But—I *would* like an old-time walk in Lover's Lane at sunset—or along the old haunted sandshore in the twilight!

Sunday, Mar. 25, 1917
The Manse, Leaskdale, Ont.

Last Monday Ewan came home with the mail and to me, waiting in the usual tense suspense, said, "Great news today." Well, it *was* great news, and it has so continued all the week. But whether it is *good* news is not yet established and until it is I shall permit myself no rejoicing. But the Germans have begun to retreat on the Western front and are still retreating. The Allies have captured all the objectives for which they fought last year, in the campaign of the

Somme. But *why* are the Germans retreating? It does not seem on the face of things that they are compelled to just now. Has Hindenburg some deep-laid scheme on hand? Does he mean to turn on the advancing allies when he has allured them from the shelter of their trenches? I fear it. On the other hand, he may be only doing, while weather conditions favor him, what he knows he would be obliged to do in a short time under less favorable conditions.

All this week we have been "visiting" frantically in an effort to overtake our work in that line before the roads break up. We have been home only one evening and I am deadly tired. It has been, for me, a wasted week.

Yesterday I read a "ten year letter"—one Frede Campbell wrote me ten years ago. I suppose she also read mine. It is a rather gruesome business—too much like opening a grave. At thirty-two I still had the courage to write such letters. Now, at forty-two, I could never dare to write another. What changes there have been since those letters were written! Frede was in Stanley then, teaching school, and I was in the old home, an unknown, obscure scribbler, past my youth. Now I am a wife and happy mother and have written "the famous book" Frede predicts and which I only dreamed of then. The ten years have made a vast change in almost everything that concerned us. And those letters were written before the war! That in itself would be change enough.

The changes for me have been for the better and I think for Frede also. But all change, even if it be for the better, has an element of bitterness in it and bitterness is something which makes itself felt above and before all other flavors.

Sunday, Apr. 1, 1917
Leaskdale, Ont.
The "break-up" came the first of the week and now we have spring, albeit a drab and muddy one as yet. The news from the western front is still fair but there are alarming rumors of a German thrust at Riga. We have been still visiting wildly, despite the condition of the roads.

This week I read Butler's "Way of All Flesh". It is a clever book but not by any means the great novel some have pronounced it. It is full of truths and half truths and yet it is on the whole a very false book. It impresses me as having been written by a man who was himself congenitally incapable of feeling any lofty or inspiring passion or even any decent, pleasing ordinary emotion. He therefore refused to believe that any other person could feel such, and proceeded to docket anyone who claimed to as a hypocrite or a fool. Real pleasure I found not in reading the book, but a certain titivating intellectual delight I did find.

Last night, being alone, I read over all Nate Lockhart's old letters—for the first time since my marriage. Their charm for me now lies in the power they possess to transport me back into the past—into a world unrent by the tragedies of the present....It is a long time since I heard anything of Nate save the fact that he was living in Estevan, Sask., was a lawyer, and had two boys. It has always been a little wonder to me that Nate should have chosen the law as his profession. I remember one spring evening twenty-seven years ago—yes, it *is* twenty-seven when Nate and I were loitering home in the twilight from some-where and holding high converse on destinies and ideals such as youth revels in. Nate, in speaking of what he would like to be, said emphatically—I recall the exact spot of the road where he said it and the stars that were glittering over the dark firs in the school woods, just beyond—"I would *never* be a lawyer! Making a living out of other people's quarrels seems to me a dirty trade."

Hum! Ha! Well, alas and alack, Nate is not the only one of that philandering couple who has been compelled or allured to forsake or compromise with the ideals we cherished then. I have surrendered many of mine.

Oddly enough, for the last eight years I have carried on a very delightful correspondence with an uncle of Nate's—the Rev. A.J. Lockhart of Winterport, Me. He is a writer of essays and verse and is known in the literary world as "Pastor Felix". Years ago Nate's possession of this uncle cast a glamor over him in my eyes. It was to me quite wonderful that I actually knew a boy whose uncle had written and published books. Nate had one of his books—a volume of poetry entitled "The Masque of Minstrels."

When "Anne" was published "Pastor Felix" wrote to me about it. Of course, he knew—and knows—nothing regarding my old love affair with his nephew. He is now an old man. His verse is rather weak but he writes delightful prose and his letters are among the most enjoyable I receive. Well, Nate's letters are re-tied and relocked away. It is not likely I will think of them again for many more years. But neither can I ever quite forget them.

This week, too, I saw a paragraph in the Charlottetown *Guardian*, under the elegant caption, "An Island Booze Fighter", stating that the Rev. Edwin Simpson had resigned his pastorate to become the leader of the Anti-Saloon Association of Rhode Island. I wonder if Ed has got tired of preaching doctrines he doesn't believe in. The last time I talked with him he told me that he could no longer believe in the divinity of Jesus; and when I asked him why he preached it then, he replied that he thought "*e*luding the people was not *de*luding them." Possibly "eluding" people grows wearisome in time.

Sunday, Apr. 15, 1917
Leaskdale, Ont.
A cold, bleak spring so far, no "lure of April days" yet. There has been a fortnight of "good" war news—with huge casualty lists. The British and French are slowly advancing on the western front, purchasing a little village or so a day with the lives for which mothers have agonized. The U.S. has formally declared war at last. I wonder if future historians will acclaim Wilson as a great statesman or a man of straw. It seems impossible to decide just now. I incline to the straw theory. He is too fine a phrase-maker to be anything else.

I went to Toronto on the third and spent a very enjoyable week. I kept the fact of my being in out of the papers so was not bored with "teas" etc. but got around quietly and saw a lot of people I wanted to see. Also did much shopping with great detriment to my purse—for the prices of things are alarming.

I spent most of my time with Mary Beal who is a chummy congenial creature. My last evening I went up to South Drive and spent it with the MacMurchy's. They are as baffling and inhuman as ever. I always feel when I am with them that I am among the inhabitants of another planet. Their mannerisms intensify with passing years and are now so strongly marked as to be much less amusing and much more disagreeable.

I dropped into Mac's and saw the cover design of *Anne's House of Dreams*—a pretty, *sellable* thing. Of course it does not in the least resemble the house or setting I had in mind but "the trade" all seem to be charmed with it and that is the main thing when it comes to "big sellers". Page has been trying his best to make trouble but the Stokes Co. seem to know just how to manipulate him. He has backed down sufficiently to ask us to "arbitrate the affair" but we have all declined with thanks. I begin to believe that all his threats have been only a gigantic "bluff" but I shall be uneasy until the book is published. He *did* try to get his Toronto lawyers to take up the Canadian end of the case but I found out that they refused, telling him he had no chance. His American lawyers may be less scrupulous.

Thursday, Apr. 19, 1917
The Manse, Leaskdale, Ont.
Another of the little heart breaks of motherhood! Chester last night moved into a room of his own—poor little man. He has always slept in his little crib in the corner of our room. Night after night I have looked on his chubby, rosy face just before I turned out the light. Always in the darkness I felt and loved his nearness. Always in the morning his roguish smiles gleamed across to me. But last night he slept alone—like a little hero, too, making no fuss about it. The change, painful as it is to me, is necessary. Stuart has been sleeping all winter with Edith; but I do not like this and he must henceforth have the crib. He is a rosy, adorable occupant—but oh, my little first-born man! Another step away from me.

We are in an orgy of housecleaning. Amen.

Sunday, Apr. 29, 1917
A strenuous week! We cleaned the library—a task involving the carrying out, dusting and carrying back of about 1200 books!—the parlor, and papered the kitchen. Friday night I was as tired as a beaten dog. But instead of going to bed as my bones yearned to do I had to dress and drive myself and Mrs. Oxtoby to Udora, four miles away, to recite at a "Maple Syrup Social" given in aid of the Methodist church there—more fool I! It was one o'clock when I got to bed.

Monday, May 7, 1917
Today I wrote to the Attorney of the Author's League and put my case re Page and the royalties into his hands. I am dubious about the outcome but I will not tamely sit down and let Page cheat me at pleasure.

The Russian situation continues precarious but the crisis seems past for the time being.

Wednesday, May 9, 1917

The news was rather depressing today. The Germans have retaken Fresnoy, captured with the loss of so much Canadian blood. It is, I suppose, only an incident—but such incidents are disheartening enough.

We were out to tea tonight and I'm afraid I caught a cold. I was over tired and there was a bitter wind. It keeps so cold. There has been no spring like this since I came to Ontario. The crop outlook is not good and this is serious. The spectre of famine is threatening the whole world and the submarine menace is growing. What will be the outcome? Prices now are terrible. Potatoes are four dollars a bag and may soon not be obtainable at any price. We allow ourselves a ration of *five* a day. Did I ever dream I should come to that with *potatoes*. I can remember when they sold for ten cents a bushel at home and even just before I was married twenty cents a bushel was a big price.

Sunday, May 13, 1917

Still cold. Stuart has been sick all the week and I have been sick since Thursday with stomach and intestinal trouble. The war news has been scanty and every day the prices go up. We finished our garden this week. Not an inch of space has been left unutilized this year.

On Monday Ewan leaves for a short trip to the Island. I have not been thinking of it for I cannot go down this year. But now that he is going I grow very homesick and wish I were going, too. When he comes back I plan to go up to Macdonald College and spend a week with Frede—and then settle down to work for the summer.

Monday, May 14, 1917
The Manse, Leaskdale, Ont.

I drove Ewan to the station this morning and saw him off for the homeland. Then I came home to find a letter from Bertie McIntyre. I have been slightly intoxicated ever since, I think, her news was so unthought-of and delightful— or rather predictive of delight. There is a strong likelihood of her coming to Toronto to live! Laura and her husband are going to move there and Bertie thinks she will come, too, if she can get a position on the Toronto teaching staff. With Frede at Macdonald and Bertie in Toronto, I should really have little more to wish for. But it will not happen—it would be too beautiful. I will not think of it or build on it lest I taste the bitterness of disappointment.

Thursday, May 24, 1917

A nice, warm, pleasant "24th" surely! It has blown a hurricane and been bitterly cold, with showers of *snow*. All this week has been cold.

On Tuesday I got the shock of my life. A letter from Frede Campbell informed me that she had been married the preceding Wednesday in Montreal to Lieut. Cameron McFarlane two days before his expected sailing on his return to the front!

I said, when the Czar of Russia abdicated that I should refuse ever to be surprised again. So I was *not* surprised by this—I was only dumfoundered, flabbergasted, knocked out and rendered speechless!

I suppose it is because I feel the thing so deeply that I write this frivolously about it. Something about it seems to hurt me terribly—the element of change and doubt that enters into it all I suppose. I knew that Lieut. McFarlane had been courting her ever since his return home on leave but she had written me more than once that nothing could come of it; and though I did not feel sure of *that* I did not dream that she would be married before the war was over— nor, it seems, did she, until about six hours before the ceremony.

It hurts me to think that I did not

"Lieut. Cameron MacFarlane of the Princess Pats"

see Frede married. We had always planned that, if she should marry, her wedding would be in this old manse where we have had such good times, and Ewan was to marry her. But plans! The war has upset a few!

Oh, I hope poor Frede will be happy! She has never had much happiness. I have always had a nasty feeling that Frede was not *meant* for happiness—that her nature was and her life must be, essentially tragic—and this in spite of all her laughter and jollity and race-of-Joseph-ness. A war marriage to a bridegroom who is on his last leave is a dubious thing.

Well, perhaps, Bertie *will* come to Toronto, now. I felt that I dare not hope that she and Frede could *both* be so near me. But if the events of the near future will remove Frede to God knows where, I may be permitted to have Bertie, that my soul be not utterly starved of friendship. But not even Bertie can fill Frede's place.

There has been rather good news from the Italian front this week and Russia is struggling terribly to pull herself together. In spite of the hurricane of rumors about a separate peace I do not think there is any real danger of that. The very real and dangerous certainty is that her army is wholly disorganized and, come the best that can, will not be anything to reckon on or with this summer.

Yesterday I took Chester to Zephyr and left him with Lily. He will stay with her until my return. Ewan returned today.

I leave tomorrow for Macdonald where poor Frede is pluckily going on with her work by way of a honeymoon.

Saturday, May 26, 1917
Teacher's Residence,
Macdonald College, Quebec

Yesterday morning Ewan drove me to Uxbridge. 'Twas a delightful day for a wonder. A fine day is such a novelty this spring. I reached Toronto at noon and stayed there until eleven. Rung in with Mary Beal and had a jolly time. Saw Balfour in the street procession. Wound up with a "movie" at the Strand at night and motored to the train afterwards. Spent a poor night as usual on the train and reached St. Anne's about nine the next morning. Frede met me and we proceeded to talk!!!

I have a nice room in the teacher's residence. Frede gave a little tea to the house girls this afternoon which I enjoyed very much.

We spent the evening in my room thrashing things over. I found out that Frede had sent a telegram to me the day she was married which I never received. This cured a little ache which I admit I had felt ever since I got her letter. I had thought that she had let three days elapse after her marriage before letting me know and that *did* hurt. I might have known Frede wouldn't do such a thing.

But I hardly know what to think of her marriage. She is eight years older than Cameron MacFarlane. It is all very well to say that he is old for his years. No doubt he is—two years in the hell of the battle front might reasonably age a man! And Frede is young for hers. Nevertheless, while 34 and 26 is not so bad 50 and 42 sounds dubious and Nature's logic is very relentless.

Again, I do *not* think Frede loves him in any real sense of the word. They have been friends for years—she likes him—but—but—but! However, it all may turn out better than I expect and little worse than I hope.

Cameron has not left Canada yet after all. He is with his regiment in New Brunswick, as all their orders were recalled after conscription was mooted. The vexing side of this is that had they known it was to be so they could just as well have come down to Leaskdale and been married as not. Poor Frede is in a rather trying position here, on a gossipy campus, amid acquaintances who are not all friends or all friendly. I think my presence is a help and comfort to her—a bit of family backing and countenance, as it were. The gods grant us all pluck and patience and good digestion! We need it.

Saturday Night. June 2, 1917
Macdonald College, Quebec

This week has seemed as long as several weeks—judging by what we have crammed into it. I have been having a delightful time—the pleasantest "vacation" I have had since my marriage.

Macdonald College is a beautiful place, especially now in the opening bloom of spring. The buildings and equipment are wonderful. I have been feeling a queer, half-resentful feeling of regret that I could not have spent some of my formative girlhood years in such a place. There is no sense in feeling resentful about it. Nobody was to blame—except the fates. Yet I feel as if I had been cheated out of something I would have enjoyed enormously and which would have been of great benefit to me. I envied the girls who sat under the trees of the campus. And *they* envied *me*, and stood in my presence with timid awe and admiration such as schoolgirls feel when they meet the writer of books they love. And so the world wags—truly "a mad, world, my masters."

I have met a great many delightful people—and some not at all delightful, but all interesting to me because I have heard Frede talk of them so much.

Sunday evening Frede and I went to St. George's church. We sat nearly at the top and as we came out we became aware that the organist—a rejected suitor of Frede's by the way—was playing Mendelssohn's *Wedding March*. There were significant smiles on several faces. If "Chippy" were trying to get a bit of revenge I must say he took a peculiar method. I think it was an abominable trick.

Frede and I spent Monday in Montreal shopping—and talking so continuously that we were "dead beat" on returning home. Tuesday afternoon a friend of Frede's gave one of those abominable teas at which I was the guest of honor, terribly bored. In the evening Mrs. Fisher gave a dinner for Frede and me in the Practice Dining Room at which the Ladies of the faculty were guests. I rather enjoyed it. The dinner itself, cooked and served by the Household Science Girls, was exquisite. But these undiluted "hen parties" are rather cloying affairs—especially when they are formal. Oh, for one agreeable, sociable rooster!

Afterwards Frede and I sat up until an unearthly hour and thrashed over her problems. We laughed so much during the process that we did not make any great headway in solving them.

Wednesday we went into Montreal and heard Balfour speak in the Royal Victoria College—and incidentally saw heaps of raw crude human nature in the crush. I was somewhat disappointed in Balfour's speech. It was commonplace—even hesitating; and he seemed to have as much difficulty in disposing of his hands as the rawest recruit at some rural "debating society." But the might of Britain was behind him and there was something about him that said "English Gentleman" very unmistakably. As we sat on the steps of the Residence that evening Frede said, "The Germans can do what they like to increase their population after the war but they'll never be able to get anything that looks like him." That's about it.

We have our meals in the College dining room—and Institutional meals seem alike the world over. Wholesome—oh, very wholesome!

We were out to tea twice this week and enjoyed it. Friday was spoiled for me by a letter from Ila saying that Carl had had his leg blown off above the knee at Vimy Ridge and was now in a hospital in England. Poor little fellow! It seems dreadful that he should be maimed for life like that. But Ila says he is very cheerful and plucky over it. I suppose he is almost thankful to escape from that inferno even at such a price.

Last night Frede and I had the most beautiful walk along the river road in the moonlight and talked of a thousand things in past and present and future. The moonlight danced on the silver river and the banks dreamed in shadow; and somehow Frede and I drew very near to each other in spirit and knew what was in each other's hearts without need of words.

The war news has been scanty this week and the Russian situation seems to be going from bad to worse. The Montreal papers give fearfully pessimistic views possibly with the idea of inducing Quebec to accept conscription. But I long for a good, optimistic "Globe" *Summary*, just to brace me up. There was an editorial in the Montreal *Star* Friday night that almost squelched me.

"Three good pals"
[*Stuart, Ewan, Chester*]

Wednesday, June 6, 1917
The Manse, Leaskdale, Ont.
I left St. Anne's at 11.30 last Sunday night. It was a cold, windy, lonely night and I felt horribly blue over leaving Frede but glad, in spite of my good times, to be going home to my darling boys. How I had longed for them! Every night after I went to bed I could feel Stuart's dear little chubby arms around my neck.

I reached Toronto the next morning, spent a satisfactory day from a business standpoint, and got on the Uxbridge train exceedingly tired, but promising myself a good rest on the way out, varied by a refreshing dip or two into a new book Mr. McClelland had given me. But I am not one to whom is allotted rest. The train was crowded and an elderly commercial traveller shared my seat. That man deliberately set out to talk me to death! He poured out on my weary ears a ceaseless stream of facts concerning politics, the war, conscription, woman suffrage, and the way he and his wife brought up their family and apportioned their income. Had I gone on to Blackwater I should have been a dead woman. As it was, I staggered off at Uxbridge with a faint spark of life still in me which a pleasant drive home with Ewan in the spring twilight fanned into a respectable flame once more.

Friday, June 8, 1917
Leaskdale, Ont.
After a weary time of inaction the war news was good today. The British have captured Messines Ridge—a notable success. The Russian situation seems to be clearing up a little.

Hugh Mustard died to-day. Ewan and I feel his death keenly. He was not only our right-hand man in the church but our warm personal friend. He and his wife met us in Uxbridge when we came here after our wedding trip and I have always remembered his hearty handshake. I feel his death as I have not felt any other death in the congregation.

Thursday, June 14, 1917
Leaskdale, Ont.
Yesterday I almost felt like running up the flag—although the flag raising spirit has pretty nearly left me. The news came that Constantine of Greece has "abdicated"—that is the Allies have finally packed him and his German queen out of Greece, bag and baggage—a year and a half too late. Venizelos will come to his own now and have a chance to retrieve what he can out of the wreck of his hopes.

Last night Edith and I drove ourselves to Zephyr where I had promised to recite at a Red Cross Social. A terrific thunderstorm came up and we had to stay there all night and had a bad time all round. Came home early this morning, rushed through my work and went to Red Cross over on the 6th in the afternoon. Oh, for my bed!

Saturday, July 7, 1917
Leaskdale, Ont.
Chester's birthday—he is five years old! It seems hard to believe that it *can* be five years since I saw that wee baby-lad of mine. He is a big, sturdy fellow, rosy and tanned, the picture of health. In some ways he has been a rather difficult child to manage—he is so determined and so full of ebullient energy. But this period seems almost over. He is now beginning to develop an understanding and self-control that should gradually make my task much easier. He is a very loyal, straightforward little soul, with a very tender heart. He seems free from deceit or low cunning— from "mean" faults in general.

We arranged to celebrate his birthday by a picnic in the woods up the old mill-race, to which we invited his bosom chums, Cameron Leask and Douglas Madill. But we had no sooner reached our picnic ground than a thunderstorm came up and we had to flee home and have our picnic on the veranda.

The war news this past week has been good. Russia has had a wonderful sort of resurrection and Brusiloff has opened an offensive that seems to be sweeping everything before it. But will it last? Somehow, I haven't much faith in the stability of Russia's efforts. Every offensive she has begun has petered out. It is

"Chums"
[*Douglas Madill,*
Cameron Leask,
Chester Macdonald]

to be hoped that this will be an exception. Yet I have little confidence in her revolutionary army.

Saturday, July 21, 1917
Leaskdale, Ont.

Verily I say unto you put not your trust in Russians. After a week of wonderful successes they are being driven back so rapidly that their retreat is alarmingly like a rout. Traitorous regiments are deserting their posts—probably bribed thereto by German gold. The situation could hardly be much worse than it is at present.

Today I got my author's copies of "Anne's House of Dreams", although it will not be "published" until August 24th. Stokes gave up his idea of bringing out a trial issue in June. I have not been worrying over the matter lately. I know Page can do nothing and I feel tolerably sure he will not be such a fool as to try.

The *House of Dreams* is nicely "made", with a pretty cover design. The latter is very illogical of course. Twenty-five year old Anne looks like a girl

"Cover Design"

of seventeen. But it is all very dainty and will "catch the trade." I do hope the book will be a success. It would be humiliating to me if it failed to make good, for I would feel that Stokes would think they had been led into giving "big terms" to an author who could not "deliver the goods." Then, too, its failure will make glad the heart of Page. Myself, I think the book is the best I have ever written not even excepting *Green Gables* or my own favorite "The Story Girl." But will the dear public think so? The Canadian advance orders are 12,000 copies—a huge advance on the numbers sold by Page, who never sold more than 3,000 and very seldom more than one or two.

The scene of the story is laid mainly at "Four Winds Harbor"—New London harbor was in my mind, though I altered the geography to suit my requirements. "Captain Jim" is a pet creation of mine. He had his first incarnation several years ago in a short story of mine published under the title "The Life Book of Captain Jesse." Some of the stories he tells were ones I used to hear Grandfather tell many years ago—especially the one about Father Chiniquy.

Sunday, Aug. 5, 1917

Somehow I feel horribly depressed. This has been a hard week. The first part was swelteringly hot. Monday, Tuesday and Wednesday nights were so hot that it was impossible to sleep in the house. So we slept outside, Ewan and the boys behind the bamboo screen on the veranda, myself in the hammock under the big apple tree that never bears any apples.

All my life I have nursed a secret wish to "sleep out." I have always wanted to go camping. Now my wish was attained. It was a beautiful clear night with a full moon in the south-west. The breeze whispered softly, the perfume of flowers floated on the dewy air—all was according to Hoyle. But alas! There were mosquitoes—scores of them. Mosquitoes don't know the horn-book of romance. I stood it until two o'clock and then retreated to the library floor.

The war news has been bad. The Russians are retreating—and retreating—*and* retreating. The whole army seems demoralized. Brusiloff has resigned or been dismissed—a bad thing, for he was a great general. Where will it end?

Wednesday, Aug. 8, 1917
Leaskdale, Ont.
Monday afternoon I went in to Toronto and met Bertie McIntyre that night in the Union Station.

"On the lawn one summer day"
[*Ewan, Chester, Stuart, Bertie, Maud*]

It is six years since I saw her last. I expected we would feel a little strange at first—that those six years would hang between us like a misty little veil. But there was nothing of the sort. We were at one from the moment of our meeting. For all the difference, our parting at Kensington Station might have been yesterday. Bert is the same dear girl, as full of fun and philosophy as ever. We came home yesterday and last night sat in the parlor until the wee sma's, settling up a number of theological and ethical problems that had lain over since our last sederunt.

Wednesday, Aug. 15, 1917
To-day Mr. Warner motored us to Lake Simcoe where we had a picnic, a delightful row, and a glimpse of an aeroplane. As I watched it calmly soaring over us I quoted to Bertie a random verse that came to my mind.

> "With the majesty of pinion
> Which the Theban eagles bear,
> Sailing with supreme dominion,
> Through the azure fields of air."

It is all very wonderful. But will humanity be any the *happier* because of aeroplanes? It seems to me that the *sum* of human happiness remains much the same from age to age, however it may vary in distribution, and that all the "many inventions" neither lessen nor increase it. After all, "the kingdom of heaven is within you."

Friday, Aug. 17, 1917
The Manse, Leaskdale, Ont.

Ewan and I drove Bertie to the station this morning and I saw her depart with a sick heart—for she is not going to stay east after all. I knew *that* was too good to be true. We have had a lovely time during her visit; but life seems lonely now that it is over.

Bertie and I had a most memorable and glorious walk at sunset last evening up the north hill and sought pictures in the clouds until we must certainly have been adjudged utter lunatics if anyone were watching us from the houses along the road—as probably someone was. We would walk along our faces fixed on the sky, then suddenly stop, grasp each other excitedly by the arm and point cloudward. No doubt when one of the Jones' cows was killed in their pasture by lightning this afternoon Mrs. Jones would attribute it to our weird incantations of last evening. But—Bertie has gone. The house is so empty tonight.

Friday, Aug. 31, 1917

After all, that was not my last taste of Bertie. Fate has been kind and has given me an unexpected box of bon-bons. When Bertie reached Toronto she found a telegram from Vancouver giving her an extra week's holiday. So Monday last I went into Toronto and stayed at Laura's till Wednesday morning. Laura, Bertie, and I took in the Exhibition and the Grand Stand show at night and we had a lovely time, which seemed to us like one of our gay old revels of long ago, when I would go into Charlottetown and the three of us would gad off to the opera for an evening's fun. It *is* so jolly to be able to shake off for a few days the everlasting incubus of Missionary meetings and mission bands and guilds, and have a little carefree enjoyment.

Earl Grey has lately died after a somewhat long illness. I felt sorry to hear it. Well, I shall not have any more heart to heart talks with him on the steps of unmentionable resorts and thereby drive his countess into agonies of jealousy.

The war news from the Western front has been fairly good this week but that from the Russian theatre has been very dispiriting. We have entered upon our fourth year of the war. I wonder how much more humanity can bear. And there were some who said, when the war broke out "It will be over by Christmas." Ewan was one of them and I can yet see his look of tolerant amusement when I said, "It will last at least three years."

Saturday, Sept. 8, 1917
The Manse, Leaskdale

The war news from Russia has been very bad this week. The Germans have crossed the Dvina and are marching on Riga with every likelihood of taking it. Of course treachery is again at the bottom of this. The Italians have been doing well and winning some important successes which may eventually mean the elimination of Austria.

Tuesday evening when I got home from a boresome "missionary tea" at Zephyr I found that my half-sister Kate had been here, having motored over from Beaverton with some of her cousins whom she is visiting there. I was sorry to have missed her, so next morning Ewan and I drove over to Beaverton. He left me at the MacKenzies and I stayed there about three hours—quite the longest three hours I have endured for many moons.

I was much disappointed in Kate—though why I should have been disappointed I don't know, for I remembered quite well what she was like when she called at the Oxtoby house six years ago. I never met so listless, dull, and uninteresting a girl. I tried my best to talk to her but no subject, personal or impersonal, seemed to hold the slightest interest for her. There was *nothing* of father about her, save a physical resemblance in eyes and nose. Neither was she much like her mother, who was a person of considerable force of character, however disagreeable it might be. I was deeply thankful when Ewan finally appeared. After chatting for half an hour we left. "And so *that* is your sister," he said as we walked away. "What an inane person." "Inane" was the very adjective.

Kate is studying nursing in Winnipeg hospital and will graduate next spring. She evidently does not care much for her work, having taken it up, I fancy, because she hated teaching and found herself "getting on" and no available man emerging from the horizon mists. Kate is about thirty. In one thing she is certainly her mother's daughter—her restless craving for "a good time" and extraneous excitement and her dislike of work. Mrs. Montgomery was one of the laziest women I ever met.

In short, my heart did not warm to Kate in the slightest degree. *We* are not "next of kin" in anything save the accident of birth.

Thursday, Sept. 27, 1917
Ewan's neuritis is no better—worse, indeed. It seems strange that nothing does him any good. Even the doses of phenacetine etc which give temporary relief in most people have no more effect on him than so many doses of water. The only thing that alleviates it even temporarily is applications of hot water.

There was some encouraging news today of a British advance—only those "advances" never seem to get very far on. And I had a dreadful letter from Amanda, bewailing her unhappiness and abusing her husband in unmeasured terms. It was disgusting. She knew what George Robertson was when, without either love or respect, she married him merely to escape "old maidenhood." If she would but control her own diabolical temper he would be good enough to her. If she does *not* control that same temper she will end up as her wretched old father did in insanity and suicide. Shall I ever forget that night after his death and the way Amanda behaved! It was enough to make one believe the old legends of devil possession. To my dying day I will see the picture of Amanda, her face convulsed with rage, shaking her fist in my face when I tried to coax her to leave the kitchen and go upstairs before the men brought in the stark dripping body they had found in Clark's pond. Grief she never felt—nothing but the most fiendish rage and fury with her father for "bringing this disgrace" upon them. Her own temper had done much to drive the poor old man to his terrible end. And I much fear me it will yet drive her to a similar one. Poor unhappy woman—who was once so nice a girl. What a tragedy her life has been and all because of the twin demons of temper and jealousy! Even yet, when I recall those old days—our walks and talks and nights and outings together—it seems to me that the Amanda I loved so much then *must* be somewhere yet and that this changeling is none of her.

Friday, Sept. 28, 1917
The Manse, Leaskdale, Ont.
Still Ewan is no better. We had all our arrangements made to leave on Monday for Boston to spend a week with Flora; but we have decided that we must put it off for a week.

I canned pears today and then went to the church in the evening and presided over the social guild—something I do not like doing when Ewan is not present, owing to the fact that prayer has to be offered.

Wednesday, Oct. 24, 1917
October so far has been a busy month. On the first Edith went away for her vacation and I had the busiest week of my life I think—doing all the household work, getting the house ready to be left, getting ourselves ready to go and doing up a lot of canning and preserving. Ewan's neuralgia improved slowly but our sleep was broken and when we started on our trip on Monday I was so tired, so utterly tired that I would much have preferred to go to bed. We left Toronto at eleven that night and got into Boston Wednesday morning. A little later we were at East Braintree where Flora—now Mrs. Eagles—and her husband have a very cosy and convenient little bungalow.

"The Eagles' Bungalow"
[*East Braintree, Mass.*]

It was very different from my last visit to Boston. For one thing there was no calling at the office on Beacon St. I sighed a little over this. That Boston trip was very delightful and Mr. Page very kind. If only he hadn't been a scamp!

By the way, Mildred divorced him last spring! I have made some ghastly discoveries of late about them, of which I had no inkling when I was their guest. Mildred it seems was Lewis' *third* wife. His first wife died it seems very soon after their marriage. He then married a Boston girl, very beautiful, accomplished and charming. Eventually she suspected him of unfaithfulness. One of his office staff was a girl who had divorced her husband—why, I do not know. Mrs. Page had her husband shadowed, found that her suspicions were correct and divorced him. He then married his new love—Mildred. They had been married about six years when I was there. Of course I knew nothing of all this then but it explains several things that puzzled me a bit when I was there. Last spring Mildred sued him for divorce—on the ground of *cruelty* and failure to provide—and got it. So that's that! He has to pay about $10,000 a year alimony to each of his two ex-wives, so no wonder he has to cheat his authors.

We had a very nice time in our week's visit, though I did not go about much because of the children. Both were very good and attracted attention wherever we went—especially Stuart, who won everybody with his delightful smiles. I spent one afternoon in Boston with Alma Macneill and we had a pleasant time.

On our way back we got to Montreal at 10 P.M., were met by Frede and her husband, and had an hour with them. Cam was leaving for the front in a few days. And yet we spent the whole hour, jesting, laughing, and talking nonsense. Somehow we could not strike another note. Cam has since left. I hope he may come back; but it seems like asking too much to expect any man to come back scatheless from that hell twice. I am glad I saw him once at least. He seems real to me now. Heretofore, he has seemed like a myth and that did not seem right in the matter of Frede's husband.

Every time I go away for a visit those miserable Russians do something to spoil it. I felt sure that trouble was coming in that quarter for I had had another of my curious "snow" dreams just before I left. Sure enough, the capture of the Riga Island by Germany followed, with its threat of an advance on Petrograd. This has not followed, however, and the incident seems almost closed. I wish I could think my dream *did* refer to it, for then I could believe that the danger was over. But, bad as it was, it somehow does not seem anything like bad enough to "justify" my dream, and I have an uneasy feeling that something worse is coming yet—the worst thing that has so far happened to Russia.

Both British and French have won some dashing local victories lately.

Tuesday, Oct. 30, 1917
St. Paul's Manse, Leaskdale
Every fall there is some catastrophe in regard to the war to embitter the waning days. Two years ago it was Serbia, last year it was Roumania, this year it threatens to be Italy. Oh, the agony of the past few days!

It has come like a bolt from the blue. All summer the Italians were gaining important victories, working their way foot by foot towards Trieste, which seemed almost within their grasp. On Oct. 25th came the first alarming rumors of a huge German offensive against the Italians. On Friday, the despatches were bad but nothing very disastrous seemed in sight. On Saturday the bolt fell. It was a beautiful day and we were enjoying ourselves out cleaning up the lawn and garden. Then the mail came with the news that the Germans had broken through the Italian line to the north, capturing 30,000 and, what was far worse, endangering the whole Italian army and all the gains of the past three years. All Saturday afternoon I worried. At night Edith telephoned down to Uxbridge to ask what the night despatches were. I did not prevent her though personally I had not the courage to do it. I have never dared, when a crisis was on, to 'phone on Saturday night and thereby risk greater anxiety for Sunday. But I let her do it, wildly hoping that the news might be better. It was infinitely worse. Sixty thousand were captured and many guns.

I passed a dreadful night. I took a veronal powder in my desperation but even it could not overcome my unrest and I got only an hour or two of troubled slumber. In that brief sleep, however, came another strange dream and, if it came from the gate of horn, Italy will not be utterly defeated. Sunday was a most miserable day. I went to church and sat with my mind pivoting on the Italian situation and spinning around it as on a wheel of torture. In the afternoon I couldn't read. I walked the floor and wrestled with principalities and powers. Sunday night I slept from sheer exhaustion. Yesterday morning I worked feverishly until Ewan left for the office. Then I could work no more but locked myself in the parlor and paced the floor in an anguish of suspense. The news was terrible—Goritz taken, 100,000 Italians taken and the whole Italian army in full retreat.

I went all to pieces. The only thing I could do was plain sewing that required no attention. So I sewed madly until five and then again retreated to the parlor and paced the floor for a twilight hour of agony. Evening brought a reaction of calmness and I was able to read but got little good of it, while torrents of rain poured down outside. I have had many bad days since the beginning of the war but all added together could scarcely equal yesterday. It was by far the worst of them all. Last night I slept poorly and all through this cold, autumnal forenoon I worked hard at routine tasks requiring little thought. When the mail came the news was slightly better. For the first time there seemed a gleam of hope that the Italian armies might yet escape supreme disaster.

Thursday, Nov. 1, 1917
Housecleaned in forenoon, went to Red Cross in afternoon and Guild at night—all in a dull maze of worry and foreboding. Cadorna seems to have rallied his men but the situation is still very critical. I foresee weeks of racking suspense. In the early days of the war we had the strength to endure it. But in this, the fourth year, when we had hoped for victory, it is very hard to bear it. The Russian collapse is mainly the cause of the Italian reverse, of course—Austria has been able to take her men from the eastern front and hurl them against Italy.

Wednesday, Nov. 7, 1917
The Italians are retreating in good order to the Piave River. A strange calm fell on me when I heard this—as if I had received also some psychic message that the worst was over as far as Italy was concerned—and this though military critics think that the Piave line cannot be held and predict a further retreat to the Adige. But the Piave line *must* hold or Venice will fall to the Hun—an unthinkable catastrophe. *They must not get it.* They must *not*!

I put faith in my message and went out to tea and enjoyed myself for the first time since that hideous Saturday night. The Canadians have taken Passchendaele—a victory that would have been blazoned in headlines a fortnight ago, but which now, in the gloom of the Italian disaster is hardly noticed.

Friday, Nov. 9, 1917
Leaskdale, Ont.
My "Russian" dream was a true one. To-day came the worst news from Russia yet—that Kerensky's government is overthrown and that the Bolsheviki is in

power led by two notorious pro-Germans. This means that worse things are to follow.

Monday, Nov. 12, 1917

Dreaded the mail unspeakably. The news in the *Globe* was fairly cheering but the *Mail* and the *World* seem to think that a retreat to the Adige is inevitable and that means that Venice—but no, I will not think it—I will not believe it. Venice *shall* be saved. There are wild mixed rumors from Russia. Kerensky is said to be marching on Petrograd. But I lost faith in Kerensky long ago. He is too weak and indecisive. Russia is on the knees of the gods. I shall give up worrying about her.

Tomorrow I go to Toronto to see my brother Carl. He is home from the front and will spend the winter in Toronto having his leg treated. Frankly, I dread going to see him, having in mind my meeting with Kate.

Wednesday, Nov. 14, 1917
The Manse, Leaskdale, Ont.

Yesterday was a very beautiful day. Ewan drove me to Uxbridge and I got on the train. Far down the car a man was reading a *Globe*. I caught a partial glimpse of the headline—*Great Battle* in *Italy*. There I sat in miserable terror and suspense. If there had been a great battle it could not have resulted in victory of the Italians or there would have been a different headline. They had lost it—Venice was lost. For God's sake, why didn't some trainman come along with papers!! If I hadn't wanted one they would have passed by the dozen. None came—none came—none came—and half the way to Toronto I sat there wretchedly trying to figure out what the whole head line was and looking, I doubt not, so dazed that the conductor glanced at me sharply evidently wondering if I ought to be out alone. Finally a newsboy *did* come, I feverishly bought a *Globe* and found, that the headline which had caused me such misery was only "Allies Prepare for Great Battle in Italy"!

The situation is very critical. On the outcome of that battle depend great issues beyond even the loss of Venice. The rumors from Russia are wild. There has been fighting and both sides claim to be successful.

I hied me up town to Rosehill Ave. where Carl was staying with his mother's cousin. He came hopping on his one leg to the door to meet me. I just caught hold of him and kissed him. No need to dread that meeting. He is father's son and my *full* brother—the dear, plucky, jolly little chap. He is *so* like father in his ways and personality, and very like him in looks, too. In short, he is just a darling. It was a great relief to me. It would have hurt me horribly if I couldn't have loved Carl—worse, much worse, than it did in Kate's case. We had a jolly afternoon together. He has father's own knack of telling laughter-provoking stories. He was so like father that I had the most ridiculous sensation that he *was* father and that I was his daughter, instead of being, as I am, quite old enough to be his mother.

I came home last night. Today there was the same old dread of the mail. I will drop dead some day when Ewan comes in at the door with it!

"Carl"
[*Carl Montgomery, Maud's half-brother, and Stuart*]

Tuesday, Nov. 20, 1917
Leaskdale, Ont.

The Italians still hold but the situation seems to be at a crisis. I feel ceaseless anxiety over it. I worked two hours at my new book today and then went to eat supper and spend the evening. We were with a nice family and I enjoyed myself after a fashion but there was always the undercurrent of worry which made itself felt continually. I laughed and talked with one part of my mind and with the other haunted the Piave front. I feel at present as if I *could not* face the war news for the rest of the week—for this week will probably decide the fate of Venice. But perhaps by morning I shall have gained from wells of slumber a little fresh strength to go on with.

Friday, Nov. 23, 1917

This has been positively a wonderful day. Yesterday we had such a storm that we had no mail so today my dread was doubled. But the news was splendid—the British have won the biggest victory of the war on the western front. Such tidings were almost intoxicating after the unbroken brew of wormwood we have been drinking this past month. And the Italians hold still. This afternoon I felt like a released prisoner. I cheerfully got ready and drove five miles through heavy snow and bitter cold to Zephyr to take supper with a family that is one of my pet detestations. I don't think I *could* have stood them had the news *not* been good. As it was I gulped them without a grimace and even looked pleasant afterwards.

Monday, Nov. 26, 1917

We drove down to Uxbridge this afternoon to hear Sir Robert Borden and Mr. Powell speak. I am especially interested in the coming election not only because it will be the most momentous ever held in Canada, not only because it will or will not show Quebec that her long day of domination is over, but because I have a vote, by the grace of my brother Carl. All Canadian women will have the vote soon. Sir Robert is certainly no orator, yet he has a forceful, direct way of speaking and what he says sticks in your memory. Powell is more flowery and eloquent—more interesting to listen to, but rather too emotional for strength. If I had not already believed every word he said I don't think he would have convinced me.

Saturday, December 1, 1917
We are having a breathing spell before the next turn of the rack. There was no especial news yesterday or today. To-night I had a treat—a quiet, undisturbed evening for reading. I am reading Lecky's "History of Rationalism". Gods, through what seas of blood and over what red-hot plough shares of torment has humanity reeled in its onward progress. Was it necessary? Could not Omnipotence have made the ascent a *little* less hard—difficult, perhaps, but not agonizing. Were the rack and stake and thumbscrews the *only* way? These questions are idle. But the mind persists in asking them.

Monday, Dec. 3, 1917
2 Nina Ave., Toronto
Came in this morning to spend a week with Mary Beal. I need the change and enjoy it, and yet it wrenches at my heart strings to leave my home and my darling boys. The war news is none too encouraging. The Germans are trying with all their might to undo the effects of the British win at Cambrai and I fear they will partially succeed.

This afternoon I gave a little talk on "The Responsibility of Women in the Future" to a chapter of the Daughters of the Empire. I dislike trying to speak in public but I did it today and tried to say as simply as possible some things that are very near my heart—especially in regard to the fate of the children of the future. I suppose I did fairly well for one of my listeners, Miss Bollert, asked me to repeat the speech tonight to the girls of the Sherbourne House Club. Mary and I dined at the club and I spoke to the girls afterwards. As a result I am "all in" tonight and have no yearnings whatever to become a platform speaker.

Tuesday, Dec. 4, 1917
2 Nina Ave., Toronto
I went to Mac's this morning and among other things discovered this curious fact. L.C. Page, after declaring repeatedly in his letters to me and his letters to his lawyers that he would "under no circumstances" have any dealings with McClellands regarding my new book, wrote to his lawyers about three weeks before the book was to be published and asked them to find out on the sly—I don't say those were his exact words but that was his meaning—if there was any chance of re-opening negotiations with them. Mr. Page's return to sanity came too late. But as he knew that the contract with Stokes was signed and the book advertised by them it is difficult to understand what chance he thought there could be for him, even supposing the unsupposable that I would have considered such a suggestion for a moment after the way he had behaved.

I lunched with Mac at the National and this evening dined at Mr. Stewart's where Carl also was. He is such a dear little chap—I like him better every time I see him.

Friday, Dec. 7, 1917
2 Nina Ave., Toronto

Yesterday at four o'clock I came out of Eaton's brilliant noisy store into the dull gray light of the late winter afternoon. I felt a little tired and dull. A newsboy went past waving a paper across which I saw a big black headline "Halifax City Wrecked". I looked at it indifferently and thought, with a feeling of disgust, "Another of those fake papers."

A few weeks ago, in the stress of the Victory Loan Campaign some enterprising canvassers brought out a fake newspaper, purporting to be published in 1921. It assumed that the present war ended in a draw. Germany recuperated and in four years time struck again—this time at a solitary Britain. The British fleet had been demolished and the paper dealt with the subsequent descent of the Germans upon Canada. Its headlines had been "Germans Land in Canada—Halifax and St. Johns in Ruins" etc. and the despatches gave the details. It was all quite clever and amusing and nearly frightened some of the good people in Toronto into fits. They thought it was genuine.

But I thought a repetition of it was rather silly and wished that the gov't had hit upon a more effective dodge for opening the eyes of Canadians to their peril. With a shrug of impatient contempt I walked down to my car corner. Here a second newsboy went past and I saw that the paper was no fake but a genuine "Star." Still, I was not alarmed. I concluded that some steamer named "Halifax City" was wrecked and although this would have been a sensation in the *Lusitania's* day it is a mere commonplace now. However, I bought a paper out of mild curiosity and opened it.

Twenty minutes later I came to my senses upon an uptown car without any recollection of how I got there. Luckily it proved to be the right one which I had boarded automatically while my brain was trying to take in the magnitude of the disaster when a steamer loaded with munitions blew up in Halifax Harbor and laid fully half the city in ruins. The loss of life is said to be appalling and the whole thing is sickening. It is hard to think that the Germans had no hand in it. It comes so pat to the moment, just before the conscription election. But in so far as appears on the surface the explosion was the result of an accidental collision between two ships.

I got here just in time to receive a bevy of Jarvis St. Collegiate girls who had asked for "the honor of an interview." I went through the hour talking like a machine, while my whole consciousness centred around the Halifax horror. Those poor girls sat in an adoring circle and gazed at me with the awed, reverent eyes of idealizing girlhood. I wish I did not feel so ridiculous in these interviews. But the contrast between my real self and what those worshippers of *Anne* believe me to be is too ludicrous. And yet there is something very sweet in the admiration of those innocent young souls. They are so uncritical and ungrudging.

Today I finished shopping. The Halifax story grows worse in each despatch. I hope Edith Russell and her family escaped. There were many killed in Dartmouth where her home is.

This evening I went and had dinner with the Aylsworths. A jolly evening. Laura has such a tang of the old stock.

Monday, Dec. 10, 1917
The Manse, Leaskdale
I had planned to come home Saturday but a terrific blizzard prevented and I could not come before tonight. It is so good to be home again. But I had a nice time in Toronto.

This afternoon when I got on a downtown car I saw a big black headline on a "*Star*" at the other end of the car. "Jerusalem surrenders to the British". I wanted to give a wild hurrah but I had to do my hurrahing internally. It is wonderful to think that the Cross once more flies over Jerusalem, after so many centuries of the Crescent's rule. Surely it will never again be displaced. After all, it is worth while to live in the days which sees the object of the old Crusades attained. Surely the ghosts of all the old Crusaders should crowd the walls of Jerusalem tonight, with Coeur-de-Lion at their head to welcome the English conquerors.

The Italians, too, are holding bravely, but the Russian muddle goes from bad to worse apparently.

"Laura"
[Laura McIntyre Aylsworth]

Tuesday, December 11, 1917
Leaskdale, Ont.
A letter from Frede today gave the coup-de-grace to a faint hope that has hitherto refused to die utterly out of my heart. She cannot come for Christmas. Poor old Uncle John is so ill she feels she must go home. She is right. But how lonely Christmas will be. And this year of all years.

Courage! "He that endureth to the end shall be saved." Verily, yes. But what about those who fall by the way? We are not all born with equal powers of endurance.

The storm-cloud is gathering on the western front. All the prophets are busy predicting a supreme effort there by Germany with the men and guns taken from the Russian front.

"Uncle John, Aunt Annie, and Frede"
[c. 1902]

We all feel like a creature cringing away from a threatened blow. God defend the right!

There is also such a constant strain of worry over the election and it intensifies now with every passing day. If the Union Government does not win Canada will be dishonored before the world. And it is so desperately uncertain whether it will win or not—the issues are so tremendous. There is no predicting the outcome from the results of past elections. No election like this was ever fought in Canada before. Estimates of the final result differ hopelessly. Let me add my predictions to the others. Shure and haven't I as good a right to prophesy as anybody? Ontario will balance Quebec, B.C. and the Maritimes will break even and the Prairie Provinces will turn the balance in favour of Union Government.

On the knees of the gods be it!

Wednesday, Dec. 19, 1917
The Manse, Leaskdale, Ont.
On Monday, Dec. 17, I polled my first vote!

I have never, I admit, felt any particular interest in politics. Perhaps this was because a woman could take only a theoretical interest anyhow. But I never felt any especial desire to vote. I thought, as a merely academic question, that women certainly should vote. It seemed ridiculous, for example that an educated, intelligent woman should not vote when any illiterate, half or wholly disloyal foreigner could. But it did not worry me in the least. And now that women have, or are soon to have, the vote I do not at all expect a new heaven or a new earth as the result. I hope and believe that certain reforms will be brought appreciably nearer by the women's vote. But I suspect that matters will jog on in pretty much the same old way for a good while yet—or if they do not, it will be owing to the war and conditions arising from it and not to the franchise.

It is rather too bad that I, who have called myself a Liberal all my life should have to cast my first vote against Wilfrid Laurier—whom at one time I thought little lower than the angels. This was simply because I was brought up that way. In P.E. Island in the old days—and even yet for that matter—one was born Grit or Tory and so remained. My earliest political recollections are of anathemas hurled at old "Sir John A." whom Grandfather Macneill seemed to regard as a demon in human form. Wilfrid Laurier was Grandfather's political idol and I, who was nothing if not loyal to my clan, worshipped him also. Our feeling was rather ludicrously like that of the old Quebec habitant in a story that used to be told at Liberal rallies!

A visiting Yankee once remarked to the said habitant, "You Quebec people seem to be crazy over Laurier. I believe you think him as good a man as the king". "Oh, yes, yes, he good as de king—yes, yes". "Well, I suppose you don't think he's as good as the Pope?" "Oh—y-e-e-s,"—more doubtfully but still with assurance, "Oh, ye-e-s, he good as de Pope." "Well, surely you don't think he's as good as God?" The old habitant scratched his head uneasily.

"No—no," he admitted reluctantly, "no, 'course he not so good as God—but"—brightening up—"but den, *he's young yet*."

Well, Wilfrid Laurier is an old man now and he has outlived his glory and betrayed his country. Why? Senility—superstition—base political cunning? It is vain to ask. Perhaps even Laurier himself does not know. But on Monday I voted, with a queer little qualm of regret and a queer feeling of disloyalty to my old traditions, for the Government which is Union but which is headed by Laurier's long rival, the Conservative chief, Borden.

The poll was held in a most disreputable old vacant store next to the manse. I append a photo of it by way of a souvenir of my first polling booth. The candidate I voted for was Major Sam Sharpe who has always been a rank "Tory". If Hogg, his opponent, had not been an equally rank anti-conscriptionist I would have found it much harder.

Having voted, there was nothing to do but wait. After supper Ewan went to Uxbridge to hear the returns and I hied me to the church where a practice of kiddies for our Sunday School concert was being held. In this occupation I contrived to pass the time with outward calmness until ten when I came home to find that Edith had been listening in on the phone and had this "news".

Sam Sharpe was in with a big majority and Ontario was almost solid for the Gov't,—*but they had done nothing in the west.*

I went to bits. If the West had gone against us, all hope had vanished. Edith went to bed. I could not work or read or sit still. So I began to walk the floor. I walked it until half past eleven when my legs gave out and I sat down perforce. I do think "politics" is too strenuous for women.

At twelve Ewan came home. I met him in the kitchen and looked at him but I did not speak. I was quite past speaking and I was as cold as ice from head to foot. When he told me that it was Laurier who had "done nothing in the West" and that the Gov't was in with a majority that was already fair and would probably be a large one. I could have sat down and cried with relief.

For the first night for a week I had a sleep untroubled by three o'clock visions of a rejoicing Kaiser and a Quebec-bossed Canada. Yesterday the full returns came in and gave the Union Gov't a majority of from 45 to 50. My prediction was about as correct as predictions usually are so I think I may count myself in Class C of the prophets. British Columbia instead of breaking even went almost solid for Union, whereas the Maritimes gave a small majority for Laurier. The rest was by the book,—Ontario matched Quebec and the West turned the scale lavishly.

It is over—and well over. I hope such an election need never be fought in Canada again.

This afternoon I got a telegram from Frede saying that her father had died this morning.

I knew Uncle John could not live long, nor was it desirable that he should, for he has been so miserable this past year. His mind was quite gone. He suffered from such terrible delusions and was as helpless as a child. Poor Aunt Annie was almost worn out and a few more months of it would have killed her.

But the news brought a sudden pang of realization of the change that had come over that old, beloved place. Uncle John Campbell was a man I always loved deeply. For no other uncle, of marriage or blood, did I have such an affection. He was the kindest, most hospitable of men. I never heard a harsh word from him.

He was 84. I cannot "sense" it. To me he always seemed to be about forty or fifty, as he was when I first knew him. He was not an intellectual man and so had poor judgment and "no head for business". But he had all the qualities that make for lovableness.

Well, he has gone. How very few of those "who danced my infancy upon their knee" are left now. I shiver, as with a sensation of physical cold when I think of Uncle John's place being vacant—when I think that never again when I go to Park Corner, will I be met by his hearty handshake and his blithe jest. When I was there last he was sadly failed. But he could still sit down in the parlor and bear his part in the conversation as he always delighted to do. "I'd rather die in the trenches than live under German rule," he repeated several times as he talked about the war....

He was never so happy as when there was a houseful of guests—especially if he was at the head of the table carving a fat goose and contriving to give everyone a special tidbit.

He has left no son who can take his place. Poor George resembles his father in nothing save his lack of business ability. Possibly a grandson may yet rise up to restore the old place and traditions. I have hopes of some of George's children, if they are not ruined in their upbringing. But oh, for the dear old days when the girls were all home and George was only a chubby little boy and Uncle John and Aunt Annie were in their prime. I am so horribly lonesome tonight—for Ewan is away and I am all alone in the dining room—that my heart aches unbearably, and I have a miserable irrational feeling that my place is "out there" with my kindred....

I look up at the picture of the home at Park Corner hanging on the wall before me—a spacious old house, built in the days when lumber was cheap and large families were to be housed. I have always liked its arrangement better than that of any other house I have ever known. I only wish I could have a house of my own like it and I would be satisfied. Roomy old hall, fine pantry, open fireplaces, large airy rooms. And I suppose that now, while I am writing here, that old house so far away is hushed and darkened and in the old parlor Uncle John is lying at rest. At last he sleeps well. God send him good slumber—and a happy awakening.

Tuesday, Dec. 25, 1917
Leaskdale, Ont.

I am glad Christmas is over. I was lonely for Frede—and very busy. As Edith went home I had all the work to do alone and a big dinner to cook, so it took all my time to get everything done. There was nothing really Christmassy about it for me. But the boys had a good time, and that is the main thing. They hung up their stockings last night and found them full of all delectables this morning. Chester still believes fervently in Santa Claus and this year Stuart has realized him—"Santy Tosh" as he calls him. I have only a very hazy recollection of ever believing in Santa Claus. I was beginning to feel very dubious as far back as I can remember.

Friday, Dec. 28, 1917
Leaskdale
This has been a hard day in many ways—hard on muscles and nerves. It was bitterly cold. The war news is none too good as the Huns are making another fierce effort against Italy and have won several important points.

Then this morning Edith told me that she could not stay longer than the first of March, as she intended to be married. I was surprised, as I had not expected it to happen so soon. I think I can get her sister Lily—but I hate changes. And I am rather sorry to lose poor Edith, too, for she isn't a bad little soul. Her two drawbacks were her untidiness and an annoying habit of making inane or out-of-the-place remarks when company was here and then bursting into a guffaw of laughter. In spite of this, however, she was really a more agreeable co-worker than Lily Reid was.

I went to a business meeting of our Red Cross in the afternoon. After supper we had a Guild Committee meeting here and then went to Guild in the church. I was very tired by this time and a certain well-meant but tactless remark made by a member of the Guild suddenly got under my skin. I came home and cried good and hard. Tomorrow I'll be all right. It's mainly nerves and fatigue.

1918

Friday, Jan. 18, 1918
Leaskdale, Ont.
I have not passed through such a week as this last since that terrible winter of
long ago down home.

For a week after my last entry it was rough and cold. Various things,
including a flare-up in the Red Cross Society were irritating. As to the Red
Cross trouble it is the first of the kind to come up since we organized two
years ago and was caused by some petty personal malice and spite among
some of the members. I think I have nipped it in the bud. I told them plainly
that if any trouble was made I would resign. This seemed to bring them into a
more reasonable frame of mind for none of them want the bother and responsibility of being president. It is disgusting to think that while our boys are
fighting and dying at the front our women cannot work for them at home
without quarrelling. And the woman against whom all this outburst of spite has
been directed has had a son killed at the front. None of those who organized
the cabal against her has anyone there. Gods, are such women worth fighting
for?

However, the various alarms and excursions of the meeting were over and
on Friday evening we drove over to Zephyr to visit a family. It was a mild
evening with a brooding sky when we went and the roads were passable. When
we left for home at eleven the worst storm I have ever known was just
beginning. It was snowing thickly, blowing wildly, and turning bitterly cold.
We were three hours covering the nine miles. Once we got stuck, and had to
get out, unhitch Queen, turn the cutter, and seek another road. We managed to
get home at last and it was well we did. All Saturday and Sunday the storm
raged, with a gale blowing sixty miles an hour and the mercury 36 below zero.
I have been in many barns that were more comfortable than this house during
those two days. My plants froze in the parlor at mid-day around the open
radiator. Stuart *cried* with the cold. I wore my overboots and a fur coat and
then was cold.

We had no mail for a whole week—but some came through today. No train
got through to Uxbridge until today. The tracks are blocked everywhere. We
drove to Uxbridge on Thursday and the roads were unthinkable.

Sunday, Feb. 10, 1918
Last Monday and Tuesday were the coldest days so far this winter—which is
saying much. Surely we are over the top now. But it has snowed more or less
every day this week and the roads are a problem. We had just one mail this

238

week—and it brought word that Hindenburg says that he will be in Paris by April first!

Hindenburg has made good his boasts on the eastern front. Can he make them good on the west? In the answer to that question lies the future of humanity and of civilization.

I was alone in the evening, tired, ill and nervous, when I read it. I walked the floor unable to reason off my dread. In my misery I resorted desperately to the old superstition—perhaps?—of opening the Bible at random and reading the first verse my eyes fell upon. With a passionate prayer I opened the book; and I read this verse in the first chapter of Jeremiah.

"And they shall fight against thee; but they shall not prevail against thee; for I am with thee, saith the Lord of Hosts to deliver thee."

Coincidence? Very likely. We shall see.

I believe that there is a great battle coming on the Western front—the greatest battle of the war—the greatest battle the world has ever seen—perhaps the last great battle it ever will see—"the day of Armageddon, the last great fight of all."

That battle will end the war whichever way it goes. Oh God, give us strength to bide it for we are weak and sorely tried!

Sunday, Feb. 24, 1918
The Manse, Leaskdale, Ont.
The blow has not yet fallen—and we wait, cringing. There are moments when I feel that I *cannot* bear the suspense any longer. In the forenoons, when I am busy and the sun shines I can force it to the background of my mind where it growls like a cornered dog. But when the day wanes and the shadows deepen and I grow tired, it comes out of its den and preys on me. The news from Russia has been very bad—Russia has quit the war and the Germans are sweeping over her undefended territory. And on the west—the ominous hush before the storm. One despatch lately says that Hindenburg has stipulated that he will take Paris if he is left free to expend a million lives. At such a price he *must* purchase some successes and how can we live through them, even if he be baffled in the end?

I wish there were no such hour as three o'clock in the morning. I generally waken then and I cannot sleep again because I see Hindenburg in Paris and Germany victorious. I never see her so at any other than that accursed hour, no matter what Hindenburg may do. But then I see civilization swallowed up in barbarism.

The only gleam of light has been the British advance in Palestine. They have Jericho now. But if Hindenburg smashes through on the west!

We have had milder weather lately and some thaws.

Monday, Feb. 25, 1918
Leaskdale, Ont.
There was no very "new" war news today. Russia is seemingly in a hopeless plight and for the rest the papers were filled up with gloomy predictions by

the war correspondents concerning the lowering offensive in the west. I suppose they have to fill their columns with something—but it is hard on our *morale*.

A letter from McClelland today says they have sold 15,341 copies of *House of Dreams* in Canada. That is pretty good.

Tonight I finished re-reading MacCaulay's History. My mind has been a good deal harrowed during the process by the war but it was calmness personified compared to my condition the last time I read it in the winter of 1910. There were a couple of weeks that winter in which I tasted all the bitterness of death—and a dreadful and lingering death. It induced a nervous breakdown to which I made reference in my journal of the time. But I did not explain the *cause* of it—I could not. The agony had been so awful that for years I could not bear even to think of it.

One Friday night in the January of 1910 I was lying awake in my old room in Cavendish. I was drowsy and comfortable and on the point of falling asleep when I happened to put my hand on my left breast. To my intense horror I felt in it a small "kernel" seemingly about the size of a pea.

All my life I had had a dread of *cancer*. I don't know exactly why for no one in my connection on either side had ever had it. But Grandfather Macneill had a morbid dread of it and was always imagining any little wart or mole which appeared on him to be cancer. His talk about it made an ineffaceable impression on my childish mind and I grew up with a deeply rooted horror of the disease and a conviction that it was the most horrible of deaths.

And now I had discovered a developing cancer in my breast. I had not the slightest doubt of that. Nor do I exactly wonder at my terror. I never slept for a moment that night. I got up in the cold and hunted out all the "doctor's books" in the house and read what they had to say on the subject. I found nothing to encourage me.

A dreadful fortnight followed. I thought I would go mad with fear and dread. I could say no word to anyone—there was no one I could say anything to. Sleepless night succeeded sleepless night—agonized day followed agonized day. I could not work—it was impossible to concentrate thought on anything. I tried to read—I had just begun on MacCaulay's History. But though my eyes followed line after line and page after page my mind took in hardly anything of what I saw. I would read for a few minutes, then fling down the book and pace the floor in restless misery. Sometimes at night I got a little sleep by dosing myself with "hop" tea. I had no drugs that might have given a temporary oblivion and no chance of getting them and the hop tea was not strong enough to overcome for any length of time my terrible unrest or soothe my tortured nerves. And the hardest thing was that I had to go about and perform certain church and social duties and affect calm and composure. I would not let anyone suspect my trouble and I ascribed my unconcealable nervousness and general haggardness of appearance to facial neuralgia. I could not think of the future. What could I do? I would have no one—*no one* to help me or stand by me. Marriage was not to be thought of with such a thing hanging over me. I decided that I would have to break my engagement. Everything in the world seemed to have become far away and indifferent to me. I moved among shadows. I remember one evening of choir practice in especial when under my surface calm I endured such agony that I made up my mind that rather than face my future I would kill myself in some way. Of course worry and sleeplessness soon produced utter nervous prostration and one thing reacted on another until I was almost insane. I could not sleep or eat or think or work. Monday, Jan. 17, 1910, eleven days after my finding of the kernel, was the most dreadful day I ever experienced in my life. I walked the floor all day in hideous restlessness. My misery reached its climax that day and that evening a reaction set in. Suddenly my restlessness departed, as if some evil spirit had rent and left me; and I felt quite calm but so physically weak I could hardly stand. For the rest of that week I suffered no more from restlessness but I felt broken—sad—helpless—a dreadful weariness of spirit. The next week I had several returns of the restlessness but none lasted so long as the first—the reactive calm generally coming after one day of agony.

I could not think of consulting the local doctor. He had a gossippy wife who told everything. My horrible secret would soon be known everywhere—a thought I could not tolerate. I could not get to town to consult a doctor there. So, soon after I discovered the kernel, I wrote the doctor in charge of the medical column in a Montreal paper asking if the kernel were likely to prove a cancer and what I had better do. Eighteen days later his letter came—I had sent the fee for a private reply. I did not dare open it just then. I had to go out to tea and spend the evening and I was afraid the contents would upset me too much. I must keep it until the day's duties were over and I could be alone with the night to face the worst. So at bedtime I opened the letter. It was very brief and I remember every line of it—I can never forget it. It shut the gates of death upon my tortured soul and opened the gates of life. "Dear Madam," it read, "the little kernel in your breast is not a cancer and my advice is to leave it completely alone."

I felt as if I had returned from the grave. Life was possible once more—hope was not excluded. But the physical effects of that hideous fortnight lasted all winter. I was tired, depressed, sleepless and nervous for many months. Not till summer did I feel like myself. As for the little kernel, it remained as it was for a couple of years and disappeared altogether after Chester was born. What caused it I do not know but I doubt if anything can ever again make me so utterly miserable—not even the discovery of a real cancer!

I have never read MacCaulay since until recently. As I read it, enjoying it hugely, now and then a poignant memory of those weeks would flash over my mind—I would see myself huddled in the old kitchen, dully reading a few paragraphs, then throwing the book down and walking the floor—repeating the alternate performance until the dull gray winter's day had worn itself out and darkness came down over the old homestead and I went upstairs alone, with death grinning at my side, to toss sleeplessly until another dreaded dawn.

Not a living soul ever knew or suspected. I got a dozen "sure" remedies for neuralgia and much sympathy on the score of it. But not one ever guessed that among them moved that fortnight a soul in torment.

Friday, March 1, 1918
The Manse, Leaskdale

Edith was married here last Wednesday and Lily Meyers reigns in her stead. It is too soon to decide whether the change is for the better or worse but I am inclined to think the former.

"Lily Meyers"

I had a curious dream last night. I dreamed I held a newspaper in my hand and across it in huge letters ran the words, "There are thirty evil days coming." Then I woke. I have had so many strange and true dreams since the war broke out that I have an abiding faith in them. And what is to come after the thirty evil days? My dream did not tell me that.

Saturday, March 2, 1918
Leaskdale, Ont.

Last night I dreamed again. I stood on a plain in France. It was sunset and the red light streamed over the plain. I held in my arms a man whom I knew, in some inexplicable way, to be dying. He leaned against me, his back and head against my breast. I could not see his face. Then he died, slipped from my grasp, and fell to the ground. I saw his face and recognized it—it was the face of the Kaiser's father—the man who, all through my girlhood, was known to me as the Crown Prince of Germany and whose pictured face, owing to his long and tragic illness, was very familiar to me.

Strange? Will the thirty evil days be followed by some disaster to the present Crown Prince—or to that Hohenzollern dynasty of which the dead Frederick was the only worthy representative? The next three months will answer that question—and we wait—and wait—and Germany masses her legions and guns on the Western front—and the world holds its breath in this awful and ominous calm.

Friday, Mar. 22, 1918
The Manse, Leaskdale

Armageddon has begun! The Great offensive opened yesterday. They have attacked the British army. Haig reports that the enemy failed to reach their objectives but says they penetrated to the British battle positions and that severe fighting continues. I do not like the sound of that last phrase but I am calm. At least, the dreadful suspense is over and a short time must decide the issue. But it will seem very long. God defend the right!

Sunday, Mar. 31, 1918
The Manse, Leaskdale, Ont.

I wonder if there has ever been a week in the history of the world before into which so much of searing agony has been crammed. I feel sure that there was not. And in this week there was one day when all humanity was nailed to the cross. On that day the whole planet must have been agroan with universal convulsion. That day was last Sunday, March 24, 1918.

The morning was fine and cold. I went to church anxious but calm. As I sat in church I wondered what I would feel like next Sunday. It would be Easter—but would it herald death or life. After the service I came home and, Lily being away, was busily preparing dinner when I heard Ewan say "Do you want to hear the latest news from the front?"

He had been reading a note handed to him after service by one of his elders. Something in his question or the tone of it filled me with dread. I snatched the letter. It was from Jas. Mustard who had come out from Toronto the night before. It said, simply and boldly, that the latest despatches had stated that the British line was broken and that the German shells were raining on Paris.

"It *can't* be true! It *can't* be true," I gasped again and again. I went all to pieces—I was nothing but a heap of quivering misery. If the Germans were shelling Paris they must have crashed through everywhere and be at its very gates! Paris was lost—France was lost—the war was lost!

Somehow or other I finished getting dinner for the rest but I never ate or thought of eating. Ewan, who is of a very phlegmatic temperament and never goes to pieces as I do, was calm though depressed and tried to encourage me, but it was a hard task even for his india-rubber optimism. As for me I writhed physically in my intolerable suffering. Oh, what an afternoon I passed! Ewan was away. I was alone, save for the children who were not old enough to realize the catastrophe that had befallen the world. I took a dose of lavender and that restored to me a small measure of self-control but that whole afternoon I walked the parlor floor, wrung my hands and prayed—"Oh God—Oh God—Oh God"—nothing else—no other words—I could utter nothing but that age-old plea—that age-old moan of supreme anguish.

If only the news had not come until Monday, I thought piteously. It would not have been so hard to endure—one could have gone somewhere—done something. So I thought then. But now I am thankful that I learned it when I did and bore my share in the world's great pain. Everywhere that day humanity was in its supreme agony—everywhere the hearts of men were failing them for fear. I would feel shame if I had spent that day in painless ignorance reading or dreaming calmly. It was better to share the pain of my fellow beings.

Ewan came home from Zephyr at five and brought with him a Saturday night *Star*. I found that the news was not *quite* so awful as it had seemed in Mr. Mustard's letter. The line *had* been broken in *one* place, before St. Quentin, but the British forces seem to be retreating in fairly good order. There was as yet no rout and the guns that were shelling Paris were seventy miles away from it—monsters hitherto unknown, spectacular enough, but rather negligible from a military point of view. But the truth was sufficiently awful. Mr. Harwood telephoned up the latest despatches that evening and they were far from reassuring. Furious fighting was still continuing. The German losses were said to be enormous—probably were. But that old sop of comfort has been served up to us too often when reverses came to be of any power now. What boots it how many they lose if they smash through?

That night I took a veronal tablet and so slept loggishly. Worked feverishly all the morning at some routine tasks requiring no thought. The mail came. The headline of the *Globe* was, "Battered but not Broken". The British had retreated to the Somme losing the territory captured in its last summer's campaign at the cost of half a million lives. The despatches were terrible. The Kaiser boasted himself of victory and the Germans had taken 30,000 prisoners.

I felt miserably depressed. Ewan and I went to Uxbridge and then to tea at Herbert Pearson's. Nice place—nice people—but they seemed as shadows to me in my maze of pain. Lizzie told me of an incredible story of a despatch that had just come through saying that the British had captured 100,000 Germans. I knew this could not possibly be true. I feared that it had been twisted in transmission and that they had *lost* a hundred thousand. This added to my distraction. But that night I slept from exhaustion. And the evening and the morning was the fifth day.

Tuesday morning I paced the floor waiting for the mail. Again the news was bad. The German advance continued and though the British line was not again broken it was pressed back and back. Back much further it could not go without irretrievable disaster. They were very close to Amiens—and the loss of Amiens would mean that a wedge had been driven between the French and British armies.

I could do nothing that afternoon and evening. I don't remember much about it. One day of anguish was becoming much the same as another. Again I took a veronal that night and obtained a little merciful oblivion. All the forenoon I worked at routine tasks.

Hitherto, when I have had reason to dread the news I never would go to the store for the mail myself. I have always felt that I could not endure reading bad news, with those men who infest country stores sitting around on boxes and counters and looking at me with curious eyes. If the news was bad I must read it at home. But on this day this hitherto strong feeling was drowned out by another yet stronger. I could *not* wait here while Ewan went down for the mail—I had borne so many of those agonies of suspense that I could not bear just that particular kind again. The "drop of water" must fall on a new place— a new kind of torture would be more bearable so I went down with Ewan to the office. It was a dull, bitter, *hard* day. All the snow was gone but the gray, lifeless ground was frozen hard. A biting wind was blowing. The whole landscape was ugly and repellent. It weighed on my soul—it seemed typical of the world in which the German hell-hounds were to be our masters. I went into the store, feeling, "Oh, if it were only over—if I had just seen the news and knew the worst." Mrs. Cook was just leaning over the counter, reading a *Globe*. The headline hung down over the counter, big and black. It was upside down to me but I read it at a glance, without even the slight effort we usually make to read letters upside down. It was,

"British and French check the Germans."

The relief was almost awful. I felt like a prisoner on the rack when they stopped turning it. But I was not off the rack. The torture might begin anytime. The situation was still crit-

"The Store. Leaskdale"

ical—the danger still horribly great and imminent. But at least the onrush of Germans had been halted—there was still a chance. I was able to work that afternoon and sleep at night. The next day's news was again reassuring but still the danger had not passed. Friday's news was bad again. Montdidier and Rosiere were taken—two important points. If the Huns advanced much beyond Montdidier Amiens must fall—and if Amiens fell the Channel ports or Paris— or both—must be given up. I was worried and upset all day. Yesterday I again went for the mail and the headline was, "Even Berlin admits the offensive checked." I exclaimed aloud "Oh, Thank God," not caring if all the loafers in Scott heard me.

And so it stands. Today was Easter and I went to church. I did not, as I had hoped last Sunday, feel rejoicing in the thought that the German offensive had failed. Alas, it had had too great a measure of success. But at least I went feeling thankful that so far it had failed of decisive success. Armageddon is not over—it has but begun. But though I doubted God last Sunday I do not doubt Him today. The evil cannot win. My dream will come true!

There has come out of this catastrophe one good—one supremely good thing. At last there is a generalissimo of the Allied forces and that man is Foch, the great French leader. It has taken this disaster to break the stubborn British repugnance to this. I believe that if Foch had been generalissimo long ago the war would have been over. May it not be too late!

On such evenings of the past week as I could read I re-read a history of Ancient Egypt by Rawlinson and found, as in all previous readings, that even the dryest details were as interesting to me as a letter from home. Always I read with the feeling of reading of a life *I* had once lived. I wonder if Egypt weaves this same sorcery over others who read of her. There is a certain couplet in *Ben Hur* which always makes me incredibly *homesick*.

"No more does the Nile in the moonlight calm / Moan past the Memphian shore."

Gods! There comes the ache! I *see* that moonlit shore, with the palm trees on the banks. I yearn for it—I could weep with very longing to see it *again*. I *must* have seen it once.

Monday, April 1, 1918
The Manse, Leaskdale, Ont.
This was the day Hindenburg was to have been in Paris. He is not there yet. But he would have been if the Huns had smashed through utterly as they

expected last week. It is a big "if"—which may yet lose the subjunctive.

To-day was a dismal blend of fog and rain and mud. The news was reassuring. The enemy has made no further progress. But most of the "critics" think there is another tremendous effort coming. This may be. I dreamed that strange dream on March first. Did the "30 evil days" mean thirty days from my dream? If so, they were out yesterday and the worst is over. But somehow I do not think so—I do not *feel* so. I think it meant thirty days from the opening of the offensive. And if this be so there is a long endurance of the rack before us yet.

In the *British Weekly* that came to-day was a very kind review of *Anne's House of Dreams* by a critic whose opinion I value highly.

Saturday, April 20, 1918

This has been a hellish week of ups-and-downs. Tuesday's news was fair. The British line held but Neuve Eglise, an important point, was lost. Still, I felt encouraged and worked with good heart. Wednesday morning just after Ewan had left the house to go down for the mail the telephone bell rang sharply. I felt that there was something ominous in its sound. It sounded like Mrs. Alex Leask's ring. They get their mail before we do, owing to their having a mailbox. I ran to the 'phone with a chill of fear. "Oh, Mrs. Macdonald," came Mrs. Leask's agitated voice, "have you seen the paper today?" "Not yet," I said, "Why?" "Oh, there is terrible news—terrible news."

I saw the British line broken at last—entirely and hopelessly broken.

"What is it?" I gasped.

"Oh, you'll see—it's terrible—it's dreadful."

She raved on like this and I could not get one word of sense out of her as to what had really happened. So I hung up the receiver and waited for Ewan. He came and the news was that Messines Ridge was lost. This was bad enough. But the line was only pushed back, not broken. As for Mrs. Leask's hysterics, I discovered that they were caused, not by the indisputably bad news of the loss of the ridge but by the Governmental announcement that all young men of military age were to be called up at once, regardless as to whose sons they were, farmers or otherwise. Mrs. Leask has two strapping slackers of military age. Hence *her* upset.

All day I was worried and depressed. In the evening we drove down to Uxbridge and got an evening paper. Again bad news—the British had retreated from the Ypres salient. That they had retreated "successfully" did not gild the pill much. Thursday the news continued bad. Friday I went to the office and waited in my usual horrible suspense. It seemed to me that I could *not* open a paper to look at the headlines and I dreaded the moment the *Globe* would be passed out to me. I was spared this. When the mailman came in he said, "The war news is better today." So I opened the paper more calmly. It *was* better The Germans had not make any further progress and the British were holding firmly against fierce attacks. Today the *Star* reviewer thinks that the crisis of this attack is over.

Yesterday the thirty days since the opening of the offensive were out.

Tuesday, May 7, 1918
Leaskdale, Ont.

Since last entry the war news has been neutral, but it is evident another attack is impending. The British have advanced in Palestine and there are warnings of another Austrian offensive on the Piave. I have been housecleaning hard all week.

To-day was something of an "epoch". Ivor Law brought our automobile home tonight. It really gave me quite a thrill. It is only very lately that I had begun to think we might have one. Seven years ago I would have laughed at the supposition.

I remember the first time I ever rode in an auto—that morning when Stella and I arrived in Boston and Mr. Nernay took us out to Roslindale in a taxi. I had several rides while there

"Our new car"

and when Ewan and I went to England we had several. We liked them immensely; but when I said jokingly to Ewan "What will your congregation say if we set up an auto," he replied, "My session would likely ask me to resign."

When I came here cars were still so much of a novelty that we ran to the window to see one going by. Now half our people have them and there are almost as many cars as buggies at our church Sunday mornings. Our old buggy was ready to scrap so we decided to get a car. It is a Chevrolet five passenger.

I don't know that I am wholly pleased. Personally, I prefer a buggy with a nice lovable horse like dear little "Queen". But I realize a car's good points also, as time and distance-savers. And one must "keep up with the procession." But I think I shall occasionally remember with regret the old days—and moonlit nights—of buggy driving. A moonlit night loses its charm in a car with its glaring lights.

Anyhow, I'm glad my courting days were over before the cars came. There is no romance whatever in a car. A man can't safely drive it with one arm! And loitering is impossible.

Wednesday, May 29, 1918

Worse news—the Germans are sweeping on to the Aisne. We went to Uxbridge this afternoon to see a military funeral. Colonel Sam Sharpe, for whom I voted last December was buried. He came home from the front quite recently, insane from shell-shock and jumped from a window in the Royal Victoria at Montreal. Thousands of people attended the funeral.

Saturday, June 1, 1918
The Manse, Leaskdale, Ont.

I spent the forenoon of this warm and windy day preserving rhubarb with my body and waiting for the war news with my soul. And it was bad! The Germans have reached the Marne again—the *Marne*! They have got Chateau Thierry—an outpost of Paris, so to speak. The afternoon was haunted for me. But in the evening Ewan motored down to Uxbridge and got an evening paper. The news was a little better—the French are counter-attacking in the Chateau Thierry region. Perhaps I shall sleep tonight after that—and perhaps I won't.

Saturday, June 8, 1918
All this week the war news has been negatively good. The Germans have made no further advance. They are quiet—preparing I suppose for a final leap on Paris.

I went into Toronto on Tuesday and stayed till last night. Had a pleasant time but always with an ache of dread in the background. I wonder if there will ever again come a time when life will be free from *fear*. For nearly four years now we have lain down with fear and risen up with it. It has been the unwelcome sharer in every meal, the unbidden guest at every gathering.

Saturday, June 15, 1918
Leaskdale, Ont.
Another week of suspense and ding-dong fighting. The news to-day was that the Germans have again been "fought to a standstill". But they are a *little* nearer Paris. Just one more spring! And what then?

June is half gone. It and May have been nightmares of months. The world is beautiful now—but the spring means nothing to me. I shall never forget May and June of 1918.

I am preparing to go "down home". It is three years since I was there. I have no feeling that I want to go—partly, I suppose, because of the war, partly because the impression made on my subconscious mind by my physically uncomfortable visit last time is still so strong. Then—I *hate* to leave home. I *like* my home so well—I am so interested in my garden and all my household doings. Last night I saw the "new star" over which the astronomical world is vastly excited just now. It is very brilliant. The general theory is that it is the product of a collision which occurred sometime in the reign of good Queen Bess. News of this disaster, signalled across space on the wings of light, has just reached us. It is curious to look at that star and realize that you are looking at something that happened over three hundred years ago. But even this event cannot dwarf into what may be the proper perspective in star systems the fact that the Germans are again but one leap from Paris.

I have never had time to resume the studies in astronomy which so fascinated me a year or two before my marriage. I wish I might have but I suppose I never shall. The memory of them is most fascinating. They gave me such a strange, *spiritual* pleasure—an *unearthly* pleasure in more senses than one. I should have liked to be an astronomer—failing that to have an astronomer among my friends. Fancy talking the gossip of the hosts of heaven! I wonder if astronomers feel as much interest in earthly affairs as other folk do. Perhaps a student of the canals in Mars would not be so keenly awake to the significance of a few yards or so of trenches lost and won on the Western front. I have read somewhere that Ernest Renan wrote one of his books during the siege of Paris in 1870 and "enjoyed doing so very much". I suppose one could call him a philosopher. I have also read that just before his death he said that his only regret was that he "had to die before he had seen what that extremely interesting young man, the German Emperor, would do in his life." If Ernest Renan "walked" today and saw what "that interesting young man" had done to his beloved France, not to speak of the world I wonder if his mental detachment would be as complete as it was in 1870.

Wednesday, June 19, 1918
The news is good—the Italians are holding splendidly. I am thankful that I will not have to leave home in the shadow of another disaster.

I am all packed up and we leave in an hour. I wish the journey were over. It is bound to be rather strenuous with two children. And I really don't want to go. I *wouldn't* go, if it weren't for the probability that if I go I can induce Aunt Annie to come back with me for a visit. She needs a change and a rest so badly but she cannot face the thought of starting out alone.

Saturday Noon, June 22, 1918
Victoria Hotel
Charlottetown, P.E. Island
Glory be, here we are. Last night we reached Sackville, three hours late. I had been worried lest the boat train wouldn't wait for us, but it did. We had a most tedious ride to Tormentine in the dark. This was the first time I had travelled over the new car-ferry route. Perhaps I shall like it when I get used to it but I found it horrible last night. There seemed to be no end to the shifts and changes, and with a heavy grip and two tired children these were not exhilarating. And amid all the men around me not one ever offered to carry that grip for me or lift a child. Certainly chivalry is not among the virtues of the majority of our Canadian men, whatever else they may possess! It was 20 to eleven the boat left Tormentine and twenty to one when our train left Borden. Luckily both lads went to sleep as soon as we got in it and slept the whole way to Ch'town where we arrived at the agreeable hour of 2.30. It was past three when we finally got to bed at the hotel.

To-day was fine and distinctly cool. The Island *flavor* is excellent. But I feel very much like a stranger in Ch'town now. It does not seem to be the town of my girlhood in any respect. I took a walk round "The Square" and tried to "think myself back" but couldn't.

The war news *seems* good but is so wretchedly mixed up and inadequate in the Island papers. At least, the Italians are still holding.

Tuesday, June 25, 1918
Kinross, P.E. Island
Saturday afternoon we went out to Bellevue and stayed till this afternoon with Rod and his new wife—who is—or was—a widow, older than himself with three children. Ewan's mother has lost her memory completely—did not know

us at all—does not know anybody. It is very pitiful. I have known so many cases like this. It makes one dread the thought of growing old.

Most of Sunday was a cold driving rainstorm. Yet I liked it. It was so thoroughly "down-eastern." We have nothing like it in Ontario. The Ontario rains have no "bite" to them—no such fine real fury and swoop. Then in the evening it cleared up suddenly and goldenly and Rod took Stuart and me to Valleyfield church where the minister preached as if he were scolding the people. But we had supper at the manse afterwards and he is good company of a sort. He is a Scotchman with a tang to his conversation which is not—exactly—wholly spiritual!

Monday afternoon Rod drove me over to Montague to see a family of my second cousins over there—Dr. MacIntyre's. The drive was delightful. Never did I smell more delicious odors of ferns and fir along the road. Yesterday's storm was an alchemist of power.

The doctor's mother was a Park Corner Montgomery—one of "Little Donald's" daughters—and a long-ago friend of my mother. She told me the dearest little story of her—a story that *revealed* her to me as nothing else has ever done—that made her *real* to me—that made me understand clearly what a gulf of difference there must have been between my mother and her two sisters. It made me feel, too, that if mother had lived she and I would have been chums—we would have understood each other.

"One day when I was in Clifton", said the old lady, "I went up to see your mother. She opened the door for me and exclaimed, 'Oh, I am *so* glad to see you. I am all alone and I just felt I *couldn't* endure it if somebody didn't come.'"

"Well, I'm here now and I'll help you out," I said. "What is your trouble?"

"Oh," Clara said, "little Lucy Maud is *so* sweet and lovely to-day and Hugh John is away and I've *no one* to help me enjoy her!"

I felt as rich as a multi-millionaire when this old old lady fished up out of the deeps of her memory, so soon to be dust, this pearl for me. How easily I might never have possessed it! My girlish mother—only 21—exulting in the charm of her baby. I have so often felt this over my own and missed Frede for nothing more than our mutual raptures of adoration over chubby little Chester and angel-eyed Stuart.

We went out for a ride in the Doctor's big "Overland" in the evening. For the motor car is on the Island at last—to stay. To be sure, there are yet two closed days—Tuesday and Friday—and some complicated Sunday regulations. But soon these will cease to exist.

In one way I'm rather pleased. I hate to hear the Island made fun of for its prejudice against cars. On the other hand I resent their presence in this haunt of ancient peace. I wanted it kept sacred to the gods of the old time. I wanted to think that there was one place in the world where the strident honk-honk of a car-horn could never jar on the scented air.

But I enjoyed my drive in the doctor's car for all that—even if we did get ingloriously ditched at the end, owing to a certain grim old dame who *wouldn't* rein her horse out to let us pass. The others were furious. But in my heart I believe I sympathized with the old girl. Had I been a spinster lady, driving along with my own nag, in maiden meditation fancy free, I believe *I* wouldn't have stirred a finger when an obstreperous car honked behind me. No, I should just have sat up as dourly as she did and said "Take the ditch or the devil for all of me!"

It all depends on the point of view!

Rod brought me up to Christy's this evening and tomorrow we go to Cavendish.

Wednesday, June 26, 1918
Cavendish, P.E. Island

It seems just as natural as ever to write that heading. Yesterday morning we came to town and had dinner with Fannie Wise. Whom should I meet there but Ida McEachern whom I have never seen since we parted in Ch'town station over twenty four years ago. Yet she had not greatly changed—a little older looking but I would have known her anywhere. She is Mrs. George Sutherland and is living in Ch'town.

We came out to Hunter River on the afternoon train and started from there with McGuigan's team as of old, on a beautiful evening. On the Mayfield hills we were overtaken by a motor load of H.R. folks who knew me and they offered transportation to Cavendish. So we crawled down and up and in, and speedily reached Cavendish—where even yet it causes a sensation when anyone arrives in an auto.

As we spun down over Laird's Hill I got a blow in the face!

Three years ago I had been horrified on reaching that same hill to discover that the beautiful living wall of spruces on the western side had been cut down. Nature has done her kindly best in those three years to repair the wrong. The wonderful beauty of that wooded slope she could not replace; but she had cured the hideousness. The piles of unslightly brush and unsightlier stumps were hidden under a lush growth of ferns and shrubs. The hill was once more beautiful in a much humbler way.

But this blow was far worse. The old school woods had been cut down!! That once green, wide, beautiful hill was an abomination of desolation of stumps. The schoolhouse sat on its crest wantonly, indecently naked. The whole sight was obscene. If I had had the power I would have spitted Garfield Stewart—the author of the outrage—on a bayonet without pity and without remorse.

It hurt me horribly—not only then, but every time I passed it. A thousand little pitiful ghosts were robbed of their habitations and haunts by the felling of those trees. Scores of tender memories were outraged and banished. That spot I had loved so much since the first day I had followed shyly my older schoolmates into its green shadows to be so desecrated!

Oh, Cavendish, I think I had better not come back to you evermore!

But here I am and half-drunken with the old charm of it. Yonder in the twilight is Lover's Lane. I shall go to it tomorrow. They tell me no wickedness has been worked there. It is well.

Saturday, June 29, 1918
Cavendish, P.E.I.

Very lovely days and very pleasant weather—very delightsome meetings with old friends—very unwriteable walks in my so-beautiful old lane. I am very happy. It is good to be here.

The war news, too, has been good. The Italians have routed the Austrians entirely and chased them back over the Piave. But, the western front still awaits the next decisive blow. I long for a *Globe* somewhat—but my hungry soul is being fed with divine manna and other longings are numbed. I had not really remembered that the sea here was *so* blue and the roads so red and the wood nooks so wild and green and fairy haunted. Yes, the fairies still abide here. Even the motor cars cannot scare them away. Do not scores of them live in the white and pink bells of the columbines growing wild just over the fence in the old orchard?

Sunday Evening, June 30, 1918
Cavendish, P.E.I.

To-day was a warm, golden-cloudy, lovable day. Myrtle, Chester and I went to the Baptist church in the morning. Verily, I have to write of a greater miracle than the motor car. The minister Mr. Piper, asked all members of any church to sit at the communion table with the others there! That, with the Cavendish hard-shells, *is* miraculous. Verily, the world *do* move!! And even Deacon Arthur Simpson has to be dragged along with it. Had anyone, twenty years ago, predicted that one day Arthur Simpson and I should sit at the same communion table *I* would have laughed in graceless disbelief and Arthur would likely have died of heart failure caused by shock on the spot. Yet it has come to pass.

However, if Deacon Arthur felt any qualms over the un-immersed "communing" with him, he was doubtless consoled by the sermon which preceded it, preached not by Mr. Piper, but by a certain Rev. Wallace, an evangelist of the old type, who has been holding "revival" meetings here for a fortnight. It was the rankest "Baptist" discourse I ever listened to—utterly unsuited to the occasion and utterly uncalled for in a Baptist church, where everyone—presumably—was a Baptist. Otherwise, it was a deliberate insult to those of another denomination. But I think I had a bit of revenge.

After the service I was speaking to people outside. Presently old Mrs. Arthur dragged me up to Rev. Wallace to be introduced. Poor old Mrs. Arthur S. always hated me as she hated my mother before me and all through my girlhood pursued me with petty malice and invective. But even she couldn't resist the temptation to sun herself in a bit of reflected glory emanating from a real live author.

She presented me to Rev. Wallace as "Mrs. Macdonald". Rev. Wallace nodded in a bored way and extended an indifferent hand as if to say, "Woman, what is your Mrs. Macdonald to *ME*?" Poor Mrs. Arthur, seeing her fireworks fall thus flat, hastily added, "The author of *Anne of Green Gables*, you know."

The most laughable change came over that man's face. First he looked surprised and delighted; then—I swear, he thought of that awful sermon—he turned a dull red. His manner was the most ludicrous mixture of embarrassment and adulation. He seized my hand again—he exclaimed fulsomely, "Did I ever think I would live to see this day?"—he piled compliment on compliment—and all the while I could see him thinking, in the back of his mind, "Oh, Lord, what an ass I have made of myself! Why did I say those things? Let me get away and kick myself."

But I did not pity him a bit. He had made statements which were false—which he must have known were false but which he thought would impose on an audience of uncritical country hearers—and he deserved what he got. May a like confusion fall on all of his kidney.

After dinner while Stuart was asleep Ernest rowed Chester, Marion, Keith and me down the pond to the shore and we had a delightful afternoon. Chester had his first experience of paddling and, though he hung back very suspiciously at first, he enjoyed it after being thoroughly initiated. Not only did the minister's son go paddling but the minister's wife went too. In the snap Ernest took of us I fondly believed I had hidden my legs—but there is an odd number, as anyone can see!...

Chester, Marion Webb,
L.M. Montgomery, Keith Webb

Wednesday, July 10, 1918
Cavendish, P.E.I.

I had a delightful sojourn at the manse. I rather dreaded going, because my last visit there, for several reasons, was not at all pleasant, though nobody was to blame. But this time it was wholly delightful. It poured rain the night I went over—the first bad rain I've had in Cavendish, but that did not matter. Margaret and I settled down to a good, soul-satisfying gossip.

The next day was fine. Some old friends called. In the evening Stuart and I had a walk in the graveyard. I felt again acutely the peculiar charm of the Island. A certain wellspring of fancy which I thought had gone dry in me bubbled up as freshly as of old. I was again a poet....

When I had tucked my two tired babies away in their bed I gave myself a little secret pleasure. Away I went alone in the twilight. I was going *home*. I walked down to the corner, whence I could see the New London light flashing against the misty sky. Then I went along the school road and climbed the fence into what used to be our old lane. I shut my eyes as I walked up along the fence through the hay. I imagined the old lane was there just as it used to be—and that the homelight was shining through the trees. But when I found myself again in the old "front orchard" it was hard for imagination to do more. There was no transforming moonlight as when I was there last. The gray twilight revealed the woeful desolation of everything. Uncle John had been murdering more trees in the grove. The old maple was gone and all the dear white birches. Through the broken window panes torn strips of the old white blinds were fluttering. The poor old home, how sad, how forlorn, how reproachful it looked!

I slipped around to the back and saw that the door was secured only by a wire easily unfastened. I did what I had never expected to do again—I opened the door and once more crossed the old threshold. I stood in the old kitchen. It was quite clearly visible. A damp odor of decaying plaster hung heavily on the air. I went through the sitting room and the parlor. In each I shut my eyes and *thought myself back* into the past. Everything was around me as of old—each picture, each chair in its place. I went up the stairs in the dark. I stood on the threshold of my old room—my old small illimitable kingdom. But I did not go in. The window was boarded up and the room was as dark as midnight. Somehow, I could not enter it. It was too full of ghosts—lonely, hungry ghosts. They would have pulled me in among them and kept me. I would have disappeared from the realm of mortals and nobody would ever know what had become of me. I was quite possessed by this absurd conviction.

But I went through the "lookout" and the north room. And I went down again and out and away. These pilgrimages to shadow land are eerie things with an uncanny sweetness. I will make no more of them.

We came to Alec's tonight.

Saturday, July 13, 1918
Cavendish, P.E.I.
We are having such a good time. The weather has been lovely, the boys good. Alec and May and I are out for fun. Our pleasantest times are after nine o'clock at night. Chores are done—the lads in bed. Then we three get into the dining room and sit around the table for a couple of hours, eating, talking and laughing. May is one of the best cooks in the world and there is no flavor like memories of old times—the preserved essence of the best of the past. The last time I was here I had a poor sort of visit, through nobody's fault, and was secretly glad to go. But this time I shall be very very sorry.

To-day was idyllic as to weather. After dinner I took the boys to the shore, stripped their legs and let them splash and wade at will, while I sat on the sand and read a novel, or dreamed dreams I thought I had forgotten the secret of.

When we got back the Stirlings came along in a friend's auto and we all went for a spin to the harbor.

This evening Alec took me in to Lizzie (Stewart) Laird's and left me there while he went on an errand. That was a rather gruesome experience. I have never seen poor Lizzie since my marriage. We used to be good friends. But about six years ago she became insane—was in the asylum for a year—and has never been her old self since. She looks so old—and is so quiet and strange. She seemed glad to see me but would not or could not talk. I don't know what I should have done if Everett hadn't been there. *He* could and did talk enough for four. I don't greatly relish his type of conversation but I was thankful for anything to tide over my ghastly predicament. Bodily illness is bad enough but illness of the mind is incomparably worse. It is as if your friend's dead body moved and spoke before you in a horrible imitation of a life that had fled. *Where was the Lizzie I used to have such pleasant hours with*? *She* was not there, wherever she was. Only once, just as I was leaving did she reappear for a moment, as a face might peer briefly from the window of a deserted house.

"You look just the same, Maud," she said in her old tone. "You haven't changed at all."

It was the only thing she had said without being spoken to. I answered laughing, "Oh, you can't see that I've some gray hairs in this light, Lizzie."

But "Lizzie" had gone. The creature who had usurped her faded body answered in the strange stilted unnatural tone she had used all the evening, "Well, they are honorable."

I came away saddened.

Wednesday, July 17, 1918
Cavendish, P.E.I.

I opened the *Guardian* with trembling fingers. But the news was reassuring. The drive seems already checked. So I went off to my afternoon at Hammond's in good cheer and had a very nice time. I missed Toff who died two years ago. But Aunt Margaret is still there, an old miracle of 95, able to do the finest and daintiest fancy work. I could see no change save that she seemed a little thinner and more shrunken. Chester eyed her with great curiosity and after we left said to me, "Mother, did you say she was 95?" "Yes," I replied. "Oh, she couldn't be, mother," he said. "That bed was very small and if she was 95 she

"Stuart, Alec [Macneill] and I"

would never be able to get into it." I suppose the poor laddie thought you went on growing as long as you live and that a person of 95 must be a giant.

In the evening Alec came for us and took us for a drive round the "shore road" to the harbor. It was delightful.

Friday Night, July 19, 1918
Park Corner

Last night, after I had got back from my walk, I said to May, "Let's call up Jane for a bit of fun tonight."

Thereby hangs a tale—or what is worse, an explanation! It is twenty eight years since I first learned to "make a table rap". We used to do it out in Prince Albert for an evening's fun. When I returned home I introduced it among the Cavendish young fry and it was the fashionable amusement of the winter. Then we grew tired of it and dropped it. About ten years ago something started it up again and one winter we had lots of fun over it. I remember some rather remarkable evenings at Will Houston's, where we got a great many rather strange answers. But I soon gave up this form of amusement—at least in public—for two reasons. In the first place, it annoyed me to have people say that "I pushed the table"; in the second place ignorant gossip got busy and circulated weird tales of dealings with devils.

I have never for one moment believed in what is called "spiritualism". Nothing I have ever seen or read has convinced me for a moment that any communication from the dead is possible by such means. But I *do* believe that the phenomena thus produced is produced by some strange power existent in ourselves—in that mysterious part of it known as the subconscious mind—a power of which the law is utterly unknown to us. But that there is a law which governs it and that the operations produced by that law are perfectly natural could we but obtain the key to them I am firmly convinced.

Although I gave up making tables rap in public May and I kept it up in private for our own amusement—and we had many an afternoon's fun out of it. We both held our tongues religiously and it never leaked out, so that ignorance and malice did not get any chance to flesh their tongues on us.

We used a little square "fancy" table in May's parlor and for convenience sake we called the power that made it move "Jane." We also assumed, for the fun of it, that spirits *were* present and wanted to communicate with us. We got no end of messages from this source—and some of them I must admit were strange enough. For one thing, they always were true to type—quite characteristic of the people as we knew them in life, or as we conceived them to be, for we did not limit ourselves in time or space and the "spirit" of "Roaring Ack" Stewart talked to us through "Jane" as freely as that of Queen Elizabeth and St. Paul—the latter always couching his message in Biblical style! I do not pretend to understand or explain it. There was one message in particular which I could never explain and which gave me a queer chill. There was a circle of us around the table that night and "Jane" was rapping out a message from Alec's father—old "Mr. Charles." It began "See to our Pensie's—", at this juncture I, who was spelling out the message, felt quite sure that the next word would be "son" or "child." The others at the table all told me afterwards that they thought the same. But the next word was "grave"—"See to our Pensie's grave."

After the others had gone May and Alec told me what I had never before heard—that Pensie's husband had never put a headstone up for her and that the grave was so overgrown with briar bushes that they could not be sure just where it was. Nobody at the table but Alec and May knew this and they had not thought of it. Nevertheless, I suppose the knowledge was in their subconscious minds....

It is a curious fact that when there are in the circle one or more people, who have never seen a table rap, even if they are not incredulous, it is a long time before it will begin. I have often sat for as long as three or four hours with a "green" circle before it would move. But once it has moved then ever after, if that same "circle" sit down the table will rap very quickly. In our old afternoons "Jane" would respond as soon as May and I laid our hands on the table; but it had been so long since we had tried it that I thought likely it would be proportionately long before the raps would begin. To my surprise, the minute we placed our hands in position the table almost *leapt up*—the impression made on both of us was that *something* was so amazingly glad to see us that it fairly bounded out in its joy.

We had an hour's fun out of "Jane". We did not call up any spirits from the vasty deep but contented ourselves with asking comical questions and putting "Jane" through all her old stunts—such as walking around the room on two legs exactly like a human being, bowing, dancing, keeping time to music etc. etc. When we finished Alec got up off the sofa where he had been lying, said "Well, there's something in you, Maud, that isn't in other people" and went to bed.

This morning Stuart and I drove over to Park Corner with Alec, and Ham Macneill brought Chester and my trunk. As we drove up under the birches Frede was at the well, fat as a seal and looking like the spirit of laughter incarnate. We've been talking ever since and our tongues are not quite worn out yet. There is enough to talk of, goodness knows—if talking would do any good. Matters here are bad and complicated enough. I see no way out and am rather sick at heart over it all. But then I'm very tired.

In spite of all, though, it is good to be here again. To adapt Alec, "There's something about Park Corner that isn't in other places"....

Monday, July 22, 1918
The miracle of the Marne has been repeated. It seems like a dream far too wonderful to be true. Again the Germans are hurled back across the Marne. It *is* the beginning of the end—I feel it—I feel it! I am *sure* the long agony is over. Frede remains somewhat pessimistic but I am suddenly borne aloft on the crest of a rosy wave of optimism.

Yesterday Life Howatt came up with his motor and took us up to Princetown—"us", being Frede, Aunt Annie, myself, Amy and Stuart. It was Aunt Annie's first trip in an auto. It was very pleasant—the day was fine and the sea beautiful. Aunt Emily is not very well—she has some heart trouble that is obscure and may be serious. We had a pleasant visit until the evening when we got into a foolish wrangle over conscription—Frede and I against Aunt E. We all got rather excited and some bitter things were said.

It was foolish—it is always foolish to argue with a woman of Aunt Emily's type. She is as narrow minded and merciless as her mother before her. We should have laughed at her and let it pass—even if she did give Frede several nasty digs all along the afternoon. We combed her down well—and were remorseful all the way home about it. "Maudie," Frede remarked to me, as we swooped in under the old trees at the gate, "if Aunt Emily dies of heart failure tonight I shall always feel that we murdered her." "The gods forfend," I said, and repented me quakingly. It wasn't worth while to have tormented Aunt Emily. But she always did continue to set my teeth on edge every time I fell in with her. And yet she can be awfully nice at times and quite jolly. Only, she has poor grandfather's fatal love of "giving digs," as he called it. He could not refrain from it—neither can she. I wonder if the satisfaction of a "dig" balances the loss of affection and friendship it entails. Aunt Emily has always felt and resented the fact that people do not give her the love and confidence they give Aunt Annie. It never seems to occur to her that the reason is in herself. I recall some things that Aunt Emily said to me when I was a young girl that I can never forget—little poisoned arrows that have rankled ever since. Yet I have no doubt she forgets she ever said them and would be amazed if she were told of them.

I suppose conscription is a sore point with Aunt Emily because she has a son who is a slacker. Jack Montgomery never tried to enlist and juggled out of the draft someway. She *must* feel it but she will not show it. Jack is a miserable specimen and I fancy his goings on are at the bottom of his mother's illness. He has a taste for low company and seems quite devoid of ambition. Yes, Frede and I were too hard on Aunt Emily—but in the dusk tonight as we sat on the north veranda we howled over some of the things we said and she said. We have not heard today that she died last night so we feel free to laugh in spite of our repentance. Frede and I can always laugh, thanks be! It is one of the strongest cords of the bond between us. If there is a lurking joke in anything Frede and I can always drag it out, hide it never so slyly. And if there isn't a joke we can make one. Aunt Annie looks at us occasionally as if to say, "Oh, when you're as old as I am you won't see much to laugh at." Well, I daresay that is true; and yet I can't conceive of Frede and I foregathering, even at seventy, and not being able to laugh—not being able to perceive that sly, lurking humor that is forever peeping round the corner of things. I am forty three and she is thirty five—old enough to be sobered. And God knows, the lives of neither of us have been devoid of sobering experiences. But when we are together we can laugh with the abandonment of sixteen.

Sunday, July 28, 1918
A beautiful day. This afternoon Aunt Annie and Dan and I drove through to Long River church. When we came back Life Howatt came up and motored us down to Mr. Howatt's for tea. We had one of those wonderful "spreads" which only Island people can—or do—get up, and which they still continue to get up despite the howls of the Food Board. In my own house we haven't had cake

for a year, but since I've been on the Island I've seen heaps of it—and eaten heaps of it, too, I must admit. We motored home under the stars and Frede and I, before we went to bed, sat down and talked everything over de gustibus.

Tuesday, July 30, 1918
Margaret Stirling came over yesterday evening and she and Frede and I had a delightful little supper together by our three selves and a good pow-wow of gossip and reminiscence.

An odd thing happened today.

I never like to sit down thirteen at a table. My reason tells me that it is only an absurd superstition. Something more primitive than reason insists on being uneasy. Sixteen or seventeen years ago I was at a party one night and sat thirteen at table. Will Stewart, one of my schoolmates was there, and he died before six weeks had passed. I have never happened to sit with thirteen from that time until today.

There is such a gang of us here, especially of children, that, since I came, we have never all sat down to any meal at once. Aunt Annie, Frede, or Ella would wait on the table and eat afterwards. Today at dinner time, however, it so happened that everyone sat down and I began to count them just out of curiosity to see how many there really were—George, Ella, Aunt Annie, John Cole (the hired man), myself, Frede, Dan, Amy, Jim, Georgie, Maudie, Chester and Stuart—thirteen.

More as a joke than anything else I said "Why there are thirteen of us at the table."

The next moment I thought, "Well, what an asinine thing of me to say! Here is Ella, expecting a baby and depressed and pessimistic as it is. If she believes in the superstition of thirteen it may prey on her mind and have a disastrous effect."

To erase any such impression from Ella's mind I laughed and said to Frede, "Frede, you were the thirteenth to sit down—the omen must be for you."

Frede had, however, jumped up and declared she would not sit at the table. I laughed again and said, "Oh, you did sit and you had begun to eat. No use in getting up now—your doom is sealed. May as well sit down and eat resignedly."

But Frede vowed she wouldn't and made off to the porch. George who, it seems, had never heard of the superstition, burst into one of his howls of laughter at us and called Frede and me fools, etc. No doubt we were. Yet somehow the trivial incident has left a disagreeable impression on my mind. What if Ella—but nonsense! I won't allow myself to think such silly things.

After we got everybody off to bed tonight Frede and I broiled ourselves a snack of beef ham and devoured it with sounds of riot and mirth. We are at one in our love of beef ham. I wonder if the spirits of the departed ever eat spirit-beef-ham.

Sunday, August 4, 1918
Park Corner, P.E. Island

It won't be Park Corner much longer. We go tomorrow—Frede, Aunt Annie, my two lads and I.

I can hardly say I'm sorry. In one way I've had a jolly time here—Frede and I together could make jollity in the realms of Pluto I verily believe. But in another way it has been rather hard. Seven children all under ten are something of a houseful. This does not mean that Chester and Stuart did not agree with their cousins—on the contrary they agreed remarkably well. But the better they agreed the more ear-splitting was the racket they made and the more fearful and unheard-of the scrapes they got into out of doors. One day Aunt Annie found them all out behind the barn thrashing a big mud puddle furiously with boughs. They were mud from head to foot. They were "fighting Germans," they told her, and the puddle was a trench!! In truth, the only times that were at all peaceful were when they had an occasional tiff and sulked for an hour or so before they made up.

Chester and Jim were especial cronies but this did not prevent them from having bitter rows on *politics*—generally after they went to bed at night. Frede and I used to sit on the stairs in the dark outside their door listening to them, doubling up with suppressed laughter over their incredible speeches.

John Cole, the hired man, an eccentric old chap, has a great admiration for Chester. Frede delights to quote his speech to her when he first saw Chester, "Never saw such legs—never saw such legs since I saw the strong old sea-captains down at Pinette. I would not be the man that crosses his path when he grows up—that would not I!"

Frede is always tickled when a compliment is paid Chester. He is her favorite. Most people are more taken with Stuart. *He* has a sunny little face, a ringing infectious laugh and an engaging personality which win him affection very readily and which will probably constitute one of his pitfalls in afterlife. Chester, on the contrary, is a rather reserved and distant little mortal and does not make so favorable an impression at first. But he has always been Frede's white-haired lad—they are both "cats that walk by themselves" and care little if other Toms and Tabbies are indifferent.

But I have wandered afar and must return to my mutton—my reasons for being rather glad to be leaving Park Corner. The real reason is the truly terrible and unhappy state of affairs that obtains here now—a state of affairs that has been gradually growing worse year by year until at last it has reached a pitch that seems to me utterly intolerable for those who live here. It seems to me that things *can't* go on like this any longer without some disaster. God himself must be tired of the situation.

In my childhood and girlhood Park Corner was one of the happiest, gayest spots in the world. Aunt Annie married Uncle John Campbell when she was 28 and he 42. I do not know that there was any romantic love on either side—certainly not on Aunt Annie's. But they were very happy together.

Uncle John's farm at Park Corner was—and is—one of the finest farm properties on P.E. Island. Two hundred acres of fertile soil, acres of fine woodland, shore rights, pond rights of mud and fishing, water on every field of the farm, a splendid orchard and a large beautiful house. The Campbells were a good old family. The original Campbell—Captain Campbell—who emigrated to Canada was a member of the Breadalbane Campbells. There is an old family tradition that he was really the heir to the earldom of Breadalbane. But he made an unhappy marriage in the old land, eventually left his wife and came to Canada, where he passed as an unmarried man and married a Miss Townsend—a cousin of Great Grandmother Macneill's. If the story were true she was certainly not his legal wife. But her right was never questioned in those days when there was little communication between P.E. Island and Scotland, even when it was desired. There may have been nothing in the tale. It sprang, I believe, from the fact that a stranger from Scotland had one day appeared and asked to see Captain Campbell, averring that he brought him news of his wife and family in the old land. Captain Campbell hustled him away and denied the story. So it rests.

His son, James Campbell, settled on the Park Corner farm. His first wife was Elizabeth Montgomery, a sister of "Little Donald" Montgomery, who died after she had borne him two or three sons. He then married her cousin, Elizabeth Montgomery, sister of "Big Donald" Montgomery, my grandfather. (It seems as if the Montgomeries must have been rather short of names in those days). It must be a rather odd sensation to have two wives of the same name. I think it would seem ghostly to me. They had a large family—seventeen children! Fancy one woman bearing seventeen children. And yet, when Aunt Elizabeth was over seventy, she told Aunt Annie one day that "she felt a strange feeling. I think it must be what you call *tired*."

Aunt Elizabeth, as we all called her, was living at Park Corner when Aunt Annie went there and I remember her very well. She lived until I was quite a big girl. She was a very sweet old lady, with remarkably large, deep-set eyes. She had been a great beauty in her youth but her life had its tragedies. When the cholera plague swept over the Island long ago she was ill in bed after the birth of one of her children. When she was able to be up it was to learn that four of her children had died in one week of cholera! Later on two of her sons were drowned in the prime of young manhood. Finally, her husband who had lived the average decent life until he was fifty, suddenly and unaccountably took to drinking and drank himself into the grave.

Some of his sons were by no means models but Uncle John Campbell was one of the best men that ever lived—kind, generous, open-hearted, moral, abstinent, and honest. I always loved him and always found in him a firm friend. Naturally, he had some faults. Intellect was not his strong point. He cared nothing for reading; emotionally he was very unbalanced, though fortunately his temper was of the best. I never saw anything like his agony of grief at the funeral of little Jacky, the oldest born of George and Ella, who died of pneumonia. Uncle John had idolized him and Frede and I had almost to drag him away from the casket by force when the undertaker went to close it. When he was about fifty or fifty-five he became "converted" at some meetings held by an emotional evangelist. Really, I think he was a little out of his head about that time. He could talk of nothing but "religion" and for two or three years bored everybody to death who went to the house. Then the wave passed as suddenly as it came and Uncle John reverted to his former self. He had always been a good man and a good man he remained to the end; but of his frantic religious spasm nothing remained save his newly acquired habit of saying grace, always prefacing it with such an unearthly groan that we graceless youngsters used to have much ado to keep from snickering outright. Uncle John's father became a dipsomaniac at fifty; Uncle John's psychical upheaval took a religious form. That was all the difference. Although he was one of the hardest working men in the world he was absolutely devoid of any business instinct. He could never in all his life save a cent. Money ran through his fingers like water with nothing to show for it. Possessing a property on which, working as he did, he should have grown rich, while living as well as need be, he not only saved nothing in his long life, but died slightly in debt, though this was George's fault, not his.

Aunt Annie has been—and is—a wonderful woman in some ways. A hard worker, a supreme cook, a splendid housekeeper. But she, too, had qualities that in the end were to make for tragedy. She had no "vision" of any sort. No ideals were ever set before her family save the most material ones. And, on the lower plane, she, as well as Uncle John, lacked thrift and business capacity. She made a great deal of money every year with her butter and eggs and poultry and never saved a cent of it. Everything was lavished on hospitality. This might have been pardonable where their own kin were concerned. But they really kept "open house" for the whole Island. They had continual shoals of visitors who cared nothing for them and simply made Park Corner a convenient house of call. It was rare that a summer day or a winter evening passed without "company". Aunt Annie was really quite proud of this, though she often complained of the hard work it involved. Uncle John revelled in playing the host. He was never happier than when seated at a long table carving up joints of meat and platters of geese and turkey. Uncle John Campbell could carve and serve after a fashion rarely seen—not seen at all nowadays. He was an artist at it—could dissect the most complicated old gobbler, give everyone a choice portion, and carry on an easy conversation all the time.

This was all very well in the hey-day. But when Uncle John and Aunt Annie grew old there was no money to fall back on. Everything had been lavished in some way. They had four children—Clara, Stella, George and Frede. Frede was the only one who was any comfort to them. Clara, the oldest, was a nice girl and rather pretty. She was good-tempered and full of fun. But her intellectual capacity was small and she had no ambition, save to be finely dressed and entertain her friends lavishly. Yet there was something very lovable about her and she and I were very dear to each other in our girlhood.

When Clara was seventeen her parents did something I have never been able to understand. They allowed that young girl, at the formative age, to go up to Boston and become a domestic servant. Many of the French River and Park Corner girls did this; it was all right for them; but for Clara it was, or should have been, unthinkable. Clara remained there until she married. She made her friends in a low class, she married in that class. What Uncle John and Aunt Annie were thinking of I cannot imagine. They both came of excellent families, with traditions of birth and breeding. One would have thought they would have been horrified at the idea. On the contrary they rather encouraged it.

Stella was clever, capable and jolly. At first her spasms of temper were not so frequent or so frantic as they afterwards became. But her parents never made any serious or intelligent effort to check it. The things Stella flew into rages over were the things Aunt Annie disliked also and therefore she found it easy to tolerate or pardon Stella's outbursts.

George Campbell was, from babyhood, a person I never had any use for. For his mother's and sisters' sake I have always taken care to "keep on his good side"—flattering his vanity and ignoring his drawbacks. As a result George has always liked me, treated me as decently as he could treat anybody, called one of his children after me—and borrowed money of me! I have considerable influence over him, as also has Frede. His mother and his wife have absolutely none.

George seemed to inherit the worst qualities of both parents, with none of their good ones. He has his father's lack of business ability without his father's industry, his father's lack of emotional control without his father's decency of emotion, he has his father's lack of taste for things of the intellect without his father's liking for society and conversation. He has his mother's intolerance of anything outside the narrow range of her experience without her kindly tolerance of things *in* it, he has her utter disregard for other people's feelings without her real regard for their material welfare, he has her lack of vision and ideals without her homely pleasure in everyday life, and her lack of any ability to judge character, without the innate dislike of taking suggestions from anybody that stood her in fairly good stead. In addition George inherited from a remoter source a taste for liquor, eventually resulting in drunkenness and immorality, a distaste for steady effort, and the temper of a fiend.

George was indulged all his life. The only son, born after two girls, he was petted and spoiled as a child. His sisters were expected to wait on him and his father never had any control over him. He matured early—used to be out half the night, driving girls about and "sitting up" with them when he was no more than twelve or thirteen. He soon began to drink. For years his mother refused to believe this and never forgave anyone who told it of him. She has learned it too well since, poor woman.

When he was twenty one George married Ella Johnston. Out of all the world *she* was the last person he should have married. Out of all the world *he* was the last person she should have chosen. It was a marriage nobody could ever understand. It was impossible to see any reason why either of them should have been attracted to the other. Ella was six or seven years older than George—a pretty, delicate little doll who had been brought up in cotton wool all her life because her father and three of her sisters had died of consumption. If she had married a professional or businessman she might have been an average wife. As the wife of a farmer, and especially of big, roystering George Campbell—well, she was a joke. She was well warned that she was marrying a drunkard. He was well warned that he was marrying a useless little doll. In spite of this—or because of it!—marry they did.

"What do you think of her, Maud?" Uncle John Campbell asked me, during the festivities attendant on the wedding.

"I think she looks like a baby astray", I replied.

Uncle John laughed.

"You've just about hit it," he said.

The inevitable happened. In six months George was tired of his wife. In a year he hated her—and she him. For fourteen years they have lived together and things have gone from bad to worse....His mother is broken-hearted, his health is wrecked. At thirty six he looks fifty—red-nosed, bald, bloated. He is in debt—he has a big family to provide for—he is discouraged—his temper is an awesome thing. He uses his wife abominably—oh, it is all utterly heart-sickening.

Ella, too, is a weakling. I pity her—I try to help her—but what is the use? All the little spunk she ever had has been crushed out of her by disappointment and child-bearing. She has had eight children—three of whom have died—and expects another. I am so sorry for the poor thing that it wrings my heart. She appeals to me constantly for advice, sympathy, and help. And I can do so little to help her.

Aunt Annie is perfectly well satisfied with herself as a mother-in-law. Yet she has been a hard one—not in deeds but in words. She has never spared Ella's feelings in anyway—she has been unjust and unfair—she blames all George's bad habits and shortcomings on Ella, stubbornly shutting her eyes to the fact that George drank long before his marriage. As a result, there is not only no sympathy between these two women who have to live together but there is thinly veiled resentment and antagonism. Aunt Annie has all that strange animosity and injustice towards "outsiders" that was so conspicuous in her mother's character. It never occurs to her that she has failed in any respect towards Ella.

But there it is. What an unhappy household, compact of bitterness and hatred and discontent! I feel all the time I am in it as if I walked on the edge of a volcano. I do not *see* the worst—I am only told of it. Since I have been here George has been outwardly decent. He *can* be quite good-humored and pleasant when he likes. George Campbell has a superficial popularity over the country—"a good, open-hearted fellow"—"his own worst enemy" etc.

The evening after I came Frede and I were in the kitchen and George came in. He sat for awhile, laughed and joked, told some funny stories, then went off to bed. Frede said to me,

"Maud, I wonder if you realize the influence you have over George?" He is a different creature when you are here. I have been home for three weeks and in all that time I haven't seen him laugh or heard him tell a joke. He has just gone about in black silence, varied by outbursts of demoniacal temper."

"I think," I said, "that when I come here George feels that something of the atmosphere of old times comes back with me—those good old times when we were all young and gay and carefree together."

If George had married the right sort of a woman—a woman something like his own sister Stella—jolly, capable, strong-willed, not over-refined, with a dash of his own temper I believe he might have developed into a passably decent citizen. As it is, things are simply dreadful here. Frede and I have talked matters over until we are black in the face—but what good does it do? We get nowhere. We seem to be in a blind alley. It seems to me that a catastrophe of some kind is about due....

The only bright spot in this is George's family. They are as nice a brood of smart, handsome agreeable kiddies as you could find anywhere. They are not like either their father or mother. If they get half a chance they will, I believe, restore Park Corner to its old status. I am very fond of them all and so is Frede. We rather feel as if the responsibility of them rests on us—that we must put our shoulders to the wheel and see that they get a chance. They are fond of us and do not resent our guidance and preachments.

Tonight, as I sat for a moment on the veranda I childishly wished that some good fairy would appear and grant me a wish. I would have said,

"Give me back the old Park Corner for an hour—just an hour. Bring Uncle John back—restore Aunt Annie to her smiling, bustling prime—let Clara and Stella be here, gay girls in their teens—let George be the little chubby, innocent boy again. For just an hour give me that olden gladness and beauty back again."

But no good fairy appeared. The clock is never turned back. I cannot have that hour out of the past. The Park Corner of today, still beautiful, still almost the same outwardly, is a terribly different place from the Park Corner of twenty years ago. And so I am not sorry that I go tomorrow.

The Manse, Leaskdale, Ont.
Thursday, Aug. 8, 1918
Last Monday morning the House of Campbell bestirred itself at a very early hour. Everybody was more or less excited—for it was an uncanny thing for Aunt Annie to be going away for a visit. Aunt Annie never gets visibly excited. That is an excellent quality no doubt but think of all the fun you miss if you are non-excitable. There's nothing quite so wonderful as dancing around a blazing fire. What matter if it end only in gray ashes? And while walking is a sure and safe mode of locomotion it isn't half as exhilarating as flying, even if you do come down with a thud.

It was quite dark when I got up. When I went out into the hall and looked out of the big hall window I saw an exquisite sight. Out to the east, over the birches and maples was a silvery red sky and floating in it what seemed like a new moon—but it was the old one in its last hours. I do not recollect ever seeing the old moon at that stage before. The colorings were so exquisite and the whole effect so fairylike and elusive that I called Frede and we watched it together delightedly, until the picture etched itself unforgettably on my brain. I have only to think of it to see it again. It continued beautiful for half an hour, the moon fading out to a wraith as the daylight deepened, and then just disappearing.

Life Howatt motored us to the station. As we left I suddenly burst into tears and cried until we reached the top of the hill. Why? I do not know. I never cried on leaving Park Corner before, though I have left it, feeling more sorrowful than I felt that morning. I was glad to be going home—I was taking with me the only people of it that I cared muchly for. And yet I sobbed uncontrollably as if I never expected to see Park Corner again.

When we got on the train the *Guardian* announced the capture of *Soissons* and all the way home every stop was punctuated with a fresh victory. The French were sweeping all before them. Very different from my last trip home three years ago to the tune of the Russian disaster. We had a very pleasant trip up to Montreal. As the car-ferry steamer was laid up for repairs we crossed by the old Summerside and Pointe-du-Chene route—which I must say I prefer.

Frede and I used to go into carefully secreted spasms of laughter over her mother's face. Aunt Annie had evidently started out with a firm determination not to betray the fact that she was not an accustomed globe trotter. No surprise or admiration or doubt or curiosity would she allow herself to betray. Her expression said plainly, "You need not suppose I am green or provincial. I know just as much as you or anybody." But she was a game old dame and enjoyed herself.

We missed the Toronto train so had to stay in Montreal all day. Left at night. Frede and Aunt A. got off at St. Anne's, as Aunt Annie was to stay a week there. The boys and I reached Toronto Wednesday morning and were met by Ewan and Mr. Fraser. We motored home—52 miles—and got here at noon. My heart was in my mouth when Ewan attempted to negotiate Yonge St. but we got on very well. It has been fairly hot since we came back and I am yet very tired.

Wednesday, Aug. 14, 1918
The Manse, Leaskdale

Yesterday morning Ewan and I rose at four and left at five to motor into Toronto to meet the Montreal train. It was dark as far as Uxbridge and we saw no living creature until we reached Stouffville. It was very delightful to fly along in the cool morning air. We got to Toronto Station at eight and Aunt Annie was on hand. We spent the day showing her Eaton's and Simpson's. I also took her to a moving picture show. I know she considered it an invention of the devil. The day was a record-breaker for heat—102 in the shade. We left for home at five and had a very pleasant drive until about two miles from home when a terrific storm of thunder, rain and wind struck us with all the force and suddenness of a tornado. In a moment we were wrapped in darkness. In Parrish's hollow a tree had fallen across the road. Ewan turned out to avoid it, the car skidded and over we went into the ditch. I screamed as we took the plunge—I felt sure we were going over the culvert. If we had we would all have been killed but fortunately we were a few feet further on, where the ditch was shallower. We crashed into a mailbox post and stopped. Out we scrambled in the downpour. I thought the car was ruined. One wheel was lying on the ground. But at least our lives were spared. Then we had to walk up that long hill lane of Parrish's in the torrents of rain and the pitch darkness lighted only by wild flashes. We stayed there until the storm abated, wet to the skin, for there was no woman in the house to get us a change of clothes. I thought Aunt Annie would catch her death. We drove home after the storm ceased and today neither of us is any the worse. The car, too, is not seriously damaged. Mr. Warner has fixed it up all right. But it has broken my nerve. It will be a long time before I feel comfortable in "Daisy" again.

Monday, August 19, 1918
The Manse, Leaskdale
I resumed work on my book today. I am not as far ahead with it as I could wish. Still, I ought to be able to finish it by the last of October. We have been having a pleasant time. Aunt Annie seems to be enjoying herself thoroughly. The war news is good. Haig's army is advancing now. They go further in a day than in a year before.

Ella has a daughter and is doing well. I feel relieved. I have been vaguely uneasy ever since that table of thirteen—which was very foolish and absurd of me certainly. But reason and feeling are two entirely different things.

Thursday, Aug. 22, 1918
The Manse, Leaskdale, Ont.
To-day we had a picnic up at the Lake. It was all very pleasant and I think Aunt Annie enjoyed it enormously. When we left to come home our steering gear broke—having, it turned out, been cracked the night of our accident. Fortunately we were going slowly in a level place so nothing dreadful happened. We had to sit on the side of the road for two hours however till we got it fixed. A sample of the joys of motoring.

Thursday, Sept. 5, 1918
Yesterday Aunt Annie and I got home after having taken in the Toronto Exhibition. Aunt Annie has had the time of her life and has admitted it. We went in Tuesday morning by train and in the afternoon went to see "Hearts of The World." It is a wonderful thing. I wanted to see it especially because a battle that Carl took part in was featured in it—the battle of Courcelette. He had told us he recognized one scene in particular by a big round hole in a brick wall. So all through the play Aunt Annie and I watched for that hole. Holes there were without number, some of them fairly round, but none seemed exactly to measure up to our expectations. Near the end came the hole—unmis-

"Aunt Annie and I on the Anderson lawn"

takably *the* hole; and we both exclaimed aloud "There's the hole!", much to the amusement of a row of young men in front of us.

This reminds me of a funny thing Frede told me. She went to see the film in Montreal. In one scene, a girl, locked in her room, secretes a knife in her stocking or some such place to defend herself. Enters a brutal German. In the ensuing struggle Frede got so excited by the realism of the thing that she suddenly stood up and shrieked at the top of her voice, "The knife is in your stocking! The knife is in your stocking!" She said afterwards that the only thought in her mind was that the girl must have forgotten the knife was there! To add to the effect, just after Frede shrieked this, the girl pulled out the knife and stabbed the German!!

In the evening, after dinner at the Walker House Aunt Annie and I went to another movie with the hectic title "To Hell with the Kaiser." It was not so lurid as its name—very good, in fact, though not in the same class as "Hearts of the World".

Yesterday morning we went out to the Exhibition grounds. Of course the cars were horribly crowded and it was funny to see Aunt Annie's face when after a breathless sprint to get on a car she found herself hanging to a strap in a jammed car aisle. It said, as plainly as words, "Has all the world gone mad?"

I think she enjoyed the Exhibition thoroughly, though, and it did her a tremendous amount of good to discover that there wasn't an apple in the fruit exhibit that was as good as what her own orchard at Park Corner could produce. I did not mar her joy by telling her that the season is late this year and very few apples as yet available. That would have been needless cruelty. I let her think Park Corner orchard could beat Canada.

And can it not, in a sense?...

Saturday, September 28, 1918
The Manse, Leaskdale
To-day came the news that Bulgaria has asked for peace terms—the first of the enemy nations to throw up the sponge. The end must be very near. All the week the news has been good from every quarter. It has been a busy and pleasant week. On Tuesday Alec Leask's and we motored to Whitby and spent a very pleasant day with the Andersons. Thursday night Ewan and I went to Uxbridge, had tea with the Willises and then went to a W.C.T.U. Medal contest in the Methodist church where I was one of the judges. I spent most of Friday at the church helping to pack Christmas boxes for the Scott boys at the front and today I spent helping Mrs. Cook address them. I am all tired out—but Bulgaria has asked for peace terms!

Monday, Sept. 30, 1918
The Manse, Leaskdale, Ont.
The Hindenburg line smashed in several places—the whole western front ablaze with victory. That was the news the mail brought at noon. I wonder if we have all dreamed it.

Spent another afternoon doing up Red Cross boxes and then we all went down to Edith's to tea. After tea the telephone rang—our ring. Ewan went to the 'phone and the word was, "Bulgaria has surrendered unconditionally and fighting on the Macedonian front ceased at noon today."

There was something dramatic in it as Ewan turned from the 'phone and told us the message.

And the first Allied triumph comes on the front that witnessed their darkest defeat in that terrible autumn of 1915. How vividly I recall the despairs and agonies of that October and November when Mackensen led his Central hordes over doomed Serbia. And now Serbia is once more free—or will be in a very short time.

Thursday, October 3, 1918
Leaskdale, Ont.
On Tuesday came word of the death of Morley Shier, a fine young fellow from our church who went overseas in the flying corps.

St. Quentin was taken yesterday—St. Quentin, that name of evil omen in the terrible retreat last spring.

And to-day is October 3rd—the day of my dream. Has it any significance? Today the *Globe* said "The big retreat has begun". The *Mail and Empire* said, "It may now be said that the battle of Hindenburg line has ended in favor of the allies." Is this enough to justify my dream? One would almost think so—I would have thought so three months ago. But now I do not know. We shall see—we shall see.

SUNDAY, OCTOBER 6, 1918
It should be written in capitals—in letters of gold. Yet it dawned in gloom and drizzle and gloomed and drizzled all day outside. The afternoon was dull. Aunty and I felt rather lonesome—at least I did. She is leaving for home tomorrow. I shall miss her dreadfully. But I think she has had a real good time. She looks ever so much better than when she came and will go home with a store of pleasant memories to refresh her. I wish she could have stayed until the end of October but I have been afraid to urge it lest she get cold travelling so late.

We were sitting in the parlor reading when the telephone rang. I went—but—could hardly believe my ears when I heard the message Mr. Harwood was phoning up. I dashed into the parlor. "Aunt Annie", I exclaimed, "Germany and Austria are suing for peace on President Wilson's terms."

Then I flew back to the 'phone and rung up everybody in the village to tell them the great news. In a few minutes our small burg was athrill with the excitement that was agitating the whole world. The telephone rang constantly. Men ran up and down the street. I got out the flag and ran it up. Then I walked up and down the parlor in my excitement. It was impossible to sit still.

"Sit down, child," said Aunt Annie—who never gets excited over anything and so has missed a tremendous amount of trouble and delight in her journey through life.

"Oh, Aunty", I said, "I have walked this floor for hours in despair and anxiety during these past four years. Now let me walk it in joy."

Mrs. Alec Leask came down and we talked it all over. Ewan came home from Zephyr and I flew out in the rain and met him at the gate.

"Have you heard the news?" I cried, hoping like a child that he hadn't, so that I would be "the first" to tell him. He *hadn't* so I had the fun of being the first. Then we had supper and a gay, merry, happy circle we were.

Of course, the war isn't ended *yet*. There may be and probably will be several weeks of dickering, during which the fighting must go on. But Germany has *asked* for peace—the haughty nation which set out to conquer the world is suing humbly to the Entente. That means that she is down and out. If a ray of hope were left her she would not do it. Yes, the great, the stupendous drama of hell is drawing to a close. The curtain has gone up on the final act. At last—at last—at last! And oh God, at what a price!

Tomorrow is little Stuart's birthday—he is three years old. It has been a long, hard, woeful three years for the world, but for him carefree happiness. He is getting to be quite a companion for Chester. I am glad of this. It is one thing I regret that there are no boys in Leaskdale that are really desirable companions for Chester. He has some little boy chums but they are rather unclassifiable. They come from respectable homes but they do not use very good language at times and I am suspicious that they are smutty little rascals when no grown up is about. But Chester can't be shut away from them. I will be glad when Stuart is old enough to be a real companion. He will "catch up" more or less every year now.

Sunday, December 1, 1918
The Manse, Leaskdale, Ont.

The war is over! Many things are over. It is "a far cry" since my last entry in October. I feel as if I had lived many years in it. Huge, epoch-making world-events have jostled each other in it. And in my own little world has been upheaval and sorrow—and the shadow of death.

On the day following that wonderful Sunday Aunt Annie and I went in to Toronto. We spent the night at Laura's and had a very pleasant time for Carl was up to dinner and stayed for the evening. The next morning I saw poor Aunty off on the Montreal train and then, feeling lonely and sad, went uptown and put in a busy day shopping.

Toronto was then beginning to be panic stricken over the outbreak of the terrible "Spanish flu". The drug counters were besieged with frantic people seeking remedies and safeguards. I didn't think much about it—really had no fear of taking it. Wednesday evening I began to sneeze and I kept that up all day Thursday. However, I felt quite well and would not believe I could be taking the flu. Ewan came in for me and we motored home that night. It was really perfect—the evening was so warm and bright, the autumnal world so beautiful. The fact that the day was warm probably saved my life. If it had been cold and I had got chilled I would probably never have got over it. For that night I took ill with flu—the deadly pestilence of which thousands have died—are dying.

At first it did not occur to me that I had the flu. Friday morning I had a cold in the head and felt sleepy and stupid but not sick. I decided to stay in bed and "sleep it off." Friday passed—Friday night—Saturday morning it was the same. I passed the day in what was really a semi-stupor. I just wanted to lie quiet and "sleep". Yet I never really slept. I was vaguely conscious all the time; but I had no feeling of illness or discomfort. Nevertheless at dusk the idea suddenly dawned on my stupid mind that something was wrong. Two days was too long to be in this condition. I asked Ewan to phone for Shier.

Dr. Shier came. He found me with a ridiculous temperature and a heart that was almost out of business. I would not—probably—have lived till morning. He gave me medicine for my heart and then tablets to induce perspiration—and went away. Later on he said that out of the 75 cases of flu he had I was the worst save one—and that one died!

I certainly don't think it was any merit of Dr. Shier's that I didn't die too. I think he did a perfectly dreadful thing in going away as he did and leaving me with no skilled attendance. I was too stupid to ask for a trained nurse but he should have suggested it. He did not—and I was left alone.

I lay there under piles of clothing—and presently sweating began. Rather! Rivers—literally—of water ran down my body. In no time my night dress and sheets were saturated. They grew cool and I was "demned moist and unpleasant." I could not face the prospect of lying like that all night. But by this time the fever had gone down and my power of thinking returned. I knew it would be an exceedingly dangerous thing to change clothing and sheets in that chilly room. Still, it had to be done. Ewan was asleep in the spare room but I got Lily up and got her to light the oil heater and warm dry sheets and nightdress by it. Then I told her just what to do, as I remembered my nurse's doing it and eventually we managed it. But once or twice I shivered with cold and—knowing what I now know of flu—I wonder that I escaped pneumonia.

I was in bed for ten days. I never felt so sick or weak in my life. The first time I went downstairs I collapsed and Ewan had to carry me up. I am still taking strychnine for my heart, my nerves are bad yet—for a month after I got up I would cry if a door slammed or if I couldn't find a hairpin when I was doing my hair!—and I have not yet been able wholly to shake off the depression and languor that is the worst legacy of the plague.

During my illness I had a letter from Aunt Annie saying that she had got home safely and that two days after she had reached Park Corner George had come down with flu. I feel anxious for I knew what George Campbell was. There would be no keeping him in bed once he felt a little better. A week later, just after I was able to come downstairs, a telegram came from Aunt Annie, saying George had died from pneumonia.

I felt very badly. Not so much because of George's death—although it was curious considering my opinion of George how much I did regret him—these family ties of blood and association are curious things—as because of my sympathy for poor Aunt Annie. He was her only son and though he was far from being what a son should be his death would be a terrible blow to her. And then, with all his shortcomings, he kept things going after a fashion. What on earth would Aunt Annie do, a woman of 70, left alone with that poor, incapable Ella and six small children under eleven. It was a black prospect and I worried greatly over it, being in a condition of body and nerve eminently conducive to worry.

I wired Stell that I would pay her expenses if she would go home but Stell wrote back a fat epistle of excuses and said she was trying to get Clara and her husband to go. What use they would be under the circumstances I could not see.

I had a wire from Frede the next day after receiving Aunt Annie's saying that she was leaving for the Island, and had no further word until Nov. 2. In this interval I slowly grew stronger, in spite of Stella's terrible hysterical letters in which she raved and ramped as if insane. Great war news also came— Turkey's unconditional surrender and the complete smashing of Austria-Hungary by the Italians. Finally, when I was sleepless over lack of word from Park Corner, came a letter from Frede. They were all sick at Park Corner, Aunt Annie and Ella from shock, the children from flu. Little Georgie had died and Maudie and Jim were very low. Frede was alone in that house to do all the work and wait on the sick. I knew her strength was not equal to it. I felt I *must* go to her assistance. Her letter came at noon. I packed a grip and caught the evening train to Toronto. I had a tedious journey, for the connections after leaving Sackville were dreadful. Tuesday evening I got to Kensington and hired a rig to take me to Park Corner through the black, cloudy night and over vile roads. Never shall I forget the stones on those Irishtown hills. But at 9.30 I reached the old house. Frede and Aunt Annie were so thankful to see me. I found the children were on the mend. All were in bed but Frede and she and I sat huddled over the stove in the dining room till midnight and talked the whole tragedy over. Like myself, Frede did not regard poor George's death as an unmixed evil. Who did? Even his mother and wife, she told me, had said they were thankful he had died a respectable death in his bed, instead of being brought home killed in some drunken row as had nearly happened several times. It is a dreadful thing when that is how a man's nearest and dearest look upon his death.

Frede and I found it comforting to talk over all the problems with each other. It lightened and clarified them. They had got a middle-aged hired man and the prospect was not so bad—if Frede and I put our shoulders to the wheel, helped Aunt Annie with advice, decided things for poor Ella and appointed ourselves guardians and mentors of those poor children. Finally we went to bed and slept.

Follow the entries made during my stay in Park Corner in a notebook.

†"*Saturday, Nov. 9, 1918*
Park Corner
Frede, Aunt Annie and I had a business seance tonight and tried to straighten out George's business affairs. They are in a terrible tangle I fear. George borrowed $2300 from me five years ago on a joint note. He always paid the interest but none of the principal. He frittered the money away—part in worthless fox stock, part God knows how—there is no record of it. Aunt Annie will give me a mortgage on the farm for it and I will never take a cent more interest from her. It won't hurt Danny when he grows up to pay the principal off that fine farm. My hope for Park Corner lies in Dan. He is a fine smart lad, industrious and thrifty—which is a new streak in the Campbells. So much his mother gave him. His worst fault is a quick temper. But he soon gets over it. He is warm hearted and loyal. Yes, I have hopes of Dan—if his mother doesn't drive him to ruin with her foolishness. She is a bigger baby than her own children. But I am sorry for her.

Frede and I work all day cleaning and disinfecting the house; then at night, when Aunt Annie and Ella are safe in bed out of hearing, we shut ourselves up in the cosy sitting room, devour snacks, and talk and laugh at our pleasure, canvassing all things in the heavens above and the earth beneath and the waters under the earth. As for our 'snacks'—well, we are good foragers. Frede and I have, neither of us, ever been indifferent to the charms of a 'good bite'— though just now it is very unfashionable to confess such a thing. One would run the risk of being called a German. Nevertheless, it is a fact and we both shamelessly plead guilty. The Park Corner chicken-bones and ham-slices have lost none of their old-time flavor and savor and delight."

†"*Sunday, Nov. 10, 1918*
Park Corner, P.E.I.
Today was wet and windy. But I found a charm in it. It is eight years since I was on the Island in November and I am enjoying it. Even its dourness and gloom have a charm.

This evening we all got in the sitting room and had a little singing of hymns while Ella played. It seemed like a pale reflection of old times. Frede and I both felt it. As we have often said to each other, there is now a strange peace about this house such as we have not felt in it since those old days. A restless disturbing presence has gone—we have a feeling as if a curse had been lifted— as if a malign influence had passed away.

All today I have found myself 'thinking back' into the past, and so perfect has been the illusion that, as I lay on the sofa listening to the music, I *was* back, twenty years ago. I was a girl of seventeen at Park Corner. Stella and Clara were about. Our beaux came driving up outside with ghostly horses. All the ties of 1918 were wraith-like. Chester and Stuart in that strange mood meant nothing to me. I did not even love them—I, who normally love them so

†LMM quotes from her notebook.

much that I fear the jealous gods. But it was not possible to love children who would not be born for nearly twenty years yet! When I told my feeling to Frede I found she felt the same. She, too, was a ghost! We sat alone and talked until midnight—and we were strangely, perfectly, weirdly happy. It will be a jolt to wake up tomorrow morning and find ourselves middle-aged women with husbands and endless responsibilities!''

†''*Monday, Nov. 11, 1918*
Park Corner, P.E.I.
Today came the official announcement of the signing of the armistice! The Great War is over—the world's agony has ended. *What has been born*? The next generation may be able to answer that. *We* can never know fully.

I picked gum on the old spruces down by the road today while I waited for the mail—and dreamed *young* dreams—just the dreams I dreamed at seventeen. They are possible to me only at Park Corner—and only in certain moods here. The lingering spell of last night is still upon me.

To-night Frede and I went out in the darkness and walked down the lane and across the pond. It was so dark we could see nothing—only feel the planks beneath our feet and sense the rippling waters below. How often have we walked together over that bridge—but never before I think on a grim, inky November night. We spoke of the armistice but without any exultation. Frede, I fancied, was dull and a little depressed.

I have never been able to picture Frede as a wife, living a domestic existence in a home of her own. I have tried. But always my imagination has met a blank wall. I have thought this was because of the uncertainty of Cam's return. But peace has come and his return is as certain as anything in the world can be certain. So I should be able to picture their life together now. I *cannot*: the paralysis of imagination still persists. I cannot rid myself of the odd, haunting feeling that Frede is not for calm domestic joys and tame house-mothering. In my thought she still 'waves her wild tail and walks by her wild lone', like Kipling's cat. That has always been her way of describing herself. It is a true one. Frede always gives the impression of one walking her chosen way alone and independent—not as Cam MacFarlane's housekeeper and sock-mender— though capable, well-trained Frede can darn socks and run a house admirably. Only—it is not of the essence of her.

She said to me one day last summer—laughing, yet with an under-current of earnest, too—'I wish I could have both the "job" and the "husband".' Even yet, I seem to feel that the 'job' really means more to her than the husband. She loves her work and has been devoted to it. I know she dreads leaving it. I fear she will not be happy or contented after the novelty of her own home wears away. This worries me. But—perhaps motherhood will come to her and make everything worth while. Oh Freddie-girl, I want you to be happy! You have had so little happiness in your uneasy life.''

†*"Tuesday, Nov. 12, 1918*
Park Corner, P.E.I.
Frede and I crawled out in the cold and dark this morning and went to Summerside where we spent a weary day thrashing out business with a lawyer. At sunset we left. As we walked up and down the station platform while waiting for our train we saw a most wonderful sunset on Summerside Harbor. And I—I looked away across to the dim, twilit shore of Lower Bedeque. I saw the old warehouse at the wharf and up beyond it the spruce grove behind, which was the house where Herman Leard lived and where I suffered hell— and heaven. Dead memories stirred in their shrouds as I gazed at it—memories whose ghosts have not walked for many a year. That winter of love and agony seems like a dream now—a dream that some one else dreamed. I have been free from its thralldom this many a year. If Herman Leard were living now and I were to meet him my heart would not beat one iota the faster. And yet— the old memories *did* stir uneasily as I looked across the purple harbor to that shadowy shore. Frede did not notice my silence or my long gaze. She knows that I once loved and that the love was a tragedy. She does not know who the man was nor where he lived. Not even to Frede have I ever named his name....

We drove home from Kensington through the cold, frosty moonlit night. As we drove up a long Irishtown hill I was suddenly impressed with the weird, striking beauty of the moonlight falling through the spruce trees along the road—alternate bars of shadow and silver. It was a road peculiar to P.E. Island. Just as the thought crossed my mind Frede said, 'Maud, have you ever seen anything more beautiful than that road before us? One never sees a road like that anywhere else.'

We got home tired and chilled. But Aunty had a good fire and a corking supper for us—and we concluded that perhaps after all things were not so much 'managed better up in Mars'. We went to bed and slept. No dream of long-dead Herman Leard disturbed my slumbers. I dreamed only of my chubby darlings in Leaskdale Manse."

*I decided that I must leave for home on Friday Nov. 15. The day before was a wild November storm of rain and wind. Frede and I revelled in it. We longed to start off for the shore where the billows were rolling wildly in—and would have gone had it not been for a dread of catching cold and being laid up.

That night was not a quiet one in the old house. We were all tired and hoped for a good sleep. But it was written otherwise in the stars. Jim set up a toothache after going to bed and wailed and howled most dismally the greater part of the night. As both Aunt Annie and his mother were up waiting on him Frede and I decided we could do no good by getting up. So we cuddled down under our blankets and, as we could not sleep, began to wile away the hours by seeing which of us could say the wittiest things about poor Jim's weird

*LMM continues the journal entry which began December 1, 1918.

noises and their probable effect on Mr. Jack, who occupied the next room. We succeeded, at all events, in amusing ourselves hugely and laughed until the bed shook.

Frede and I have never been in any predicament or situation yet where we could not beguile the tedium or lighten the gloom by mutual jokes. We both seem to possess the knack of saying things that, at the time and under the circumstances, seem excruciatingly funny, though if they were written down or repeated in different surroundings they would not be at all mirth-provoking. At least, we turned what would otherwise have been a long and dreary night into a perfect orgy of fun.

Friday was fine and Danny drove me to the station in the afternoon. Poor Aunt Annie put her arms about me when I said good-bye and sobbed.

"Thank you for coming to me, Maudie. I could never have plucked up spirit again if you hadn't."

But it was Frede it worried me to leave. I am not easy about Frede. Her heart is not acting right. It has never been strong since the typhoid. I wish she would give up working now and rest till Cam comes home.

I came away sadly: yet I did not feel as I had felt when I left in the summer. The foretokened valley of the shadow had been passed. Two of the thirteen who sat at the ill-omened table that day were gone. Superstitious or not, never again will I, if I can avoid it, sit thirteen at a table!

I stayed all night in Summerside and left at six the next morning, through the gloom and chill of the first snowfall. My journey home was uneventful. I reached Uxbridge Tuesday night and Ewan met me with the car. It was wet and dark. As we drove into the yard Stuart and Chester came tearing out, flung themselves into the car and devoured me with kisses, shouting wildly, "'My *dear* little mother—my *dear* little mother." It was good to be back in their love again. And it was good to be home. But I miss Frede so much— more than ever this time, I think. In Frede I find both emotional and intellectual companionship. Very rarely is that found in one person. Apart from Frede, and in a lesser degree, Bertie MacIntyre, I know it not. The people I have loved best have not measured up to my standard of intellectual comradeship.

I settled down to work at my book as soon as I could. It *must* be finished by New Years. I hate a despotic date like that. It takes all the pleasure out of the writing.

Stella writes that Clara has had flu-pneumonia and nearly died but is recovering now. I am coming to feel a physical cringe whenever I hear the name of "Spanish flu". It has been worse than the "Black Plague" of old time. Ewan has had another bad attack of neuritis this past week but seems to be improving now.

It has been a hard, dreary fall enough. But the war is over! And that means so much that we have not yet grasped what it *does* mean. We don't realize it. The sudden cessation seems uncanny—as if one had gone to sleep in one planet and wakened up in another.

I am sure no one could feel more profoundly thankful that the war is over than I—I am sure that no one, except the mothers and wives, could have felt it more keenly. And yet the truth is that everything seems flat and *insipid* now, after being fed for four years on fears and horrors, terrible reverses, amazing victories, all news now seems tame and uninteresting. I feel as if I had been living for years in the midst of hell; and then suddenly found myself lying on a quiet green meadow stretching levelly and peacefully to the horizon. One is thankful—and bored!

It is strange and blessed—and *dull* not to dread the coming of the mail every day—not to open the papers tremblingly and after a quaking glance at the headlines turn greedily to the "War Reviewed" column. Somehow, there is a blank in life. I suppose it will gradually fill up.

The Kaiser has abdicated and fled to Holland. Likewise Son Willy. Germany is a republic. What a downfall for the man who, four years ago set out to conquer the world—to succeed where Napoleon failed. Byron's lines, written on Napoleon a hundred years ago, read to-day as if written for William Hohenzollern, especially the following verses.

'Tis done. But yesterday a king,
And armed with kings to strive,
And now thou art a nameless thing
So abject—yet alive!
Is this the man of thousand thrones
Who strewed our earth with hostile bones
And can he thus survive?
Since he, miscalled the Morning Star,
Nor man nor fiend has fallen so far.

The triumph and the vanity,
The rapture of the strife—
The earthquake voice of victory
To thee the breath of life,
The sword, the sceptre, and the sway,
Which man seemed made but to obey
Wherewith renown was rife—
All quelled! Dark spirit, what must be
The madness of thy memory!

Has there ever been a man so universally hated as William of Germany? Has any one man before in the history of the world been the ultimate cause of so much agony, heartbreak and death? Well, as I heard an old lady say once,

"If the devil doesn't catch a man like that what's the use of having a devil?"

Sunday, Dec. 8, 1918
Leaskdale, Ont.

To-day was Sunday and for once I flunked. I was simply too tired to go out. The responsibility of training the S.S. children for the annual Christmas concert has been mainly shuffled over on me this year. It is an imposition. I have more than enough to do as it is. I am president of the Red Cross, President of the Mission Band, President of the Social Dept. of the Guild both in Leaskdale and Zephyr and secretary of the W.M. Society. That is not enough forsooth but the work of training for the concert must be imposed on me, too! I was over at the church with the children all yesterday afternoon and came home at the point of tears. I have not been strong since I had the flu and any strain or over-exertion seems to play me right out. So I stayed home today and rested— and thereby, I believe, glorified God.

Tuesday, Dec. 17th, 1918
The Manse, Leaskdale, Ont.

The S.S. concert has been called off, owing to another outbreak of flu in the vicinity. I am glad for I dreaded it all. I haven't the strength for it. But I grudge the wasted afternoons I have already put in at the practices. If I had just had that time to rest! Oh, I want a rest! I've been really happy and contented during these past seven years but I have worked very hard and ceaselessly all the time. I bore three children in four years and there has been the four-year strain of the war. It has worn me out. I feel tired *all* the time—I *never* feel rested. I know what I would do if I could—go to bed and stay there for a fortnight, seeing nobody, talking to nobody, doing nothing but just lying flat!

But even this small boon is not to be compassed just now. And there is more worry ahead. Yesterday I got a letter from Mr. Rollins, my Boston attorney, saying that my case against Page Co. was to come up in January. I have to go down for it. This thing has been dragging on for two years and it is going to be settled at last. But even if I succeed I shall just have to file another suit; and I anticipate nothing but legal conflict with the Pages the rest of my life. It is a pleasant prospect, truly.

I must make arrangements to go to Boston "on business." The parish must not suspect that "the minister's wife" is mixed up in lawsuits against her publishers. They wouldn't think I was fit to run the mission band if they knew! Seriously, it wouldn't do for them to know. It would excite no end of gossip, even if most of them didn't think that all the parties in a lawsuit are tarred with the same brush.

Thursday, Dec. 26th, 1918
Leaskdale, Ont.

I am glad Christmas is over. It seemed such a *disappointing* day. I had hoped early in the autumn to have Frede here for Christmas once more but George's death made that impossible. For me it was a poor sort of day. I have been nervous, depressed and headachy for a week and it culminated last night in a blinding, old-time sick headache. But the boys had a good time and that is the main thing now—that the children should be happy and enjoy the day. We had their tree for them and they were wild with delight, dear little souls.

I finished my ninth book *Rainbow Valley* the day before Christmas. I am so thankful it is done. Everything has dragged so since I had the flu. It isn't as good as "Anne's House of Dreams"—in my opinion—but still averages up pretty well of its kind. But I'm tired of the kind. I've outgrown it. I want to do something different. But my publishers keep me at this sort of stuff because it sells and because they claim that the public, having become used to this from my pen, would not tolerate a change.

Nevertheless, if I ever get a little more leisure and a little renewed physical and nervous strength I mean to try my hand at something different.

Lewis Page is a queer mortal. Before my break with his firm they always sent me a parcel of books at Xmas. After the break they sent no more as was to be expected, and I certainly did not think they would ever do it again. Yet today came a copy of "Sunset Canada", an expensive travel book, and with it, not the firm's card as aforetime but L.P's personal one and written across it in his own fair hand "Merry Christmas and Happy New Year. L.C.P." Quite free and easy! Especially for the man I'm suing in the Mass. Court of Equity for cheating and defrauding me! Wonder if he is trying to heap coals of fire on my ungrateful head!

1919

Friday, Jan. 3, 1919
Leaskdale, Ont.

Today our Red Cross Society disbanded. This indecent haste to close down has a reason behind it. Normally we should have carried on our work all winter at least. But for over a year trouble has been brewing in that society. I have felt that I was walking on the edge of a volcano which might erupt at any moment and cause, not merely a Red Cross row, but a congregational one. The trouble was over our treasurer, who is suspected by some—quite unjustly, I feel certain—of diverting some of the money collected to her own purse. It started brewing last winter but I headed it off then and have been sitting on the lid ever since. But I knew that there was bound to be an explosion at the Annual Business meeting and I have been looking forward to it with dread for many moons. But when the armistice was signed I saw my way clear and I worked out a little scheme which resulted in the disbanding today. If we tried to keep up the society there would be a venomous quarrel and no good work would be done—for the treasurer would be offended and leave and without her I know not what we could have done. She is the only woman in the place with any executive ability and she has worked like a slave cutting and planning. Not one of the women who have criticized and slandered her could, or would try to, take her place. In view of all this I felt it was better to disband the society peacefully and in good repute "before the smouldering scandal broke and blazed." So it came about as I desired; and those very women who have gossipped about Mrs. Lapp and said they would leave the society had she been retained as an officer voted her the thanks of the society for the good work she had done! For the love of Allah, what is human nature made of? Is there any sincerity anywhere?

One day last summer Frede, after telling me of some intimate friend at Macdonald who had betrayed her confidence, exclaimed passionately,

"Maud, upon my word there's *nobody* true—except *you*. You are the only person I've ever found whom I could trust absolutely."

Alas, there *are* very few people whom we can absolutely trust. In youth we fondly believe most friends are true; but after we suffer repeated disillusions and betrayals we grow wiser and more cynical.

Saturday, Jan. 4, 1919
Leaskdale, Ont.

We had a nice pleasant evening of reading at home tonight. This is by no means a frequent occurrence. One or both of us must very often be away in the evenings—or we have company here—or work to do which cannot be set aside for the best of books. So we heartily enjoy an evening when we can settle down easily and read, with a plate of russet apples or a box of chocolates within easy reaching distance. We generally sit in the parlor. It is the pleasantest room in the house. Frede always called it "a

"Corner of Parlor"
[*Leaskdale Manse*]

summer room"—I think because its good lighting and green carpet and pale yellow walls, and the pink touches in the decorations give it a woodsy, gardeny aspect. Our big china dogs sit gravely on either side of the bookstand and Daffy generally wanders in, too, and goes sedately to sleep on the coyote skin rug or a rocking chair. Daffy will be thirteen years old in April, yet his eye is not dim nor the pluminess of his tail abated. The only sign of old age that I perceive in Daffy is that before he jumps up to his favorite basking place on the kitchen window-sill he sits a little longer than formerly gazing somewhat wistfully up at it before he makes his spring. I expect Daff-o-dil "feels in his bones" that all is not as it used to be. Oh, Daffins, it is not—neither with you nor me. Much water has flowed under the bridges of the world since that spring evening thirteen years ago when I carried you home from Alec Macneill's in a little covered basket. You howled every step of the way and everybody who met me on the way smiled broadly.

Daffy and Frede's old "Maggie" have been the longest-lived cats I ever knew. "Maggie" died about ten years ago, being then seventeen. She was like one of the family at Park Corner and Frede adored her. The two grew up together. Frede and I always loved cats. Where we got the liking is a mystery for our fathers and mothers and our grandfathers and grandmothers on both sides detested them. There was a fine breed of cats at Park Corner—they were always so big and fat and furry. Maggie was gray and white, and had more brains, emotion, and personality than quite a few humans have. She had an enormous number of kittens in her lifetime. Maggie certainly replenished the earth with kittens and fine little bastes they were too. Maggie finally got caught in a rabbit trap and was injured so badly that she had to be killed. I wrote some "In Memoriam" verses for her and Frede had them printed on a card with Maggie's picture. I have it framed in the library. Frede took Maggie's sad death very keenly to heart. It was hard that she should have died in such a way but I don't think she would have lived much longer in any case. During that last year she had got very deaf and had shrunk almost to nothing—a tiny handful of bones in her faded fur. I remember that I was up at Park Corner one autumn day before the winter of her death. Frede was away teaching school and I think Maggie, though well fed and cared for did not get much petting— Aunt Annie having no real liking for cats. I looked down to see her sitting at my feet looking up with imploring eyes. At once I took her up on my knee, cuddled and stroked her, talked to her and made much of her. She sat on my knee purring loudly and looking up into my face. Her eyes were absolutely uncanny. They haunt me to this day. They were not the eyes of an animal—they were *human* eyes. In them was exactly the expression I have sometimes seen in those of some poor old woman who has been neglected and overlooked when somebody sat down beside her and talked to her as if it were a pleasure or showed her some little attention such as younger women receive as a matter of course. Verily, it is hard *not* to believe that Maggie had a soul. Who knows? Perhaps long and intimate association with a loving human companion may, and sometimes does, develop a soul in an animal. Perhaps over beyond the dark valley Frede and I will find old Maggie again, plump and furry and kind in eternal youth. I don't think we would either of us feel perfectly at home in heaven if there were no adorable kittens frisking about the little grassy alleys leading down off the golden streets or snoozing on the window sills of the many mansions.

But I can't quite believe that Daff will go to heaven. He is such a weird, uncanny creature in many ways—absolutely diabolic. He *may* go on living—he has got so in the habit of it—but not in heaven. Yet he can't be banished to hell either. There must be some nice shadowy limbo where gray ghost cats can prowl and "walk by themselves."

Grandma, who never liked cats, grew quite fond of Daffy in her old age and was very good to him. But she would never tolerate his staying in the house at night. Only on the very coldest stormiest nights of winter would she connive at letting him go down cellar for the night. Most nights out he must go. But on fine summer nights Daff used to outwit her. One moonlit night long ago I remember waking up in my old room, with a nightmare-like feeling that persisted after waking. Seeing a round blot of darkness on the white spread I put out my hand and touched a warm, breathing body. Daff was curled comfortably up on my stomach sound asleep. He had evidently climbed up on the kitchen roof, found the window of the north room open, and came straight over to mine. After that I always left the north window open at night as long as it was possible at all and Daff never missed his tryst but always spent the wee sma's curled up on the bed at my feet. The "front passage" door being always securely shut no one was ever any the wiser....

Daff has his own odd ways. He does not like—never has liked—petting. He seems to resent it, even from me. Once in a while he does me the honor of jumping up on my knees and going to sleep—of late years I think he has done it a little more frequently. He never purrs, except when he is very hungry. *Then* he will come and sit by me and purr loudly. So he *can* do it and it is provoking that he will not because I love to hear a cat purr. It is the most utterly satisfied and comfortable sound in nature.

In the late twilight is Daff's unchanciest time. I have been afraid of him then with good reason. Several times when I have been standing beside him in the dusk, admiring him—for he is always incredibly handsome then—when, without any warning, he would give one tigerish spring at me, striving to bury teeth and claws in my leg or arm and not giving over until I batted him soundly over the head. At such moments he seemed possessed. Again, he would be most kind and companionable then. Many a night long ago, when I would be coming home on my lonely way after dark and had just turned in at the old lane Daff would spring down from the fence where he seemed to have been waiting for me and frisk around my feet up the lane. He was my familiar in many twilight rambles. We hunted Halley's comet together, I remember—at least, I hunted the comet. Daff, I suspect, was more interested in field mice, as evidenced by his sudden eager springs into the big fat clover "buttons" in the hayfields.

It was the funniest thing in the world to see Daff chase his tail—a habit that he kept up till he was quite old—four or five years. He would go around after it so fast that he seemed to be a mere revolving ball, growing madder and madder as it escaped him until when he did succeed in catching it he would bite it so furiously that he shrieked with pain, and then pursue it with more vicious rage than ever, biting and squealing and snarling, till he became too enraged to go on.

The first winter and spring we were here Daff always slept at the foot of our bed. But he never would come near the room after Chester was born and never has to this day. Daff knew his nose was out of joint and he was not going to play second fiddle to anyone.

Daff and Frede are very fond of each other, but he does not stand any nonsense from her either. One day, the last Christmas she was here, she was sitting in the kitchen, her legs crossed and her feet stuck out, displaying a pair of very nice new silk stockings. She was dressed to go somewhere. Daff was sitting on the kitchen window sill, and Daff was looking very cross because Stuart had been teasing him. Daff can *look* cross in every muscle and stripe and whisker. Frede and I began to make fun of him and he knew it and got crosser than ever. At last Frede said, "Daff, I firmly believe that you are a German spy."

Daff—this is an actual fact—deliberately got down from the window, deliberately walked across the floor to Frede, deliberately turned his tail to her, *and* deliberately sent a *shower-bath* over her fine silk stockings! Madam Frede had to go upstairs and dress from the skin out. We simply shrieked with laughter. I never saw Daff, or any cat, do such a trick before. And he did it with such devilish coolness and malice with an expression that said plainly, "I will teach you to call *me* names, my lady!"

Tuesday, Jan. 7, 1919
The Manse, Leaskdale, Ont.
Sat up till one last night arranging the correspondence I have to take to Boston as evidence in the trial. Went to W.M.S. in afternoon and then we went out to tea and spent the usual evening of boredom. To-morrow I must spend getting ready for my pleasure excursion. I wish it were all well over—but wishes boot not. The only thing to do is to set my teeth and go on with it to the bitter end. I have *not* informed the parish that I am going to Boston on litigation. They would probably think I had been doing something dreadful. Lizzie Oxtoby would take a new lease of life in gossip. So I have lavishly informed everyone

that I am going down on "business connected with my old book contracts". Could anything be a more definite statement of fact? There is really no way of hood-winking people like telling them the plain truth!

Friday, Jan. 10, 1919

I am flying through the night on the Boston express. Yesterday I left home in a snowstorm and reached Toronto at ten. I had planned to stay there until morning but reports of trains belated by snow made me feel that it might be better to go right on to Montreal that night and take no risk of losing my connections next day. So I tore madly around, got a berth and left on the eleven o'clock train. We pulled into Montreal this morning. Frede was to meet me in the evening and we expected to have a precious half hour between trains. I 'phoned Macdonald and Miss Hill said Frede had gone to Ottawa for the day but would be back at night and asked me out to spend the day. I went and had a delightful visit with her and Miss Phelp. In the evening I returned to Montreal. Frede's train was due an hour before mine started but it was delayed by the storm and so I never saw her at all. A few minutes ago at Rouse's point I got a wire from her explaining the cause of her delay. I am disappointed at not seeing her. But I may be able to stop off a day on my way back.

Sunday, Jan. 12, 1919
East Braintree, Mass.

I arrived in Boston yesterday morning and spent the day with my attorney, going over evidence, etc. We are bringing suit upon two points. (I.) That the Pages owe me a thousand dollars on the reprint edition of Green Gables and (II.) that the selling of the reprint rights to Grosset and Dunlap without my consent was a fraud on my interests. We are certain that we won't win this point because I practically endorsed the reprint by accepting the checks for it. But it will give the judge something to give Page, if he wants to be impartial and he will then be the more likely to interpret clause (I.) in my favor. Moreover, we will gain a good idea of where we stand when the *Avonlea* suit comes on, because in the case of the Avonlea reprint I have *not* accepted any checks and so have not endorsed it. I shall be perfectly satisfied if I win the first point.

I like Mr. Rollins. He is nice and seems a shrewd, level-headed fellow.

Last evening I came out to Braintree and am here in Amos and Flora's cosy little bungalow. There is something very fascinating to me in this little house on this New England hill-top. Their "den" is especially cosy.

Monday, Jan. 13, 1919
East Braintree, Mass.

Had my first experience in a court of law today. It was very interesting. Judge Jenny is on the case. The Pages were in court but gave me a wide berth. I was shocked at Lewis' appearance. It is 8 years since I saw him and I had expected to see him 8 years older. He looks sixteen years older. He was formerly a handsome man. His good looks have almost vanished. Well, one can't live the life he has lived and escape the penalty. George Page hasn't changed at all, as far as I could see. Lewis was examined and swore to at least three deliberate lies.

The Page lawyer is a Mr. Nay who is an elderly man and very nice, too. After the Pages had gone out he came up and smiled amiably "I hope, Mrs. Macdonald, that you realize that my opposition is purely professional. You wrote a wonderful book etc."

But this won't prevent him from grilling me in his best style in the witness box tomorrow morning.

Tuesday, Jan. 14, 1919
East Braintree, Mass.

A very hard day. Mr. Rollins and I went up to the court and Lewis Page was again in the box. Swore to more lies. He was very nervous all the time—kept moistening his lips and fiddling with his watch chain. After him, my turn came. I was in the stand about half an hour and swore to the very opposite of Lewis P. It remains to be seen whom the judge will believe. I left the witness box, feeling as if I had made every possible kind of an ass of myself. But Mr. Rollins said to me as I went out, "You should be on the witness stand all the time if you enjoy it. You made a capital witness."

Perhaps the judge thought so, too. At any rate he made it rather clear in what he said after I was through that he meant to give me the first point. Evidently the Pages realized this, too, for before we left the courtroom their lawyer came across with an offer to compromise the suit by buying out my entire rights in the books of mine they publish.

I had thought of this as a possible solution of my troubles and a good way out. But I had not expected the Pages would offer it. They certainly would not have done so if they had not at last realized that I had a legal grip on them and was not to be bluffed or frightened into foregoing it. They offered me $10,000. I smiled at this but said I would talk it over with Mr. Rollins. I did some mental figuring and decided that if the Pages would give me $18,000 I would sell out to them. It is nothing like the value of my books—or what would be their value in a different firm. But with a pair of scoundrels like the Pages, a bird in the hand is worth half a dozen in the bush. I can invest this money and the yearly interest will amount to as much as the yearly royalties would. So I said $18,000. Their lawyer smiled in turn. Oh, no, they would never do that. *Might* come up to $13,000—not a cent more. I smiled last and came away. I will not budge an inch. But non-budging is hard on the nerves. I was wretchedly tired when I got home. A reaction has set in and I am all in small pieces. But I'll gather up the fragments and face the Pages with restored morale tomorrow. Amen and amen! I shall win because I can afford to lose and the Pages can't. They are as desperately anxious to be rid of me as I am to be rid of them. *I* have discovered them to be conscienceless and reputationless rogues whom I cannot trust; *they* have discovered *me* to be a woman whom they cannot bluff, bully, or cajole. They know if I win this suit I will at once file another with still better chances of winning.

Thursday Night, Jan. 16, 1919
East Braintree, Mass.

I am in pieces again—but nevertheless I have fought a good fight—and won! Yesterday morning Mr. Rollins and I again hied us to the Equity court. Mr. Nay came suavely up and told us that the Pages would give me $17,000 for a settlement. I smiled once more and said "Eighteen". "Then the case must go on", he said. "They will not give it." "So be it," said I. It went on; the lawyers made their pleas and the judge announced, not exactly his formal decision but what his decision would be. As we expected, he gave the second point to Page on the ground that I had authorized the G. and D. transaction by accepting the checks; *and* he gave me point one—the original point on which I had gone to law. The disputed thousand was mine—and all the other thousands which might hinge upon that phrase in the contract in future.

Nay came up and talked aside to Rollins. When we left the court Rollins said, "We've got them good and scared. Nay says their $17,000 offer still stands." "Eighteen", said I. Mr. Rollins laughed. "I think you'll get it," he said.

I left him and went to meet Alma Macneill. We had lunch in a Chinese restaurant for the fun of it, then went to a movie. I stayed all night with Alma and then went up to Mr. Rollins' office this morning. He had a grin on.

"They have come up to the eighteen thousand," he said.

Vici!

The formal agreement is to be drawn up tomorrow. I went to a movie and then came home. I am so tired. I don't know if I can pick up the pieces once more or not.

Sunday Night, Jan. 19, 1919
East Braintree, Mass.

I spent Friday and yesterday dickering with the Pages—or rather with George Page, for Lewis, evidently, will not face me. George not having told me so many direct lies is not so shamefaced. But Lewis pulls the wires behind the scenes and makes all the trouble he possibly can for me.

When my volume of short stories "Chronicles of Avonlea" was mooted, I sent Lewis Page all my short stories up to date. He made a selection from them for the "Chronicles" and returned the rest to me. But now it appears, from Nay's letter on the subject, that, with characteristic thievery he kept copies of them. These old "culls" he now proposes to publish and I'm afraid he can— and will—publish them whether I agree or not, because the most of them were not copyrighted in the U.S. Among them, however, are two or three—and these the best—which were copyrighted and which he therefore cannot use without my consent. In order to obtain that consent he is willing to bind himself not to publish the book in a year during which I am to bring out a new volume. If I do not bind him thus he is quite capable of publishing those stories this spring and cutting the market for my new Stokes book which comes out in August. He must be prevented from doing this and I am the more willing to consent from the fact that I would never want any other publisher to publish those stories for they are poor stuff. Consequently I give up nothing of value to myself and I tie a pair of scoundrels down so that they can do me the least possible harm whereas if I left them loose they could—and I feel certain would—do me a good deal.

So I have consented but I have made them agree to several minor details which made them grit their teeth. The consequent agreement is rather a curiosity in the way of legal agreements I think. It is not yet signed however, as one or two more points have to be settled but surely tomorrow will see the end of it.

We have had a very pleasant Sunday. Mr. and Mrs. Viles have been here—cousins of mine. Christie Viles was a daughter of Uncle Charles Crosby. I never even met her until the last time she was here and she is so much my senior that she seems more like an aunt than a cousin. I feel absurdly disrespectful when I call her "Christie." She is a very fine looking woman—a feminine edition of the old Senator, resembling him much more strongly than any of his daughters. Her mother, Aunt Jane, did not resemble him at all. These family likenesses are very curious things. For instance, Chester, who is really very much like his father, has the eyes and brows of my mother, while Stuart has my father's eyes absolutely. There are times when Chester's expression gives me an absolutely *ghostly* sensation, as if eyes long closed in death were looking at me.

My dear little boys! How I long to see them tonight! How glad I shall be when all this vexatious law business is disposed of and, free at last, I hope forever, from the incubus of the Pages, I shall hasten back to my own dear home.

I had a letter from Frede Friday night, regretting having missed me and urging me to stop off on my way back for a day or so. I must try to arrange it and have wired her to that effect.

Friday, Feb. 7, 1919
Leaskdale, Ont. The Manse
On Saturday, January 25th, at seven o'clock in the morning Frederica Campbell MacFarlane died of flu-pneumonia in the infirmary of Macdonald College at St. Anne de Bellevue, Quebec.

There, it is written! and I feel a strange relief. I have so dreaded the writing of it.

Oh, my God, can it be true? It is unbelievable—impossible! It is too hideous to be true!

It is true! And my heart is broken! Oh, how can I go on living?

On the morning of Monday, January 20, I went into Boston again and spent most of the day wrangling with Geo. Page and Mr. Nay over the details of our agreement. Another characteristic bit of *Pageism* came to light. I discovered that the Page Co. has *not* got the copies of those stories. I suppose they wanted me to think they had lest, if I knew the truth, I would not have let them publish them. Nor would I; but having consented I will not be shyster enough to withdraw now. They said they wanted me to send them the copies they had sent me back. I told them this was impossible as I had destroyed them but I would send copies of the original magazine stories. (The copies I had sent them had been changed somewhat to fit into the Avonlea atmosphere.) They said this would be satisfactory but we could not get all the resulting details worked out that day, so I finally left and went out to Wakefield to spend the night with my old namesake and correspondent of long years, Lucy Lincoln Montgomery. I had a very enjoyable evening but shortly before bedtime Flora rung me up on the phone saying that a wire had come from Frede—to whom I had written, asking if such-and-such a day would suit her plans for me to call at St. Anne's. The wire said that she had "flu" but had two good nurses and was "very comfortable", and wanted me to stop off on my way home whatever day it was.

I did not feel the least alarm over this news. I was possessed with the idea that "flu" was only really dangerous if there was carelessness or lack of attention and I knew there was no fear of either in Frede's case. So I went to bed and I slept soundly and well—the last good sleep I was to have for many a dreadful night.

But I dreamed a strange dream. I thought I had arrived home. In my absence workmen seemed to have torn the whole inside of my house to pieces and to be making it over. Everything in the way of furniture and household gods seemed to have utterly disappeared. I ran upstairs to my room. It was likewise empty and had been made over to half its old size. This seemed to me a terrible blow. I felt broken-hearted. My dear home was all bare and changed. My own room had narrowed down to a mere closet. And where were all my treasured possessions? With a bitter sinking of spirit I said to myself, "Everything has gone and now I have to set to work to furnish my house all over again." And as I stood, gazing blankly at the new bare unpainted rooms around me I awoke.

I never thought of connecting the dream with Frede. Instead, I thought if it meant anything, it referred to the fact that Ewan had been asked if he would accept a call to a certain congregation. Possibly the dream meant that we would go—and so life be changed.

But now I know that it meant Frede's death. And has it not come true? Is not my house of life left unto me desolate—is not the inmost shrine of my heart narrowed down? Does not everything seem gone from me? Am I not left to furnish forth my soul's habitation afresh—if I can?

Tuesday morning I spent again with the lawyers and Friend George and got things so far along that it remained only to draw up the agreement formally and sign it. After lunch I went with Lucy Montgomery to Cambridge where we attended a meeting of some literary club and I gave a reading from "The Golden Road" and had a very enjoyable time. Professor Dallas Sharpe motored me home and I arrived at Flora's very tired out—but—oh!—very happy. The Page matter was virtually settled. The next night I would leave for home,

Frederica Campbell

spend a day or two at Macdonald with convalescent Frede, then hie me happily home to my own dear boys. I spent a pleasant, cosy evening in the "den" and at eleven o'clock I was ready for bed.

Suddenly the telephone rang. Flora answered it—it was a call for me.

Sick of soul I went to the 'phone. I knew it must be bad news. The message was delivered—briefly—mercilessly. Miss Hill sent it—Frede was seriously ill with pneumonia. They wanted me to come at once.

It fell on my heart like a knell of doom. "She will die—she will die," I moaned. I paced the floor in anguish—I went to my room wondering how the night was to be put in—and the next day. For I could not get into Boston early enough to catch the early morning train to Montreal. Oh, that night! The torment of my suspense was so hellish that when, about five, I felt myself dropping into the slumber of exhaustion, I *willed*, with a fierce intensity that I should *dream the truth* about the termination of Frede's illness. I had a queer forbidding idea that I was *doing wrong* in this—laying violent hands on the future—a different thing from a dream that came as an unsought gift or warning from the Keepers of the Gate. But my pain was so great that I did it—and I *dreamed*.

In my dream I had arrived at the outside of the Apartment at Macdonald and the only way to get up to it was to climb up the steep wall by iron spikes which were driven into it, after the fashion of the spikes on telegraph poles. I began to climb with frantic energy. Half way up my toilsome ascent I heard a terrible cry above me and I thought "Frede is dead". I redoubled my efforts—I reached a sort of open casement and looked in. I beheld a long hall. In the centre on a kind of bier lay Frede, with nurses and doctors standing around. "She *isn't* dead," I shrieked in agony. I rushed forward and flung myself over her. She *was* dead—I wakened.

From that moment I had no *real* hope of Frede's recovery. I *knew*. I had willed to tear aside the veil that hides the future and my punishment was the torture of the vision.

Flora and I went into Boston after breakfast and I went to Rollins' office and with him to Nay's. I was resolved that neither Nay nor George Page should see my suffering—so I preserved outward calmness. While we sat in Nay's office awaiting Page, Nay began to talk of Kipling and spoke of a poem of his in "The Brushwood Boy" which he said had always appealed strongly to him. He took out a notebook and read it. I bit my lip and clenched my hands under cover of the table to keep from screaming. It was "The City of Sleep" and the first time I had ever heard it had been when Frede had recited it to me one evening in my old room in Cavendish over ten years ago. I could see her sitting in my rocking chair—I could hear her voice lingering caressingly on the lines, "We must come back with Policeman Day / Back from the city of sleep."

Nay read the poem all through and I listened—and kept my calm and my senses! George Page came—the agreement was signed—my twenty thousand dollar check (including the royalties due) was in my hand. How gladly would I have torn it into bits and scattered it to the winds if only by so doing I could buy Frede's life! Pshaw! Frede could *not* die! Scores of people had recovered from pneumonia—even flu-pneumonia. I would go to Macdonald—I would find her better—we would yet be talking laughingly over my fright, as we had done after her typhoid.

But underneath—I knew—I *knew*!

I went back with Rollins, settled up, and said good-bye. "You have been a good client," he said. "You knew your mind. There was no wobbling with you." Yes, I had known my mind—I had matched my wits against roguery and won—but my victory was bitter in my mouth. What did it matter—what did anything matter? Oh, if with that twenty thousand dollars I could buy instant transportation to Macdonald College! How could I live until the next morning!

I rejoined Flora and we went to visit friends as we had promised. The afternoon dragged intolerably away. But even the tortures of the rack ended at last for the martyrs—and at last I found myself on the Montreal train. I prayed for just one thing—that I might see Frede *once* more—speak to her *once* more. I *must* have that or I should die, too. If I could just reach St. Anne's before it was too late!

I took veronal and so had a few hours of heavy drugged sleep. I arrived in Montreal just in time to catch the St. Anne's train. When I got off at the station at St. Anne's Miss Kirby—Frede's assistant—met me. I forced myself to utter, "How is Frede?" and even as I spoke I knew that Frede must be living still or Miss Kirby would not be smiling.

"She had quite a comfortable night and the nurses think she is a little better this morning," was her reply.

Frede was still alive! In my reaction from my sickening terror I trembled so that I could hardly stand. We walked up the street and turned in at the big entrance gates, where Frede had so many times gone in. I was suddenly hopeful and in good spirits—on the surface. After all, had that dream meant anything? Had I not dreamed it because my mind was so full of the matter and my dread so great?

I had breakfast in the apartment with Miss Hill, who was or seemed to be quite hopeful. She has always been a close friend of Frede's and is

*"The entrance gates,
with Boys' Building beyond"*

a very sweet woman. I can never forget her exceeding kindness and thoughtfulness to me in all those terrible days. Miss Phelp was there, too—another remarkably fine and sweet and clever woman whom Frede had loved and whom I had met several times before.

After breakfast I went over to the college infirmary and, shrouded in mask and overall, was admitted to the ward and then taken to Frede's room. I found her very ill and again my heart sank. This was not typhoid, where the tide of life, however low it ran, might be turned by some sudden exhilaration or pleasure that stimulated Nature to another and supreme effort. Frede always had said that I saved her life in typhoid. Perhaps I did. Dr. Gordon said she began to improve from the moment I arrived. Perhaps it gave her just the fillip needed to start her on the upgrade. But I had no such power now. This was a grislier foe.

But she was very glad to see me, poor darling! She was no longer alone among strangers, even though they were kind and attentive strangers. Once more those brave, kindly, clever eyes lighted up with welcome as they met mine—as they had done hundreds of times in the past—as they would never do again. She did not know she had pneumonia—she thought it was only the flu. The doctor would not allow her to be told, fearing she would give up utterly. I think this was a mistake—I think she should have been told. But so it was.

I sat beside her and tried to soothe and encourage her. She had been delirious all night but she was perfectly sensible then. I found her terribly worked up and worried over some unkind, abusive letter that wretched Stell had written her a short time before. When I wrote Stell that afternoon I told her plainly that I should never feel the same to her again if Frede died. But to Frede I made light of it. "Don't worry, you foolish dear. You know perfectly well what Stell is. She is not worth a second thought."

She was worried over many things—her mother, the situation at Park Corner, Cam's prospects etc. I tried to calm and encourage her—I think I succeeded. As of old she turned to me for advice and assistance—and thank God I did not fail her—I never failed her—we never failed each other!

I take up my pen again, after a wild outbreak of tears. I must go on with this—must get it over. If I "write it out" perhaps I will be better able to endure my pain.

I was permitted to sit by her and talk to her on condition that I did not let her talk very much. I told her all my news—that I had won my suit with Page and so on. I told her a little joke—one of Stuart's funny sayings over which we had laughed at the manse supper table the last evening I had been at home. We had pancakes and maple syrup and the edge of the one Stuart was eating had been crisped in the frying. He tried vainly to cut it with the spoon. "Mother," he said plaintively, "*how* do you cut pancake bones?"

Frede gave her little characteristic laugh when she heard it. That was the last time I was ever to hear Frede laugh. Never, never again! Oh, Frede, heaven must have needed some laughter and so you were taken.

She took off her wedding and engagement rings and gave them to me. "Keep them for me till I get better," she said. Her poor finger had grown so thin that they worried her, for fear they might drop off. I remembered how she had proudly shown me her engagement ring that morning I arrived at Macdonald after her marriage. Cam had given it to her just a few hours before their marriage.

I spent most of the afternoon with her. Went over to the apartment for dinner and returned. We talked over "the problem of Stella" and as usual arrived nowhere. Dr. Gordon arrived from Montreal. I had sent for him. He told me that she was very ill—that he was gravely anxious about her, but that he thought she had "an equal chance." It was scant food for hope but I fed avidly on it. I know now that, although I had asked him to tell me the exact truth, he had not quite done so. He had spoken more hopefully than he felt. I heard later that his parting words to Dr. Helso had been those old ones of doom—"Well, while there's life there's hope."

I said good-night to Frede and went over to the apartment, the nurse having promised to send for me if any change for the worse set in. I was very tired after two bad nights and I fell into a heavy sleep almost at once. It seemed but a few minutes—although it was about two o'clock—when I became conscious that Miss Hill was bending over me saying that the nurses had phoned, asking me to come over—that there was a change for the worse.

I got up and dressed. I never hoped again. Miss Hill and I left the apartment, went down and down and down those interminable flights of stairs through the echoing, ghostly corridors, passed through the long "covered way" whose icy chill struck to my heart like a waft of death, and through the long corridor of the Women's Residence to the Infirmary. Frede was lying in the stupor-like sleep induced by an injection of morphine. Her breathing had grown heavy and stertorous. The nurse feared that she was already in the coma that precedes death.

All the rest of the night I walked up and down the corridor outside Frede's room in the grip of hellish torment. Frede dying! I could *not* believe it—and yet I *did* believe it—I knew it was so. *How* can human beings live, or keep sanity, through what I endured that night. Why should they *have* to live through it? Why does God send us the blessing of great love and then send it away? *Is* it God—or some malignant Power of Evil who hates love and happiness and is mighty enough to destroy it in spite of the Power of God? Vain questions! I did not ask them that night—one question only I asked, over and over in my ceaseless pacing, "Oh God, how can I live without Frede?"

At five her breathing changed again—and again for the worse. The night nurse was a Miss Patterson. I did not like her—she seemed a hard, unsympathetic woman; but I must say she was skilful and attentive. The day nurse was a Miss Ince—a girl from Barbadoes—a very tall woman with snow-white hair. Yet I do not think she was much past girlhood. Her personality was very charming and individual.

"Miss Hill"
[*of Macdonald College, Montreal*]

At six Frede wakened out of the morphine sleep, muttering in delirium. From then until seven we thought her dying. I stood by the bed and watched while the nurse strove to rally her, feeling as if I were in some hideous nightmare—or in some narrow cell of torment from which my agonized soul looked out on what was passing around me.

At seven Frede rallied. She became conscious and her pulse improved. But I knew there was no longer any hope. It was only a question of time. I dragged myself back to the apartment, forced myself to swallow a few mouthfuls of food and returned to the Infirmary. Frede was lying calmly on her pillows. I bent over her and asked her how she was. "I feel fine," was her answer. I would rather have heard the complaints of the day before. *That* would have meant nature was still fighting. *This* meant that she had given up the struggle.

The day dragged away. Frede took little notice of anyone. She muttered to herself incessantly; but when I spoke to her she always answered clearly and rationally. At dusk, as I sat beside her bed she made the only reference to her condition that she made that day. "My breath is getting very short," she said. The fact did not seem to alarm her. I went out while the nurses prepared her for the night. Then I went back and walked softly up and down the room, clenching my hands and praying wildly and despairingly. Then poor Frede came back once more—*for the last time*—from the Valley of the Shadow. And she make a little joke—the last of all her gay and merry jests. Oh, Frede!

"I would like to see Stell with the influenza," she said. "The specific gravity would go up to 90."

"Specific gravity"—Frede and I had made a jest of it for many a day. Poor Stell was always writing that a certain "specific gravity" had gone up so many degrees, in every upheaval of her nerves. Frede and I had tossed the phrase back and forth like a ball in our meetings. And now!

I made myself laugh. "It certainly would," I said. The tears were pouring down my face under that stifling mask. Oh, my friend—*my friend*!

Miss Hill and the nurse insisted that I should take a veronal pill and lie down in the adjourning room. I did not want to. But, as they truly said, I owed a duty to my children and I could do nothing for Frede, who had sunk back into her muttering semi-stupor. I realized this and allowed myself to be led away. Miss Patterson said she would wake me at the slightest change.

I took the tablet almost greedily—it would mean a few hours blessed oblivion and relief from pain.

At five o'clock I was called. I sprang up and hurried in. The end was coming. I bent over Frede and asked her how she felt. "Fine", was her response, firm and clear. But the brave heart was almost worn out—it was failing—failing. She lay, muttering and unnoticing, but to the last my voice had power to bring her back for a moment.

"Frede," I said, "I am going to write to your mother today. Have you any word to send her?"

"Yes. Tell her I want to know exactly how her hand is," she said.

This was a commonplace message. It came from the conscious mind. The next was different. It came up from the subconscious deeps.

"I think I'll write to Cam, too," I said, as soon as I could control my voice. "Is there anything you would like me to tell him?"

"No, only that I wish for him the courage of the strong," she replied.

I walked up and down the room a few times. There was yet something I must say to her—but I must put it in such a way that it would not alarm or shock her with any sudden realization that she was dying. Such a realization could serve no good purpose now—and it might worry her. Yet I *must* remind her of a certain promise in words whose significance she might not grasp just then but would when—and *if*—the freed, conscious and intelligent spirit was released from the clogs of the failing body.

....We made a compact. When in the course of years, few or many, one of us died that one was to come back and appear to the survivor *if* it were possible to cross the gulf. I *must* remind her of this.

Again I bent over her. "Frede," I said earnestly, "you won't forget your promise to come and see me, will you?" "No," she said. "You'll be sure to come, won't you?" I insisted. "Certainly," she said, clearly and loudly. It was her last word.

But oh Frede, you have not come yet. The dead *cannot* return or you *would* have come. I cannot—I *cannot* bear it.

I sat down beside her. I was sick to my soul with agony. Oh, is there not after all something in that old superstition that the Immortals who control our destinies are jealous beings—jealous of a too-great love or a too perfect friendship which makes us too much like them?

Poor Frede seemed unconscious of all that went on. Yet once she put out her poor thin hand, her hand that had been so beautiful and shapely—one of her best points—and laid it on my arm as if appealing to me to help her—to me, who was so helpless. I could do nothing for her—nothing—I, who would have done anything. I took her hand and held it until she drew it away again in a sudden restlessness.

Her breath grew shorter and shorter. At seven it ceased. She died as peacefully and gently as a tired child might fall asleep. *She died*. And I live to write it! Frede is *dead*. "After life's fitful fever she sleeps well." But *I* wake and must face the dreary years without her. I *must* live as long as I can for my children's sake. I must live—without that blithe comradeship, that intellectual companionship, that faithful, earnest friendship—live, knowing that Frede will never come again under my roof—that never again will come to me a letter addressed in her old familiar hand—that I will never hear her laugh—never save up a joke to tell her—never walk with her again under the Park Corner birches or over the old bridge in the summer twilight! How *can* I go on living when half my life has been wrenched away, leaving me torn and bleeding in heart and soul and mind. I had *one* friend—one only—in whom I could absolutely trust—before whom, I could in Emerson's splendid definition "think aloud"—and she has been taken from me. Truly, as has been said, in such an instance as this "it is the survivor who dies". Yes, Frede, you did not suffer the pangs of death. It was *I*—*I*—as *you* would have suffered had it been I who went away!

She died just as the eastern sky was crimson with sunrise. She "went out as the dawn came in"—like old *Captain Jim* in my *House of Dreams*. When I realized that she was dead I stood up—I felt Miss Hill's arms around me—I heard her whispering at my ear, "Look at the sunrise—look at the sunrise." It was one of those absurd things people say, in a desperate effort, I suppose, to be kind and inspirational. I could have shrieked with derision at it. The sunrise had no message for me. I went out of the room with an unbearable agony tearing at me. Tears had ceased to flow and I had not that relief. If I had been alone my anguish would have found vent—and so relief—in screams. But I must not scream out of consideration for the others there. I crushed back the impulse to shriek—I went into another room and sat down on the bed. Suddenly I found myself laughing. In a moment my hysterical peals of laughter were ringing through the hall.

I have never before in my life had hysterics—and I have always felt a little contempt for women who have had them. Well, I ask their pardon.

I laughed—and shook until the bed shook under me. Miss Hill put her hands about me and held me tightly. The nurse, seeing that I was trying to check my horrible laughter said, "Don't try to keep it back, Mrs. Macdonald. It will injure you if you do." So I laughed on.

Well, Frede and I have always laughed. It has been the key note of our life together. So there was an ironic fitness in the fact that I mourned her with laughter.

The nurse finally brought me a drink of some stimulant. I drank it and regained my self control. The next moment I fell asleep on the bed exhausted.

Miss Hill had presently to awaken me to ask me what dress they should put on Frede. We decided on her pretty "Khaki-kool" one. And my thoughts went back to the time Frede bought it. It was in May 1917, when I was with her at Macdonald just after her marriage. Her bridal had been too hurried to include a trousseau and it was necessary for her to get a new dress for the social functions which were to come off in our joint honor. We went into Montreal for the day and scoured the stores for a suitable dress. For a long time we could find nothing; but at last a clerk brought out a sample dress of the new fabric "Khaki-Kool" and we were both delighted with it. Frede tried it on. It became her from every standpoint. "You will make no mistake in taking it, Frede," I said. "It will be suitable for anything, except a dance or a formal dinner."

Suitable for anything—ay, even for a shroud! Dear God, it is well that the future is hidden from our eyes.

I took off the mask and overall and went back to the apartment. The hideous suspense was over; the still more hideous certainty had to be faced.

All that day I walked the floor of the beautiful living room—all the next interminable day I walked it. I could not sit down. Miss Hill and Miss Philp were consideration itself. They did not torment me with platitudes of consolation(?)—they did not urge me to "rest". They knew no rest was possible for such pain as mine.

I walked—and walked. Tears came freely at last but brought no relief. I "thought forward"—I lived out the allotted span of human existence in a few hours—*without Frede*. All the pain that should have been spread over many years—all the loneliness—all the longing—was concentrated in those hours. And I saw my whole past friendship with Frede in a series of vivid pictures, which burned in upon my consciousness and with them the unbearable torture of realizing that I would never see them in life again—Frede sitting in my old room at Cavendish, sleeking her beautiful black hair before my mirror—Frede squatted on the floor of her room at Wedlocks discussing the universe—Frede standing laughing at the well at Park Corner—Frede setting bread in the old porch—Frede hunting for snacks in the pantry—Frede with "Sonny Punch" in her arms—Frede at my Christmas table, flushed and handsome, flirting with Fraser—Frede coming to meet me in Montreal station in that old homespun suit of hers—Frede sitting by my kitchen fire with Daff in her lap—over and over and over again I saw her—and knew that I should never so see her again.

At dusk Miss Ince came over and told me that the casket had been closed— she had thought it better not to send for me. I was shocked by this—I found that I had unconsciously been looking forward to seeing Frede *once more*. For a moment I felt that I could not bear *not* to see her—I *must* see her. But it was no longer possible. With a shiver of agony I resigned myself to it. After all, perhaps, as Miss Ince said, it was best. I think perhaps they were all afraid I would break down again if they had sent for me. They need not have so feared; but I don't think I would want to remember Frede's dead face—cold, unresponsive, pallid—"that sad shrouded brow"—no, it was better not. And yet how I hungered—and hunger—for that denied last look! In life Frede and I never said good-bye to each other. We had made a compact to that effect—we both hated saying "good-bye"—and we agreed years ago that we would never say it—we would always part with a laugh and a gay wave of the hand. On the November afternoon when I last left Park Corner Frede sprang on the back of the buggy and came down with us to the road. She wore her green "Household Science" uniform. As she dropped off I said "Well, Freddie, when shall I see you again?" "Oh, I don't know," she said—and she ran back up the old lane. There was no good-bye—and there was to be none now. Frede had gone on and I was left. Her work was done—mine, it seemed, was not.

One of the windows of the living room looked across the campus to the college rink. That Saturday evening it was aglow with electric lights and gay with whirling figures. I thought it a little strange. When death was on the campus—and the death of a member of the faculty at that—I thought it would have been more appropriate if the customary sports were omitted until after the funeral. As I looked at the gay skaters I asked that old, stupid, selfish question. "*How* can they be enjoying themselves there while Frede is lying *dead* in that dark room yonder?" The old, old question—how can there be light if *our* sun is blotted from the heaven? "Oh, never morning wore to evening but some heart did break", but the rest of the world is none the less gay for that.

I walked—and fought for some little transient respite from torture in foolish childish visions and pretendings. Fred wasn't dead—the door would open presently and she would pop in with her gay laugh—it was all some dreadful dream—some silly mistake—how nice it would be to waken!—how we would laugh over the blunder and my tragic suffering over it! To *waken*—yes, that was it—waken up in the Braintree bungalow again and know that Frede was alive and I was going to see her at Macdonald in a day or two and talk all our family and personal problems over with her. Oh, to waken!

Household Science staff, Macdonald College. Frede is the second woman standing.

I dreaded going to bed that night but when I did I slept at once and unbrokenly till morning. Then I got up and lived through another day of horror. My pain seemed *physical* as well as emotional. It wrung my body with actual pangs. People came and went and were sympathetic. They were shadows—shadows! When one of the Macdonald professors heard of Frede's death he exclaimed, "Oh heaven, what a loss to the country!" But I thought then only of *my* loss.

Monday brought a different form of martyrdom. Frede's body was to be taken to the Crematory in Montreal for cremation.

Frede and I had often, years ago, talked, as we talked of every other subject under heaven, of the best way of disposing of "worn-out fetters that the soul had broken and thrown away." We were both agreed that the proper and sanitary way was by cremation and we both declared that when we died we wanted to be cremated. With me this was merely an academic opinion. But Frede seemed to feel very deeply on the subject. She had a horror, she said, of being buried alive; and she had another horror of the slow process of decay in the grave. She often adjured me to see that she was cremated if she died before I did. I promised lightly enough—I had little fear then that Frede would go before me.

When Frede was dead Miss Hill told me that when Frede first knew she had flu she asked for pen and paper and wrote out instructions for her cremation if she did not recover. Miss Hill said she was a little delirious at the time and appeared to think she might not have meant it. But I, remembering our old compact, knew that she did when I looked at the few faintly scrawled words "If I die I hereby direct that my body be cremated. Frederica MacFarlane"— the last words she ever wrote; and though I did not know how Aunt Annie and Cam would feel about it I determined to carry out Frede's last wish and ordered the arrangements made for it. I am satisfied that I did it. But for my own part, although I still believe and always will believe, that cremation is the right way to dispose of the dead, I shall never ask that it be done in my own case. *It is too hard for the living*. It is far harder than giving our dead to the earth. *Then* one seems to possess them still in a measure. But in cremation they seem absolutely gone—*nothing* is left—the sense of utter desolation is dreadful.

On Monday morning there was a brief funeral service in the reception room of the Girls' Building. Mr. Lancaster, the minister of the St. Anne Anglican church conducted it. He had been a personal friend of Frede's and she had attended his church. Then we drove to the station and waited for some time for the train. The casket was before us, covered with flowers—my sheaf of red roses among them. On the evening before Frede died a friend had sent her a beautiful pot of freesias with a note referring to some mutual joke regarding "favorite" flowers. It suddenly occurred to me that, with all our interchange of opinions, I had never heard Frede say what her favorite flower was. I asked her then; and she answered, in the strange, clear, decisive fashion she employed in those last, semi-conscious hours, "A red rose!" It was a good choice. I might have known it. The red rose was just what Frede, the vivid and dramatic and intense, would like best. So I ordered the red roses for her casket—the last thing I could do for her. Oh, Frede!

We went into Montreal—we drove up the mountain—up—up—up. As we passed the gateway of the crematory grounds the bell in the belfry just beside it began to toll. I felt as if each toll smote on my brain like a physical blow.

Was that melancholy sound for Frede, the laughing and the brilliant? It had nothing in common with *her*.

Presently I found myself standing between Miss Hill and Miss Philp in the little hall of the crematory, with the palms and blossoms on either side. The casket was before us and Mr. Lancaster was reading the burial service—"ashes to ashes—dust to dust"—do human love and companionship end so? Was all that had been Frede pent up in that black box before me? Or was her spirit by my side, pitying my anguish—suffering in her inability to reach and comfort me? Wild tormenting thoughts rushed through my mind—then concentrated in one weird obsession. Frede was lying in that box—*dead*—and if I bent over her and *told her a joke she would not laugh*. This realization beat in upon me and tortured me. Over and over and over the thought repeated itself—"she wouldn't laugh"—yes, she must indeed be dead if she wouldn't laugh! This sounds ridiculous I suppose. It was the keenest anguish I had ever experienced in my whole life.

The service was ended—the ashes were sprinkled on the casket. Suddenly the grim black doors in front opened—the casket was pushed through them—they closed. What an unbearable moment! All the suffering of the past five days was repeated and concentrated in it. To see those doors close *between us* was far harder than hearing the clods fall on the coffin in the grave. It symbolized so fearfully the truth that the doors had closed between us for all time. I was here—Frede was there—between us the black blank unopening door of death.

I went back to St. Anne's. I made arrangements for sending Frede's ashes to Park Corner for interment in the old plot at the Geddie Memorial Church, beside George and his little son. Three who sat at that table of thirteen are gone. Is the tale fulfilled?

Tuesday I faced a task I knew must be done, though I shrank from it with cringing. I did not see how I could do it—but done it had to be. Accompanied by Margaret MacFarlane—Frede's sister-in-law, who had arrived on Sunday evening—a nice girl—I went over to Frede's room in the Men's Building. It was not the pretty gray-and-old-rose room she had occupied in the Teacher's Residence when I was with her at the time of her marriage. Owing to the coal famine the teachers had had to give up the residence and move over to the Men's Building. The room had been disinfected and aired but otherwise was just as Frede had left it. I stifled a moan of agony as I looked around. The room was so full of her—her favorite pictures on the walls,—mine, Aunt Annie's, Margaret Stirling's, and one I had given her of the old home at Park Corner, enlarged and framed. Her pen and her books lay on her desk—her little toilet articles on her bureau, everything stabbed me.

What was the thing that hurt me most? Another ridiculous thing. On a table behind a screen were the remnants of some little supper poor Frede had cooked up for herself some evening when she had come in late from a country trip, hungry and tired—likely that very last evening when she had returned from her fatal trip to Waterloo. She hadn't eaten it all—in a small dish was a pitiful little scrap of cold bacon—cold bacon—yes, that *did* hurt the most. Frede and I had

had so many of those little chummy, delicious bed-time snacks together.

I had felt very helpless over the problem of just what to do with Frede's belongings. Therefore it was a great relief to find, in the drawer of her writing table, a letter addressed to me and her mother and Cam. She had written it in October when the first flu panic had fallen on Macdonald. It began, "Dear Maud or mother or husband." Was it only because Cam was overseas and because she knew I would be the likeliest one to find the letter if she died? Not altogether I think. My name came first to her instinctively—before even that of the mother she loved but who had cruelly misunderstood her in her earlier years and before the boyish husband who had caught her fancy in the glamor of his uniform and his overseas experience, coming into her life at a psychological moment of loneliness. No, *I* came first—the old friend to whom she had always turned in her hours of need—to whom she turned at the last when the shadow of what might be fell over her.

The letter made our task simpler—nothing could make it easy. We spent the whole day going through her possessions and assorting them according to her wishes. The wedding presents from Cam's friends to his people—her books and his letters and gifts to him—the rest to her own people. I worked and cried until I was almost blind—everything rent my heart—the pretty things she had been given or had bought for her expected home—the hats and dresses I had seen her in so often—the cards I had sent her since my marriage, full of little intimate jesting messages only we two could understand—little clippings, little snaps I had sent her and which she had kept like precious treasures. Oh Frede, I wonder if anyone will ever go over *my* possessions with the agony that was my portion when I went over yours. I hope not—I believe not—for I will leave none behind me to whom I will mean what you meant to me—no, not even if my husband outlives me. For men do not feel these things as women do.

On Wednesday we finished our task and packed everything into boxes and trunks, most of them to go to poor Aunt Annie. Frede had directed in her letter that I was to have "first choice" of her little treasures but I took very little. I needed nothing—to use anything of Frede's would always wring my soul.

When Frede married I gave her a beautiful silver tea and coffee service. She had taken great pleasure in it—I am glad to think of that now—and always used it proudly at her afternoon teas. I took this back and have packed it away. Some day Chester, if he lives, may marry and then I shall give, or cause to be given to him his "Aunt Frede's set". I believe that is what would please her most. She loved Chester so—her old "Captain" of his baby months. I know there is no living human being she would rather have get it.

I also brought home her "Good Fairy." That morning in May when I arrived at the Teacher's Residence Frede took me up to her room and delightedly showed me her "first wedding present"—a pretty little bronze statuette called "The Good Fairy" which had been given her by two of the staff. Being her first wedding gift it seemed to have a special significance. She always kept it on her bureau. I shall put it somewhere where I shall see it often and perhaps in days to come it will give me pleasure and not pain.

Among Frede's little bits of jewelry were a pendant of peridots and pearls and a pair of drop earrings to match. They were given her by an ardent lover of hers in the west—an Ed Willetts. She liked him very much—she was very near marrying him. But somehow she found she couldn't—and didn't. I brought the pendant and earrings home with me and packed them away. I don't know yet what disposal I shall finally make of them. Perhaps one of the little girls at Park Corner shall have them some day. Or perhaps some misty little unborn bride of Stuart's may wear them. She will not be haunted as I would be by visions of Frede as I saw her at my Christmas dinner table two years ago, laughing and jesting with Fraser, her cheeks flushed, her eyes black and brilliant, the pendant glistening on her breast, the earrings caressing her cheeks.

Miss Hill and Miss Stuart had together given her a little set of afternoon tea cups and saucers of old-fashioned design. Miss Hill said she thought Frede would like me to have that so I brought it, too. The rest of her gifts went to Park Corner.

When I returned to the apartment Wednesday night I found that my martyrdom was over. The fierce flame of torture had at last burned itself out—and gray ashes were over all my world. I was calm and despairing.

I left on the 11.20 train. It bore me away into darkness. There was no Frede behind—no Frede anywhere in the world—nothing but a little handful of ashes. *Where was she?* That wit, that strength, that vivid, brilliant personality—*these* could not be gray ashes—these must be somewhere in existence still. But nowhere where I can reach them—see them—feel

"Frede" (x) and Macdonald Group

them. And therefore, as far as my world is concerned, lost to me.

I reached Toronto in the morning and spent the day doing some necessary shopping. I came home Friday—have been home a week—a gloomy, bitter week. I can do nothing in the day—at night I cry myself to sleep. This house seems so full of Frede—everything is connected with her—everything tortures me. I think of her constantly. I realize, as never before, how intimately the strands of our lives were woven together. Does Stuart say some quaint, funny thing I find myself thinking "How Frede will laugh when she hears this," *before* the new consciousness that she is gone can prevent it. I find a passage in my reading that arrests me—"I must send this to Frede"—"how Frede will enjoy this." Some of the things that have rent me with the keenest pangs are absurd enough, too—for life always mixes up tragedy and grotesqueness. Today when I was hanging up my beef hams to dry I broke down and cried because Frede could never come to taste them. "Maud," she used to say, "I love you but even if I hated you I would come to see you for the sake of getting some of your beef ham."

It seems to me now that Frede and I must have been intimate and congenial friends all our lives. It seems to me quite unbelievable that I was 28, with a lifetime of bitter experiences behind me when Frede and I found each other. Yet such was the fact.

In my journal of the winter I spent at Park Corner in 1892 Frede's name is not even mentioned. This is not perhaps to be wondered at. I was then seventeen—practically a young woman with my head full of the beaux and parties and amusements of budding bellehood. Frede was a child of eight. Naturally there could be little in common between us. The strange part is that I have so little recollection of Frede during that winter. This is odd, because she was always around and one would think that vivid, magnetic personality of hers must have been manifest even in childhood to a sufficient extent to impress itself on my memory. It did not, however. I scarcely remember Frede at all, though I do remember that I used to make her frightfully mad by teasing her about "Mel Donald", a little freckled urchin of her own age who went to school and whom Frede hated. She always got in a baby rage when I teased her about him and I am afraid I was mean enough to delight in doing it rather often. I should think she must have hated me. In fact, I believe she did; but also she accorded me a reluctant admiration. "In spite of my hatred I thought you very handsome," she once told me laughing, and averred it was one of the chief delights of her small existence that winter to get into my bedroom when I was dressing to go out or entertain company, and sit curled up on the bed to watch me while I combed and curled and frilled and plumed myself. I have no recollection of this. I was too full of the egotism of early youth to think about her and no prescience came to me of what this small, black-haired, sallow-faced mite was to mean to me in the future.

I might remark that this same "Mel" Donald, who was a second cousin of our own, later on developed into a quite smart and nice-looking young man and an excellent friend of Frede's. They were very intimate and congenial, though there was never any "lovering" between them. Frede outlived her hatred both of Mel and me!

Years passed. Frede grew up; I grew older and sadder and—let us hope—a little wiser. I must of course have seen Frede whenever I was at Park Corner. The first mention of her in my diary is in the winter of 1893, when I speak of her popping out of Park Corner school to greet me one day, when I called there on my way over to Aunt Annie's. The next mention is not till December 1898, when I speak of having been at Park Corner and finding it changed. "Cade and Frede are away. Only Stella is left." There is a note in this as if I missed Frede, which must have meant that we had been more companionable but if so I have no memory of it. At this time Frede was at P.W.C. In 1899 I mention a summer visit to Park Corner, where I had a pleasant time "as Frede and Stell were both home." But it was not until August 1902 that Frede and I "found" each other. Our friendship seemed to open into full bloom in a single night. Before that we were mere acquaintances; after that we were to each other what we were to be for over seventeen, beautiful, unmarred years of comradeship and understanding.

I recall the night distinctly. It was a hot night. For some forgotten reason we all three occupied Stella's room. Stell herself slept on the floor. Frede and I were in the bed. We began to talk confidentially each finding that we could confide in the other. Stell was furious because our chatter kept her from sleeping, so we buried our heads under the blankets that sweltering night and whispered to each other all our troubles—I, the woman of 28, Frede the girl of 19. We discovered that our souls were the same age! She told me her love troubles—I told her mine. In those years love troubles seemed to us to be the only things worth worrying about. We both had had bitter and heart-rending experiences. We talked, until dawn. Many times I have regretted the fact that nearness and darkness have betrayed me into confidences that were foolish and unwise. But neither of us ever regretted the mutual revelations of that night—never did we wish a word unsaid. From that hour we were—as Aunt Annie writes me that Life Howatt said when he heard of her death—"part of one another." Oh, Frede, Frede!

Frede taught in various schools and in 1905 she came to Stanley. She was comparatively near me then and we met quite often. It was a boon to me beyond price in those hard, lonely years. I could not have endured them without Frede's sympathy and encouragement and jolly companionship. When I made a hit with *Green Gables* and saw a little money assured my first determination was to help Frede. She was, I knew, tired and discouraged, seeing nothing before her but endless, monotonous years of teaching country schools for a mere pittance. I insisted that she should go to Macdonald or McGill and I would pay her way—I told her I wanted to "help her little ship to come in." After much urging she assented. She chose Macdonald and Household Science. She had a busy, happy two years there and led her class in graduation. She spent a year in Red Deer College, Alta. and then went back to Macdonald as Demonstrator to the Home-Makers' Clubs of Quebec. She did a wonderful work there and won recognition as one of the cleverest women in Canada. She was specially fitted for such a work, for not only had she the brains, training and personality for it, but she had the practical upbringing on the farm which enabled her to have a complete understanding of all the problems of farm life—an understanding no city-bred woman could ever attain. She had hosts of warm devoted personal friends—and a few virulent enemies, for a certain class of people hated her truth and sincerity and her clear-eyed and uncompromising penetration of their shams and hypocrisy.

Frede, like myself, had a somewhat lonely and misunderstood childhood. She was "different" from the rest of her family. She was, as she expressed it, "the cat who walked by herself." Her sisters were a good deal older than she and George was no kind of a companion. She has often told me that her mother "never loved her," until the older girls left home and Aunt Annie was forced to turn to Frede for companionship in her loneliness. Frede, not being a mother herself, was mistaken in this. Aunt Annie *did* love her; but it was only the love of maternal instinct. It is certain she never understood her. Frede was an odd, lonely, homely little thing. Homely? Yes, especially in childhood. Frede was always the plainest of the three girls. Her enemies called her ugly but she was never *that*. There was always too much spirit and character in her face for that. She had beautiful thick glossy black hair, greenish-gray eyes that, like mine, had the Montgomery trick of seeming black at night, owing to the dilation of the pupils, and a fine figure. But her features were irregular and her complexion—her worst point—sallow and freckled. Yet I have seen Frede look positively handsome. As in my own case her appearance depended vastly on the way her hair was arranged. In evening dress, with flushed cheeks and brilliant, mocking eyes, Frede had a certain *beauté du diable* that was fascinating. I have seen her look exactly as she does in this picture of her, holding a flower, taken at the time of her marriage. But ordinarily the one below, snapped in a

Jean Fraser and Frederica Campbell in Greenhouse, Macdonald College

Macdonald greenhouse with a friend, is truer of her. I think it is the truest picture of Frede she ever had taken. In spite of her plainness, Frede found admirers and lovers wherever she went—her wit, vivacity and magnetic personality assured that.

Frede was clever from childhood. She passed for First Class License at Prince of Wales when only fourteen. If she could have gone on there or soon after to McGill or Dalhousie she would have had a brilliant college career. The thing should have been done. But there never was any ready money; and neither Uncle John nor Aunt Annie seemed to have any ambition for their family beyond giving them enough education to enable them to "earn their own living" in a very humble way; George squandered enough on horses, new buggies and carouses every year to have paid for Frede's college course. It is a maddening thing to think that a girl

with Frede's brains and in a home where the inmates ought to have been comparatively wealthy had no chance. She could not save enough to send herself to college out of the wretched salaries paid to teachers then—$180 or $230 a year.

She taught near home at first in Sea View and Irishtown. She was always a marked success as a teacher—later on Dr. Anderson said she was the best teacher in P.E. Island. She had in a marvellous degree the power of drawing out and inspiring her scholars. They invariably worshipped her.

When she was nineteen she had her unhappy love affair—the real tragedy of her life. She met and passionately loved my cousin, Will Sutherland, then a young doctor in his first year of practice. It would have been an ideal marriage. They were suited to each other perfectly. As the wife of the successful man Will has become Frede would have been in her element. She would have made him an ideal wife. But it all came to nothing. I don't know that Will cared for Frede. Sometimes I think he did! But he was already engaged to a girl he had met during his medical course. She was a Catholic and a trained nurse. He married her a year or two later, much to his mother's grief. I have met her. She seemed a rather likeable common girl—not to be mentioned in the same breath with Frede. But perhaps Will really loved her and is happy with her. Frede and I never knew—never will know. Frede eventually outgrew her unhappy love for Will. But it marked her for life. She was never quite the same again. Her cousin, Jim Campbell, went with her for several years. Frede was very fond of Jim. She never loved him but she might have married him if he had not been her first cousin and uneducated. When she was out west Ed Willetts was wild about her and never gave up hope of winning her until she was married. When she went back to Macdonald she had another quite serious affair with Dr. Walker, a very clever and interesting man but, as far as I have been able to discover, a very untrustworthy one. He, too, was engaged to another girl of whom he was tired. Frede, I think, thought he would have married her if it had not been for that. But I doubt it. They eventually quarrelled; later he broke his engagement and married a third girl. It was something of a blow to Frede at the time but later on she realized that she had had a fortunate escape. It had not gone nearly so deeply with her as in the case of Will. She realized that her infatuation for Walker was an unwholesome one and could never have resulted in happiness. She always saw quite clearly with her brain what manner of man he was, in spite of the fascination he exercised over her for a time.

Well, it is all over. It has been my privilege to possess for seventeen years a rare and perfect friendship—something that is very rare in this world, especially between women. Perhaps some day I may be thankful that I had it even at the cost of losing it. Just now the agony seems too great a price to pay. When I went through Frede's things I found in her desk some little pen and ink sketches she had made. They were of no value to anyone but me so I brought them home with me. I am going to put them here in my journal to keep them safely. To me they are full of Frede.

It has been dreadful to write all this out. On every page I have had to stop and cry my heart out. And yet there has been a strange sad comfort in it—as if it brought me nearer to Frede to write thus of her—as if death and the grave were cheated for a little while. Oh St. Paul, you never lost anyone vitally dear to you or you would not have shouted so magnificently "Oh death where is thy sting? Oh grave where is thy victory?" The sting is that we lose our comrades out of this life—the victory that we can never see them again on this side of the grave.

Well, I must make an end now and face life without her. I am forty-four. I shall make no new friends—even if there were other Fredes in the world. I have lived one life in those seemingly far-off years before the war. Now there is another to be lived, in a totally new world where I think I shall never feel quite at home. I shall always feel as if I belonged "back there"—back there with Frede and laughter and years of peace.

Sunday, Feb. 9, 1919
Leaskdale, Ont.
I had such a ghastly dream about Frede last night—the first time I have dreamed of her. I was at Macdonald College in a large upper room. Several people were in it—Miss Philp, Miss Zollman, Miss Hill and several strangers. Frede was lying on a couch, alive, but seemingly very ill. I went over to Miss Philp in a far corner and said to her in a whisper "What does this mean? Didn't Frede die?" Miss Philp, with a look of horror on her face pointed to Frede. *"That"* she said, "has been here ever since you went away. Now you know as much about it as I do." I went back to Frede. I felt none of the horror which seemed to entrance the others. There had been some awful mistake—but Frede was still alive and must be cared for. I gave her a drink of milk and then endeavored to tuck the bedclothes warmly around her. Suddenly I found that I held, not a quilt but a coffin lid and that I was pressing it down on her while she struggled feebly beneath it. I woke in horror and have been haunted by it all day.

Friday, Feb. 14, 1919
Have been very lonely and heartsick all the week. So many letters come which wring my soul. Some of them are from my friends sympathizing—mostly with the old stock platitudes. Some from friends of Frede, ranging from the Atlantic to the Pacific, begging me to write them and tell them about her death. Each and all say the same—they never knew a friend like her and never will again. I must write them—but oh, it is hard!

Saturday, Feb. 15, 1919
The Manse, Leaskdale, Ont.
It would be easier for me if I were living in some place where nobody had ever heard of Frede. She was so well-known here and everywhere I go people ask me about her death. Some betray such a heartless curiosity regarding details and ask tactless questions that are like a stab to me. Today I was up to see the old Oxtoby girls and Lizzie raved about Frede's being cremated—"it was so barbarous." I told her curtly that it was Frede's own wish and dying request. I felt I was foolish to let the strictures of an ignorant and narrow-minded old maid hurt me—but everything hurts me now.

Monday, Feb. 24, 1919
The Manse, Leaskdale, Ont.
Tonight we were out to tea at a near neighbor's, so took the children. When we came out Stuart looked up at the begemmed sky and exclaimed, "Oh, see the beautiful stars!"

I think Stuart has inherited my love for natural beauty. I doubt if Chester has—at least, so far he has given little indication of it. I think he "takes after" his father in this respect. The beauty of the world of nature means nothing to Ewan. He seems to be as totally unaware of it as a blind man. I remember that Chester once, when he was about four, exclaimed as we were driving along a very pretty wooded road, "Oh, see the dear little tiny darling road." But never since have I heard him make any reference to pleasure in natural scenery. I hope it will develop later. One who has it not misses so much out of life. I am anxious for both of them to possess it for I consider it one of the greatest of happiness-yielding gifts.

The two boys are amazingly unlike each other. Chester is of a very reserved nature. He is much harder to understand than Stuart, who is frank and open. He gives an impression—and always has—of unyielding *sturdiness*. Stuart gives the impression of beauty and charm. Physically he is a very lovely child, so clear and rosy his skin, so brilliant his large blue eyes. He worships me with a strange intensity. This isn't vanity—or maternal idiocy—or anything but a simple statement of fact. Chester is very fond of me with the average boy's love for his mother. But he is quite as fond of his father. Stuart, on the other hand, seems to care nothing for anyone but me. "My *dear* mother", he exclaims passionately, throwing his arms around me, "*do* you like me?" He is never happy away from me—he cannot bear that a cloud should come between us for a moment. He is rather jealous and does not like even Chester to kiss and hug me. He will push him away, exclaiming, "*You* have a father. This is *my* mother." Why he should not feel that he has a father too, I cannot understand for Ewan has always made quite as much of him as of Chester. But "*my* mother" seems to be the only person in the world for whom, as yet, Master Stuart has any real love. He centres all his affection on me—alas, I fear he has inherited from me something besides my love of beauty—my passionate intensity of feeling and my tendency to concentrate it all on a few objects or persons unspeakably dear to me.

Friday, Feb. 28, 1919
The Manse, Leaskdale, Ont.
I had a wild, distracted, incoherent letter from Ella today. I really fear that woman is going out of her mind. She has always been in the habit of pouring out her woes to me in letters and I have always sympathized with her and tried to give her as good and sensible advice as was in my power, for I have been keenly alive to the bitter things in her lot, as well as the weakness of character, or rather of mentality in her that rendered her incapable of grappling with them. But she is really going too far. I am ready to assist her in real difficulties but I cannot have her dumping a lot of purely imaginary troubles on me like this. I have written in answer rather sharply, simply because I think she needs a bit of a tonic and will pull herself together the better for it. I do not think I have been harsh or impatient but I have told her a few plain truths that may act as a bracer. Her letter spoiled my day and made me unhappy. Frede and I used

to share the "problem of Ella" as we shared "the problem of Stell" and now I have no such assistance.

Ella entreated me to "burn" her letter. I did not and shall not do it. I shall keep it to justify my own, should the necessity ever arise. Some bitter experiences in the past have taught me the wisdom of this.

Saturday, March 1, 1919
Leaskdale, Ont.
Today was a raw, surly day with wind and showers—quite lion-like. But we have had a wonderful winter. It has been more like one long spring. There has been no snow and hardly any cold weather. Cars and buggies have run all winter. It is well that it has been mild for we could not get any coal at all and have had to burn wood. It is not suited to a coal furnace and we have been almost smoked out. Nevertheless we are thankful to have any fuel at all.

Tonight I was casting up my financial accounts for the year. I find that I am worth about fifty thousand dollars now, and have earned by my pen since that first wonderful three dollars of 1896 about seventy five thousand dollars. How the thought of possessing such a sum would have made my eyes stick out twenty four years ago! It is not a bad showing, considering my initial equipment—my pen and the scanty education I managed to get. If I could only have had a couple of thousand of it twenty five years ago when I wanted so much to take an Arts Course! But it does not matter much now. I daresay I would not have done any better, if as well, if I had got the B.A. degree I hungered for. "There's a divinity that shapes our ends"—yea, verily. We are only clay in the hands of a mysterious Potter, who will not give us even the sorry comfort of knowing at the time the reason of our anguish.

Monday, March 3, 1919
The Manse, Leaskdale, Ont.
Wrote during the forenoon and then drove to Uxbridge over very bad roads and read a paper on Astronomy to the Hypatia Club. Had tea with Mrs. Sharpe and came home in the evening. After nine I read till bed-time—my only time for reading. My book was a novel called "The Blue Germ" and a very fascinating yarn it was, though its ending was weak. I fancy the man who would suddenly make human beings immortal *would* rather make a mess of things, especially in a world where every custom and law is based on the fact of mortality. After all, wouldn't immortality be rather boring in the long run— say, a few million of years. Even a soul, I think, must get tired and want a rest from "the fever called living", just the same as the body.

Friday, March 7, 1919
Leaskdale, Ont.
Have been haunted all day by thoughts of Frede. Some days are more like this than others. This house is so full of her. I can't even make a cake without a stab of agony for my recipe book is full of the Macdonald College recipes she gave me. And in every room I see her in some favorite position—she haunts

my dining room table, sitting opposite the mirror and looking into it according to the habit about which Ewan used to tease her. She had the habit, though it was not born of vanity.

Tuesday, Mar. 11, 1919
Another day of bitter loneliness for Frede. Oh, it is so unbearable to think she is nowhere in the world—not even in the old Geddie Memorial graveyard at Spring Brook. There is nothing *there* but a little handful of gray ashes.

Yet am I not wholly desolate. Tonight, Chester, when I was undressing him, suddenly looked gravely up in my face and said "I don't know how I could live without you, mother." It is rare that he shows his affection like that. It comforted me. Life can't be *un*livable as long as one is necessary to somebody's happiness.

I began work on my tenth novel today. It is to be another "Anne" story—and I fervently hope the last—dealing with her sons and daughters during the years of war. That will end *Anne*—and properly. For she belongs to the green, untroubled pastures and still waters of the world before the war.

Wednesday, March 12, 1919
The Manse, Leaskdale
We were out to tea tonight. I found it dreadfully hard to keep up my end of "small talk" and appear bright and interested. I was dull, depressed, and lifeless—as if the "youth of the soul" were gone, as well as the youth of the body. These pastoral visitations are rather dreadful to me just now.

Had a paper from Miss Philp today containing a sketch of Frede. Could I ever have pictured myself reading Frede's "obituary?" How she hated that word—"that fat and unctuous and objectionable word." I remember once, many years ago, telling Frede that I did not believe that I would live to be old. "I have a feeling," I said, "that early middle life will see the end for me. I cannot see myself *old*."

"*I* can", said Frede with a shudder. "I can see myself a wrinkled, shrivelled old woman." But her vision of herself was never to be. She went away in her prime of womanhood. Yet she had *lived* more in her thirty five years than most women do in ninety.

Shall I live to be old? I have, as aforesaid, never felt that I would. Yet Frede was wrong in her "feeling"—I may be wrong in mine. It doesn't matter, if I can only live long enough to see my boys educated, well-started in life and—if the fates are kind—happy in homes of their own.

Saturday, Mar. 15, 1919
Leaskdale, Ont.
A chilly day—and a dreary one. I had a letter from Ella today—abjectly apologizing for her wild letter of a few weeks ago and evidently very frightened that she has "lost my friendship" because of it. I will reassure her on that point but I think the little alarm has proved salutary. My plain speaking has braced her up temporarily at least—but I fear only temporarily....

Saturday, Mar. 22, 1919
The Manse, Leaskdale

I have been dull and nervous continually. And the event of yesterday will not help me. Our little black mare "Queen" got kicked last night, had her leg broken and had to be shot. We have had her ever since we came here and she seemed like one of the family. She was such a dear little thing, with every good nag quality—speedy, gentle, trusty. Last evening was heart-rending. I cried all the evening....I have never had much to do with horses, although I was brought up on a farm. Grandfather was a man who never let anyone have a horse to drive anywhere if he could possibly help it.

After his death Uncle John coolly took possession of grandmother's two horses, worked and used them, but was so disagreeable about letting me have one to drive that after two experiences of it I never again in all the years I lived there asked him for one. I walked or stayed home. "Doctor," Alec Macneill's horse, and "Miss Flo", Lou Dystant's pretty mare were two nags I was very fond of. I never cared for any other horse until we got Queen. She has been a great pet and this cruel ending has hurt me horribly. What is the use of loving anything? It only means more suffering.

Sunday, Mar. 23, 1919
Leaskdale, Ont.

Alone this afternoon I read all Frede's old letters. I felt impelled to do so. Lately I have been so tortured by the thought that I can never again look forward to getting a letter from Frede. So I got out all her old letters. The reading of them was not painful—on the contrary, it was a comfort and a strange, bitter pleasure. While I read them Frede was *alive*, she existed—she was somewhere in the world. The vivid personality behind those letters *could not* have been blotted out....

Many things in the letters hurt me, of course—especially the little instances of her solicitude for me scattered through them. Writing me before Stuart was born she said, in urging me to take things easier and spare myself a little, "I know of no woman who works so hard as you do and takes so little recreation. Missionary meetings and Guilds and visits in Zephyr are *not* recreations!"

Again, in the same strain she wrote, "Maud, I want you to remember that you are Ewan's wife and Chester's mother and my dearly beloved friend and we cannot do without you. I have lived in a great many houses and I have never known a woman who considered her husband's work as you do."

I think what hurt me so keenly in these was the fact that there was no one left on earth to understand or note these things.

In one letter from Sturgeon, written one winter when I was not feeling well she said, "I tremble to think of what the world would be to me without you."

Oh, Frede, you never had to learn it. It is I who must find that out.

Ella writes me that she has called her baby "Frederica MacFarlane." I am glad of this and will remit many things to Ella because of it. I like to think that in days to come there will be another Fred Campbell at old Park Corner. Little Maud is not much older and the two will be companions for each other as Fred and I were before, I hope. Fred has no other namesake. She hated her name—"Frederica Elmanstine." She was called after the German wife of an uncle who had married in a western state. Yet, somehow, the odd striking name suited her odd striking personality. Frede couldn't have been a Lilian or a Jennie or a Mary.

Speaking of namesakes I have six—Christine Maud Agnew, Anita Maud Webb, Maud Dingwell, Maud Beaton, Maud Campbell, and a small Maud Quigley here in Leaskdale. I had a small French namesake also—"Tennis" Doiron down home called one of his numerous progeny after me but the poor little thing died last winter from an epidemic of diptheretic sore throat.

I wish that Frede had left a child—that her life went on in something. Perhaps Cam would have let me have it. Upstairs I have a trunkful of pretty baby clothes. When I looked them over last spring I thought, "Some day Frede may have a baby and I will send her these." But they will never be worn by a little child of Fred's. When we were together at Macdonald after her marriage she said once, speaking of my two boys, "I hope I'll be as lucky as you." But last fall at Park Corner she spoke in a different strain. She said if it were not for Cam's sake she would not care if she never had a child. "It was too much risk—they might turn out changelings as George had done etc. etc." I think she felt that she had not the strength, physical or emotional, for motherhood. Her intense life had exhausted both.

Thursday, March 27, 1919

Yesterday I had to go to Lindsay to a "Presbyterial" meeting. Worse still, I had to take a fat stupid old dame of the parish with me. We came back to Uxbridge late in the evening and had a dreadful drive home through the pitch dark night over the worst roads that this part of the country has known for years. Had it not been for Ewan's flashlight I don't think we would ever have got home. It was half past nine when we reached here. Do you think I could then go to my welcome bed? Verily, no, I had to dress up and go to a wedding reception. Ewan said he was too tired to go and I knew the people in question would be offended if one of us didn't go, so I was the victim. I went up with the Cooks and had to sit there until three o'clock in the morning before old J.C., who is seventy, could tear himself away from the scene of revelry. I talked to scores of the women who were sitting around the room in rows, until I felt like a machine that just talked on without any volition. My head ached, my back ached, my mind and soul ached. I talked hens and eggs and markets and high prices and roads and all the other entrancing subjects for "conversation" which prevail hereabouts—at least, when "the minister's wife" is present. I have a suspicion that when she isn't they talk racy and malicious and interesting gossip and enjoy themselves much better. But alas, ministers' wives dare not meddle with gossip else would their tenure in the land be short and troubled.

Saturday, Mar. 29, 1919
Leaskdale, Ont.

Tonight I enjoyed the treat of a "good read." I read "The Twentieth Plane", the book which has made such a sensation in Toronto. I was much disappointed in it. It was absolute poppycock—utterly unconvincing. And I was so ready to be convinced for since Frede died I would give anything if I could only be convinced that she still exists and that there might be a faint hope of getting some communication from her, even by the medium of the ouija-board. But my intellect absolutely refused any credence to the so-called "revelations" of "The Twentieth Plane". As a stunt of the "subjective mind" or whatever strange occult power is responsible, it *is* rather remarkable. But as a proof that communication is possible with the spirits of the dead it is nil. There was a certain enjoyment in the book, though, because it is really exquisitely funny—all the funnier because it is so deadly serious. The "pink twilight" and the "orange sun" of the Twentieth Plane don't appeal to me, and the "bill of fare" which the departed eat is farcical—"synthetic beef tea" and "juice of a rice product"!! Ye gods, if one must eat in the world of spirits I would prefer something more appetizing. How Frede would have howled over that! What fun we could have had if we had read this book together!

In the whole book there was only *one* thing that seemed to me rather inexplicable on any hypothesis other than that of a communication from another world. But I have a long long way to go before I can believe that the spirits of the dead can spell out messages on the Ouija board or that they live in an eternal pink twilight on synthetic beef tea.

But I will say that Dr. Watson is choice in the spook company he keeps. There isn't a single non-famous spirit on his calling list, except his mother. Shakespeare and Plato and Wordsworth and Lincoln etc. etc. etc. jostle each other for a chance to expound through the Ouija board—and all use precisely the same literary style and a very awful one at that. There don't seem to be any grocers or butchers or carpenters on the Twentieth Plane—though one would think that a few butchers at least would be needed to convert the synthetic cows into the synthetic beef out of which the synthetic beef tea is made!

The denizens of the Twentieth Plane never by any chance "go to bed." They invariably "retire to the silken couches of rest."

I think I will retire to my silken couch of rest!

Tuesday, Apr. 1, 1919
The Manse, Leaskdale, Ont.

Yesterday and today have been bitterly cold with high, tempestuous winds. Ewan was away last night, so I took both the boys to bed with me, fearing that the little creatures would be cold in their own bed. We snuggled cosily down; myself in the middle, Chester on the right, Stuart on the left, and listened to the wind howling outside. I love to have them sleep with me—I hate to think of the day when they will be too big. They are such delicious little souls in bed—so plump and warm and soft and cuddlesome, with their whispered confidences and their sleepy kisses.

Sunday, April 13, 1919
Leaskdale, Ont.

Last Monday I went into Toronto and stayed a week. I had much shopping and business to attend to, and I also wanted a little change for a tonic—something to stimulate me a little. I had "sagged" all the previous week—was depressed and nervous—thought constantly of Frede and cried about her all the time I was alone. This cannot continue if I am to have strength and energy for my work and duties. So I went to town and feel much better for it.

I stayed with Laura and we had pleasant evenings. There is no one like one's own. I invested in a good Victrola while in. I have never had any musical instrument in my home since I was married. When I left Cavendish I gave my old organ to the Sunday School there. I intended to get a piano but there was so much else to get that the first years of our marriage slipped away and I did not get one. Then the war came and while it lasted I did not think I ought to spend any money for unnecessaries. Now that it is over I felt I must have something. But for some time I have grown out of concert with the piano idea. I have no daughters; none of us have any musical gift. Rarely does anyone come to the house who could play well enough on one to give us real pleasure. On the other hand, the Victrola records bring the best music of the world into your home; I think it will be a splendid thing for the children; and as a means of entertaining visitors it is far ahead of a piano nobody could play. So a Victrola I did buy me. The agent was of the usual slick type and was very anxious that I should be made aware of all the good points of the machine. Pulling out a little contraption at the side he said confidentially, "You see, if you want a little *dance music* some Sunday evening and *don't want it to be heard on the street* just pull this out—so."

I had a vision of myself sitting in the Leaskdale manse parlor some Sunday evening, when Ewan was away preaching to the Zephyrites, listening to "dance music" with the soft pedal on!!!

Just to see if it would be possible to make an agent shrivel I said smilingly, "I am a minister's wife so I don't expect to have *much* occasion for dance music on Sunday evenings."

I shall never be absolutely certain whether he blushed a little or not. But the odds are against it.

I spent Tuesday evening with Marshall Saunders and we talked shop and Page. He was her first publisher also and cheated her without pity and without remorse. The man must simply have an obsession of dishonesty. Most certainly he could make more money by being honest. Wednesday evening I went up to see the MacMurchys and spent quite a pleasant evening talking with Marjorie who was in one of her agreeable moods.

Thursday I attended a luncheon given by Mr. McClelland at the National Club. Several nice and interesting people were present but conversation was annihilated by Mac's announcement that the new Copyright Bill—which has passed the Commons and is in Committee in the Senate and which we have all been considering a most excellent thing—will, if passed in its present form, simply ruin Canadian authors for a time at least, because they will not be able to secure copyright in the U.S. Horrified, we all began questioning and exclaiming and kept it up the entire luncheon. Life is certainly one darned worriment after another.

On Friday evening Laura, Ralph and I had a very interesting seance with the Ouija board. A wave of Ouijaism has flooded Toronto as a result of the publication of *The Twentieth Plane*. Honest dealers in Ouija boards have made small fortunes.

A rather strange thing happened. When we asked if any spirits were present the answer was—as usual—"Yes". "Frede" was present and wanted to speak to "Maud". This is the ordinary thing at seances like this. I was minded not to go on. I did not believe that Frede was there—and yet—I did hunger so for some communication from her. Why not try? So I crushed down a certain distaste and asked Ouija to give me the message.

Ouija thereupon began spelling out rapidly. In passing, I may remark on the curious fact that whenever *I* am present at a Ouija seance the Power that moves the pointer always spells *phonetically*. As I have not heard of this occurring when I am not present I must conclude that the reason is in me. But why? I have always detested the idea of phonetic spelling and have virulently opposed the idea all my life.

To resume:—Ouija spelled out,

"Has she cashed the second check?"

I was rather staggered. Certainly it was not the sort of message I had expected from Frede—or whatever power or personality was imitating Frede. Who was "she"? And I had no idea what "the second check" referred to. I asked of Ouija, "*Who is she?*" "Miss B.A. Hill" was the reply. Now, Miss Hill's initials are A.E. I did not know this at the time but I knew one of her initials was "A". Neither Laura nor Ralph knew of the existence of Miss Hill, so this answer *must* have come either from my subjective mind or from some outside intelligence. I said to Laura, "When I see Miss Hill I will ask her what it means." Instantly Ouija began to spell and spelled, "Trust a clear appearance, dear Maud." I then asked, "Shall I write Miss Hill or wait till I see her?"

Answer. "Better visit her. Her talk will convince you that I am right. Trust your uncle F.C."

Laura and Ralph laughed at the "uncle", thinking it nonsense. They did not know that in our family circle we have always called Fred—and she called herself—"Uncle Fred", as a little joke on her masculine nickname. But she *never* called herself, or was called, "Uncle *F.C.*"

I then asked if when I saw Miss Hill, I should ask about that "second check" or wait until she introduced the subject herself.

Answer. "Just let her talk."

I asked. "Where shall I see her?"

Answer. "Tomorrow at Uxbridge. She is on her way now."

Up to this time I had been feeling rather weirdly credulous. But now I knew this was not the truth. I knew perfectly well that Miss Hill would not be in Uxbridge the next day. However, I asked,

"Where shall I see her in Uxbridge?"

Answer. "Willis' drug store. Good-night dear Maud."

That ended Frede's communication. I did not—could not—believe it came from her. Yet it gave me a queer comfort—as if I really had been talking to her. I *knew* Miss Hill would not be in Willis' drug store. Yet when I reached Uxbridge Friday evening I induced Ewan to drive up to Willis' through the vile mud, alleging that I wanted to get some notepaper.

I did *not* find Miss Hill there!

Now *whence* did that message come? Why was part of it a lie? And is there any meaning or truth in that "second check"? Shall I ever know?

We had some other funny communications. The Aylsworth Ouija has, it seems, a great spite at Laura and always says something sarcastic to her. As soon as we stopped asking questions it started in of its own accord.

"Now Laura will dance. Tee-hee!"

Really, one could almost hear the sardonic chuckle. Laura said teasingly, "But, Ouija, I have no music. I can't dance without music." "Oh, Maud will whistle," retorted Ouija.

Again we all asked Ouija to tell us our worst faults. Ouija promptly told Ralph and Laura theirs but all I could elicit was the mysterious remark,

"Ewan knows."

Ralph's father, Dr. Aylsworth, believes that the power behind Ouija is a demonism. He may be right. But evidently some demons have a sense of humor!

Wednesday, Apr. 16, 1919
The Manse, Leaskdale

We have had five dark, dull, wet, cold, *wicked* days. Again I have been depressed and heartsick. Last night I cried half the night about Frede and when I fell asleep I had a horrible dream of seeing her drowning and trying vainly to rescue her. The gloom of it has been over me all day.

Today I had a letter from Stell. She was married on April 11 to Lowry Keller who is just home from France. I have been expecting it. She told me about him last fall and a week ago I had a letter from her saying he wanted her to marry him at once. She has been engaged for nearly fifteen years to Irving Howatt. Twice she has been all ready to be married and he put her off on the plea of not yet being able to afford it. He certainly was badly pinched in the real estate slump that followed the outbreak of the war. But I think he was long ago tired of Stell. Her complaints and hysterics would wear out any man. But he behaved like a cad—as poor Frede said on her death bed. It is just as well she has dropped him.

And so "the problem of Stella" is solved. I am thankful. I don't think I could have borne it alone. Her husband will now be responsible for her vagaries and aberrations—*he* will have to endure her complaints, her aches, her agonies, her threats of suicide, her spasms of temper. He is madly in love with her at present. Let us hope it will last. Anyhow, Stella Campbell is now Stella Keller. Escape from old maidenhood, a home, support, companionship may work a change for the better in her neurasthenic outlook. But one thing is certain—she will always find plenty in life to grumble about. And heaven help L.K. if he ever tries to counter her.

Wednesday, April 23, 1919
Leaskdale, Ont.

Last Friday Cameron MacFarlane came for the Easter week-end and stayed until yesterday.

I think I understand now why Frede was taken away. It does not lessen my grief but it has lessened my rebellion. She would never—could never—have been permanently happy with Cameron MacFarlane.

When she married him I feared much more than I hoped. I thought—and think—that I understood how it came about. Cam was home from the front and felt lonely and out of place. The girl he had been engaged to had been very disagreeable about his enlisting in the first place and eventually had broken off her engagement on the score of it. He met Frede frequently; they had always been friendly; he found her sympathetic and jolly and imagined himself in love with her.

Frede was also lonely and disillusioned. She had begun, as she had confessed to me the preceding Xmas, to experience the bitterness in the lot of a woman whose youth is almost gone—the social neglect, the heart's loneliness, amid the crowd of younger girls. She was caught in some measure, too, by Cam's uniform and the romance of a "war marriage." All these things combined to hurry her into it. Then the excitement and pleasure of being a bride hypnotized her into thinking she was happy.

Before I met Cam some things I had heard others had said of him, some unconscious betrayals by Frede herself made me suspect that there was not much in Cam from an intellectual point of view. When I met Cam that night in Montreal for a brief time—well, I certainly did not dislike him but quite as certainly he did not attract me in any way. Since then we exchanged occasional letters and his letters had as little effect on me as his personality. They never made me feel in the slightest degree acquainted with him. I regretted this. I felt it would be a tragedy if I could not like and feel at home with Frede's husband—if I continued to have that baffling feeling of strangerhood.

Well, Cam has been my guest for five days. He is a puzzling personality. I cannot decide whether he is painfully deep or painfully shallow—but I think the latter. He was in excellent spirits. Once or twice he referred to Frede very flippantly. One time we had been talking of Aunt Annie's sore finger and I told him of the tendency all that family had to blood-poisoning and added, "I remember that Frede had a troublesome wart on her finger two years ago and she burned it off with nitric acid and that gave her blood-poisoning." Cam laughed and said—and in Lily's presence at that—"Served her right for being so vain as to try to burn it off."

I felt as if I had been struck in the face.

There were two or three more such incidents. But I would have found some excuses for Cam in his youth—he really belongs to another generation—if it had not been for his behavior on Monday evening.

The two old Miss Oxtobys were in their own way very fond of Frede, who always went to see them when she came here and was always nice to them. Naturally they wanted to meet her husband. So old Miss Mary toddled down here Monday afternoon. Cam was away with Ewan for a motor drive so Miss Mary asked me to bring him up in the evening. When Cam came home I told him. I did not expect he would want to go for enduring boredom is *not* one of his strong points; so I was agreeably surprised when he said heartily "Sure I'll go," and I forgave him many things I had resented.

We went up; we stayed about half an hour; and I never felt so bitterly ashamed and humiliated in my life.

Cam behaved during the whole call, like an absolute *buffoon*—I can call it by no milder term. If he had been a stranger to me I would have said, "That man can't be in his right mind." Every question those poor old souls asked, or every remark they made, he insulted them by a flippant or irrelevant reply. He said things that were in the vilest bad taste. For example—I had been speaking to Miss Mary of Lily Shier, who had been ill, and I remarked to Cam, "She was a maid of mine. I have married off two of my maids from the manse."

"Good!" said Cam. "I wonder what kind of luck you would have if you tried your hand on me." This from a man whose bride had died three months ago!

I tried to get him away but could not. He was enjoying himself too much for that. When I hinted that it was late he laughed loudly and said, "Oh, yes, I suppose these *young ladies* want to go to bed. That's the advantage of being single—you can go to bed when you please."

The "young ladies," who are well over sixty, must have liked this.

Finally I did get him up—then he suddenly pranced around to the corner where Lizzie O. was sitting, got behind her, and bent over her. I swear I thought he was going to kiss her and I believe she thought so too for she jerked to one side like a flash. Cam, however, only whispered something to her— what it was I'm sure she doesn't know yet for she was too much upset by his caper to take it in. Then he said, with another guffaw,

"But then you know I'm just as happy as if I were sane."

I got him out then.

"Say, didn't I shock them!" he chuckled, as we went down the walk.

I was literally cold with rage. I wanted to say with biting sarcasm,

"Oh yes, you shocked them—and me—if that is anything to be proud of. You have repeatedly insulted two old women who were friends of your wife, you have disgraced Frede's memory, you have shamed and humiliated me before the members of my husband's church and you have made an unforgettable ass of yourself. Chuckle—do! It's well worth it."

But I was not going to quarrel with Frede's husband. I said nothing. I walked down the road beside him tense and silent. But I made a resolution that I would never ask him to my house again; and I knew that death had been a friend to Frede—had undone the mistake of her marriage to this crude, conceited, ill-bred boy who was not and never could be "of the race of Joseph." Frede, my darling, I would rather you were dead than unhappy even though it means my lifelong loneliness.

Cam left yesterday. I feel that I do not want to see him again. Somehow I resent his having any share in Frede when he was so unworthy of her.

When Cam wrote me after Frede's death he said that in one of her recent letters to him she had said she "wished she were dead." Why, he did not know—she was to tell him when she saw him. On the day before her death she said to me, "Maud, I should never have married Cam when he urged me to." I thought then that it was mere delirium—but now, I do not know. I think she had realized her mistake and had begun to dread the life before her. But she has gone—my brave, gay, gallant girl—and her going sits very lightly on her bridegroom.

Friday, May 9, 1919

A typical day. Worked hard all day, carrying the books out of the library preparatory to cleaning it. Then in the evening when I was horribly tired and should have gone to bed I had to motor to Zephyr instead and give a programme for the Social Guild. Didn't get home until nearly one and am now too tired to sleep.

It didn't rain today for a wonder. It *has* rained almost every day this spring and been bitterly cold also. It is so difficult to get housecleaning done. We have been struggling with it for three weeks and are only at the library now. I seem to have so little strength mental or physical to grapple with it this spring. I waken in the morning tireder than when I went to bed. I seem to have only one real wish—to lie down somewhere and sleep for a month. Perhaps I would "catch up" then.

"Road to School"
[Leaskdale]

Chester began to go to school last Monday. In a way I hated it—it seemed that I was giving him up to the world—as if he were no longer mine. He goes to the school in along the side-road. It is too far away for him to come home to dinner, which I much regret. It is also a very small school which is another drawback—and the teacher is a sleepy mortal named Miss Brent—which is a third.

He seems to like it very well, so far as we can find out—for Chester, like his father, never tells anybody anything of his own accord!

Sunday, May 11, 1919
Leaskdale, Ont.
Another rainy, gloomy, dull Sunday. I did not feel well enough to go out today and yet it was a bad thing to be here alone all day. I felt nervous and depressed. Last night, too, I heard a horrible thing.

Miss Fergusson, the nurse I had when Chester was born, was married soon after to a Mr. Jenkins of Montreal. Last winter she died of flu, leaving three little children. This has haunted me all day. What fun she and Frede had here together that happy summer! And now they are both dead!

"C's school"

Wednesday, May 21, 1919
The Manse, Leaskdale
This afternoon Lily and I were busy housecleaning when Chester suddenly arrived home from school. I almost fainted at sight of him. I thought his eye was out. He was a dreadful sight. Blood was running down over his face from two cuts above the eye. The flesh was black and swollen; the eye was closed and—most terrifying thing of all—blood was oozing out between the lids. What had happened to the child's eye inside?

The boys had been playing down at the brook at noon recess and Chester had been struck, accidentally by a stick, or rather an old, dried, many-pointed root flung by a chum. I got the poor frightened child to bed and sponged off the blood. But those drops continued to ooze out between the lids and after supper we sent for the doctor.

"Off to school"
[Chester]

Dr. Shier arrived at dusk with one of his characteristically reassuring remarks! "I hope the eyeball isn't cut."

He said it with such dark significance that I, upset and nervous enough already, felt as if he must think the eyeball *was* injured. He examined Chester and said he must give him a little chloroform in order to be able to open the eye. Chester has never had any chloroform and I could not know how it might affect him. Reason told me that he would probably be all right; but that did not prevent me from going to pieces nervously. I made Ewan go up with Shier for the examination. Once I could have gone—but since the flu I have *no* nerve. I *could* not go. Instead, I shut myself up in the parlor and sat right down on the middle of the rug with clenched teeth and hands to wait.

"Oh, if Frede were only with me!" I moaned. Then I thought, "Perhaps she is. If human personality survives death I *know* that Frede would come to me in any crisis. But I want to *know* it."

Daff had come in and was sitting gravely over by the door. I recalled reading that animals are aware of presences which human beings cannot sense. Perhaps it was also true that those presences could influence animals. If Frede were with me could she make Daff do something which would prove her presence to me? I thought for a moment. I would ask for some unlikely thing—something that Daffy would never think of doing normally.

"Frede", I whispered pleadingly, "if you are here *make Daff come over to me and kiss me.*"

Daff *never* offers any caresses or seeks or enjoys petting. Yet it is the actual truth that hardly had I spoken when Daff walked gravely across the floor to me, lifted his forepaws and placed them on my shoulders, and touched my cheek with his mouth. Moreover, he did it twice.

Written out thus, the thing looks ridiculous. Why do such experiences always seem ridiculous when written or told? Perhaps because they should *not* be written or told—only lived. There was nothing that seemed ridiculous at the time. Instead, I felt sure that Frede *was* there with me and had made our old furry comrade the medium of her message. The conviction brought comfort and strength and calmness.

Presently Dr. Shier came down and said Chester had come out of the ether and he had found that the skin of the eyeball was cut but did not think there was any further damage. He could not be sure for a few days, however. So there is no sleep for me tonight I fear.

Friday, May 23, 1919
The Manse, Leaskdale

After two days of intense worry we are assured that Chester's eye is not seriously hurt and that the skin of the ball will heal up without scar or disfigurement. We finished housecleaning today and I am very thankful. We have been at it a month....

Saturday, May 24, 1919
The Manse, Leaskdale, Ont.

"Queen's weather" for the 24th. Today was delightful—so bright and warm. Lily took a holiday and went to town but my holiday consisted in working hard from blushing morn to dewy eve—and after—finishing up the little left-overs of housecleaning before the F.M. meetings began. I managed to do it and then got supper for Dr. Drummond of Hamilton, who came tonight and is to preach tomorrow. He is a very nice and intellectual person but I am too tired to enjoy his company. I envy the fairy tale princess her hundred year nap. How glad I shall be when this coming week is over and I can have a little leisure and rest.

September 1, 1919
The Manse, Leaskdale, Ont.
"A summer of leisure and rest!" That was what I hoped for and looked forward to when I wrote on May 24th. It has a very ironic sound now in view of the hideous summer I have passed through—the most dreadful summer I ever lived in my life—the horrible climax to a horrible year of illness and grief and worry. 1919 has been a *hellish* year. I am so hopelessly tired—too tired ever to get rested again. I've got too far behind with rest—I can never catch up. At least that is how I feel just now.

Well, to tell the tale. On the Sunday after my last entry all went well. We motored to Zephyr with Dr. Drummond and after the service took him to Uxbridge. Ewan seemed perfectly well and in excellent spirits. On the preceding Friday he mentioned that his "headache and weakness was coming back." He was referring to the winter he spent in Glasgow, when he had suffered continually from headache, and insomnia. At the time I knew of the headaches and insomnia but I did not know of the "weakness." When he came home in the spring he seemed perfectly well and assured me that his trouble was merely the result of not "being acclimated." I thought this a peculiar thing but as he was quite well again I ceased to worry, having no realization of what his malady really was.

When he spoke that Friday of his headaches returning I felt anxious but it seemed to pass away very quickly and all Sunday and Monday he seemed perfectly well. Monday morning he took Dr. Drummond away and brought back Mr. Rae of Unionville and Mrs. Dodds of Sonya who were to be the speakers that night. In the evening Mr. Rae spoke here while Ewan took Mrs. Dodds to Zephyr. They returned at 10.30. I made tea for them and we sat up until nearly one talking. I never saw Ewan seem better. He was as jolly as any of us. That night, as Mr. Rae had the spare room I took Mrs. Dodds in with me and Ewan slept with Chester—or rather, went to bed with him for, as he told us at the breakfast table, he had not been able to sleep at all. This in Ewan was surprising for he generally sleeps like a log. What was still more unusual and which should have alarmed me if I had realized the full significance of it, he had risen in the night, dressed, and gone for a long walk up the north road. I felt vaguely uneasy over this extraordinary proceeding but Ewan seemed as well as usual all day and quite cheerful and jolly. He went with Mr. Rae to Zephyr at night and slept well afterwards. Nevertheless, he seemed dull at breakfast and spoke of a headache.

From that out the rest of the week seemed like a dreadful nightmare to me. We had company right along and I had to conceal my anxiety and plan and manage and laugh and talk as if nothing were the matter. Wednesday forenoon we motored to Uxbridge. Ewan went to the manse while I did some shopping. It was warm and I was very tired. When I went down to the manse I found Ewan complaining of headache again. Somehow, there was something about him that worried me—I could not tell what it was. We brought Revs. Smith and Lawrence, the speakers of the evening home with us, also old Mrs. Collins, who is "Mrs. Nickleby" in the flesh. She is hard to endure at any time but when one is tired and possessed by worry she is intolerable. She talked incessantly and inconsequently, detailing to me all the items of her recently deceased husband's illness and death, even to the kind of underclothes she put on him to "lay him out." I talked to her with one corner of my mind and wrestled with my dread in the other corners. Ewan was very dull at supper time. He took Mr. Smith to Zephyr and when they came back he sat dejectedly in his chair, looking dully before him, taking no part in the conversation at all. By this time I was feeling terribly alarmed and anxious although as yet no realization of the nature of his malady had dawned on me. Ewan did not sleep that night but got up and went out walking again. Smith and Lawrence departed and Mr. Lord, his son Lieut. Lord, and Mr. Mutch came. Ewan sat among us in silence and gloom. He got someone else to motor Mr. Mutch to Zephyr and remained at home lying in the hammock. He would not or could not talk and my pleadings to go and consult a doctor were in vain—no doctor could do him any good, he declared moodily. He alternated between fits of dull apathy and spells of restless walking.

Friday night Mr. Brydon was our guest. When Ewan took him to Uxbridge in the morning I insisted on his going to Dr. Shier. Dr. Shier told him he had a "nervous breakdown" and must go away for a change. Ewan said he would not do this. Dr. McKay came that night. I made Ewan take a veronal tablet. This made him sleep but he was no better next day. In the evening we motored Dr. McKay to Wick where he was to speak. On the way back the night was beautiful and moonlight. I was too tired and worried to talk and sat silent in my corner. As we neared home Dr. McKay said, "What a pleasant, restful drive this has been!" I smiled bitterly. It had been for me an hour of the most horrible unrest and worry. Dr. McKay and others supposed Ewan's trouble to be physical—a little breakdown which a short rest would put right. I could not believe it. Ewan had been perfectly well right up to that week and he certainly had not been working hard all winter. Ewan is not the type of man who overworks—he "takes things easy" in all respects.

But I was determined to find out what was wrong. I pleaded with Ewan until he at last confessed the truth. He said he was possessed by a horrible dread that he was *eternally lost*—that there was no hope for him in the next life. This dread haunted him night and day and he could not banish it.

Never shall I forget my despair when I discovered this. I had always known it as one of the symptoms—*the* symptom—of religious melancholia. Unutterable horror seemed literally to engulf me. Was my husband going out of his mind? He had every symptom given in the encyclopedia on that type of insanity. It was one of the things I had always had the most deeply rooted horror of. Every trouble I had had in my life seemed as nothing beside this. I do not know how I lived through the days that followed.

I made other discoveries. This was not Ewan's first attack. When he had gone to P.W. College at about eighteen he had had a slight attack. Six or seven years later at Dalhousie college he had suffered from it for two years—though in a much milder form than this. Then that winter in Glasgow he had had a very bad recurrence—and now this, the worst of all.

I was horror-stricken. I had married, all unknowingly, a man who was subject to recurrent constitutional melancholia, and I had brought children into the world who might inherit the taint. It was a hideous thought. There *was* a ray of light, though, in the fact that he had recovered from the former attacks—he might recover from this one, too.

Dr. McKay went away the next morning and I was thankful. The nightmare of guests was over and I could wrestle with my terrible problems. I did not know *what* to do. Never was I in such a terrible position. That day was fearfully hot. I tried to put in a little bit of garden for Ewan declared he could not work and would not try. That night I felt sick with despair. Ewan lay in the hammock, his eyes staring before him, his mind possessed by that horrible, unnatural idea. I sat by myself in the dusk in the corner of the veranda and cried bitterly for Frede. If she were only alive! She was the only human being to whom I could have gone with my trouble and my fear. I was determined no one else should know of it if it were possible. For Ewan's own sake and the childrens' the impression must not get abroad that his mind was unbalanced. It would ruin his prospects. I talked to the people of his headaches and insomnia but I fenced the world from him as much as I could lest the other deadly thing should be suspected.

Ewan slept one night out of three naturally. The other two he did not sleep unless he took veronal. I induced him by tearful pleading to give up going out for walks before daybreak. I knew if he were thus seen wandering around people would begin to wonder and suspect. As for me, I hardly slept at all. A plague of heat and mosquitoes was also upon us. Some days Ewan would seem a little better and be able to interest himself a little in reading. But for the most part he sat or lay in gloomy silence. He was so utterly unlike himself that he seemed to me like a stranger. He never took the slightest notice of the children and seemed to have absolutely no interest in them or anything. I suppose in a way this was reasonable enough. Granted that you believed completely—and *felt*—that you were doomed to hell fire for all eternity—that hideous old mediaeval superstition which Ewan normally believed in no more than I did—you wouldn't feel much interest in anything else.

Hour after hour in the long nights I would get up—I was sleeping with Stuart in the spare room—and tiptoe down the long hall to the door of our room, listening with suppressed breath to find if Ewan were asleep. If he was I went back and dozed a little myself. If not then I slept not. Oh, what nights of horror those were when my dread was too great even to find relief in tears. And at dawn the birds would sing madly and joyfully outside and I would ask myself in dreary incredulity if it could be the same world it had been two weeks before this awful thing swooped down—when we had been so busy and eager and—by comparison at least—so happy. Was it not some hideous dream? Oh, if I could only waken!

Some days or nights stand out in my memory of this time unique in horror. One was, the first Sunday night after the Forward Movement meetings, when Mr. Fraser of Fenelon Falls supplied for us. Ewan seemed a little better in the forenoon but would not go to Zephyr with Mr. Fraser. He got Alex Leask to take him. After dinner one of the most dreadful thunderstorms I have ever seen came up. I was almost terrified by it. Ewan took no notice of it or me but walked the floor wrapped in his own morbid thoughts. The rain came down in a sort of cloud-burst—a perfect river rushed down the hill and swept our garden out of existence in a twinkling—the garden I had worked so hard to get in, doing all the digging and preparing myself. I was so tired—so worn out—this seemed the last straw. I burst into tears and sobs. Ewan looked at me unsympathetically and said if that was all the matter I had very little to cry about.

The very hardest part of my trial was this same lack of sympathy on Ewan's part. My sufferings mattered nothing to him. His attitude was "You do not believe that I am to be damned or that you are so I do not see why you should worry." I was absolutely alone in my despair. I was never in all my life so wretchedly unhappy as I was in those awful days when I went about trying to work and plan and smile with that fear that was not to be mentioned hanging over me.

Ewan went to bed that night at nine. I sat on the veranda until 10.30 and talked to old Mr. Fraser. It was a beautiful silvery moonlit night—such a contrast to my inner misery.

At the end of a fortnight Ewan was no better and I decided that something must be done. I could not get him to go to Toronto and consult a specialist. "I don't want a doctor—I want a minister" was the absurd reply he would always make when I urged it. I thought it over and decided that he must go away for a change. I could not go with him. The children must be looked after and besides Stella was coming in a few days on her way to the Island so I could not leave. But if he went to Flora's he would be looked after and I could write her to get the opinion of a nerve specialist. Ewan was unwilling to go—it involved an effort which he declared he was too weak to make. The delusion of weakness possessed his mind equally with the other—or rather, as the specialist later told me—was the result of it. The subconscious mind produced the belief in weakness to secure him against any effort that would necessitate his dragging his attention from the hideous subject he was worrying over. But I was resolute. I made all the arrangements and literally forced him to go.

The evening before he went we motored down to Uxbridge for some household supplies. Ewan seemed a shade better when we got there and after our errands were done he suggested some ice cream. We went into an ice cream parlor. It was crowded with gay laughing people. We sat down at a table. Ewan stared fixedly before him all the time we were there. I could not swallow the ice cream. It choked me. I got up, got him out and we started for home. It was a hideous drive through that beautiful blossomy spring twilight. Ewan would not talk and I could not. I crouched in the car with only one wish in my mind—if I could only spring out of the car and run away across the fields—run till I dropped—anywhere—anywhere—if I could only escape the fate that seemed to be drawing nearer—nearer all the time like a menacing shadow. When we got home I flew upstairs, shut myself in my room and broke into crying that was almost hysterical. "I *can't* bear it—I *can't*" I moaned, over and over again. Presently Ewan came up. He seemed to feel for me a little. "Oh Ewan, come back to me—come back to me," I sobbed. "I will—yes, I will," he answered agitatedly. "Don't cry, dear—I'll come back." But ten minutes later he was again sunk in gloomy reverie, lost to all realization for any external matter.

The next morning we went to Toronto. From the time we left Ewan never spoke unless I spoke to him. It was a hard journey. In the Union Station Waiting room we found Stella, just arrived from Los Angeles. I may say that I paid her way from California to P.E.I. and back, in order to give Aunt Annie a little comfort and cheer. But there is nobody to give me any of that, now that Frede is gone.

I had not seen Stell for nearly six years. Before Ewan's illness I had been looking forward with pleasure to her visit. Now I wished her a thousand miles away. She had, I knew, never liked Ewan. She *must not* suspect what the real trouble was. I poured a tale into her ears of Ewan's headaches and insomnia—all perfectly true—but said nothing of his mental state except that he was in low spirits over his breakdown.

Stell and I left for home on the afternoon train. Ewan was to leave for Boston on the night train. He seemed a little brighter when he bade us good-bye but I never had a heavier heart than when he got off the train. I clung to the hope that the change might arrest the progress of his malady and turn him back to normality. But the hope was a very faint one and I was sick at soul.

Nevertheless, the ensuing ten days were easier in many ways than the preceding fortnight had been. I was not constantly tortured by the sight of Ewan sitting in gloomy, unheeding reverie. I did not have him on my mind like an incubus all the time. And at night in spite of my anxiety I slept well—something I sadly needed to do—and did not spend the night lying miserably listening for tip-toeing from room to room like an uneasy ghost. Then Stella helped considerably, for between her frequent spasms of growling over the heat and mosquitoes—which were certainly pretty bad—and her aches and pains—which were non-existent except in her own hypochondriac imagination—she could be and was as jolly and full of fun as of yore. Then, too, it was a pleasure, spiced with sadness, to be again with someone with whom I could talk over old times, old friends, old foes.

As for Stella's prospects in life I have some painful doubts. Her husband seems to be a good fellow; but she does not love him and it is easy to see that she is far from contented with affairs as they are. Given her temper, tyranny, selfishness, and delusions of illness I foresee rocks ahead for their matrimonialship.

We sat up most of the first night thrashing out various family problems and talking over all that had happened in the six years since we parted last. I had a fair sleep afterwards with poor little Stuart cuddled close to me. The next day I was busy all day preparing for the social Guild which was held here at the manse. The guests sat on the moonlight lawn and I moved the victrola to the front door and gave a victrola programme. I had to dress and smile and chat as if I had the lightest heart in the world. Had Ewan's malady been some physical illness I could have shown my anxiety. But as it was I must hide it. When I had put a record on I would slip out to the darkened kitchen and walk the floor until it was time to go back, praying desperately. Where was Ewan and how was he? He should be in Braintree. How had he stood the journey? What would the news be in his first letter? These questions tortured me. But I smiled gallantly—have I not had good training in so smiling most of my life?—while the fox gnawed.

The worst hours of that week were when I went down to the office to get the mail. It was worse than the days when I waited for the war news. I don't know which I dreaded most—to get a letter from Ewan or not to get it. I had hoped that on Saturday I might get a card written from Montreal but none came and this made me feel that he must have been very miserable when he arrived there. After I went to bed, having smiled all the evening lest Stell should suspect—I *would* not have *her* think that my husband was going insane—I had a breakdown and a bitter cry. The next day—Sunday—was very hard. It was so terribly and unseasonably hot. I was unhappy—dispirited in mind and not too well in body. On Monday a note came from Ewan. It was not very satisfactory and did little to disperse my worry and dread. It said briefly that he had arrived in Braintree the night before "much exhausted" but felt a little better that morning. I afterwards discovered that he had reached Flora's almost in a state of collapse, after a dreadful journey of mental suffering—which, no matter how irrational the cause, must have been terrible. It must be more awful than we can realize to be haunted by the dread that you are doomed to an eternity of torment. In his normal state of mind Ewan does not believe any more than I do in that blasphemous old idea of a "hell of fire and brimstone." But he was not normal and all the gloomy teachings he had listened to in his childhood from ministers of the old school had taken complete possession of his thoughts. I have heard him mention more than once the impression made on him long ago by a sermon one of those ministers preached on "hell." I believe that sermon is responsible for his delusion—as such sermons have been responsible for many tortured hearts and souls.

I had no letter again until Wednesday when another brief dull note came. He said merely that he had been to see a specialist and nothing else. I spent the rest of the day in agony of mind and in a miserable physical condition with a burning, tingling sensation all over my body—the protest, I suppose, of tortured nerves.

The next day Ewan's note said he felt a little better and had slept well the preceding night. This helped me through the day. Again on Saturday another note came saying that he felt "a little better." How I grew to hate that phrase! He was always "a little better"—but never really any better. He said he would have to stay five weeks at least.

On the following Monday—June 23rd—I went to Toronto with Stella. She left on the night train to Montreal and I saw her off with a sense of relief. Then I went to the Carls-Rite and spent a poor night, half sleepless and tormented by bad dreams of Ewan. One of them was very awful—he was looking at me through a barred window and weeping—the horror of it wakened me and I slept no more.

I came out on the 8 o'clock train and came up with the mailman. I found two letters from Ewan. I opened the one which had come the day before and it held good news. Ewan wrote that he felt better than any day yet. Cheered and encouraged I opened the other. He said he was very miserable—the specialist was doing him no good—he was going to try an osteopath—the whole brief, disconnected epistle reflected the gloom and turmoil of his distracted mind. I threw myself on the bed and cried bitterly. But I could not indulge in the relief of tears long. There was work to do. I changed my dress and went downstairs to get a bite of dinner.

Just as I reached the foot of the stairs the telephone bell rang. I went to take the message. My heart stood still with a horrible fore-knowledge when I heard that there was a telegram for me. It was from Flora and said, "Ewan is no better. Can you come at once?"

I hung up the receiver. Now that the blow had fallen I was calm and collected. I thought quickly and clearly. I *must* go. I must leave those two poor little boys in Lily's charge and go. She was a good girl as girls go—but to leave my children alone with her! Still, there was nothing else to do. Flora would not have sent for me unless the need was urgent. My own belief was that Ewan had finally gone completely insane. But I did not think about *this* then—it must be considered later. The first question was—how soon can I get to Boston? If I went on the evening train from Uxbridge I would catch the second train to Montreal. But I knew that that train very often missed connection with the Boston train leaving Montreal in the morning. Then I would have to wait in Montreal all day and could not get to Braintree until Thursday morning. But if I could catch the two o'clock train from Uxbridge I could connect with the first Montreal train and get to Boston by Wednesday night. It was a quarter past one. Could I catch that train? I could and did.

I had no money. I 'phoned the Dominion Bank Manager to have a hundred ready for me. I asked Mr. Warner to motor me to Uxbridge. I flew upstairs. In fifteen minutes I was ready, and Lily had tossed a few necessities into my grip. We left at twenty five to two and reached Uxbridge in twenty minutes. I did not think much as we tore down the Seventh at a breakneck pace in that old Ford. My mind was concentrated on catching that train—later on thought would come. I caught the train. All the way to Toronto I was calm and did not suffer much. Feeling seemed numbed or held in leash by the need for prompt action. We got in at four. I had to wait until 7.20. I sat in the crowded station and wondered if anyone else in the passing throngs faced just what I did. I had eaten nothing since my 7 o'clock breakfast. I went into the lunch room and got a sandwich and a cup of tea. But I could not swallow one morsel of the sandwich. It stuck in my throat. I gulped down some of the tea. It was a rank black brew and scalding hot but it gave me a little needed stimulation. At last, after what seemed years of interminable waiting I found myself gliding out of the dingy old Union Station on the Montreal train just 24 hours after I had seen Stella off on it.

Then my composure failed me for a time and I broke down and cried bitterly. This relieved me somewhat and when I regained self-control I got the porter to make up my berth. It was an upper one—I could get nothing else on such short notice and indeed was lucky to get that. It was the second time in my life that I had to sleep in an upper berth. The first time was twenty nine years ago when I went out west with Grandfather Montgomery. I spent my first night on a train in an upper berth—and slept as little that night as this. I dozed brokenly for a couple of hours and then lay there till daylight. When morning came I found the train was an hour late and I was racked with anxiety lest I miss the Boston train after all. But I did not—fortunately, for I *could not* have endured waiting all day in Montreal. I had however only fifteen minutes to get my ticket and have my grip checked—no time to get even a cup of tea. It mattered little—I was not hungry; but when the Boston train pulled out I realized that I was weak from lack of food. I had eaten nothing since my breakfast at the Carls-Rite the preceding morning.

That day was beyond any comparison the longest and most horrible I have ever spent in my life. The train seemed to crawl. I tried to think—to plan—but it was impossible. My mind refused to work. If Ewan had gone out of his mind completely *what was I to do*? I had *no one* in the world to go to for help— neither father nor mother nor sister nor brother. If this horrible thing had happened—and I fully believed it had—the only thing to be done was to put Ewan in some good sanitarium and go back to the children. Our home would have to be broken up and we must go—where? I asked myself a hundred questions—I could not answer them. A hundred sickening possibilities haunted my distracted thoughts. I could not read. I bought a magazine and forced myself to look at it but the lines made no sense. At twelve I went to lunch and forced a few mouthfuls down. Somehow it seemed to me that my distracted state of mind must be reflected in my personal appearance and I shrank from the sight of the other passengers in the car, even though I knew the feeling to be absurd.

At one station, I remember, a bride and groom got on—just newly married, as was evident from the rice on their hats. They sat before me. She was very young and very pretty. They were both insultingly happy. My thoughts went back to my own wedding day nearly eight years ago, and the thing that flashed first into memory was something that had happened as we drove to the station. Not long after we left Park Corner a *hearse* came out from a sideroad and drove on ahead of us, on its way back to Kensington from some funeral. That ill-omened thing headed our procession all the way to the station. We never got quite close enough to pass it. I was not superstitious and we all laughed at the "bad omen." It came back to me now and haunted my mind like a black raven. As for the gay little bride and groom I owed them no ill will nor felt any but I hated the sight of them—they seemed so to emphasize the bitter contrast between my feelings and theirs.

Well, even to those who were stretched on the rack or bound to the stake came an end of torture. At eight I reached the North Station at Boston, caught a street car and got across to the South Station, to find that the Braintree train had just left and I must wait until 9.15 for the next one. I sat down in the waiting room, passed and repassed by throngs, not one of whom I knew. I was sick, tired, racked with anxiety. But that hour passed, too. At ten I got to Braintree, found a cab, and drove to the little bungalow on the hill. I steeled myself for the worst—in a few minutes I would know all. As we drove up to the door a light flashed up in the porch where they had been sitting in the twilight and I saw Ewan coming down the steps with a smile!

The reaction from the horrible dread from which I had suffered ever since getting that telegram left me so weak and trembling that I could hardly stand. I clung to him, asking tremulously, "Ewan, how are you?"

"I have felt better today than I have for four weeks," he replied.

For the time being I was almost light-hearted. The relief at finding him sane and better was so indescribable that I will not try to describe it. I got in, greeted Flora and Christy Viles—who was there—got washed and dusted and sat down to supper. I was hungry now and ate heartily. We were all quite gay and Ewan seemed indeed more like himself than he had been since the attack came on. Afterwards, as I helped Flora wash up the dishes she told me what a terrible time they had had on Monday and most of Tuesday. Ewan had walked the floor ceaselessly, wild with unrest, declaring that there was no hope for him—that he would never be better, and so on until poor Flora was nearly distracted. Tuesday morning he had asked her to send for me—"she may as well know the worst" he said. So Flora had sent the telegram. Then, Tuesday night, Ewan had taken a turn for the better. For the first time since he had arrived in Braintree he had slept naturally and all day had felt well. Christy said she believed his malady had passed the crisis—and indeed, in spite of all that came afterwards I believe she was right. Certainly, he was never anything like so bad again.

After we went to bed he told me of his attack. He said he had had *a vision* of himself and the children in *hell*. Well, I knew that *that* had been absolute insanity while it lasted. The question was—would it return—and last longer?—or was that the crisis and had he turned back finally to comparative sanity? After he had talked out his troubles and I had soothed him as best I could he slept four hours and I slept not at all. In the first place I was too tired and nervous. In the second, I was frightened to go to sleep lest a movement of mine in sleep should waken him—and it was so terribly important that he should sleep. But his sleep was certainly anything but sound or restful for his body was full of nervous jerks and twitches and he sighed, moaned and moved continually.

The next day he seemed fairly well until dinner time. Then we went in to Boston, as he had an appointment with Dr. Garrick, the nerve specialist whom he had consulted.

We walked down to East Braintree station through the little wood path down the hill which I trotted over so often last winter. On the way silence descended suddenly on Ewan. At the station he walked the platform restlessly. All the way in he was in the old black reverie. In vain I urged him to pull himself together—in vain I pled and reasoned. The nature of his malady was such that he could not make an effort—will was paralyzed. The noise and crowds of the South Station made him worse. The roar of the subway as we thundered through it tortured him. When we finally reached Commonwealth Ave. Ewan was worse than I had ever seen him. I felt almost distracted with anxiety and terror. *What* was it I was fighting? If I only knew my foe!!

We were half an hour ahead of time, so we sat down on one of the seats of the boulevard. Ewan's head fell on his breast. He was in the deepest gloom—nothing I could say or do roused him in the least. I said some bitter things—hoping to make him angry—I believed it would do him good if he could just become really angry. But it had no effect—never had any effect. All through his illness he was never in the least angry or vexed, no matter what provocation he had. This was abnormal for although Ewan is in the main a good-natured man he can be angry enough on occasion.

On either side of us rolled past an endless stream of fine cars filled with fashionably dressed people. Not *all* in that procession could have been happy or carefree—no doubt many of them carried anxieties and problems as bitter as mine. But they all *looked* happy and prosperous and I felt as if I were alone in my world of misery—hopeless and heartless. Life could not be faced.

On a seat not far away a man was sitting. He, too, seemed to be down and out. He was shabbily dressed and he sat, leaning forward moodily, never glancing up, the picture of dejection. I think he was some poor derelict, out of work and utterly discouraged. Anyway, I felt that the three of us all looked and felt alike.

It is a curious fact—that when I am badly upset in mind, worried and nervous, I always feel *dirty and dishevelled*—as if I were physically unclean and untidy. I was not—I was neatly and carefully and quietly dressed, but I felt like the veriest drab and shrank from the eyes of every passerby as if he must notice and wonder over my unkemptness.

At last the hour of our appointment came and we went in. I liked Dr. Garrick immensely. He impressed me as being a strong, kind, competent man. After he had seen Ewan he took me away for a short talk. I knew Ewan had not told him about his conviction of having "committed the unpardonable sin" and so forth—so I told him the whole facts of the case. He said frankly that the case puzzled him. The idea about his future fate which haunted Ewan was one of the hall-marks of insanity but he was inclined to think that Ewan's malady was simple melancholia.

"On the other hand", he said, "we must face the possibility that it is manic depressive insanity." He told me not to argue with Ewan on the subject of his "phobia" and *not to let him out of my sight*. My heart sank like lead at this hint—it seemed to voice a fear I had not dared to face though I knew it had been lurking in my mind from the very first. He went on to say that possibly the malady had a physical cause which might be found in the condition of the kidneys which were not functioning properly, as analysis showed. More than half the poisonous elements were being retained in the system. Whether this were a cause or an effect, Ewan must drink all the water he possibly could. He also gave me some chloral tablets to produce sleep.

Then we left. I felt very wretched. Ewan did not even ask me what Dr. Garrick said. He was in terrible mental distress all the way home. It was like a nightmare to me but we got to Flora's at last. Ewan continued miserable all the evening. I broke down and cried hopelessly, to Flora's dismay. After I had sobbed myself calm I rose up, grimly determined to renew the fight, made Ewan take a drink and a dose of chloral and went to bed myself.

It was the next day that I began to write notes for my journal, partly by way of easing my mind by the old resource of "writing it out." These entries I will copy here. They reflect with tolerable accuracy my summer that I had hoped would be "quiet and restful!"

†"*Friday, June 27, 1919*
East Braintree, Mass.
30 Dobson Road
Last night I took a veronal tablet. I have kept veronal by me for the last fifteen years. Dr. Jenkins prescribed it for me once. Realizing fully the danger of forming a drug habit I have never allowed myself to take it, save in cases of great emergency, and I considered this one, since I am almost exhausted from my recent loss of sleep. So I took my tablet and went to sleep in the 'den', on the lounge by the long low window. It was no use to think of going in with Ewan. I would not sleep myself and I would very likely disturb him. I had one night of blissful oblivion, at least, though I woke early this morning. Ewan slept three hours after the first chloral tablet last night and three hours more after a second. He seemed bad all the morning until ten. Since then he has seemed better. Once he called me 'Pussy'—the old nickname he has never used since the beginning of his trouble. Also, this afternoon he read three hours unbrokenly and seemed really interested. This, too, is a new and good sign. I make him drink water mercilessly, compelling him to swallow a brimming goblet every hour. Ewan himself would never take anything. His argument is that his trouble is that he is 'outcast from God' and drugs will not help that. So I have to make him take his medicines etc. I carry the glasses to him and stand over him until he drinks it. It is no light ordeal either for the water here is miserable stuff. Flora does not have ice and the water is tepid; also, being filtered, it is flat and insipid. I loathe it and long for a drink of the cold sparkling water from my good old Leaskdale pump."

---

†LMM quotes from her notebook.

†"*Saturday, June 28, 1919*
30 Dobson Road
East Braintree, Mass.

Today was cool—such a beautiful change from the 'hot wave' in which we have been sweltering. I had to take veronal again last night. But I feel encouraged about Ewan. Last night he slept five hours without any drug. All the afternoon he has been reading. Once he made a small joke—again he read me something out of the paper—he asked for and read a letter that I had received—he spoke about Chester and wrote a note to him—all small things in themselves but tremendously significant when compared to the utter absence of all such indications this past month.

This evening it was necessary that I should go somewhere to buy a few necessities to supplement the scanty contents of my hurriedly packed grip. So I motored to Quincy with the Reids. In spite of the improvement in Ewan I hated to leave him. All the time I was away I was worried and so nervous I could hardly sit quietly in the car and compel myself to talk composedly to the Reids. When we reached Quincy we separated and I made my purchases alone. Then I went and sat down on the low stone wall surrounding a church green and began to read a magazine which I had bought. Presently a policeman came up and ordered me off none too politely. The church people, he said bluntly, had told him not to allow people to sit on the wall.

I don't think I hurt the wall much by sitting on it—there was no visible dent in the granite when I got up. For of course I did get up. One doesn't dispute with a policeman. But this trifling incident had an exaggerated effect on me, owing to my worn-out condition. At another time it would have either angered or amused me. Now it hurt me—hurt me bitterly. As I walked away the tears came to my eyes. Foolish as they were I could not check them. I was surrounded by a gay Saturday night mob of strangers. I was dreadfully tired—so tired that I could hardly stand—and to be ordered off that wretched wall was really the last straw. I shall detest Congregational churches forever.

I walked wearily up and down for half an hour—and it seemed half a year—before the Reids came. When we got home I found Ewan standing on the corner talking to a group of men—something he had not done for a long time—never since he came to Braintree. He came to meet me with a smile. I had been dreading to come back and find him plunged in gloom again—I felt that I could not endure it if he were. But it was so blessedly different from what I had feared. Later on Flora told me that while I was away he had been chatting to her quite brightly of old friends and old times and seemed quite like himself. Oh, if this only lasts! I feel better now than I have for a long while and I am hungry for the first time for a week."

†"*Sunday, June 29, 1919*
30 Dobson Road
East Braintree, Mass.

....The Dobsons called in the evening. Their daughter, Mrs. Marston, has the most awful voice I ever heard in a human being—high-pitched, shrill, raucous.

It caused me actual physical pain in the raw state of my nerves. My relief was enormous when I saw her finally walk out.

Another hopeful sign in Ewan—he *criticized Amos* to me today—rather deprecatingly, it is true, as if he were doing something very reprehensible. Still, he *did* criticize him. Amos deserves it. He is an intolerable bore. When I am well and easy I don't mind him but just now he grates on the raw. He is one of those people who are always trying to start an argument just for the sake of argument and he is everlastingly trotting out some ancient 'heresy' which he plainly thinks must prove very shocking to anyone so orthodox as he evidently supposes a Presbyterian minister and wife must be. If poor Amos only knew how out-of-date his questionings are to me—the hoary old problems of Cain's wife and the seven-day creation and all that. I used to humor him in the winter and argue away as solemnly as if I thought all his queries brand-new and startling, but I haven't the patience for that now and I feel like shrieking or throwing something at his head when he begins. This afternoon he started up on 'the unpardonable sin'—of all subjects in the world, the very last one I want referred to in Ewan's hearing just now. Why, it might tear open afresh something that was just beginning to skin over. I choked Amos off so quick that he has been in a dazed condition ever since, not knowing just what happened to him or why."

†*"Monday, June 30, 1919*
East Braintree, Mass.
....I had a letter from Lily today—a very ill-spelled and ungrammatical epistle but the most eagerly welcomed one I ever got in my life—for it told about my dear little boys—that they were well etc. It is so dreadful to be separated from them like this...."

†*"Tuesday, July 1, 1919*
E. Braintree, Mass.
Last night I went in with Ewan because when I sleep in the den, the getting up and prowling about of Amos at four always wakens me and I cannot get to sleep again. He has to leave at six and he is so slow that it apparently takes him two solid hours to dress and eat his breakfast. Flora, too, is given to night prowling owing to her chronic indigestion. So I went with Ewan hoping for a good-night's rest but I was out of the frying pan into the fire. Ewan slept, though very nervously, but I could not sleep at all. I was afraid to move a muscle, so great was my dread of waking him, and I grew numb and cramped. Sleep was impossible. I heard millions of sounds—trains incoming and outgoing with grunts and puffs and shrieks, motor cars chugging and honking, and each and every sound got on my nerves because of my dread that it would wake Ewan. Plainly, there is nothing for me but the den.

Today was terribly hot. I had a letter from Stell, written on her way home. She saw Cam in Montreal and he had said, in referring to Frede, 'Well, we had a ripping good time while it lasted.' And again, that he 'wasn't going to carry any excess baggage'—meaning a second wife!—'for awhile.'

I sometimes wonder if Cam is quite normal. He really doesn't seem like any sane person I have ever known.

This afternoon I went to Boston where I found the heat terrific. I had a good talk with Dr. Garrick. He was delighted to hear that Ewan's abnormal ideas had disappeared so quickly. The trouble was only simple melancholia he said, and Ewan was probably over the worst. I went away with a heart wonderfully light compared with my previous visit. To be told your husband has religious melancholia *is* good news when you have been dreading to hear that he has manic depressive insanity! Everything is measured by contrast in this world. I almost enjoyed my hour of shopping in spite of the dreadful heat and mugginess. Under all, of course, was the undercurrent of dread lest I should find Ewan worse again when I got home. But he was all right.

Tonight I have felt a peace that almost amounts to exhaustion. For the first time since May 28 I feel off the rack. There seems no longer any reason to fear that Ewan will become violently insane. I feel as if I had been lifted out of hell. Tonight I lay on the couch out in the porch, utterly relaxed in body and mind, limp, inert, resting absolutely. I cannot describe the wonderful release from intolerable torture and fear."

†*"Thursday, July 3, 1919*
E. Braintree, Mass.
I slept miserably last night owing to heat, a sore throat, and prowlers. Ewan slept fairly well but complained of nightmares. The heat today was such as I have never experienced. The thermometer was 101 and with it humidity and general mugginess. Flora, too, was not well all day—very nervous and inclined to crying spells. She is really a chronic neurasthenic, poor soul. Between the two of them I felt as if I were going to fly to pieces myself. We have been three rather uncanny people."

†*"Monday, July 7, 1919*
East Braintree, Mass.
Friday was a day of breathless heat—we sat and sweltered. Saturday was worse. At noon Mr. Viles came to motor us over to Newton for the weekend. It was a beautiful drive and not unpleasant in spite of the heat, as the motion kept our faces dry and we could endure it better.

The Viles live in a very old house—200 years old. It was dusty, musty and 'old'-smelling. Christy is an untidy housekeeper. But she can at least get up a regular old 'Montgomery' meal, and there is nothing the matter with her cooking.

We went to bed in a large old room upstairs and in spite of the heat and mustiness I hoped for a decent sleep, for I had slept very poorly the two preceding nights. It was not to be. The house was built at one of the busiest motor corners in Newton. Until two o'clock an unbroken stream of cars tore by and as the corner is a dangerous one every car honked or shrieked or yodelled according to its horn. I might as well have tried to sleep in Pandemonium. The strange part is that Ewan slept and all the racket never woke him, although he sighed, moaned and turned from side to side continually. Worn out from loss of sleep I began to suffer from an annoying form of nervousness—a sort of 'burning unrest' in which the unrest is of the nerves and the burning sensation physical—especially in my feet. I have seldom passed a more unpleasant night. But a thunderstorm at dawn cooled the air and yesterday was much pleasanter. But I was miserable all day with suppressed nervous unrest and was glad when we got back to Braintree. Then I found a letter from Stell that got under my skin. She said 'her mother thought she or Clara should have Frede's peridot necklace.' There is gratitude for you! After all I've done for that family and the hundreds and hundreds of dollars I've given them—after paying Stell's expenses for her trip home. I was sick with disgust. The minute I go home I'll pack that necklace up and send it to Aunt Annie. If I choose to keep it, they could do nothing. That letter of Frede's to me, since it was written and signed by herself, was a legal will in the province of Quebec and has been probated as such. In it she left me 'first choice' of all her things. Yet I took little. She owed me $140 dollars which I had lent her to pay some bills and in her 'will' she directed her mother to pay this out of her life insurance. But I told Aunt Annie I would not take it and let her have all the Insurance. And this is how she behaves. Of course Stell put her up to it—Stell's greed and selfishness is abnormal—but the whole thing sickened me. I broke down and had a good cry—after which I felt much better. What a relief tears are!

Today was cool and pleasant—such a blessed change. It is dear little Chester-boy's birthday. He is seven years old today. It is the first birthday we have been separated. I had a letter from Lily today. Both boys are well. But at times I shiver over the thought of them—two little creatures only 7 and 3½ away up there, a thousand miles away from me, absolutely alone, save for a servant girl and some kind neighbors. Why, they might take ill and die before I could get to them—they might be killed by a car—but it doesn't do to entertain or encourage thoughts like these. I resolutely put them away. But when I am tired or nervous they creep in. I can't hear the 'phone ring without a dreadful feeling—born of the time when I got the wire of Frede's illness last winter; and if it turns out to be someone asking for me I turn sick lest it be a wire from Leaskdale with bad news.

Ewan's head continues to bother him considerably and that worries me. But thank God, there is no return of his delusions."

†"*Thursday, July 10, 1919*
East Braintree, Mass.
The preceding days have been cool and livable. Ewan has kept better and sleeps pretty well—better than I do, indeed. Last night I slept very little but lay and watched the full moon as great dark clouds sailed over her. The effects were very fine. I thought of many things as I watched them—events of long-past years, friends gone over, buried hopes and fears and loves and hatreds. After all, life has been in the main a hard thing for me. What happiness I have had has been far out balanced by suffering. Yet I have always found life interesting and I have never wished to stop living, save in temporary moments of torture.

There is always the lure of something further on—something in hiding just around the next bend—to lend spice to it. It may be only a trick—it has always seemed to be a trick hitherto—but it serves.

Flora and I went into Boston this afternoon to see the much advertised movie 'The Fall of Babylon.' Like the curate's hackneyed egg it was very good in spots. The siege of Babylon was wonderful. But the heroine, the so-called 'mountain maid' was nothing but a very sophisticated chorus girl and there was never for a moment an illusion of anything else.

We came home very tired and found E. reading and in pretty good spirits but with a handkerchief tied around his head. I always hate to see that flag of distress appear."

†*"Thursday, July 17, 1919*
E. Braintree, Mass.
I know just how a wretched little mouse feels when it has crept a little bit away from the clutches of the cat and is pounced on again.

Both Ewan and I slept poorly. He got up very early, dressed, and came out, determined to go out walking. I pleaded with him until he consented not to go. I dared not let him go out alone after what Dr. Garrick had said. All the forenoon he was dull and I was heartsick from worry. After dinner we had to go into Boston to consult an oculist about Ewan's eyes as Dr. Garrick had ordered. It was another terrible trip. Ewan seemed to be and declared he was as bad as he had ever been. Owing to the car strike we had to walk from the station to Commonwealth Avenue and the clatter and traffic of the streets seemed to upset Ewan completely. At one time I thought he would simply collapse on the street. I did not know what to do. I took him into a drugstore and got a dose of aromatic ammonia for him. It did not do him any good. His 'weakness' was not real, but merely a delusion, so not to be acted on by drugs. At last he yielded to my pleading and consented to make another effort. He admitted that his terrible ideas regarding his destiny had returned. This seemed to me the worst of all. There is something about it that paralyzes me. It seems so unnatural—so morbid—so alien to the world of reason and sanity. I feel so powerless before it—as if I were menaced by a foe whose face I could not see—by something creeping upon me in the dark—formlessly, shapelessly horrible.

We got the visit to the oculist over. Somehow I got Ewan down to the station again and on the train. We got to Braintree—we walked home. I had kept up until this. Now my strength gave way. I went to Ewan's room, flung myself on the bed and cried despairingly. My agony at last seemed to pierce even Ewan's apathy and he roused himself a little and vowed he would fight against the gloomy suggestions of his malady. But I have given up hope entirely.

We were to have started for home next Monday. How eagerly I had looked forward to it! Now it is out of the question to think of going. Oh, my poor little boys!' "

†*"Friday, July 18, 1919*
East Braintree, Mass.
Last night I gave Ewan chloral twice before twelve and it had no effect on him. Then I gave him veronal and he slept. I took veronal myself but it had little effect. I only dozed fitfuly. This morning I felt as if I *could not* get up. But I had to. As the day wore on I felt a little calmer. Ewan seems better again. He is quiet but not moody. It is possible that this attack will not last as long as the others but I am afraid to hope.

We spent most of the afternoon sitting down under the oak trees of the woods on the hill and talking. Ewan seldom tries to 'talk out' his dreads. It would be better for him to do so and I always encourage him when he takes a notion to. Yet it is very dreadful to hear the things that possess him. They are so appallingly irrational and absurd.

I had a letter from home today. Chester had a bilious spell. He was better but the news has added to my anxiety. Mr. Dobson motored me to Quincy tonight to get more chloral for Ewan. I had hoped he would not have to use it again."

†*"Tuesday, July 22, 1919*
East Braintree, Mass.
Wet and muggy. Ewan and I went in to Boston as he had to see his oculist again. I was half sick with dread lest I should have another such experience as I had last time and the strain was dreadful. But he did not and kept at least as well as when we left home. Nevertheless, I was expecting every moment that he would 'slump', and I went like a cringing dog expecting a second lash.

We went first to see Dr. Coriat who is the author of several books on nervous disorders. His personality did not appeal to me. I did not like him at all. But he said Ewan would be quite well by the fall.

This gave me a little courage to go on with. We then went to see Dr. Garrick, who also spoke hopefully and I felt much better psychically when we came away. But physically the trip home was almost the last word. It was 'rush hour.' The subways and station were simply packed solid with sweating crowds. I felt as if I would smother in the heat and odor. The possible effect on Ewan worried me too. But he did not seem to mind it half as much as I did. I am almost worn out and feel as if the only thing that would do me any good would be to get away out in some lonely waste place and shriek at the top of my voice for half an hour."

†*"Wednesday, July 23, 1919*
East Braintree, Mass.
....Ewan's glasses came in the mail and were broken. This meant that I must hie me into Boston and get the lens replaced. The oculist, by the way, found a bad astigmatism in both eyes and says that Ewan has only had half sight all his life...."

†*"Saturday, July 26, 1919*
30 Dobson Road, E.B., Mass.
Last night, after I lay down on my couch by the den window I had a cry over the thought of Frede. The pain of her loss is coming back to me as the later pain subsides. I slept only from twelve to three.

Ewan seems well. We went into Boston and saw Mary Pickford in 'Daddy Long-Legs.' It was very good and Ewan laughed heartily over it. He has not laughed like that since May. It is a good sign. I feel sure he is really recovering but he is far from normal yet."

†*"Sunday, Aug. 3, 1919*
....This may be our last night here. I dread the journey home terribly. But Ewan is anxious to be home and I think if he can get there it will be better for him. He seems to be craving to get back to his work. There will be more there to take up his attention and keep him from brooding. And oh, I will be so thankful to get home!"

*On Monday evening, Aug. 4, we left Braintree. Ewan had been dull that morning but was better in the afternoon and seemed fairly well when we left. Flora went to the North Station with us. I parted from her with real regret. Flora is a stupid, uncultured, uninteresting woman but she has a heart of gold and she was kindness itself to us this summer.

Our train left at 7.15. I had taken a drawing room so we were by ourselves. There *are* times when a little money makes life easier. *What* would we have done this summer if we had nothing but Ewan's salary to depend on? If I had had financial worries on top of everything else it would have been the last straw....

†*"Tuesday, Aug. 12, 1919*
Leaskdale, Ont.
I have been exceedingly busy trying to get things straightened out. Hosts of people have been coming to see Ewan, of course. I am woefully sick of going over and over the same routine of information re 'kidney poisoning' etc. Ewan seems real well mentally. But last night he woke at one in a cold clammy sweat, such as he has had two or three times before this summer. I do not like it."

†*"Thursday, Aug. 14, 1919*
I have had to resort to the spareroom to sleep. If I stay in my own room I simply can't sleep for fear of waking Ewan. Last night I got a good sleep. So did Ewan but for two nights before he had to take chloral. I am so sick of the sight of that brown bottle with its little white tablets. Ewan has not been so well these two days past. He is dull again.

---

*LMM continues the journal entry which began September 1, 1919.
†LMM quotes from her notebook.

As for me, I have begun work on my new book. I hope the ending will be more auspicious than the beginning. But it is time I got to work for I've done nothing all summer."

†"*Saturday, Aug. 16, 1919*
The Manse, Leaskdale
Today Ewan had the handkerchief around his head again. How my heart sank! Yet this evening he was much better again. So it goes—up and down, forward and back. I am still the mouse in the claws of the cat."

†"*Sunday, Aug. 24, 1919*
Ewan has seemed pretty well all this week. He has slept without drugs and been quite cheerful. Lily has been away for a week of her vacation so I have been very busy. Miss Chapman, sub-editor of *McLeans Magazine*, spent Wednesday here, to get material for an article on me and my 'career'. I talked brightly and amusingly—and watched Ewan out of the corner of my eye, wondering how he felt. That is my existence now.

'Rainbow Valley' is out. The cover design is very pretty. My ninth novel—and I don't feel a particle of interest in it!

Frede will never read it!

One of the stories she would have recognized. It was the one of Mary Vance chasing Rilla Blythe with a codfish. Chester and Amy Campbell were the originals of that and Frede was never tired of laughing over it with her Macdonald cronies. The only other bit of 'real life' in it is the ghost the children saw on the dyke. Of course that is the old ghost that Well and Dave Nelson and I saw, which turned out to be grandmother with a tablecloth.

This afternoon I was alone and bitterly lonely. I took a wild spasm of longing for Frede. It seemed to me that I *could not* go on living without her—and that it was no use to try."

†"*Wednesday, Aug. 27, 1919*
The Manse, Leaskdale, Ont.
Ewan motored to Toronto to the Exhibition today. I never feel easy when he is away alone. But I could not go with him this time.

Today I happened to pick up and open at random an old scrapbook containing reviews of my books. A clipping caught my eye, written in 1910. Some editor had written me, asking some questions about my views on 'Canadian Literature' and in my reply I find the following paragraph—rather significant in view of what has come since.

'*I do not think our literature is an expression of our national life as a whole. I think this is because we have only very recently—as time goes in the making of nations—had any real national life. Canada is only just finding herself. She has not yet fused her varying elements into a harmonious whole. Perhaps she will not do so until they are welded together by some great crisis of storm and stress. That is when a real national literature will be born. I do not believe that the great Canadian novel or poem will ever be written until we have had some kind of baptism by fire to purge away all our petty superficialities and lay bare the primal passions of humanity.'*

When I wrote that I had no premonition of the Great War. But if I had known what was coming I could hardly have described it better. Many a prophet's reputation has been made out of less! It remains to be seen if the rest of my prediction will come as true. I believe it will, but it may take twenty—thirty— forty years before it is made manifest. The great Canadian literature will come from the generation born of this conflict not from the generation that fought through it."

†*"Sunday, Aug. 31, 1919*
The Manse, Leaskdale, Ont.
Ewan came home last Thursday night. He seemed tired and admitted that his head had troubled him a good deal while away. He was duller on Friday than he has been since coming back. Last night again he was very dull. I got dreadfully blue. At times I feel that I cannot bear any longer this alternation of faint hope and sickening despair. If Ewan does not soon recover he must resign and I must get a house somewhere where I can make a home for the children while he goes to a good sanitarium for treatment. I can think of no other solution. It is very disheartening. He seemed so much better when we came home and for a week afterwards."

*So this has been my summer! Well, I've lived through it and kept up for my children's sake.

Later on.
After writing the above I went into the library and found Ewan sitting in his arm chair gazing gloomily before him. I made him confess that he is again haunted by conviction of eternal damnation. I went upstairs to my room, shut the door and cried wretchedly. This is the one thing I cannot endure. I can help him fight headache and insomnia but this other thing seems so unnatural that it fills me with such horror and repulsion that I can't face it. I can't help it—it always turns me against Ewan for the time, as if he were possessed by or transformed into a demoniacal creature of evil—something I must get away from as I would rush from a snake. It is terrible—but it is the truth.

Tuesday, Sept. 2, 1919
Leaskdale, Ont.
Ewan slept last night without drugs. I went to the spareroom, so slept well and feel better. Ewan went away today for a visit to Sutton. I dreaded to see him go; and yet it was a relief. I am good-for-nothing when I see him sitting

---

*LMM continues the journal entry which began September 1, 1919.

gloomily around, a prey to dejection and delusions. When I don't see him I can at least work, no matter how heavy my heart is.

Last winter I began to copy my whole journal into a set of volumes all the same size. My journal, beginning in the fall of 1890, has been written in various "blank books" of equally various shapes and sizes. I resolved to copy it as aforesaid. It will mean a great deal of work and will take a long time, for I can only spare fifteen minutes a day for it. But it will be a satisfaction when done. I shall be careful to copy it exactly as it is written but I mean to "illustrate" it as I go along with such photos of the scenes and people who figure in it as I possess. How I wish I could have had in childhood and girlhood, a "kodak" such as almost everybody now has. But of course such things were unknown then.

I find that when I am copying those old journals I feel as if I had gone back into the past and were living over again the events and emotions of which I write. It is very delightful and a little sad.

Today I was copying my account of the "peanut party" we had in one of poor Prof. Harcourt's classes. At the time I thought it good fun. But if I were to write an essay on "Things I Am Ashamed To Remember" that peanut party would be one of them. Harcourt was a nonentity and his classes were farces. The time we spent in them was absolutely wasted. But all this did not justify us in such a performance. I was not one of the ring leaders—I merely followed. But I enjoyed it, so I am condemned. I was a little beast—we were all little beasts.

A few years ago a brother of Prof. Harcourt's, who is a missionary in India, was here for a visit. He was a fine-looking, very agreeable man, with a decided and charming personality—a great contrast to Prof. Harcourt who always gave me the impression of a sneak—and a weak sneak at that. But if he had been ten-times sneakier that peanut party would still remain something to be ashamed of.

Wednesday, Sept. 3, 1919
Leaskdale, Ont.
Worked hard all day, then went to Guild at night and read a paper I had written. There were only a few there and I felt that the time and trouble the paper had cost me was practically wasted.

While I was writing my "fifteen-minute stint" of old journals today I found a reference to "Sam Wyand's field." Instantly fancy took wing and I was back among scenes that have now vanished from the face of the earth.

"Sam Wyand's field"—a most unromantic name for one of the most beautiful little spots I have ever seen—a spot to which in my childhood I gave the love I afterwards gave to Lover's Lane. For years "Sam Wyand's field" spelled Arcady for me—to this day it shines in memory like a land of lost delight....

I have made myself wretchedly homesick by writing all this and visualizing the memories evoked. It has been so real to me that it has filled me with a bitter longing to be in those spots once more—to taste the inimitable flavor of the wild fruit, to lie amid the sun-warm grasses, to hear the robins whistling, to tiptoe through the lanes of greenery and fragrance in the summer mornings of those faraway years. When I wrench myself away from their idyllic memories to the bitter, carking reality of life at present I sicken at the contrast.

Thursday, Sept. 4, 1919
The Manse, Leaskdale, Ont.

A pleasant day, filled up for the most part by the preserving of two huge kettlefuls of plums. I like this sort of work, however. Only, it takes so much time—and the Government won't extend the day to thirty six hours!

Tonight in copying my old diary I found a mention of Norman Campbell. Poor Norman! His life ended in tragedy.

Norman Campbell, when I knew him at P.W.C. and later, was a nice jolly fellow whom I always liked. We were "good pals" and where Norman and I were at any time laughter made a third. After teaching school for a few years Norman went to Charlottetown and took up the study of law. He passed in due time and was admitted to the bar. Meanwhile he had become engaged to Miss Ross, the matron of the P.E. Island hospital. Most of his friends thought it an odd match for she was his senior by at least fifteen years—literally old enough to be his mother. But Norman seemed happy enough and their marriage was on the point of coming off when Norman suddenly broke down with "nervous prostration"—at least that was the name given out. The real truth was—though this did not leak out for several years and may not be known to his family to this day—that it was the oncoming of the terrible insanity which is consequent on syphilis. Sometime poor Norman must have tampered with forbidden fruit— and paid a terrible price. He went home to his father's "for a rest"; but it was evident erelong that his mind was giving way. The last time I was at Mary's she told me of his condition and what a dreadful time they had with him. I forgot how long he lingered—a few years—and then died. So closed a life that promised fair—gay, merry, clever Norman. It hurts me when I think of it. There are such terrible tragedies in life—things we never dream of when we are young. I recall Norman as I knew him—Norman laughing with me in the hall at MacMillans—Norman terrifying the soul out of my body with his weird ghost stories one dark night when a gang of us were out driving in Donald E's old pung—Norman and I dancing together all night in the maple-roofed pavilion on the night of Mary's wedding—Norman whisking me out to see the sunrise after it and kissing me unblushingly because he had a glass or two of Scotch courage in him after the Highland fashion at weddings and so was quite ready to dare anything. It was the only time he ever kissed me for there had never been any sentiment between us. And, as always, a jest on his lip and a twinkle in his eye. Somehow I cannot connect *that* Norman with the Norman Mary described to me—the furtive, unshaven creature, slinking furtively about the house, snarling at his friends, refusing to eat at the table but tearing food found in odd corners—repulsive, idiotic—mind, heart, civilization gone. "The wages of sin is death." The life and death of Norman Campbell was a terrible commentary on that merciless old text.

Sunday, Sept. 7, 1919
....Tonight I feel as if I were beating my hands against a stone wall. Oh, how hard I have tried lately to convince Ewan that his gloomy fears are irrational and foundationless—I have tried every way—argument, "suggestion" entreaty, scorn, sympathy. I might as well have saved my breath. Nothing has the slightest effect. Reason has no power over the delusions of an unsound mind.

Wednesday, Sept. 10, 1919
The Manse, Leaskdale
Ewan was dull all day but on the whole seemed better than yesterday. There was no outburst and he did not seem so restless. But he complained a good deal of his head.

This evening we were playing Halma in the library when old Lizzie Oxtoby came in. She is a person in whose presence I always feel unhappy and defensive at any time so her effect on me in my mood of tonight may be imagined. I felt as if I would fly into little pieces every moment of her stay. I talked desperately to cover Ewan's moody and noticeable silence and oh, how thankful I was when she went away!

Thursday, Sept. 11, 1919
Ewan was very dull all day. We had promised to go over to John Lockie's on the fourth to tea and we left about five. When we got there Ewan excused himself and lay down on the sofa, saying his head was aching. I sat and sewed and talked to Mrs. Lockie. At supper Ewan was very gloomy. He could not or would not talk. Before the meal was done he excused himself and went back to the sofa. There he fell asleep and, in spite of the talk around him—for Mrs. Lockie had several other guests—he slept soundly on. I recognized this as something new, for never before this whole summer has he slept anywhere but in his room and the slightest sound would make him moan and turn if he did not actually wake. When he woke he sat up and made a joke—the first I have heard him make for a long time. As we drove home he said he felt better. I feel hopeful once more.

Saturday, Sept. 13, 1919
I have again almost given up hope. Ewan was as bad today as I ever saw him. He had to take chloral twice last night. He did not get up until noon and then was very dull. When I went up to my room to dress for the Mission Band I found him lying on the bed, evidently given over once more to his delusions. I felt as if I could not endure it. Though I knew it was no use I implored him for the thousandth time to banish such false and blasphemous ideas. "You have assumed responsibilities," I said. "You have brought two children into the world—"

"Yes, and I wish from the bottom of my heart I never had," he exclaimed bitterly.

That was more than I could bear. I felt as if a knife pierced my heart. That Ewan, who has always been so fond and proud of his boys, should say *that*—

and if it were *not Ewan* who said it—well, that was a deeper horror still! With a choking cry I flung myself on the couch. I cried blindly. It was my darkest hour. Ewan got up and went out saying, "Well, I must go to meet Smith I suppose. Your idea is that I must go on till I drop."

This did not hurt me. Ewan never says such things in his normal condition of mind. But I cannot get over what he said about the children. It seemed so hideous. It is just because those horrible delusions of his make him believe that they are eternally lost as well as himself and so he wishes they had never been born.

Well, they never would have been born if I had known that Ewan was subject to constitutional recurrent melancholia for I believe no one has a right to bring children into the world who may possibly inherit such a curse. But now I cannot and do not wish them unborn.

After he went I got up, bathed my face, set my teeth and went to the Mission Band where I cut and sewed Shaker flannel patches for a hospital quilt with the children for an hour. Then I came back, walking through the beauty of the warm golden afternoon like a lost spirit through a heaven in which it has no part. Ewan is not back from the station yet. He has gone to meet Captain Smith who is to preach for him tomorrow and will be here until Wednesday. I dread it. Capt. Smith is an old P.E.I. acquaintance and I hate to have such see Ewan as he is now, lest they suspect his mental condition and scatter the news broadcast. I have kept the mental side of Ewan's trouble a secret from all but Dr. Garrick and I cannot bear the thought of anyone knowing it, especially the people I know down east. Stella, too, is coming next week. I feel like a caged creature. Turn where I will there is nothing but dungeon bars.

Sunday, Sept. 21, 1919
Leaskdale, Ont.

Is it only a week since my last entry? Yet what a difference. For what seems like a miracle has happened. Ewan is—or seems to be—*absolutely well*. It seems too good to be true. And I cannot help fearing that the recovery has been too sudden to last. Yet the onset was sudden. And he recovered just as suddenly from the attack he had that winter in Glasgow.

Last Saturday when he left to meet Captain Smith at the station he was very very miserable. Two hours later, when he returned, he was well. That is all there is to it.

When he returned with Captain Smith he seemed quietly cheerful and talked easily about old times—as he and Capt. S. knew each other well down home. After supper we all motored over to Jas. Mustard's and stayed for an hour. Ewan seemed his old self, laughing and joking. When we came home he started up the victrola, something he has not done since last spring. That night I slept in my own bed but lay awake most of the night, afraid to move as usual. But I noticed a change in Ewan's sleeping. For the first time he never sighed or moaned in his sleep, although he moved a good deal and woke twice. He kept well all day. Sunday night I slept on the box couch and slept well. When Ewan got up in the morning he said, "This has been the first night since last May that I have slept a *real* sleep and felt rested on waking." That day I felt a lightness of heart long unknown to me.

Captain Smith stayed until Wednesday and we enjoyed his visit very much. About twenty years ago Edwin Smith was the minister in Kensington and Long River. I never met him but as the Park Corner folks were in his congregation I heard of him frequently through them. I always felt a certain unusual interest in him because it was hinted abroad that he was a writer of articles and so I felt professionally akin. He was then a young man, lately married, very handsome and clever. The first time I saw him was on the occasion of a meeting of Presbytery in Cavendish during the "church row." Fan Wise and I were standing in the hall porch looking at the ministers on the platform, Edwin Smith among them. "That man is too good looking to be a minister," whispered Fan. Later on he preached in the new church on the occasion of Ewan's induction there. He was then settled at Cardigan; after that he went out to Alberta and when the war broke out was

"Rev. Edwin Smith, M.A."

settled in Tilsonburg, Ontario. He had always had a hobby for sailing and wherever possible he kept a yacht. He had studied navigation and qualified as a captain. When the war broke out he offered his services to the British admiralty and was accepted. For four years he has been an officer in the British navy, commanding a flotilla of submarine chasers. He had adventures galore and did such good work generally that he was personally thanked and decorated by the king.

The war was ended and he had to doff his gold stripes and return to civilian life. His nerves are rather shaken and he is at present agent at Oshawa for the Imperial Life Insurance Co. I very much doubt if he ever goes back to the pulpit—which is rather a pity, since he is a very good preacher.

I had expected to see a good deal of change in him. He is by now fifty years old. But he looks about 35. There is not a thread of gray in his thick black hair, not a line on his lean, handsome, almost boyish face, not a trace of stoop or stodginess in his slender, upright figure.

Ewan Macdonald and Edwin Smith

He entertained us brilliantly with his tales of adventure. He is certainly a rather universal genius, for he can preach, talk and write wonderfully well, is a Fellow of the R.A.S. of London, and is full of personal charm and magnetism. I rather think he lacks steadiness of purpose, with all his gifts, and so has been surpassed in his professional career by men who were far his inferiors in mental capacity.

On Wednesday Ewan and I motored him to Oshawa. The day was fine. Ewan was in excellent spirits, and we had a delightful time. We came home in the evening, Ewan was as cheerful and merry as of yore, teasing me, and calling me "Pussy" and "Monkey." He seemed perfectly well and said he was.

I hardly know myself. The burden I have carried all summer has suddenly slipped from my shoulders and I think I feel a little light-headed—as if I were flying rather than walking. I cannot describe my feelings. It is easier to write out pain than joy. I feel as if twenty years had been knocked off my tale of birthdays.

Stella came last night. We motored down to meet her and all the way home and all the evening Ewan teased and bantered her as of old. Then she and I talked until twelve, of the incidents of her summer at home and the many seemingly insoluble problems of Park Corner.

Ewan preached today and had no difficulty in doing so. Oh, if it only lasts! I would not re-live this past summer for anything that might be offered me.

I must be a pretty wiry creature. When I was a child I was supposed to be delicate. I don't think I really was. Because my mother died of consumption I think people got the idea that I must necessarily have inherited delicacy of constitution and the fact that I was subject to rather severe colds spread and deepened the impression. I have not had an easy life and yet, since I left childhood behind me I have not had a serious illness. And now, after a summer of unceasing care, worry, and hard work an Insurance Co. finds me a "first class risk"—heart, lungs, kidneys, blood-pressure all normal. That isn't too bad.

I took out $20,000 on my life. That will provide for the boys' education if anything happens to me.

Monday, Sept. 22, 1919
Leaskdale, Ont.

I spent the morning doing up grape jelly. After dinner Ewan and Stella and I motored to Sonya to say goodbye to the Dodds who are leaving there—to my regret, for I like Mrs. Dodds and we have been quite chummy. Then we went to Uxbridge to meet George Millar, a P.E. Island pal of Ewan's who was coming out from Toronto for a brief visit. This evening we had a grand seance of fireworks on our lawn. I got them in the spring, intending to have them for Chester's birthday in July. But we were away then and since our return I have not felt much like fireworks until lately. So we had the fun tonight.

Sunday, Sept. 28, 1919
The Manse, Leaskdale, Ont.

We have had a most enjoyable week, motoring everywhere we could find an excuse to go. Capt. McGillvary came last night to speak on the Prohibition referendum. He is a young chaplain who was overseas—very good fun and he and Stell and I have had much laughter together.

Stell goes tomorrow and I feel badly over it. We have had a very jolly week—a week that seemed like a bit of olden times. It is long since I have laughed so much and so often and so light-heartedly. I think it was because the mirthful side of my nature has been so completely repressed this summer. When it was again released it shot up like a spring and vibrated tremendously to the currents of life. In a little while it will revert to its normal level and life will be sober enough again but for this week it has had full sway.

Anyhow, Stell and I have had a joyous week of mirth and good feasting together. When all is said and done, she is of the race that knows Joseph and the only person in the world, now that Frede is gone, who can enter with me into its heritage. She has been pretty well this time—fewer growls than I have ever known in her—and when Stell is in good humor there could not be a jollier companion. I hate to see her going so far away, where we can never meet save at intervals of years. But it seems to be my Kismet to go through life thus and I must e'en make the best of it.

Thursday, Oct. 2, 1919
The Manse, Leaskdale

Ewan didn't sleep very well last night—sighed and moaned a good deal. This has made me feel anxious all day. I wrote two hours this morning and put up grape juice in the afternoon. In the evening we motored over to Zephyr to re-organize the Guild there—which of course slumped this summer when we were not able to shoulder it along. Midway in the big swamp, two miles from everywhere, a tire blew out, and as our jack, as usual, was not in working order we had a devil of a time getting the spare on. I'm all tired out.

Saturday, Oct. 4, 1919

Today I heard Ewan going through the hall shouting, "Last call for dinner in the dining car." It seemed good to hear the threadbare old joke again though in days past it often "got on my nerves" by reason of its vain repetition. I hadn't heard it since last spring and it meant Ewan was feeling O.K.

I was busy all day preparing for a visit to Toronto. I am going in Monday to spend a week with Mary Beal and am looking forward to it eagerly. It will be *good* to be free of responsibility for a few days—no meals or meetings to plan etc. etc. etc. Ordinarily I like my household routine very well and enjoy carrying it out with the systematic planning that enables me, as Frede used to say, protestingly, "to do three women's work." But we all like a little playtime....

Wednesday, Oct. 8, 1919
2 Nina Ave., Toronto

This is "the end of a perfect day." The weather was glorious. Mr. McClelland, and Mr. and Mrs. Stewart and I motored out to Oakville today on the Hamilton Highway and had dinner in the evening at the Mississauga Golf Club House. Before dinner we went over part of the links and I played my first round of golf. Made a fearful mess of it, of course, but felt the fascination of the game. I have always thought that golf is a game I'd love if I ever had a chance to learn and practise it. But then I've never had a chance and never will have.

The scenery about the Mississauga Links is charming. I have seldom seen a more beautiful bit of landscape than the valley below the club house.

Thursday, Oct. 9, 1919

Today Mary gave an afternoon tea for me. My soul loathes afternoon teas. May the devil fly away with the individual who invented such a form of entertainment. But for Mary's sake I went through the motions gracefully— togged myself up in a French gown of shot pink and green taffeta and honiton lace, which I don't often get a chance to wear, strung some "jools" on myself and pinned on the inevitable corsage bouquet and receiving smile. I stood most of the afternoon shaking hands and saying, "I'm glad you do" to women who told me they loved my books etc. and whom I probably will never meet again and won't recognize if I do. And this is in the year of grace 1919! How long does it take a world to learn how to live?

But Mary was happy because her tea was a great success of its kind and so wisdom is justified of her children.

We wound up by going to see "Mickey" tonight, a movie which is attracting crowds and is hailed as a wonderful performance. It really bored me to tears. I could howl and tear my hair to see what should be a simple, innocent, artless "backwoods" girl played by a sophisticated movie star who rolls her eyes and indulges in the vulgar pantomime of a Broadway soubrette. It really doesn't "go" at all.

Monday, Oct. 13, 1919
Leaskdale, Ont.

We have been having some fairy-like autumn days. Last Friday I wound up my shopping orgy, paid the bills—"some performance" nowadays, believe me!— and went to Mr. McClelland's for dinner at night. Met Mr. and Mrs. Hatheway, rather nice people. Saturday night I came home amid the Thanksgiving mob— no joke in Toronto's old station. Marshall Saunders, author of *Beautiful Joe*, came out with me for the week end. A clever woman but a bit of a bore—talks too much and overloads her conversation with irrelevant detail. I was quite reconciled when she left this morning. Lily has gone for her second week of vacation and I shall be trebly busy for a time. Chester walked "around the block" with Douglas Madill this evening—a distance of five miles. Quite an exploit for a kiddy of seven. He was quite tickled and wrote in his diary about it. He has kept a little diary for a year now. Whether he will keep it up when I cease to be the moving power I know not but he is quite interested now. Dear boy, I hope he will never need a journal for what I have needed mine—the outlet of pain and bitter experiences which none shared with me and which I could tell to no other confidant.

Wednesday, Oct. 15, 1919
The Manse, Leaskdale, Ont.
Beautiful weather. Ewan motored to Toronto yesterday and didn't come back till tonight, so the lads and I were alone last night. I forgot to lock the doors but we slept none the less soundly and nobody ran off with us.

Copying my old diary tonight I came to a mention of Mamie Simpson. Poor Mamie—the only one of those old Cavendish schoolmates of mine who took the road that leads down to death. Mamie and Emma Simpson were the two daughters of "Charlie" Simpson by his first wife. A man who is known all his life as "Charlie" is classed by that fact. Charlie S. was a notorious bigot in his religious opinions—he was of that sect which arrogates to itself the title of Christians and is known to those outside the pale as "Campbellites." In Charlie's opinion you were damned if you were not immersed—or if you played cards or danced. *His* girls were brought up to abhor such things; but it never worried him a particle that his girls were out on the roads, or "sitting up" with every Tom, Dick and Harry for all hours of the night.

Mamie was the older and was considered a very pretty girl. She was gay, merry, free from malice; everyone liked her. In the apt country phrase you "always heard her before you saw her"; she always had a new beau on the string—harmless, silly flirtation at first—then indiscretions—then hinted scandal. It never broke into open flame but in a few years poor Mamie's reputation was fly-blown. She went to Boston and erelong the inevitable followed there— open shame, rapid degradation. She has been the mistress of scores of men, she has been in the reformatory, in the brothel. Her name is never mentioned in her old home—she has never returned to Cavendish—never will. "'Tis an old tale and often told." But in spite of that I think there are worse women in God's sight than poor, good-hearted, wrongly-trained, misled Mamie Simpson.

Friday, Oct. 17, 1919
The Manse, Leaskdale
Twenty-four years ago I wrote in my diary, "I wish I could have lots of books." Looking at my library today one would suppose that I had attained my wish. In truth, I have. I have more books than I have convenient room for. But alas, I have not the time to read them, save by a hungry dip and bite now and then. So am I much the better off by reason of my granted wish? And will my children, who will have these hundred of books to revel in, get any more pleasure and nutriment out of them than I got out of the few well-chewed ones of my youth?

Saturday, Oct. 25, 1919
Leaskdale, Ont.

Today I realized that I have been feeling better these last few weeks than I have felt at any time since I had the flu a year ago. I have not felt tired or dragged or headachy. I have been full of vim and energy. I have slept well and wakened refreshed. The gods grant that it continue.

Last night I copied a lot of my old diary. It is like living over the past again and I always come back to the present with a little sense of unreality. Some of those old entries hurt me, too. For example here is one, apropos of a visit to Pensie's home "What a dear old place it always is! Always the same and always certain of a good time." Alas, it is many years since it ceased to be "the same." Charles and "Mrs. Charles" are gone. Pensie has been dead for several years, her gay, ready, if not over-intelligent laughter, forever stilled. All the girls and boys have gone from the old place, save Russell, who was the one I never liked. His wife, Maggie Houston, is an odd, unamiable person, and to go there now is so little like what it used to be in the gay days of old that it is almost farcical.

Ches Clark figures quite frequently in the records of that particular time. Ches and I were always excellent friends. We were never "beaux" though he occasionally drove me or walked home with me. We were simply "pals." In 1897 Ches went out to B.C.—and has never been home since. At first when he went out there he was coming home every "next year." But the years came and went and he returned not. And now he can never come back to the Cavendish he left—it is no longer in existence.

Ches was married a few years ago to some lady he met out there. They have no family and I have an idea that she is a good deal older than Ches. He always liked mature friends and sweethearts. I was four or five years older than he and so were all the girls he went with. I would like to meet Ches and have a talk over old times but it is not likely our paths will ever cross again. "Lem" too—I have just been copying the entry of his proposal. Well, as I predicted, Lem did not die for love. In no very long time he was going about with several other girls. I don't know why all his affairs with them came to nothing. Eventually he left Kensington and went into a store in Ch'town. There he met Maggie Sellars, a very pretty girl, and, I have heard, a very nice one. They became engaged and Lem went out west, set up in business for himself, and married his Maggie. Since then he has drifted out of my ken. He has no family and I have heard that he was not especially successful in business, but that last is mere rumor and may not be true.

Tuesday, Oct. 28, 1919
Leaskdale, Ont.

I have been reading Marshall Saunders' latest book "Golden Dicky" to Chester, a chapter every night when he goes to bed. He has been keenly interested in it. Tonight I was reading a somewhat pathetic chapter detailing the adventures of a lost and starving dog. Suddenly I was interrupted by a bitter cry. Looking down I saw the child's face convulsed. "Oh, mother, I can't bear it," he sobbed.

"Why, lad," I said, "it's going to come out all right. Billy isn't going to die. She's going to find a good home and a kind mistress very soon." "Are you sure?" "Yes." "Well, just read me the part where it says so right off before you finish this chapter."

I never saw a child so keenly sensitive to accounts of suffering. He is even more so than I used to be—too keenly sensitive I fear....

Saturday, Nov. 8, 1919
The Manse, Leaskdale, Ont.
Chester has a knack of saying odd little things. He goes over to George Leask's every morning for our milk. It was very sharp this morning and when he returned he said, "Mother, when I got the milk and left Mr. Leask's I just kneeled down on the ground and asked God to make it warmer but when I got out of the gate it was just as cold as ever."

Last night he developed a sudden fondness for celery. When I said, "How is it you can eat it now when you have never liked it before?" He said gravely "I can eat celery now because God put the power into me."

I wonder if I made many queer speeches when I was a tot. If I did they were not recorded or remembered, save two, which I often heard told by way of a joke—something I did not at all relish. One day when I was very small an aunt asked me if I would go and bring home her turkeys from the shore field. I responded gravely, "I am afraid it would excite ridicule."

I remember saying this but I have no recollection of the other speech with which I am credited. There was company to tea—"quality folk"—Mr. and Mrs. Archibald, with another minister and wife who were visiting there. I came in late, very hot, breathless, and dishevelled. I had been down to the mill brook with "Katie", Uncle John's French servant girl, to water the cows. Grandma asked me why I was so late and I gasped out, "Katie and I went to water the cows and we had to chase *that bloody heifer* for nearly half an hour."

Consternation!

Of course, I was merely repeating a phrase I had heard Katie use. The French "hired help" of those days were given to swearing. For that matter, I would not have known that "bloody" was a "cuss word." Nor, indeed, could I ever understand why it should be so considered until little over a year ago when I learned that it was, in that usage, not an adjective at all but a corruption of the old oath, "By our Lady"—"By'r-l-dy"—"bloody."

The other evening I heard Chester explaining "marriage" to Stuart. "A man and a woman go to a minister and he *preaches a sermon to them* and then they're married."

Friday, Nov. 14, 1919
I feel half sick with despair. Thursday morning was cold and gray. Ewan and I motored to Glenarm, a distance of thirty miles, to visit Rev. Mr. Smith and family. I enjoyed the drive for Ewan seemed quite well and I thought my

anxiety of the previous night groundless. But after dinner he complained of a headache and from that on I was worried. We had supper at Woodville with the Brydons and then motored home through a very black dour night. Ewan still complained of his head but seemed cheerful enough. Last night, however, he wakened at four and could not sleep again. He admitted that his "phobia" had returned. This was dreadful news to me.

It has been a terrible day—dark and cold and windy. I had to work at cleaning the dining room. Is the winter to be like the summer? I *cannot* face it here alone if it is—no, I cannot!

Saturday, Nov. 15, 1919
Leaskdale, Ont.
Another day and evening of something sadly akin to utter despair for me. Ewan had a poor night. I had to get out the chloral bottle again—I had so hoped I had put it away forever—but even it did not give him sleep. He had a poor day—headache and depression. I worked doggedly all day. The hardest thing I had to do was go over to the church in the afternoon to help with a practice for the S.S. Christmas concert. It is a job I dislike at any time and today it did not seem to me that I could face it. But I set my teeth, went over, selected and allotted recitations and dialogues and drills and kept my gnawing fear in the back of my mind. It got its revenge when I came home in the early autumn twilight. I shut myself in the dark parlor where no one could see me and the children could not find me and had a bad half hour. This evening after I had got the children to bed I sat here by the table, too despairing even to read. Oh God, I cannot face a winter like last summer!

Wednesday, Nov. 19, 1919
Leaskdale, Ont.
Last night Ewan had to take two doses of chloral but this time they worked and he got a good long sleep from them. I slept with Chester, who has a bad cold and sore throat, that I might keep him warm and covered. I slept little for outside a cold fierce gale was blowing and the shutters kept rattling and banging. Besides, my bitter thoughts haunted me. How long the night seemed! It was very cold all day. Ewan stayed in bed all the morning and seemed very dull all day. I am keeping up the bromide treatment and will give it a fair trial. I worked hard all day getting the kitchen cleaned.

A copy of the *Canadian Bookman* came today with a splendid review of *Rainbow Valley*. It would have pleased me very much if it could have pierced through the fog of worry that surrounds me.

Friday, Nov. 21, 1919
The Manse, Leaskdale
Again I feel encouraged. Ewan slept well from 10 to 5.30 without any chloral and seemed more like himself all day. Mr. Forbes, a visiting missionary, came for over Sunday. I had expected he would bring his wife with him and I dreaded it under the circumstances but fortunately she did not come.

Saturday, Nov. 22, 1919
Again Ewan slept well and seemed much better all day. I went to S.S. practice again this afternoon and came home tired and dispirited from trying to get the children into line. Ewan and Mr. Forbes were away. It was dark and cloudy and cold. I found it very hard to compel myself to go to work. I wanted to go upstairs, fling myself on the bed and just give up. But I didn't—instead I went to work.

Had a letter from Nora Lefurgey—Mrs. Edmond Campbell—today. She lives in B.C. and has three children. She wrote a gay, happy letter. Such letters are a little bitter to me now, in my own dread and unhappiness.

Stokes also wrote me that *Rainbow Valley* is to be translated into Danish and Swedish.

Tuesday, Nov. 25, 1919
Leaskdale, Ont.
A cold snowstorm. In the afternoon we went to Allan Gray's to tea.

There are people who seem to take all the beauty, color, rhythm, sparkle and courage out of life and leave it ugly, gray, flat, dull and cowardly. The Grays are this kind of people. When I came away and drove home through the cold wintry night I felt depressed and cowed. We have to go back to the buggy now and so the drive home was slow and cold and dreary. I suppose I am feeling the reaction of my fortnight on the rack. Or else Mrs. Gray's "sweet supper" consisting of nothing but jam, pie and several kinds of poorly made cake has damped my spirits! No wonder they are dull and depressing when they live on such stuff.

Wednesday, Nov. 26, 1919
The Manse, Leaskdale
This morning Ewan, Chester and I drove to Uxbridge. It was bitter cold and it did seem very slow progress after skimming down in the car. But we've just got to resign ourselves to it and make the best of it. I shall not growl over this if other things keep bearable. Chester had to have his two lower front teeth taken out as the second ones were pushing through behind them. I try to keep

Brock Street East, Uxbridge

sharp tabs on my children's teeth in order to secure as regular a second set as possible. I have several of his first set filled in order to keep them in place so that the gum might not shrink and crowd the new ones. I have felt badly all my life from the ugly, crowded crooked appearance of my teeth—at least of the lower ones—which might have been remedied if they had been attended to early enough. Of course, I inherited teeth with a tendency to be crooked from father but much might have been done to straighten them if they had been taken in time.

I have always envied people with nice white even teeth—something rather rarely seen. However, I have most of my own teeth yet and that is something to be thankful for. One's own teeth, even if they are ugly, are really better than a beautiful false set.

We got home in time for dinner and I spent the whole afternoon in writing a paper for Zephyr Guild tomorrow night and in arranging a "scrapbook" programme for our Leaskdale guild tonight. Then after supper I went to the Guild and "ran" it. Now I'm home, good and ready for bed.

Thursday, Nov. 27, 1919
Leaskdale, Ont.
I worked at Book 10 all the forenoon. Then after dinner got ready and went to Zephyr and had tea at Frank Walkers—a performance almost as depressing as our visit to Gray's. To be sure, they are not quite as "gray" as the Grays but they are ignorant and trivial. Mrs. Walker told me she thought Ewan was "too fat" for real health and that his cough was "terrible" etc. He is no fatter than he has been for years and his cough is a temporary one owing to a bad cold he has contracted. But that sort of thing is depressing when one is rather down anyhow. I remember the first time I was ever there. It was in the winter before Chester was born. Mrs. Walker knew my condition, which was perhaps the reason why she entertained me with the cheerful accounts of three women she had known who had all died in childbirth. I did not let it worry me. I knew there was a certain element of risk but I knew also that only a very small percentage of women die in childbirth. Besides, my sense of humor was in good working order then and it really amused me. But now when I am not feeling especially cheerful such a hostess rather gets on my nerves. I was quite willing to exchange her conversation for even the dark night and rough roads of the way to the church. Then, when we got there, there was no guild after all and I might have spent my precious two hours yesterday much more profitably. We came home over that long bleak hilly road. Ever since I came here those night drives home from Zephyr have been the bane of my existence. I get here chilled to the bone, tired and disgruntled. But a good hot drink and the consoling prospect of soon being cuddled down in a warm blanketty bed with a blessed hot water bottle have raised my spirits somewhat.

Sunday, Nov. 30, 1919
Leaskdale, Ont.
I am forty five years old today—not a particularly exhilarating fact. I don't look forty five—strangers usually guess my age as 30. My hair is still dark in general effect, my complexion is reasonably fresh and I have no wrinkles, owing I suppose to faithful cold-creaming and massage every night as well as to a series of facial muscle exercises I invented myself and practice regularly every day. And I don't *feel* forty five—at least, I don't feel as I once supposed a woman of forty five must inevitably feel. But I *am* forty five and life must be on the down-grade henceforth. One may as well look the fact in the face, distasteful as it is, and make the best of it. After all, most of the time I shall forget that I am forty five, or any age, and then it will not matter.

"Making the best of it"
[*Maud and her cat*]

Last night we had one of the worst hurricanes that Ontario has had since 1896. The wind was terrific. It shrieked through our keyhole like the whistle of a steam engine. We are so well sheltered in this little dale that we seldom feel a wind but last night we got enough for a year in one capful. I sat here alone and tried to read but I was very lonely and so my book seemed savorless.

This afternoon was dull and cold and bitter. I copied down a goodish bit of my old journal. Lou Dystant's name figured in it conspicuously.
Poor Lou! Of all the men who have loved me he was the slowest to recover. He did not marry until two years after I did. Then he married a nice girl and lives at Ellerslie and has a daughter....

Friday, Dec. 5, 1919
Leaskdale, Ont.
Ugh! Those boys were here again for practice tonight. My nerves are frayed out. Ordinarily I like training small fry to do these things but these lads are certainly very raw material. One chap sat on the rocking chair and rocked fiercely all the time. One slumped down on his chair and it seemed impossible to get any energy into or out of him. I wanted to stick a darning needle into him to see if he could really feel or jump. One was pert and "Smart Aleckish." All were gigglers. There wasn't one nice or nice-mannered boy among them. I kept my patience admirably and put them through that dialogue until my head grew dizzy. Then I packed them off. It is 9.30 now and I am going to read

Gibbon for awhile to take the taste of raw cub out of my soul. I am on my third volume of him now. It is about twelve years since I read him through before. I read one volume, then I plunge into the most frivolous novel I can find by way of getting back to normal. He is so big and massive that he seems to suck one's individuality clean out of one—swallow one up like a huge, placid, slow-moving river. As I march with his stately procession of forgotten heroes and forgotten fools I get the uncomfortable feeling that I am as insignificant as a grain of dust amid so many centuries of "baffled millions who have gone before." And I know I am—but it is an abominable feeling and one not to be tolerated, because it makes life impossible and silly.

Sunday, Dec. 7, 1919
The Manse, Leaskdale
Seven days of December gone, praise be. Not that I am in any hurry to get to the end of my forty-sixth year, thank you; but this winter is just something to be endured. This week has been very cold and gray and depressing. Our coal is poor so our house is not comfortable. Ewan, though fairly well, does not seem like his old self yet and I go in daily fear. I am lonely. I miss Frede hideously these gray days. Last night as I sat here alone I cried chokingly. If she were only somewhere in the world—if I might only hope to get a letter from her! But there is only blank and silence.

Cam is going to put on her tombstone the epitaph I selected.

> "After life's fitful fever she sleeps well."

It is the one I want on my own when I die. And I trust I shall sleep well—and dreamlessly. For I think it will take me a long while to get rested.

Monday, Dec. 8, 1919
The Manse, Leaskdale
Got home from a cold drive to Uxbridge to find a letter from Stell, all growls as usual and coolly demanding the loan of $2500 to start up a chicken ranch. That girl seems to be entirely without any sense of shame. She borrowed $1000 from me eight years ago, promising to pay 5% interest—and has never paid one cent. Yet now she asks for another loan, as if I were a bank on which she could draw at will. I am getting tired of lending money to her and her pals and never getting even interest on it. When I was poor and struggling nobody ever lent me a cent to help me along. I thought when Stell got married I would surely be free henceforth from her appeals and demands for money but I shall never be free from her. She has come to be a most disgusting compound of falsehood and effrontery and I'm out of all patience with her and her gang.

There, I've got that out of my system and feel better—and disposed to think I've stated it a bit too strongly. After all, old Stell is "one of us" and I suppose I must help her out. Perhaps she'll get on her feet and do better after this. But it is her callous taking-for-granted behavior that nettles me—as if I had no purpose in life than to earn money to help her out.

And I can never forget the way she behaved last summer about Frede's necklace.

Friday, Dec. 12, 1919

Tonight I had to go to Zephyr to give readings at a concert in aid of the Library there. One interesting feature of it—to me—was a little play which some of the scholars gave, taken out of my book "The Golden Road"—the chapter containing "Great Aunt Eliza's visit." They did it very well and I really enjoyed it. The performance gave it a freshness which, for me, the printed page lacks.

But my evening was spoiled by the fact that Ewan's head bothered him a great deal and that he was staring at vacancy part of the time, immersed in gloomy reflections, instead of listening to the programme.

Saturday, Dec. 13, 1919

This was a dull gray lifeless day all through without a gleam of sunshine without or within—except a letter from Bertie which only made me feel so hungry for a talk with her that it made matters rather worse than better. I wrote in the forenoon and finished the skeleton of Book 10. After dinner I went to concert practice—a lifeless, dragging performance where everything seemed at loose ends and everybody seemed waiting for somebody else to go ahead and do things. After it was over I made a call on an old lady who may go into the kingdom before me but is a doleful inhabitant of this world. She sucked out what little "grit" I had left in me and I came home feeling like a squeezed orange.

The truth is, I'm starving for a little companionship. For eight weeks I've been mewed up here without one living soul near me who is any kin whatever to the race of Joseph. Ewan, in his present quiet, dull state of mind is rather worse than no company at all. So I'm utterly alone, and once in a while, when a dull, lifeless twilight is wrapping itself over a dull lifeless gray world I give up in a sort of despair and mutter, "I *can't* go on."

But my givings-up never last very long. When I get rested and cheered up by a bit of a dip into some interesting book—or even by a dose of confession in this, my diary—I rise up again and resolve to endure to the end. This little outburst here has quite refreshed me.

But oh, if I could only write to Frede or get a letter from her. That would keep life wholesome and normal. How I dread the thought of Christmas—the first Christmas on which I cannot hope to get even a greeting from Frede. Never again will she spend a Christmas with me. Christmas can never again mean anything to me but a day which must be made gay for the children's sake but which will only make me glad when it is over and done with.

Wednesday, Dec. 17, 1919
The Manse, Leaskdale

Life in weather as cold as these past three days have been is not life but mere existence. Monday and Tuesday were bad enough but today was still worse. This morning it was 16 below zero and we could not get the house warm. All day we have shivered and sighed. Mental work was out of the question. So I put on a sweater and *overboots*—for the kitchen floor was so cold that water froze on it at noon—and compounded my winter's supply of mincemeat. Now it is bedtime and I am glad. I shall go to bed with a hot water bottle and get warm.

Thursday, Dec. 18, 1919

I shut the manse door tonight behind those boys and said a fervent thanks-be. This was the last night of practice for them and I hope I'll never have such a gang to train again.

It was much milder today—we got the house warm—and life seemed a shade less gray.

I had a letter from Clara, giving some details of Stell's goings-on. Poor Stell—and yet when I think of some of the lies she has told Clara in order to cheat the latter out of her share in poor Frede's little leavings—I turn sick at soul.

Clara wrote that she had been to see "Anne of Green Gables" on the screen. Page, by the way, sold the movie rights last summer. He would never sell them as long as we were in partnership because he would have had to share up with me. I knew he would do it as soon as he was free. He got $40,000 for the film rights. My share would have been $20,000—a nice sum to be cheated out of!!!

Mary Miles Minter is playing *Anne*. I've seen her in other plays. She is very dainty, very pretty and utterly unlike my gingery Anne. Clara wrote that she did not like the film at all and that everyone else was disappointed. The reason seems to be that their "favorite characters" are not included in the cast. Now, these characters do little in the books, but *talk* and unluckily talk can't be reproduced on the screen. Only the characters who *do* something can appear there. I do not expect to like the film myself—I never yet have liked any film I have seen that was reproduced from a book I had read. Nevertheless I am very curious to see it. Clara says Los Angeles turned out *en masse*—that she never had to stand so long in line in any city in her life to get a ticket.

Sunday, December 21, 1919

I was so tired last night I cried. Yesterday morning I got up tired. I had company coming for tea so I made cake and salad and did a hundred or so odd jobs. In the afternoon I went to the S.S. practice, came home, got supper, as Lily was busy with concert preparations—and then hurried back to the church and stayed there till eleven helping with the rehearsal. The children were noisy and silly—the grown-up performers seemed more anxious to get off into corners and hold hands than attend to practising. I felt like wringing their necks, as I smiled sweetly at them and suggested this or that. And these girls, mark you, are not young. Some of them are nearer 30 than 20 and all are old enough to have some sense. When I was a girl my chums and I had our good times, driving with and talking to the boys, and I admit we all flirted a little, but we did not make asses of ourselves in public, especially when we were supposed to be working. When I came here eight years ago the then set of young people were sensible, well-behaved boys and girls—at least, the majority of them were and they kept the rest in order. But they are married or gone—the generation in power at present seems to be devoid of sense, ambition, executive ability. Consequently I came home feeling worn-out, cheap, out of place, *declassé*, discouraged—and as aforesaid I cried. This morning I was so tired I could not go out to church. I rested all day as well as I could and tonight I feel more courage and a determination to see the wretched thing through since I have put my hand to the plough.

Another volume of my journal finished. It covers less time than any of the others—less than four years. But in those four years have been crowded a lifetime of emotions. Since I began this journal the war has ended—Frede has died. I will begin a new volume with the bitter certainty that in it there will never be any Frede, save in my memories. It will record no footsteps of hers on my threshold, no laughter of hers at my fireside. The Gates of Life and Death have opened and shut between us—I on this side, she on that. Perhaps, when the night of the universe is over she and I will find each other again. But I want her now.

(END OF VOLUME 4)

Monday, December 22, 1919
The Manse, Leaskdale, Ont.
Sometimes—fortunately—things we dread turn out to be quite pleasant. I have been dreading the S.S. concert at Zephyr to-night—especially the long cold drive there and back in the buggy. But it was not cold. To-day was very mild and when Ewan and Chester and I left after supper we positively enjoyed our drive over. Owing to the skim of snow the night was not dark. The road was good, the trees and fields and groves pleasantly suggestive and eerie and elusive, as if full of elfish secrets. Chester chattered amusingly and I enjoyed the drive. The concert and Christmas tree was also nice. Chester recited, Ewan read and acted as Chairman. I gave two readings and also read the Cottar's Saturday Night while it was shown in a series of tableaux—so I think the Macdonald family did its duty and quite deserved the nice fat goose which was hung on the tree for it. The first and only goose we have ever been given, as it happens!

The drive home was just as pleasant as the drive over. I was not tired—or rather my tiredness showed itself in a certain exaltation of feeling and imagination, such as I sometimes experience when I am really much fatigued. My drive home was a seven-mile-film of brilliant adventures of fancy.

Tuesday, Dec. 23, 1919
The Manse, Leaskdale
Thanks be, the S.S. concert is over. We had a fine night, a good crowd, and a programme that seemed to please. To me it seemed a two hours' nightmare for besides looking after Chester and Stuart I had to arrange dialogues and "run" tableaux and evolve order out of the chaos behind the scenes. And under all this ran a current of dull worry over Ewan who had seemed duller to-day than

usual. So it was a very different evening from last evening and when it was over I gathered up my chattels, rounded up my boys, and came home through the thickly-falling snow, with a profound thankfulness that it was over.

Wednesday, Dec. 24, 1919
I was busy all day preparing for Christmas, with very little heart in it. I made pudding and doughnuts and thought of Frede incessantly. Tonight when I was dressing the Christmas tree for the boys I broke down and cried. It was the first Christmas since Chester was born that there was nothing for him from "Aunt Fred." I felt an unbearable sense of desolation. Frede, *where are you*? Three years ago tonight we were together—you were here in my home, a guest for the last time. I remember that when you went away I felt a strange loneliness and desolation such as I had never felt before when you went....

Thursday, Dec. 25, 1919
Leaskdale, Ont.
The saddest, dreariest Christmas I have ever spent is over. I am thankful. I got up in the bitter, cold, gray morning and—for Lily had gone home—got breakfast while the boys exulted over their tree. Then I cooked the dinner and had so much trouble over it, owing to a smoking stove and an oven that *wouldn't* get hot that my nerves went to pieces. It was two before we had dinner and four o'clock before I got the dishes washed. By this time one of my headaches was fully underway and I had to take an aspirin tablet and lie down. In an hour the aspirin had worked and the pain was gone, but I was exhausted physically and mentally. I had seen no living soul outside of my own family all day. The outer world was gray and cold. Ewan was dull and complained of his head. There was no mail—nothing to cheer, stimulate, or encourage. But it is over— my first Christmas with no Frede in the world. The children had a good time and that is the main thing with me now.

These headaches of mine have been periodic occurrences for the past twenty-three years. Up to the time I was twenty-one I never had a headache, save when I was catching some disease such as measles or scarlet fever. But after that winter in Bedeque I began to have them regularly. Their origin is nervous and was probably due to the rack of suppressed passion and suffering on which I was stretched that winter. I tried everything in the way of medicines and doctors to no avail. For ten years I suffered miserably from them, never getting any relief from the pain until, after hours of suffering, I vomited bile. Then it ceased and left me exhausted for a day. Worse almost even than the pain was the day of depression, languor and general nervous unrest which always preceded it.

About thirteen years ago I heard of aspirin and tried it. It worked like magic and since then I have not suffered over much as a tablet will almost always cure me speedily. But it is of no use to take it until the pain comes-the boring pain over the left brow. All the preliminary discomfort I must endure. To-day would not have been so hard if my nervous misery had not robbed me of the strength to bear the worry and loneliness bravely.

Friday, Dec. 26, 1919
Leaskdale, Ont.
Today I felt unusually well. Always after my headaches I do—as if something that had been pressed down by pain had rebounded with redoubled energy. Mr. Fraser was here to tea and the bit of intellectual companionship resulting was just the stimulation I needed and gave me courage to carry on. I won't cry myself to sleep tonight.

Sunday, Dec. 28, 1919
....Today in copying my old journal I came to the part dealing with my first month in Belmont and the doings of Fulton and Alf Simpson. Really they were an absurd pair—or rather Fulton was absurd. The two geese quarrelled over me and never spoke to each other all winter. Fulton never forgave me for not appreciating him. He turned against me and hated me as bitterly and unreasonably as he had loved me. Some years later he married a Miss Taylor—of St. Eleanor's I think. They have—or had at last reports—three daughters and are living at the old place in Belmont.

Alf has never married—not because he did not get his first love but solely, I am afraid, because nobody else would take him—nobody he wanted anyhow. His uncouth appearance was against him. Yet I always liked Alf—indeed, to be frank, I was quite a little bit taken with Alf that winter we went about together in Belmont. It did not go very deep—and as he was quite out of the question for anything serious I nipped it severely in the bud and no one, least of all Alf himself, ever suspected it.

I had always supposed that likely Alf thought bitterly enough of me, too. But a few years ago, just before Aunt Mary Lawson died, he was up to see her, and in speaking of me he told her that he had never met anyone in his life he liked as well as me. So he must think kindly of me. He lives with his mother at St. Eleanor's and the last report I heard of him was that all he was interested in was the piling up of money. Perhaps that may be the criticism of jealousy: or it may be true, all other aspirations having been thwarted and other passions starved.

Of Ed I never hear much. He seems to roam about a good deal. The last time I was home I heard Myrtle Webb saying that she thought the reason "Ed hadn't been more successful was that his conceit spoiled him. He could get a good church easily but couldn't hold it long."

His wife is a clever, talkative woman, quite a dab at public speaking. They have no children. This must be a disappointment to Ed. But he would never have had children, no matter whom he married, I believe. When I was engaged to Ed I did not know enough of men to realize what was lacking in him, but I know now that there *was* something lacking and I believe that was why, though I did not understand it, I felt such a mysterious repugnance to him.

Monday, Dec. 29, 1919
Leaskdale, Ontario

I finished Gibbon's "Decline and Fall" this evening. It is the third time I have read it, but the first since my marriage. I hardly think I shall ever find time to read it again. It is a monumental piece of work. I know of no historian so coldly impersonal as Gibbon. He seems more like a machine recording history than anything else I can think of. This makes for the proper impartiality; but it is also largely accountable for what, after all, must be called the monotony of his style. Almost the only portions of his history in which we get a glimpse of Gibbon himself—the intellect behind the machine— are in his famous chapters on Christianity and—such a coupling!—his sprinkling of sly, spicy, smutty stories. Naturally these—the chapters, I mean—are therefore the most interesting part of the work, since only personality makes anything interesting. As for the aforesaid scandalous little anecdotes—well they haven't a Puritan flavor— but now and then a *little* risque seasoning is agreeable! But it is a seasoning easy to overdo and an overdose is nauseating. Gibbon doesn't overdo but his smirk, as he pens a choice tidbit, rather gives the effect of a Satyr leering suddenly around the columns of Karnak.

1920

Sunday, Jan. 4, 1920
The Manse, Leaskdale, Ont.
This finishes a week of bitter and unbroken cold—zero at the best, 20 and 22 below at the worst. I could count on my two hands the hours I have been really warm this week out of bed. Our house is miserably cold; we have poor coal this year and can't ever get the best out of it because our flue needs cleaning so badly and smokes vilely. I tried to get Ewan to clean it in November but the apathy of his malady was on him and I couldn't get him to do it. But it *must* be done soon for we can't go on living like this. I am sitting here by the dining room table with a thick sweater on and an oil heater burning beside me and my feet are like ice. I really haven't suffered so from cold since my winter at Frasers' in Belmont.

Ewan has seemed rather better this week. Out in company he is quite cheerful. But at home he is very dull and certainly not a stimulating companion. I cling to the hope that when spring comes he may get well again as he did the year he was in Glasgow. But sometimes the dread possesses me that his melancholia has become settled and I ask myself dully if I can face years of this kind of life.

Tuesday we drove to Uxbridge in the cold and then out to tea at Jas. Mustards'. Wednesday and Thursday evenings we also had to spend out and in no case was the pleasure of the evening among dull people great enough to compensate for the cold drives and late hours. Besides, though Ewan is quite cheerful when out most of the times he is occasionally *distrait* and shows by his vague remarks how little attention he has really been paying to the conversation, and this wears terribly on my nerves, so that when I reach home I am woefully tired physically and bedraggled in soul.

I had only two days in this week on which I could do any work on my book.

Friday morning we started out in the forenoon for a day's visiting at Zephyr. It was intensely cold with a bitter penetrating wind blowing from the northwest, right in our teeth. I never drove out on a worse day. But I was not cold myself. I had put on sweaters and coats and furs until I was a shapeless mass and I had a sizzling hot brick at my feet which kept me warm. So I buried my nose in my collar and forgot the outside world in a series of reflections upon this astounding new discovery of the nature of light made by Einstein which is going to utterly revolutionize most of the beliefs held by scientists for two hundred years. It is a curious thing that this upsetting discovery should come just at a time when almost everything else that made up our old world is being upset, revolutionized, or torn to pieces. The result will probably be in the end a very wonderful era of development in everything.

But whether light be matter or vibration there was not enough of it coming from anywhere on Friday to warm up our planet—on our part of it at least—and when we finished our drive of eight miles I was beginning to get so cold that I could not have detached myself from the material world around me much longer.

We had a good dinner—roast duck etc. etc. I have never been one of those who consider "a liking for a tasty bite" something to be rather ashamed of. Frankly, I'm very fond of a good table. I keep one myself and I like to sit down to one. It is an old Montgomery tradition and when I hear anyone say, "I don't care what I have to eat," I conclude that that individual is either lying, or is a pale anemic creature of very little use and no charm or force in the world. And I have mostly found that this conclusion was borne out by the facts of the case. So, though I would certainly not have driven to Zephyr on such a day for that, or any dinner alone, still, since I had to go, the "savory meat" was a bit of compensation which I welcomed very cordially.

We went to another house to supper. Then Ewan went to a business meeting of the Guild but I had reached my limit. I was tired out with making endless small talk on harmless and incombustible subjects and with taking off and putting on overshoes, overstockings, hat, veil, muffler, extra underskirt, sweater, suit coat, fur coat, two pair of gloves and a muff. So I hied me to Lily Shier's where I lay on the sofa till ten, resting and silent. At ten we left for home. The wind was in our backs which made every difference; my brick was beautifully hot; we drove though a fantastic fairy world where moonlight was shining through a very thin skim of cloud and the fine, floating mist of snow falling from it. As Ewan had relapsed into quietude I again went roaming in an ideal life of adventure and brilliancy and the drive home was a pleasure.

I did not go out today. I have had a strenuous week and another still more strenuous is ahead of me. So I resolved to stay home and rest up a bit.

It is 1920. 1919 has gone—the most terrible year of my life—the year of Frede's going—the year in which I discovered that my husband was subject to recurrent constitutional melancholia. I hailed its dawn gladly. The war was over—I looked forward to a year of peace and old time pleasure and freedom from gnawing care. But what a dreadful year it has been almost from the first! So I shrink from 1920. I think I will never again welcome in a New Year with gladness or anticipation.

Monday, Jan. 5, 1920
The Manse, Leaskdale
This morning it was 23 below zero. I spent the forenoon making eats for a meeting of the Guild executive here tomorrow night. This evening Lily and I and the boys went to a "shower" at Alec Leask's, held for Ada Marquis, one of our girls who is to be married Wednesday. Ewan had to go to Zephyr and, as Stuart could not walk home in the snow I had to wait until everybody was ready to go before I could get a chance home. It was long after twelve and I

was bored to tears and envious of Chester and Stuart who had fallen asleep—and then had to be waked up and dressed, limp and cranky. I'm home now, have got them tucked up in bed and come to my journal for a bit of companionship while I'm waiting for the water to get hot for my faithful bottle—without which the mistress of Leaskdale manse would have been found several times this winter frozen all stiff and stark.

Speaking of that, however, I hope for better things after this. This afternoon, driven to desperation, Lily and I went to work, took down the kitchen pipe and burned the chimney out with newspapers and coal oil. It was a long process and very vile in the early stages when the smoke poured out at every crevice and filled the house with gloom and vile odors. But in the end we got it done. Then, while the place still reeked and I was a sight for gods and men with soot and grime the door bell rang and I had to go, for Lily was wrestling with the problem of the spare room where soot had fallen on bed and carpet. The caller was a "stylish" Christmas visitor who had been sojourning in Leaskdale and was the last person I expected or desired to see just then. But I dressed my smutty features in a smile and took her into the parlor where I talked to her as if I had no other thought on earth. When I finally shut the door behind her, I muttered a profane "Good riddance." But when Lily rekindled the fire it burned gloriously with a heart gladdening draft—and so once more we fare forward.

Chester, by the way, is undergoing the pangs of his first love affair—at the mature age of 7½. A few weeks ago he informed me that he had "picked out a girl to marry" when he grew up, adding in strict secrecy that she was "V. Harrison"—the full name, I presume, being too sacred to desecrate by utterance. Since then he had alternated between hopefulness and spasms of despair lest the said V. Harrison prefer Douglas Madill after all. One day he informed me with sparkling eyes that she had called him "My dear little Chester." Another day he confided to Stuart that he just couldn't help winking at Velma whenever he looked at her. But today he sighed to me that he was afraid Douglas would get her. "I suppose I didn't tell her soon enough," he concluded mournfully.

As for the said Velma, to my eyes—but then perhaps I'm jaundiced!—she is a coarse featured, rather bold little girl, aged ten, quite devoid of charm or beauty. But kissing goes by favor and evidently Chester finds her desirable extremely.

Chester and Stuart are occupied these days poring over their Christmas books. Stuart as yet cons only pictures but Chester is quite a remarkable reader for his age. Indeed, he reads too much, I fear. I am anxious lest he injure his eyes. I had to put a decisive stop to his reading in bed. If I let him he would read there until ten o'clock—as he did one evening when I had company. I supposed he had been asleep for hours and was horrified to discover him at ten lost in the adventures of Peter Rabbit and Bobby Coon and Ol' Mistah Buzzard.

Both the boys seem to have inherited my good memory. I am glad of this. I had been afraid that they might "take after" Ewan in this. His memory is very poor—abnormally so indeed. This has been a serious drawback to him in every relation of life, especially in his profession and in society. Nothing that he reads seems to stick in his memory at all, so that, as far as any enrichment of intellect or life goes, he might just as well not have read it. But Chester and Stuart seem to remember everything easily and long.

Wednesday, Jan. 7, 1920

All day I worked hard getting ready a supper for Ada Marquis and her husband, who came here at five this evening to be married. Ordinarily of course I don't get tea for the couples who come here to be married. But Ada has always been a particular friend of mine and there were other reasons why I wanted to give her a nice little send off. So I made salad and cake and biscuits etc. and fixed up a pretty table with pink-shaded candles etc. and all went off well—on the surface. But Ewan was very miserable all day and especially so this afternoon, restless and gloomy. He hasn't had such a bad attack for a long time. This evening, after I had helped Lily wash and put away all the dishes I broke down and cried. But tears never seem to relieve me now. They only give me a throbbing headache.

Friday, Jan. 9, 1920

....Tonight when I put the boys to bed Chester said eagerly, "Are you going to read us a chapter of Hiawatha tonight, mother?" Ever since he was two I have always read to him when I put him to bed—just the Peter Rabbit series etc. But lately I have been reading selections from the poets. "Hiawatha" seemed wonderful to me when I was a child. I revelled in it and never tired of it. I haven't read it for many years and I confess it seems rather poor and thin now. But Chester seems to find it full of charm and it is wonderful how much he understands of it and how he loves it.

Tuesday, Jan. 13, 1920
The Manse, Leaskdale

A missionary meeting this afternoon and one of Stella's letters full of growls and complaints spoilt today. I led the meeting and tried to put a little life and inspiration into the programme but the sight of that circle of stolid, fat, uninteresting, narrow old dames would have put out any poor little fire of my kindling. They just sucked all the animation out of my soul.

But tonight I read Tarkington's "Seventeen" and laughed as I haven't laughed for years over a book. It isn't a very subtle book—it has no great literary charm and it verges on caricature. But it *is* so excruciatingly funny and the laughter it gave me a boon. It flooded my drab soul with a rosy light and entirely headed off the fit of nervous crying with which I had expected to end the day.

Friday, Jan. 16, 1920

About this time two years ago we had a terrible three days of bitter cold. With the exception of those three days today has been the coldest I ever endured in my life.

Yesterday was very frosty and the house was not comfortable. But I managed to work a couple of hours at Book 10 in the forenoon. In the afternoon we went to Zephyr a-visiting. Although so cold that my lashes froze it was calm and bright, so the drive over was not so bad, thanks to furs, a brick and so many clothes that I felt like a Dutchwoman. The folks we visited were fairly nice, too, had a good warm house and a good supper. Ewan seemed better than he has been for a long time. After supper we went to Guild. Partly owing to the bitter night, partly to the fact of a carnival at the rink, and partly I daresay to the fact that a family in the village has developed smallpox, only four were there besides ourselves. However, we had Guild and then started home. My brick was cold and the drive home through the white and iron night was not pleasant. How many of those miserable drives we have had home from Zephyr in the past eight years! I detest that merciless road with its never-ending hills. But we got over them and when we came to Quigley's Hill I was only rather chilly and not positively cold. Quigley's Hill is what "David's Hill" in Cavendish used to be—a place that fills up on the least excuse of a drift. It was badly filled up last night and the road was very sidelong. All at once we went over and landed in snowbank. Luckily our mare halted and we got up but then she got into soft snow and it was some time before Ewan could get her through it to the road. It was lucky everything was not smashed up. By the time we got in again I was ready to cry with cold hands and feet, and, what was far worse, Ewan's heart began to act badly, as a result of his plunging in the deep snow. I was distracted with anxiety but by the time we got home he was all right again. We got in, I got a hot drink for both, a hot water bottle and presently we were in bed, comfortable and warm. But this morning—Lord, how I hated to get out. It was dark—it was cold—my muscles ached from the cramped drive. But up I got—got dressed—got the boys dressed—and got down. But I got *not* warm. In spite of a good furnace fire the house has been barn-like all day. Our oil heater is out of whack so we could not supplement the furnace by it. My feet were cold and I developed chilblains. Chilblains are not romantic. The heroines in novels never have them. But they are cussed things for torment. For three hours tonight I "suffered the tortures of the damned" as Stell is so fond of repeating. But I got the boys tucked up in bed, and there they are sound asleep and cosy and rosy, the darling little creatures. I could fall upon them and eat them.

Ewan and I are in the parlor now. It has got comfy at last. Daff is asleep on his pet rocker. My chilblains have ceased from troubling. A north-east snow storm is howling outside. I fear we are going to be blocked up. But we have a roof over us, a house not colder than most barns, and plenty to eat. We might be worse off. Let us be cheerful and apply Nyal's Mentholatum.

Sunday, Jan. 18, 1920
The Manse, Leaskdale
Zero again. Went not forth as it was too cold to take Stuart out and it was Lily's turn to go. I finished copying Volume One of my journal today. I have found it an interesting task. Writing it, much more than reading it, brought

back all the past very vividly. I seemed to be living it over again as I wrote it day by day. The next volume will not be so pleasant—at least the first part of it, for it deals with my engagement to Edwin Simpson. I heartily dislike the thought of "re-living" that, even in illusion.

Saturday, Jan. 31, 1920
Leaskdale, Ont.
This has been a *damnable* day. Bitter cold—20 below zero—and a sharp east wind blowing; a gray, wintery world; chilly house, worry over some matters connected with the Page Co. and this book of old stories they are bringing out—and a persistent dull headache which even aspirin did not relieve. The headache made everything else harder to bear, for it prevented me from indulging in my usual solace of imaginary adventures.

This power of mine has been all that has saved me many times in my life from absolute break-down. I can imagine things so vividly that it seems to me almost exactly the same as if I were *living* them, and it has the same, or largely the same stimulating physical effect on me as the real adventures would have— I really thrill and glow and delight and exult—and so I have always been able to escape from "intolerable reality" and save my nerves by a double life. It is a power for which many a time I have been profoundly thankful; but when I have a headache, or any too-insistent worry, I lose it—I can still imagine things in an intellectual way, so I might compose a story but I can't *live* them, and so I get no good effects from them—no antidote to the numbing grayness and monotonous discomfort.

Had two letters, one from Stell, and the other from some unknown, sixteen-year-old worshipper who addresses me as "Dear Wonder-person." The letter, full of girlish enthusiasm and hero-worship, was a pleasant antidote to Stell's usual compound of growls and egotistic complaints about trifles.

January goes out tonight. It has been the coldest January on record in Ontario. I think there were no more than three days when the mercury was above zero. And Arthur Mustard on the side road has been quite positive that we would have a thaw *yet*. "I've never seen a January without a thaw and I've seen hundreds of them!" he averred. But he has seen a thawless one at last.

There is one bright spot in all this gloom—Ewan has been *much* better these last two weeks. He seems almost well except that he has occasional spasms of headache—or rather of the nervous discomfort in his head which it is convenient to call by that name. It is possible that he will soon be entirely well again I must hope it, at least.

This evening I was looking over an old blank book in which I used to copy little quotations and epigrams that took my fancy. Some of them are really very good; this, for instance:—

"In that curious compound, the feminine character, it may easily happen that the flavor is unpleasant in spite of excellent ingredients."

Most true—and just as true of masculine as feminine I think. How many excellent men and women I know, most excellent and good and moral people in whom the flavor is unpleasant—or, which I think is really worse still, in whom there is no flavor at all. And some quite wicked folks have a delightful flavor. Who was responsible for the mistakes in mixing pray? Did the cook nod?....

Oliver Wendell Holmes says a lot of wise things. "A woman would rather talk with a man than an angel any day."

Of course she would! Why not? For one thing, she wouldn't know what to say to an angel. She couldn't talk the gossip of heaven and it is inconceivable that he would be interested in that of earth—or even in tidings of new discoveries and uplift movements. For, myself, I am sure I should be extremely uncomfortable with an angel. But I have not yet found anything much pleasanter than talking with the right kind of a man—except—but I won't write it. My descendants might be shocked....

"It is not everybody" says Charlotte Bronte, "even among our respected friends and esteemed acquaintances, whom we like to have near us, whom we like to watch us, to wait on us, to approach us with the proximity of a nurse to a patient."

No, not everybody—very, very few. No wonder the gods of old always veiled themselves from humanity. And what torture it is to have people come too near us—physically, mentally, socially—who don't belong to our household of faith.

Barrie says many good things. Here is one of his which has always appealed especially to me. "The keenness with which she felt necessitated the garment of reserve which they who did not need it for themselves considered pride."

No one ever said anything truer than that. If we feel very keenly we *have* to wrap our feelings from sight. To betray them, blood-red and raw, would be indecent. The world despises you if you show it your feelings—and hates you if you don't!...

"Our natures own predilections and antipathies alike strange. There are people from whom we secretly shrink, whom we would personally avoid, though reason confesses they are good people. There are others with faults evident enough beside whom we live in content, as if the air about them did us good."

Bronte again. She was a wonderful psychologist. But she only put into those clear words what we have all found and realized—and what none of us can explain. "As if the air about them did us good." Oh, excellent comparison! I wonder if, in verity, people don't give off subtle exhalations of personality which affect their atmosphere. There is a girl in our church against whom I can say nothing—against whom nobody can say anything; yet I am uncomfortable in a room if that girl is in it and want to get out if possible. She has a stronger effect on me in this way than anyone I have ever encountered—and I have met at least a round half dozen to whom I have felt this apparently causeless and certainly inexplicable antipathy....

"Life," says "Ouida" in one of her novels, "never gives two opposite sets of gifts to the same recipient: it never bestows both the king's dominion and the peasant's peace." Amen! One cannot have imagination and the gift of wings, along with the placidity and contentment of those who creep on the earth's solid surface and never open their eyes on aught but material things. But the gift of wings is better than placidity and contentment after all.

In Olive Schreiner's *African Farm*—which long ago was one of my wonder books—is a very fine and unforgettable paragraph on love:—

"There are different species of love that go under the same name. There is a love that begins in the head and goes down to the heart and grows slowly; but it lasts till death and asks less than it gives. There is another love that blots out wisdom, that is sweet with the sweetness of life and bitter with the bitterness of death lasting for an hour. *But it is worth having lived a whole life for that hour*.

There are as many kinds of love as there are flowers; everlastings that never wither; speedwells that wait for the wind to fan them out of life; blood-red mountain lilies that pour their voluptuous sweetness out for one day and lie in the dust at night. There is no flower that has the charm of all—the speedwell's purity, the everlasting's strength, the mountain-lily's warmth; but who knows whether there is no love that holds all—friendship, passion, worship?"

Yes, I think there must be a love which embraces them all—but it is rarer than a blue diamond. Most of us have to content ourselves with far less. I have loved different men in vastly different ways; but I have never loved any man with the whole force of my nature—with passion and friendship and worship. They have all been present repeatedly but never altogether in any of my loves. Perhaps it is as well, for such a love, in spite of its rapture and wonder and happiness, would make a woman an absolute slave, and if the man so loved— the *Master*—were not something very little lower than the angels I think the result, in one way or another, would be disastrous for the woman.

And yet—such a love might be worth disaster. One would always have its memory at least. My own love for Herman Leard, though so incomplete, is a memory beside which all the rest of life seems gray and dowdy—a memory which I would not barter for anything save the lives of my children and the return of Frede.

So there you are! Who knows?....

Ruskin says,

"Taste is not only a part and index of morality—it is the *only* morality. The first and last and closest trial question to any living creature is 'What do you like?' Tell me what you *like* and I'll tell you what you *are*."

Well, let us see. What do I like?

I like my own children and all nice, fat, clean babies anywhere. I like *all* kinds of books if they're well written whether they are religious or philosophical or sentimental or cynical or humorous or exaggerated or indecent. I like writing books myself. I like cats and horses and some dogs. I like curling breakers, woods and mountains and stars and trees and flowers. I like nicely furnished houses. I like good Victrola records and the music of the violin. I like pretty china and glass and old heirloom things. I like a cosy bed and a tight hot water bottle. I like to be kissed by the right kind of a man. I like jewels and pretty clothes. I like doing fancy work and I like cooking and I like eating the nice things other people cook. I like motoring and driving and walking. I like a systematic life with occasional dashings over the traces. I like open fires and moonlit nights. I like nice chatty letters. I like compliments. I like to see a person I dislike snubbed. I like my own looks when my hair is dressed a certain way. I like a snack at bed time. I like going out to dinner. I like helping other people and I like to be very independent of help myself. I like sunsets and pictures and sea bathing. I like keeping a journal. I like reading old letters. I like housecleaning—I *do*! I like entertaining the race of Joseph. I like day-dreaming. I like going to concerts, good movies and plays. I like—or used to like before I wedded a minister—dancing and playing whist. I like reading the Bible—most of it. (I like the folk-lore of Genesis and the drama of the Exodus and the gorgeous furnishings of the tabernacle and the doings of the kings and the good maledictions of the Psalms and the warm imagery of the Song of Solomon and the cynicism of Ecclesiastes and the worldly wisdom of the Proverbs and the idyll of Ruth and the blazing fire of the prophets and the wonders of Jesus' teaching and the poetry of Revelations.) I like listening to good sermons. I like gardening. I like good spruce gum. I like my husband. I like people to like me. I like a good joke. I like rainy days. I like old homesteads. I like people who agree with me. I like chocolate caramels and Brazil nuts. I like—or liked in pre-prohibition days—Miss Oxtoby's dandelion wine. I like perfumes. I like a little gossip with carefully selected people. I like shopping at Eaton's.

There now, Ruskin, tell me what I am....

Tuesday, Feb. 3, 1920
In copying my old journal tonight I found the following passage. Writing of having drifted away from old beliefs I said, "I have not yet formulated any working belief to replace those I have lost."

Since those days I *have* formulated a belief—or rather one has seemed to take shape within my mind slowly and relentlessly as experience and comparison and reflection have forced me to certain conclusions. I *know* quite clearly what I believe but I have never yet reduced it to black and white. Let me see if I can do so now.

I believe in a God who is good and beautiful and just—but *not* omnipotent. It is idle to ask me to believe in a God who is *both* good and omnipotent. Given the conditions of history and life the two things are irreconcilable. To believe that God is omnipotent but *not* purely good—well, it would solve a good many puzzling mysteries. Nevertheless, it is a belief that the human soul instinctively shrinks from. Well, then, I believe in God who is good but not omnipotent. I also believe in a Principle of Evil, equal to God in power—at least, at present—opposing hideousness to His beauty, evil to His good, tyranny to His justice, darkness to His light. I believe that an infinite ceaseless struggle goes on between them, victory now inclining to the one, now to the other. So far, my creed is the old Persian creed of the eternal conflict between Ahrimanes and Ormuzd. But I did not take it over from the Persian. My own mind has compelled me to it, as the only belief that is in rational agreement with the universe as we know it.

I believe that if we range ourselves on the side of good the result will be of benefit to ourselves in this life and, if our spirit survives bodily death, as in some form I feel sure it will, in all succeeding lives; conversely, if we yield to or do evil the results will be disastrous to us. And I admit the possibility of our efforts aiding to bring about sooner the ultimate victory of good.

That victory will come—perhaps not in the time of our universe—perhaps not for the duration of many such universes—but eventually evil, which is destructive, will be conquered by good and remain in subjection for age-long duration. Perhaps forever; and perhaps all eternity devoid of *all* evil would be tiresome even to God, who, like us, may find in struggle a greater delight than in achievement—a greater delight in contest with his peers than in unquestioned supremacy over vanquished foes. Perhaps alternate light and darkness—the alternate waxing and waning of evil must follow each other through the unnumbered, the innumerable eons of Eternity, even as night and day follow each other in our little system.

This is my creed, it explains all which would otherwise puzzle me hopelessly; it satisfies me and comforts me.

Orthodox Christianity says reproachfully, "Would you do away with my hope of heaven?" The hope of heaven is too dearly balanced by the fear of hell and the one thing implies the other. I believe in neither: but I believe that *life* goes on and on endlessly in incarnation after incarnation, co-existent with God, and Anti-god, rejoicing, suffering, as good or evil wins the upper hand. To me, such an anticipation is infinitely more attractive than the dull effortless, savorless existence pictured to us as the heaven of rest and reward. Rest! It is a good thing; but one does not want an eternity of it. All we ask rest for is to gain fresh strength for renewed effort. Reward! Even in this life reward once tasted, soon loses its flavor. Our best reward is the joy of the struggle.

Saturday, Feb. 14, 1920

This has been a week when, as far as my personal bit of life goes, Ahrimanes has been in the ascendent. On Wednesday Ewan came down with his old foe, neuritis, in back and shoulder, and has been lying helpless in bed ever since, unable to move an inch without agony. Wednesday and Thursday I was very miserable myself with a slight attack of flu. Yesterday was a really dreadful day. Lily and Chester came down with flu. I was hardly able to drag around, do the work, and wait on the sick and helpless. Fortunately Mr. Warner did the outside work, feeding horse and hens etc. so I did not have to go out. It was a bitter-cold, dull-gray day spitting snow. So was to-day. I got no sleep last night with Chester and tonight Stuart is taking the flu. I am worried constantly over the Page affair, I am ill and tired. I have spent four lonely desolate evenings when I think I would have gone quite crazy if it had not been for old Daffy, who cuddled up to me and purred, "Take a brace. We've weathered many a storm together and we'll weather this one." Really, the cat was no end of a comfort to me. I would get a nurse to help out if only one could be got. But such a creature is unobtainable owing to the prevalence of flu everywhere. Half the people in the congregation are down with it.

I had a letter from Mr. Rollins to-day but I have not yet opened it. I shall leave it till tomorrow. If I can get some sleep to-night I shall not be so nervous and so easily upset and shall be in better shape to face whatever news or opinion it contains.

The Page matter is briefly this: George Page told me in 1919 that they did not have copies of the 1912 versions. In December last he wrote me, giving me notice according to our agreement, that they were going to publish the stories in 1920 and informed me that they had "found" their copies of the 1912 versions after all and would use them. I instantly saw that I had been tricked. They had those stories all the time—I know that now perfectly well—but did not dare to tell me so because they knew I would not let them use them without my revision. Now they claim the contract gives them the right to use these stories.

I did not want these stories to be used for two reasons. In the first place Anne is mentioned in two or three of them, and this will be a violation of my agreement with Stokes; in the second place there was a good deal of material in those versions which did not appear in the original magazine stories. When Page sent these stories back to me I used this extra material in my following books; and now to have a volume of stories come out apparently repeating this material will make me ridiculous. So I put the matter into Mr. Rollins' hands and will bring suit if necessary to prevent the Pages from publishing that book from any MSS except the MSS I authorized. What scoundrels they are!

Sunday, Feb. 22, 1920

I sent for the doctor for Stuart last Sunday for I was afraid the child was developing pneumonia. But he is better and I think we are all improved. Lily and Chester are up. Ewan's neuritis is better but he is very dull and depressed. The weather has been exceedingly cold and Mr. Rollins writes me that Page refuses to be good—which means that they are going ahead with the book. I feel very draggy but have sought to while away the dismal hours by reading Prescott's "Conquest of Mexico." Cortez was a wonder of determination and "grit." But to what end?

I am blue and disheartened.

On Friday I went in to Toronto and saw *Anne* on the screen at the Regent. It was a pretty little play well photographed but I think if I hadn't already known it was from my book, that I would never have recognized it. The landscape and folks were "New England", never P.E. Island. Mary Miles Minter was a sweet, sugary heroine utterly unlike my gingery Anne. *Matthew* was a dear but totally unlike the *Matthew* of the book. *Marilla* was a commonplace female who says *"Ain't"*, instead of the dour, rigid *lady* of my conception. A skunk and an American flag were introduced—both equally unknown in P.E. Island. I could have shrieked with rage over the latter. Such crass, blatant Yankeeism!

The play has had an enormous success and I don't get a cent from it!! Well, I wish the Pages joy of it.

I came home yesterday morning and was nearly frozen. Rollins writes advising me to take no action until the book is really published. I would prefer to go ahead at once and settle the question of their right or no right.

Friday, Feb. 27, 1920
The Manse, Leaskdale

Rose betimes and got my fires on in furnace and range because all had gone out in the night. Lily and I between us have had to "run" the furnace this winter because Ewan has gone to bed at 8 and stayed in bed till 11 or 12 next morning all winter. His strange indifference to his duties as man of the house is one of the symptoms of his malady. Lily seems better today but can't do anything yet. I managed a chapter of Book Ten and got on fairly well.

I had a letter today from a man in the U.S. who felt it laid upon him to write and tell me that he had been dreaming "Patrick Grayfur" was alive, said P.G. being the cat in "The Story Girl." Also a letter from some pathetic ten-year-old in New York who implores me to send her my photo because she lies awake after she goes to bed wondering what I look like. Well, if she had a picture of me in my old dress, wrestling with the furnace this morning, "cussing" ashes and clinkers—if not aloud, in my heart—she would die of disillusionment. However, I shall send her a reprint of my last photo in which I sit rapt in inspiration—apparently—at my desk, with pen in hand, in gown of lace and silk with hair just-so—Amen. A quite passable looking woman, of no kin whatever to the dusty, ash-covered Cinderella of the furnace cellar.

Wednesday, March 3, 1920

Cold keeps. Ewan is home and seems much better. Lily is slowly improving. I suppose we shall get through somehow. But "getting through" is not living. I go through the days now, dreading a 'phone ring, because I am expecting a wire any day saying that "Further Chronicles of Avonlea" is published. And if that happens I am in for another lawsuit—for I will not let the Page Co. put a trick like that over on me and get away with it scot-free. Yet I loathe the thought and whenever the 'phone rings I turn cold with apprehension....

Tonight I finished copying that part of my journal dealing with Herman Leard. It is a relief. I will not be further tortured by the upleaping of fires that have long seemed only white-ashes.

Friday, March 12, 1920

....Something I was copying in my old journal made me think of Pensie Macneill tonight. Poor Pensie! We were such chums in those dear childish days. I thought she acted strangely to me at the time of her marriage and after she went to New Glasgow I did not see her often. She died about eight years after her marriage of tuberculosis, having literally worked herself to death. The summer before she died I talked with her at her old home where they were having a family reunion of children and grandchildren. I spoke to her about her looking so thin and advised her to take things easier and give herself a chance. "Oh, Maud, my life is broken," she said pitifully. I went to see her one evening shortly before her death and we talked over all our old merry times. She did not then know she would not recover but I knew it and the knowledge made our evening a rather ghastly farce to me. "Friend after friend departs."

Sunday, March 14, 1920
Leaskdale, Ont.
Two more hard days—to-day especially so. Yesterday the house was so cold I could not write. A letter came from Mr. Rollins. I knew there was fateful news in it of some kind and dared not open it till bed-time, lest it unfit me for work. After I had had my final "rassle" with the furnace I read it. It contained a copy of a letter to Mr. Rollins from Mr. Nay, Page's lawyer, stating that the Page Co. would use the 1912 versions and fight the matter out. I had expected nothing else but the certainty was a blow. I could not sleep all night and today has been very hard for me. Ewan seems not so well again and made a mess of preaching. I feel pessimistic and discouraged, but a good cry tonight has helped a bit. Tears generally relieve. It is when I am too worried to cry that I have the hardest times. Well, well, cheer up. "Even this will pass away." The lane *must* turn sometimes—but it has been a long one indeed.

Monday, Mar. 15, 1920
The Manse, Leaskdale, Ont.
Some questions Chester asked me to-day reminded me that in our class at Prince of Wales College one day, the question of being able to move the ear by voluntary action of the muscles came up. The professor said that animals all possessed it but human beings, as a general thing, had lost it. Then he had all the members of the class try it. Out of the big roomful were only two who could "waggle" their ears—myself and a Trainor or Kelly scion of Irish blood. I can still do it quite easily. Am I then a case of atavism? It is a disgrace or a gift to be able to wiggle your ears by their own muscles? Anyhow, it doesn't seem of much use to me. I don't suppose I could paralyze Page's lawyer by suddenly shaking my ears at him!

Friday, April 9, 1920
There is no longer any doubt—or hope. Page has published the book from the 1912 versions. I have wired to Rollins to proceed. I feel I am foolish—I fear my chance of winning is not good, considering the unscrupulous character of the men I have to deal with. They will swear to any lie they safely can. I will likely lose and throw away a lot of money. But there is *something* in me that *will not* remain inactive under injustice and trickery and to satisfy that I am driven to this. Besides, the Page Co. need a lesson. They have traded for years on the average woman's fear of litigation and the fact that very few authors can afford to go to law with them, especially when they can't expect to get money out of the result. They have done the most outrageous things to poor authors who can't afford to seek redress. I want to teach them a lesson, even if I can't obtain my rights. But I hate the thought of it all. Fortunately it will not take long—not more than a day or two, Mr. Rollins says. So the agony will

be short if sharp. Really, the worst aspect of the case to me is that I will have to come into the presence of Lewis and George Page again. I despise them so—I shrink from their atmosphere as from pollution. It is painful to think of them—how much more to be in the same room with them. But I can surely endure it for a day or so.

Saturday, April 10, 1920

Page sent me a copy of the book to-day—"Further Chronicles of Avonlea." It is got up to resemble the Anne books in every way and is an evident attempt to palm it off on the public as an Anne book. They have put a red-haired girl on the cover as appears on all the Anne books—another evasion of the terms of our agreement. But everything is so skillfully done that it will be very hard—impossible, I fear,—to bring it home to them. They have also mangled one of the stories by crude interpolations, in one of which a character is made to do an absurd and impossible thing. This reflects on my literary skill. But what else could one expect of such a firm? I was a fool ever to let them have the stories in the first place. I did it to oblige them—and this is the result.

Friday, Apr. 23, 1920
The Manse, Leaskdale, Ont.

It is one o'clock. I have been up all the evening writing business letters, after a busy day of papering Chester's room. Ewan was very poorly up to yesterday but seems much better since. Probably the crisis of this attack is over. But I suppose others will follow.

I had a letter from Cavendish to-day in which the writer said that Uncle John was tearing down the old house. It gave me a nasty pang. Yet it might as well be—it was falling into ruin. Yet—that dear, old, beloved spot—my old room— to go into nothingness! It cannot be helped—it is foolish to feel it—but it hurt someway—just as it would hurt to see the body of one we loved destroyed though the soul be gone. But is not life one pang after pang?

Sunday, May 2, 1920
Leaskdale, Ont.

There is nothing to say about to-day except that it was fine and cold, that I went to church, and that I am going to bed now at nine o'clock for the sake of getting warm.

Tuesday, May 4, 1920

Today I wrote a chapter of my book, house cleaned, and attended the W.M.S. Had a very nice letter from an English school teacher about my books. Tonight I spent an hour copying my old journal. Something in it reminded me of old post-office doings in Cavendish. There is no post-office there now—naught but post-office boxes strung whitely along the roadsides. Much more convenient, no doubt. Yet I think something is lost in the way of friendliness. At least, I was always glad that we kept the post-office—even apart from the assistance it was to me in sending away—and getting back!!!—MSS. in secrecy. Hardly anyone would ever have come to the house if we had not had the post-office. As it was, in the evenings, especially the winter evenings, the neighbors would come in for the mail and stay to talk politics and news with grandfather and each other around the old kitchen. Occasionally, too, a boy friend, who would never have dared to come otherwise, ventured to linger for an hour or so and chat to me. Pensie and Amanda used to come on summer nights and furnish an excuse for me to get out for a walk, "going a piece with them"—"down the church hill" and up "as far as David's gate" with Amanda, or "down to Will Laird's gate" with Pensie.

Wednesday, May 5, 1920
A letter from Stella to-day tells me that she is pregnant. Now for months of wildly complaining letters!

But I'm sorry it has happened. Stella is not young and it may go hardly with her. In spite of everything it would make a big blank in my life if Stell should go utterly out of it. This will be a dull worry all summer now. Well, what is life but worry—my life anyhow? I've never been free from it since I was twenty—never will be free from it again I suppose. If it is not one thing it's another. The only thing to do, I suppose, is to "carry on" and play the game.

Sunday, May 9, 1920
Leaskdale, Ont.
Have been reading Byron's *Life*. Don't like the man as well as I like his poetry—for *I do* like Byron's poetry very much. It thrills some chords in my being as no other poet can do. Byron is out of fashion—but he is immortal for all that. Passion is always immortal and he touched too poignantly all its notes, of spirit as well as sense, ever to be forgotten. But his letters make a disagreeable impression on me. They give me a sense of unreality and posing. And his life—what a series of tragedies it was! For himself and the women entangled in it. He was a being of storm-cloud and lightning flash—beautiful, ruinous, transient.

Friday, May 14, 1920
Had a wire from Rollins to-day, saying that the case will come up May 20. So I must even hie me to Boston. Fortunately I won't have to stay long. Rollins says the case won't take more than a couple of days. I would hate to have to be long away from home and my dear boys....

Thursday, May 20, 1920
East Braintree, Mass.
I left home last Monday and reached Braintree on Tuesday night. Yesterday I conferred with Mr. Rollins and today our case opened. I was in the witness stand most of the day. Page's regular lawyer, Mr. Nay, could not—or would not—take the case and they have a Mr. French—a very able fellow and a "trick" lawyer. I don't think he found me so easy a subject to handle as he seemed jauntily to expect at first. I dislike the man: he is a cad; Judge Fox

called him down very sharply once for something he said to me. But he rouses a combative instinct in me—and that is well. I can fight well when I am goaded to it. From to-day's developments I rather fear the case will take some days longer than we thought. But if I get home by June 1st it will not matter. I am tired tonight—a nervous tiredness that will not let me rest.

Friday, May 21, 1920
The case goes over to a Master. Mr. Rollins gave George Page a drilling to-day. They have suppressed a certain letter of mine which George Page swears was destroyed at my request—an absolute lie. The suppression will not do them any good, no matter how they camouflage it.

Tuesday, May 25, 1920
East Braintree, Mass.
Had a tedious day in court. Yesterday Rollins was cross-examining George Page all day but as French "objected" to almost every question and the two wrangled it out to the Master nothing got very much "forrarder." George Page told a few more lies. I used to think he was not quite so conscienceless as Lewis but I find I was mistaken. When court closed I went out to Concord Square and spent the night with Alma Macneill. Had a nice time but under it all felt the strain of worry. Also, a recalcitrant tooth had begun to bother me.

Our case did not go on to-day as the Master had to have the day off for some reason or other. So I came home and spent the day nursing a bad cold, a bad tooth and a bad worry.

Friday, May 28, 1920
East Braintree, Mass.
I have heard of "the maddening delays of the law." Now I am experiencing them. Yesterday morning I wakened at four o'clock and threshed the case over in my mind till six—as if that would do any good. But I cannot help it and occasionally an idea of some importance crops up in the welter of my thoughts.

I went in yesterday and found that Mr. Mellen was still ill and no likelihood of the case going on this week. The delay is getting on my nerves. I can't eat at all and am beginning not to sleep....

Wednesday, June 2, 1920
East Braintree, Mass.
Couldn't sleep till late and wakened early. Had a very hot, intolerable day but tooth is better so I begin to hope I'll escape ulceration. An ulcerating tooth and a lawsuit together is a very bad blend. Rollins 'phoned at one that they must get a new Master as Mr. Mellen cannot go on with the case. This means heaven knows how much more delay. I felt almost despairing. But I read and crocheted alternately the rest of the day. I have got a set of Maupassant's works from Mr. Dobson. One wearies of his "eternal triangle" but in some respects

his style is very wonderful. But he is obsessed by sex and cannot write about anything else.

This evening I am very upset and nervous. I feel a childish, impatient desire to be *free from worry* after such a continuance of it. I'm just a baby tonight, that is exactly what I am. Only I'm doing all my howling and kicking and squirming inwardly. Outwardly I smile and talk to Flora on the weather and to Amos about future punishment—a theme on which he seems to like discoursing. Future punishment, indeed! I am more concerned with present punishment. God knows we are all punished enough in this life for our misdeeds. Only—it seems to me that it is *weakness* that is punished—not *wickedness*. The weak suffer—the strong go free. The Pages are the scamps in this affair—they have cheated and lied right through—yet they are not worrying over the case I'm ready to wager—never think of it except academically. I know I am foolish to do so either. After all, no matter how the suit goes, the consequences will not be very dreadful. But I cannot help it. It is the uncertainty of when I am to get home that is worst. And the whole business is so distasteful to me—French reacts upon me as a rattlesnake would. I hate and fear him.

Friday, June 4, 1920
East Braintree, Mass.
Went in as usual. I am sick of that train ride and loathe the sight of East Braintree station. Court opened again today. Master Sampson seems to be a nice gentlemanly man but I have an idea that he is rather narrow and literal. George Page was in the chair all day and Rollins screwed some rather important admissions out of him. I have had no word from home for several days and I have a half frantic feeling about the children.

Besides I keep worrying over the days when French will begin to cross-examine me again. There is no reason why I should worry. I have nothing to tell but the truth. But in this case so much—everything in fact—depends on mere memory. And it is so hard to recall exactly everything that happened in those long negotiations of 1919, just as and when it happened.

Much of the misery of my life—just as much of the pleasure—has been caused by my habit of living everything over beforehand. It is never half as bad—or half as delightful—when it really, comes. When I finally find myself in the chair with French glaring insultingly at me I know I shan't mind it at all, my spirit will flash up at his challenge and I shall thrust and parry vigorously. But this knowledge never seems to help me much beforehand. I feel just now as if I *couldn't* face next week.

Monday, June 7, 1920
East Braintree, Mass.
I have had to take veronal these last few nights to get any sleep at all but such sleep is very unsatisfactory. We had only a morning session of the court to-day as the Master had to be absent in afternoon. George Page admitted a certain important allegation of mine in his evidence. Nevertheless, I felt blue until, as

we left the courtroom Rollins astonished me by saying, "I think we've won our case. I was afraid we couldn't get Page to admit that."

Rollins should know—but it seems to me that we are very far short yet of having established our case. The Page defence is yet to come and Rollins doesn't even yet know their capacity for lying as I do. Nevertheless his opinion cheered me up and I came home in a better mood and pleased Flora vastly by being able to eat some supper. It is three weeks since I left home—and it seems three years.

Tuesday, June 8, 1920
East Braintree, Mass.

I slept well last night for which praise be. But to-day was unsatisfactory. Most of the time was wasted by French and Rollins wrangling over the admissibility of certain questions and it did not seem as if we made any progress at all. Rollins is depressed again,—thinks "the Master's mind doesn't get his—Rollins'—ideas." I worked hard all my spare time to-day tabulating certain statements for evidence. When I came home I found a card from Lily saying that Ewan had not gone away after all. This worried me. I had spoiled Ewan's vacation—and he needed it so badly. I felt as if I couldn't endure this on top of all my other worry so I fled to my room and had a good howl.

Thursday, June 10, 1920

Yesterday George Page swore to some rather dreadful lies. How can he? I used to think Lewis was the champion liar of the firm but George can equal him. To-day I had to go on stand and Mr. Rollins examined me. In a way I dread his examination worse than French for of course *he* doesn't arouse my fighting instincts and I am so afraid of getting mixed up in my many recollections of 1912 and 1919 and all the different revisions and MSS. of those wretched stories. Yet Rollins says I am an excellent witness and make a good impression on the court. That may be—but I always leave the stand feeling that I have made an incredible ass of myself and smeared everything up. Then when I get Miss Dowd's typed report and read it over it seems quite unbelievable that those clear-cut and definite statements can be mine.

So I came home, tired, worried, miserable, unable to eat or think of anything but myself in the chair tortured and badgered by French—disgraced—put to

"Home again"

shame—all especially absurd. I know he cannot do it—but still I am obsessed with a sort of hypnotic terror that he can.

Will I *ever* get home? That peaceful, vine-hung manse and green, maple-shadowed lawn seem an unattainable heaven just now—something I'll never see again. The truth is, I'm very far from normal just now and as a result I have lost every particle of my sense of proportion. This case looms up before me in grotesque exaggeration, shutting out everything else from my view. I *know* this—but I cannot *feel* it—and consequently I am obsessed.

Friday, June 11, 1920
Had to take veronal again last night. I hate taking it but I cannot face the ordeal of the day without some sleep. I spent to-day in the chair examined by Mr. Rollins. French raged and uttered vain things but we got our evidence in. Mr. Rollins' persistency and imperturbability are things of wonder to me. I never saw anything like his poise. Nothing disturbs it—he never shows the slightest impatience or irritation, even when French is acting in a fashion that would aggravate a bronze Buddha. When, after a long wrangle, the Master decides against him, Mr. Rollins, instead of striding madly about the room, as does French, bows and says suavely, "Very good. I'll try again," and proceeds to ask the very same question in a different form, until finally French is wearied out and the Master appears to think, "I may as well save time by letting that question in, since this man will keep on until he does get it in somehow." In this respect Mr. Rollins is admirable. But in other respects I fear he is hardly a match for French. He has not as good a memory for one thing and cannot anticipate and prepare for the moves of our opponents as does French. It is certainly all amazingly interesting—this battle of wits—and if I were not the toad under the harrow I should enjoy it. But as it is I am conscious only of the torture.

After court closed Mr. Rollins said, "I think we have them on the run," but I feel he is too sanguine.

I lunched to-day on a glass of milk because it could be easily swallowed. The heat and crowds in the South Station were dreadful tonight and I had to wait a long time for a train. Got so homesick and *children sick* that I could scarcely endure it.

Monday, June 14, 1920
After a veronal sleep I went to Boston and was cross-examined by French all day. As per usual, when fairly "up against it" I could fight well—without nervousness or fear. I came home exhausted but not so worried and spent the evening reading Maupassant. I wonder if he believed that there was *one* decent woman in the world. Well, he died insane—so his point of view on life is not to be taken too seriously.

Wednesday, June 16, 1920
East Braintree, Mass.
Court did not sit yesterday—another delay—so I slept well, and went into Boston through this damp, muggy morning, going as usual down that pretty, lovable little woodland path to whose appeal I cannot respond. French cross-examined me all day and got nothing for his pains. Mr. Rollins says he never saw a better witness than I am. He is blue, however, because he thinks we won't get much in the way of damages. I don't care a hoot whether we do or

not. I want to get an injunction against that book and teach Page a lesson in square dealing. But I see no prospect of the case being concluded this week and I came home frightfully depressed over the prospect, or rather the no-prospect of getting home. Guess I'll never get there. For the rest of my life I must get up at 6, trot down through the woods to that East Braintree station, go to Boston court-house and be put to the question by French. At least that is exactly the way I feel.

Friday, June 18, 1920

Yesterday was a public holiday so there was no court, but I had to go to Boston to mail an important letter as the p.o. here was closed. On return found a wire from Ewan saying that all were well, not to worry etc. But I felt very restless and near absolute collapse. Had veronal sleep last night and went to Boston this morning in a pouring rain. French grilled me all day but didn't advance much. Rollins says he went back. Those three grave lawyers and myself wrangled all day over the question of the exact color of *Anne's* hair and the definition of "Titian red." Ye gods, it was funny! The big table was snowed under with literature and prints to prove or disprove. Years ago, when I sat down in that old kitchen at Cavendish, that rainy spring evening, and dowered *Anne* with red hair, I did not dream that a day would come when it would be fought over like this in a court room. It would be deliciously amusing—if it were not so beastly horrible. French was determined to prove that Titian hair was dark red and that I knew it was dark red. I didn't. I always supposed Titian-red was a sort of flame-red and I stuck to it through all his badgering. Rollins dug up an encyclopedia in which Titian hair was defined as a "bright golden auburn" and the Master said it had always been his impression that Titian hair was the hue of burnished copper! And so on!

The *raison-d'etre* of all this is the red-headed girl's picture on the cover of the book.

Mr. Rollins and I went to see the big Ringling circus tonight—I having never seen a circus. It was worth seeing—though having seen it I don't fancy I'll ever want to see another. The animals were good. There was a magnificent Bengal tiger pacing restlessly and endlessly up and down.

I know exactly how the poor brute felt!

Tuesday, June 22, 1920

All day yesterday and the forenoon of to-day I was on the stand. Then my torture was intermitted for a time and Mr. McClelland took the chair, having come down to witness in my behalf in the matter of damages. Lewis Page came into court for the first time—to hear what Mac would say I presume.

When we left the court a deputy served a writ upon me to the effect that the Page Co. meant to sue me in September! As there is nothing else they can sue me about it must be for "false and malicious litigation" in the present suit. Rollins says they can do nothing and as I have had plenty of experience of their empty threats in the past it does not really worry me. They want to frighten me if possible into a compromise. They shall not do it. I'll fight them all the more determinedly for such a contemptible proceeding. Rollins seems to be amazed that "a reputable lawyer like French" would do such a thing. But it is my opinion that there is very little French would not do if he thought he could get away with it.

Nevertheless, the incident has added a little more to my discomfort. There is always the possibility that Lewis Page, who is the most vindictive man on earth, will go to any extreme, even if he knows he goes to certain defeat, in order to inflict worry and vexation upon me.

I lived on "milk shakes" all day. I've forgotten what it is like to feel the slightest desire for food.

Wednesday, June 23, 1920
East Braintree, Mass.
Even veronal could not make me sleep past three last night. When I went in Mr. Rollins said, "I have been thinking over the matter and I think I can promise you you won't have any serious trouble."

"Anyhow," I said, "I am not going to let them bluff me into surrender." "You are a good fighter," said Rollins. "After a summons like that you came here this morning looking as pink and pretty as if you hadn't a care in the world."

You see, I don't tell Mr. R. of my sleepless nights and nervous unrest. But I'm *not* a good fighter—or I wouldn't feel so. I'm only a good bluffer. I sailed into the court-room, bowed coolly to French, flashed a gay smile and "good-morning" at the Master, laughed and jested aside with Miss Dowd. French and the Pages did not find me flattened out, if they expected it.

McClelland was cross-examined this morning and French made mince-meat of him. I have been wondering why Rollins persisted in regarding me as "a splendid witness" until I saw a solid, middle-aged business man like McClelland go all to pieces under cross-examination. I feel he has done our cause more harm than good. It was Rollins' idea to send for him. I had a feeling against it somehow but gave in. It would, I believe, have been better if I hadn't. The court did not sit this afternoon.

Thursday, June 24, 1920
Had a good cry last night and as a result slept well. Nothing like a good howl for calming distracted nerves. Mr. Morrow came on from New York to-day and testified. French could not rattle or brow-beat *him*. In the afternoon I went on the stand again. French tried to trap me twice with two inordinately long and involved questions, the meaning of which was fearfully hard to follow. But I saw the trap and avoided it. That man is a fiend. Nevertheless, he is the right sort of a lawyer to have if you want to win. I do not really think Rollins is a match for him.

I continue to feel worried and depressed—though only about not being able to get home. I have ceased to care whether the case is lost or won. My whole summer is spoiled—and Ewan's, too, which is worse. I had planned to spend August on the Island but I'll have to give that up. After having wasted all this time down here I can't go away again—supposing I ever *do* get home.

Friday, June 25, 1920
East Braintree, Mass.
I was again on the stand all day. Hitherto I have kept my temper amid all French's grilling but to-day he made such an insulting remark that I flared out in anger. "I will not allow you to make such a statement to me, Mr. French," I flashed out at him. And Mr. French, realizing, I suppose that he had gone too far, muttered a sort of apology and dropped the subject. Rollins says the Master flashed a quiet smile of enjoyment at him during this passage at arms. French isn't popular with other lawyers and they rather enjoy his discomfiture. Rollins was pleased as Punch today over some change in the Master's point of view which he had discovered. I am not enough of a lawyer to grasp its significance and should not have considered it worth getting excited about. But I came home tired completely out. Those hateful, crowded streets—that hateful South Station! I fear my *morale* is giving way completely. Soon I won't even be able to "bluff." The thing that I can't bear is the wretched uncertainty of how long I must be here. If I only *knew*—if I could only say, "I must endure to a certain date"—I *could* endure it.

Tuesday, June 29, 1920
Got through to-day by help of bromides. Mrs. Hayden and Mrs. Stone were here—friends of Flora. The latter is a thin, Christian Science lady, wearing three necklaces, who asked me dreamily if I "ever worked against mental trouble?"

I did not ask her to explain the process!

I wonder what effect the Christian Science methods would have on French! Let me see. Evil does not exist—French is evil—therefore French does not exist!

What could be clearer?

I think it would be fine to see Mrs. Stone in the witness box, cross-examined by French. No, it is cruelty to animals even to think about it.

Wednesday, June 30, 1920
East Braintree, Mass.
At last my acutest martyrdom is over. To-day French finished cross-examining me and Rollins closed our case for the present. The defence opens tomorrow. I want to go home but Rollins thinks it is of extreme importance that I should hear the evidence for the defence. So I must stay a few more days longer. Then I suppose I'll be able to get home—but I don't believe it.

July 1, Thursday, 1920
French opened his defence to-day, with three witnesses. One of them told two point-blank lies. But we have no means of *proving* them lies and Rollins regards it as "dangerous testimony" unless we can break it down in cross examination and seemed blue. The witness swore that I *was told in his presence* during the

1919 negotiations that Page had found most of the 1912 versions but not all. This is an absolute falsehood. George Page told me distinctly that all they had were newspaper copies. I remember, too, though I did not catch the significance at the time, that he made the statement when and where nobody but myself could hear him.

I came home blue, and worried all the evening. I am in such a bad state that, in spite of my wild longing to be home, I have at the same time an odd feeling of *dread of going home*—of having to take up my routine duties again while feeling quite unfit to cope with them.

Friday, July 2, 1920
East Braintree, Mass.
Rollins was flat this morning—so flat that he said he did not believe it would be profitable to fight the case longer and suggested we ask for a compromise. I vetoed this flatly. I told him I did not care whether we lost the suit or not. I would fight it to the end and pay the piper cheerfully rather than humble myself to the Page Co. So Rollins acquiesced and we went up to the court-room. He crossed the witness, with the result that the latter went to pieces, floundered helplessly, and "couldn't remember certainly" about anything—couldn't say anything more than that it was "probable" I had been told Page had the 1912 stories. So, Rollins says his testimony will not be so damaging after all and is quite encouraged again. He also extracted another bit of important evidence from another witness. Lewis Page was in the chair in the afternoon and told a few lies too many for he contradicted George flatly on some rather significant points. I simply cannot understand how even he could sit there before me and tell the atrocious lies he did.

Tuesday, July 6, 1920
Court sat this afternoon and Lewis P. reeled off a few more perjuries. Mr. Rollins says I can go home on Friday. I don't believe it. I shall have to stay here forever beyond any doubt!

Wednesday, July 7, 1920
I couldn't sleep till late last night but for the first time since coming here my thoughts were pleasant and normal—and what a delightful sensation it was! I slept till it was time to get up and went to Boston feeling a *faint enjoyment* of external things once more. Lewis Page was in the stand to-day again and Rollins thinks he got some important things out of him.

There will be only one day more of it for me. I am afraid to believe this—for fear something happens again to prevent it—and *that* would break me all into little bits. I should "vanish, leaving not a rack behind."

This is dear little Chester's eighth birthday—and I am away again. Last year Ewan and I were both away. I got him a little wrist watch for a present.

Thursday, July 8, 1920
East Braintree, Mass.

I felt *afraid* of to-day and literally trembled with dread as I went to the court-room, lest something happen that I could not get away. Lewis Page was in the stand and we were treated to an odd outburst. Evidently I am not the only one who has "nerves." When Mr. Rollins was questioning him he stood somewhat near Lewis. All at once the latter bounded to his feet, his face suffused with passion, and exclaimed,

"Mr. Rollins will you have the goodness to stand further away from me. Your personality is so offensive to me that I cannot endure to have you standing so near me"!

The whole scene was peculiar. I have become convinced that Lewis Page's mind is not sound. I would not be surprised to hear at any time that he had become quite insane. He is certainly not normal.

The matter of *Anne's* red hair came up again and was re-threshed.

Rollins was greatly encouraged by to-day's developments. But I have made up my mind that the suit is lost and I am not going to think about it any more. All I want is to get home to my children.

"Blessings on thee, barefoot-boys!"
[*Stuart and Chester*]

When four o'clock came Lewis Page and Brother George and their precious French went out, and as their backs disappeared I breathed a fervent prayer that I might never see their faces again.

I came back to Flora's, feeling that I had scrambled out of Hell, though the reek of the pit was still upon me. I came up the little path through the woods and found it sweet and friendly and alluring. This evening I spent happily packing up and preparing to go home. I have a strange, dream-like sensation that I am going back to a place I lived many years ago. It would not surprise me at all if I found on getting home that Chester and Stuart were grown up!!

Saturday, July 24, 1920
Leaskdale, Ont.

The first few days of this week were hard. I seemed to be as neurasthenic as ever and Ewan was miserable again. Then I just suddenly got well and have been so ever since. I don't worry about the case—I eat and sleep well—and to-day I wrote a chapter of my book and found that I could get on all right. When I discovered that all other worries ducked under cover and I am my own woman again.

Thursday night just when Ewan and I were both feeling very rotten, Captain Smith motored in and in no time had us both cheered up. There seems to be something infectiously healthful about his personality—you simply *catch* optimism from him. He stayed all night and we had a very pleasant evening. He and his family are living at Whitby now, so we can be neighborly, as it is only 30 miles away....

Captain Edwin Smith

Monday, July 26, 1920
The Manse, Leaskdale

I am keeping well. And I seem to feel so deeply now the peace and rest of my home after that hideous strain in Boston. It is like heaven. Ewan seems well and in fairly good spirits. Last night he remarked that he felt better than he had for a long time.

Had a charming letter to-day from some Miss O'Connell of Washington, D.C.—who vows she isn't a Sein Feiner—telling me that her father at 85, a retired U.S. army officer, enjoys my books so much and is at present afraid that he won't live long enough to read the next one! I suppose uncharitable people would say the poor old gentleman is in his dotage! But I prefer to think otherwise and feel happy in such a compliment.

I had another letter from a little U.S. girl, asking the old, old question, "Is Anne a real girl?" I must have been asked that literally a thousand times since *Green Gables* was published.

Sunday, Aug. 1, 1920
Leaskdale, Ont.

....Laura told me an item of gossip tonight which at first made me inclined to rage and utter vain things. Then my sense of humor got the upper hand and I laughed instead. She and Bertie once met Aunt Hattie at some social function in Vancouver and the lady gushingly informed them that *she* was the inspiration of *Anne*!!!

This is atrociously funny. Aunt Hattie, that cold, shallow, childish, selfish, hopelessly uninteresting woman, whom I have always detested and who alternately snubbed and ignored me during her few visits to Cavendish during my childhood and girlhood, the "inspiration" of *Anne*!! I cannot imagine two beings more hopelessly different in every respect. Poor Aunt Hattie! Her vanity was always patent and egregious but I should scarcely have supposed that even she could imagine that she was Anne.

Ewan has been miserable enough these past three days.

Monday, August 16, 1920
The Manse, Leaskdale, Ont.

Laura and family went away today after a very pleasant visit. Laura and I had a good time. Mac is a dear little fellow and was beloved of Chester and Stuart, but Miss Pat is an *enfante terrible* and my hand has yearned to spank her with no uncertain spanks. I was truly thankful to see the last of her and her freaks and tantrums.

"Laura and I"
[*Laura Aylsworth*]

I have had an exceedingly strenuous fortnight of visiting and being visited, picnics, barn-raisings, funerals, missionary meetings and guilds. Now I hope to settle down to quietness and peace and get in some good work on my book. I am at the twenty eighth chapter now and ten more will finish it, I hope. I loath writing against time like this.

It seems to me that my life nowadays is simply one mad rush to overtake work that "must be done" in a dozen different departments of existence and that I never "catch up", leaving me with a sense of breathlessness and failure that is depressing. I cook and sew and mend and train my children and write novels and endless letters, and run three societies and make innumerable parish visits and garden, and advise and can berries and encourage Ewan and entertain endless callers and shop and plan menus and take snapshots all mixed up together pretty much as enumerated, with countless interruptions thrown in, and undercurrents of worry over several things running all the time. Sometimes I feel quite desperate. I get up at seven and generally work until twelve at night. Then usually my sleep is broken by E's unrest or some little need of the children. I think something must change—or bust! Well, once my book is done I *will* take a little rest.

Sunday, Aug. 22, 1920
The Manse, Leaskdale, Ont.

Last Saturday morning, while I was writing in the parlor Lily came in and said that Daffy was over at Mrs. Leask's *dying*. I tore madly over and up to their barley field where my heart was nearly broken to see my dear old pet lying limply on the stubble. I thought he was already dead but when I gathered his chilling body up in my arms he opened his eyes and mewed faintly. I thought he had been poisoned but when I got him home I discovered that he had been shot—accidently by some ground-hog hunter, no doubt, as there is nobody round here who would do it purposely. He lived for two hours while the children and I hung over him in an agony of tears. Then he died. There are not many human beings who are mourned more sincerely than he was. To me it was a real tragedy—the last *living* link with the old life was gone. Daffy was not a cat—he was a *person*, and had more individuality than seven out of ten human beings. He was fourteen years old last spring—the age limit for cats. But, except for a little slowness in the matter of a jump, he showed no sign of age and would, I feel sure, have lived for several years yet if he had not been thus done to death. He was with me through all the most vital years of my life—the years of my literary "arrival", the years of marriage and of my children's birth. I miss him woefully. He had so many favorite spots according to the season that this place seems haunted by him. Everywhere I look I see Daff. When I came home from Zephyr the other night there was no big gray cat waiting for me on the back platform and running nimbly before me to the door, as Daff always did. I could not keep the tears back as I came in alone. I have had him so long I cannot realize that he is dead. We buried him behind the asparagus plot on the lawn—old Daff, with his plumy tail, his distinctive markings, his wild glowing eyes—my old companion of days and nights of long ago, my faithful furry comrade through the many lonely evenings of the past two years. I feel a sense of desolation and loneliness. Ewan says, "Get another cat." I don't want another cat. No cat can ever again be to me what Daff was. One day when Laura was here I showed her the snapshots of Frede, Miss Ferguson, and Daff, taken together on the walk and I said "Only Daff is alive now of the three." *Now* they are all gone— those three who were here that happy summer day eight years ago. Frede loved old Daff so—I think I loved him doubly for her sake. "He was a cat—take him for all in all / We shall not look upon his like again."

Good-bye, Daffy, old friend.

I am writing furiously at my book these days and getting on pretty well.

Stuart came to me to-day and announced that he had "made a poem." When I asked what it was he responded,

"Who did that?
It was Oxtoby's cat."

Well, it rhymes, anyway. Stuart has not begun with *vers libre*. May he never finish with it. *Vers libre* aggravates me beyond my powers of expression.

> I feel
> Very much
> Like taking
> Its unholy prepetrators
> By the hair
> Of their heads
> (If they have any hair)
> And dragging them around
> The yard
> A few times,
> And then cutting them
> Into small, irregular pieces
> And burying them
> In the depths of the blue sea
> They are without form
> And void,
> Or at least
> The stuff they produce

Is.
They are too lazy
To hunt up rhymes,
And that
Is all
That is the matter with them.

Tuesday, Aug. 24, 1920

To-day I wrote the last chapter of "Rilla of Ingleside." I don't like the title. It is the choice of my publishers. I wanted to call it "Rilla-My-Rilla" or at least "Rilla Blythe." The book is fairly good. It is the last of the *Anne* series. I am done with *Anne* forever—I swear it as a dark and deadly vow. I want to create a new heroine now—she is already in embryo in my mind—she has been christened for years. Her name is *Emily.* She has black hair and purplish gray eyes. I want to tell folks about *her*.

And I want—oh, I want to write—something entirely different from anything I have written yet. I am becoming classed as a "writer for young people" and that only. I want to write a book dealing with grown-up creatures—a psychological study of one human being's life. I have the plot of it already matured in my mind. The name of the book is to be "Priest Pond." If I had only time to go to work on it—time and leisure. But I haven't as yet. The boys are too young—there are too many insistent duties calling me—I can't give up my profitable "scrics" until I have enough money salted down to give the boys a fair start in life—for my "real" novel will not likely be a "best seller."

Monday, October 18, 1920

How can a month have slipped away so fast?....In September I had a letter from Mr. Rollins in which he said French had filed a declaration of suit for "malicious litigation," but added that I need not worry as he was tolerably sure it would never come to anything. That remains to be seen. I know what the vindictiveness of Lewis Page is.

We have had a wonderful autumn—more like summer than autumn. I do not remember anything like it—warm golden days and summer-like nights.

Thursday, Dec. 2, 1920
The Manse, Leaskdale

I left home on Tuesday Nov. 3 for P.E. Island, having decided to run down for a brief visit to see poor Aunt Annie. I reached Breadalbane on Friday night which I spent with the Stirlings. Margaret and I sat up and talked most of the night, having a very hilarious time as of old. The next day I motored down to Park Corner.

It was in some ways a very painful experience. To be there without Frede or Stella—to know that Frede would never be there again. I felt like a ghost, revisiting a world I had once lived in, with no fellow-ghost to keep me company. There was *nothing* of the old life left, except Aunt Annie. The house is full of youngsters who call me "Aunt Maud" and look at my diamond rings and my silks and laces as I used long ago to look at those of the city aunts who came to visit us in Cavendish. To them I am a somewhat fascinating mysterious outsider from an unknown world—*not* anyone who belongs to Park Corner....

When I reached home I found both Chester and Stuart down with whooping cough *and* chicken-pox. Fortunately they are not very bad with either.

Saturday, Dec. 11, 1920
The Manse, Leaskdale
Have just returned from Chatham, whither I went on Wednesday to give readings from my books to the Women's Canadian Club there. I had a delightful time and met some very nice people. When I rose from my seat on the platform to begin my readings the whole large audience rose to its feet. The tribute thrilled me—and yet it all seemed as unreal as such demonstrations always seem to me. At heart I am still the snubbed little girl of years ago who was constantly made to feel by all the grown-up denizens of her small world that she was of no importance whatever to any living creature. The impression made on me then can never be effaced—I can never lose my "inferiority complex." That little girl can never believe in the reality of any demonstration in her honour. Well, perhaps it is just as well. Likely it is very effective in keeping me from *developing symptoms* of *swelled head*.

Monday, Dec. 13, 1920
Leaskdale, Ont.
I began writing again to-day after a holiday of two months. I have begun to collect material for my "Emily" books and I also want to do a few short stories and some verse. Poetry was my first love in literature and my deepest. I enjoy writing it more than anything else.

To-day I finish reading Mrs. Asquith's autobiography. No wonder it has set English society by the ears. I don't see how she dared. But the book is *real* and so is very intriguing and interesting. But there is nothing vital in it. I doubt if it will live when the generation it castigates or betrays has passed away.

Mrs. Asquith's analysis of herself has been much commented on by reviewers. Some praise it highly. Others say it is not so frank and thorough as it claims to be. I agree with the latter. I do not believe any human being can—or would if he could—make a thorough and absolutely frank analysis of himself or herself. Even if one could be sufficiently detached to be able to do it one wouldn't. There are some faults that we all are willing to acknowledge; some that the frank ones among us will acknowledge and *some* faults—I believe in *everyone*—which nothing would induce us to admit. I do not think one person in a thousand sees or knows his own real faults—and perhaps his own virtues. But the thousandth *has* the power of *getting outside* himself and *looking on* at himself as at another person, and he *does* know himself in weakness and strength.

I believe I have such a power myself. But I could not, even in these diaries which no eye but mine ever sees, write frankly down what I discern in myself. However, I will go as far as I can and endeavor to do what Mrs. Asquith has endeavored to do—describe and analyze myself. It will be amusing and interesting.

I will begin with myself physically. I am of medium height—about five feet five inches, but somehow usually impress people as being small—probably because I am delicate featured and have been, until lately, very slight. My feet are quite large in proportion to my size—I wear number fours—but they are said to be "perfectly shaped" and I have a high instep and a good ankle. My figure has generally been described as "neat." I hate the term but I believe it is true. Lately I have been filling out and getting plump. My hands are exceedingly small. I wear a 5¾ glove but could wear 5½. If my hands were plump they would be very pretty, but they are too thin for beauty, especially when I am cold. *Then* they are absolutely scrawny. When I am comfortably warm they look plumper and being white and soft have sometimes been complimented. But they are not pretty hands. I use them a good deal in conversation and I believe my gestures are animated and graceful. I have pretty, well-turned delicately made wrists but my arms and elbows are too thin.

My hair was golden-brown in childhood but turned very dark brown when I grew up. It has quite a few gray hairs in it now but not yet enough to destroy the dark effect. It has always been very long—quite to my knees—and thick, although in late years influenza and maternity have thinned it somewhat. It is absolutely straight but has been noted for its gloss. When it is dressed properly my head looks very well-shaped.

My complexion has always been good, though at times rather pale. When I am excited I flush up, sometimes even to crimson. My skin is very soft and fine and when I was a girl my nose was freckled. My forehead is too high but I have good arched eyebrows. My eyes are not beautiful in color, being a grayish blue, but the lashes are long, the expression good. By artificial light the pupils always dilate and people who meet me then go away and assert that I have dark eyes. It is a family peculiarity. Bertie and Laura MacIntyre have it, too. My lids when down-dropped are pretty, and so I have always passed as having beautiful eyes which I really have not. I have been accused of "making play" with my eyes but I never do this consciously.

My nose, viewed from the front is not bad, looking quite straight, but in profile it is poor, being crooked. My cheek bones are high and my cheeks slightly hollow. My teeth are very poor, being crowded, crooked and rather yellow. I do not show them very much, except when I laugh. Then I show my upper gum—very unbecomingly. I have a very small mouth—the smallest mouth I ever saw. It is red, pretty, and "sweet" but I do not like it and would have preferred a larger one. My chin is small and pointed. It does not recede but it is rather a weak chin. My ears are quite good.

And what of the general effect of all these features? Well, it varies tremendously. When I have my hair dressed becomingly, drawn low over my forehead, and am excited enough about something to redden my cheeks and darken my eyes I candidly state that I believe I am a very pretty woman and have been told so times without number. On the other hand when my hair is combed off my forehead, plain and straight I am not even good-looking. Now a really pretty woman is one who looks pretty at all times. So I am not really pretty. I only *look* pretty when I am properly "done." Old rose and salmon, pinks, creams, and yellows become me in colors and I look well in black, brown and navy.

My enemies accuse me of being "fond of dress." The charge is perfectly true. I am very fond of pretty dresses, hats and jewels and cannot enjoy myself if I do not feel well-dressed. I don't like to be in any company where anyone is better dressed. I do not feel happy when I am *alone* if I am not prettily dressed. I am especially fond of lace, pearls and diamonds.

I am not bad-tempered and never go into rages but I am inclined to be impatient when people or things don't "measure up" to my ideals and then I say sharp things—which I am immediately sorry for and worry over afterwards. I am easily hurt by my friends and am not as wholly indifferent to what those outside my circle think and say of me as I would like to be. I am not easily offended but when I am I never forgive. I withdraw myself with a cold dignity and avoid the offender contemptuously henceforth. I would never seek to inflict revenge on anyone who had injured me but I do not feel sorry when fate does it. I am entirely free from deceit and it hurts me to pretend to anything. I hate ructions and disturbances and I go too far and yield too much to avoid such things. I would never knowingly hurt a friend's feelings. I am very loyal in my real loves and friendships and very intense and passionate—too much so. I am too extreme in all my feelings. The pleasures of sense make a very strong appeal to me but have always been kept in check by a certain fastidiousness of choice in me and by the fact that it is only one man in a thousand who has any appeal for me. I have strong will and a determined ambition. I am very persevering. I believe I am naturally truthful but I can tell a lie without worrying over it when people meddle in what isn't their business. I am distrustful of people and suspicious of their motives. Externals make too deep an impression on me and have too great an influence over me. I am jealous in so far that I cannot bear to have anyone I love love another better than me but I am not jealous in regard to other matters. In thought I am independent and would be so in action if it did not injure anyone dear to me. I am energetic and systematic. I am inclined to worry too much over certain things. I am keenly sensitive to all forms of beauty. Ugliness inflicts anguish on me. I have a keen sense of humor and am a fairly good conversationalist with certain people. With others I am dumb. I am reserved to the world, but very frank and open to real intimates. I can hide my real thoughts, feelings, and opinions very skilfully when I want to. Perhaps this is why there are so many different opinions of me floating about. I like the admiration of men. I like luxury and leisure, though my ambition has always spurred me to hard toil and unceasing activity. I dislike change and am very conservative. Yet I am not bound by conventions. I am physically a great coward, intellectually quite fearless; morally about half and half. I am petty and small in some ways and quite big and generous in other ways. I am very impatient of any control.

"I walk where my own nature be leading,
It vexes me to choose another guide."

I am not vain or conceited but I am very proud. I am too much given to acting on impulse and I attach too much importance to unimportant things. I have a keen sense of justice, both in regard to myself and to other people. I want to "play fair" but I want others to play fair, too. And I want to win the game. I have no self confidence and have always been greatly hampered by this. I am very healthy in body and mind. I have a very vivid imagination which has been a great blessing and also a great curse. I dread physical pain terribly, yet when it comes I seem to bear it tolerably well. I can see quite clearly into people—or *feel* quite clearly, since my understanding of them seems to be more of intuition than of mind. My feelings are very easily touched by the distress or suffering of others. I hate to inflict suffering on others, yet when I am keenly annoyed I can say very cruel things. I like to rule—to be "boss", yet not enough to fight for it. I have a remarkable memory but as for reasoning power—I don't know. I was a dunce in geometry, a star in algebra, fairly good in arithmetic. I am a good sewer and a good cook. I want to do everything *well* or not do it at all. I am lacking in equanimity and moderation. I am generally in a turmoil of some kind of feeling—joy, sorrow, worry—and I am inclined to go to extremes in everything though maturity has toned this down somewhat or rather controlled it to some extent. I can't haggle over bargains. Mr. Rollins said I was a good business woman but I am not. That is, I am theoretically, because I can see clearly but I lack some stamina or backbone necessary to standing out for what I see. I think my "inferiority complex" is to blame for this. The idea at the back seems to be that my merchandise can't really amount to much and I ought to be thankful to take what people give for it. In childhood I had very deep religious instincts but I do not seem to possess them now. I am not in the least spiritual—that is, in the ordinary meaning of that word. I am a good, intelligent and patient nurse in sickness, except when anything offends my stomach and then I am useless. But I do not like nursing. I am tolerant of almost anything except deceit, deliberate cruelty, and bad manners. I have better manners in company than I have at home.

Well, that is all I can think of now except a few things which I know quite well of myself but which nothing would induce me to admit. I wonder how this analysis would compare with one which an *unprejudiced* person who knew me for many years would write. But that, I suppose, is a comparison which will never be made.

Monday, Dec. 27, 1920

This morning a wire came from Lowry Keller saying that Stella had a son the day before Xmas. I am much relieved as I had been feeling very anxious about her. I hope her child will make a difference in her outlook on life generally and divert some of her monstrous egotism into other channels. Her letters this past year have been awful.

The baby is named Ewan Campbell. When Stell was here last fall she and Ewan made a crazy compact that the "first boy" was to be called after him. Stella did not then expect she would ever have any children but the unexpected has happened and she has kept her "agreement."

1921

Sunday Jan. 16, 1921
The Manse, Leaskdale

This has been a busy, typical average week. For my own amusement I jotted down in my note-book a detailed account of my doings throughout the whole week. I will copy it here. My descendants may read it with interest and my great-great-grandchildren may use it as a peg on which to hang compassionate opinions as to what country ministers' wives did back in the old-fashioned days a century ago!

Last Monday morning I rose at 7.30 and dressed by lamplight—a thing I always hate to do. There always seems to me something dismal about getting up before daylight. Luckily, with the lengthening days there will soon be an end of this. And luckily also the house was warm. We have good coal at present—and so we have had no real winter yet. So it is a heartening difference from last winter—that most hideous winter of all my winters here.

Having dressed and got Chester up and dressed—a more strenuous proceeding still—I went downstairs and prepared his school lunch and after breakfast got him off to school. He is, I think, getting on pretty well at school and likes it pretty well—better than I did at his age. He has quite a long distance to walk and the school is small and the teacher a very commonplace young girl. But at his age this does not so greatly matter. He is an inveterate reader and reads far more mature books than I did at eight years. And he has more books than I had when I was eighteen—a whole bookcasefull. I have given him a good many and Mr. MacClelland very generously sends him many new volumes. Stuart and he read together and learn the poems that take their fancy, and then spout them at all times and seasons until we are sick and tired of them. At present they are at Drummond's "Leetle Bateese", quite undaunted by its dialect, and they say it very well. I have to answer about a thousand questions per day in regard to every subject concerning this world and the next. Chester having gone, I washed the breakfast dishes as I always do every wash day. Then I gave Stuart his writing lesson. He reads so well, having practically picked it up by himself, that I no longer give him reading lessons. Then I "tidied up" all over the house, arranged the books in Chester's bookcase, mended a torn cushion, and sewed for half an hour at an underskirt I am making—a false economy of the "penny-wise-pound-foolish" kind. It would pay me much better financially to put the time on my writing. But there are some things in me, inborn and confirmed by long years of necessary, careful economy lang syne; and one of them is an inveterate hankering not to waste anything. I had a good, full, old-fashioned skirt of shantung silk with embroidered design. As a skirt I could no longer wear it but the material was excellent and I could not resist the urge to make use of it.

Then I got the vegetables ready for dinner and dressed for visiting. After dinner we drove to Uxbridge where I did a lot of shopping and then dropped into the Hypatia Club for half an hour. I enjoyed this. I am a member of that club but rarely can get down to its meetings. After leaving Uxbridge we went to John Taylor's for tea and spent a rather dull evening, which I improved by crocheting at a strip for an afghan. I get considerable fancy work done during these pastoral visitations. Fancy work is something I never touch at home now. I am, as always, very fond of it and it reconciles me to the many deadly tedious evenings I have to spend thus. Nevertheless I grudge them. It would be so delightful if I could have the time thus wasted for reading or a little recreation. For it is wasted. Nobody is done any good to. The vanity of the family so visited is appeased or flattered—*they* have not been overlooked by "the minister and his wife." That is all. Why then do we go—or why do I go? Well, my reason is this. If I did not go they would be rather "sore" and they would visit it on Ewan as well as on me. They would begin to find fault with him and the end would be that he would either be unhappy here, or have to leave. Now, Ewan is not the type of minister who finds it easy to get a new congregation that would suit as well as this. He always makes good as a pastor, once he is scttlcd, but to gct settled is a different matter—thanks to the absurd and abominable system the Presbyterian church has for settling its ministers! How I hate the thought, either of his getting discontented here, or of his having to go somewhere we might not like to go. So in order to do all I can to prevent this I visit as much as I can to keep them in good humor and pleased with their slaves of the manse.

When I came home from the Taylors at 10.30 I had a bad half hour of rebellion over certain things. Then I recovered my self-control and went to bed at 11.

Tuesday—early rising as per usual and Chester's lunch made ready. Then, with due housewifely care I took a batch of hams out of my pickle barrel and put a fresh batch in—neither a romantic nor a tragic proceeding. But I am fond of ham and one cannot live on tragedy and romance, so somebody must do the pickling. Then I put away the purchases of the preceding day and shut myself up in the parlor to write for two hours. Then I put the house in order and dressed. After dinner I walked up the hill to Mrs. Jas. Blanchard's where the W.M.S. met. When it was over I came home, mended for half an hour, wrote a little, helped Chester with his home work, taught Stuart a recitation for Guild and gave him a lesson. After supper I wrote a paper for Guild on "The Duty of Saying Pleasant Things," wrote letters to Clara and Bertie, copied my old journal until 9. Then read Grote's *History of Greece* until bedtime.

Wednesday morning: Rose at 7.30. Got ready Chester's lunch and tidied house. Then I made a crockful of brine for pickling tongues and wrote two hours. After which I did mending, sewed for an hour, copied journal, wrote a letter and dressed.

At supper we had a domestic laugh. Lily was having a squabble with Stuart—she has "a poor way" with children—and finally said pettishly, "Well, I'll leave you to your mother. She'll have to straighten out your manners." Whereupon Chester, who always sides with Stuart when the latter counters Lily, remarked gravely "I think my own manners have a *slight curve*."

After supper I put the boys to bed, read to them as usual, then went to Guild and read my paper. The work in the Guild is not as pleasant as it was in our first years here. Then we had quite a fine class of young people in their twenties. They had considerable initiative and helped us a good bit. These have all married or gone. The Guild we have now is composed of young people in their teens and they seem unusually giddy and entirely lacking in aspiration. I don't decry young folks for wanting and having a good time. But they seem to care for nothing else. I can't discern any germ of anything else in the lot we have now. And there is not to be found the two or three superior ones who sometimes leaven a whole society. They all seem to be on a dead level of dullness and vapidity. I came home at 9.30 more or less discouraged, and put a lot of old hens, which Lily had killed and dressed, into a tubful of salt and water to be ready for the next day's canning. Then I read Mrs. Browning's poems for half an hour and had an anguish of my own special brand for a time, too.

Thursday:—Rise at 7.30. Chester's lunch and house as usual. Then Lily and I spent the forenoon cutting up the aforesaid old hens and packing the pieces into glass sealers. After which I sorted out my linen closet, mended several things, made a saucepanful of cranberry sauce, and cleaned the fragments of meat off the boiled hen carcases, out of which the fragments I concocted a very nice "jellied chicken" mould for supper. I spent the afternoon in attending to the canning of the hens, thus transmogrifying them into "canned *chicken*"—and prepared all the ingredients necessary for a big fruit cake; hemmed a pair of pillowslips, gave Stuart a lesson, copied old journal, sent a batch of MSS away to be typed, and then read from 9 to 10.30 in Mrs. Wharton's "The House of Mirth." "And so, to bed."

Friday:—Rise and make rise; C's lunch; Hang up hams for drying, tidy house, compound fruit cake, bake it in afternoon with gratifying success. Then I did a lot of odd jobs, wrote up the minutes of the W.M.S., sewed half an hour, gave Stuart lesson, wrote a letter, copied journal, read half an hour, put boys to bed, read to them, and then, everybody being out of the way, I painted the library door which has needed it for some time. I was through at 8.30 and rested from my labors and read till bedtime.

Saturday I could sleep blissfully till ten to eight and there was no small boy's lunch to prepare. I put my fruit cake away, turned my hams and tongues, wrote two hours, got lunch for Ewan who was going away, washed a bunch of embroidered doilies, and dressed. After dinner went to Mission Band. Got home at four, peeled a tongue I had previously boiled, ironed doilies, sorted out a trunk of stuff upstairs, entertained a caller, got the children to bed, blacked the family shoes, wrote a letter, wrote in journal, and read rest of evening—what little "rest" remained.

This morning we slept till 8.30. Lily was away—it was stormy—Chester had a headache. So I thought I could brave public opinion by staying home all day. I did, and wrote letters and read and got the meals. So endeth the week. I am done as I always am these winter evenings. Ewan is rarely home. Since his illness he seems not to care, or be able, to read much, as he used to do, and generally goes out to visit someone in the village. If he is home he goes to bed. So I sit alone, not even having old Daffy for company now—alone with books and dreams. For I dream still—I must or die—dream back into the past and live life as I might have lived it—had Fate been kinder. I cannot dream of the future now—I dare not....

Monday, Jan. 17, 1921
The Manse, Leaskdale
A hard day. In the first place I did not get much sleep last night partly owing to the tremendous wind that kept shutters and windows banging and rattling all night and partly to some physical discomfort, and got up feeling tired and nervous. In the second place, it was bitterly cold—the first real cold day we have had this winter and as a result the manse has been uncomfortable despite a good furnace fire and we have all been shivering and goose-fleshed. As Chester was not very well yesterday I thought it wisest not to let him go to school today. It was too cold for him and Stuart to go out. Usually they get on very well together but today—well, I suppose the general chilliness got on their nerves as it did on older people's and they teased and squabbled and bickered, matters being complicated by the presence of little Ruth Cook who had been sent down here this afternoon because of the arrival of a new baby at her home. Even when the three children were on good terms, they made a frightful noise and got into one kind of mischief after another until my head ached. Finally Chester had to be punished. I had, as usual, to do all the disciplining myself. Ewan has never, since the boys were born, attempted to teach or train them in any respect, not even in the truths of his religion. Everything, from morals to manners, has been left to me. It was a bitter moment in my life when I was forced to accept the fact that *all* the responsibility for the teaching and training of my children was to fall on me. I accepted and make the best I can of the situation. But the lack of the training a wise and judicious father can give is a terrible want in a boy's education and one no mother can wholly supply. Ewan is very fond of his children but his only idea in connection with them seems to be romping with them when he is disposed for it. And he has done little even of that since his trouble began. There was a time when Chester and Stuart were babies and I was finding all rapture and sweetness in motherhood, that I hoped earnestly I would have more children, and was deeply disappointed that I did not. But these past two years I have been well satisfied that I have no more. Under different circumstances I would have liked at least six children if I could have had them—but not as matters are.

Then this was the day of the annual congregational meeting and as usual Ewan came home from it blue and discouraged. I do not know if Leaskdale is worse than other rural charges in this respect—probably not. But I do know that, since I came here, there has never been one cheerful, optimistic, encouraging annual meeting. I dread the day every year and especially now when Ewan is dull enough anyway.

And now, having got this all out of my system, I begin to feel a little less pessimistic. After all, our house is generally pretty comfortable; and Ewan is never stern or harsh or unjust with his children; and our boys are hearty, healthy little chaps with no very dreadful faults, as far as they have yet developed; and there has never been any friction in the congregation between people and minister or minister's wife. So things might be worse. But I shall take a hot water bottle to bed with me tonight!

Thursday, Jan. 20, 1921
The Manse, Leaskdale
There is nothing to write concerning today. It was just the ordinary one of ceaseless work. But I feel so lonely and sick at heart tonight that I come to my old journal for comforting, as many times of yore. There is no one else I can go to. I have no friend near me to help me in any way. And if I had I could not go to her and say, "My husband is in the throes of one of his attacks of recurrent melancholia. He has lain around the house all day, either gazing into space with a wild, haunted look in his eyes, his hair on end, his very features so changed as to make him look like a stranger to me, or chanting hymns from the hymnal in a singsong way that makes me feel like rushing out of the house and screaming, so intolerable it is to me in its childish futility and still more because of the state of mind it reveals in him." I cannot say this to *anyone*. No one must know, for Ewan's sake and the children's as well as my own, what his trouble is as long as I can keep it secret. ...

Sunday, Jan. 23, 1921
Leaskdale, Ont.
Last night I read over a packet of Laura Pritchard's old letters. I had to laugh a little over some of them, in which Laura poured out her affection for me. I read the first four pages of one of them aloud to Ewan and howled over his puzzled, half-jealous question, "What fellow ever wrote such stuff to you?" It *did* read exactly like the outpouring of a very badly smitten lover!

A stranger, reading those letters, would certainly form a very unjust idea of Laura's personality and character. He would be sure to think she was a gushing, sentimental girl, whose sole ideas were dress and beaux. Nothing could really be further from the truth. Laura was really a merry, sensible, hard-working and unselfish girl; and the most of her "flirtations", like the majority of my own, were little more than a few walks, drives, and dances, well sprinkled with badinage, with the young men we met casually in society for a few weeks or months.

Laura got through with her flirtation in due time and married Andrew Agnew. They have had a very happy life together. I have not heard from Laura since 1917. Then she had five children—three boys and two girls. Her oldest son was in France. When I was down in Chatham I met a lady whose old home was in P.A. She told me that the Agnews had had business reverses and had gone to live in Saskatoon. I was very sorry to hear it. It must have been very hard for Laura to leave the lovely new home they had planned and built, and the town where she had lived all her life. But up to that time she had had a life of such happiness as few women have, I think, and it seems it is not permitted to anyone to have sunshine from first to last. In some way or another we have to pay.

I would like very much to see Laura again. She was the most dearly loved friend of my teens. But I question if we could be to each other now what we once were. Laura, from her letters, does not seem to have changed much. I have changed immeasurably. I could never now pour out to her all my thoughts and feelings as I once could. I have become too reserved to reveal my feelings to anyone. No, I don't think Laura would satisfy my demands on friendship now—not after having known Frede—not after having had my soul seared in sorrow and pain and passion for thirty years while Laura has walked only the hedged paths of happy, protected girlhood and wifehood. She would not know my language and I should have forgotten hers.

Laura (née Pritchard) and Andrew Agnew [Prince Albert, Sask.]

Tuesday, Jan. 25, 1921
Leaskdale, Ont.

Two years ago today Frede died. Two years ago! Bright, brave spirit, whither have you fared since you went out through the sunrise? Shall we meet again? Or shall we take up again "the fever called living" in new incarnations of flesh? There are some moods when this idea appeals to me more strongly than aught else. And there are other moods when I am afraid—afraid!

Sunday, Jan. 30, 1921
Leaskdale, Ont.

In writing over my old diaries I have recently copied out the "Oliver Macneill" section—and I'm afraid I laughed a bit over it—or over the memory of the frantic Oliver. He went back to Dakota when he found he couldn't get either me or Campsie. We corresponded occasionally that winter—Oliver used to send me a "much" of "poetry" he had composed himself—addressed to me and extremely sentimental. It was *not* "free verse"—*that* much could be said in its favor! Oliver could mostly find a rhyme whether it was a very suitable one or not! He also sent me a volume of poetry for Christmas—*not* his own—entitled, "To Thee Alone," and full of verses fairly reeking with sentimentality.

The next summer Oliver again visited the Island. We had a few more frantic scenes. I remember one in particular back in the woods near Lover's Lane when Oliver sat on the trunk of a fallen tree and declaimed bitterly, "I could *never, never* have believed that a woman could take such a hold on a man as you have taken on me." But I had quite recovered from the physical infatuation he had once cast over me and he could not bind the spell again. So I laughed at him and advised him to marry Lucy McLure, a second cousin of mine and a willing damsel. I did my best to make the match—the only time I ever tried my hand at matchmaking—and I all but succeeded. I think I *would* have succeeded if only Lucy had had more hair! Her scanty tresses jarred so horribly on Oliver's sensibilities that eventually he decided against her and married Mabel Lea of Summerside—one of my old Belmont pupils, by the way. His Aunt, Mrs. Allan Fraser, made *that* match and Oliver decided to take Mabel because, so he told me, she reminded him a little of me!! I never heard from or about him after his marriage.

This part of my old journal was largely written under the blight of those dreadful attacks of neurasthenia from which I used to suffer in winter. I don't wonder at it—when I recall those ghastly months of loneliness and worry and solitude. I don't quite know how I escaped with my reason. Life is strenuous enough still and holds many baffling and perplexing problems yet; but at least I do not have to wrestle with such periods of nervous agony. What should have been the best years of my life were years of such ghastly, long-drawn-out loneliness and suffering as make me shudder in the recollection.

Thursday, Feb. 10, 1921
....Last night I sat down and computed the number of dollars I have made by my pen since that day in Halifax twenty five years ago when I got my first check—five dollars for a story. The result totals up to about one hundred thousand dollars. Not such a bad total, considering the equipment I started out with—my pen and a knack of expression. If Pages had not been rogues I should have had at least fifty thousand more. But it's not so bad. It's a pity it doesn't mean happiness. But perhaps my children will reap the happiness from it that I cannot have. And perhaps they would be better off, and more ambitious and successful if they had to scramble along and struggle as I did. That seems often to be the way in this mad world.

Saturday, Feb. 12, 1921
The Manse, Leaskdale
I've had an exasperated afternoon—the result of a letter from Stell coolly demanding more money!!!

Last spring I loaned her $2,700.00 to buy a cotton ranch. She was going to make a fortune in cotton—very glowing reports—and would give me as security a joint note signed by her husband and his *brother*—said brother being a well-to-do man. They would pay me back in the fall plus interest etc. I had little faith in their success but I lent her the money for Aunt Annie's sake. She sent me a note signed by herself and her husband—worth the paper it was written on and no more, since neither of them has a cent. I was furious over such a trick but still I said nothing. They had a fair cotton crop but the bottom fell out of the market. They could not sell nor pay me any interest. Still I said nothing. Three weeks ago I had a curt cable from Stell, ordering me to send $350 to pay her hospital bills. I said "once more", for Auntie's sake, and said nothing. Today comes a letter demanding that I loan them several thousands more to enable them to hold on until "a big oil boom" makes their land worth "$1,000 per acre."!!!

Poor Stell is not in her right senses, that is all. As for me, the breaking point is reached at last. I am done with wasting money on her. She and her husband can go to work and earn money for their own financing. Counting the loans I have made Stell—not to mention the hundreds I've *given* her—and to her friends the *Howatts* at her request, I have ten thousand dollars out, from which in eight years I have never received a cent of interest, and have very little hope of ever getting even the principal back, for the security is not good and none of them have anything behind them. Ten thousand is my limit to waste money. I have written Stell a letter which may bring her to her senses. She will be furious no doubt but I am past caring. The break had to come sometime—it may as well come before I waste any more money on her, the insolent, ungrateful spendthrift that she is.

Monday, Feb. 14, 1921
Leaskdale, Ont.
Today Ewan came to me in the library, put his arm about me, and told me I had brought a great deal of joy into his life and that I was "the dearest little wife in the world." Poor Ewan. His life is gloomy enough now in the shadow of his malady; but I am glad I have made him happy, apart from that. At least, I have not failed in everything, as in my discouraged moods I am sometimes inclined to think I have.

I finished a short story today—"The Tryst Of The White Lady"—a fanciful little thing.

Wednesday, Feb. 23, 1921
The Manse, Leaskdale
Have been very busy this past week—but when am I not busy? And I should be—and am—very thankful that I can be busy—that I can plan and dovetail and overtake things. Only at night I am just a little too tired.

Lately in copying old diaries I came to "the Grey Time," as Bertie McIntyre used to call it—and laughed again over the seance Earl Grey and I had on the McPhail w.c. steps. There was a sequel to that confab which was amusing enough and which I don't think I ever wrote about in this journal. Three years later I was on the Island and came up from Uigg station with Janetta McPhail— Dr. McPhail's sister who had been there that night. She said she had always wanted to see me to tell me about it. Thereupon she did tell me the tale as follows:—

When Earl Grey and I had disappeared that evening Mrs. McPhail went to Janetta in distress, saying that she was afraid the countess was upset about something, as she was walking restlessly up and down the veranda and would not join any of the various parties of sight-seers about the grounds. Janetta said, "Oh, don't worry, mother. Lady Grey must be bored, of course, and can't find much entertainment here. I'll go and ask her if she would like to lie down a few moments before dinner."

Accordingly Janetta went to the veranda where the Countess was striding fiercely about and said politely, "I am afraid your excellency is tired. Would you like to lie down etc."

"Her Excellency" paid no attention whatever to Janetta's question. But she halted before her, took her arm in a savage clutch, and demanded in an intense tone,

"*How old a woman do you think Miss Montgomery is?*"

Naturally, Janetta was flabbergasted by such a totally unlooked-for query. Moreover, she didn't know my age; but recollecting that I had been to P.W.C. shortly after one of her brothers had been there she made a guess at it and stammered out, "I think she must be about thirty-five."

"Oh," said the countess in a tragic tone, "I had hoped she was at least forty."

And with this she dropped Janetta's arm and resumed her agitated pacing on the veranda.

Poor Janetta did not know what to do. But to her intense relief the Earl and I now hove in sight on our way back. The countess saw us also and flew down the steps and through the orchard to meet us, while Janetta thankfully washed her hands of the matter.

I remembered that the Countess had met us in the orchard and had whisked the Earl off without even a glance at me. I thought it rather odd and very rude of her, but concluded that it was probably my ignorance of the way of the English aristocracy that led me to think it so. It certainly never occurred to me that her ladyship was jealous. *My* conscience was clear. *I* certainly hadn't been trying to "vamp" the earl. I don't think Earl Grey, with his bald head and his squirrel teeth, could have flirted if he had tried. He didn't try to flirt with me, at any rate.

I howled over Janetta's story and concluded that Lady Grey—who seemed older than the earl and was certainly no beauty—must be the victim of a morbid jealousy which tortured her whenever her husband paid any attention, even of the most harmless character, to another woman. Something I heard later on at Macdonald College confirmed this. Some person, speaking of Earl Grey laying a cornerstone somewhere, remarked. "The Countess wasn't with him." Another lady said, "It's a wonder she would let him out of her sight that long." So evidently "Elsie" kept pretty strict tabs on friend husband and didn't approve of him decoying middle-aged authoresses to the steps of mysterious houses back of cherry orchards!

Saturday, Mar. 5, 1921
Leaskdale, Ont.

Most of last week I was busy reading the proofs of "Ingleside." Also had a letter from some locality called "Myrtle Station" entreating me to go down and "give a missionary address" in their (Methodist) church on Easter Sunday evening!

I declined!

Monday I went in to Toronto and stayed till Thursday doing spring shopping. Came home Thursday night and had a drive home over terrible roads of frozen mud. I wonder if I shall ever be able to live near a station. The drive was further "en-wretched" for me by the fact that Ewan said a letter had come from Stokes complaining that "*Ingleside*" was "too gloomy", and wanting me to omit and tone down some of the shadows. *Also*, subtly intimating that I had not "taffied up" the U.S. enough in regard to the war—this last being the real fault, though they did not like to say so bluntly.

Well, I didn't and I won't! I wrote of Canada at war—not of the U.S. But I have felt worried by the matter. I do not like to feel that my publishers are dissatisfied with my book. Mac liked it—said it was a good story and would sell well. This last is what Stokes doubts—and he has made me doubt it.

But I had a nice letter from Mrs. Estey, stating that Dr. Logan of Acadia University, recently lecturing in St. John, said that Canada had produced "one woman of genius"—that "L.M. Montgomery" in the opinion of eminent critics "equalled or surpassed Dickens in her depictions of child life and character."

Ha—hum! No, I'm not a genius but thank you all the same, Dr. Logan.

Mrs. Willis of Uxbridge writes me that they want me to give them an address at some cantata performance round Easter on "Jerusalem, Past, Present, and Future." I told Mrs. Willis I didn't know enough about the past or present of Jerusalem to be worth telling, and had no conceit of myself as a prophet.

Saturday, March 12, 1921
Leaskdale, Ont.

Last night Ewan and I went down to a Hypatia Club in Uxbridge. The roads were undescribable and my courage almost failed me. But I wanted to go for two reasons—I thought it might do Ewan good, for he has been very dull all the week, and as I had not had any real social evening since my Chatham visit early in December I was hungry for a "function." So I got out my little-used evening dress and went. And we had an exceedingly nice time—almost nice enough to compensate for the roads.

Had a letter from Stell today—pretty squiffy. I was rather amused. I know she was literally boiling with rage. But I am the one person in the world she doesn't dare insult or quarrel with because she owes me so much money. So she dare not give way to it and it nearly kills her. Clara writes me that Stella doesn't seem to have much love for her baby. I had thought as much from her letters. She only refers to the baby to complain of him. Stell really has no affection for anybody. Like all mentally unbalanced people she is completely centred on self. Poor creature. I had hoped that the child's coming might cure her of her neurasthenia and bring her back to normality. But it evidently has not done so—probably it came too late in life—and what is to become of her I don't know. The poor wretch who has married her has an awful life of it, so Clara says, and I can well believe it. He was wildly in love with her when he married her, completely duped by her surface jollity; but I fear he has had a rude awakening since. Poor Stell is a nightmare to us all. She is the most terrible example I have ever seen of what unchecked indulgence in bad temper and selfishness can bring a person to.

Sunday, March 13, 1921
Today I finished copying my Cavendish diary—and so seem to have come to "modern history" in my life. I have lived over those old years in thus writing them over—relived them more vividly and intensely than I have ever done in reading them. I am a little sorry that I have finished with them. The last thirteen years of my life there were certainly not happy years, and parts of them were violently unhappy. Yet there were many hours of happiness and sweetness in them, too,—the happiness of a loved work and success in that work, the happiness of wonderful communions with sea and field and wood—and I tasted this happiness again in writing over those years.

Lucy Maud Montgomery, c.1918

There are many different happinesses—and we never have them all at once—because that would be perfect happiness and that is something the gods do not allow to mortals. We have some at one period of our lives and yet others at another. Perfect happiness I have never had—never will have. Yet there have been, after all many wonderful and exquisite hours in my life.

Notes

1910

February 11 "CONSUMING THEIR OWN SMOKE". Thomas Carlyle, *Sartor Resartus*, II, ch. 6. MY FIRST TWO VOLUMES. Selections from the first two handwritten volumes of Lucy Maud Montgomery's journals are published in *The Selected Journals of L.M. Montgomery*, vol. I (Toronto: Oxford, 1985). ORMUZD AND AHRIMANES. Zoroastrian twin-deities: the lord of good (usually Ormazd) and the lord of evil. AMANDA MACNEILL. A cousin who had been LMM's closest friend in schooldays. ZODIACAL LIGHT. Faint illumination of the sky, surrounding the sun and elongated as a band of light on each side of the sun. In the northern hemisphere it is best seen at twilight in February and March. **February 19** ROYALTY CHEQUE. LMM recorded all payments in an account book, now at the University of Guelph. The total royalties for 1909 (paid in 1910) for *Anne of Green Gables* were $5396.53; the rest came from first royalties for *Anne of Avonlea*. MY NEW BOOK. *The Story Girl* was begun in June 1909 and finished in August 1910. Its heroine enchants a happy circle of cousins with tales of the Island. **March 19** KILMENY. *Kilmeny of the Orchard*, the story of an artistic girl who is voiceless, published by L.C. Page, Boston. An early version had run in serial form in the Minneapolis *Housewife* in 1908. SWEDISH EDITION OF ANNE. *Anne pá Grnkulla*, translated by Karin Jensen (Lund: Gleerup, 1909). Three other translators and three other publishers have also brought out Swedish editions of *Anne*. **March 23** ALEC MACNEILLS. Alec was a second cousin, son of Charles Macneill, and brother of Pensie, LMM's school friend. A genealogical chart of LMM's family appears in Volume I of *The Selected Journals of L.M. Montgomery*. HEATHEN IN TRINIDAD. The Presbyterian church in nearby New London maintained a mission in Trinidad, British West Indies (BWI). **March 29** FREDE CAMPBELL. Frederica, daughter of LMM's Aunt Annie (Macneill) and Uncle John Campbell of Park Corner, was a first cousin, nine years younger than LMM; she became LMM's dearest friend in the next few years. **April 4** "LOVE'S LABOR'S LOST". The title of Shakespeare's play (1598); LMM misquotes it as *Love's Labor Lost*. SAMPLERS. A square of embroidery, displaying a girl's efficiency in needlework. (LMM misspelled the word as "samplars" in the manuscript.) THICK AS AUTUMN LEAVES IN VALLAMBROSO. Milton's *Paradise Lost*, I, 1.302. **May 2** LAMBREQUINED. Draped with curtaining material. **May 23** HALLEY'S COMET. A star with a tail of gas and dust, orbiting between Mercury and Venus, appearing to observers every 76 years. The comet is named for the English astronomer, Edmund Halley, who observed it in 1682. In 1910 Halley's comet was three times closer to earth than in 1986. NORMAN WILLIAM. William the Conqueror, who defeated the English army in

1066 at the Battle of Hastings, inaccurately called the Battle of Senlac Hill by historians before 1895. "GET LEAVE TO WORK". From Elizabeth Barrett Browning, *Aurora Leigh* (1857); LMM quoted the same lines in 1900 at the time of her father's death. MY NEW BOOK. *The Story Girl*. **July 11** MARGARET ROSS. One of the three women whose names had been linked with Ewan Macdonald's by local gossip before his engagement to LMM. DR. PRINGLE. The Rev. G.C.F. Pringle (1873-1949) later collected his Yukon stories and published them as *Tillicums of the Trail: Being Klondike Yarns told to Canadian Soldiers Overseas by a Sourdough Padre* (Toronto: McClelland, 1922). UNCLE LEANDER. The Rev. Leander Macneill was LMM's uncle, elder brother of her mother Clara Macneill Montgomery. **August 14** SOPHY SIMPSON. Sister of the Rev. Edwin Simpson, to whom LMM was engaged in 1897-8. LOVER'S LANE. LMM's favourite walk, behind the schoolhouse to the Webbs' (present day "Green Gables"). **August 21** MACDONALD COLLEGE. Affiliated with McGill University and situated at Ste-Anne-de-Bellevue. Sir William Macdonald, a Montreal manufacturer and businessman, born in Prince Edward Island, in 1905 founded and endowed the College for the teaching of Agriculture, Domestic Science, and Pedagogy. **September 6** LIEUTENANT GOVERNOR ROGERS. The Hon. Benjamin Rogers (1837-1923), a long-time Liberal, had retired from active politics in 1904; he was appointed ninth Lieutenant-Governor of Prince Edward Island, 1910-15. EARL GREY. Albert Henry George Grey, fourth earl, was Governor-General of Canada, 1904-11. He urged the government under Wilfrid Laurier to strengthen imperial ties, supported drama and music festivals, and donated the Grey cup for national championship in football. CH'TOWN. Abbreviation for Charlottetown, the provincial capital, 33 km from Cavendish. "MISS FLORA MACFLIMSY". From "Nothing to Wear", a verse by the American comic writer William Allen Butler, in *Two Millions* (London: Sampson, Low, 1858): "Miss Flora Mac-Flimsy of Madison Square / Had thousands of dresses but nothing to wear." MR. [John] HILLMAN. Owner of the forge at the western end of Cavendish. **September 7** PIERCE MACNEILL. Another cousin: his house at the crossroads was the original of Mrs Rachel Lynde's in *Anne of Green Gables*. HUNTER RIVER. The nearest railway station. THE VICTORIA. A hotel in Charlottetown. BERTIE. Beatrice McIntyre, LMM's Charlottetown cousin, to whom *Kilmeny of the Orchard* is dedicated. DR. [Andrew] MACPHAIL (1864-1938). Professor of the History of Medicine at McGill, essayist, editor of *The University Magazine*, Prince Edward Islander, and Imperialist. He changed the spelling of his name from McPhail to Macphail; LMM refers to him as MacPhail. He wrote a well-known book, *The Master's Wife* (1939), about his parents and their life in Orwell. ORWELL. In the eastern part of PEI; part of this community has been restored as a tourist site. The Macphail home is now the centrepiece of the Sir Andrew Macphail Provincial Park. **September 11** AUNT MARY LAWSON. Sister of LMM's grandfather Alex Macneill; *The Golden Road* (1913) is dedicated to her. **September 16** MRS. [James] SUTHERLAND. Isabella Henderson Sutherland was an aunt by marriage to LMM's cousins Will and John Sutherland. The original entry in the journal for this date was excised and replaced, perhaps to eliminate some family gossip. UPPER PRINCE. A fashionable street in Charlottetown. JUDY

GALLANT. Member of a French-speaking community near New Glasgow. "FAL-
LACIES". Macphail's *Essays in Fallacy* (New York: Longman, 1910) comments
critically on contemporary feminism, education, and theology. CUTHBERT. Bertie McIntyre's brother; another first cousin. VERE DE VEREISH. Ultra-aristocrat-
ic; from Tennyson's "Lady Clara Vere de Vere". There is also a de Vere in
Walter Scott's *Anne of Geierstein*. JUDGE AND MRS. FITZGERALD. Rowan Fitzgerald (1847-1921) was Justice of the Supreme Court of PEI; his wife was Agnes
Tremaine Fitzgerald. PREMIER AND MRS. HAZARD. The Hon. Francis Longworth
Haszard (1849-1938), a lawyer and magistrate, led the Liberal party in PEI to
become the tenth Premier and Attorney-General, 1908-11; his wife was Elizabeth DesBrisay Haszard. MR. ARMORY. The Charlottetown paper gives this
name as "Amery". The *London Times* ran his story about Lord Grey's Charlottetown visit in its midday edition on September 15. BROCK. Reginald Walter
Brock, F.R.C.S., born the same year as LMM (1874), had been director of
Geological Survey in Ottawa since 1907. LORD PERCY. Alan Ian Percy (1880-
1930), later eighth Earl of Northumberland; aide-de-camp to the Governor
General of Canada, 1910-11. Lord Percy's mother was the daughter of the
Duke of Argyll, and his father was A.D.C. to the King. Young Lord Percy
had already served with distinction in South Africa and the Sudan. PERLE
TAYLOR. A friend from Dalhousie University days; her brother was married to
Mrs James Sutherland's daughter Marion. EARL OF LANESBOROUGH. Charles
John Brinsley, seventh Earl of Lanesborough (1865-1929), was military Secre-
tary to the Governor General of Canada, 1909-10. He had succeeded to the
title in 1905. MAYOR ROGERS AND HIS WIFE. Benjamin Rogers, Sr, wholesale and
retail hardware merchant, was mayor of Charlottetown 1910-12. He was a
nephew of the Lieutenant Governor; his wife was Mary Trenaman Rogers.
PROFESSOR MCNAUGHTON. John MacNaughton (1858-1943), born in Scotland,
taught at Queen's University (1908), McGill (1908-19), and the University of
Toronto (1919-25). COLONEL OGILVIE. Canadian military aide-de-camp. The
vice-regal party also included Dr Macrae, Mr Douglas Sladen, and the Hon.
John Agnew. PICTOU. A port in Nova Scotia, across the Straits of Northumberland from Charlottetown, PEI. **September 21** CHOLERA MORBUS. This name for
an epidemic disease (usually spread through infected water supplies and dormant since the 1880s in Canada) was LMM's hyperbole for ordinary influenza.
November 29 MR. PAGE. Lewis Coues Page (1869-1956), prominent Boston
publisher; his firm, L.C. Page & Co., at this time also published Bliss Carman,
Marshall Saunders, Charles G.D. Roberts, and many other Canadian authors.
Page had been in publishing since 1891, with his own firm since 1897. LMM
consistently refers to him as "Louis" Page; perhaps her error stems from the
fact that he signed all his letters to her "L. Coues Page". MUSSON BOOK CO. A
Toronto publishing firm, founded in 1894, Canadian agent for L.C. Page, and
for the British publisher Hodder and Stoughton. Charles J. Musson had sug-
gested to LMM that Page was not giving accurate accounts of Canadian sales.
In 1913 Hodder & Stoughton made Musson a Managing Director of their
Canadian subsidiary and in 1921 purchased the Musson Book Company. REV.
MR. GREEN. The Rev. Wm I. Green of New London was a missionary in

Trinidad, BWI. STELLA CAMPBELL. LMM's first cousin, sister of Frede, Clara, and George, and daughter of Uncle John and Aunt Annie (Macneill) Campbell. LUCY RITCHIE. Another first cousin, daughter of Uncle John and Aunt Emily (Macneill) Montgomery of Malpeque. MR. LAIRD. Farmer next door; the father of several of LMM's schoolmates. S'SIDE. Summerside, PEI, where the ferry-boats leave for Pointe du Chêne, New Brunswick. ST. JOHN. At this New Brunswick city the Canadian Pacific Railway joined the American line; the train crossed the border at St Croix/Vanceboro. ELECTRICS. The Boston subway for electric trams, which began construction in 1895, connected with surface and elevated lines; a single fare would take a passenger over 100 square miles. TREMONT TEMPLE. A Baptist church in central Boston; Cortland Myers (1865-1941) was its pastor 1893-1921. GEORGE PAGE. Like his brother Lewis, George had been in his stepfather's firm, Estes and Lauriat, and in Joseph Knight Co. THE BINDING CLAUSE. LMM's contract bound her to offer Page first refusal on her subsequent work for five years on terms established at the time of publication of *Anne of Green Gables*: 10% royalties on the wholesale price, rather than 15% on the retail price (as was usual for successful authors). DEP'T STORES. Filene's and Jordan Marsh were the major department stores in Boston in 1910. "THE CHOCOLATE SOLDIER". Operetta by Oscar Strauss based on George Bernard Shaw's *Arms and the Man* (1894). In this production the heroine's part was played by Alice Yorke, a Canadian actress. LUCY LINCOLN MONTGOMERY. An American verse-writer (no relation to LMM) who lived at 4 Jordan Avenue in Wakefield, Mass. GENERAL GOODALE. Greenleaf Goodale (1839-1915) had served in the Civil War and in the Philippines; he retired in 1903. MRS. SLOCUM. Probably the wife of William Frederick Slocum, born in 1851 in Grafton, Mass., and President of Colorado College 1888-1916. NATHAN HASKEN DOLE (1852-1935). Author of 11 books, editor of the *Encyclopedia Americana* and of many volumes of poems and letters, translator of the work of Tolstoy and others. LMM owned a copy of his edition of the poems of Robert Burns. Ten years later, Dole wrote an introduction to *Further Chronicles of Avonlea*. CHARLES FOLLEN ADAMS (1832-1918). He had been publishing humorous poems in German dialect since 1872; Page had published his *Leedle Jawcob Strauss and other Poems*. J.L. HARBOUR (1857-1931). Jefferson Lee Harbour, a native of Iowa, had been associate editor of *Youth's Companion* 1884-1901 (covering the years when LMM's first publications appeared in that journal). He was the author of over 700 short stories and was also a popular lecturer. HELEN WINSLOW (1851-1938). Editor and publisher; connected with women's clubs; author of 11 books, including *Spinster Farm* (1908) and *Woman for Mayor* (1909). ABBIE FARWELL BROWN (1860-1935). Editor of *Young Folks' Library* since 1902, and author of many books for children, such as *The Flower Princess* (1904), *Brothers and Sisters* (1906), and *Friends and Cousins* (1907). ELLEN DOUGLAS DELAND (1860-1923). Her popular girls' books included *Josephine* and *The Friendship of Anne*. BASIL KING. Born in Charlottetown, but long a resident of Cambridge, Mass., Basil King (1859-1928) was an Anglican priest who wrote a great many novels with moral themes, including *The Wild Olive* (1910). "SUMMER WIDOWERS". "A Musical Panorama in 7 Views" by Glen MacDonough and Baldwin Sloane.

CHATEAU-YQUEM. Chateau d'Yquem, a wine from the Sauternes area in Bordeaux, France. MRS. MOUNTAIN; MRS. MORRISON. Mrs Benjamin F. Mountain of Roxbury, Mass.; Mrs James Kay Morrison of Winthrop, Mass. THE CANADIAN CLUB; THE INTERNATIONAL CLUB. No longer in existence in Boston. Besides the Boston clubs, there was a Canadian Club at Harvard University. REV. MACLEOD HARVEY. McLeod Harvey was pastor of First Presbyterian Church, Worcester, Mass. "POTENT WISE AND REVEREND SIGNIORS". *Othello*, I,iii,76. (Shakespeare makes them "grave" rather than "wise".) LEXINGTON. A town 11 miles northwest of Boston; site of the first skirmish in the American Revolution, April 1775, moments before the "shot heard round the world" was fired at Concord. HANCOCK-CLARKE HOUSE. A historical museum house in Lexington, where Samuel Adams and John Hancock stayed on the eve of battle with the resident parson Jonas Clarke. LMM misspells as "Hancocke". CONCORD. 19 miles northwest of Boston, birthplace of revolutionary action; in the 1840s the home of Ralph Waldo Emerson and Henry David Thoreau. MRS. DANA ESTES. Grace Page, widow of a noted journalist and diplomat, had remarried in 1884; Estes, the founder of Estes & Lauriat publishing company, died in 1909. THOMAS WENTWORTH HIGGINSON. Dean of American essayists, author of over 30 books including biographies of Longfellow and Whittier. Page was the publisher of Higginson's *The Afternoon Landscape* and *The New World and the New Book*. **December 26** MRS. GASKELL'S NOVELS. Elizabeth Claghorn Gaskell (1810-65), novelist and wife of a minister, raised social issues in *Mary Barton* (1848), *Ruth* (1853), and *North and South* (1855). Her biography of Charlotte Bronte (1857) is also still read. MR. MACDONALD. LMM had been engaged to marry the Reverend Ewan Macdonald since 1906. After a period of study in Glasgow, and two years in churches in Bloomfield and Bedeque, PEI, Macdonald had been called to a parish in Leaskdale, Ontario, early in 1910. As a young man he signed his Christian name as Ewen, but later switched to Ewan. Both spellings appear on his tombstone. "ROMOLA". George Eliot's historical romance (1863) about the duty of self-sacrifice. **December 31** BLISS CARMAN (1861-1929). In 1910 this popular New Brunswick poet was settled in Connecticut. *The Pipes of Pan* was published in 1906.

1911

January 27 LUCY. LMM's first cousin Lucy Macneill was the daughter of uncle John Macneill. MR. WEBB. Ernest Webb (1880-1950) had married Myrtle Macneill, a grandniece adopted by David and Margaret Macneill. His house is now the Green Gables museum, the central feature of the National Park at Cavendish. THE SPECTATOR. Founded in 1828, this weekly newspaper was the most highly respected London journal of the period because of its political and literary criticism. "QUICK AS THE SLAUGHTERED SQUADRONS". Lines from a hymn based on Judges 8 and Isaiah 9. "The race that long in darkness pin'd" by J. Morison, published in *Scottish Translations of Paraphrases*, 1781, was still in use in Presbyterian hymnaries in 1911. HOOD. The English poet Thomas Hood (1798-1845). **February 5** BARRIE. The Scottish novelist and playwright, J.M. Barrie (1867-1937). GEORGE ELIOT. LMM consistently misspells the name of this favourite novelist (Mary Ann Evans, 1819-1880) as "Elliot". "WE NEEDS MUST LOVE THE HIGHEST". From Alfred, Lord Tennyson, "Guinevere" (1859), l.660. ADAM BEDE. In this novel (1859), Adam tries to help Hetty, the child-murderer; he loves Dinah, the Methodist preacher. **February 24** "SLEWY..." Roads where a driver could swing involuntarily round. **March 4** GRIPPE. French term for influenza. LAURENCE HOUSMAN. Best known as a writer of plays and fairy stories, Laurence Housman (1865-1955) was the brother and biographer of the poet A.E. Housman.

1912

January 28 THE MANSE, LEASKDALE. The home assigned to the minister at St Paul's church is still in use in Leaskdale, a farming settlement 93 km northeast of Toronto. The village had been named in 1857 after the Leask family, who owned the saw-mill and grist-mill near the crossroads. GEO. R. George R. Macneill, who lived at the Cavendish crossroads, was LMM's second cousin. †**April 12, 1911** MCKAYS. John Mackay of French River was the son of Donald and Matilda (Macneill) Mackay (Pensie's sister). CAINE'S "MANXMAN". *The Manxman* (1894) by Hall Caine was a favourite novel of LMM's youth. †**July 18, 1911** ROB ROY. A novel (1817) by Walter Scott. †**July 19, 1911** MR. MACMIL-LAN. George Boyd Macmillan had been a correspondent since 1903. LMM's letters to him are collected in *My Dear Mr. M: Letters to G.B. Macmillan*, ed. F.W.P. Bolger and Elizabeth Epperly (Toronto: McGraw-Hill Ryerson, 1980). In 1925 LMM would dedicate *Emily of New Moon* to Macmillan, "in recogni-tion of a long and stimulating friendship". †**July 22, 1911** OBAN, STAFFA, AND IONA. A village, and islands, in the west of Scotland described in Walter Scott's *Lord of the Isles* (1804). LMM used many details from the honeymoon section of her journals in the autobiographical series reprinted as *The Alpine Path* (Toronto: Fitzhenry and Whiteside, 1975). Many of the photographs that illus-trate this section were shaped to fit into a stereopticon viewer. †**July 30, 1911** AYR. Birthplace of Robert Burns. "COOK" GUIDE. Thomas Cook and Son, found-ed 1841, was the major travel agency based in England. TROSSACHS. A wooded glen in the southwestern highlands of Perthshire, extending from Loch Achray to Loch Katrine; popularized for tourists in Walter Scott's *Lady of the Lake* and *Rob Roy*. LMM consistently misspells as "Trosachs". CYSTITIS. Inflam-mation of the bladder. RIZZIO. David Rizzio (1533-66), suspected of being the lover of Mary Queen of Scots, was murdered in her supper chamber at Holy-rood Palace. †**August 6, 1911** ABBOTSFORD. Palatial home of Sir Walter Scott in southeast Scotland. KIRRIEMUIR. J.M. Barrie's birthplace in northeast Scot-land. The "Thrums" novels included *Auld Licht Idylls* (1888), *A Window in Thrums* (1889), *The Little Minister* (1891) and *Sentimental Tommy* (1896). †**August 13, 1911** ALLOA. East of Stirling, in central Scotland. BERWICK. On the east coast, at the border between Scotland and England. MARMION. *Mar-mion: a Tale of Flodden Field* (1808), a poem by Sir Walter Scott. †**August 20, 1911** CARLISLE. Border town on the west coast. GRANDMOTHER WOOLNER. LMM's great-grandmother, Sarah Kemp Woolner, mother of her maternal grandmother Lucy Woolner Macneill. FLODDEN FIELD. Scene of a battle between

Scottish and English forces, September 9, 1513. KESWICK. In the Lake District, in northwestern England. †August 27, 1911 LEEDS. In the Midlands of England. CHINA DOGS. "Gog and Magog" remained part of LMM's household, and are now in the University of Guelph collection. The others purchased in 1911 were inherited by David Macdonald, LMM's grandson. September 3 LONDON. London entries also itemize visits to Trafalgar Square, Hyde Park, Westminster Abbey, the Crystal Palace, Kew, Hampton Court, the Zoo, and Temple Church. The entries are brief and colourless. VANITY FAIR. The novel (1848) by William Makepeace Thackeray. †September 10, 1911 WARWICK. In the central region of England. "UNWEPT, UNHONORED, AND UNSUNG". Walter Scott, *Lay of the Last Minstrel*, VI, 1: "Unwept, unhonour'd, and unsung". †September 18, 1911 THE PITMAN FIRM. A British publishing house, specializing in business publications, which had developed from the nineteenth-century enterprises of Sir Isaac Pitman, pioneer in short-hand systems. BEERBOHM TREE. The famous actor-manager, Sir Herbert Beerbohm Tree (1853-1917), produced *Macbeth* in London in 1911, using a stage setting of unusual magnificence. DUNWICH. A coastal town between Lowestoft and Aldeburgh in Suffolk, one of the most easterly of the English counties. AUNT MARGARET. Margaret Woolner Mackenzie, mother of Tillie Mackenzie Houston. [January 28, 1912] MARJORIE MACMURCHY. Marjory MacMurchy worked on the Toronto *News*; she had been President of the Canadian Women's Press Club since 1909 and her essay, *A King's Crowning*, was published in 1910 by Briggs of Toronto. She had written to LMM when *Anne of Green Gables* came out and the two writers had met in 1910 when MacMurchy visited PEI. UXBRIDGE. An Ontario town 75 km northeast of Toronto, nearest to LMM's new home in the village of Leaskdale for banking, groceries, and medicine. Established before 1809 by settlers from Pennsylvania, Uxbridge was incorporated as a town in 1885. MARY AND LIZZIE OXTOBY. The Oxtoby family had come to Canada from Yorkshire in 1837 and settled in Leaskdale in 1845. William Oxtoby was a prosperous farmer and blacksmith; the Misses Oxtoby lived in a frame house on the corner of his farm, directly across from the Presbyterian church. ZEPHYR. Another small settlement, ten km northwest of Leaskdale, settled by the early 1850s, and growing in the 1880s when the railway went through the village. LEASKDALE CHURCH. St Paul's Presbyterian congregation had been formed in 1862; the original church built in 1864 was served by the minister of Chalmers Church, Uxbridge, until 1880, when Leaskdale joined Zephyr as a joint charge; a frame (wooden) church was built in Zephyr in 1881. In 1906 a new brick church was built in Leaskdale, where the old church, shed, and hall had been. It is still in use. THE MANSE. Stucco over brick, this two-storey house four doors north of the Oxtobys had been built 25 years earlier for the Rev. A.G. McLaughlin (whose wife was a Leask) and had been the home of four ministers before the Macdonalds moved in. †October 3, 1911 A RECEPTION IN THE CHURCH. This reception is fully described in *L.M. Montgomery as Mrs. Ewan Macdonald of The Leaskdale Manse 1911-1926*, comp. Mrs. Harold Clarke (Leaskdale, 1965). HUGH AND JAMES MUSTARD. Grandsons of Hugh Mustard, one of the 12 settlers of the township in 1831. JOHN MUSTARD. LMM's teacher and suitor in Prince Albert,

Northwest Territories (NWT), now Saskatchewan; in 1911 he was a Presbyterian Minister at Dufferin Street Church in Toronto. †**October 13, 1911** KATE. Hugh John Montgomery's daughter by his second marriage. BEAVERTON. A town on Lake Simcoe, 37 km north of Leaskdale. P.A. Prince Albert, NWT, where LMM's father had lived and raised a second family. †**October 22, 1911** CROQUINOLE. A popular table game involving movement of markers on an octagonal board. PHIZ'S. Slang for "physiognomies": faces. †**October 24, 1911** LARES AND PENATES. Latin: household gods. **[January 28, 1912]** HEPPLEWHITE. George Hepplewhite (d. 1786) designed furniture in a delicate and graceful style. ZELLA COOK. Church organist since 1902; the Cook family had come from England to a farm west of Leaskdale by 1868. HOBSON'S CHOICE. No choice at all: Hobson (d. 1631) was a London carrier who offered no choice of horses. MRS. GEO. LEASK. George Leask ran the grist mill; he was one of the three sons of the original Leask who emigrated from Aberdeenshire. THE CANADIAN WOMEN'S PRESS CLUB. Founded in 1904; LMM became Vice-President of the Toronto branch in 1912. "MARIAN KEITH". Pen name of Mary Esther Miller MacGregor (1876-1961), also a recent bride of a Presbyterian minister stationed in Galt, southwest of Toronto. *Duncan Polite* (N.Y.: Revell, 1905) was a very popular regional idyll about old-style Presbyterian Scots in Ontario. "Marian Keith's" other novels published by this time were *The Silver Maple* (1906), *Treasure Valley* (1908), and *'Lizabeth of the Dale* (1910). JANE WELLS FRASER. President of the Toronto Women's Press Club; she worked with Presbyterian Publications in Toronto. JOHN DREW (1853-1927). A major American actor of the day, Drew played in *A Single Man* by Hubert Davies. THE KING EDWARD. This elegant hotel at 37 King Street East in downtown Toronto designed by Ives Cobb with E.J. Lennox was built 1902-3. MR. AND MRS. BEER. G. Frank Beer, 54 Glen Road, Toronto, a financier who was president of the Alton Realty Company, was born in Bedeque, PEI, in 1864, attended Prince of Wales College, and married Annie Weeks of Charlottetown. THE NATIONAL CLUB. A private men's club founded in 1874 with premises at 109 Bay Street, Toronto. REV. MR. MCKAY OF WICK. W.A. McKay was minister at Blackwater Junction, near the village of Wick, eight km east of Leaskdale. MARGARET ROSS. LMM's Cavendish friend, wife of the Rev. John Stirling. REV. MR. FRASER OF UXBRIDGE. An old friend of Ewan Macdonald's, James R. Fraser, M.A., of Chalmers Church, Uxbridge, was the interim moderator for the local presbytery when the Leaskdale pulpit was left empty in 1910; he probably suggested that Ewan Macdonald preach for a call there. "CHRONICLES OF AVONLEA" A collection of stories (Boston: Page, 1912); in some "Anne" plays a peripheral part. Dedicated to the memory of Tillie—Mrs William A. Houston. **March 28** "PITCHY". Dirt roads in the country broke up into pot-holes as the ice and snow melted. Roads became impassable during the spring break-up. MRS. URQUHART. Sarah Heise Urquhart. Her husband John was a carpenter and also the township assessor; his family came from Rosshire, Scotland, before 1837 and were among the families that founded the local Presbyterian Kirk. **April 30** A SECOND "STORY GIRL". *The Golden Road* continues the story of two Ontario boys who travel to Prince Edward Island to join their cousins, including Sara, the gifted storyteller. **September 22** LITTLE SON. Chester Cameron Macdonald, 1912-1964. MISS FERGUSSON. Isabella W. Fergusson, graduate nurse from the Toronto General Hospital. DR. MCMURCHY. Dr Helen MacMurchy, the sister of Marjorie MacMurchy, had a Toronto practice at 133 Bloor St East, Toronto. DR. BASCOM. Dr Horace Bascom practised in Uxbridge until 1912. He and another doctor had arranged for telephone service between Leaskdale and Uxbridge in 1910. HUDSON'S "LAW OF PSYCHIC PHENOMENA". T.H. Hudson's book, subtitled *A Working Hypothesis for the Systematic Study of Hypnotism, Spiritism, Mental Therapeutics, etc.* (Chicago: McClung; London: Putman, 1893) went into its 34th edition in 1912. **September 26** CHLOROFORMED A CAT. LMM used this incident in *Anne of the Island*, ch. 16; but in the story the cat survives the chloroforming. **October 7** FRICASSEED. Fried and served with sauce. **December 1** EUMENIDES. Greek name for the Furies. **December 16** RED DEER. A town 166 km south of Edmonton, Alberta. "THE RACE THAT KNOWS JOSEPH" An inversion of the biblical phrase, Exodus 1:8, regarding the Egyptian king who "knew not Joseph". MRS. REID. Lillis May Reid, daughter of George Harrison, was the widow of Arthur Wesley Reid. **December 31** "AUNT JANE OF KENTUCKY". "Aunt Jane Allen" is a character in the *Samantha* stories (c. 1890) by Marietta Holley.

1913
February 22 THE HYPATIA CLUB. This Uxbrige club, dedicated to "stimulating literary taste and intellectual culture", had been founded by a group of university graduates in 1907; membership was limited to 20 women. The name Hypatia (a neoplatonic philosopher and daughter of Theon of Alexandria) was also the name of the heroine of Charles Kingsley's novel, *Hypatia* (1853). LMM attended meetings in 1912 as an honorary member and in 1913 gave a paper on Hawthorne's *Scarlet Letter*. **May 6** DEAR LITTLE SON. In 1937 the words "Oh dear God!" were added to the journal at this point. Always a difficult child to manage, Chester had become a serious worry to his parents by the time he was a young adult. **May 21** THE GOLDEN ROAD. This novel (Boston: Page, 1913) was dedicated to the memory of Aunt Mary Lawson. **June 29** ON THE 6TH. County roads were laid out on a numbered grid. Leaskdale was on the seventh concession road of Scott township. "YE SHALL KNOW THE TRUTH". St John 6:32. **July 3** BELLEVUE. Ewan Macdonald's family home, in the eastern part of Prince Edward Island. "KATIE MAURICE" AND "LUCY GRAY". Imaginary playmates: see the entry for January 27, 1911. †**August 3** JACK LAIRD. One of LMM's best friends in school days. †**August 6** GEORGE HENRY. George Robertson, the Mayfield farmer who was Amanda's husband. [**September 27**] MARY BEATON. A second cousin, Mary (Campbell) Beaton, had roomed with LMM in Charlottetown in 1893-4. THE WALKER HOUSE. A Toronto hotel at Front and York Streets near the railway station (across York Street from the present Union Station). A THIRD "ANNE" BOOK. The story of Anne at college, tentatively titled "Anne of Redmond", but eventually published as *Anne of the Island*. CAVENDISH POST OFFICE. LMM's grandfather Alexander Macneill was postmaster 1870-98, her grandmother succeeding him 1898-1911 with LMM as Assistant Postmaster. A new post office was opened in 1973 at Cavendish to

handle tourist mail. SIC TRANSIT GLORIA MUNDI. Latin: "Thus passes the glory of the world." **October 18** PARALYSIS AGITANS. Parkinson's Disease. **November 1** THE WOMEN'S CANADIAN CLUB. A club with branches in cities and major towns, founded in 1907 to sponsor speakers of national importance. The Toronto branch of the club had 921 members in 1912-13. FORRESTERS' HALL. A hall belonging to the Independent Order of Foresters. MRS. DICKSON. Mrs George Dickson was President of St Margaret's College, a boarding and day school for girls at 144 Bloor Street East. REV. DR. GANDIER OF KNOX. Alfred Gandier (1861-1932) was Principal of Knox Theological College, which is affiliated with the University of Toronto. **November 16** DR. SHIER. Dr Walter C. Shier of Uxbridge had become the Leaskdale physician, following Dr Bascom's retirement.

1914

January 3 PANSY BOOKS. Moralistic books for girls by Mrs G.R. Alder, published from 1876 on by Ward, Lock & Co., London. SCYLLA AND CHARYBDIS. Between two dangers: based on the Greek legend of a monster and a whirlpool that made the Straits of Messina hard to navigate. **January 10** GROTE'S "HISTORY OF GREECE". This valuable study of legendary and historical Greece was published in London by George Grote (1794-1871) over a period of ten years, 1846-56. GODEY'S LADIES' BOOK. The most popular American women's magazine of the 19th century, *Godey's Lady's Book* was published from 1830 to 1898. UNDINE. A romance (1811) by Baron La Motte Fouqué. **February 25** BARSET SERIES. Anthony Trollope's six Barsetshire Novels were published between 1855 and 1867. **March 22** MRS. NORMAN BEAL OF UXBRIDGE. Mary Beal was the daughter of Mr and Mrs Isaac Gould. The Beal family had owned an important tannery in Uxbridge, managed since 1902 by N.R. Beal, but the business was destroyed by fire in 1912. Mary Beal had been the Vice-President of the Hypatia Club in 1911-12. "PEG O' MY HEART". This popular comedy by Hartley Manners opened in New York in 1912 and launched numerous road companies. **April 15** THE BOOKMAN. A conservative New York literary magazine (1895-1933). JEAN INGELOW. An English Victorian poet (1820-97) whose best-known poems were "Divided" and "The High Tide on the Coast of Lincolnshire, 1571". LYTTON. Of Edward Bulwer-Lytton's novels, LMM's favourite had been *Zanoni* (1842). **April 18** ANNE III. *Anne of the Island*, still tentatively called *Anne of Redmond*. **June 28** STEWART FORBES. Born in 1886, and ordained in the Lindsay presbytery, Forbes served in Honan, China, as a Presbyterian missionary. Of his $1,200 missionary salary, Zephyr contributed $387, Leaskdale $413, and the Macdonalds $400. THE S.S. PICNIC. Annual end-of-year event for the Sunday School. Presbyterian Sunday Schools had been active in Canada since 1811, when the first one was founded in Brockville. **August 5** WAR. Virtually all the historical details noted in the Journals about the war of 1914-18 reappear in LMM's novel *Rilla of Ingleside*, written 1919. (This novel will be referred to in these notes as *Rilla*.) A GLOBE. The Toronto *Globe*, a morning daily newspaper founded in 1844. A SERBIAN. Gavrilo Princip, a Serbian student, assassinated the heir to the Austrian throne on June 24, in protest against Austro-Hungarian repression of southern Slav nationalism.

"THE SHOT HEARD ROUND THE WORLD". From Emerson's "Hymn Sung at the Completion of the Concord Monument", referring to the opening of the American Revolution. MRS. AUBIN. An Uxbridge nurse. **August 30** MONS. A Belgian canal-town, near the French border, where the extreme right-wing of the German army, advancing towards the British channel, defeated the British on August 23; for Canadian soldiers, the war would also end at Mons, which was recaptured on November 11, 1918. **September 5** GOD'S FINGER. In *Rilla*, ch. 8, this same phrase is used by the Presbyterian minister, Mr Meredith. **September 8** GENERAL FRENCH. Field-Marshal J.D.P. French (later Earl French) commanded the British Expeditionary Forces until late 1915. THE MARNE. The Marne River rises in the northeast of France and joins the Seine in the suburbs of Paris. British forces retreating from Belgium and French forces retreating from Verdun joined to hold the line at the Marne and save Paris (*Rilla*, ch. 8). **September 12** HIDEOUS STORIES. German soldiers terrorized Belgian civilians to cut down resistance to the drive through Belgium to France. Stories of atrocities against Belgian women and children were publicized in the world press. **September 21** WHITBY. A town 40 km southeast of Leaskdale. **October 13** ANTWERP. The major North-Belgian commercial city, to which the government had withdrawn from the capital, Brussels, in August. Antwerp remained occupied until 1918 (*Rilla*, ch. 10). **October 30** TURKEY. Turkey's declaration of war meant the opening of a third front in Asia Minor against the Allied armies of Russia. ARMENIAN MASSACRES. In 1894-6 Armenians (chiefly Gregorians and Protestants) were massacred, on suspicion that they planned to overthrow the Sultan of Turkey; European powers abstained from intervention then, and again in 1909, when the "Young Turks" stepped up the massacres. **November 19** DIXMUDE...THE YSER...CALAIS. Dixmude, a Belgian town of 3,460, was held by a force of 5,000 Belgians while the Yser River was dammed and sluices were opened to flood the countryside, creating the "Flanders mud" into which the armies settled for a winter of trench warfare. The French port of Calais, across the English Channel from Dover, was the object of the German army drive on the western front (*Rilla*, ch. 10). **November 20** ANNE OF REDMOND. Retitled *Anne of the Island*, this novel deals with Anne's four years at Redmond University, and draws on LMM's memories of her year at Dalhousie in Halifax, 1895-6. **December 7** LODZ. A manufacturing and rail centre in Poland (which in 1914 was a Russian territory). Russian forces evacuated Lodz on December 5, halting the Allied movement against Germany on the eastern front until spring (*Rilla*, ch.10). **December 10** FALKLAND ISLES. A group of British islands in the South Atlantic, 250 miles east of South America, where British ships were repaired and provisioned. A naval victory on December 8 against a German Squadron under Admiral Graf von Spree ended Germany's bid for control of the outer seas. **December 19** MRS. [Felicia Dorothea] HEMANS (1793-1835). The collected works of this popular English poet, issued in 1839, included "Casabianca" ("The boy stood on the burning deck...").

1915

January 1 K. OF K. Kitchener of Khartoum: Horatio Herbert, Earl Kitchener, hero of campaigns in Egypt, South Africa, and India, had recently been appointed Secretary of State for War. CARL. Hugh Carlyle Montgomery, born in 1893, son of Hugh John Montgomery and his second wife Mary McRae Montgomery. "HE GOES TO DO..." Walter Scott, "The Lady of the Lake", IV,x. (In *Rilla*, ch. 6, Rilla uses the same quotation when her brother enlists.) BATOCHE. A Métis settlement in present-day Saskatchewan, headquarters of Louis Riel from July 1, 1884-May 12, 1885, when General Middleton's forces (including Hugh John Montgomery as a volunteer militiaman) defeated the Métis in the uprising now known as the North West Rebellion. "WITHOUT SHEDDING OF BLOOD..." Hebrews 9:22. "STRUGGLE OF ANTS..." Misquoted from Tennyson's "Vastness": "What is it all but a trouble of ants in the gleam of a million million of suns?" HARVEY GOULD (1857-1943). The village of Uxbridge was originally called Gouldville; Gould Bros store sold groceries, feed, etc. **January 6** THE TRENCHES. From 1915 to 1917 men on both sides dug hundreds of miles of trenches, living in these dugouts out of enemy sight, but engaging in sporadic forays "over the top" (*Rilla*, ch. 11). **January 17** BILLY SUNDAY. An American Presbyterian revivalist (1862-1935), flamboyant in the pulpit, estimated to have made a million converts to his version of evangelical fundamentalist theology. RIZPAH. A poem by Tennyson—the monologue of a mother who collects the bones of her son from the gallows to bury them in consecrated ground. **March 19** THE DARDANELLES. Once called the Hellespont, this channel between the Aegean Sea and the Sea of Marmora commands the approach to Constantinople (now Istanbul) from the Mediterranean. The British opened a campaign here to relieve Turkish pressure against Russia in Armenia. After a year-long attempt at invasion, British troops were evacuated, after losses of 130,000 dead, wounded, or missing. **April 11** "STRENGTH AND HONOR..." Proverbs 31:25. **April 26** LANGEMARCK. A village in Belgium near Ypres. The Germans had delivered the first gas attack in this area on April 22nd (*Rilla*, ch. 12). **May 30** LUSITANIA. British passenger ship, destroyed by a German submarine on May 7, with a loss of 1,198 lives, including 113 Americans. A note of protest from President Wilson created a crisis in the American determination to maintain neutrality. **June 7** KINROSS. Ewan's sisters Annie Macdonald Gillis and Christie Macdonald McLeod lived at Kinross in the eastern part of Prince Edward Island. PRYSMYSL. The fall of the Polish fortress of Przemysl lost the Russians a pivotal point in their line against the Austro-Hungarian and German armies. In *Rilla*, ch. 10, LMM uses this "unpronounceable" name as an example of the impingement of European place-names on the consciousness of people on the home front. **June 18** EATON'S. The T. Eaton Company, 190-218 Yonge Street at Queen, was at this time Canada's largest department store. **August 6** THE FALL OF WARSAW. Russian withdrawal from the Vistula River after the fall of Warsaw marked the re-establishment of German power in the part of Poland that had been under Russian domination since 1863. **September 24** SERBIA. In 1915 after pressure on the Russian front had lessened, Germany assembled an army in Hungary to cross the Danube near Belgrade. A general advance in

October, assisted by Bulgarians from the east, overran Serbia. This situation is discussed in *Rilla*, ch. 17. CONSTANTINE OF GREECE. The King, who succeeded to the Greek throne in 1913 after his father's assassination. His wife, Sophia of Hohenzollern, was a sister of Kaiser Wilhelm. **October 26** ANOTHER...SON. Ewan Stuart Macdonald, 1915-1982. AN UXBRIDGE NURSE. The nurse in attendance was Mrs Martha Nicholls Austin. **November 29** GALLIPOLI. The peninsula north of the Dardanelles. THE GUARDIAN. Charlottetown paper. LMM clipped items of news about her home province and entered them in scrapbooks, now at the University of Guelph. "THE SCHOOLMASTER'S BRIDE". This title appears in LMM's ledger list of short stories, but no record of its publication has been found.

1916

January 3 EDITH MEYERS. Daughter of John R. and Lillian Meyers of Zephyr. BAGDAD. Baghdad, an ancient city on the banks of the Tigris in Asiatic Turkey (it is now the leading industrial city in Iraq); a British force from India was engaging the Turkish army in Mesopotamia (now Iraq). **February 4** PARLIAMENT BUILDINGS. The centre block, the Houses of Parliament, had just been destroyed by fire (not by "German incendiaries"), leaving only the magnificent Library. **February 16** "PRAY YE THAT YOUR FLIGHT..." St Matthew 24:20. **February 28** VERDUN. An ancient French town on the Meuse River in northeastern France, near the Lorraine border, centre of a fortified region that had not capitulated during the German push of 1914. In 1916 German forces under the Crown Prince targeted Verdun with heavy artillery bombardment. **March 11** "THE MOVING FINGER WRITES". From Edward Fitzgerald, "The Rubaiyat of Omar Khayyam", st. 71. **March 21** MCCLELLAND AND GOODCHILD. The publisher of LMM's books in Canada was founded by John McClelland and Frederick Goodchild in 1906; George Stewart's name was added in 1914; Goodchild resigned in 1918, and the firm, then at 42 Adelaide Street West, became McClelland and Stewart. **April 12** BRITTON PUBLISHING COMPANY. Eventually Constable of London got the British rights to the next book. **April 20** TREBIZOND. A port on the Black Sea in Turkish Armenia. **April 26** SINN FEIN. Gaelic for "We Ourselves": the name of an organization that advocated in 1905 the establishment of an independent Irish Republic. In early 1916 it agitated for an immediate rising against British rule, setting up continued resistance until the Irish Free State was established in 1933. AUTHOR'S LEAGUE OF AMERICA. Founded in 1912, it had over 1,500 members in 1916. **May 1** KUT-EL-AMARA. A Turkish town, important for the defence of the Tigris. **May 25** "HE THAT ENDURETH..." Matthew 24:13. ("He that shall endure unto the end, the same shall be saved.") **June 10** BATTLE OF JUTLAND. The major fleet action of the First World War, which took place on May 31 off Denmark. The British lost 14 ships and 6,000 men; the Germans, 9 ships and 2,500 men. W.F.M.S. Branches of the Presbyterian Women's Foreign Mission Society were founded in Halifax and in Toronto in 1876. It was enlarged to include Home Missions in 1885, and renamed the Women's Foreign and Home Mission Society in 1910. The Leaskdale Society was founded in the 1880s. ORKNEYS. The ship that was carrying Kitchener to a conference with Russian leaders hit a German mine and sank off the northeastern tip of Scotland. **June 17** CHURCH UNION. Debate concerning possible union of Presbyterian, Congregationalist and Methodist Churches in Canada, to be decided on a church-by-church vote, led to the formation of the United Church of Canada in 1924-5. ANNE'S HOUSE OF DREAMS. The fourth novel in the "Anne" series concerns Anne's early days of marriage and motherhood; a sub-plot presents a passionate but inhibited woman, tied to a dead marriage. Dedicated to "all the readers who have loved Anne." **July 30** MY AILMENT. On June 30 LMM noted another attack of cystitis. THE SOMME. This river flowing through the Picardy area of northwestern France had been reached by the Germans in 1914. After a year of stalemate, the Allies began a series of battles here in July 1916. APPLETON'S. A major American firm since the 1840's, Appleton's, the first American publisher of *Alice in Wonderland*, also published *Uncle Remus*, and many other bestsellers including the novels of LMM's favourite Hall Caine. STOKES. The F.A. Stokes Company was a less well-established publisher, but one of rising importance, especially in the new field of detective thrillers. ANNIE FELLOWES JOHNSTON. Annie Fellows Johnston's *The Little Colonel* was a bestseller of 1896, first of a popular series. MRS. PORTER. Eleanor Hodgman Porter first published *Pollyanna* in serial form in the *Christian Herald* in 1912; L.C. Page published it in book form and sold over a million copies. **August 1** RUPERT BROOKE (1887-1915). A poet of exceptional promise who died of blood-poisoning while on active duty and was buried at Scyros. LMM used a quotation from Brooke as an epigraph for *Anne's House of Dreams*. **August 8** WELL NELSON. One of two orphaned brothers, Wellington and David, who lived with LMM's family for several years during her childhood. **August 19** TARNOPOL. An Austrian town near Lemberg, on the eastern front. **September 2** ALLAN MUSTARD. Son of James and Jennie Mustard, and nephew of the Rev. John Mustard; served overseas 1917-19. **September 4** DNEISTER. A river in south-eastern Europe running through Austria and Russia to the Black Sea. CLERY; GUILLEMONT. Villages near the Somme where repeated attacks hammered the German line. **September 9** WARSAW. A town in Indiana described in an entry (omitted here) as "a pretty town of 5,000", near the Winona Lakes. Ewan Macdonald's brother, Dr Angus Macdonald, was head of a private hospital in Warsaw. **October 5** MRS. LAPP. Probably Mrs George Lapp. The Lapp family had come from Germany via Pennsylvania in the 1840s. TAG-DAY. The sale of paper badges in aid of the Red Cross brought in $50 at the Scott Fair on October 10th. **October 17** MARSHALL SAUNDERS (1861-1947). The author of the international bestseller *Beautiful Joe*, she had moved to Toronto from Halifax in 1914. Her most recent book was *Boy, the Wandering Dog* (1916). HISTORY OF THE PAGES. LMM retells the story of the Pages' marital troubles three times in her journal. **November 11** "THE WATCHMAN". *The Watchman, and Other Poems* was published in Toronto by McClelland, in London by Constable and in New York by Stokes; 159 pages. MACKENSEN. August von Mackensen, Prussian field-marshal commanding the German army on the eastern front, was now fighting in the Drobudja, a Romanian territory on the Black Sea. Romania had declared war against Austria-Hungary on August 27, 1916. **November 24** FOUR COPIES. Three carbon copies of the typescript had to be corrected individually in pre-photocopy days. **November 30** BUCHAREST. The capital city of Romania. A SLEEPING POWDER. This is the first reference to what became a life-time habit of self-medication. KIRLZBABA PASS. Through the Carpathian Mountains. **December 10** ASQUITH GOVERNMENT. Herbert Henry Asquith, who had been Liberal Prime Minister of Britain for nine years, formed a war-time Coalition Government in Britain in 1916; his ministry was shaken by the rebellion in Ireland, the loss of Lord Kitchener, lack of success on the Somme, and the crushing of Romania. MRS. LOCKIE. Elizabeth Imrie Lockie of Zephyr. Her husband Robert died in 1916. The Lockie family had come from Scotland by 1841, and had helped found the Zephyr Presbyterian Church. **December 10** ILLUSTRATED LANTERN AFFAIR. Illustrated talk, using pictures projected from a "magic lantern"—lens fitted to a box holding an electric light bulb. RECRUITING SPEECHES. In December the Scott Township League on Resources Committee (a recruiting organization of which Ewan Macdonald was President) was authorized to raise 45 men as a township quota. LLOYD GEORGE. David Lloyd George had been Chancellor of the Exchequer before the war, Minister of Munitions, and head of the War Office in the Asquith administration. **December 13** GERMANY HAS OFFERED PEACE. On December 12 Germany sent notes to President Wilson and to the Pope expressing a desire for peace. The Allies replied on December 29, rejecting the note as "devoid of sincerity and of substance". **December 16** BUZEU. The town of Buzau is 100 km north of Bucharest. **December 18** SERETH. This river rises in Moldavia, Romania, and joins the Danube near the Russian border. **December 21** WOODROW WILSON. President of the United States since 1913, Wilson was re-elected in 1916 on his policy of keeping the U.S.A. out of the war. On December 18 he sent identical notes to the Allies and to Germany asking for a statement on their terms for ending the war. Wilson's series of notes, from 1914 on, is emphasized in *Rilla*, chs. 11, 16. KIM. A novel (1901) by Rudyard Kipling about an orphan boy's life in India. **December 31** QUEEN'S WEATHER. English folklore held that Queen Victoria always brought good weather when she visited.

1917

January 5 EVERYWOMAN'S WORLD. A Toronto-based magazine that commissioned from LMM a series of six autobiographical sketches, which appeared from June to November. They were republished as *The Alpine Path*. MR. CHISHOLM. Arthur M. Chisholm (1856-1902) attended the Nova Scotia School for the Blind from 1872 to 1879, graduated from a conservatory of music in Berlin in 1884, and became a popular teacher of music at the School for the Blind in Halifax. He married Jessie Lawson of Pictou, N.S., in 1890. NATHAN LOCKHART; WILLIE PRITCHARD; LEMUEL MACLEOD; EDWIN SIMPSON; IRVING HOWATT; ALEC MACNEILL; JOHN SUTHERLAND; LOU DYSTANT; FULTON AND ALF SIMPSON; HERMAN LEARD; JOE STEWART; HENRY MCLURE; OLIVER MACNEILL. see entries on these young men in Volume 1 of *The Selected Journals of L.M. Montgomery*. UDORA. A village eight km north of Leaskdale. **January 10** A NEW BOOK. *Rainbow Valley*, a novel about Anne's children in the pre-war years, and about a family of motherless children in the manse next door. **January 20** HATTIE SMITH.

"Miss Gordon", LMM's favourite teacher at Cavendish public school; *Anne of Avonlea* was dedicated to her. **January 22** GOLDWIN LAPP. One of the three young men to whose memory *Rainbow Valley* is dedicated. He was killed in 1916. **February 3** SOCIAL CONGRESS. A Social Service Congress, organized in Toronto by John George Shearer, a Presbyterian, brought together groups concerned with social problems. SUBMARINE WARFARE. The submarine was a new weapon. British submarines had been active in the Baltic and at the Dardanelles. In December 1916 Germany warned the Allies of a decision to wage "unrestricted" submarine warfare. In protest, on February 3, 1917, the American ambassador left Berlin. In spite of anti-submarine devices and manoeuvres, the 148 German submarines came close to breaking British power in 1917. MR. DOMINICK. The agent for Stokes, the New York publishing firm which brought out American first editions of all LMM's subsequent work, with the exception of *Further Chronicles of Avonlea*. Stokes arranged for a cheap reprint edition of *Anne's House of Dreams* (1917) with the New York firm of A.L. Burt; but Grosset and Dunlap, the New York publishers with which Page had always arranged cheap reprints, also brought out a cheap edition in 1917— another cause of LMM's irritation with Lewis Page. **February 6** THE TIGRIS. River in Mesopotamia (Iraq), giving access to Baghdad and the Persian gulf. An Anglo-Indian force was attempting to recapture Kut. **February 10** ROYAL-TIES. The hold-back of $1,000 became the basis of LMM's first lawsuit against L.C. Page. **February 18** 22 BELOW ZERO. This temperature on the Fahrenheit scale is equivalent to -30 degrees Celsius. **February 25** THE ANCRE. A French river flowing north from the Somme. PEPYS. Samuel Pepys' *Diary*, written 1660-9, was deciphered in 1825 and published 1893-6. On March 10, LMM reported reading a modern parody: *Diary of the Great Warr*, by "Samuel Pepys Jr.", with Watson M. Williams (illustrator), a light, satiric account of the first year and a half of the world-conflict. **March 4** SUFFRAGE TO WOMEN. In Britain a parliamentary bill enfranchising women was introduced on March 28, 1917, but British women were not given the vote until the summer of 1918. In Canada the Wartime Elections Act, 1917, gave the vote immediately to mothers, wives, or sisters of men on active service (a gift offered in hope of swinging the pro-conscription vote). In the United States the 19th Amendment to the Constitution, granting Woman Suffrage, was ratified in September 1920. **March 16** ABDICATION OF THE CZAR. Nicholas II abdicated in favour of his brother Michael, who declined the throne; the Romanov power ended on March 15, and a Provisional Government was established. **March 18** "A HILLTOP ON THE MARNE". A novel (1915) by Mildred Aldrich, subtitled "Being Letters Written June 3-September 8, 1914". "MY HOME ON THE FIELD OF HONOUR." Frances Wilson Huard's personal narrative, published by McClelland in 1916. **March 25** GERMANS RETREATING. Withdrawing from their position on the Somme, the Germans established themselves behind the new defensive "Hindenburg Line", running through Douai, Cambrai, and St Quentin. HINDENBURG. Paul von Beckendorf und Hindenburg, who had been commander of the German armies of the east, succeeded Erich von Falkenhayn as chief of general staff. **April 1** RIGA. Riga (which became the capital of Latvia in 1920), a major Baltic port, ranking second to St Petersburg as a Russian port for foreign trade. "THE WAY OF ALL FLESH". A novel (1903) by Samuel Butler, on the tyranny of parents. "PASTOR FELIX". The Rev. A.J. Lockhart (1850-1926)—uncle of Nathan Lockhart, LMM's schoolfriend, and a Methodist minister in Maine—published four books of poetry between 1887 and 1919, and a collection of poetry and essays. EDWIN SIMPSON (1872-1949). The man to whom LMM had been engaged in 1897-8. ANTI-SALOON ASSOCIATION. Temperance societies had proliferated during the war, some working to promote Prohibition legislation, others focusing on education. In the United States the Anti-Saloon League attacked liquor saloons as having dangerous political and social power in local communities. On August 1, 1917, Congress proposed a National Prohibition Amendment. Rhode Island, where Edwin Simpson worked, was one of the last three states to ratify this amendment. **April 15** MACMURCHY'S. Marjorie MacMurchy had published *The Woman—Bless Her* in 1916. **May 7** ATTORNEY OF THE AUTHOR'S LEAGUE. Their Counsel was B.H. Stern of New York. **May 9** FRESNOY. Fresnoy had been captured on May 3, Vimy Ridge on April 9. In the struggle for Verdun, the Germans were striking at all points along the Meuse River. **May 24** CAMERON MACFARLANE. Lance-corporal N.C. MacFarlane joined the first University Company of the Princess Patricia's Canadian Light Infantry in May 1915 and arrived overseas in July 1915. The university group was mustered at McGill to fill the ranks decimated by the first poison-gas attacks at Ypres in April 1915 when only 150 "Princess Pats" survived out of 828. As Sergeant and Acting-Lieutenant, MacFarlane fought at Cambrai and at Canal-du-Nord, where the Regiment lost its commanding officer, most of its junior officers, and 60% of its men. He was gazetted Lieutenant in October 1918 and demobilized in March 1919. **May 26** BALFOUR. British Foreign Secretary A.J. Balfour headed a mission to the United States in April-May, then proceeded to Canada, where he addressed Parliament. CONSCRIPTION. The Canadian Expeditionary Force had been recruited by voluntary enlistment until 1917. After Vimy Ridge, Prime Minister Robert Borden determined to find replacements for the thousands of dead and wounded by establishing compulsory military service. In spite of the heroic record of some French-Canadian units, there was general hostility to conscription in Quebec. **June 2** ST. GEORGE'S CHURCH. The Anglican Church in Ste-Anne-de-Bellevue, near Macdonald College. MENDELSSOHN. Jakob Ludwig Felix Mendelssohn-Bartholdy (1809-1847), German composer. LMM misspells as "Mendelsohnn". ROYAL VICTORIA COLLEGE. The women's college of McGill University, founded 1899. The R.V.C. building is on Sherbrooke St in downtown Montreal. ILA. Ila May Montgomery, Carl Montgomery's sister—LMM's half-sister. **June 8** MESSINES RIDGE. One of a chain of heights between Armentières and Passchendaele. **June 14** VENIZELOS. Eleutherios Venizelos, pro-Allied Greek statesman, returned to Athens after the dethronement of Constantine on June 27. **July 7** BRUSILOFF. Alexei Brussilov, commander of the armies on the southwestern front, took supreme command in May 1917 after the Russian Revolution. **July 21** "THE LIFE BOOK OF CAPTAIN JESSE". LMM's short story was published in *Housekeeper* magazine, August 1909. **August 5** ACCORDING TO HOYLE. Edmund Hoyle (1672-1769) systematized the rules for the game of whist. His "laws" remained in force until 1864; the phrase "according to Hoyle" remained in general currency, meaning "following the best authority". **August 8** SEDERUNT. The sitting of an ecclesiastic or other assembly, from the Latin: "they sat". **August 15** MR. WARNER. The Warners lived next door to the manse. Isaac Warner ran the Leaskdale blacksmith shop. LAKE SIMCOE. A large lake 42 km north of Leaskdale. AN AEROPLANE. Successful flight had begun in 1909 with the Wright brothers. Wartime need for spotters and fighters had accelerated aeronautical research. A plane flying over Zephyr was noted in the local paper in August 1917. "WITH THE MAJESTY OF PINION..." From Thomas Gray, "The Progress of Poesy" (1754). **August 31** LAURA'S. Laura McIntyre Aylsworth, a first cousin—sister of Bertie and Cuthbert, and daughter of Aunt Mary (Montgomery) McIntyre. THE EXHIBITION. The Toronto fall fair had been officially named the "Canadian National Exhibition" in 1912. Grandstand shows in 1917 featured a tableau depicting a night attack on "Hun dugouts" by Canadian forces, and a spectacular pageant set in Quebec City at the time of Confederation, with 1,200 performers. **September 8** THE DVINA. The Southern Dvina River rises near the Volga, and flows northwest to the Gulf of Riga, off the Baltic Sea. **September 27** PHENACETINE. Para-acetamino-phenotol, a drug used as an antineuralgic, relieves migraine, rheumatic, and neuralgic pain. **September 28** FLORA. Ewan Macdonald's half-sister; his father's daughter by a first wife, Flora; married to Amos Eagles of Braintree, Suffolk County, Massachusetts. **October 30** ITALY. Fighting against the Austrians in the Carso "was going badly", to quote Hemingway's *Farewell to Arms*, set in this period. On October 26 the Italians began the retreat to the River Piave. Besides the known dead and wounded, 230,000 soldiers were missing. VERONAL. A barbiturate: Diethylmalonyl urea, used for insomnia, mental disturbance, alcoholism, and disorders of the heart, lungs, and kidneys; dangerous in overdoses. THE GATE OF HORN. In Greek legend, the gate through which true dreams come; false dreams come through the gate of ivory. GORITZ. Gorizia, a town on the border between Italy and Austria, halfway between Udine and Trieste. **November 1** CADORNA. Count Luigi Cadorna, commander-in-chief of the Italian forces from 1914 until November 1917. THE RUSSIAN COLLAPSE. A military coup attempted in September by General Kornilov failed, there was mutiny in the Baltic fleet, and revolutionary zeal swept the country. **November 7** THE ADIGE. A river in Italy south of Venice. PASSCHENDAELE. This Belgian village was an essential holding-point in the renewed British push in Flanders. The Canadian capture of high ground near the village closed this third movement on the Ypres/Yser salient. **November 9** KERENSKY. Alexander Feodorovich Kerensky, who had been Russia's Minister of Justice before the Revolution, emerged as head of the first Provisional Government until the Bolshevik rising in November. BOLSHIVIKI. "Bolsheviks" is Russian for "Majority". **November 14** ROSEHILL AVE. The cousin on Rosehill Avenue, Toronto, was Viola (Mackenzie) Beauchamp, 1887-1977, niece of Mary McRae Montgomery. **November 23** BIGGEST VICTORY. The British Third Army under General Byng won the battle of Cambrai on November 20, largely through the surprise use of tanks. **November 26** SIR ROBERT BORDEN (1854-1937). The Prime

Minister from 1911 to 1920, as head of a Union government, fought the 1917 election on the Military Service Act and won. MR. POWELL. Charles B. Powell, Conservative Member of Parliament for Ottawa, 1898-1905. **December 1** LECKY'S "HISTORY OF RATIONALISM". W.E.H. Lecky developed an essay on "The Declining Sense of the Miraculous" into the opening of his *History of Rationalism* (1865). **December 3** CAMBRAI. A town in northern France. The Germans were able to bring reinforcements to retake Cambrai because of the end of hostilities on the Russian front. DAUGHTERS OF THE EMPIRE. The Imperial Order Daughters of the Empire (I.O.D.E.), a patriotic organization of Canadian women, was founded in 1900. SHERBOURNE HOUSE CLUB. A club for young women, especially nurses, at 104 Sherbourne Street in downtown Toronto. **December 6** "HALIFAX WRECKED". This was the famous Halifax Explosion caused by the collision in Halifax harbour of the Norwegian freighter *Imo* and the French munitions ship *Mont Blanc* at 9 a.m. on December 5. The resulting explosion devastated the city. JARVIS ST. COLLEGIATE. A high school in central Toronto. Dr MacMurchy had been its principal, 1872-1900. EDITH RUSSELL. A first cousin, daughter of Aunt Emily (Macneill) and Uncle John Montgomery. **December 10** JERUSALEM. Palestine had been under the rule of the Ottoman Turks since 1516. Under General Allenby, British and French forces outflanked and defeated the German/Turkish forces and captured Jerusalem. **December 11** "HE THAT ENDURETH...". A favourite biblical quotation; see the entry for May 25, 1916. **December 19** WILFRID LAURIER (1841-1919). Leader of the Liberal Party since 1897, and Prime Minister of Canada from 1896 to 1911. Himself a supporter of Canada's participation in the war, he nevertheless realized that conscription would be unacceptable to most French Canadians. In *Rilla*, ch. 18, an unattractive dog is named "Wilfrid Laurier". GRIT OR TORY. Slang for Liberal and Conservative respectively. SIR JOHN A. (MACDONALD) (1815-1891). Conservative Prime Minister, 1867-73; 1878-91. HABITANT. A farmer in the Province of Quebec. LMM misspells as "habitat". MAJOR SAM SHARPE (1873-1918). Born near Zephyr, a lawyer twice elected Member of Parliament for Ontario North (as Conservative, 1908, and as Unionist, 1911); he raised the 116th Ontario County Battalion and led it overseas.

1918

February 10 "THE DAY OF ARMAGEDDON...". From Rudyard Kipling's poem, "England's Answer". **February 25** MACAULAY'S HISTORY. Thomas Babington Macaulay, *History of England from the Accession of James II* (1849-61). LMM consistently misspells as "MacCaulay". **March 1** LILY MEYERS. Lillian Meyers of Zephyr; her sister Edith had married Dave Lyons. The Meyers family had come from Switzerland in the 1850s; Jacob Meyers of Zephyr was a County Councillor. Lily later married William Cook, brother of Zella Cook Mustard. **March 2** THE [former] CROWN PRINCE OF GERMANY. Not Crown Prince Rupprecht— since 1917 Commander of German Armies on the Western Front—but the late Prince Frederick of Prussia, husband of Victoria, the Princess Royal of Great Britain; he became Emperor in March 1888, but died three months later, and was succeeded by Kaiser Wilhelm III. **March 22** HAIG. British Field-marshall

Douglas Haig had commanded the British army in France since 1915. **March 31** LAVENDER. Oil distilled from lavender flowers, dissolved in spirit of wine, was a traditional remedy for disorders of the nerves. ST. QUENTIN. From this point in northwest France the Germans made swift advances toward Amiens on the Somme River, with the aim of pushing British forces back towards the Channel ports. MONTDIDIER, ROSIERE. French villages in the Somme area south of Amiens: the limit of the German advance westward in 1918. SCOTT. The name of the township in which Leaskdale is located; in Ontario (now Durham) County. In 1984, Scott became part of Uxbridge Township. FOCH. Marshal Ferdinand Foch had commanded French forces at the Marne (1914), at Ypres (1915), and the Somme (1916). To stem the German advance, he was nominated in April to co-ordinate British-French efforts, and by May 1 was also recognized as commander-in-chief or generalissimo by the Belgian, Italian, and American governments. ANCIENT EGYPT BY RAWLINSON. George Rawlinson published histories of the seven great monarchies of the Eastern world (1862-76). *BEN HUR.* Lew Wallace's novel (1880) is subtitled *A Tale of the Christ.* **April 1** BRITISH WEEKLY. A family journal, the *British Weekly and Christian World*, was founded in 1886 and published by Hodder & Stoughton. The review (March 7, 1918), entitled "A Sunshiny Novel", was signed "A Man of Kent", a pseudonym of Sir William Robertson Nicoll, the editor. **April 20** NEUVE EGLISE. A Belgian village near the northern limit of the German push toward Calais and Dunkirk. **May 7** IVOR LAW. Ivan Law, whose father, William, had been a local wagon-maker, opened a car dealership in Zephyr. LMM mistakenly refers to him as "Ivor". AUTOMOBILE. Motor-cars had developed from Daimler's petroleum-fired motor of 1885. During the war the Americans became pre-eminent in car manufacture. In 1917 Canada came next after the U.S.A. in number of cars per capita: between 1915 and 1919 cars in Canada increased 279%. **May 29** THE AISNE. A river and a frontier Département in the northeast of France. **June 1** THE MARNE. In 1914, when the Germans crossed the Marne River, they had come within a few miles of Paris, but they were pushed back to a line running from Reims to the Meuse River north of Verdun. On May 31, 1918, they again crossed the Marne southwest of Reims. CHATEAU THIERRY. A town 100 km east-northeast of Paris. In 1814 Russo-Prussian forces were defeated here by Napoleon. **June 15** THE "NEW STAR". Independent observers discovered Nova Aquilae III on June 8. Since 1888 developments in theories of gravity and radiation and in instruments and photometric techniques had greatly advanced astronomy. ERNEST RENAN (1823-92). French author of *The Life of Jesus* (1863) and other works. The same allusion to Renan's comments on the Kaiser appears in *Rilla*, ch. 30. **June 25** ROD. Ewan Macdonald's youngest brother Roderick, of Bellevue, maintained the home farm. DR. MACINTYRE. John Donald MacIntyre, M.D., a graduate of McGill, who practised in Montague as a "country surgeon" until his death in 1925. CLOSED DAYS. A complete ban on automobiles had existed in PEI between 1908 and 1913. In 1913 autos were permitted on the roads on Mondays, Wednesdays, and Thursdays, except in some communities still totally "closed". "Closed days" lasted until 1919. A SPINSTER LADY. In one of many examples of LMM's direct dependence on journal materials, *Rilla of Ingleside*, ch. 27, presents a variant version of this anecdote. CHRISTY'S. Ewan Macdonald's eldest sister, Christie Macdonald McLeod of Kinross. **June 26** FANNIE WISE [Mutch]; IDA MCEACHERN [Sutherland]. Classmates from Prince of Wales College days. **July 19** "SPIRITUALISM". Psychical research or spiritualism grew to unparalleled proportions during the war, perhaps because of the nearly universal experience of bereavement. **July 22** LIFE HOWATT. Eliphalet Howatt, younger brother of Irving, a friend from Park Corner days. **July 28** THE FOOD BOARD. Under the direction of a Food Controller, the Canadian Food Board coped with food shortages at home and in the army overseas by regulating prices, controlling distribution, and rationing. DE GUSTIBUS. "According to taste" (Latin). **July 30** THIRTEEN AT A TABLE. Writing seven months later to George Macmillan in Scotland, LMM copies this entry almost verbatim (see *My Dear Mr. M.*, pp. 90-1). The changes show the way the author used her journals and her correspondence to sharpen memory and style. **August 8** SOISSONS. A medieval French cathedral city on the Aisne. **August 14** SIMPSON'S. Across from Eaton's at Yonge and Queen Streets; these were the principal department stores in downtown Toronto. **August 19** HAIG'S ARMY. Under Haig, British forces, including the Canadian Corps, moved to break the Hindenburg line in the direction of Cambrai-St Quentin; meanwhile the newly arrived American army, supported by the French on their left, drove to break through the German line north of Verdun. **September 5** "HEARTS OF THE WORLD". A film—directed by D.W. Griffith, and starring Lillian Gish and Robert Harron—about British soldiers in the trenches; it was made at the behest of the British government. COURCELETTE. A battle fought in 1916. In *Rilla of Ingleside* LMM uses it as the place where Rilla's brother Walter is killed. Another young man in the book is called Carl; still another loses a leg in battle. THE CARS. Electric street-cars had begun to replace Toronto's horse-drawn cars in 1861; the Toronto Railway Company, operating between 1891 and 1921, included a line into the Exhibition grounds. In 1921 the Toronto Transport Commission amalgamated nine separate electric tram systems. **September 28** W.C.T.U. The World's Women's Christian Temperance Union was founded in 1883, based on the American W.C.T.U., founded in 1874. **September 30** OUR RING. On rural telephone lines each house was assigned a recognizable signal combining long and short rings. Leaskdale had been on the Uxbridge-Scott phone line since 1907. **October 3** MORLEY SHIER. Born in 1894, Morley Roy Shier was a public-school teacher who became an aviator and Flight Lieutenant in the Air Force; he was the second of the three young soldiers to whom *Rainbow Valley* was dedicated. The third was Robert Brooks, of Zephyr, who died August 8, 1918, while LMM was in PEI. She misspelled Brooks' name in the dedication, as "Brookes", perhaps thinking of Rupert Brooke. THE MAIL AND EMPIRE. Toronto daily morning paper, founded February 1895, by the union of two earlier daily papers. **October 6** IN CAPITALS. This is the only time the dateline is written in capitals in this volume of the journals. *Rilla*, ch. 33, gives October 6 as the date for celebrating victory. PRESIDENT WILSON'S TERMS. On Jan. 8, 1918, President Woodrow Wilson had expounded 14 points for peace: open covenants; reduction of armaments; free trade; free seas; evacuation of Russia, Belgium, Romania, Serbia, and Montenegro; independent Poland; restoration of Alsace-Lorraine to France; autonomy of peoples in Austria-Hungary; readjustment of Italian frontiers; and the formation of a league of nations. THE ENTENTE. The Allies, originally France and Great Britain, had been tied since 1904 by an "Entente Cordiale"; it was enlarged in 1908 to include Russia in a "Triple Entente". **December 1** SPANISH FLU. A pandemic outburst of influenza, attributed by France to Spain, by Spain to France, and by America to eastern Europe. The disease involved catarrh, high fever, and prostration. Prevalent in the summer of 1918, and appearing first in the armies of the Entente, then in civilian populations in England, France, Italy, Spain, and Portugal, it was followed by a more malignant universal wave in the fall and winter of 1918-19. DR. SHIER. Dr Walter C. Shier of Uxbridge—the son of James Shier of Leaskdale and Udora, and uncle of Morley Shier—was Coroner for Ontario County by 1919. "DEMNED MOIST AND UNPLEASANT". Mr Mantalini, in Dickens' *Nicholas Nickleby* (1838-9; ch. 34), threatens to become "a demd, damp, moist, unpleasant body!" STRYCHNINE. A poisonous alkaloid, used in minute doses as a nerve-stimulant. †**November 11** KIPLING'S CAT. From "The Cat that Walked by Himself" in Kipling's *Just So Stories* (1902). [**December 1**] BYRON'S LINES. From Lord Byron's "Ode to Napoleon Buonaparte". **December 17** MR. ROLLINS. Weld Allen Rollins (1874-1952), a graduate of Dartmouth and Harvard, specialized in corporate law and was counsel for many large companies, including General Motors. MY CASE. LMM was suing her publishers over their failure to pay her full royalties on *Anne of Green Gables*. ANOTHER SUIT. A separate suit was to be filed over Page's proposal to bring out *Further Chronicles of Avonlea*. **December 26** RAINBOW VALLEY. This novel (1919) deals peripherally with Anne's children, but focuses on the livelier children of a dreamy, widowed minister. SUNSET CANADA. Subtitled *British Columbia and Beyond*, Archie M. Bell's book (Boston: Page, 1918) was part of the series "See America First". MASS. COURT OF EQUITY. LMM uses this term to refer to the Suffolk County Court in Massachusetts where her case was first tried. It was later appealed to the Supreme Judicial Court of Massachusetts. Her case was heard as a "bill in equity". Equity is a form of adjudication meant to grant relief from the strictures of law on the grounds of natural justice and fairness.

1919

January 10 MISS HILL. Anita Hill was Head of the School of Household Science at Macdonald College, Ste-Anne-de-Bellevue, from 1917 to 1920; she then married Whyley Baird and moved to Nappan, Nova Scotia. MISS PHELP. Bessie M. Philp, a lecturer in the School of Household Science, became its Head in 1920. She died in 1941. **January 12** GROSSET AND DUNLAP. Founded in 1899, this firm had long been the chief reprint publishers in the U.S.A. **January 13** JUDGE JENNY. The Hon. Charles Francis Jenney (1860-1923), appointed Associate Justice to the Supreme Judicial Court of Massachusetts on September 24, 1919. Former Member of the Massachusetts House of Representatives and of the State Senate and lecturer in Law at Boston University. MR. NAY. Frank

Nelson Nay, born 1866 and educated at Harvard and at Boston University; member of the law firm of Bates, Nay and Abbott from 1907. **January 14** MY ENTIRE RIGHTS. The case was settled when Page agreed to purchase all LMM's royalty rights in all her books published by him. (Part of this contract covered short stories submitted in 1912 for *Chronicles of Avonlea*, but set aside by Page at that time. This clause would lead to further litigation.) The price agreed to was $17,880. This agreement cost LMM the rights to royalties on later stage and screen versions (1919 and 1934) of her novels. **January 16** THAT PHRASE. The original contract referred to her right to royalties on reprint editions. VICI. Latin for "I have conquered", quoting Julius Caesar. **January 19** MINOR DETAILS. The 1919 contract specified that in publishing *Further Chronicles of Avonlea* Page would not change the stories so as to introduce "Anne Shirley", would not use any picture suggesting "Anne", and would not advertise the book as an "Anne book". UNCLE CHARLES CROSBY. Married to Aunt Jane Montgomery, sister of Hugh John Montgomery. **February 7** PROFESSOR DALLAS SHARPE (1870-1929). This clergyman was Professor of English at Boston University, an editor of *Youth's Companion*, and author of many books about wildlife in forest and field. "THE BRUSHWOOD BOY". Rudyard Kipling's uncanny story about precognition, from *The Day's Work* (1898). MISS KIRBY. Laura Kirby (later Mrs H. Porter) was on the Macdonald College staff 1918-19. "AFTER LIFE'S FITFUL FEVER..." *Macbeth*, III, ii, 22. KHAKI-KOOL. Twilled cotton cloth, manufactured at the end of the war in the same weight as summer uniforms, though usually not in the same earth-colours as khaki. "WORN-OUT FETTERS". From Henry Wadsworth Longfellow, "The Slave's Dream" (1842). WATERLOO. A town in the Eastern Townships of Quebec, where Frederica MacFarlane had gone to a Women's Institute meeting. SEVENTEEN BEAUTIFUL...YEARS. The manuscript has "fifteen...years"; LMM corrected this detail when she typed a short version of her journal late in her life. HOME-MAKERS CLUBS OF QUEBEC. In honour of Frederica's work as Superintendent of Quebec Women's Institutes from 1913 until her death in 1919, Macdonald College still offers a Frederica Campbell MacFarlane Prize of $100, open to students from rural districts of the province. The Women's Institutes of Quebec have raised money for this fund annually since 1920. DR. ANDERSON. Alexander Anderson was Principal of Prince of Wales College. DR. WALKER. Dr John J. Walker acted from 1908 to 1914 as Physician to the Men's Building. (There was a female doctor for the women students.) **March 1** "THERE'S A DIVINITY..." *Hamlet*, V,ii,10. **March 3** MRS. SHARPE. Col. Sam Sharpe's widow, Mabel Crosby Sharpe, was the granddaughter of Joseph and Mary Gould of Uxbridge. "THE BLUE GERM". A novel by Martin Swayne (N.Y.: Doran, 1918)—a fantasy about a magic cure for all diseases. **March 11** MY TENTH NOVEL. *Rilla of Ingleside*, dedicated to the memory of Frederica Campbell MacFarlane. The novel ends in spring of 1919, when demobilized soldiers returned home. **March 29** "THE TWENTIETH PLANE". A novel (London: Low, 1919) by Albert D. Watson, subtitled *A Psychic Revelation*. **April 13** VICTROLA. Record-player manufactured by the Victor Company. OUIJA-BOARD. Lettered board, used to receive messages in spiritualistic seances. THE NEW COPYRIGHT BILL. Legislation to provide a comprehensive copyright law, which would permit Canada to apply for admission to the revised Berne Convention governing international publishing rights. The need for a strong bill rose partly from publishing practices in the United States (not a member of the Berne Convention); but while it offered some protection against piracy, it also limited the power of authors to control licensing of their own work in the U.S. **May 9** SCHOOL. School Section 8, Leaskdale, was a one-room frame school. Miss Irene Brent taught for two years, followed in 1920 by Elva MacKay. **May 24** THE 24TH. "Empire Day", a Dominion holiday established in honour of the birthday of Queen Victoria. F.M. MEETINGS. The Forward Movement was a program of evangelism, service, missionary education, and social concern, formally accepted by the General Assembly of the Presbyterian Church of Canada in June 1919. DR. DRUMMOND. The Rev. Dr Drummond of Hamilton, early in favour of the union of Presbyterians and Methodists, changed his stance and revived the idea of a federation rather than a union. **September 1** HIS MALADY. Ewan Macdonald's malady appears to have been a major affective mood disturbance, resulting in depression, loss of normal involvement, decreased energy, and a sense of guilt—accompanied by changes in appetite, sleep, and weight. MR. RAE. The Rev. J.W. Rae (1852-1930) was minister at Newcastle, 80 km southeast of Leaskdale. MRS. DODDS. Her husband, the Rev. Thomas Dodds (1869-1941), was minister at Sonya (20 km east of Leaskdale). REVS. SMITH AND LAWRENCE. The Rev. W.G. Smith (1865-1935) was minister at Glenarm, 50 km northeast of Leaskdale; the Rev. S. Lawrence (1863-1953) at Duff's Church near Guelph, 200 km west. All these people were speakers implementing the Forward Movement. MR. BRYDON. The Rev. Walter Brydon of Woodville later became Principal of Knox College. DR. MCKAY. The Rev. Dr R.P. MacKay, D.D. (1847-1929), Moderator in 1911 and later a leader of the Church Union Movement—not Mr. MacKay of Blackwater (Wick). ETERNALLY LOST. Obsessive thoughts of death, a usual part of major depression, were linked in Ewan Macdonald's case with the Presbyterian concept of "election": because man's original sin was so great, a just God could not save many humans from eternal punishment after death; but a merciful God might, by His mere will and pleasure, elect to save a few. A Presbyterian in a state of depression could easily assume that he was beyond God's mercy and doomed—justly—to eternal wrath. THE ENCYCLOPEDIA. In the *Encyclopedia Britannica*, 11th edition (1910-11), LMM could read, under "Insanity", of "the delusions of a melancholic patient...hearing voices...delusions of unworthiness and unpardonable sin". FENELON FALLS. A community about 100 km northeast of Leaskdale, between Cameron Lake and Sturgeon Lake. "OLD MR. FRASER". The minister of Fenelon Falls (not the Rev. J.R. Fraser of Uxbridge). CONSULT A SPECIALIST. Toronto would have been a good centre for treatment, but consulting a specialist there would have made it impossible to maintain secrecy about Ewan Macdonald's malady and thus to protect his appointment. FLORA'S. Ewan Macdonald's sister, Flora (Mrs Amos Eagles), living in Braintree, Mass., could provide a place for him near Boston, which was at this time a major centre, with Vienna, for the treatment of mental disorders. The Massachusetts General Hospital had a world-famous branch for mental and nervous diseases. "THAT SERMON IS RESPONSIBLE". The quality of Ewan Macdonald's disturbance suggests that his was not a *reactive* neurosis— a response to an environmental factor—but an *endogenous* one, in which genetic factors play an important part. AN OSTEOPATH. A practitioner of manipulation of the mechanism of the body, especially the bony structure, designed to break up lesions. Osteopathy was founded in the U.S.A. in 1874; the Massachusetts College of Osteopathy was one of seven such colleges established by 1919. Physical disorders accompanying the onset of mental disease, including impairment of muscular power and derangement of the stomach and bowels, could be interpreted by an osteopath as the determining causes of Ewan Macdonald's nervous disorder. A VISION. Untreated depression can bottom into psychotic delusion and cause the victim to lose touch with reality. DR. GARRICK. Nathan Garrick (b. 1885) was Instructor in Neurology, Boston University Medical School, 1917-23. His home and office were in an apartment building at 416 Marlborough Street, Boston. MANIC DEPRESSIVE INSANITY. Disease of the brain, as distinguished from affective mood changes; manic episodes would be part of a depressive syndrome, whereas in systematized delusional insanity hallucinations persist and destroy connections with reality. THE KIDNEYS. A functional disorder common to the onset of mental disease. In states of depression there are deficiencies in excretions. CHLORAL. Chloral hydrate, a hypnotic, used to induce refreshing sleep; it was thought to be addictive at this period. Modern treatment would use a drug of the tricyclic group as an anti-depressant, or lithium, a mood-stabilizer, unless the kidneys were diseased. †**June 28** QUINCY. A town five miles south of Boston. †**June 29** THE DOBSONS. Neighbours of Flora and Amos Eagles. †**July 7** NEWTON. A Massachusetts town, five miles from Braintree. †**July 10** "THE FALL OF BABYLON". This film—directed by D.W. Griffith and starring Constance Talmadge and Elmer Clifton—was originally made as part of the film *Intolerance* but was released as a separate feature in 1919. A stub in LMM's scrapbook shows that she saw it at the Colonial Theatre. †**July 22** DR. CORIAT. Isidore Coriat (b. 1875) was a frequent contributor to medical journals on subjects relating to nervous and mental diseases, to psychopathology and to psychoanalysis; he taught Neurology at Tufts Medical School and other Boston colleges. His office was in the same building as that of the younger Dr Garrick. Dr Coriat's books included *The Hysteria of Lady Macbeth* (1912), *The Meaning of Dreams* (1915), and *What is Psychoanalysis?* (1917). †**July 26** "DADDY-LONG-LEGS". This 1919 film starring Mary Pickford, showing at the Tremont Theatre, was based on Jean Webster's novel (1912) about an orphan girl who was adopted and sent to college by a secret benefactor. †**August 14** MY NEW BOOK. *Rilla of Ingleside*, the story of Anne's family during the war years. †**August 24** MISS CHAPMAN. Ethel M. Chapman (1888-1976) wrote an article, "The Author of Anne", for the section on "Women and Work" in *Maclean's*, October 1919, pp. 102-4, 106. MCLEANS MAGAZINE. *Maclean's*, published in Toronto and founded in 1905 by J.B. Maclean—it was given its present name in 1911—since 1914 had featured Canadian themes and personalities. From 1914 to 1917 *Maclean's* had republished many of LMM's early short stories; from 1918 on they published her new stories, *e.g.*, "Garden of Spices", March 1918. **September 2** SUTTON. A nearby town on Lake Simcoe. PROF. HARCOURT. George Harcourt was Professor of Agriculture at Prince of Wales College, Charlottetown, 1891-4; he moved to Alberta and in 1917 became Assistant Dean of Agriculture, University of Alberta. **September 4** NORMAN CAMPBELL. A second cousin on the Montgomery side; a friend from Prince of Wales College days. **September 10** HALMA. A checkers type of game, played on a board with 256 small squares. Each player tries to move his pieces into the "yard" diagonally opposite. Chinese Checkers is a modern game derived from Halma. **September 11** JOHN LOCKIE. J.H. Lockie, son of Robert and Elizabeth Lockie, was the Secretary Treasurer of the United Farmers of Ontario at Zephyr. **September 13** SHAKER FLANNEL. Soft white cloth napped on both sides, originally made in grey shades by the Shaker religious community. CAPTAIN SMITH. Edwin Smith, born in Nova Scotia in 1884, attended Dalhousie College, Manitoba College (B.A. 1894, M.A., 1903), and, in 1897, Pine Hill Theological College—Ewan Macdonald's college. Smith married in 1897 and had seven children; he was minister in Kensington and in Cardigan, PEI (1900-1909), and in Tillsonburg, Ontario, until 1914. He joined the Princess Pats, then became the first Canadian to gain a commission in the Royal Navy. After the war Smith became a free-lance writer and in 1930 earned a Ph.D. in Indiana. **September 21** "CHURCH ROW". In 1901, when the old Cavendish Presbyterian church had to be torn down, there was a sharp difference of opinion about the best place for relocating it. **September 28** PROHIBITION REFERENDUM. In 1918 a wartime measure had stopped the manufacture and importation of liquor; referenda were now held to extend this measure and to ratify provincial prohibition laws. **October 4** "LAST CALL FOR DINNER". The cry of dining-room stewards as they moved through the railway cars. **October 8** MISSISSAUGA. Then a village, now a major city at the western edge of Toronto. **October 9** HONITON LACE. English lace. Queen Victoria wore honiton lace at the marriage of her daughter to Frederick Wilhelm of Prussia. WISDOM IS JUSTIFIED. St Matthew 19. "MICKEY". This film, directed by Mack Sennett, starred Mabel Normand. **October 13** DOUGLAS MADILL. A friend of the Macdonald boys, he was raised by Richard and Jane (Madill) Oxtoby. A LITTLE DIARY. At a later difficult period of his life, Chester did indeed keep a journal, which is now in the Montgomery collection at the University of Guelph. **October 15** MAMIE SIMPSON. The next long entry (October 16; omitted here) retraces the family history of the Macneills and the Simpsons. **October 28** "GOLDEN DICKY". Subtitled *The Story of a Canary and his Friends*, Marshall Saunders' 23rd novel (N.Y.: Stokes, 1919) continued her series of animal stories, sequent to *Beautiful Joe* (1894). **November 8** "BY OUR LADY". The *Oxford English Dictionary* does not corroborate this derivation of the term. **November 14** MR. SMITH. The minister at Glenarm was the Rev. W.G. Smith (1865-1935)—not Edwin Smith. WOODVILLE. A town 30 km northeast of Leaskdale. **November 19** BROMIDE. Bromine, naturally combined with potassium, was considered the safest and most generally applicable sedative for the nervous system; it was used for all forms of morbid mental excitement. **November 19** CANADIAN BOOKMAN. A literary journal taken over in 1921 as the official organ of the Canadian Authors' Association. **November 22** DANISH AND SWEDISH. *Rainbow Valley* was also published in Dutch (1921) and Norwegian (1922). **November 15** ALLAN GRAY. A farmer (1863-1943) and a leading member of the Leaskdale Presbyterian Church. **November 27** FRANK WALKER. A farmer, member of the Zephyr church, and president of the Scott Agricultural Society in 1921. **December 5** GIBBON. Edward Gibbon's *History of the Decline and Fall of the Roman Empire* (1776-1788). **December 18** "ANNE"...ON THE SCREEN. The first film version of *Anne of Green Gables* (1919) was directed by Wm Desmond Taylor. MARY MILES MINTER. Her career was ruined by scandals connected with Taylor's death in 1922. **December 22** COTTER'S SATURDAY NIGHT. A poem of Scottish family life by Robert Burns (1786). A later entry (January 28; omitted here) records more readings at a Burns' birthday evening—a popular festival in many Canadian towns. **December 25** ASPIRIN. Compounded of salicylic acid and acetic acid, aspirin was developed during the war for fever and pain relief, replacing phenacetine in common use. **December 29** KARNAK. Theban ruins in central Egypt near Luxor.

1920

January 4 EINSTEIN. Albert Einstein's publications on the theory of relativity began in 1905; the generalized theory was published in 1915-17. Predictions based on Einstein's theory that a ray of light from a distant star will be bent as it passes the sun were tested in 1919 during an eclipse. **January 5** PETER RABBIT AND BOBBY COON. *The Tale of Peter Rabbit* by Beatrix Potter (1866-1943) was first published in 1901, *The Adventures of Bobby Coon* by Thornton W. Burgess (1874-1956) in 1918. **January 9** "HIAWATHA". Poem by Henry Wadsworth Longfellow (1807-1882). **January 13** "SEVENTEEN". A sentimental novel (1916) by Booth Tarkington. The previous entry (January 12; omitted here) reports equal enjoyment in reading *The Secret Orchard* (London: Macmillan, 1908) by Agnes and Egerton Castle. **January 16** CHILBLAINS. Itching sore on foot or hand from exposure to cold. NYAL'S MENTHOLATUM. Camphor-like substance used to relieve pain from neuralgia. **January 18** VOLUME ONE OF MY JOURNAL. LMM copied her early notes into legal-sized lined ledger books. Her first volume covered the period from 20 January 1890 to 19 April 1897. **January 31** BOOK OF OLD STORIES. *Further Chronicles of Avonlea*, published by L.C. Page, was brought out by agreement in a year when there was no other new LMM novel for sale in the United States. The 1919 contract had given Page the right to publish a group of stories written by LMM before 1912, "revised or not revised as she may see fit." LMM revised them in 1919, removing references to "Anne". Page now proposed to publish the earler versions, in order to exploit the connection with the popular heroine. LITTLE QUOTATIONS AND EPIGRAMS. These are quoted from the writings of Oliver Wendell Holmes (1809-1894), Charlotte Brontë (1816-1855), J.M. Barrie (1860-1937), "Ouida" (1839-1908), Olive Schreiner (1855-1920), John Ruskin (1819-1900). **February 14** THE 1912 VERSIONS. In 1912 LMM had sent Page the manuscripts of 28 short stories. These were revised versions of earlier work published in newspapers and magazines. Of these, 12 stories were published as *Chronicles of Avonlea* (1912). Page—in spite of the 1919 contract—now chose several others in their 1912 versions for publication. **February 22** PRESCOTT'S CONQUEST OF MEXICO. W.H. Prescott, *History of the Conquest of Mexico* (1843). **March 15** "WAGGLE" THEIR EARS. In other entries (omitted here) LMM discussed at length another of her physiological oddities: the ability to make wallpaper go in and out of focus. **April 9** ROLLINS TO PROCEED. LMM's lawyer began a lawsuit against L.C. Page & Co., by filing a Bill in Equity in the Superior Court of Massachusetts, on April 24, 1920, seeking to force Page to withdraw *Further Chronicles of Avonlea* from the market and to assign damages and an accounting of profits from its unauthorized publication and sale. **May 9** BYRON'S LIFE. Probably the Hon. R. Noel's *The Life of Lord Byron* (London: 1890), or Ethel C. Mayne's *Byron* (N.Y.: 1912); the 1921 republication of *Astarte* (1905) by Byron's grandson, the Earl of Lovelace, revived interest in the Byron story. **May 20** MR. FRENCH. Asa Palmer French (1860-1935) was District Attorney for the South East District of Massachusetts 1901-6, and U.S. Attorney for the District of Massachusetts, 1906-14. **May 21** A MASTER. LMM's suit was referred by the Superior Court to a Master—a parajudicial officer appointed to meet the parties, hear their evidence, examine their exhibits, and report his findings to a judge of the Superior Court. **May 28** MR. MELLEN. George Henry Mellen (b. 1850) was the Master first assigned to the case. **June 2** MAUPASSANT. The famous French short-story writer Guy de Maupassant (1850-93). **June 4** MASTER SAMPSON. Harry LeBaron Sampson (1878-1971), educated at Dartmouth and Harvard, had been a partner since 1914 in the law firm of Hutchins and Wheeler. **June 18** A PUBLIC HOLIDAY. Memorial Day. **June 18** "TITIAN RED". A colour associated with the Italian painter Titian (Tiziano Vecelli, c. 1487-1576). The point at issue was that the 1919 contract stated "No picture of 'Anne Shirley'...shall appear in or on said proposed book." The cover of *Further Chronicles of Avonlea* featured a red-haired girl, suggestive of Anne. **June 24** MR. MORROW. Agent of the Stokes Company, the publisher of LMM's books in the United States. **July 7** "VANISH, LEAVING NOT A RACK BEHIND". Misquoted from *The Tempest*, IV,i,48: "dissolve...leave not a rack behind". **July 26** NOT A SEIN FEINER. In spite of her Irish name, Miss O'Connell disavows membership in the Sinn Fein, the revolutionary group in Ireland. **August 1** AUNT HATTIE. Wife of LMM's uncle Chester Macneill of Vancouver, B.C.—where LMM's cousin Bertie McIntyre had once lived and worked. Laura McIntyre Aylsworth was Bertie's sister. **August 22** VERS LIBRE. French for "free verse": without rhyme or regular metre. **August 24** EMILY. The first of the three "Emily" books was published in 1923. **December 11** CHATHAM. A city in southwestern Ontario, 410 km from Leaskdale. **December 13** MRS. ASQUITH'S AUTOBIOGRAPHY. Margot Tennant, second wife of H.H. Asquith, Liberal Prime Minister of Great Britain, 1908-16, published her frank and indiscreet *Reminiscences* in 1920, probably setting back her husband's hope of regaining power in 1921.

1921

January 16 DRUMMOND'S "LEETLE BATEESE". One of the humorous and sentimental dialect poems of W.H. Drummond (1854-1907), which purports to render the broken English of French Canadians. First published in 1897, it became a very popular recitation piece. GROTE'S "HISTORY OF GREECE." George Grote, *History of Greece* (8 vols, 1846-56). MRS. WHARTON'S "HOUSE OF MIRTH". Edith Wharton's novel (1905) of social life in New York. **January 20** HIS VERY FEATURES SO CHANGED. LMM's description of the physical changes occurring during Ewan Macdonald's attack has been characterized by modern authorities in psychiatry as remarkably accurate and typical. **January 23** LAURA PRITCHARD. A friend in Prince Albert during LMM's year there (1890-1). **January 30** OLIVER MACNEILL. A cousin from Dakota whom LMM found attractive at the time of his visit to Cavendish in 1909. **February 10** THE NUMBER OF DOLLARS. This is a generally accurate computation of LMM's royalties, according to her scrupulous account books, now at Guelph. THIS MAD WORLD. An interpolation, "Oh yes, yes!—1942", was added to this phrase—not in the manuscript, but in the typescript—in the year LMM died. **February 14** "THE TRYST OF THE WHITE LADY". This story was published in *Maclean's*, August 1922. **February 23** EARL GREY. See entries in this volume for September 6 to 16, 1910. **March 5** "INGLESIDE". *Rilla of Ingleside*, the story of "Anne"'s grown-up children, was published later in 1921. **March 5** DR. LOGAN OF ACADIA. John Daniel Logan (1860-1929)—university professor, poet, biographer, essayist—later edited, with Daniel French, *Headwaters of Canadian Literature* (1924). **March 13** COPYING MY CAVENDISH DIARY. The present Oxford volume opens with final passages in the record of LMM's Cavendish years (to June 24, 1911), as a prelude to her "modern history".

Omissions

All the entries that have been deleted, either in part or in total, are listed below. An asterisk after the date indicates that the deletion is only partial.

1910: Feb. 15, 28; Mar. 21, 31; Apr. 3, 24; Aug. 10, 26; Sept. 10, 25, 30; **1911**: Jan. 15, 17*, 22*, 27*; Feb. 5*, 6*, 15; **1912**: Jan. 28; †Apr. 12, 1911, †May 7, 1911, †May 23, 1911, †May 24, 1911, †May 26, 1911, †May 27, 1911, †June 5, 1911, †June 8, 1911, †July 2, 1911, †July 19, 1911, †July 20, 1911, †July 30, 1911, †Aug. 6, 1911, †Aug. 13, 1911, †Aug. 20, 1911, †Aug. 27, 1911, †Sept. 3, 1911, †Sept. 10, 1911, †Sept. 18, 1911, †Sept. 24, 1911; Dec 1, 16, 19; **1913**: Feb. 1; May 1*; June 10*, 11*; July 4, 6, 7; Sept. 27*; †July 25, †July 30, †July 31, †Aug. 3*, †Aug. 6; Nov. 10; **1914**: Jan. 10*; Feb. 11, 16, 19; Sept. 26; Nov. 4, 12; **1915**: May 6*; June 9, 11, 18*, 27*; July 6, 11*, 18*, 24*; Aug. 7, 31; Sept. 22, 25, 27; Oct. 3; **1916**: Jan. 4, 31; Feb. 3, 10, 16*; Mar. 9; Apr. 1, 11, 18; June 1, 2, 10*, 12, 30; July 3, 6; Aug. 8*, 13*, 19*, 29; Sept. 4*, 9*, 14, 17, 18, 20, 21, 24*, 27; Oct. 4, 10, 12, 17*, 21, 23, 24, 25, 27, 28, 30; Nov. 8, 15, 16*, 20, 21, 25, 27; Dec. 11, 12, 14, 15, 18*, 19, 27, 31; **1917**: Jan. 1, 4, 6, 9, 11, 15, 20*, 27, 29; Feb. 4, 8, 9; Mar. 7, 10, 12; Apr. 1*; May 6; July 1, 29; Aug. 11; Sept. 16, 23, 25; Oct. 31; Nov. 3, 6, 8, 15, 18, 21, 24, 29; Dec. 5, 19*; **1918**: Jan. 5, 31; Feb. 1; Mar. 16, 23; Apr. 6, 14, 15, 27, 30; May 11, 17, 30, 31; June 17, 20, 30*; July 3, 10*, 16, 18, 19*, 20, 27, 29; Aug. 30; Sept. 5*, 19; Dec. 27; **1919**: Feb. 8; Mar. 6, 15*, 24, 28; May 4, 23*; †June 29*, †June 30*, †July 2, †July 15, †July 19, †July 20, †July 21, †July 23, †July 25, †July 27, †July 30, †Aug. 2, †Aug. 3*, †Aug. 10; Sept. 3*, 5, 6, 7*, 8, 9, 12, 29; Oct. 4*, 6, 16, 28*; Nov. 12, 16, 17, 18, 20, 24, 28, 30*; Dec. 9, 19, 24*, 28*; **1920**: Jan. 6, 8, 9*, 12, 14, 25, 28, 31*; Feb. 23, 25; Mar. 3*, 8, 12*, 21; Apr. 17, 19, 30; May 5, 14*, 22, 26, 28*, 29; June 1, 3, 13, 19, 20, 26, 28; July 5, 10, 17, 24*; Aug. 1*, 23, 28; Oct. 18*, 21; Dec. 2*, 4, 13*, 26, 29; **1921**: Jan. 16*, 20*; Feb. 1, 2, 3, 9, 10*, 11; Mar. 8, 13.

A Note on Dates

L.M. Montgomery occasionally entered the incorrect date/day when writing up her journal. Using a perpetual calendar, we have changed her erroneous dates (italic) to the correct dates/days (shown in brackets).

Monday, May *2*, 1910 [3]; Wednesday, Sept. *21*, 1910 [22], Sunday, Sept. *25*, 1910 [26]; Thursday, Sept. *29*, 1910 [30]; †"July *22*, 1911 [20]; Saturday, Sept. *12*, 1914 [13]; Saturday, Oct. *23*, 1915 [26]; Saturday, March *11*, 1916 [12]; Friday, Dec. *7*, 1917 [6]; Monday, Dec. *10*, 1917, [9]; Saturday, July *13*, 1918 [14]; *Friday* Night, July 19, 1918 [Tuesday]; *Tuesday*, July 30, 1918 [Saturday]; *Wednesday*, Apr. 16, 1919 [Monday]; Friday, Oct. *17*, 1919 [19]; Friday, Apr. *9*, 1920 [8]; Monday, August *16;* 1920 [15].

Index